WORLD
RELIGIONS

WORLD RELIGIONS

AN INTRODUCTION

CHARLES R. MONROE, Ph.D.

Prometheus Books

59 John Glenn Drive
Amherst, New York 14228-2197

Published 1995 by Prometheus Books

Inquiries should be addressed to
Prometheus Books, 59 John Glenn Drive, Amherst, New York 14228–2197.
VOICE: 716–691–0133, ext. 207. FAX: 716–564–2711.
WWW.PROMETHEUSBOOKS.COM

03 02 01   8 7 6 5

Library of Congress Cataloging-in-Publication Data

Monroe, Charles R.
    World religions : an introduction / Charles R. Monroe.
        p.   cm.
    Includes bibliographical references and index.
    ISBN 0–87975–942–9 (pbk.)
    1. Religions. 2. Religion—History. 3. Church history.
BL85.M66   1995
291—dc20   94–40049
                                                                      CIP

Printed in the United States of America on acid-free paper

Thirty years of teaching history to variegated, multicultured groups of college students taught the author that the seeds of religious bigotry and conflict flourish in a soil enriched by myths and historical ignorance. It was this lesson that inspired the writing of this book. However, the execution of the inspiration is a tribute to the love and support of my wife, Edith; my daughter, Marilyn; my son, Eugene; and his wife, Lynn Lewis.

Contents

1

A Universal Human Experience

Since the origins of the human species no human being has been without some form of religion. Religion serves a basic human need. It is an essential element for life and its survival, as essential as air, water, and food. Man was created to be born, to live a span of life, to propagate his kind, to dominate the earth and all that is in it, and then, in a few seconds of geologic time, to die. Death is man's eternal enemy. Although intelligent humans know that death is inevitable, most still hope that victory over death can be won in an afterlife of immortality.

Man hopes to retain his hold on life by finding security or salvation from the many death-causing forces that surround him in his various environments. One environment is the external world of the cosmos, the forces of nature, the motions of the planets, an environment with the dual possibilities of sustaining and destroying human life. This external environment experiences catastrophic storms, floods, earthquakes, volcanic eruptions, disease, famines, threats from plants and animals, and, of course, man himself, in the form of murder and war.

Man lives also in an internal environment, the world of mind, the conscious, the subconscious, and the unconscious, a world composed of emotions, feelings, ideas, and dreams. Man has within himself self-destructive, suicidal forces that emanate from his biopsychological structure. Fear and anger may be as destructive to the human person as famine and earthquakes. These internal forces, often referred to as demons and evil spirits, drive humans to destroy themselves or to destroy one another in a competitive struggle for survival on earth. Failure to meet the competition successfully leads to suicide, conditions of mental pathology, or mass killings in war and riot.

Man's struggle to maintain life has caused him, like the biblical Job to ask many questions: "Why is man born into this world of struggle and death?" "Why must man be a victim of this cycle of life and death?" "How can I escape the terrors from the external and the internal environments." "What is life?" "How did creation happen?" Throughout human history, man has sought to find answers

9

to these and other basic life questions. Unfortunately many of the questions are unanswerable, and, as Job learns at last, only God knows. Some answers are found through the intervention of science, but probably the majority of life's questions still belong to God's realm of knowledge, the province filled by religion.

Wise men have sought answers to the puzzling questions of the universe and life by pursuing two avenues in the search of truth or wisdom. One is the way of the scientists, the use of rational thinking, deductive and inductive reasoning, and scientific tools to find truth. The other way is the use of intuition, meditation, prayer, mystical feeling, visions, dreams, revelations from God, magic, prophecy, and faith, in which the final proof of truth comes from transcendental experience.

The first route to truth is used by scientists. The second is used by theologians, prophets, and saints. Modern theologians living in an age of science are trying to harmonize science and religion, to develop a modern religion that can accommodate both revelation and the truths of science. Exponents of a scientific religion, sometimes called Cosmic or Process theology, include Albert Einstein and philosopher Alfred North Whitehead.

Western religions tend to be more rationally oriented than Eastern religions, although every religion relies more on faith than science in the search for truth. But in all world religions there are a minority of believers who reject all aspects of rational thinking and rely wholly on the truth of emotional and mystical experiences. A mystic finds God not in obedience to a creed or some church institution, but in his own power to know God from within his own resources, from the depths of his soul or heart. The mystic knows God's presence when he feels a "warming spirit," a sense of ecstatic joy, an urge to join God in a mystical love of all of God's creatures, or when he says jubilantly, "I have found God."

The answers provided by theologians, prophets, and seers constitute the substance of religion. A simple definition of religion might state that it describes how mankind relates to God. William James in his *Varieties of Religious Experience* defines religion as the "feelings, acts and experiences of individual men in their solitude so far as they apprehend themselves to stand in relation to whatever they may consider divine."[1] Joseph Campbell defines religion as a "linking back" to the sources of all life.[2] Hippolyte Taine, a nineteenth-century French historian, describes religion as a metaphysical poem married to faith. "In every society religion is a precious and natural organ; man needs to think of the infinite and true world; if it suddenly failed, they would feel a great sad void in their soul and would hurt each other the more."[3]

Religion is concerned with the supernatural power of the Creator, the inevitable forces of nature and of the spiritual world, and how humans react to these mysterious and supernatural forces. Religion is essential for human survival. Voltaire is reputed to have said that if God did not exist, then man would have to invent God. Freud claimed that religion is so basic to human survival that it is innate, that humans have an instinct to believe in and to worship a god or gods. Man may rely less and less on God and religion as humans use reason and science to discover the secrets and mysteries of creation, but also at no foreseeable time in the future will human beings be able to dispense with a belief in a god who loves us, heals us, and promises eternal peace in heaven after death. More difficult than defining religion is defining God, the subject matter of religion. Some theologians and scholars claim that God cannot be defined, a view expressed by St. Augustine, Plato, Buddha, St. Thomas Aquinas, and others.

Conceptions of God

The God phenomenon is beyond the realm of physical sensation. God is beyond time and space, beyond all conditions that set the limits of human sensation. Hence, God is described as being transcendent, beyond human thought, and beyond the human's test tubes. But human curiosity and pragmatism demand a common-sense explanation of God, one that mere mortals can understand. Thus God is often depicted not as an invisible force but as some anthromorphic being, living somewhere in space, the sky, the earth, on some planet, or in some mythical place called heaven.

God has been given many different forms and names. Sometimes God is called the Great Father, the Mother Earth, Jehovah, Brahma, Allah, the Spirit of the Mountain, or, by twentieth-century physicists, the presence of electrons and protons. In a recent presentation of modern physics, *The Dark Side of the Universe*, James Trefil concludes that we do not know what makes up 90 percent of the universe but we do know it is not something we have ever seen before, and perhaps that 90 percent is God. James Gleick, in an article entitled "Science on the Track of God,"[4] suggests that most scientists today view religion with less suspicion than formerly, since modern concepts of the ultimate stuff of creation seem to give some support to a belief in God. Gleick cites a statement by Alan Lightman that "the greater the scientist, the deeper is his faith. . . . You might say that the scientist sees God as a mathematician."

Composer Leonard Bernstein, in a poem written for his seventieth birthday says, "For want of a clearer conception of the inconceivable beginningness, the lineage of a star, the key, the ultimate Creative Mind, he calls it God."[5]

The father of astronaut Scott Carpenter wrote of God: "Yet I cannot conceive of a man endowed with intellect, perceiving the ordered universe about him, the glory of a mountain top, the plumage of a tropical bird, the intricate complexity of a protein molecule, the utter and unchanging perfection of a salt crystal, who can deny the existence of some higher power. Whether he chooses to call it God or Mohammed or Buddha or Turquoise Woman or the Law of Probability matters little."[6]

These traditional forces are called conventionally in the English language *God*, or in Greek *Theos*, or in Latin *Deus*, or in Chinese *T'ien*. All human groups have their own name for God, their own image of God, their own place or location for God, and their own understanding of how a person can communicate with God. Some gods are male, others are female; some are sexless and some are the essence of sexuality. In some cultures God is one (monotheistic), but in other cultures God is plural or many (polytheistic). God may be pictured as a human, an animal, a plant, or some geometric, abstract, nonrepresentational figure. In general, God has always been and will always be a supernatural, transcendent force before creation, beyond the reach of man's intellect, but never beyond the faith of man to believe that God is the ultimate source of power and wisdom. The multitude of names and attributes possessed by God is illustrated by Hans Küng in his *Does God Exist?* (p.627): "Not only Muslims in Allah, but also Hindus in Brahma, Buddhists in the Absolute, Chinese in Heaven or in the Tao, are seeking one and the same absolutely first, absolutely last reality, which for Jews and Christians is the one true God Jehovah."

Another concept about the nature of God is found in pantheism, a belief that God is found in all things, a belief that is typical of most primitive or cosmic religions. Pantheism was best expressed in philosophical terms by Spinoza: "God is in the world and the world is in God. Only one divine substance, God, but inaccessible to us. God is not outside of the world but in the world, the cause of all things." The eighteenth-century deists, the apostles of reason, men like Voltaire, Diderot, Rousseau, Locke, Jefferson, and Franklin sought to find God in nature through the media of reason and science. God is made visible to man through the process of evolution, the orderliness and precision of nature's laws and planetary movements, and the beauty found in all of nature. In one sense the "New Age" cult of the 1880s may be pantheistic when it proclaims "God is within you. You are God."

As a rule scientists cannot accept the Genesis account of creation as a literal, historical fact. The story is only one more mythical explanation of creation similar to the explanations given by many other cultures for the process of creation. Nor can scientists conceive of man being the image of God. Yet the majority of human religions do picture God in a human form, a superman figure, a Father person, a human God endowed with all power, all wisdom, the dispenser of justice, benevolence, rewards and punishments both here on earth and in the afterlife. Frequently this Man-God is one that man can manipulate, cajole, or even outwit as man seeks to win from God favors, privileges, good fortune, and death to his enemies. This God concept is one that many scholars and rational people cannot accept. The human being has been endowed with the capacity to love and to hate, with the freedom to choose either option as one's intelligence and sense of justice, or will, dictates.

Scientists cannot accept the biblical record for the age of man on earth, a date often given as ranging from six thousand to ten thousand years. Current scientific evidence suggests that the universe may be fifteen billion years old, and the human species has been on earth for 100,000 years.[7] Even if the Genesis account of creation is scientifically incorrect, it in no way invalidates the universal belief that the creation process is beyond the understanding and control of the human mind. To say that God (whatever God is) created the universe and all that is in it, is still a fact, no religious myth.

In the beginning knowledge about God was found in oral traditions handed down from generation to generation. When the gift of writing came to man these explanations were written into sacred texts. Although each group of worshipers will differ in details as to how God created, the underlying essential elements are found in all of the myths or scriptures. All sacred books contain instruction on proper or moral human behavior, rewards and penalties for disobedience to divine law, concepts of the nature of the soul and its destiny after death, the processes by which man can communicate with God and God can make known his will to his created creatures, and suggestions for how man can live in harmony both with the divine will and with the human social group.

Are the sacred scriptures man-made myths or are they the revelations from God to those human interpreters on earth who are called prophets, like Isaiah or Buddha, or even Joseph Smith, or among more primitive people their witch-doctors, medicine men, or shamans? It all depends on one's perspective or belief as refined through generations of religious tradition and study.

Soul and Spirit

Closely related to the concept of God are the concepts of soul and spirit. For most humans God, soul, and spirit are often bound together as almost indistinguishable elements. Are soul and spirit simply other aspects of the nature of God? Christian Scientists, for example, view soul and spirit as being God. Primitive religions seem to discover God as a spirit. St. Paul spoke of the human person as being formed of three elements, body, soul, and spirit. The body represents both the human body and the physical aspect of the Christ that later becomes the body of human followers of the Christ, the Church, the symbol of Christ's body here on earth.

The soul represents the personality of the human person which, in turn, represents the divine person of the Christ. It is the force that gives life and action to the human person, and that is regarded as never dying, hence it is the part of the human that survives after death, leaving the body to find its eternal, immortal existence with God.

The concept of spirit as something different from soul is rejected by many writers, who believe that soul and spirit are identical forces. But if a distinction is to be made, then spirit becomes that aspect of personality we know as a conscious motivating force, or will within the person, or, within the Church, the Holy Spirit, the will to bear the burdens of a Christian life for Christ's sake.

If distinctions are to be made among the concepts God, soul, and spirit, then one might conjecture that soul and spirit are manifestations of God as God operates upon and within the human person. What the difference is between soul and spirit may be debatable, but an attempt, though hazardous, will be made. The soul seems to represent the divine element within the human person, namely the nonmaterial aspects of personality, one's intelligence, emotional structure, the system of drives, or whatever else can be included in the term "ego" or psyche. Spirit represents the life-giving, life-driving forces within the personality, such as the will to live and to act, the *élan vital* that is extinguished at death.

The Jewish concept of the soul holds that God creates a separate soul for each person that enters the human embryo sometime after conception. The Jewish word for soul is *nefish,* or the breath of life. Within the soul is the spirit, or *riah* (wind), or the life force. Upon death the soul goes with the body to the grave or *sheol.* Eventually the soul will depart from the body to await a final reunion with the body at the time of the resurrection.

In Christian theology soul and body are separate entities that become joined at the moment of conception. St. Thomas Aquinas, St. Jerome, Peter Lombard, and John Calvin believed that the soul enters the body at the time of conception, a belief that antiabortionists use in their assertions that abortion is a form of murder. Since the soul is not destroyed at the time of death, a belief has developed that the soul is transmitted from parent to child, hence original sin is transmitted through the soul to the children of the parents. A related belief is that the soul contains one's destiny. This view gives rise to the doctrine of predestination, a belief associated with the theologians St. Augustine and John Calvin. Upon death the soul and the body are separated, with the soul continuing to live on to enjoy the blessings of heaven, or the cleansing process in purgatory, or the torments of hell. In hell the soul will not be destroyed for it must remain there to await the final judgment and the resurrection, when the soul and the body will be reunited.

Neo-Platonists, including the Christian theologian Origen, believed that the soul exists before creation, that it never dies, and that it is always in the process of being reborn or reincarnated. While the soul represents the divine element in the person, the spirit provides the motivation for action. Since Jesus received the Holy Spirit at the time of his baptism, it is believed by Christians that the same spirit enters the human personality upon baptism.

Among the Greeks, as taught by Plato, the soul is a distinct entity from the body or the material world. The soul transcends matter. The great Soul (God) existed before time and creation in the form of the Logos or Word, that is, the patterns by which God created all things on earth and in the heavens. The Logos or soul represents the totality of God's power and will. The soul enters the human body after conception, but it always remains a separate part of the person. Upon death the soul then returns to its original source, where it awaits further births and rebirths.

Most Islamic theologians believe that each individual person has a soul created by God, but, like Greek Platonists, they say the soul is created before the body. When later God breathes (*ruh*) life into the human body the soul enters the body, and it remains a part of the body until death. Then the soul leaves the body until the Day of Judgment, when body and soul are reunited. Hindus recognize the existence of a soul in the form of a world or universal soul, called Brahman. When Brahman enters the human body it becomes *atman* or personal soul, the presence of God. Upon death the soul must be released from the body so that it can return to Brahman, the Godhead.

Buddhism denies the existence of any soul. Each person is a special creation with its own special intellect, will, and personality. Since Buddhism believes there is no afterlife, no heaven or hell, no God, the ultimate end of the body is the complete annihilation of all human attributes. When this happens the person has reached or attained a state of reality, that is, a state of nothingness or *nirvana*. The physical body and the material world are, after all, only illusions of reality or *maya*. Hence there is no soul to live on into eternity.

Among primitive religions God is known as a spirit force within all aspects of nature. Thus the number of Gods or spirits could be infinite, and the term "pantheism" is used to describe the existence of God in all things material. God-spirits are the creative and controlling forces on earth, and they determine man's fate on earth. All things on earth are endowed with spirits, some of which are good, others evil. The good spirits are to be honored, worshiped, and given gifts. The evil spirits are to be appeased unless somehow they can be destroyed. Of all of the elements of God's creation, the planets have given man more of the spirits than other parts of the universe. Among the ancient civilizations the sun god has been the prime object of worship in the religions of Egypt, Babylonia, the Mayans and Incas of South America, and many others. Even the Hindus worship a sun god, Surya.

The Varieties of Religious Experience

Often the question is asked, "Why do people have so many different forms of religion?" A ready response would be that as children we inherit our religious beliefs from our parents. Do most human beings have a free choice in selecting their religion? History suggests that very few people have chosen their religions freely. In the Western democracies, such as the United States, freedom of religious choice does exist politically. But even in the United States the majority of people have inherited their religion from the family and the social environment in which they grew up as children. In the United States today there is evidence that religious preferences move in cycles. In the 1980s the popular trend was toward a more conservative, fundamental form of Protestantism. Many Americans tend to follow the current trend by joining some conservative church. Some persons are converted to a particular brand of religion by a process of education or persuasion. A dynamic teacher, priest, or evangelist may be so convincing that people will join his or her form of religion. Many religions bear the name of a great missionary-teacher, or prophet, who was so persuasive as to cause some persons to go and follow him, such famous personalities as Jesus, Mohammed, and Buddha. At other times a person may experience some emotional crisis in his or her life, a death or other catastrophic event, that motivates the person to seek shelter in the arms of God or religion. A few persons have found their preferred religion while engaged in a deep trance, or in a long period of meditation, or some intense emotional state, and in a sudden burst of enlightenment, in a vision perhaps, the person discovers God or Truth. This sudden conversion experience is typical of those persons who say that they have been "born again." However, rarely is a person reared in a Christian environment converted to Buddhism, Islam, or some other religion unlike Christianity.

History indicates that in most instances one's religion is a product of one's social environment, especially the family. In many instances in history a person had no choice but to accept the religion of the ruler, tribal chief or king, or suffer the consequences, often death.

An interesting story is told of how Russia became a Christian nation following the Greek Orthodox brand of Christianity. An early pagan czar, Vladimir, in A.D. 987 sought to find a better religion for his people. First he sent an emissary to the Muslims. The emissary returned and told the czar that Islam had one God and his prophet was Mohammed, but, best of all, they had a paradise with many beautiful virgin girls who could give men great pleasure. This was most acceptable until Vladimir was told that the Muslims were not permitted to drink alcohol. The czar declared, "The Russians cannot exist without that pleasure." So Vladimir requested that an emissary from Rome should come to visit him. The pope sent an agent, who informed the czar that Christianity had one God, one who had created all things in the world. But when the agent said that Russia's gods were only wooden images, Vladimir sent the agent away at once. Vladimir liked the idea of one God, so he sent for a Jewish agent to tell him about Judaism. But when he learned that the Jews were condemned to wander over the earth for all of time, he sent the Jew away. Then the Greeks sent Vladimir a philosopher who related to him the history of the world and the torment in hell for nonbelievers The czar was so impressed that he sent an agent to Constantinople to see for himself the Byzantine churches. When the agent saw the beauty of Hagia Sophia, he believed that he had seen heaven. The agent returned and convinced Vladimir that he and the Russian people should accept the Greek Orthodox Church. It became the state religion until the Russian Revolution.

The Function of Religion

Any analysis of the phenomenon of religion must answer the question, "Why does mankind need religion?" Before the eighteenth century it would have been a daring skeptic who would ask such a question. The person would risk the charge of heresy and death at the stake. By the nineteenth century the forces of science, rationalism, and religious tolerance had made it possible for a few persons to suggest that God and religion were irrelevant and unnecessary for human happiness. A Karl Marx or a Friedrich Nietzsche could suggest that religion was the opiate of the people, that in an age of science and reason God ought to be dead for he could serve humanity no longer.

The reality is that mankind has always had religion, and one must assume that religion does serve the needs of mankind. Since man is a curious, thinking creature who wants to know the answers to many puzzling questions, perhaps religion's usefulness is that it provides some of the answers. In the eyes of a scientist today some of the answers given by religion may seen ridiculous, but for most people they have been rewarding and helpful.

Man wants to know about creation, about reproduction and growth, the reality of incessant change, why life is followed by death, and what follows death. He wants to know why man must suffer pain, famines, disease, and a thousand other forms of suffering. If there is no better answer than that it is God's will, we wonder if the scientist can furnish better answers. Science can give us better answers in many areas of human endeavor, but there remains a host of questions that science today cannot answer. Science can explain the creation process in terms of the "Big Bang" theory, it can reduce material substance to minute particles of atoms, protons and neutrons, but the question that only God can answer is why and how creation really occurred.

But religion has a greater function than to answer questions, helping mankind survive the perils of life, especially the periods of war and violence. If man were to live in the proverbial Hobbesian world of anarchy and beastly greed and conflict, where man is free to prey upon his neighbors with no restraints, then the human race would disappear from the face of the earth. Man's most powerful urge is not sex, but to survive and avoid death. In a sense religion can be defined as the bearer of the gift of love for others, for love is the enemy of death. Religion is the social cement, the social gravity, that permits humans to operate in a community of harmony and peace. Religion provides the underpinnings of human morality and justice, of law and order, and of those social frameworks that we know as the family, the community, and the tribe or state. The survival motive includes also the impulse for sexual reproduction of the species. Religion gives support and protection to those forces of nature that provide mankind with food, protection from the storms of nature, and especially protection of the environment. Primitive people, living close to nature, knew they must protect the environment. The avoidance of death depends upon the capacity of God's bounty to provide the necessities for good health and long life, accompanied with the wisdom provided by man's intelligence. It is no wonder that primitive peoples made sacred the reproductive processes of all life, human, animal, and plant, for unless the sanction to be "fruitful and multiply" was fulfilled, death might well be the victor in the struggle for existence. All human societies have incorporated into their religions controls on the conduct of sexual behavior. All religions celebrate sexuality and fertility with appropriate rituals, sanctions, and symbols of reverence. Not only is human reproduction given divine reverence, but also the reproduction of plants and animals necessary for human survival. The Hindus revere the cow, Native Americans the buffalo and maize, Persian Mithraism honored the bull, and Orientals consider rice to be a fertility symbol. All societies have religious rites and rules to control marriage, birth, the onset of puberty, and the conditions under which sexual activity can be expressed. No culture grants complete freedom in the exercise of sex, even though some sexual practices approved in one culture may be deemed sinful and unlawful in other cultures.

But of all the human actions that religion seeks to control the most important is man's aggressive impulses to dominate other humans and to destroy them in the struggle for dominance. The history of the human race has revealed that violence, murder, and war has been more evident than peace and love. Unfortunately religion, theoretically an enemy of violence, has been responsible for much of the war and misery found in human history. Religion is the great force or cement that binds a given human group together. The greater the commitment the people have for their religious beliefs, the stronger and more powerful that group will become. If religion were to be destroyed, as happened in the course of the French and Russian Revolutions, then man would have to invent a substitute religion in the form of national patriotism, communism, or democracy. When religion and national patriotism or ethnic and national pride are joined together, then a powerful potential exists for revolution and war. Western Europe's Thirty Years' War (1618–48), a war fought between Protestants and Catholics, killed three million to four million people. The war between the Hindu Tamilis and the majority Buddhists in Sri Lanka during the 1980s is another one of the many religious wars in human history. Religion carries a mixed message to the human race, a message of love for all mankind as well as the message that my religion is better than yours and that I must prove it even by war. The movement toward religious toleration has been one of long struggle, and the goal of all religions to have peace on earth is far from being achieved. Among Christians religious toleration became necessary with the birth of Protestantism and the multiplicity of Christian sects.

Man knows that he does not live by bread alone. There must be more to life than mere physical survival while awaiting the inevitability of death. Seldom does man welcome death, even for an ideal cause, martyrdom or war. Religion provides another function for mankind's journey on earth. It answers the question of the mystery of death, and the greater mystery of what happens after death to man's body and soul. Mankind loves to live and to survive the many hazards of life while on earth. But mankind wants to believe that death is not the end of life. There must be an afterlife somewhere in the earth, in heaven, or in nirvana, we know not where. Among primitive people the afterlife world was assumed to be somewhere on earth. So corpses were buried with the common tools of earthly existence—food, water, clothes, and sometimes animals, plants, and slaves. Primitive people feared the return of the spirits from their dead ancestors, hence ancestral spirits had to be appeased by appropriate religious rites. If possible the dead body had to be protected from the elements by burial in caves and tombs, perhaps to await a future day of resurrection.

Most advanced religions in the Western world accepted the belief that the body after death ought to be preserved, a practice carried to an extreme by the ancient Egyptians. Jews, Muslims, and Christians all sought to preserve the body even though they knew that it was the soul that was imperishable. Yet there lingered the hope that somehow the physical body might also join the soul in a resurrection experience. In ancient Crete the graves were equipped with rainpipes so that the dead could satisfy their thirst. Platonists, Hindus, and Buddhists could accept the cremation of the body as proper since only the soul would survive death, destined to be reincarnated in some other body, human or animal, depending on the degree of evil possessed by the body of the original soul. Thus religion provides explanations for man's pain and sorrows on earth, proper care for and disposition of the body upon death, comfort and hope for the bereaved left behind, and the promise of a new life after death.

Finally religion inspires mankind to seek a more ideal world, "heaven on earth," a utopia in which people of all races, religions, and classes can live on earth in brotherhood and peace. War and violence among men will cease forever. No longer will humans need the sanctions of God and church, the laws and governors of the state, or the threat of violent punishment from any human source, to live in a state of peace. If man could follow the ideal human model exemplified by Jesus, or Moses, or Buddha, or Mohammed, or Confucius, the ideal human state could be realized. One universal moral precept that might bring to earth the ideal human society is the Golden Rule—Do unto others as you have them do to you. Or, as Confucius said, "Do not do unto others what you would not have them do unto you." Or, as Buddha said, "Hurt not others in ways that you yourself would find hurtful," or, as Islam declares, "No one of you is a believer until he desires for his brother that which he desires for himself," or, as Taoism says, "Regard your neighbor's gain as your own gain," or, as Hinduism says, "Do naught unto others which would cause pain if done to you," or, as Judaism states, "What is hateful to you, do not to your fellowman."

Thus for most, if not all human societies, religion becomes a part of the daily life and conduct of its members from birth to death, and even after death. Religion is a primary regulator of human behavior. It provides cohesiveness for the human group, and it minimizes the passions and violent nature of the human being.

The Problem of Evil

A question arises: Why are people evil and cruel? If a good God created man, why then is man evil? How can one God in a monotheistic religion have created both good and evil? In a polytheistic religion with many gods it is easy to have both good and evil gods, evil gods identified as Satan, the Devil, demons, or evil spirits. For example the Zoroastrian religion solves this dilemma of good and evil by providing for a god of goodness or light and a god of evil or of darkness. Job's query of God, "Why are good men punished for evils they did not commit?" might be answered: a good God, Jehovah, created mankind with the freedom of will to choose between good and evil. Therefore, man became evil when the first humans, Adam and Eve in Eden, then without sin, chose freely to disobey God, committed the sinful act that condemned all future generations to a life of sin until that future when they might be redeemed by a divine savior. In the eyes of St. Augustine redemption will come when all humans on earth live in the City of God, a theocracy in which a church or religion will order the lives of humans according to the laws and dictates of God.

Clergy, Ritual, and Dogma

All religions have ways to communicate with the supernatural powers, from which humans hope to receive beneficial blessings, or, if not blessings, then a minimization of the pain and destruction the supernatural powers can inflict upon them. First, the supernatural or God power must be cast in a form and language that mere mortals can understand. God must be depicted in words and images familiar to the common people. God is best pictured in a human form, often represented in the image of a prophet or teacher, or as pictures and statues of a human form that is God.

Secondly, special and mysterious knowledge about God beyond the comprehension of the average human needs an interpreter, one with a special insight to God's world. These special persons are the priests, the rabbis, the mullahs, the gurus, the shamans, the witch doctors and other specialists in the knowledge of God.

Thirdly, these God communicators have access to the sacred scriptures, the songs and myths, the rituals, the music and dance, the prayers and sacred words, all things which go into the structure of a given religion.

Fourthly, an aura of mystery and magic, the ability of intermediary agents to ignore or override the laws of nature is needed to convince believers that they live in the presence of God.

Fifthly, the people need to acknowledge the presence of God by some visible and audible response, such as prayers of thanksgiving, festivals and pilgrimages, bowed heads and clasped hands, kneeling or sitting in a special position, as in Hindu meditation. People demonstrate their love for God by acts of charity, or chastity, or physical suffering, or erecting a holy temple, synagogue, or church in honor of God. The use of water, candles, fire, the burning of incense or other perfumes, the wearing of special garb, usually white, as a symbol of purity, enduring the pain of scarification or circumcision, and a host of other rites and rituals are found among the religions of the world.

Finally, all religions have a code of ethics that tradition says came from the gods. Moral laws and ethical codes promote the well-being of the group, be it a family, a clan or community, a tribe or a nation, through acts of charity, mutual aid, and a body of fellow men who are willing to give their lives in times of struggle and war to protect their God and their fellow men. However, the moral law needs institutions to assist the divine power in commanding obedience to the law. Even Buddha, who saw no need for a church government or a priesthood, found that it was necessary to organize monasteries with rules and rulers if his message was to be expanded and perpetuated. Therefore, religions need rules and laws, prescribed dos and don'ts, with a body of judges and governors who can execute the laws and provide the appropriate penalties for disobedience. If the law and the governors are inadequate to command obedience, then a church would hope that the power of the state could join with the powers of the church to secure a more obedient religious society. The most potent law-enforcing weapon a religion has is not the temporal forces on earth, but the fear of divine punishment on earth as well as in the hereafter.

Fundamentalism vs. Critical Inquiry

A troublesome issue for religions today is to decide whether religion and its interpretation of the God-power is writ in stone, forever to be accepted as the only truth, never to be changed, or whether religion, like other aspects of life, over the passage of time evolves into new forms with new concepts of truth. Change seems to be the one constant in God's creation. Is religion an exception? Should twentieth-century man be free to interpret old religions in the light of new knowledge gained through the study of science and technology? For most of Christian history science and religion have been in conflict, since Christian leaders believe that Scripture is inerrant and not subject to change. A student of the Judeo-Christian religion must be aware that the God in the Old Testament is not the same God depicted in the New Testament. A wrathful, commanding Jehovah became a loving, forgiving Father. Albert Einstein in his *The World as I See It* (1935) speaks of three stages in the evolution of the Judeo-Christian God. First there was the fear stage, when Jehovah was a wrathful God who punished sinners harshly. Next appeared a morality era, in which the fear of God's wrath was modified by transferring obedience to God's will, which might be capricious, to God's law, the Mosaic law. Then came the love concept, as preached by the later Jewish prophets and Jesus Christ. God is found in the practice of love relationships to all human kind, the brotherhood-of-man ideal.

The fact is that religions do change, even though slowly and reluctantly. How many Christian seminaries in the 1800s offered courses in comparative religions? Probably none. The study of religion as historical science, even the critical study of one's own religion, came first in the late 1800s. The beginnings of a scientific study of Christianity occurred in the 1800s. German scholars, Friedrich Schleiermacher and David Friedrich Strauss, in the early part of the nineteenth century began historical studies of the life of Jesus and the history of the Christian church. Since then more critical studies have been made by Albert Schweitzer, Rudolf Bultman, Dietrich Bonhoeffer and many others. Yet many Christians refuse to recognize change and the need for historical analysis of Scripture and dogma. In his novel *Rogers' Version,* John Updike suggests that man no longer needs a God to be proved by reason and science. Instead people want to know God through faith, the world of mystery and the supernatural. Yet the issue of change, evolution, and science creates great tension not only in Christianity today, but also in the Jewish and Islamic faiths. Fundamentalist Christians charge that the enemy of religion is not only atheism and communism, but also "secular humanism," a term that seems to describe the views of modern liberal Christians who wish to bring Christianity into the twentieth-century world of science, people who have a vision of a world brotherhood of man, free from the scourge of war and religious strife.

In the modern world there are those religious skeptics and critics who denounce all religions as superstituous nonsense, rendering more harm to the human race than good. In the United States probably fewer than 10 percent of the population hold such extreme views. Even though half of Americans do not attend any church, most claim to believe in God and religion.

The serious critics of organized religion are the atheists and agnostics. Atheists deny the existence of God since sensory experiences cannot confirm it. Yet no atheist denies that there exists some force or power beyond man's power to control. Probably the most current version of atheism is expressed by Karl Marx and other communists when they declare that, since "religion is the opiate of the people," eventually the nonsense of religion and church will be replaced by science. Closely related to atheism is the belief that, "I am not sure about God." Agnostics doubt the existence of God since God cannot be proved by scientific analysis. They do not say that God does not exist. The door to God's wisdom is not shut completely. A small crack in the door is left open.

One new development in modern religion is an ecumenical movement among the major world religions to come together in a recognition of their mutual right to exist in harmony and equality. The hope is that the concept that one's religion is always the best can yield to the position that all religions serve a common goal and hence all are worthy of common respect and the right to live.

Another development in modern religion is the attempt to join science and religion in a new "cosmic" or "process" religion. Cosmic theology is found in the writings of Albert Einstein, Alfred North Whitehead, Harvey Pothoff, and Mortimer Adler. In his *How to Think About God,* Adler seeks to prove the existence of God by reasoning that since the cosmos is in existence, it had to have a cause, and since cosmos continues to exist, with no finite limits to its time, and in no future time does cosmos seem to experience death or a state of no existence, then whatever caused cosmos must be God or a supreme being. However, mankind has no way of knowing whether God is limited or unlimited in his power, or whether God is just, kind, loving, moral, forgiving, or anything else. Since cosmos is caused by God, cosmos continues because of God's love for his creation and that compels God to continue the existence of cosmos.

The basic tenets of a cosmic religion are:

1. Life and all therein reflect the cosmic view that the earth is a minor, minuscule part of the total universe, and that man on earth is no longer lord and master of the earth. Man is only one of God's creations, and he must learn to live within the limits established by God.

2. The universe is energy, always alive and in flux. Human existence is one of constant change and unpredictability. Man must learn to live with change, and to pronounce change good.

3. Cosmic God is not anthropromorphic. He is not a father figure. God

has no human aspects, no ears to hear or eyes to see. God created the universe and the natural laws of science. God is but another term for atoms, electrons, gravity, the movement of the planets, and all the other phenomena of nature. God is limited by the dynamics of the universe. He cannot be manipulated by human intervention. The laws of nature apply in all aspects of life, thus miracles are ruled out as valid explanations for any event or condition.

4. In the cosmic view God cannot answer or solve problems. Prayer can only induce humans to use their intelligence more effectively to solve their problems and to create a happier world. Prayer did not cure the disease of polio. The intelligence of Jonas Salk did. Prayer awakens people to the needs and pains of the world. Meditation opens the mind not so much to God as to the deeper meanings of human existence and how human needs can be met by human intervention.

5. Traditional Christians charge that cosmic religion removes Christ from the religious scene. Cosmic theologians reply, "Not at all." Christ's message of love, charity, and peace are universal human values that will never perish, for if they do then mankind will perish in the flames of greed and violence. Harvey Pothoff in his *God and the Celebration of Life* (p. 50) gives the essence of cosmic religion in these lines:

> The time has come to challenge the axiom that theology deals only with the fixed, the permanent, the unchanging. The time has come to seek an understanding of the meaning of God in relation to a dynamic, relational, and evolutionary world, and to rethink the doctrine of God, man, salvation, and related doctrines in terms that reflect contemporary perception of the way things are.

Ecumenism and One World Religion

In a shrinking world caused by better communication, transportation, international trade and business alliances, and new and better personal relationships formed across the boundaries of national states, the time is arriving when the leaders of the world's religious communities need to come together and seek means by which all religions are better understood and tolerated and common goals are projected. Until the religions of the world can find peace and mutual cooperation within their own ranks, then the chances for peace among nations in the realms of politics and economics seem remote.

The twentieth-century Christian world is seeking ecumenical movements to bring together the Protestant denominations that split over the slave issue. Catholics are seeking closer relations between Roman Catholics and Greek Orthodox Catholics. Roman Catholics and Protestants are making moves to understand each other better. Pope John XXIII invited Protestant observers to Vatican II and Roman Catholics and the Anglican Church in England have held exploratory meetings looking forward to some future reconciliation. Similarly, Jews, Christians, and Muslims have found that they can meet and explore avenues for better understanding between the faiths.

Throughout history a few idealists have had a vision of "One World, One Faith." Perhaps Jesus offered the world this hope of one faith. Certainly St. Augustine in his *City of God* projected the possibility of one religion and one world, albeit a Christian one. The eighteenth-century deists dreamed of a universal religion based on science and reason. Thomas Jefferson sought to find a God more universal and more in tune with the new sciences than the God Jehovah. The deists found their God in the forces of nature or natural law and reason, a religion beyond creed and a personal God. The deist God was the supreme creator of all things and the prime mover of all things. Utopian visionaries like Francis Bacon or H. G. Wells have offered the hope that mankind can come together and share the problems and blessings of the world in a world state and a universal faith.

In a search for a common world faith, one that might combine the best attributes of all major world religions, the ideal of a world brotherhood of man and peace on earth, perhaps the Bahai faith is a model. The Bahai faith was born in the nineteenth-century from the teachings of a Persian (Iranian) prophet, Baha Ullah ("Glory of God"), who lived from 1844 to 1892. The son of a wealthy public official, he claimed that he was a divine prophet in line with prophets like Jesus, Mohammed, and Buddha. He proclaimed the unity of all religions and universal peace for humanity. The Bahai tenets have been summarized in the book *Great Themes of Life,* by Eric Bowes. Bahai declares that all humans, regardless of race, are equal in the eyes of God. Both sexes are equal. There shall be no slavery or discrimination because of race. All humans worship one God, but God must be found by each person individually, and not through the intervention of a priesthood or an institutionalized church. Religion must be in harmony with reason and science. Universal education and a universal language are prerequisites for a universal faith: the ultimate goal for humans on earth is world peace, the abolition of war, and the distribution of the world's resources on a more equitable basis. Bahai temples are built in the form of a hexagon, reflecting the unity of the six major world religions. Two of the best known Bahai temples are located in Haifa, Israel, the world headquarters for Bahai, and in Wilmette, Illinois, a Chicago suburb. Probably no more than four million people have joined the Bahai movement. Most members are found in Iran, Western Europe, and the United States. In the United States Bahai has appealed especially to black people. Since 1979, when Ayatollah Khomeini and his Shiite revolutionaries came to power in Iran, Bahai followers have been persecuted severely there. Over two hundred have been executed, and many of Iran's original 300,000 Bahai followers have fled.

The dream of one world, one religion, one language, and a world free from the terrors of fear, greed, and war is by no means about to be realized. Even unity among Christians, divided by hundreds of different sects, each firmly convinced that their interpretation of the gospel of Christ is the only true one, is unlikely in the foreseeable future.

2

Prehistoric Cosmic Religions

Ancient Roots

Most humans view their family history favorably and with pride, unless they suspect that dark shadows of shame would be revealed if they investigate too closely their ancestoral heritage. By analogy, some Christians hesitate to explore the religions of early humans, pagan religions, lest they find that the prehistoric and pre-Christian religions contributed many of the beliefs and practices of the Christian faith. In Christianity a historian can find many pagan "carry-overs" such as the celebration of Halloween, a fall New Year's festival of the ancient Britons; or the celebration of Christmas, which nearly coincides with the winter solstice, marking the time when light and fertility begins its annual return to Earth. This sun celebration is an almost universal event recognized by all religions. Examples include May Day, an ancient spring festival of the Celts honoring the May Queen, goddess of fertility, the may pole being a phallic symbol; Easter, which also has its origins in a pagan fertility celebration of the spring solstice, or a reenactment of the Greek Dionysian sexual orgy symbolized by the use of eggs and rabbits.[1] Other pagan rites borrowed by Christians are a host of purification symbols, baptism, holy water, the burning of incense, and the wearing of white garments. The veneration of saints and the exorcism of evil spirits have pagan connotations, and some historians see a link between the Christian Eucharist and the Persian worship of the bull, a symbol of God power, when a bull would be sacrificed and its blood drunk in a sacred rite called taurobolium. In this manner man became a part of God.

The religions of early man are usually called "prehistoric" or "primitive." "Prehistoric" suggests religion belonging only to Stone Age people when in reality many peoples in Africa, Asia, Australia, and the Americas worship prehistoric-type gods. Even Japanese Shintoism retains many elements characteristic of a prehistoric religion. The more common label for the religions of early man is

25

"primitive." But too often the word implies something inferior or even evil. It would be a mistake to assume that the religion of the native American Navajos, which has served them for thousands of years in a satisfying manner, is somehow inferior. In his 1959 *Cosmos and History,* Mircea Eliade has suggested a better term, "cosmic religion," religion characterized by finding God or the divine in all things created in nature, the universe, the solar system, the earth, all living creatures, plants and animals, the human species. The "cosmic" world is populated by a host of spirits that dwell within all of God's handiwork and that control the destiny of man from birth to death. It is from the spirit world that humans derive the means for survival here on earth and after death in the other world.

The continuation of life is found in the worship of human ancestors and in the sanctity of the family and the reproductive process by which life is passed on to future generations. The use of the term "cosmic" for the religions of early man should not be confused with the twentieth-century liberal interpretation of Christine doctrine that hopes to unite science and religion in a harmonious and acceptable manner.

Knowledge about prehistoric cultures and religions is limited to what archaeologists and paleontologists can "dig" from fossil beds, caves, and graves—such items as bones, stone images, ornaments, tools, and cave wall paintings. Since religion is primarily a construct of mental images and emotions it is most difficult to extract the psychological essence of ancient religions from cold stone and bone. Scientists must either use controlled guesswork or rely on the visible evidence drawn from living cultures that are today in a state of development; these cultures are similar to the cultures and religions of early man. Therefore, students of cosmic religions rely heavily on these living cosmic societies, which are found largely in the undeveloped parts of the world. Also it must be assumed that oral traditions were passed on from generation to generation over a period of thousands of years in a reasonably faithful, accurate manner, so that there is a good link between modern primitive and prehistoric peoples.

Genesis: The Modern Account

If a contemporary prophet were to write a new Genesis, a new account of creation, he would begin with the claim that God created the universe some fifteen billion years ago, when the "Big Bang" released all of the essential building blocks for the creation of all things, living and not living. These building blocks consist of many forms of pulsating energy, atoms, electrons, protons, neutrons, anti-protons, pulsars, quarks, and undoubtedly many other particles yet to be discovered. Under certain conditions those material objects evolve into what we know as suns, planets, mountains, streams, plants, animals, and those creatures we call humans.

Some two and a half billion years ago on earth these minute particles had gone through a sufficient number of levels of combination to give birth to simple, one-celled creatures. A billion years ago a larger, more complex nucleated cell became the essential structure for all plants and animals. Four million years ago a human-like primate, a hominid, appeared in Africa. This creature was the first to walk upright, but it was still more ape than human. About three million years ago a more advanced man-creature appeared on earth, homo habilis, who was a tool-using animal. The best remains of homo habilis were found in Tanzania by Richard Leakey in 1968. Over the passage of time these creatures ceased to exist; only their fossilized bones remain.

About one and a half million years ago, homo erectus appeared on earth, an animal more like man than ape. These prehuman beings were more intelligent than earlier manlike animals, and could use fire and more complex tools. They were the first "humans" to populate the earth when they migrated from Africa to southern Europe, known there as the Neanderthal man, and to China and Java.

Some one hunded thousand years ago there appeared a fully evolved human being, fully erect, even more intelligent, who could make and use even more complex tools, such as stone axes and knives. This creature learned to domesticate plants and animals such as dogs, cows, and horses. These creatures were called homo sapiens, the wise men. By ten thousand years ago homo sapiens had moved from Africa to all parts of the world, even to America. Their cultures evolved from Old Stone Age to New Stone Age, then to a Bronze age, and eventually to an Iron Age. Through these ages successively more superior tools and weapons were fashioned, enabling man to dominate the earth. Man learned to spin and weave, to make boats and shelters, to plant crops and acquire surplus foods, and to express the joy of beauty in jewelry, painting, and sculpture.

Scientists disagree as to where on earth homo sapiens first appeared. Both African and Asian "Edens" have their proponents, but the evidence is shifting in the direction of an African origin. Current thinking is that homo sapiens moved from central Africa to southern Europe, then to Asia Minor, from there into Asia, and from Asia across the Bering Strait to America. Over the period of a hundred thousand years homo sapiens evolved into the several racial types found among modern men. In the same manner unique social and cultural patterns evolved, included marriage and family structures, forms of religious worship, and social organizations and governments.

The Earth as Mother Goddess

Prehistoric people were aware of their dependence on natural forces in the environment for their survival. Nature provided the plants and animals for their food. Early man learned to fish and hunt for his food. Later Neolithic man found that farming provided a more abundant supply of food than fishing and hunting did. No matter how man secured his food he believed that his bounty came from God or nature, and he learned to give thanks and reverence to the nature gods for it. Mother Earth, the direct source of food and shelter, was the first goddess to be worshiped. As a female figure, the earth goddess was seen as the source of all creation, even human reproduction. The natural configurations of the earth, mountains, valleys, rivers and oceans, were seen as life-producing forces. In India, the river Ganges became a sacred object since its origins were said to have come from the head of the god Shiva. The Havasu Indians in the Grand Canyon of Arizona regarded the Havasu Falls as a symbol of their gods. The Plains Indians of North America believed that the buffalo was a sacred being, and if the buffalo was ever to be destroyed, then the gods would destroy the Indian way of life.

Mother Earth was a symbol of fertility for prehistoric people. The earth goddess was portrayed in stone images as a pregnant female with bloated breasts and abdomen. Such images, "Venus" figures, have been found in burial sites across Europe from France to Russia.

Many of the early religions have represented Mother Earth in the form of a female goddess. In Egypt she was Isis; in Phoenicia and Syria she was Astarte (Easter); in Babylon she was Ishtar; in Greece she was Demeter or Aphrodite; and in Japan she was Amaterasu. It was from Mother Earth that primitive people derived their subsistence, and it was from Mother Earth that these people found the creation of the human race, or, at least, their human origins.

Today feminist groups are quick to point out that not always was the human species ruled by male patriarchs, despite what might be the divine order as portrayed in the Bible and the Koran. In the societies that worshiped female deities the social system was matriarchal, one in which the family line of descent was traced through the mother and not the father, and the mother played a dominant role in decision-making processes.

Merlin Stone concluded, "After reading these and numerous other studies on the subject, there was no doubt in my mind of the existence of the ancient female religion, nor that in the earliest of theological systems woman was deified as the principal and supreme divine being. . . . That this religion preceded the male religion by thousands of years was also quite evident."[2] The historical record of religions in the Mediterranean area and the Orient would indicate that female deities prevailed until sometime in the late Neolithic era, that is, about 3000 to 2000 B.C., when migrations of northern tribes of Indo-European people moved into the regions where female Goddesses prevailed and replaced them with male deities. With the dominant male gods came also a social structure that placed husbands and fathers over wives and mothers. A patriarchal system of control, both in the state or tribe and in the family, replaced the former matriarchal system of control. For example, in India the Indo-European or Aryan tribes from Persia entered India and conquered the native, dark-skinned tribes who worshiped female goddesses, the most revered one being the goddess Devi. Worship of Devi was replaced by that of the warrior Gods Indra and Rama.

Christianity and Islam derive their patriarchal orientation and male-dominant social system from the ancient Hebrews, who, in turn, may have inherited their preference for a patriarchal society from contacts with various Indo-European cultures. Hence, Judaism and the Old Testament tend to depict the symbol of womanhood, Eve, as an evil temptress who lured the male Adam into a condition of mortal sin, which condemned all of his progeny to a life of sin and separation from God. Eve is cast into a pit of pain and slavery, always to be ruled by her husband. In her book *The Language of the Goddess,* Marija Gimbatas reminds us that in Greek mythology the poet Hesiod relates the story of Pandora, a parallel to the evil Eve. Pandora was created on orders from an angry Zeus, who sought revenge upon Prometheus, the first man born of a mother goddess, for giving fire (civilization) to mankind. Pandora represents the fall of womankind from power and the rise of a male-dominated society in which male divinities supersede the once dominant female goddesses.

Early Ritual and Beliefs

Anthropologists believe that most primitive peoples buried their dead with special services and rites, all of which suggests that these early men had a special concern about death and what happens to the body and soul after death. Often the corpse was placed in an east-west axis, as if the body's soul would follow the course of the sun across the sky. Prehistoric corpses might also be covered with a red dye, which might represent blood, a symbol for life on earth and life after death. The Mayan basketball game was a symbolic struggle between Mayan heroes and the lords of death, played in the hope that the heroes would conquer death. At Stonehenge in England is found a gigantic monument, perhaps astronomical as well as religious, erected in memory of the dead. American Indians in Mexico, Central America, Peru, and the United States built pyramids to house and memorialize the dead. Egyptians built elaborate pyramids and cliff tombs to preserve and to honor the bodies of deceased ancestors, especially those of royal and noble ancestry.

Although these early primitive or cosmic cultures for the most part did not possess the art of writing, there is nonwritten evidence that these people had some basic concepts about life and death. Beliefs were orally transmitted from generation to generation in the form of myths, sagas, and songs. These cosmic cultures recognized the need for special persons to interpret the world of God to them. Persons gifted with special powers and knowledge would be priests, shamans, sorcerers, and witch doctors.[3] All of these specialists not only had knowledge about gods and spirits, but possessed magical powers by which they could protect their people from all harm or punish evil forces. A special gift was the one of prophecy, the ability to foretell the future. Animals were believed to be messengers of the gods. The Aztecs used the eagle, Egyptians and Hindus used snakes, and the Jews regarded doves in this way.

Cosmic religions recognized that some external forces, beyond man's control, were responsible for all of creation. The sun was most often given first place among the natural forces of creation. These forces would be given human forms as gods and goddesses to which humans could relate. The central god among the Egyptians was the sun god, Ra; the Babylonians worshiped Shamash, a sun god; and the Greeks recognized Apollo as a sun god. American Indians also made the sun a central object for worship.

Not only the sun, but all of the life-giving natural elements, earth, the other planets, the sky, rivers, mountains, plants and animals were objects for worship. Of all the evidence left by cosmic men the most intriguing is the cave wall drawings of animals found in the caves of Niaux in the Pyrennes mountains, the Pech-Merle and Lascaux Caves in southern France. Cave drawings are found also in the Altamira Caves of Spain, plus some two hundred cave sites scattered throughout Europe. What do these animal drawings represent? Why were they made? Are they only drawings to satisfy the urge to create? Were they messages to the gods? Were they hex signs placed on the hunted animals so that they might be more easily killed? Or are they symbolic representations of the spirit world that was thought to dwell within the bodies of the animals? No one knows for certain. Many of the drawings of bison, deer, and horses seem to represent pregnant animals, so they may be symbols of fertility. They may also represent some sacred relationship between man and his gods. The drawings may be expressions of gratitude for the food provided by the animals and their spirits, or they might be expressions of guilt for having killed a brother creature. Among the Eskimos whenever a seal is killed the hunter must perform a ritual sacrifice over the body of the seal before carving the body for food. Some scholars have suggested that the caves may have been temples for worship in which the animal spirits could be honored. Only a few drawings of humans have been found and among them more images of men than of women. At least these early cave dwellers were reasonably talented artists, the forerunners of later Michelangelos and Rembrandts.

Cosmic religions evolved sacred songs, music, dances, magical incantations and prayers, sacrifices, of both animals and humans, all of which were designed to communicate with and to please the gods. The Aztecs sacrificed virgin girls to appease the gods. The priests or shamans might tell the future by examining the entrails of animals, or by throwing dice, or by the use of hallucinatory drugs. The peyote ceremonies of the Navajo Indians is a good example of how cosmic religions use special drugs to enhance the spiritual emotions and visions of the worshipers. The peyote ceremony pays tribute to all of the sacred elements in nature, such as fire, water, and air. At the conclusion of a daylong ceremony food is served, each peyote devotee takes a small amount in a symbolic act of saying "amen" or "thanks to God."[4]

All cosmic religions have common modes of relating to their gods and spirits. There is reverence expressed for the forces or spirits of nature on which their lives depend for food, shelter, and protection from natural catastrophes. Special thanks are offered to the gods for the blessings of fertility, the reproduction of plants, animals, and children. Then man needs the possession of magical skills by which he can assure his survival and minimize the dangers to life. These include special incantations, prayers and songs, and the use of spiritual specialists. Cosmic people had concern for the care and disposal of the dead, a concern that might also reveal the hope for an extended life into eternity. In his *Worship of Nature* (*The Golden Bough*) James Frazer says that early man believed that all of nature was alive with unseen spirits, like the pantheists who find God in all things of nature. Usually, however, one special spirit or god was given a superior position over all other spirits, a first step toward the worship of one God, or monotheism. Edward Tylor thought that ancient man considered the spirits of the universe, a belief in which he called "animism," to live in the human body, and to continue to live after death, thereby causing the living to revere dead ancestors. In truth, we can never know for certain what cosmic men in prehistoric times really believed about the gods, their world, and how man relates to his fellow men.

If knowledge of prehistoric cosmic religions were limited to what has been collected from caves, tombs, and fossil beds, then all that could be written about the religion of Stone Age people would be that they had some awareness of the forces in nature over which they had no control; that they believed in the presence of spirit forces within the animals upon which they depended for food; that they thought spirits could control the reproduction of animals and humans; that they believed that spirits of dead ancestors must be appeased by proper burial rites and that ancestral spirits must be honored; and that perhaps they had some concept of an afterlife. For the details of cosmic religions we must resort to those available sources found among peoples living today in remote parts of the world whose religions may resemble the religions of prehistoric people. Or we must study the written records of ancient people whose religions were also in the cosmic stage of development.

Space permits the presentation of only a few samples of cosmic religions from both the past and the present day.

Modern Descendants of Prehistoric Religion

SHINTOISM

Japan's Shintoism, which was the state religion until 1945, is a type of cosmic religion that gives value to a large body of well-educated people today. Shinto means the "way of the gods." It is a religion that finds in the beauty and symmetry of nature manifestations of the gods. Divinity is found in all of nature, from Mt. Fuji to cherry blossoms, bonsai trees, and formal gardens. All aspects of nature (*kami*) are to be worshiped, including things beyond man's control. A sun goddess of fertility becomes the principal object of worship. This goddess, Amaterasu, is reputed to be the founder of the ruling dynasty in Japan, hence Shinto became the state religion. The essence of Shintoism, *kami,* is the divine spirit representing those things that seem to have properties of mystery, are awe inspiring, and have superior power. This is found in all things in heaven and on earth—mountains and rivers, sun and moon, animals and plants, and human beings. Persons who possess power, like the emperor, become the ruling class, hence there is a divine basis for a ruling class in the feudal period of Japanese history. Shinto accepts the material world as good, while Buddhists view the world as evil, yet both religions are practiced in Japan.

Shinto erects shrines and temples to several deities, the most famous in honor of the goddess Amaterasu, located at Ise on the south coast. Since Shinto gives great respect to ancestors, Japanese homes have altars for shrines for daily prayers. Special holy days are observed. An important one is New Year's Day when the gods come to earth. The people welcome the arrival of the gods with special prayers, gifts, feasts, and the drinking of sake.

Shinto has no Bible or special statement of creed. Shinto respects other religions, especially Buddhism, since most Japanese observe the rites of both religions and pray at both shrines. They frequently celebrate weddings in Shinto temples and funerals in Buddhist temples. The Buddhist Todaiji shrine at Nara is a very popular shrine. Shinto has little idea of any life beyond death. If anything the afterworld is a dark and evil place.

Before World War II emperor worship was a patriotic duty, but since then Shinto has been limited by American fiat to being a religion separated from the state. Shinto identification is confined now to its temples, shrines, and order of priests. Shinto temples are marked by a Tori gate before the entrance way. In Japan there are over one hundred thousand shrines and temples and over two hundred thousand priests who wear white robes. In general the priesthood is hereditary. Sons inherit the father's position. The chief function of a priest is to offer prayers to the gods for blessings for the people and to preside at weddings and festivals such as the Gion Festival, held annually in July in Kyoto.

NATIVE AMERICAN RELIGION

Other forms of currently living cosmic religions can be found in Africa, the South Pacific, and America. Those closest to home are the primitive, cosmic forms of religion among the six hundred or so tribes of North American Indians. Although many Native Americans have left their tribal homes for new ways of life in American cities, most continue to live on tribal reservations in remote areas isolated from the contamination of the prevailing Christian, capitalistic world of the white man, judgments made in terms of Native American cultural values. It is true that Native Americans have accepted many aspects of the non-Indian world, such things as tools, weapons, farm animals, cars and trucks, and obnoxious recreational addictions to alcohol and drugs. However, in general the Native American world has refused to accept those religious, ethical, and personal values that most modern Christians consider of unquestionable value. Throughout the period when the Christian way of life has impinged on their ways, Native Americans have universally resisted the efforts of Christian missionaries.

Often where it appears that the missionaries have had some conversion success, a closer analysis reveals that Christianity is only a thin veneer covering the heart and soul of traditional beliefs. For some years I was a teacher in an Indian mission college in Oklahoma. I was invited to attend the funeral service of an Osage Indian student. His parents were nominally Catholic, so a Catholic service was held in the morning. In the early afternoon came a Baptist service. Finally in the late afternoon came a service held in the cemetery, where the Osage Indian rites were performed. It was this service that would truly promise eternal peace for the boy's soul. The graves were covered with a small wooden dog-like house for the rest and protection of the souls.

My experience teaching Native American high school and junior college students representing thirty or more different tribes ranging from Alaskan Eskimos to the many tribes throughout the continental United States taught me that Native Americans have difficulty when asked to behave as white Americans do. They have trouble accepting the Puritan concepts of sexual morality. To them premarital sex is no unredeemable sin, nor are illegitimate children. But the one point of greatest conflict is the inability of the individual Native American to resist the pressures of the social group, be it the family or the larger tribal society. Native Americans are oriented to the values and welfare of the group, whereas the majority of Americans accentuate the value of personal freedom and individual achievement. It was frustrating for me as a non–Native American to teach classes where the students were unable to give responses, either verbal or facial, to the comments I made or the questions I posed. In class the students acted as if they were stone images, yet in a one-to-one relationship I found them alert and interested, with a real sense of humor. Only by written exercises and examinations could student reactions be discerned. The students were silenced by the social pressure to never excel above any other member of the group. There prevailed a predominant sense of democratic equality, a social condition that recognized women as being equal with men, and the less able as being equal to the more fortunate in ability and wealth.

The Native American has much in common with the views of the environmentalists concerning how mankind should use the resources God has given them. Christians were commanded to use and to dominate all of God's creation on earth, the plants and animals, the forests and the exhaustible resources of coal, oil, and iron. For the Native American the natural heritage is sacred, and great care must be taken to minimize its abuse. Land is not to be sold and committed to private ownership, for all land belongs to the tribe. In the manner of St. Francis, Native Americans share their love for the birds and animals; all creatures are our brothers and sisters. In Native American religions many animals possess sacred powers, and hence must be protected as if they were divine. The food-producing deer and buffalo, the eagle, the serpents, the sly fox, the bear, and the beaver were among the animals most frequently endowed with spiritual powers for good. Among the southwestern Native American a favorite symbol of evil was the coyote, famous for being deceitful and tricking people into being evil. The sun, the moon, the sky, Mother Earth and all therein and thereon were gods to be worshiped. Although all Native Americans accept some form of a cosmic religion and have many rituals, myths, and divine beings in common, each tribe will have its own interpretations and variations. Hence for a more detailed account of a typical

Native American religion, let us look at the Navajo tribe. It is the largest Native American tribe, about 170,000 people living in a large area that covers parts of Arizona, New Mexico, Utah, and Colorado.

Originally the Navajos lived in northwestern Canada. They migrated to their present location about A.D. 1300. They and their cousins, the Apaches, were roving nomadic hunters who were able to conquer the peaceful, agricultural Pueblo Indians of the Southwest. Over time the Navajos assimilated with the Pueblos, intermarrying and absorbing the agricultural mode of living. Hence the Navajos became sheep-herders, small-scale farmers, basket and blanket weavers, and silversmiths. However the Navajo religion remained largely unchanged.

The name, Navajo, meaning "people of the big fields," was given to them by the Spanish. The Navajos refer to themselves as the "Dineh," "the People." Navajos see themselves as people chosen by their gods to live at the center of the universe in a land called "Dinetah." Like most humans the Navajos want to know about their origins and how they came to be on earth, so they have a Genesis story, of which there are several versions. In the beginning of the People, all life lived in a dark, misty world somewhere in the bowels of the earth, in the First World. Into this dark world without sun or moon was born First Man and First Woman from ears of corn. When the wind blew the breath of life into an ear of white corn there arose the First Man, a symbol of power, intelligence and light, born on the most sacred east side of the world. From the west side came the First Woman, born from an ear of yellow corn. She represented darkness and death. Hence corn or maize becomes life for the Navajos.

But life in the First World became intolerable as the People quarreled and fought. So First Man and First Woman and all other creatures move upward to the Blue or Second World. Here First Man encountered many new animals, and some of them First Man killed. Then First Man learned that these animals could bestow upon him blessings so he restored the slain animals to life. In this world there appears the tricky Coyote, the source of evil and trouble. Coyote caused so much dissension that the People moved upward into the Yellow or Third World.

In this world there was a great river and from this river Coyote had captured a baby water monster. The gods were so angry that a flood was sent to destroy all creatures. By good fortune or favor of the gods a strong reed or stem sprouted from the water. This reed became the way by which the People (animals included) could climb to the safety of a higher world, the Fourth World, or the Glittering World. After all were saved Coyote was prevailed upon to return the baby monster to the river, after which the floods receded.

The Fourth World was to be Paradise, a land of peace and plenty. Locust was the first one to claim this good land. First Man and First Woman brought soil from the Third World, which was used to build five mountains, four of which were placed in line with the compass points, east, west, north and south. East was to be the most sacred of all points, the place from which the sun was to rise. These four mountains become the boundaries of Navajo territory. For example, the south is Mt. Taylor; the west is today's San Francisco Peaks; the east is the Sangre de Cristo Range in Colorado; and the north is Hesperus Peak. In the center was built a mountain, the center of the universe, called the Mountain, around which moving was done. In this manner the Land was defined and made sacred; it is the most sacred trust from the gods. No one shall desecrate or despoil the Land, a trust that modern environmentalists could endorse and emulate.

The People had come from a world of darkness and they needed to have light. With the aid of Coyote's intelligence First Man and First Woman created the sky, then filled it with stars. But more light was needed so the sun and the moon were set in the sky. But how were the sun and the moon to be moved across the sky? Two carriers in the form of horsemen were found who were willing to move the sun and the moon, but at a considerable price from the People—the advent of death. For every day of service the carriers demanded that one of the People (animals) must die. Thus death for the Navajo becomes a part of the natural way. Death does not come as a price the human race must pay for original sin. For the Navajo the only life is the present one. There is no afterlife, no place for the administration of rewards and punishments, for acts done during one's lifetime.

Once the People had light it was time to plant the seeds that First Man and First Woman brought from the Third World. Turkey offered multicolored corn seeds, and Big Snake provided the seeds for melons and pumpkins. Then a house for the People was needed. So Talking God taught the People how to build separate houses for men and women, and a house that is reserved for religious services. This house, a hogan, is a representation of the world of the four sacred mountains. Each corner of the hogan must be placed in line with the cardinal points of the compass, with the door facing toward the east, the sacred land of the rising sun. A domed roof covers the hogan with a hole through which the fireplace smoke can leave, but also so family spirits can arise to the sky. In the meantime the four seasons had been created, and everything seemed to be in readiness for the appearance of human people. But great trouble descended upon the People, the curse of licentious sex and adultery.

One day First Man caught Turquoise Boy having sex with First Woman. The People were in doubt, not knowing what to do. So First Man called together some of the leaders for advice on what to do. The decision was that the sexes must be separated, so the men left to live across the river from the women. Four of the overactive sexually males, Turquoise Boy and three others, were left to satisfy the women. After days of a sexual orgy the four men were exhausted and impotent. The women wanted the men to return, and the men needed the women. However, before the People could be one again, both men and women had to undergo purification by taking a sweat bath.

But the Fourth World remained in torment. After the sins of sexual excess terrible monsters appeared in the Land. No peace could be found until the monsters were destroyed. Also there remained the need for the creation of true human beings, the Navajos of today. Legends differ as to how the humans arrived. One version says that First Man and First Woman married and soon had twin hermaph-rodite sons who matured in four days and gave birth to children who matured in four days who also had children, in short order, so the population growth exceeded all expectations.

Another version is more complex and contains also the solution to the problem of the monsters. One day First Man found a baby girl, wrapped in a cloud, whose father was Dawn. This girl, named Changing Woman, grew to womanhood, and when she reached the age of puberty First Man and First Woman designed a special initiation ceremony into adulthood for her, a ceremony still used by the Navajos, one called "Walking into Beauty." Soon Changing Woman gave birth to twin sons fathered by the Sun. When later the boys had grown to men they wanted to visit their father. With directions from Spider Woman the twins overcame many obstacles on the way and eventually met their father. The Sun at first refused to recognize them as his sons. They had to prove their strength and wisdom to be worthy of their father. The father designed a number of difficult tasks for the twins, among them that they must return to earth and slay the evil monsters. In the manner of St. George slaying the dragon, the twins killed all of the monsters, and they were accepted by their father as heroes.

Now that peace had come to the Land, human people could be created to inhabit it. Changing Woman solved the problem by creating from her body the first four Navajo clans from the skin of her breast, her back, her right arm, and her left arm. Each clan was given a guardian animal spirit, the Bear, the Lion, the Bull Snake, and the Porcupine. The Land, Dinetah, the Fifth World, became the Navajo world of today. All of nature is divine and sacred. All of God's creation, the universe, the earth, the other planets, the animals, the plants, and all human belong to one inseparable chain of life, the manifestations of the Breath of Life, the wind.

Religion serves as the bond that ties the Navajo people to their environment. The forces of nature, the spirit forces, are symbolized and ritualized by prayers, chants or songs, dances, symbolic paintings in the sand, even daily tasks such as farming and weaving.

Peace of mind and body, as well as peace within the community depend upon a rigorous observance of the sacred rituals. Even health comes from main-taining a proper balance between the physical and spiritual aspects of the human person. Illness comes not from germs, but from imbalance within the soul of man-kind. Medicine men, with the aid of professional chanters or singers, singing hun-dreds of different chants and with the aid of priestly artists who fashion their sand paintings according to prescribed formulas, effect cures that even modern medicine recognizes as having some merit. The Navajo way of life continues to resist the encroachment of the white man's Christian, individualistic, and capitalistic systems of how human beings should live.

A popular and sympathetic portrayal of Navajo culture and religion has been written by Tony Hillerman in three novels, the latest being *Coyote Waits*.

NORDIC RELIGION

Another cosmic religion, although no longer in existence, is the religion of the ancient Norse or Viking people. Jacqueline Simpson, in her 1980 book *The Viking World*, portrays the old Norse religion as it was told in the legendary sagas or Eddas. Three gods, Thor, Odin, and Frey rule the other gods, the entire universe, and all of mankind. These deities represent the cosmic forces of nature. The chief god was Odin, a sun god, a god of wisdom, of war, and of courage and magic. He carried a spear and wherever he traveled he was accompanied by eagles and wolves, all symbols of power. Odin was also the god of death and the ruler of the underworld or Valhalla. The souls of the hero warriors, killed in battle, were carried to Valhalla by the female Valkyries. In Valhalla the fallen souls were regaled with wine and beautiful Valkryie maidens, a most enticing reward for bravery. Odin was also the patron saint of kings, sages, and poets. The name Odin, sometimes spelled Woden, is the basis for the name of the day of Wednesday in the Christian calendar.

The son of Odin, Thor or "thunder," the basis for the name of Thursday, was a sky god, similar to the Greek god Zeus. He controlled the storms and as such he was the patron god of farmers and sailors. Thor was also the guardian of the law and justice. Oaths sworn to Thor were sacred oaths symbolized by a ring in the form of a hammer. The hammer would give protection from all evil forces, such as dragons and giants.

Frigg, the mother of Thor, was the earth goddess. Balder, another son of Odin, symbolized mortal man. But mortal man lost all hope for immortality when he went to the underworld, ruled by Hel, for he was never to be released to return to earth. Loki, a fire god, was the source of all evil and the father of Hel, the female ruler of the Underworld.

Thor's wife, Sif, was the goddess of the crops. Freyja was the goddess of fertility, love, and peace. Her twin sister, Freya or Frija (the basis of the name for Friday) was Odin's wife. Freyja was symbolized by figures of men and women dancing as well as by an erect phallus, a common ancient fertility symbol.

In general, Nordic worship occurred in open fields or forests, places identified with nature. A few wooden temples were built but none have survived. Priests were used to conduct burial services, offer prayers, forecast the future, and conduct human and animal sacrifices. Bodies were buried with the owners' tools, dogs, horses, and food for use in Valhalla. Some burials were made by placing the corpse in a ship and then sinking it at sea, this being a tribute to the gods Hel and Balder. Cremation was also used since the Nordics believed that fire could carry the soul to Valhalla. Burial sites were often marked with wooden posts and vertical slab of stone.

From the old Nordic beliefs the Scandinavian people have inherited a rich collection of folklore and legends recounted in the Icelandic Eddas and the Norse sagas. These myths suggest that these ancient people were most superstitious, for they attributed great powers to dragons, trolls, ghosts, and spirits. Trolls lusted after children and they would steal them from their parents. Devils came from fiery Hell to lure people into sinful ways. Fairies, water sprites, and ghosts could perform magic that might bless people or might cause disasters and death. The challenge before all people was to win the favor of the good spirits and to appease or to avoid the evil ones.

RELIGION ON FIJI ISLAND

Another cosmic religion is found among the inhabitants of Fiji, an island in the Pacific. Ronald Wright, in his 1986 book *On Fiji Island,* describes the religion of these Polynesian and Melanesian people. Although their nominal and official religion is Christianity, the basic beliefs continue to be in the ancient natural gods and spirits. So often the religion of primitive people presents an outer skin of Christian faith, but underneath the old gods still prevail.

The supreme god of the Fijians is a snake, Degel, who created all of the universe. Fiji was seen as the center of this universe, hence it was the largest and most powerful of all lands in the world. Many religions proclaim that their native land is also the center of the universe. The Fijian people pay some respect to their Christian faith by reciting the Lord's Prayer, reading from the Bible, and listening to a sermon from the pulpit decrying their ancient, sinful ways, which must yield to the Puritanical standards of the Christian missionaries. In the eyes of the missionaries Degel becomes the Devil and is replaced by the Christian god Jehovah. But out in the after-church world, when the natives return to their thatch huts, Degel again rules supreme.

VOODOO

The voodoo religion of the Haitian people illustrates another form of a cosmic religion. Voodoo was brought to Haiti by African slaves who were imported to work on the sugar plantations. The term *voodoo* is derived from an African word for god or spirit. Today voodoo is the national religion of Haiti, although the official state religion is Roman Catholicism. Voodoo has continued to survive in Haiti since the 1600s despite the efforts of French rulers and Catholic missionaries either to destroy it or to reduce it to the status of a minor cult. Instead voodoo has conquered Catholicism by permitting the people to go to church, accept the sacraments and the holy days, but retaining the soul of the people for the voodoo gods. Voodoo has served as a bond of unity among the Haitian slaves whenever they attempted revolts against their masters. Voodoo played an important role in the popular revolt against the dictatorial rule of "Baby Doc" Duvalier in 1986.

In the voodoo faith a host of spirits and gods controls man's destiny. The supernatural forces are found in the sky, the mountains, the streams, and in the life forces of plants and animals. They also reside in the bodies of living people and of dead ancestors. Ancestor spirits are special messengers from the living to the gods. Christ, the Virgin Mother, and the many saints have been incorporated into voodoo worship. The Good God, Bendye, has been transformed into Jehovah. The ancestral spirits are said to belong to Lucifer's army of benevolent angels who descend from heaven to earth to assist man in his efforts to survive. They are the intermediaries between man and the gods.

Voodoo, like other religions, has constructed an elaborate set of practices and rituals that solicit the aid of spirits for mankind's benefit. Voodoo has no set of scriptures or an organized church government, but it does use priests, both male and female, to instruct the people in the proper ways to communicate with the gods. Priests are called "mama" and "papa," while the people are "children" who address one another as "brother" and "sister." Special rituals celebrate births, marriages, and deaths. Much use is made of magical objects or charms. Animals are sacrificed and special prayers and chants are performed to bring good luck, good health and prosperity, and good fortune to find a good marital partner who will produce many children. Spirits may be rewarded for their favors with prayers and gifts of food. The gods are also favored with abundant and exuberant displays of joyful songs, dances, and loud beating on the drums. At times the frenzied rejoicing attains such heights of joy that the participants are literally possessed by the spirits of the dead ancestors. People drop to the ground, deep in a state of trance, rolling and twisting in the ecstasy of their spiritual intoxication. Such possessed people are called "zombies" and they are deemed to have special powers to do both good and evil to the people about them.

NATIVE AUSTRALIAN RELIGION

Native Australians have a cosmic form of religion that typifies many of the religions of both ancient and modern people. Stanley Breeden describes the culture of an aboriginal tribe living in the Kakadau National Park in northern Australia.[5] For over twenty thousand years the Gagudji people have lived in this area. Their story of creation relates how in the beginning the world had no shape. It was only a soft glob of matter until the arrival of Dreamtime, a female form that arose, like Venus, from the sea. She created the earth and the sea, the people, their language, and all of the plants and animals, the crocodiles and sea eagles, the trees and the grass, and all other living things. Once all creation was completed creature-spirits came to dwell in a white rock, named Warramuuuungundji, which became a place for worship called "Dreaming Sites." In this rock is found the original energy of creation, a force that rules man and puts him under obligation to protect the environment—man is under penalty not to injure the environment because the environment was created by God. The spirit in the rock is often depicted on cliff walls. Upon the death of a person the body is buried so that the spirit is free to return to its motherland, while the body will return to earth.

Many hundreds of cosmic-style religions are found today among less developed peoples. The few examples of cosmic religions summarized here typify most of the others. A common thread woven into the fabric of all cosmic religions is the recognition of the divine element in all things of nature. God is everywhere and in everything. This belief in the divinity of things created and existing in nature links the cosmic religions to modern nature devotees, the deists, the pantheists, the Spinozan philosophers, and twentieth-century environmentalists.

In a final recognition of the truth and validity of cosmic religions it is worth reporting that in 1986 Pope John Paul II invited representatives from all world religions to meet in Assisi, Italy, the birthplace of St. Francis, to celebrate the "oneness" of all of God's people. Representatives from 160 religious bodies responded to the invitation. Some conservative Catholics and Protestants protested the inclusion of "pagan" groups, as a "hellish abomination." However some of the "pagan" spokesmen uttered most Christianlike sentiments, as for example an African animist who said, "Almighty God, the Great Thumb, we cannot evade in tying any knot, the Roaring Thunder that splits mighty trees, the All-Seeing Lord upon high who sees even the footprints of an antelope on a rock mass here on earth—You are the cornerstone of peace." Or a Crow Indian medicine man who said, "I pray that you [Great Spirit] bring peace to all my brothers and sisters of the world."[6]

3

River Valley Religions: Babylon and Egypt

By 3000 B.C. most of Africa, Europe, and Asia had become home to a vast number of diverse tribes, racial groups, and cultures. Humans had emerged from Stone Age and Cro-Magnon types of homo sapiens to more civilized levels of humans. Man had learned to use a plow, to domesticate animals and plants, to manufacture cloth wares, to build stone and brick homes and temples, and to convert oral sounds into symbols that can be impressed on brick or clay, or engraved in stone. With the invention of writing begins the historical or literate era of human history.

As centuries pass mankind begins to live in social units larger than family, clan, and tribe, as monarchial states with systems of law and government begin to develop in the fertile river valleys of Babylonia and Egypt. These rich valleys can produce a surplus of goods to be traded to other peoples in far-off lands. People now begin to live in towns and cities away from rural villages. A larger food supply can support larger populations and a surplus of wealth to support military forces, which can be used to expand royal territory, conquer neighboring lands, and make slaves of the conquered people. The social systems develop class systems and a specialization of labor: rulers, priests, noble landowners, soldiers, merchants, craftsmen, peasant farmers, half-free serfs, and, at the bottom of the social scale, the indispensable slaves. Until the invention of steam power no rich civilized country could afford to abolish the institution of slavery. So new religious systems replaced the simple, outdated cosmic religions. The gods now had to bless the royal monarchs, the new, class-organized social system, slave labor, and war.

Looking back on how man evolved from primitive cosmic religions, a cynic might ask, "How much better is a civilized human than one not so civilized?" An eighteenth-century romantic, like Rousseau would say, "No progress, only regression." Early, cosmic-age man, when compared with his later progeny, was indeed a noble savage, an ideal human living in freedom, equality, and peace.

The realm of religious experience changes slowly and painfully compared

41

to the relative ease with which material aspects of life can change, but change it does to accommodate the needs of new lifestyles.

The river-valley religions have special value for the modern world in that traces of their heritage can be found in Judaism, Christianity, and Islam today. The invention of writing has permitted modern scholars to learn much detail about the religions of Egypt and Babylonia. The Egyptians left us their scripture in the Book of the Dead; the Babylonians gave us their epic of Gilgamesh; and the Zoroastrians of Persia left their hymns of Zoroaster. Probably an absolutely correct account of these old religions is impossible since translations of these writings may be in error. But recent archaeological finds have added information that confirms much of what we think we know.

All of the river-valley religions worshiped the cosmic or natural forces of nature, the sun, the moon, the sky, the earth and the life-sustaining elements found in water, soil, and air. Religion's main function was to give humans a sense of power to control their environment for better survival conditions. The powerful forces of nature were endowed with human form and personalities that were able to speak to humans. The gods had intellect, human emotions and desires, and the entire gamut of human virtues and frailties.

As the river-valley societies enlarged their territories by conquest and their governments prospered, the ruling monarchs began to claim to be descendants of the gods, endowed with their wisdom and power. The moral taboos of each religion became the laws of the state.

In these kingdoms agriculture was the predominant source of wealth, so Mother Earth was transformed from an invisible source of fertility to a human female figure, a goddess such as Isis in Egypt and Istar in Babylonia. The domesticated animals on which agriculture depends were worshiped as other gods. The cow and the bull became important deities.

The Cult of the Bull

In Egypt there is a tomb of bulls near Memphis and the great pyramids. In a large underground tunnel are hundreds of granite burial crypts into which embalmed bulls were placed. Over the years most of the mummified bull bodies have been removed or destroyed, but the tombs are as indicative of the bulls' divine status as the pyramids are of the pharaohs'. The Egyptians worshiped many animals in addition to the bull—jackals, hippopotamuses, crocodiles, cats, falcons, and many others—but the bull was the most sacred of all. The bull god, Apis, represented both the life force in all of reproduction and the absolute power of the god-kings. Apis was the incarnation of the god Ptah, the creator of the universe. Only one god-bull could rule at a given time, and when the reigning bull died, as in the selection of a Tibetan Buddhist chief lama, the Egyptians had to conduct a search for the divine bull from among the living bull calves at that time. The chosen sacred bull then became the object of worship.

The deceased bull then, like the human body after death, joined Osiris in the underworld.

Worship of bulls was practiced in Crete, Sardinia, and Malta as well as in Persia. In the Minoan civilization of Crete, developed about 2000 B.C., excavations reveal many bull statues and pottery decorated with bulls and young men engaged in bull jumping and other acrobatics with bulls. Archaeologists have unearthed a large palace in Knossos, Crete, built by a ruler, King Minos, who was reputed to have had a bull for an ancestor. The bull was celebrated in royal processions, which were intended to promote human fertility. Greek legends tell that the Greeks had to send annual tributes to King Minos in the form of seven young men and seven young women who were to be sacrificed to the Minotaur, a half-man, half-bull beast. Bulls were pictured frequently on palace walls, and the powerful bull was said to have caused earthquakes and volcanic eruptions. It is no wonder that the bull god ruled the pantheon of gods.

Bull worship spread to Cyprus and the Aegean provinces in Turkey. In Ephesus, St. Paul had to compete with pagan bull worshipers for converts to Christianity. In Ephesus archaeologists have found female statues on which the body is covered with round egg-shaped objects. First it was thought that these protuberances were eggs, symbols of fertility. Now scholars believe these shapes are really bull testicles. Similar female statues are found in Greece, thought to represent the goddess Artemus or the Roman goddess Diana, both goddesses of fertility.

The bull cult spread also to Persia in the form of Mithraism. In the pre-Christian era and in the first three centuries after Christ, Mithraism was a popular cult in the eastern Mediterranean, where it was an early competitor with Christianity for converts. Mithra, a major god, was born in a cave. When he became a man he captured a wild bull, took it back to his cave, and killed it. From the blood gushing from the bull's throat, all creatures on earth were formed. Mithra, however, was only one of several Persian gods. The supreme Persian god was Ahura Mazda, a sun god and an ally of Mithra. Followers of Mithraism identified themselves by wearing a religious replica of a bull testicle with a scorpion hanging from it. Mithraic temples were built underground, where secret rites were performed. Members of the cult would dress in animal skins and dance around an altar. The central act of worship was the sacrifice of a bull, after which the communicants drank its blood. One wonders if this sacrificial act in any manner set a precedent for the Christian Eucharist.

Mithraism had a special appeal to athletes, soldiers, and hunters, all persons who admired feats of courage and strength. Finally, Mithraism offered its adherents the promise of a savior who would come to save the human race from sin by destroying evil with fire. The birthplace of the savior would be made known by the appearance of a star in the East, which would lead wise men, the magi, to the birthplace.

Earth and Sun

Although polytheistic religions endowed many animals with supernatural powers, none were given the supreme place among the many gods. The most honored positions were given to members of the solar system, usually either the sun or the earth. Mother Earth was given special reverence since it was earth that provided the food supply, and for this Mother Earth was always a fertility symbol or goddess. Judaism, a monotheistic faith, also gave earth a special measure of reverence. Earth was man's homeland, whose fruits man was to enjoy and over which man was to exercise dominance. Even the early concepts of the solar system placed the earth at the center of the universe. The sun revolved around the earth, according to the Greek Ptolemaic system, which prevailed among scientists until the Copernican sun-centered universe was conceived in the sixteenth century, something Christian theologians resisted for centuries.

In most polytheistic religions the sun god is at the top of the hierarchy of divine beings, for the sun represents power, a masculine attribute, while the earth represented submissive femininity and weakness. In her book *Man and the Sun* Jacqueline Hawkins writes that there is scarcely any religion that does not give first place to the Sun Deity. Common sense, no need for science, is sufficient reason to accept the fact that the sun is an indispensable source of energy for man's survival on earth. The fear that the sun might vanish someday has cast a deep sense of anxiety among humans since the day we began to think about the sun. Native Americans worshiped the sun, sometimes designated it as a sky god. The more advanced American native civilizations, the Mayans, the Aztecs, the Toltecs, and the Incas, all were sun worshipers. A visitor to a Christian service today in a Central American nation like Guatemala or Nicaragua, or even Mexico, can identify pagan remnants of sun-oriented religions. Mayan gods became Christian saints. The churches were built on the sites of Mayan temples.

Babylon

Among the Babylonians of the Tigris-Euphrates river valley the sun god was the major focus of worship. The sun god Marduk played a prominent role in the Babylonian account of creation. He created man, although Marduk in turn had been created by the supreme god of the sky, Enlil. Over time, Marduk became the god who represented the high power of the state. In the Babylonian religion two versions of creation are given. An original version described a female goddess, Chaos or Tiamat, as the source of all things. The story relates that a group of male gods in the sky conspired to kill Tiamat and impose upon the world a male ruler. The young god Marduk was selected to kill Tiamat, who lived in the form of a dragon. When Marduk approached Tiamat, he blew wind into her mouth, blowing her into parts, out of which Marduk fashioned earth and heaven. Another version has Tiamat as the source of creation.

The pantheon of Babylonian gods included Anu, the sky god; his son Enlil, god of air and storm; Enki, god of fresh water and the underworld; Ningirsu, a female goddess ruling over agriculture; and lesser gods including the sun god, called Utu by the Sumerians and Shamash by the Babylonians; the moon god, called both Nanna and Sin; and Inanna, goddess of fertility, love, and the cycles of reproduction, life, death, and rebirth or resurrection. Later Inanna became associated with the morning star, Ishtar. As the goddess of love and fertility, she was said to return to the underworld each winter, thus causing the death of the vegetation and the cold of the season. In the spring she would return to earth, after being ransomed by her lover Tammuz, thereby bringing new life to all living things. In a vague sense here is found an early version of the resurrection experience. The Babylonian Ishtar and Syrian Astarte become forerunners of the Egyptian goddess Isis, the Greek Aphrodite, and the Roman Venus.

Eventually Marduk, an agent of Enlil, becomes the supreme god over all, and, being most powerful, also the god of war.

The chief god of the Assyrians, who follow the Babylonians as the rulers of the Mesopotamian Empire, is Assur, a sun god. He is symbolized by a "tree of life," which was worshiped in the form of a palm branch placed on the altar in a jar of water. Is this a source for the use of palm branches on Palm Sunday?

Mesopotamian religions left traces in later religions. The forces of nature became represented in human forms as superhuman beings. The monarchs of later empires found their strength in an identification with gods and goddesses, especially sun gods. Government, royal prerogatives, systems of law and justice, and the social-class order were often attributed to the will and dictates of all-powerful sun gods. The Mosaic code can trace its ancestry to the Babylonian code of King Hammurabi, which used revenge as its basic principle of justice, "an eye for an eye, a tooth for a tooth." The imperial ruler became the high priest and was sometimes revered as a god, who rules over both heaven and earth, and whose will no earthly being dare question. The notion that the king is a divine monarch had its most recent expression in Emperor Hirohito of Japan.

Gods and kings required temples in which to live and statues to represent them to the people. So temples and monuments were erected to the god-kings. In Babylon the temples were built in the form of a stair-step pyramid, a ziggurat, on top of which would be placed an altar, a place nearest to heaven, where the priests could offer prayers and gifts to the gods.

Virgin sheep were often sacrificed to appease the gods. Female prostitutes were used by the priests in a religious rite to promote human fertility. The family was patriarchal, one in which women were to be ruled by their husbands, and where women's sole function was to produce children and to care for them.

The heritage from Babylonian religions includes the use of priests to offer prayers and to sacrifice animals for the gods' sake. A host of superstitious beliefs has come down to us today from Babylonian religion, such as beliefs in magical powers, astrology, numerology, divination from animal parts, ghosts, vampires, and exorcism. The concept of body purification through the use of water and the taboo on eating unclean foods are both of Babylonian origin.

Finally a rich source of literature, legends, and myths, come to us from Babylon. The *Epic of Gilgamesh* relates the story of a hero, Gilgamesh, who seeks to find a cure for death. In his travels he is told the story of a flood and the salvation of the human race by means of an ark into which humans and animals are brought to safety, later to repopulate the earth. Eventually Gilgamesh is given a magic herb of immortality. However, he carelessly leaves the herbs on the shore of a pond while he bathes. A serpent comes by, swallows the herbs, and the moral of the story is that man is doomed to die. Here is another serpent who brings evil and death to the human race.

Another more detailed version of the Flood story also very similar to the biblical account of Noah's ark is found in the *Legend of Atrahasis*. It begins by describing Enlil, god of storms, destruction, and agriculture, complaining that too many people are living on earth. They make so much noise that he cannot sleep. So Enlil orders disease and famine to come to destroy the people. This tactic does not work, so he orders a great flood to come. This plan is thwarted when Enki, god of underground fresh water, purification, and irrigation, intervenes by having an ark built by which the people are saved. Enlil becomes very angry so Enki arranges a truce by which disease, famine, and barrenness afflict the people, thereby keeping down their numbers.

The Babylonian epics also tell the story of how man was created. The original story related how man was created from earth or clay that was mixed with the blood of Marduk. Therefore, man was a blend of the earth and the divine. In the process of birth both the god Enki and the goddess, Ninmah, the birth attendant, were responsible for the creation of man. Both sexes were involved in the creation of man. However, later versions of creation omitted Ninmah from the story. By 1000 B.C. Enki alone created mankind.

The Mesopotamian epics also relate that Eve was formed from a rib, that judgment of man's sins would be made by Marduk in the underworld. Furthermore, they answer the question asked by Job, "Why are good men punished by God?"— only Marduk knows. When Abraham emigrated from the land of Ur in Mesopotamia about 1800 B.C., he took with him a religion that borrowed heavily from the Mesopotamian heritage. The story of the Flood and Noah's ark, the Ten Commandments, all have Babylonian antecedents. The story of the hunter Nimrod is similar to that of Gilgamesh, who is two-thirds divine and one-third human.

Egypt

The other major river-valley civilization was Egypt. It has left modern scholars with an extensive written record of Egyptian religion,[1] which is supplemented by many archaeological collections from tombs and pyramids. From the burial sites have been recovered many tools, pieces of furniture, chariots, foods, clothing, and ornaments buried with the embalmed bodies of royalty and nobility. The existence of these physical remains, from a civilization highly developed two thousand years before Christ, yields great knowledge of Egyptian religious beliefs and practices. Hence by reading the written language, in hieroglyphics or translations thereof, as recorded in such sacred scriptures as The Book of the Dead, religious hymns and prayers, one can reconstruct the ancient Egyptian religion in much detail.

Egyptians had a profound belief in the reality of an afterlife for both humans and certain sacred animals such as cats and bulls. Since the deceased body would life in the afterlife it would need to have the same physical necessities as the live body needed on earth. The pyramids near Cairo and the cliff tombs near Luxor were homes for the dead. Since it was necessary to preserve the human body from decay, Egyptians early in their history learned the art of mummification, the word for which is derived from the Arabic word, *mūmiyā,* meaning to be encased in a bituminous or tar substance. The process was successful in preserving the physical body for centuries. A desert climate with a dry atmosphere also contributed to the preservation process.

The pyramids were tombs built above ground. Some seventy are known to exist today. The pyramid-building era extended from 3000 B.C., to about 1500 B.C., along the Nile river near Cairo. The pyramids are symbols of the sun god in the form of a four-sided triangle. The Great Pyramid of Giza took a hundred thousand men working for twenty years to complete. It was placed in an exact line with the compass points, with the tomb entrance facing north. The pyramids wre truly masterworks of architecture, astronomy, mathematics, and engineering.

At Luxor, along the west bank of the Nile are high, sheer cliffs of sandstone. Here were cut out of the cliff walls many tombs for royalty and nobility. One of the most famous and also smallest is the tomb of the boy king Tutankhamen. The tomb chambers are empty today, except for the sarcophagus and mummy of the king, but they contained a huge number of articles of daily use stacked in an extremely small space. The contents of the tomb have been removed to the top floor of the Cairo Museum and the entire floor of a large building is given over to a display of the contents of the tomb of King "Tut." The single most memorable object in the museum is the gorgeously ornamented breast plate that covered the king's body. In the Luxor tomb one remembers best the walls, mostly green, painted as if it was only yesterday. On the tomb walls are depicted, as in other royal tombs, the story of how the soul is transported to the underworld for judgment.

The burial tombs were designed to protect the sacred bodies from both physical deterioration and robbery. In most respects mummification was a more successful objective than prevention of grave robbery. Most of the tombs were sacked and desecrated soon after burial, the contents being stolen, sold, and scattered throughout the Western world. For some reason the tomb of King "Tut" escaped this fate, although there is some evidence that robbers may have found it, but did not take its contents.

The resurrection theme is basic to the Egyptian religion, a theme best told in the life of the god Osiris, and his sister-wife Isis, a story to be related later. The Isis myth also suggests the mystery of a virgin birth, or an asexual process of reproduction. There exists the possibility that Christian views on resurrection and the virgin birth may have been influenced by Egyptian beliefs.

The Egyptian pantheon of divine beings, as with many early religions, was based on the forces of nature or spirits found in nature, such forces that created the universe and continue to control and move the universe through the cycles of life and death applied to everything from the stars and solar systems to all forms of life on earth. The process of the creation of new life and the maintenance of life become the essence of most religious systems. The number of gods and goddesses in Egyptian religion, as with the Mesopotamian religions, is legion, a half hundred or more, if all deities, major and minor, are counted. Each local province or tribal group had its own set of gods. As Egypt became a united empire, local gods were replaced by the gods and goddesses of the ruling dynasty. Some of the local gods were retained with new names. For example, the sun god, the chief god, bears the names of Ra, Re, Atun, and Aton. All of the deities represent some element of nature, or some source of energy that has the power to bless or destroy man. In turn man must be able to communicate with, and, if possible, to control the gods.

Space forbids any detailed description of the many Egyptian gods. In the process of evolution the Egyptian family of gods had origins similar to the gods of other lands. Natural forces were given either human or animal attributes. The animal gods most commonly worshiped were the bull, the cow, the cat, the falcon, the ram, the crocodile, and the jackal.

The chief god was Ra, the sun god. Ra was born out of the sea (Nun) by his own creation. In turn Ra gave birth to a son, Shu, and a daughter, Tefnut, who together gave birth to Geb, god of Earth, and Nut, a sky goddess. Nut became the wife of Geb, her brother, and they give birth to Osiris, Seth, and two daughters, Isis and Nephthys. Nephthys became the handmaiden to Isis. Seth represented the forces of evil, destruction and death, while Osiris became the god who gave life, protected virtue, ruled the underworld, and judged the dead souls. Of all gods, Osiris was the most loved. Osiris was the god of the ancestors, the god of resurrection, and the guardian of eternal life or *ka*. Osiris became a model for other resurrected saviors, the Sumerian Dumuzi, the Babylonian Tammuz, the Caananite Baal, the Hittite Telapinush, the Persian Mithra, and perhaps the Christian Jesus.

Osiris and Isis brought forth Horus, the falcon god, who represented courage and leadership. The pharaohs were the incarnation of Horus, who was also the chief aide to Osiris in ruling the underworld and judging the souls of the dead.

Egyptian myths relate the origins of other gods. The sky goddess Nub, symbolized as a cow, was the protector of the earth. The five stars of heaven were her children. The moon was the brother of the sun, and he was deemed to be god of learning. Mayet, the daughter of Ra and Thoth, was the goddess of truth and justice, the giver of civilization, the source of balance between good and evil, and the patron of scribes and writers. Thoth was represented as a dog-headed baboon. All priests and judges paid homage to Thoth, for she presided over the courts of law.

Another myth of creation credits the god Ptah as having created out of his own mind, by the Word (like Plato's Logos) all of the deities, all things on earth and in the heavens. Ptah's wife, Seknut, was a lion-headed goddess who wore a solar disk on her head. She was the goddess of destruction and war, the one who destroyed the enemies of Ra.

The sun god, by one story, received his power from a sacred beetle or scarab, Khepri. It is Khepri who causes the sun to rise and set each day, just as the beetle rolls his ball of dung across the earth. As mentioned earlier, the bull god Apis, was the source of power and fertility, the soul of the creator god Ptah, and the divine essence in the ruling pharaoh. Apis's soul, upon death, joined Osiris in the afterworld.

A momentous religious innovation occurred during Egypt's eighteenth dynasty, when a young ruler, Akhenaton IV or Ikhnaton (his original name was Amenophis) had a vision of a monotheistic religion with only one supreme God. Akhenaton planned a new capital to be built at Heliopolis, the center for his new religion of love, the equality of the sexes, and the brotherhood of man. He had many of the enlightened virtues of Jesus, which were expressed in his hymn, "The Sun Hymn," which can be found in our libraries today. This hymn has been compared to Psalm 104. The young pharaoh was weak and epileptic so his reign was relatively short, eighteen years, and his dream of a new religion, never popular with the established priests and bureaucrats, was replaced following his death. Akhenaton's wife was the beautiful Neferteti.

Until the Egyptian religion was replaced first by Christianity and later by Islam, Ra remained the supreme ruler of the Egyptian pantheon. It was from Ra that the pharaohs derived their absolute power. Temples and pyramids were erected in honor of Ra. Obelisks, phallic symbols, the image of Horus, the falcon god, over temple doorways, and the sacred scarab, all caused the people to remember their debt to Ra and the pharaoh.

The daily worship practices included prayers and gift offerings in the homes. But the larger religious services were conducted by the priests in temple worship, and on the occasion of funerals and seasonal festivals celebrated in the honor of those deities who were connected directly with the event. The festival of Amun celebrated the memory of the dead pharaohs; the festival of Min celebrated the fruits of fertility, both of the royal couple and of the harvest of the crops; and the festival of Sed remembered the unification of Egypt under the pharaoh Menes. The priestly caste was numerous, powerful, and hereditary.

The temples became wealthy landowners, and the priests were the administrators and benefactors of this wealth, and the possessors of much political power in the government of the country. Women played a secondary role in the priesthood, but the fact that they played any role suggested that women in Egypt enjoyed a higher political and social status than was generally accorded to women at that time. Women were known to have been rulers, notably Queen Hatshepsut, whose large funerary temple near Luxor indicates the measure of her power.

Religious texts such as the Book of the Dead and the "Wisdom Literature" record a standard of moral ethics quite as high as is found in the Mosaic code. Forgiveness of sins, love of fellow man, moral virtue, patience, wisdom, justice, avoidance of murder and theft, were all the good deeds for which unrighteous souls would be judged and punished in the hereafter. The Book of the Dead, a guidebook for the dead as they journey to the underworld of Osiris, describes the judgment of the soul by Osiris. The heart of the deceased is placed on a scale with Truth in the other balance pan. If Truth and the heart are in balance, then the soul will go to a place of eternal happiness. If the balance is unfavorable, then the soul will go to a place where a monster will destroy the evil one.

In many respects the most interesting feature of the Egyptian religion was the emphasis placed upon life after death, and the divine judgment of the soul for the commitment of earthly sins or the practice of moral virtures. The judgment of the souls also implied the reality of bodily resurrection, at least for the gods and the pharaohs. At first it was believed that only the pharaohs, among humans, could inherit immortality, but later it was believed that mere mortals could join Osiris.

Concern for the dead became the motive for embalming the dead, creating enormous tombs for the dead, and using impressive funeral rites that seem to be the prime purpose for religious worship. The burial tomb, no matter what type or size, housed both the body and the soul of the deceased.

Although the god Ra was king among the gods, the most popular deities were Osiris and his sister-wife, Isis. In this divine pair could be found the seeds for a belief in a virgin birth and a bodily resurrection. Isis was the model wife and mother, like the Virgin Mary, and her husband, Osiris, was the ideal husband and father. Osiris was the god of civilization, fertility, the crafts, and agriculture, all things deemed necessary and good. Osiris and Isis provide the most interesting myth in the collection of Egyptian literature.

The myth as told by the Roman historian Plutarch, in brief, reads as follows: The story begins with a feud between Osiris and his jealous brother, Seth, who threatens to destroy all of civilization and Osiris for being denied his share of the kingdom. The father of both brothers, Geb, thought that Seth was an irresponsible person who would make a poor ruler, so he gave all of the kingdom to his favorite and good son, Osiris. Osiris was lured by Seth to a banquet where he was tricked into getting into a chest destined to be Osiris's coffin. Osiris entered the coffin whereupon Seth and his aides nailed shut the coffin lid. The coffin was then thrown into the Nile River, where it eventually floated into the Mediterranean Sea. The coffin drifted to the shore of Byblos in Phoenicia. In the meantime Isis set forth to find her husband. A protective angel, Buto, took her to Byblos, where she found the coffin imbedded in a giant cypress tree. The tree had been cut to make a pillar in the king's palace. For a time Isis was hired to be a nursemaid to a royal child. Later Isis is revealed to be a goddess who is seeking her husband, Osiris. The king responds to her plea to release Osiris from the pillar, which he does. The king gives her a boat to return with Osiris to Egypt. Isis grieves that she has no children, so on the way with the dead Osiris she miraculously conceives a child by Osiris. The child eventually becomes the god Horus. When Isis arrives in Egypt Seth discovers that she has the body of Osiris. In anger he cuts the body into fourteen parts and scatters them throughout Egypt. Isis searches the kingdom for the scattered parts and recovers all of them. By anointing them with a sacred oil she is able to resurrect the body to life.

This myth becomes the source for a belief in a judgment of the soul after death, the possibility of a resurrection of the body to eternal life, and the possibility of a virgin birth. The Isis-Osiris myth may be the single most important legacy left by a pagan religion.

The location of heaven or the underworld is never clear. Is it in the sky or under the earth? The evidence seems to prefer the earth location. It was also believed that the pharaohs went to a sky heaven, where they joined Ra in continuing to rule over Egypt. As to the fate of the souls of the common people, that remains uncertain. However, the common people identified most with Osiris and Isis, and it was this pair of gods that have the promise of immortality and resurrection, probably for all people.

Osiris was the giver of life and of life after death. His suffering on earth, even death, atoned for man's sins, provided that mankind lived virtuous lives. In a sense Osiris replaces Ra as thge supreme god. It is to Osiris as much as to Ra that the priests direct their prayers and magical incantations. The priests, loyal to the god Ra and his counterpart on earth, the pharaoh, explained to the people that Ra's powers were given to Isis and Osiris, and then to their son, Horus, who, in turn, bestowed divine power upon the pharaohs. Horus is the protector of the pharaohs from the evil power of Seth. Horus promises that if the pharaoh is harmed or destroyed all of creation will be destroyed by Ra. Hence the theocratic and absolute rule of the pharaohs, the landed nobility, and the priests must be perpetuated forever lest all of Egypt and its people be destroyed. Egypt had perfected a model for future alliances between church and state by which peace and order might guarantee the security of the people and the salvation of their souls in heaven.

4

The Greek Gods and the Hellenistic Cults

For most people who live in the Western world, Osiris and Marduk are not household names. But Zeus, Apollo, Venus, and Athena are recognized readily by anyone who studies Latin or Greek in high school and college. Greek and Roman civilizations are fundamental ingredients in the development of Western civilization. Although the gods of Greece and Rome contributed little to the theology of Christianity, certainly Western language, literature, philosophy, science and government owe much to their classical heritage. Alan Bloom in his *The Closing of the American Mind,* a 1987 bestseller, offers severe criticism of contemporary American higher education for neglecting the study of the classics, the part of the curriculum that provides knowledge of the humanistic and ethical aspects of our civilization. Before the twentieth century no college-educated person escaped the requirement of having a major portion of his or her studies in Greek and Latin, an extensive knowledge of Greek philosophy, and more than a mere acquaintance with the Greek gods and heroes.

The Greek myths described the lives and acts of the gods, Homer's *Iliad* and *Odyssey* recounted the heroic episodes of the Trojan War, and Greek drama presented both the comedies of Aristophanes and the tragedies of Aeschylus, Sophocles, and Euripides. Perhaps the Greek gods had little influence on Christianity, but the philosophy of Plato did contribute greatly to the thinking of St. Paul and the Apostle John.

The story of the lives and escapades of the Greek gods and goddesses, of their marital and sexual relations, and of their many feuds and intrigues requires volumes, or a year's study in a university classics department. The Greek list of divine beings is long, many of whom cannot be mentioned in a brief discourse. Each community in early Greek history had its own gods and goddesses. The area that is now Southern Greece was divided by mountains and the people remained somewhat isolated in their own valley villages. Later the small communities become consolidated into larger city states, usually through conquests. Before the rule of Alexander the Great in the fourth century B.C. Greece never was a single state or nation unified under one government and motivated by a national spirit.

A summary of the early Greek religion finds three dominant characteristics. First, the earliest record of religion in Greece finds that it was a typical cosmic form of nature worship in which all elements of the natural world were thought to be inhabited by spirits, that were sometimes represented in human form. Before the Hellenes, the Greek ancestors, arrived, the central god figure was a female, Mother Earth, known as Demeter. She was known also as Aphrodite in Corinth, Artemis in Ephesus, and later as Hera, the wife of Zeus. She was a symbol of fertility, of renewal causing the annual cycles of seasons, the goddess of agriculture and vegetation, and also the goddess of human sexuality and reproduction. It was the latter power of Demeter to cause St. Paul in Romans 1:26 to say of the Corinthians, "Their women exchanged natural relations for unnatural" (Revised Standard Verson).

In addition to Mother Earth the other natural forces in the Universe were given divine properties. The sky, the sun, the moon, the other planets, the storms, the process of changing seasons, fertility, and death were each honored with an appropriate deity. Before 1500 B.C. Greece was invaded by tribes from the north, the Hellenes, who brought with them a sky god, Zeus, who married Hera, the earth goddess. The marriage of the sky and earth would seem to guarantee a perpetual cycle of fertility and population of all species on earth. Zeus became the chief god, the father of the other gods and goddesses, the proprietor of man, the wise and just god who gave direction to mortal man so that his kind would survive the hazards of life.

Secondly, the Greek religion was anthropomorphic, one in which the supernatural forces were represented as humans, endowed with intelligence, emotions, good and evil motives, physical strength, and beauty. All of these human qualities were to be expressed in the manner of gods, that is, with superhuman powers that defy the apparent laws of nature. For the gods all things were possible. In some respects the Greeks caused their deities to be so like humans—they committed all the possible sins—that is would be easy for the Greek philosophers to transfer the divine qualities of the gods to humans, who resembled the gods so much.

Thirdly, as with all religions, the Greeks had to create a special class of laborers, the priests, to interpret the will of the gods and to communicate with them. The prime function of the priests was to appease the gods, to propitiate them by the use of proper prayers, rituals, and magical acts. The priests presided over the shrines and altars, the religious processions, the athletic events, and the festivals with dances and music and the offering of animal sacrifices to the gods. In fact, the magic, the foretelling of the future by astrology and divination, and the use of sacred words, and all of the ways of communicating with the gods found in any cosmic religion could be found in the early Greek religion. However, one should note that the Greeks permitted the individual person and family to bypass the priests, and make their direct contact with the gods. Community or church worship was not typical of the early Greek religion. The family altar was the usual place of worship for both the Greek and Roman families.

The Greek Pantheon

The history of the Greek pantheon of gods and goddesses is long complex. Tradition relates that in the first stages of the evolution of the universe there was Chaos, out of which earth (Gaia) was formed, as well as love (Eros), Uranus, the sea, and the mountains. From Uranus and Gaia arose six Titans, six Titanides, and three hundred Giants. After Uranus there came his Titan son, Kronos, who was to rule the universe. From Kronos and Rhea, the sister of Kronos, came six children, Demeter, Hestia, Hera, Poseidon, Hades, and Zeus. Kronos feared that his children might overpower him so he swallowed them. However, Zeus was saved by his mother from the anger of Kronos. Later, when Zeus had grown to manhood he waged war against Kronos and the Titans. With the aid of the three hundred Giants, Zeus forced Kronos to accept defeat and to disgorge his five swallowed children. Thus Zeus, the sky god, became the supreme ruler of all of the gods.

One legend tells the story that Zeus was fashioned from clay by Prometheus, a Titan's son, and that he was given life by his daughter, Athena. Later Zeus punished Prometheus, who gave fire and civilization to man, for being too friendly to man. However, Prometheus continued to give fire (civilization) to man, so Zeus bound Prometheus to a rock as punishment, from which punishment he was freed by Hercules. Zeus was credited with bringing evil to mankind when the goddess Pandora, clothed as a woman in the Garden of Eden, opened her box of evil, containing plagues, pain, and sin, and thus doomed mankind to suffer them all.

Zeus married his sister, Hera, and began the family of the Greek gods. Zeus would rule all of creation, but, unlike the Judaic Jehovah, he was not the creator of all things. Hera became the guardian of family, marriage and protector of women, a role that Juno would play in the Roman religion. Hera had one special gift, that of self-reproduction.

Her son, Hephaestus, was the product of a virgin birth. Each year Hera renewed her capacity for virgin births by bathing in the spring, called Canthus. Like many good wives in the human family, Hera was beaten and betrayed by her husband many times. However, she remained faithful and loyal to Zeus while giving birth to three children, Ares (Mars to the Romans), god of war, Hephaestus (Vulcan) god of the forge, and Hebe, goddess of youth.

Closely related to Hera as the protector of women and the guarantor of fertility was the goddess Aphrodite (Venus). She was the daughter of Zeus and Dione, according to the *Iliad,* and the wife of Hephaestus. Another myth says Aphrodite arose from the sea, which was saturated with the semen of Uranus after he had been castrated and his sexual organs were thrown into the sea. Aphrodite shares with Eros the capacity to incite gods, humans, and all animals to engage in pleasureable sexual intercourse so that all concerned will continue their kind.

Anyone who has visited Athens and the monumental temple ruins of the Parthenon on the Acropolis (hill) will learn that Athena, the ruling goddess of Athens, was honored by the construction of this beautiful marble temple to house a wooden statue of Athena, all richly adorned with gold. Athena was born from the head of Zeus, wearing a suit of armour and carrying a sword. At first she was only a war goddess, like Ares. Later she became the protector of Odysseus, a man of great wisdom, and as such she was the goddess of wisdom. She was the patron saint of technology, invention, and engineering. Athena is said to have inspired the art of pottery making, shipbuilding, and the invention of the ploughshare.

Apollo, a sun god and son of Zeus, became the guardian of agriculture, protector of Justice and the law, and the god of prophecy as the ruler of the sacred cave or oracle at Delphi, from which place future events could be predicted. Apollo drove across the heavens in a chariot marking a path for the sun to follow from horizon to horizon. As a sun god he symbolized light and purity, cleanliness, and medicine. His son, Asclepius, became the protector of all doctors. Apollo had more than one sacred attribute. He was the god of physical beauty, of the intellect, of music and poetry, and of youth. He is pictured as armed with a bow while posing in the nude.

Poseidon (Neptune to the Romans) became the ruler of the sea and protector of sailors. Hephaestus, the ugly crippled son of Hera, became the blacksmith who held the secrets of iron technology, fire, and magic. In one story Haphaestus caught his mistress, Aphrodite, in bed with Ares. To punish them he cast a net over them, making them look foolish and guilty.

The goddess Artemus, always the virgin, became the protector of virgin girls, pregnant women, and hunters. Hermes (Mercury), son of Zeus, is the god of the flock and of shepherds. He also protects cattle, and for some unknown reason, he protects thieves and lucky gamblers. Hermes was known for his travels, wore golden sandals, and guided travelers along the road to their destination. As the traveler's companion he is given the duty to accompany dead souls to Hades. He was also the personification of wisdom, and the holder of secret knowledge (gnosis) that could unlock the mysteries of the universe. As such he was the favorite god of the philosophers.

Two other divinities who play major roles in the Greek religion are Demeter and Dionysius. Both are related to the Eleusinian Mysteries. Demeter, a sister of Zeus, was goddess of grain. Her daughter by Zeus was Persephone, who was captured by Hades and taken to the underworld, signifying the end of the growing season. But each spring Hades was persuaded to let her return to her mother, and thereby begin a new cycle of growth on earth. But each fall she had to return to the realm of Hades.

Dionysius, son of Zeus and mortal Semele, daughter of the king of Thebes, was born twice, once by Semele and again from the thigh of Zeus. Thus he was both man and god. Each spring he disappeared only to return each winter. His winter return was welcomed by a celebration in December, the winter solstice.

The return was marked by much feasting, drinking, playing of games and sports, and the exchange of gifts, all of which resemble the Christian celebration of Christmas. This festival may have contained the promise of an equally happy life after death. Thus Demeter was the goddess of both fertility and the promise of life after death. She was a most popular goddess for she promised the people much joy in sexual orgies and feasting. She promised both happiness and hope for the future. She was also the goddess who promised people an escape from the fear of evil and terror of their gods by indulging in wild intoxication and ecstatic visions.

Demeter and Dionysius became the gods of the Mystery Cults, of which there were three important ones: the Eleusinian, the Orphic, and the Dionysian. These cults practiced secret services and rites, conducted often in the woods or caves. In their services secret knowledge or gnosis (mystery) would be given to the initiates. The revelation of divine knowledge would be accompanied by ritual drinking, dancing, hallucinations, and sexual pleasures.

Many more divine personages could be added to the Greek pantheon, but the principal players have been introduced.

Notions of the Afterlife and the Religious Cult

One further element in all religions is the perplexing problem of how to explain the inevitability of death and what happens to both body and soul after death. The Greeks did believe in a life after death, but this life was thought to be lived in a dark, joyless place. The Greeks were uncertain whether this afterlife was located underground, or on an island, or in a land beyond the setting sun. In all instances it was a world of darkness to which the soul was guided by Hermes to the shores of the river Acheron (one branch of which was the river Styx). The soul was carried across the river by a boatman named Charon, who released the soul to Hades, brother of Zeus and the ruler of the underworld. For the heroes a special place of happiness, the Elysian Fields, was reserved. Here the heroes enjoyed a life of fun and feasting. For the ordinary mortals, their souls would be judged by Hades. If the soul was condemned for being evil, it was sent to a place of eternal punishment, deep down in Hades, to be tortured by the Furies. If the soul was judged to be good, then it was sent to the realm of the Blessed.

The everyday religious observances of the ancient Greeks were similar to those of other early religions. Since the people were at the mercy of the gods for their daily survival, religion designed practices that would placate them, such as prayers, incantations of magic words, and animal sacrifices. Also performed were ritual ceremonies, which might include music and dancing, sexual intercourse, and the keeping of temple prostitutes to ensure the reproduction of the human race and its food supply. Man would seek to outwit the gods by the performance of magical tricks or resorting to the Delphic Oracle for knowledge on how to please the gods. Although the Greek gods seemed to have been made in the image of man, there was little direct communication with the gods. Each family had its special altar for worship; there was no intimate, loving relationship with the gods.

One might wonder what role gods played in the daily life of the Greeks. The gods did not impose upon the people any strict code of morals. Apollo did represent an ethical code of justice and morality, but, in general, the gods left humans to their own fate. Luck, fate, and predestination played a major role in determining a human's success in life, as well as his final destination after death. So far as the gods were concerned life on earth was dark and hopeless, as dark as the afterlife in the realm of Hades and Persephone.

Greek Philosophy

As Greek civilization evolved, the importance of the gods declined. There arose a new philosophic concept that man could rule his own destiny, that he could choose freely among the options presented to him, and that his own intelligence was sufficient to secure a good and safe life, better than could be secured through prayer and magic. Protagoras in the fifth century B.C. declared that "man is the measure of all things." It is true that Judaism and Christianity believed that God gave man the gift of free will or choice, but the option of free will was always limited by the degree to which man was obedient to God.

Of the many Greek philosophers, perhaps the most influential was Plato. According to Plato's philosophy Truth, or ultimate reality, was not in material things, subject to change and impermanence, but in the invisible, spiritual forms, the Ideas or Logos, which are permanent. Logos preceded creation, the highest Logos was the Idea of Good. Plato did not call Good God. But for practical purposes, Plato's God was the Idea of Good. The abode of Good might be conceived as being in heaven or wherever the souls of men might find an eternal resting place. Plato saw mankind as being both material and spiritual, but only the spiritual part was Idea.

Plato had thought of creating a new religion, but his disciples would create a system of religion called neo-Platonism. The most important disciple was Plotinus (A.D. 205–270), who taught that there is the possibility of a mystical union of man with God, that is, the Idea of the Good. In other words, the soul of man after death can join another, nonmaterial world, not a physical union, but, as St. Paul said, "A union of a new body, the soul, with God." This union would be effected through a mystical process called Love or Eros. Citing St. Paul again, "Things that are seen are transient, but the things that are unseen are eternal. (2 Corinthians 4:18)

If any single theme permeates Greek philosophy it is that man is a thinking, reasoning being who has the power, independent of the gods, to make his own decisions, for better or worse. He alone is responsible for the choices he makes, and if the choice proves to be in error, then man must suffer the consenquences.

One Greek school of philosophy, best expressed in the life of the Roman Emperor Marcus Aurelius, stressed the importance of a life ruled by reason, free from passion. Stoics rejected the Dionysian and Epicurean philosophies of living for the pleasure of the day. The good life was one disciplined by reason, reasonably ascetic, and marked by intense self control. The Stoics recognized that there were limits to man's ability to control his passions and his destiny. If life soured and the pain was great then man might pray to the gods for relief. However man must never display anguish, but suffer the pain in a stoical manner, with no visible sign for others to see. A less severe code of ethics was expressed by Aristotle in his concept of the "golden mean" as being a guide to an ideal lifestyle. The concept of the golden mean was that it was good to avoid the extremes of righteousness or evil, but attempt to pursue a middle course between the extremes. Virtue then is a state apt to exercise deliberate choice, bring in the relative mean, determined by reason, and as the man of practical wisdom would determine. It is a middle way between the faulty one, in the way of excess on one side and of defect on the other. But Virtue finds, and when found adopts the mean.[1]

Mystery Cults

At the time of Jesus and his message of love, Palestine was ruled by the Roman Empire and heavily influenced by Greek philosophy and the mystery cults. Greek mystery cults were popular at the time of Jesus. These cults (the "mystery" came from a Greek term meaning to keep one's hands over the mouth so as not to reveal secrets) introduced man to a closer, more intimate relationship with the gods by means of using secret rituals and prayers. Mystery cults had in common the practice of transmitting this secret knowledge about the gods, in the form of initiations rites. In no case was this secret knowledge to be given to anyone who was not a cult member, in the same manner that a fraternal organization of college youth or Masons will not reveal their secrets to others. Each cult had its special initiation rites, dramatic performances that insured that the initiate would never forget the experience of becoming a member. Once a member, he would always enjoy a blessed hereafter for all of eternity.

The mystery cults all had a number of purification rites designed to rid the soul of evil or unclean elements. A common purification rite used water, a symbol of purity, by either bathing in water or using water in a baptismal rite.

Different mystery cults had their special objectives and ritual acts. The Orphic mystery rejected the libertine practices of the Dionysian cult by practicing a severely ascetic daily life, wearing white robes, abstaining from eating meat, and living a celibate life, all of which were thought to secure a place for the soul in heaven. Man was believed to be both body and soul, with the soul destined to live forever in a cyclical process of reincarnation. Only Orpheus, the son of Apollo, could offer an escape from this rebirth cycle. Orpheus was god of music, a strict ascetic, eating no meat, abstaining from sex, and living a purified life.

The Dionysian mystery was most sensual, anything but ascetic. The essence of Dionysian worship was the celebration of a god who was twice born or "reborn," but also born of a human mother. Of all of the gods, Dionysius was one most easily approached by humans. The celebration of a god who was reborn and returned to earth each spring was a happy one for it meant a good harvest for the new year. Moreover, Dionysius was a link between life and death, for if a god returns to earth from death, then man has hope that he too can be resurrected from the dead. The Dionysian celebration was Bacchian in nature, including wild nightly orgies, intoxication by wine, and convulsive dancing, until the communicant attained a state of emotional madness. But this was always a divine madness, a sign that the person was filled with the spirit of the god. Dionysius was a popular god for he was the god of the dance, the satyr plays, and Greek tragedy. In some respects a Dionysian frenzy has its counterpart in the religious ecstasy of an intoxicated, charismatic Christian, a believer, one might say, in the mystery of Christ.

Even the celebration of Christmas can be traced to the Roman celebration of the winter solstice or Saturnalia, when it was supposed that Dionysius returned to earth.

The Eleusinian Mystery also promised its adherents immortality, since Persephone returned each spring from Hades. This mystery celebrated the lives of Demeter and her daughter, Persephone. The "Hymn to Demeter" describes the mystery rite by which these goddesses gave immortality to mankind, as well as bountiful crops each year. Sacred festivals were held at Eleusis, near Athens, with parades, dancing, feasting and drinking, display sexual symbols, and finally special rites used to memorialize the dead. These rites also established a sacred link between sex, birth, the fruits of agriculture, and the dignity of dying with the promise of immortality.

5

The Greek Gods Become Roman

As early as the sixth century B.C. Greek gods and culture had begun to enter the Italian peninsula. First the Etruscans in northern Italy had made trade connections with the Greek cities and found that the Greek gods would be useful companions to their native spirits and gods. By the fourth century B.C. the Romans were trading with the Greeks and so they began to adopt the Greek gods and other aspects of Greek culture. By the second century B.C. Rome had become a powerful, expanding military state. By the time of Christ it had become a world empire, extending its boundaries from Britain to Parthia, and from Egypt northward to Palestine, Greece, Syria, Persia, even to the Tigris River bordering Parthia. By 146 B.C. Rome had conquered Macedonia and by 32 B.C. Egypt. When Rome finally conquered the three eastern kingdoms that had inherited the Alexandrian empire after the death of Alexander the Great in 323 B.C.. Rome became the possessor of a hybrid population. Each had its own language, religion, and culture, and each segment of the empire contributed cultural elements to the others, thereby creating a new, Hellenized culture. The Hellenic age owes its existence to the exploits and rule of Alexander the Great, 356–323 B.C. King Philip of Macedonia, father of Alexander, had by military force united the warring and independent city-states of the Greek peninsula. Alexander used his father's resources to expand the kingdom to the Indian borders, including all of Asia Minor and Egypt. Not only was Alexander a great soldier, but he was a man with a vision of one world under one ruler. He dreamed that he could join together the mixed races into one people. He married his soldiers to native women, and he set the example by marrying a Persian woman, Roxanne. He dreamed that a one-world culture could be created. He built a number of cities, fifty or more, which were to become regional centers for the propagation of the arts and sciences, however, using the Greek language and retaining Greek culture as the foundation. Alexander's most famous city, Alexandria, was built on the Nile delta. For several centuries, just before and into the early Christian era, Alexandria was the world's most noted center for learning, art, science, and theological discussion. Not to be overlooked among the wise decisions made by Alexander was that a god-king could become a great cohesive force to bind together many diverse peoples, especially when the people were in awe of divine persons. Hellenistic culture found its inspirations coming from a variety of sources including, Greek religion and philosophy, Judaism, Persian Mithraism, and the Egyptian gods, Ra and Osiris.

Before any further review of the Hellenic era is made, the religious experiences of Rome should be surveyed.

Roman Religion

The first people to live in Italy were the Etruscans, who occupied northern Italy. In general, the Etruscans, like other people who had a cosmic type of religion, worshiped the forces of nature, spirits, some good and some evil, some with human attributes, and some resembling plants and animals. Sacrifices were made to the several gods so that the people might win their favor and thereby have bountiful crops and many children. The dead were buried in well-designed granite tombs, along with their tools and other worldly possessions. Perhaps the Etruscans had some concept of an afterlife. Some of the Etruscan gods took the names of corresponding Greek gods and goddesses.

The Romans before the fifth century B.C. had a religion similar to the Etruscans in that it possessed a number of gods and spirit forces. At first these supernatural beings were considered to be forces without human characteristics, but later they took on human form. As the Romans extended their empire to the east, Greek culture and religion became a part of the Roman way of life. The first Roman god was Mars, a war god, a sun god, and a god of fertility. Two other early Roman gods were Jupiter, akin to the Greek Zeus, and his wife, Juno, parallel to the Greek goddess Hera. Jupiter became the patron god of Rome, while Juno became the guardian of the home and women, both young and old.

As Rome became more involved in the Greek world through trade and war, more of the Greek deities were adopted as Roman ones. The names would be changed, but their special functions in the Greek religion were retained in the Roman religion.

The Greek deities most honored were those deemed the most powerful in Roman eyes. Jupiter and Juno were the supreme deities, while Mars, god of War, was next in line in the power hierarchy. Venus, Greek Aphrodite, was goddess of love, Apollo the god of healing, and Minerva, the Greek Athena, became the goddess of wisdom. Many other gods and goddesses were listed in the Roman pantheon.

Roman religious services and practices resembled greatly those found among the Greek religion. Perhaps the Romans placed more emphasis on home worship than the Greeks, although in both religions the center of worship was before the altar in the home and before any altar in a public place. The special guardians of the home and family were the vestal virgins. The goddess of the hearth was Vesta, whose altar was attended by virgin girls and women. Roman priests, like Greek priests, employed magic tricks, including astrology, amulets and charms, and magical words and prayers, all used for the purpose of warding off the evil spirits or the wrath of the gods.

The Roman attitude about death was also taken from the Greeks. The Romans, like the Greeks, had no certain convictions about the hereafter, or what happened to one's soul or if the souls were judged. However, the Romans did honor dead ancestors by observing "All Souls" Day in February.

The Roman Empire and Christian Persecution

The Roman religion developed one non-Greek feature, namely that it permitted Roman rulers to use the power of the gods to unite a great empire under the banner of a divine emperor.

It was a Roman republican, Julius Caesar, who converted the aristocratic Roman Republic into a military dictatorship, and it was his successor, his nephew Octavian, who, in 31 B.C., changed the dictatorship into a divine emperorship. His title, "Augustus," suggested an alliance with the gods. Being a divine ruler, Augustus Caesar (and all of his successors) was treated like a god. Oaths were sworn in the emperor's name, coins and banners were stamped with the image of a divine king, and most importantly, all Roman citizens, regardless of their own religious beliefs, were required to swear fidelity and obedience to the one god king, the emperor of Rome. Jews and Christians would be punished and persecuted, not so much for their religious faith, but for their refusal to swear allegiance to the Roman emperor.

Christian writers have probably exaggerated the degree to which Roman Christians were persecuted. Frequently during the first three centuries after Christ Christians who were killed by the Romans were elevated to the status of sainthood, a status in which the martyred souls became quasi-divine agents for expanding the Christians message and intensifying the degree of Christian commitment to the Lord Jesus Christ. However there is much evidence to confirm the possibility that Christians were in fact usually punished and killed for their "atheistic" and treasonable beliefs. Before A.D. 250 there are only three recorded instances of Christians being persecuted in a mass campaign.[1]

Most Christians were punished as individuals for treasonable or criminal acts, not because they were Christians. The first large-scale persecution of Christians occurred under Nero following the burning of Rome in A.D., for which he (falsely, of course) blamed the Christians. Under the Emperor Domitian, 89–96, another mass persecution took place. However, the more serious anti-Christian campaigns occurred under the Emperors Decius and Diocletian during the latter half of the third century. One last effort to eradicate the Christian faith in the Roman Empire was attempted by the Emperor Julian, A.D. 361–363. Julian sought to outlaw all Christian groups and practices and to restore all of the former Roman gods to their rightful place in the power structure of the Roman state. His efforts ended in failure, and soon after Christianity would become the state religion.

In general the Roman state was reasonably tolerant of both Christians and Jews. Certainly after the destruction of Jerusalem in A.D. 70 the Jews were no longer a nuisance to the Roman Empire. The Christians, however, became an increasing problem to the security of Rome. At first the Romans more or less ignored the puny Christian movement. Roman officials viewed the Christians as just another quarreling sect of Jews. Moreover the early Christians were for the most a collection of poor peasants, artisans, and slaves, the "riff-raff" of the Roman population. Since they were powerless, without money, arms, or prestige, why should Romans fear the wrath and revenge of their God, their Christ? A few Roman writers, such as Galen, the physician, Celsus, a conservative intellectual, and Porphry, a Platonic critic, did see a danger in the Christian movement (see Robert Wilken, *Christians in the Roman Empire,* for more information on these men).

Most Roman rulers followed a "let live" policy toward the Christians. So long as Christians paid their taxes, refrained from acts of treason and rebellion, and obeyed the Roman law they were tolerated as second-class citizens.

At times the Roman emperors might attempt to deny their divine heritage but the religious patrons, priests, and writers continued to proclaim the emperors as divine beings. Legends would relate the myths that the emperors were descendants of the founders of Rome, Romulus and Remus, who, in turn, had descended from Venus, goddess of fertility.

Like the Greeks, the Romans saw in religion a vital, effective form of social control, a guide to good morality that would ensure a stable and peaceful society. So these Roman gods placed their blessings not only on the emperors and on Roman law and government, but also upon the established class system, the patriarchal society and family, the institution of slavery, and the superiority of the Roman citizen and state. All other peoples were barbarians. If anyone wished for the freedom to find their own god or gods and to have a personal relationship with their god, this was not in the Roman set of values.

Religious rites were acts of patriotic devotion to the state. Appointed Roman priests were agents of the state. They were appointed for life, unlike all other governmental positions. It was their duty to guide and instruct the people to follow the correct paths of devotion and obedience. The priesthood had two classes: the "pontifices," who controlled the vestal virgins and the sacrificial rites to the Roman gods; and the "augurs," who communed with the gods for information on what was to be the divine destiny of mortal man. One can suspect that the ruling emperors were assured that the "augurs" would always relate the proper words.

Hellenism

The story of the Roman religion must include the impact of the developing Hellenistic culture upon events in the Roman Empire. The empire had provided centuries of relative peace and freedom for competing religions to seek their claims to the souls of the Roman people. Christianity, along with several other religious groups from Egypt and the eastern realms of the empire, despite official disapproval of these alien sects, continued to find adherents. Trade was stimulated, and with the traders went the Greek language and culture. As Greek culture impacted on non-Greek people, so the Greek way of life was affected by them. Hellenistic culture, therefore, was an amalgam of a number of cultures, not unlike the American cultural mix. (For a study of the Hellenistic legacy to Christianity, see Frederick C. Grant, *Roman Hellenism and the New Testament*.)

By the fourth century B.C. the glory days of the Greek civilization were waning. Internal civil wars and the Persian invasions had weakened the Greek city states. Alexander's empire had distributed Greek ideas and the Greek language to the far corners of his empire. In turn religious cults and gods from the several parts of the empire began to contribute their ideas to the Greek world. The empire became a melting pot of many religions: Judaism, Mithraism, the cult of Isis and Osiris, neo-Platonism, and, eventually, Christianity.

During the Hellenistic era, the fourth century B.C. to the first and second centuries A.D., certain religious trends developed. First there was a trend toward monotheism, a trend that of course favored Judaism and Christianity. Another trend was the search for a more loving God to whom people could pray directly, without need for any intermediary agents, priests or seers. A god like Zeus, living on top of Mt. Olympus, seemed remote and unapproachable. If there was any need for a messenger to God, then this agent should not be a man, but a divine being, a savior, or the Greek Logos.

The Greek philosophers had claimed that man was master of his own fate. He was by virtue of his intelligence and reason a god unto himself. The thinkers of the Hellenistic period were not so sure of man's ability to save himself. To them man was not the measure of all things. God still ruled the universe, and his power still governed the course of nature's movements and the destiny of mankind.

Another theme found in the literature of the Hellenists is a haunting desire to find a better world beyond this one on earth. It might be possible to fashion a utopian paradise on earth, a new Zion, but more likely man had a better chance to find the good life in heaven. The search for a world of bliss appealed especially to the poor masses and slaves, probably 90 percent of the Roman population. The promise of a good life in eternal peace and happiness, free from pain, was a powerful incentive for religious leaders to pursue this goal of eternal peace in Heaven.

These religious trends provided a formula for remodeling old religions or creating new religions. But why wait for death to enjoy the beauty and peace of heaven? Why not have heaven on earth? There arose an apocalyptic vision of some divine agent coming from heaven who would rid the world of sin and war, even, perhaps, free the conquered nations from the burdens placed upon them by the Roman Empire. Captive peoples like the Jews, wished to speak their languages, maintain their traditional customs and religions, and reestablish their former state of self-government. The burden of paying taxes to Rome strengthed the religious and political movements desirous of being rid of Roman rule, either by revolution or by divine intervention.

Isaiah's concept of a "suffering servant" was an early Judaic belief that it was possible for a savior to come to free mankind from sin and captivity by a foreign power. A new Jerusalem was a divine possibility. The book of Daniel portrays in greater detail how God would come to earth to free the Jewish people from foreign conquest. This "savior" concept reached a peak among the Jews during the post-Alexandrian reign of Antiochus IV, 168–125 B.C. Antiochus tried to impose upon Israel a Hellenistic version of Judaism. He sought to modify the Torah by converting Jehovah into the god Zeus. He also tried to outlaw the rite of circumcision and to abolish many of the Jewish holy days. Orthodox Jews, led by the Hassidim, or Pharisees, began a revolt against Antiochus. From the time of the revolt, which began in 168 B.C., until Pompey captured Jerusalem in 63 B.C., Israel enjoyed a brief period of relative independence. The book of Daniel, written about 164 B.C., reflects Jewish faith in the reality and power of a divine savior to save Israel from its enemies. Daniel saw a Zoroastrian type of dualistic battle between God and an evil sea monster. A Mithraic bull was used to symbolize the divine savior. The gist of the Daniel prophecy was to say to the Jews that God would come in the form of an anointed savior to restore the kingdom of Israel to its former glory.

One Jewish party, the Zealots, believed that with God's help a successful war could be waged against the Romans. The majority of the Jews preferred to bide their time, to make a temporary truce with their Roman masters while awaiting the arrival of the promised savior from heaven.

Other captive nations, Egypt, Syria, Armenia, Persia, and the Greeks, like the Jews, had similar aspirations for the restoration of their independent status.

The Hellenistic search for a more intimate relationship with God was given some credence if one notes the changes in the nature of the God, Jehovah, from Mosaic times, when God was a just but demanding patriarch. He was far from the loving, compassionate God portrayed by the later Jewish prophets, Micah, Hosea, Isaiah, and others. The mystery cults mentioned above sought to give the worshiper a sense of personal touch with God. Another religious movement, Gnosticism, which existed from about the first century B.C. to the third century A.D., preached a gospel that man could be saved from sin by the acquisition of secret knowledge, or gnosis, an idea held by the mystery cults also. Gnosticism was an outgrowth of Zoroastrianism and Orphic mystery beliefs which held that the earth and mankind are evil, and that only the forces of light or good can overpower the forces of darkness or evil. In the books of Acts and Luke there are related the actions of Simon Magus (Magi or Magician), who preached the coming of a more humane, loving God who could relate to the human condition. Simon was probably a follower of Gnosticism who tried to unite Greek philosophy and Hebrew theology into a new interpretation of the nature of God. Gnostics saw God as being indefinable, absolutely perfect and immaterial, pure spirit with no human attributes. The material body is evil, as is all material substance. Man, therefore, must avoid contact with all material things if he is to know God. The soul must be freed from the body if there is to be immortality for the soul.

The Gnostic god is both male and female: the sexes are deemed to be equal. But this god is not the creator of the universe, like Jehovah, who created an evil thing. In fact creation was an accident more than any planned act of God. Creation gave birth to sin and ignorance. It is only the secret knowledge held by the Gnostics that can redeem man from sin. But God, the good spirit, is not the ultimate being, that is the Logos, the Platonic Idea, which existed before God and above God. As with the mystery cults, the Gnostics believed that some intermediary with God would be needed to provide the link between man and God. They saw Christ as being this agent to reveal God to man. However, Christ was never human, being only pure spirit. Gnosis or knowledge was obtained by a system of rituals and prayers, practiced in a state of intense, irrational emotion that would permit man to receive Holy Wisdom and to know God.

Another Hellenistic religion was Neo-Platonism, a religious derivation of Platonic philosophy. Reality was not in the material world, which was only an illusion of reality. Reality lay the realm of Ideas or Logos, the divine pattern by which all things in the world were created. The highest Idea, Goodness, became the equivalent of God. All humans could aspire to attain Goodness by living a life of morality and creating an ideal society for the promotion of virtue. The souls of the dead, if good, could never die; at some future time they could be resurrected to join another body. Neo-Platonists also believed that if the soul could be released from the painful body, then the world could be freed from pain and sin by the miraculous intervention of a divine power that would come to earth, destroy all evil, and build a new world of peace and goodness. Thereupon, the world would be ruled by Logos or wisdom, or God.

More and more during the Hellenistic era people hungered for some escape from earthly miseries caused by Roman rule. Many of the religions and cults believed that the souls of humans were immortal, and that the future resurrection of body and soul to life on earth in a new, idealized condition was possible. No single religion could better incorporate the several religious trends found in the Hellenistic era than Christianity, which may be a factor in explaining the success of the Christian church.

Yet one idea among Hellenistic philosophers, like Aristotle and Plato, was that chance or fate has as much to do with man's future destiny as faith in God or the power of reason and free choice. Among the common people not given to theological debate or philosophical speculation, a belief in the powers of chance, the god Tyche, was an attractive one. The Roman writer, Pliny the Elder, wrote of chance that "We are so much at the mercy of Chance that chance is our God."[2] Life is a gamble, a throw of the dice, and no one, even the gods, can guarantee mankind the ideal of peace and prosperity.

The Hellenistic period of history, filled with many diverse religious and cultural movements, furnished a fertile environment for the birth of a new world religion, Christianity.

6

The Chinese Way of Life:
Taoism and Confucianism

For over two thousand years Confucianism, Taoism, and Buddhism have been integral parts of the Chinese culture. The first two are indigenous to China, while Buddhism came as an import from India in the second century A.D. Buddhism is treated in a separate chapter so repetitous detail will be omitted from the discussion of Chinese religion. It will suffice to say that Buddhism was introduced by Buddhist missionaries, and that, although it was resisted, even persecuted, by the ruling classes as a threat to the peace of Chinese society, it received a warm reception from the masses of the people. Buddhism promised the poor and oppressed classes release from the pain of earthly existence. Neither Confucianism nor Taoism offered much hope for eternal salvation of the soul or a peaceful afterlife. By the ninth century China had over 44,000 Buddhist monasteries and 260,000 monks and nuns.[1] After the ninth century Buddhism no longer experienced significant growth, but it was destined to remain a major aspect of the Chinese religious experience.

As for other imported religions only Christianity and Islam sent missionaries to China. Neither was successful in winning the allegiance of more than a minority of the Chinese people. In the seventh century Nestorian Christian missionaries made their way into China, but their efforts were soon nullified when Chinese authorities began a campaign of persecution. It was not until the thirteenth century that Roman Catholic missionaries, Jesuits, Dominicans, and Franciscans, came to China but within a century Chinese authorities had banned all Christian activities. In the sixteenth century Jesuit missionaries were again active in China. In 1582 Matteo Rici came to Macao and by 1601 he had arrived in Peking. The Chinese officials accepted him with tolerance so long as he did not preach his religion. He was welcomed for what Western science and technology could give to China. But above all Christian missionaries had to divorce themselves from any efforts to encourage the political and economic control of China by Western powers.

69

Protestant missionaries appeared in the eighteenth century, but never did Christianity become a significant form of worship in China. A century after Ricci there were probably fewer than 250,000 Christians in China.[2]

Islamic missionaries were more successful than the Christians. The first Islamic missionaries arrived in the late seventh century, and a century later Islam had gained the souls of Central Asian people. Although Islam failed to dominate all of China, it did become the largest minority faith in China, and the majority faith in Northwest China.

When China came under Communist control in 1940, vigorous efforts were made by the government to suppress all forms of religious worship. Communism was to become the national faith. On the surface the antireligion campaign seemed to be successful. Temples and churches were destroyed. Religious schools and charitable agencies were closed. Any public expression of any religious act risked imprisonment or exile to the countryside doing hard labor. However, quietly, in the hearts of the common people, the traditional worship of three ancient faiths continued. Since the death of Mao Tse-Tung in 1976, religious restraints have been relaxed, temples and churches have reopened, and the people who wish to worship, whatever their particular religion, may do so.

Prehistoric Chinese people, had, like other primitive human beings, a cosmic religion in which natural, cosmic forces were worshiped. The gods were spirit forces found in nature, the sun, earth, moon, the several planets and stars, or those forces that created the world and all therein and that continue to control the destiny of human survival. These early people realized that they must learn either how to control these external spirit forces or how to escape them if control was impossible. Soon there appeared among the people professional interpreters of these forces, astrologers who read the heavens and the stars for what messages they may have for mere mortals.

The earliest known records of ancient Chinese religion came from excavated animal bones dating to the Shang Dynasty, 1523–1028 B.C. On these bones were inscribed messages that the diviners were to reveal to the people. During the Chou Dynasty, 1028–256 B.C., religion became more sophisticated, more ritualized, more directed by a priestly class, and more subordinate to the ruling emperors. The Chou family conducted a rebellion for power against the Shang in which they justified their rebellion by declaring that it was ordered by a "Mandate from Heaven." China's rulers became divine beings, demi-gods if not gods. There was now a belief that the universe was composed of a three-tiered power structure, with heaven or t'ien at the top, then earth, and at the bottom man. Even though man was at the bottom, it is significant that Man was included among the ruling forces of the universe. It is important to note that both Confucianism and Taoism are less concerned about heaven and salvation than is Christianity, and more dedicated to the idea that man's welfare on earth is of major importance.

Heaven became the supreme god or authority, and since the emperor had his mandate from heaven and had to obey the mandates of heaven, it was logical that all other Chinese had to submit to the rules of the king-god. In this chain of command we find the origins of a society in which order is paramount, and where order prevails there appears to be a peaceful society living in a balanced state of static harmony. For centuries this mode of government was the ideal one.

In primitive times and idea arose that worship of the dead ancestors of royalty was necessary. The ancestor spirits were among the controlling forces that determined whether man lives or dies. As the society became more developed, with the arrival of a feudal nobility who would share power with the emperors, then the noble ancestors would be revered as well, and eventually ancestor worship became an established part of Chinese religious life for all of the people. Ancestor worship is a further bulwark to guarantee a static, balanced, harmonious society.

The concept of a balanced society was reinforced by a philosophical explanation of how the universe operates, a concept given the name of yin and yang. Although the universe is in a state of constant change, it is not a straight line of change from one state of being to a better state, or from a simple to a complex order, but a cyclical change, rotating in cycle after cycle, of opposing forces of creation and destruction, positive and negative, or yin and yang, always finally striking a state of balanced harmony. Yang represents power, a positive force, heaven, and the male element. Yin is the weaker force, the negative, the earth, and the female element. Through the interaction of the yang and yin forces all of creation is brought forth into a world of harmony.

These early religious concepts become a permanent part of Chinese society. The concepts of obeying the moral laws of heaven and the dictates of divine kings, of ancestor worship, of maintaining a static, balanced social system, and of placing human welfare on Earth above any desire to save souls, would all be incorporated into the philosophical systems of Confucianism and Taoism.

For the masses of illiterate peasants the observance of the religious life might be found primarily in the presentation of gifts to the shrines of the many deities, the saying of ritualist prayers, the seeking of good fortune in magical charms and rites, and observing the proper times as dictated by the stars for planting crops, arranging marriages, building homes, and a host of other daily tasks.

Chinese family life has been molded by its religious systems and traditions. Nora Waln, in her 1933 book, *The House of Exile,* has related her experiences in China living with a wealthy middle class family for several years. Waln, a Philadelphia Quaker, came to China as a young secretary for The Young Women's Christian Association. Her husband was a British consul agent for a large bank, which gave the couple some access to important Chinese families, from whom Waln had the opportunity to learn about Chinese customs and religion. Waln served as a tutor for the children of one of these families. The family had eighty members, all presided over by the elder patriarch. It was an extended family in which parents, grandparents, children, uncles, aunts, nieces, nephews, and cousins all lived together. This family was close to the Soong family, whose daughtters became the wives of two Chinese rulers, Sun Yat Sen and Chiang Kai-Shek. It was a crime almost greater than murder for any family member to dishonor the family name in any manner. The misdeeds of any family member would bring dishonor upon even the ancestors. Disobedience of the ruling patriarch meant action, banishment forever from the family home and use of the family name. The offender would be barred from any position of trust or good employment.

Family property was owned in common. Marriages were arranged by the parents of the prospective bride and groom. All family members were responsible for the sins of each member. However, no child was ever illegitimate; all were honorable members of the family. Widows were to remain confined to their quarters until they remarried, an event that was expected and desired. The woman's primary function was to bear children. To fail to have children was to have a failed marriage. It was a death sentence for a woman to commit adultery, but for the husband to have mistresses and illegitimate children was neither a sin nor a crime. During pregnancy no woman could be imprisoned, so valuable was each child. A divorced woman could never marry a man who bore the same family name.

The eldest son inherited the father's position and wealth upon his death. A funeral ceremony was a most impressive event. All three religions, Buddhism, Taoism, and Confucianism, would participate in the funeral rite. Death was a time of joy and celebration, for now the soul of the deceased was free to enter heaven. Buddhist and Taoist priests would bless the coffin and then accompany the funeral procession to the burial site. Along the way gifts and money would be thrown to the mourners. The eldest son carried the spirit tablet, a symbol of the family's ancestors, and after the funeral, the tablet would be placed in the family's hall of ancestors. Cymbals would play and paper horses, houses, and people would be burned as symbols of good fortune for the soul in heaven. After death a sixty-day mourning period would be observed, during which time all family members would wear white clothes and shoes.

Waln's Chinese family worshiped in Confucian temples, where prayers and hymns of praise were offered to Confucius. Lighted lanterns and music celebrated the glory of their Lord. In all Confucian temples there would be a tablet bearing the inscription, "When Fan Che asked Confucius the question, What is humanity?, he replied, To love man. When he was asked, What is knowledge?, he said, To know man. He who desires to know man first knows God."

China's two indigenous religions, Confucianism and Taoism, began more as philosophical utterances than as revelations from God. However, over the years both sets of ideas became for the common people religious systems with temples, priests, rituals, and supernatural phenomena related to sacred legends. Neither religion has had any impact on non-Chinese people, with the exceptions of the Japanese and the Koreans. Neither religion had missionary agencies to propagate their faiths among the Western nations of the world. But both religions were destined to have great influence on Chinese life for centuries. Chinese ethics, politics, family life, education, art and literature, in fact, the entire fabric of Chinese culture reflects these religious systems. A few people in the Western world know something about Confucianism, especially the wise and witty aphorisms attributed to Confucius. Taoism, by contrast, is alien to rational Western minds. It is an abstract, mystical, and transcendental religion akin to Buddhism. Confucianism seems rational, more down to earth, with common sense ideas that most people can understand. It has a system of moral codes so similar to the Ten Commandments that the Christian people could feel kinship to Confucian ethical conduct.

Both were products of philosophies of the sixth century B.C., Taoism perhaps preceding Confucianism by a few years.

Taoism

Followers of Taoism claim that Lao Tzu, the founder of Taoism, was a teacher of Confucius, even though the birthdate of Confucius is given as 604 B.C., while the date for Lao Tzu is uncertain, perhaps 551 B.C. Some scholars doubt that he ever lived, or, if he did, they think that he was only one of several authors of the book of Taoism, the Tao-tei Ching ("The Way and the Power of Life"). Scholars tend to agree that the basic beliefs of Taoism were made and collected into book form two to three centuries before Lao Tzu, or even before 2000 B.C. Lao Tzu was probably a petty government officer, and also a teacher on how to live a good life with a good government. Almost nothing more of his life is known. It is said that Lao Tzu claimed, "I am the Tao, the Truth, the Life." He stressed the need to live in harmony with nature. Everyone could be a master, that is, learn how to live in peace, free from stress, by following man's instincts to obey the rules made by society and government. Goodness or virtue come from within one's self.

Legend has filled in the missing chapters in the life of Lao Tzu. One story relates that he was born of an immaculate conception, his father was a star, and that he was carried in his mother's womb for eighty-two years. He was already an old, white-haired man when he was born. He was reputed to have lived the life of a hermit for many years. During these years he sought to find a body of followers, but with little success. So he left his native land by riding on a buffalo on his way to Tibet.

At the entrance to the Tibetan gate, the gatekeeper tried to persuade him to return to China. Lao refused but he did yield to the gatekeeper's plea to write down his thoughts on the good life. Thus the most important source for Taoism, the Tao-te Ching, was written.

Lao Tzu left no church, no priests and missionaries, no rituals and services, nor anything that might have convinced his followers that his message of peace was of much importance. Yet "the Way" did become a major Chinese religion, which eventually developed a creed, rituals, and an organized religious institution with priests and teachers to guide the faithful. As with Buddhism the most devout followers found that Taoism, a mystical religion, is best studied and practiced in the quiet solitude of a monastery. Taoism requires a body of followers who are intelligent, with the fortitude and patience to engage in prolonged periods of meditation and abstract thought. For the ordinary, working masses who must struggle diligently even for survival, Taoism would not be the best choice for religious participation. Hence the more simple and practical teachings of Confucius had greater appeal and reception among the majority of the Chinese people.

Taoism can be defined as a religion with three levels of comprehension. At the highest, most philosophical level, Taoism attempts to define the ultimate reality of existence. This reality is beyond comprehension by the sense organs and the reasoning mind. Reality is that which is behind all of creation, and the place to which all creatures return after death. Tao is the creative force for all of creation. Mankind and all other aspects of nature are one and the same. Tao is energy, that which energizes all substances, all of life, akin to Bergson's *elan vital,* or the physicist's reduction of all matter to pure electrical energy. Knowledge about Taoism is not found by research and study, but by the practice of meditation. Meditation has the power to release the invisible energy of the subconscious mind to reveal the truth in an instant, intuitive act of illumination or enlightenment. In brief Tao, like the Buddhist Brahman, is spirit, infinite and eternal, hidden but always present, existing before God and creation, the creator of good and evil. It is never born, never dies, but is always within the human person.

At a lower level Taoism is the expression of the mystery of nature, the mystery of the planets that move with precision and predictability as Tao comes into action. Life and death move in cycles, just as the sun rises and sets, and the seasons come and go. Always in nature the conflicting elements, the positive and the negative elements, seek to find a balanced harmony. The Chinese express the duality of life that stems from the invisible creator, Tao, as the competition of complimentary opposites, yin and yang. These two competing energies are found in all things, but both must be kept in balance as in Aristotle's "golden mean." Excess of either energy is harmful. Yang is masterful but with justice, while Yin is passive and merciful. Yin and Yang are always in a state of interaction, but also always seeking to find a state of balance. When the two forces are in balance within the human personality then the perfect, ideal human will exist. The goal of the Taoist is to live in harmony with Tao, with nature, and with all creatures. All things follow the rules of Tao and Tao only follows itself. Hence it is impossible to improve nature, the world, human beings, or even oneself. Be what you are in peace, humility, and the acceptance of life as it is now Tao is not only a spirit force, for it has the capacity to be clothed in flesh and in all of the material aspects of natural things. But always Tao, the spirit, will prevail over the physical, material elements found in the natural world, for Tao will never die.

At a third level, a human level, Taoism becomes the way to a good life, or the way of the perfect human. Mankind must live in harmony with all other beings, human or nonhuman. The ethical aspects of Taoism operate on two levels: that of the philosophical mystic who seeks to find Tao or truth by living a disciplined life in a world isolated from all other humans, from all sensual pleasures, a life of denial and poverty spent meditating on the matters of life and death. Since man is God, the only way to know God or Tao is to know oneself, and that knowledge comes only from the deep recesses of the mind or the "spirit self," discovered through the medium of meditation. The other level is the way of the common man who will use the traditional paths to God's wisdom, namely through the intervention of priests, rituals, and the building of a religious establishment or church.

Pure spirit can be known only when the physical human body is purified of all sensual desires, sex, wealth, power, self-pride, and fear. Perfection is destroyed when one seeks fame and fortune and worships at the feet of temporal gods. Perfection will come only to that person who has quelled all desires, mastered his emotions, become totally unselfish, and lived a clean life. When a person chooses to live a celibate life of poverty in a monastery where master teachers can teach the truth, then one begins to learn how to travel the way. The road is long, hard, and demanding. For one who has not shared this lifestyle, it would be impossible to understand what radical change in one's daily life would be required. Taoist teachers give instruction to the novices in the practice of yoga techniques, breathing exercises, and even the control of sexual intercourse so as to avoid having an orgasm.

By the second century A.D. Taoism had become a religion for the common people also. However, for those Chinese people who were struggling for a bare existence, most of whom were illiterate, the abstract, mystical nature of Taoism would need a major reconstruction. Taoism took on the formalized, ritualized patterns of worship similar to some forms of Christianity or Hinduism, or even the cosmic religions of primitive man. For popular Taoism, the principal altar for worship was within the home. External worship would be within special temples and before sacred shrines, where formalized prayers were recited, gifts of food and money were offered, magical incantations and physical gestures were performed, and priests were available to receive confessions of sins, religious instruction was offered, and the messages of the stars could be interpreted. Money could be paid to the priests for their blessings, given to ensure more babies, or rain for the crops, or cures for illness, or finding good fortune in a game of chance. Popular Taoism had little need for asceticism, meditation, and philosophical study of the Taoist books. It was a mixture of Taoism and the traditional cosmic religions. Tao, the invisible spirit force that energizes all of creation, for the common people was located in the sky, or in heaven, where lived a hierarchy of gods and spirits ruled over by a Jade Emperor and a female deity, the Queen of Heaven. Many of the gods represented former real-life emperors. Emperor gods ruled all corners of the globe, south, east, north, and west. Tao also was thought to be an ocean of pure void that gave birth to two dragons, male and female, which caused the cycles of change on earth, moved the planets, caused the change of seasons, and brought to the people the cycle of birth and death. The earth was described as being a square planet, whereas Heaven was a round form more suitable geometrically as an abode for the gods and spirits. Also in heaven could be found the evil demons, the ghosts of the dead ancestors, and all other forces that might destroy mankind. However, these dire evil forces did not dwell within pure Tao.

Good Taoists accept nature and all that happens on earth as a part of human existence. Like the flow of water down the river, which accommodates itself to the course in which it is forced to move, bending when necessary, running swiftly or slowly as the river changes its elevation, and, as the river ends its course and flows into the ocean, so one must accept the defeats and victories along the way; whatever hand fate deals one in the card game of life, so be it; when death comes one has the assurance that the soul flows into the ocean of Tao where the mystery of rebirth in a new creation will occur.

Taoist ethics prescribes the ideal formula for living a good life. The essentials are simplicity, patience, and compassion. Moral laws or commandments are unnecessary since virtue comes from within oneself. Love the world and all therein, love others as one loves him or herself, said Lao Tzu. He said, "Cease this talk of benevolence and righteousness and the people will be benevolent and kind."[3]

Taoists reject all forms of competition and the need for material wealth and success. A simple life, like the one enjoyed by Thoreau at Walden Pond, living in harmony with nature, accepting the reality of polarized forces, yin and yang, will yield happiness and contentment to all humans. Taoists find no value in striving to find ultimate, absolute values for good and evil, or right and wrong. All values are relative, so what purpose do concepts of good and evil have? Life and death are not opposite states of being, for death is only the continuation of life. Those persons who are left behind after the death of a loved one should not mourn but rather rejoice knowing that nature's or Tao's plan for life has been fulfilled.

Taoists preach nonviolence. They oppose the use of violence or war as a means of settling disputes. Lao Tzu said, "Even the finest arms are instruments of evil: An army's harvest is a waste of thorns." Rulers need to be compassionate and love peace. To rejoice in a victory over an enemy is a sin.

In the nonreligious areas of Chinese culture Taoism profoundly influenced art and literature. Since Taoists find God or the supreme spirit in all things of nature so they found God in the beauty of nature, in its landscapes and forests, in the birds and animals, and like St. Francis of Assisi Taoists proclaimed all living creatures as man's brothers and sisters.

In summary, the ideal Taoist accepts life as it is, good and bad, the painful and the pleasurable. Man makes his own heaven and hell. The Taoist way of life offers such counsels as: Learn to control the passions for nothing is essentially good or evil. Keep all things in balance according to the principles of yin and yang. Life is in a state of constant flux. Learn to accept change. A person finds salvation within his or her inner self. There is no need for a divine intercessor, hence priests and churches are irrelevant. Live by wisdom, not by commandments. Good government comes not from rulers but from within oneself. Rules are no substitute for that deep inner instinct to do right, for that is how we become like the master, Lao Tzu.

Confucianism

The one religion most closely identified with China is Confucianism. Many non-Chinese people know about Confucius and his wise sayings with those moral endings. Historians hesitate to classify the teachings of Confucius as a religion since they seem to be a set of moral axioms rather than religious dogmas. Confucius minimized the traditional aspects of religion, such as seeking salvation through the intervention of the gods, or by the manipulation of the gods through the use of prayer and miracles. However, since Confucius based his ethical teachings on the law of the cosmos or heaven, the claim is made that he did establish a new religion. So, as time passed, Confucius's message did become a religion, with all the customary attributes of priests, liturgy, rituals, prayers, and worship practices.

Confucius, meaning "king of the master," was born 551 B.C. in Qufu, a city in Shantung Province. His father died when Confucius was three, and his mother was left with only modest means to care for her family. So as a boy Confucius learned early in life what hard work was, and how painful poverty can be. He was a bright boy who learned readily. At first he was employed as a minor government official, but soon he left this work to become a tutor. He believed that all people had an instinct to learn and to love others, that could be developed through education and practice. It was through the means of education that a better society could be realized.

Confucius aspired to become a high-ranking government official, even to be a prime minister, so that he could have the power to construct a model state in his home province. His quest for such a position over a ten-year period was in vain. Confucius died in 479 B.C. believing that his life had been a failure. Soon after his death, however, his house was made into a shrine. Subsequently, the shrine became a temple, and on the same site many temples were eventually built, the last in A.D. 1724. The descendants of Confucius were given honors, nice homes, and wealth. His heirs were known as "princes of letters." They were exempted from taxes as well as given title to the lands surrounding the Confucian temples. The students of Confucius became leaders in government, and during the Han Dynasty, beginning 210 B.C., Confucian moral precepts, along with Buddhist and Taoist principles, were incorporated into Chinese law. These legal principles served the Chinese state for more than two thousand years, until banned by the Chinese Communist Party in 1949. Later the Communists destroyed the Confucian temples at Qufu. Since 1976 the counterrevolution has restored the temples and opened them to visitors. Whether Confucius will ever regain his "divine" status is unknown, but that Confucianism will survive to remain a significant force in the Chinese way of life is certain.

Confucius was motivated to seek moral and political reforms for his country to mitigate the endless series of civil wars and violence that dominated the sixth century B.C. Wars among competing feudal princes had devastated the land, killing thousands of people and even entire populations in some regions. Thousands were put to death by rival warlords. Government officials were notoriously corrupt and lazy. China was living in a state of Hobbesian violence and immorality.

Confucius believed that human beings were naturally born to be good, and to have a potential to love others, only if they had a good, compassionate ruler. If China were governed by moral leaders then the country would become a peaceful, law-abiding state. Confucius also believed that earlier in Chinese history the people had been ruled by an enlightened ruler, the Duke of Zhou, who lived some two hundred years before Confucius. This duke was deemed to be a model prince, so Confucius planned to use him as a pattern for all good kings in the future.

The teachings of Confucius are found in a collection of sayings called the Analects, which contain twenty books of sentence- and paragraph-length comments, many of which are familiar to Western readers. The Analects, the Confucian Bible, would eventually be supplemented by interpretations and commentaries written by Confucius's students, a most famous one being Mencius, who lived a century after Confucius. Like his master, Mencius was a famous teacher, who, like Confucius, failed to find good employment in the government. His ideas are found in *Works of Mencius*.

The first principle of Confucianism is that a just society must first have a just ruler, or one who rules by the dictates of heaven, or one who rules by the principles of *jen,* meaning love and virtue. Originally jen was found only among men who were from the class of aristocrats, those men who practiced courtesy and compassion for their subjects. Confucius refrained from using jen as a synonym for love, for his ideal society was based on a social class system, not on the principle of brotherly love for all men. The benevolent ruler was not to be chosen by the people. He had to come from a family of noble ancestors who lived by a set of moral guidelines that had been derived from the historical analysis of how good rulers had ruled in the past.

Confucius answered the question, "How can mankind live together in peace?" by saying, "Mankind has an instinct for group harmony in the manner of ants and bees, but this instinct has to be developed through education. The moral person is not one who obeys the gods, but one who obeys the laws of the land." An ideal government is neither a theocracy nor a democracy. The best government comes from a benevolent despotism. If the government is just, then the citizens will behave accordingly.

As important as government is, much more important for the peace and survival of the nation is the nature of the family and home. If family life is good, then government and society will be good. However, it is the ruler who must set the example for the ethical standards of the nation. Confucius had great respect for the value of education and the best schoolhouse was the home. Confucius said, "Those who are born wise are the highest type of people; those who become wise through learning come next; and those who are dull but still will not learn are the lowest type of people."[4]

Also great is the man who knows his country's history, its arts and literature, and above all the art of peace, not war. Education will enable the government to recruit wise persons to do its work. Until the Communist revolution government posts were filled by the use of competitive examinations that placed a premium not on the functions of government, but upon knowledge of the classical literature, the main core of Chinese education.

Confucius taught that all people should obey the Golden Rule, but he never went so far as Jesus, who said that we should love our enemies as we love ourselves. Confucius did say that injuries done to you by an enemy should be returned with a combination of love and justice. Moral families produce moral children, hence an ideal family must have honor and respect for parents, grandparents, all blood relatives, and the highest honor must be paid to dead ancestors. To dishonor the family is the most major sin of all, a sin so black as to warrant suicide.

Underlying all of his axioms and wisdom, Confucius developed a comprehensive system of philosophy that he described as the observance of Five Right Relationships. Four of the relationships were family oriented: father–son, elder brother–junior brothers, husband–wife, and honoring parents and family ancestors. The last was obedience to the rulers.

In addition Confucius included five basic principles. The principle of jen was the first. Jen is the greatest of all virtues. It is an innate quality that motivates people to have respect for all humans, and for all things in nature, animate and inanimate. Confucianism had little concern for the afterlife or the affairs associated with heaven. It is said that Confucius did pray to the gods, but since he never found a true god he dismissed the value of worship to any god. Since we know so little about life on earth, Confucius said, why should we spend time trying to understand the mysteries of God, the spirit world, and death?

The second principle is *li,* the model by which humans are to react to one another in an act of communication or a social relationship. Li prescribes how people are to speak to each other, how to use the proper words, and how to avoid the use of obscene and demeaning words and gestures. It is the Chinese Emily Post guidebook on proper social manners, those qualities that entitle humans to be called "ladies and gentlemen." Li also includes the doctrine of the golden mean or *chung yung,* the Middle Way. Confucius would be no spokesman for the Puritan standard of morality, for he found virtue in the moderate enjoyment of pleasures, fame, wealth, and marital sex.

The third principle, *chung-tzu,* defines the nature of jen as being primarily a term to describe the right relationships among humans, and then finding the correct words to express these relationships. Such terms as "the supreme good" or "true manhood," or the "ideal gentleman" would be examples of good jen.

The fourth principle is *te,* the art of government. Te provides the rules for a good ruler, one who can command the respect of his subjects. The good ruler desires peace. He avoids war if possible, by seeking diplomatic negotiations and compromise with his enemies. He treats his subjects with charity and compassion, but he does not coddle or pamper his people.

The final principle is *wen,* the study and practice of the arts of peace. A nation that loves beauty, the aesthetic values found in art and poetry and music, will find it easier to pursue peaceful international relations. A moral nation becomes a model for other nations in a mutual search for peace.

Confucianism has had a tremendous impact on how the Chinese live their daily lives. Western progressives, who value a fluid, changing society, would charge that China has been harmed by Confucianism, which places a premium on retaining a static culture that venerates ancestors and holds fast to a rigid caste system. However, the ancient Chinese pattern of life is changing as it yields to external pressures from the Western nations, which represent democratic principles and economic capitalism. The advent of Chinese Communism struck a heavy blow to the traditional patterns of Chinese life. Two political and social revolutions, the revolution of Sun Yat Sen in 1910 and the Communist revolution in 1949, broke some of the traditional shackles, but if one could measure the social temperature of the Chinese society it would reveal that the old way registers a higher degree of influence than any of the Western economic, political, and religious systems that have been imported into China.

Other Cultural Influences

China has produced a host of philosophers and religious teachers over the many centuries of its history. In addition to Confucius and Lao Tzu, one other teacher deserves mention: Mo Tzu (479–381 B.C.) Mo Tzu was a rational philosopher who sought to replace a class-based society with a democratic, egalitarian one, in which all people, including women, would enjoy equal social status in both the eyes of the gods and of the government. By the use of logical reasoning Mo Tzu attempted to prove that a god of will ruled the universe, and that this god, like Jesus, taught that he was a god of love, and that all people should love one another. The greatest good that any person could do was to sacrifice one's own interests and render service to others.

Mo Tzu was also an early pacifist. He preached nonviolence and avoiding the use of war, yet he was realistic enough to know there are times when a nation must defend itself from the aggressive acts of other nations. The voice of Mo Tzu was heard by few Chinese people. His message of love and social equality was no match for the louder voices representing the traditional values of an aristocratic, class-oriented society that found comfort in the teachings of Confucius. When the Han Dynasty came to power Confucianism was declared to be the state religion, a position that was rarely disputed throughout Chinese history.

However, when the Communists came to power in 1949, they designed a new social and religious order. Since Communists accepted the Marxist dictum that religion was the opiate of the people and should be abolished, all religious institutions and practices were outlawed. In reality what happened was that religious worship was placed in a deep freeze while awaiting a future time when it would be restored to a new era of acceptance. Even though temples and churches were closed, the need for religious worship remained in the hearts and minds of the people with loyalty and affection for the traditional gods and their counterparts on earth.

After the death of Mao Tse-tung, the driving force behind the revolution was gone. Mao's successors, Deng Xiao Peng and Zhou Enlai, were more concerned with economic and political reforms than the eradication of old religious systems. Gradually after 1985 religious restrictions were relaxed. Temples and churches were reopened and people could worship in public. However, freedom of religious worship remains severely restricted. All religious bodies must refrain from any political action that might be interpreted as treasonable. Christian churches are forbidden to proselytize among the Chinese people for new members. However, in recent years Christian churches have had more success in recruiting new members than they ever had in pre-Communist years. Christianity has had its greatest appeal among those Chinese people who are educated, middle class, and have some Western contacts, such as family relatives living abroad or engaged in various commercial enterprises with Western nations.

A serious handicap for the Catholic church in China is the limitation of children to one or two per family, which necessitates the use of some form of birth control, which Catholics oppose vigorously. Christian churches offer little threat or competition to the traditional faiths found in Confucianism, Buddhism, Taoism, and the long-standing popular or folk religions, which serve many of the poor working class and peasants in China. As of 1990, the number of Christian believers in China is officially given as 5.5 million Protestants and 3.5 million Catholics, a very small number in a population of over one billion people.[5] Other estimates claim that the real total number might be two or three times greater, but even then the Christian population remains only the proverbial drop in the bucket.

7

Hinduism

Of all of the major religions existing today, Hinduism is the oldest. No record contains a date for the beginning of the religion that became India's way of life. Primitive elements of Hinduism date back to two thousand years before Christ, when northern Aryans from Persia invaded India and conquered the native people, who spoke a Dravidian language. These people worshiped, as most other cosmic-religion people did, by honoring the spirits of nature, especially Mother Earth. Scholars are uncertain as to how much or what the Dravidians contributed to Hinduism. As for the Aryan invaders, who spoke an Indo-European language related to most Western languages, there is no doubt. The Aryan culture and religion became the Hindu way of life.

Hinduism is the national religion of India, although today it is not proclaimed as a state religion. Many branches of Hinduism are recognized today, including the Dharmas, Sanatanists, Harijans, Sikhs, and many more. As with Christians, where there are many different sects who all recognize the primacy of Jesus Christ, so the many branches of Hinduism worship the same god or gods as found in the spirit of the Arya-Dharma. Arya-Dharma represents the highest ideals of mankind, namely to propagate the message of love and brotherhood among all men. Hindus define the God-spirit as being universal, eternal and the creator of the universe. God is without form and name, but so God can be understood by common people he is given human form and attributes. True religion is found among those humans who practice forgiveness (except for the enemies of religion), those who refrain from theft, anger, murder, and those who are honest, disciplined, charitable, and just towards other humans. The sum total of all the virtues that God commands of mortal men is called *dharma,* another word for religion.

The history of India and Hinduism is inseparable. Religion permeates every aspect of Indian life, its social structure, its family mores, its economic structure, its moral principles, its political system, and its attitudes toward non-Indian societies and states. No other religion has integrated its basic tenets into a more complete system for the guidance and control of a total society than has Hinduism for India. Both Judaism and Islam resemble Hinduism in that they would dominate their worlds in much the same manner wherever possible.

The term "Hindu" is a word coined by Europeans to describe a set of religious beliefs held by the Indian people. It is not the name by which Indian people describe their own religion. In 1969 the Indian state did recognize "Hinduism" as the proper term to describe the beliefs of the majority of Indian people. Other religions that arose from Hinduism are Buddhism, Jainism, and Sikhism. The name "Hindu" comes from the Indus river, which flows from Tibet, through Pakistan on to the Arabian Sea. In sixth-century Persia some Indian people lived along this river, and they were called by the Persians, "Hindus."

Today the religious composition of India is approximately 83 percent Hindu, 11 percent Muslim, 2.5 percent Christian, 2 percent Sikh, 7 percent Buddhist, 3 percent Jain, and less than 1 percent for all other groups. Only a few Jews, fewer than fifty thousand, live in India. Among the eighty million Muslims, the majority are Sunni. They are mostly from the poor untouchable caste, the Harijans. Although the untouchables have equal rights under the Indian constitution of 1949, old prejudices continue. Hence the Harijans hope to find in Islam the freedom denied by the Hindus. India's twenty million Christians trace their origins to the missionary work of St. Thomas, who went to India only seven years after the crucifixion of Christ.

The antiquity of Indian culture is revealed when one sees how closely Hinduism is tied to the early worship of natural forces. One is struck by the reverence the people have for rivers, mountains, and animals. These natural objects are endowed with spiritual power and have been given human form. The most sacred natural object to be found in India is the river Ganges and its principal city, Varanasi (formerly Benares). Varanasi is to the Indian people what the Vatican in Rome is to Roman Catholics. Hindu mythology tells how the Ganges was born when the water goddess, Ganga, flowed from the heavens through the long hair of the god Shiva, so that the souls of the people might be freed. The Ganges becomes "Mother Ganges," a divine being. To bathe in the Ganges and to drink its water is to experience the highest form of worship. To have the body of a deceased relative cremated on the banks of the Ganges at Varanasi is a guarantee that the soul, released from the body by fire, will go to heaven. Some forty thousand bodies are cremated annually, adding an estimated five thousand tons of ash and body parts to pollute an already heavily polluted river, a condition that greatly concerns the Indian government. Thousands of devout pilgrims come daily to bathe in the Ganges, a holy rite if not a sanitary one.

If a Western visitor to India expects to find in each village a white church bearing some religious symbol, then that person will be disappointed. In large cities one will find Hindu temples. Some are old and delapidated while others, like the Shri Lakshminarain (Birla) in New Delhi, are new and beautiful. Temples are not places for congregational worship. They serve to remind the people that the gods do live and are to be served. It is true that worshipers do enter temples to pray and meditate. Some may be seated in the lotus position (for Hindus this position is preferred to kneeling or bowing heads) for hours at a time, as if in a trance. Connected with temples are religious teachers, gurus or priests, to give instruction to the people. Priests are seldom seen in public, quite unlike the saffron-robed monks in Thailand.

Hindu worship is primarily a home form of worship, so a visitor to India will not see throngs of people going to worship on any special day of the week. On certain festival days public celebrations could be witnessed. A most obvious sign of worship is seeing countless number of pilgrims trudging along the roads, carrying a few personal items and gifts for the gods, such as food, flowers, and holy water, in knapsacks on their backs. Hundreds of shrines and many temples are built in honor of innumerable, some say a million, gods or more, and these divine places attract the pious Hindu.

Eleanor Munro has written an interesting account of her travels in search of the shrines to which pilgrims of all faiths go to pay their respects to their gods in her 1987 book *On Glory Roads*. Chapter one relates the Hindu experience. No place provides a more holy experience for a Hindu than to go to Varanasi and bathe in the Ganges, or to be able to carry the ashes of a deceased loved one to be cast into the holy river. A temple built on the Ganges, the Ladder to Heaven, dedicated to Shiva, is one of the best-known temples. Inside the temple is an altar on which there is a phallic object, Shiva's power of fertility, arising erect from a base to represent his wife's vulva. Near Allahabad, where the Yumana and Ganges rivers unite, pilgrims come to celebrate the winter solstice and the return of life by bathing in the rivers. Near Bengal at Behubanesevar, is one of India's finest temples, The Lord of the Three Worlds. Nearby is the Black Temple of Konnarak.

Other famous temples are the cave temples of Ajanta, some temples carved out of rock walls at Ellora, the temple of the sun god Surya, the cave temple at Badami near Mysore, the Bhu Vanesh Vara temple in Orissa, and a large temple at Kanch Puram. Not in India, but one of the world's finest monuments to the Hindu gods, is Angkor Wat in Cambodia, now Kampuchea. In visiting the Taj Mahal, a Muslim tomb, I was impressed by the large number of Hindu pilgrims who regard this beautiful architectural creation by man as a place to honor a Hindu god. In general Hindus tend to be tolerant of other religions. In the temple city of Brindaban, south of Delhi, is another Muslim-built temple that has become a Hindu shrine.

Hindus celebrate many festivals in honor of the several gods. Lord Krishna's birthday in September is a national holiday. A spring festival in honor of the god of love, Kama, is a fertility occasion on which the people enjoy reckless pleasure. A fall festival honors Durga, a female deity who is another form of Shiva's wife, a warrior goddess who fights off evil demons and offers protection to girls and women.

Probably the most visible sign of Hinduism to an outsider is the presence of innumerable cows roaming freely on the streets and in parks. I recall entering a shop on Connaught Circle in New Delhi when I had to step over a sleeping cow in front of the entrance. Motorists and pedestrians must yield to the sacred cow, which always has the right of way. An injury to a cow would cause injury to a god. Cows, although not used for meat, do provide other benefits, such as milk, dung for fuel and plaster for the walls of homes, and cow urine, which is used as a medicant.

Western Christians visiting Hindu temples and shrines are often shocked when they view sacred images of the gods and goddesses displayed in the nude, not even with the proverbial fig leaf, and often engaged in erotic embraces, obviously sexual ones. The penis is a common religious symbol. For example, girls of marriageable age may be brought to a temple where a special rite is performed to prepare the bride for the marriage bed. Yet Hindu people, in daily life, are as prudish as Christian puritans. The showing of the nude body is taboo. Childbirth is deemed to be unclean, and the parents must refrain from sexual intercourse for a period of time after a birth, seven days if the baby is male and thirty days if it is female.

Again it needs to be emphasized that Hindu worship is a family affair, observed before the altar in the home. Veneration of the gods, or a special household god, is performed by following sixteen rituals in which the god is welcomed into the home as a guest. Thus he or she is to be served by washing hands and feet, dressed and perfumed, and then presented with gifts, such as flowers, incense, lighted lamps, and food. A concluding prayer for both the god and the family guru or teacher is offered.

The Hindu religion has its origins among the Aryan people who lived in Persia and around the Caspian Sea. They brought their religion to India when they entered about 1500 B.C., as well as their Sanskrit language and a rich sacred literature called the Vedas, songs of wisdom. The Vedas, the Hindu Bible, contain the essence of Hinduism, that is, worship of one Supreme Being, Brahman, the source of all life in the universe, and also the soul of man, called *atman.* Atman seeks to attain its highest level of merit after death by suffering a series of cyclical births and rebirths until the soul reaches a state of moral perfection, when it will be ready to join the perfect Brahman in heaven.

A Brief History of India

The first inhabitants of India were dark-skinned members of an Austro-Asiatic family that spoke a Dravidian language, a language still used by the Tamil people of southern India and Sri Lanka. The native people of India are thought to be the source for the later caste of untouchables. What Hinduism received from these Dravidian people is uncertain. It is thought that their civilization was considerably better than the invading Aryans. However the Aryans had better weapons and military skills, a fact of life many civilized societies have had to suffer. The Dravidians were nature worshipers who gave the sun and Mother Earth prime positions of reverence.

By the sixth century B.C. India was a part of the Persian Empire and so remained until the Greek Macedonians under Alexander the Great conquered Persia in the fourth century B.C. Then the Indians came under the influence of Hellenistic culture. After the dissolution of the Alexandrian Empire, India began to establish independent life divided among many feudal princes. Eventually stronger rulers overcame their weaker neighbors until a central government ruled most of India. India reached its height of power under the Emperor Ashoka, 268–233 B.C. Ashoka was instrumental in the spread of Buddhism from India to China and other Asian lands. He also furthered the worship of Hinduism when he made the Hindu virtues the ruling guides for his kingdom.

The political history of India for the next thousand years was a story of disintegration, internecine feudalistic wars that opened the way for powerful Muslim or Mogul rulers from the north to move into India. From the eleventh to the fourteenth centuries A.D. Muslim rule reestablished unity and order to the Indian continent. Famous Mogul rulers have left their mark on India. A peak of Muslim glory and cultural achievements came during the reign of the Emperor Akbar, A.D. 1556–1605. He fostered an era of peace, cultural enlightenment, and prosperity. He built a new capital city at Fatehpur Sikri (City of Victory), which is now a place for tourists to view the ruins of an ambitious dream. After sixteen years, a city of notable buildings had to be abandoned for the lack of an adequate supply of water. Akbar's wisdom was demonstrated when he sought to bring to India one religion, representing all faiths. He invited scholars from Hinduism, Jainism, Islam, and Christianity to meet in a search for a common religion.

After the reign of Emperor Aurangzeb, 1658–1707, the Mogul era went into decline. Hindu and Sikh princes rebelled and gradually reasserted their independence. However, India was left a country broken and divided, easy prey for exploitation by the commercial companies of France and England. After the traders came the armies, and India became the colonial possession of the French and British Empires. By 1767, after the Seven Years War in Europe, France lost her colonial empire in both India and North America. For a hundred years England continued to dominate Indian politics. At first English control was exercised through the agency of the East India Trading Company and a series of fortuitous treaty arrangements with the many native princes. This deceptive form of control over India was brought to an end by the Sepoy Rebellion of the native troops, who refused to fight with weapons that offended their religious beliefs. England ruled India profitably from 1857 until 1947, when Britain granted independence to India. It was truly the jewel in the crown of the British Empire. The rule of the British Raj and the influence of British culture on Indian life is told graphically in the novels of Rudyard Kipling and E. M. Forster.

India's struggle for independence after World War I is familiar to most American students. The life of Gandhi and his passionate devotion to the cause of freedom for India using the Christian principle of nonviolence or passive resistance caused Gandhi to become a model for worldwide revolutions using the civil disobedience type of resistance. The civil disobedience campaigns of American blacks in the 1960s, led by Martin Luther King, Jr., took their inspiration from Gandhi.

After World War II, India was granted its independence by Britain, which was too weak to continue to resist the nationalistic aspirations of the Indian people. Modern India, though free, continues to be plagued by internal dissension and mass poverty. The leadership of Prime Minister Nehru and his successors has done much in the past forty years to develop better agricultural practices so that India has become almost self-sufficient for its food supply. Industrialization has also made good progress. Yet the masses of Indian people, still living on small farms in rural villages, barely eking out a subsistence living, present an almost insurmountable problem for the Indian government. But India has other demanding problems that threaten its national unity and strength. No sooner had India won its freedom from colonialism than its Muslim provinces declared their own independence. The resulting state, Pakistan, itself later split apart, its eastern portion forming Bangladesh, probably the poorest of all the states in South Asia. In the 1980s India faced rebellion from another religious group, the Tamils in south India and Sri Lanka, who seek their freedom from the Buddhist majority in Sri Lanka. India has another, even more serious problem with the Sikh minority in the Punjab, northern India. The Sikhs there are the majority in this province and they are fighting for either self-rule or preferably an independent Sikh nation. Finally, the Muslim minority left in India is also restless. A recent conflict has developed over a temple in north India that Hindus claim is of significant Hindu religious importance.

Indian Influences on America

For most Americans the Orient remains a land of mystery. American schools teach children about their European heritage, regardless of where their parents were born. American concepts of Hinduism and Buddhism are both in error and negative. These ancient religions are usually treated as only pagan superstitions, barely worth study or respect. Americans do know much about Japanese cars, but almost nothing about Shintoism or Zen Buddhism.

Americans had some slight introduction to Hinduism when in the mid-eighteenth century, a philosophical and literary movement called transcendentalism arose among a few New England intellectuals such as Ralph Waldo Emerson, Henry Thoreau, and Nathaniel Hawthorne. The other Hindu connection is related to the Hare Krishna movement, which has grown in the United States since 1960.

The transcendentalists were seeking to find a good philosophical foundation for American democracy and individual freedom, one that was relatively free from sectarian dogmatism and national bias. The transcendentalists borrowed from Hinduism and Buddhism the idea of an "over-soul" God, ultimate reality, invisible, all-powerful, the creator of all in the universe, the source of all life and energy present in the world, and also the soul of man. The over-soul has no human attributes nor can it be reached by human intervention or prayer. Man must learn to know the universal soul by a form of transcendent knowledge revealed not by study and reason, but only by the process of immediate illumination or intuition. The soul of man, a part of the Great Soul, is sufficient guide for human conduct. Laws and government, moral codes and eternal penalties, are scarcely necessary. Man was created self reliant, Master of his own destiny, born to be a citizen of democratic America.

The Hare Krishnas are most often seen in public places, especially airports, dressed in saffron robes, offering their literature for sale. More often than not, these young men and women are brushed aside by the passing public as nuisances.

In *The Spiritual Supermarket* Robert Greenfield has related briefly the goals of the Hare Krishnas. They seek to save man from sin or the evil forces in the world. They chant a mantra, "Hare Krishna, Hare Rama," which, when translated, means "Krishna is Lord in Bliss, Rama is Lord in Strength."

Some Americans have read about an Oregon-based community or Hindu ashram, led by a Hindu guru, Raj Neesh. This ashram had over 60,000 acres of land and 125 followers. Since the community was charged with sexual misbehavior by its Christian neighbors and also the guru's flight to India to escape criminal prosecution in the United States, the Oregon ashram has been abandoned. Sally Belfrage has written of her brief encounter with a Hindu ashram in Poona, India in her 1981 *Flowers of Emptiness*. The Poona ashram is ruled by the same Oregon guru, Bhagwan Raj Neesh. She found the practice of meditation to be a positive force for self-improvement, but the leadership proved to be questionable and untrustworthy.

In 1982 the Philadelphia Museum of Art brought to the United States a display of Indian art entitled "The Manifestations of Shiva." Since Shiva represents many different divine beings, artists have a field day representing him according to their own interpretation. Shiva is usually portrayed as a person with many arms and a third eye in the center of his forehead. He is portrayed also as a bull, a heroic warrior, an amorous lover, a dancer, a naked ascetic, or even as an abstract phallic statue. His wife, Nandi, a sex symbol, is shown with massive breasts and long, outstretched arms with slender fingers.

Hindu epics furnish the theme for a modern drama, *The Mahabharata*. Peter Brook has dramatized this epic poem, which is fifteen times longer than the Bible. A 1985 review in the *New York Times* says the drama shows that there is "a certain world harmony, a Cosmic harmony, that can be either helpful or destroyed by individuals, and so one must try to discover what his place is in the Cosmic scheme, and how he can help to preserve it, knowing that the Cosmic harmony is always in danger, and that the world goes through periods of terror or greater danger. . . . What is the role of the individual? Must one act or withdraw from the game?"

Today in larger cities and around large university campuses, Americans can locate a Hindu mission, study center, or, place for meditation. In Denver one can find the Divine Light Mission, where one can learn about Hinduism and the technique of proper meditation. Instruction in meditation tells one to chant a mantra while placing the middle finger against the corner of one eye, then concentrate on one spot, the third eye in the center of the forehead. Also placing the thumbs in both ears will cause music to be heard as the mantra is repeated producing a sound like "so-hum."

It can be difficult for the Western mind, trained to think in terms of rational, scientific processes, to understand the mystical, intuitive, truth-seeking methods used in the Hindu religion. Such mystical concepts as reincarnation and the transmigration of souls are not everyday ideas discussed in the Judeo-Christian home.

There is no single, clear-cut source of religious information on Hindu beliefs, such as is found in the Bible or the Muslim Koran. Hinduism is not just one set of beliefs. Many different sects, worshiping different gods, characterize Hinduism. The absence of any dogmatic, absolute tenets of belief enable Hindus to be tolerant of other religions, unlike Western religions that claim to be the only chosen universal road to salvation.

Hindu Literature

Hinduism does have a body of sacred literature, myths from the point of view of non-Hindus, from which can be derived the essential elements of Hindu belief. In these sources, like the Greek myths and legends, are found a mass of poetic expressions that praise the gods, explain the origins of the universe and man, and define the relationships between man and the many gods. Many of the religious stories relate how the forces of good and evil battle one another for control of man's soul.

The principal religious sources are found in the Veda epics, the Upanishads, the Puranas, the Laws of Manu (the first man), the Bhagavad-gita, and the Ramayana story. But the one most significant source of knowledge of Hinduism is the Mahabharata epic. This voluminous work is to Hinduism what the Bible is to Christianity.

The Vedas (meaning "knowledge") were among the earliest of written records, written in Sanskrit, a language belonging to the Indo-European family of languages, between two thousand and one thousand years before Christ. Orthodox Hindus believe that these sacred scriptures were handed down to man from the one supreme god, Brahman, although the earliest Vedas make no mention of such a thing. The Vedas are written in the form of prayers, hymns, magical formulas, in poetic style, with prayers often ending with an amen, "That thou art." There are four groups of Vedas, Rigveda, (royal veda), Samaveda, Yajurveda, and Atharvaveda. The longest and most important veda is the Rigveda. It contains over a thousand hymns to the many nature deities worshiped by the early Aryan Hindus. The early deities were the nature spirits or gods, the sun, the moon, Mother Earth, fire, water, air, the rivers, the mountains, the animals and plants, or all of God's creatures including the most noble creation of all, mankind. The principal Hindu gods and their battles are described. Many of the early gods will be downgraded or eliminated in later Hindu scriptures. The principal god, Varuna, is made the sovereign god. He, as many gods, have different forms, first a sky god, then later a serpent god, Naga, and a sea god who fights sea monsters. Indra, second in line, is a war god who fights against evil dragons, and he is also a popular fertility god. Other gods are Agni, god of fire, and source of light and supernatural powers; Soma, a moon god, and a source of a plant juice, which, when drunk as a potion, produces an ecstatic state of intense joy, thereby linking man to the gods; and two others gods, who at first were lesser gods but in later versions of Hinduism became the major ruling deities, Shiva and Vishnu.

The three other vedas are of lesser value. The Yajur veda tells the faithful how to conduct sacrifices to the gods; the Samaveda provides the many chants to be used in worship; and the Atharvaveda lists the magic spells and incantations that are useful for healing the sick.

The basic tenets of Hinduism are set forth in the Vedas: the existence of one supreme godhead conceptualized as the universal soul, which is found in all things on earth and in man is identified as the soul. The yoga techniques are also given by which good deeds or *karma* will conquer those evil forces, greed, lust, and anger, all being the enemies of life. In addition the four stages of life development from birth to death are spelled out. These stages come from the Laws of Manu, who was the first man, and who decreed the social caste system for India.

The Upanishads variously translated in the English as "Sitting With a Master," "The Wisdom of the Gurus," or "The Approaches," are a collection of parables, dialogues and maxims that attempt to explain in deeper, more philosophic terms the Hindu concepts of soul (atman) and its relation to the universal soul, Brahman. In the Upanishads there is presented the idea of *samsara,* or reincarnation, the life process by which an endless cycle of births and rebirths must occur before atman, the human soul, can find its ultimate destination in unity with the absolute reality or soul, Brahman. Brahman is in all humans in the form of the personal soul, atman. Much of the Upanishads is given to instruction in how this merger of Brahman and atman can occur. The process of liberation from evil or karma comes from God's deliverer, *moksa.* Moksa is the way of salvation, not by sacrifices, ascetic living, giving to charity, and engaging in formal rituals, but by way of gnosis, secret knowledge gained by the practice of meditation and yoga technique.

The Puranas, or "Antiquities," were written during the thousand years after Christ. There are eighteen principal puranas, in which further information is given on the nature of the gods, how man was created, the penalties in hell for being sinful, the rewards for virtuous living, and honor to the god Vishnu as being the highest form of Brahmanism.

Other, less philosophic epics are the narrative tales about the gods as told in the Ramayana and the Bhagavad–Gita epics. The Ramayana story relates the adventures of a good god, Rama, and his wife, Sita. Sita is abducted by a rival evil god, Ravana. Later Sita is returned to her husband by a monkey god, Hanuman, and his army of monkeys. Rama and Sita become the models for an ideal marriage and family. In the Ramayana story is found the idea of predestination, a belief that man has no control over his life's destiny. Whatever happens will happen, and all that man can do is to accept his fate while paying homage to his past lives.

The Bhagavad–Gita has been called the gospel of Krishna. An excellent presentation of the contents of this epic has been written by A. C. Bhaktivedanta Swami Prabhupada in a book *Bhagavad-Gita As It Is* (International Society for Krishna Consciousness, 1972). The most famous section of the Bhagavad–Gita is a poem, "The Celestial Song," that praises eternal values and life as being much more important than life on earth, or value in material things, or even death itself. Five heavens are described, in which four gods are found: the lowest heaven, the abode of Indra, is peopled with dancing girls; next highest is the heaven of Shiva, then comes the heaven of Vishnu, decorated with pools of lotus flowers; then comes the heaven of Krishna, with more dancing girls; and finally, the best of all heavens, the dwelling place of Brahman.

The Bhagavad–Gita is basically a dramatic story of the god–warrior Arjuna and his companion charioteer, Krishna. As Arjuna enters into battle with his enemies, the Kauravas, he hesitates to fight since he does not want to shed blood. Krishna reveals himself to be the supreme lord and advises Arjuna to do his duty as a warrior. Death must never prevent anyone from doing his duty, or performing unselfish acts, or refraining to accept his destiny as a disciplined self who will eventually be at peace with Brahman.

The Laws of Manu represent the Hindu Ten Commandments, the rules by which society is organized and governed. These laws outline the social custom for marriage and family life, the duties of women, ascetics, and kings, or, in brief, the rules for daily life, the good life of virtue, or that which Hindus call *dharma,* the right path to virtue. The Laws of Manu instruct the Hindu people how to recognize the four stages of development in all human lives and how to mark these life passages by observing the appropriate rituals and ceremonies. The first stage is birth itself. A number of rituals receive the infant into the world, rituals that regulate the relationships of child to parents and parents to each other during the period of infancy. Before infancy is past, a final act of initiation into adulthood occurs between the ages of seven and fourteen, a ritual not unlike the Jewish bar mitzvah.

The second stage occurs at the time of marriage, at which time the marital couple takes a vow to bear children, to support the grandparents, and to remain loyal to the spirits of the dead ancestors and to the gods. The third stage comes at the age of retirement, when parents put behind them the daily cares of family and work, and begin their preparation for the final rewards that come with death. As a preparation for death people are expected to devote more time to study of the holy scriptures, perhaps with the aid of a guru or teacher, and to the performance of acts of charity and helping the less fortunate. Finally comes the stage of death, a happy event since now we are leaving behind the pains of life on earth and beginning the long journey of reincarnation to join a life of peaceful bliss with Brahman.

Another Hindu epic, the Mahabharata (Great Bharata), written about 1100 B.C., tells the story of a long war between two Indian tribes for the control of India. According to legend this war happened about 1500 B.C. This war between the tribe of the Pandavas and a related tribe of Kauravas was recorded by the elephant god, Ganesh, as it was told to him by Vyasa, a mythical poet, born of a virgin mother. It is one of the longest epics known, containing some hundred thousand couplets, ten times longer than Homer's *Iliad* and *Odyssey*. The tale concludes with an eighteen-day battle in which all participants are killed except for five Pandavas brothers, and their allied god, Lord Krishna. Krishna's involvement in the war and his role in Hinduism's family of gods is told in the later portions of the epic, the Bhagavad–Gita ("Song of the Blessed Lord"). A principal heroic character among the Pandavas is Arjuna, Krishna's protege. Arjuna was a famous archer and warrior who was taught by Krishna to be a brave warrior and a noble, benevolent ruler, a model for the kings of India.

A Kauravas warrior, perhaps equal to Arjuna, was Karna, but one who represented the forces of darkness and evil, or hell, while the Pandavas were the rulers in heaven.

The long war finally ends with the destruction of the world, after which the world will be reconstructed as a better world in the manner of the Hindu concept of reincarnation.

One character of interest in the Mahabharata is the perfect man, Bhishira, who was given by the gods the freedom to choose the time of his death, provided he remained celibate all his life. This tale seems to refute a popular misconception that Hinduism encourages an excess of licentious sexuality.

In the Mahabharata can be found the essence of Hindu religion and culture. Guidelines are established for the conduct of government, family and social institutions, moral codes, the mysteries of life and death, Hindu philosophy, and the ultimate fate of man's soul in the afterlife.

Creation Myths, Cosmology, and Pantheon

Hinduism also has its mythical explanations for the origins of the universe and of all living things. However, the Hindu belief that their land is at the center of the universe and that its inhabitants have been chosen by the gods to be the preferred race of all human beings is not peculiar to the Hindus, for most human groups have claimed the same measure of divine superiority. For the Hindus the legendary land is probably in the region of the Himalaya mountains. On the highest of the mountains, Mount Meru, dwell the Hindu pantheon of gods. Mount Meru is surrounded by four lesser peaks, and around the five peaks, like a giant wall, are other mountain ranges. This land of mountains, in turn, is enclosed by seven oceans. From the ocean waters came the life spirit, *amrita,* when the total universe, resting on the back of a giant tortoise, was twisted and turned by the sea waters as a powerful serpent, Naga, directed by the god Vishnu, churned the waters into a sea of milk. It is this spirit of life over which the gods and the demons will later fight for control. Hindu temples, like Angkor Wat in Kampuchea, often use this mythical concept of the universe as a construction floor plan. One major tower, with four adjoining smaller towers, all enclosed by a wall, in turn surrounded by an "ocean," in the form of a large moat filled with water.

Hinduism also has its concepts of heaven and hell. Heaven points skyward to Mount Meru, while hell descends into the bowels of the earth. The torments of hell, as described by Dante in his *Inferno,* are equaled by those in the Kauravas-ruled hell. However, the Hindu concept of the afterlife differs markedly from the Christian. In Hinduism all elements of the human personality are lost upon death, whereas in Christianity the human personality remains intact, even to the degree that the living might expected to be in communication with the dead. Hinduism views the soul as being separated from the human personality and returning to its original elements, monads or atoms, which dissolve and then unite with the universal soul or being, or with Brahman.

Although the torments of the Hindu hell may be as severe as those in the Christian hell, at least in the Hindu version of hell the soul has a much better chance to escape. Those souls sent to the Christian hell are doomed for the rest of eternity to remain there. But in the Hindu hell the soul remains in hell only until the evil deeds or karma are burned away. Once purged of sins, as in the Christian purgatory, the soul is released to seek another reincarnation in a new life form. The most vile sinners may be reborn as a rat or vulture, or, even worse, as grass, a bush, or even a rock. The least offensive sinners have the chance to become someone better than they were during their last life on earth.

From the many legends and myths, and Hindu sacred literature, the basic tenets of the Hindu religion can be derived. Hinduism found its origins in a primitive pantheistic worship of nature. In the cosmic universe there exists the unity of all things, above and below, material and nonmaterial. Each part of the universe, organic and inorganic, is an expression of God's creativity and power. The material world is deemed to be a shadow or an illusion, *maya.* Reality, as in Plato's concept of reality, is found only in the ideal, spiritual realm. The human mind is so limited that it cannot comprehend the unity of all creation or the eternal Brahman. Man can see only small bits and pieces of the total existence. Hence, Hindus do not consider Brahman as a god to be worshipped.

If one accepts the existence of a creative force, the ultimate creator, as God, then Hinduism might be called a monotheistic religion. However, in the minds of the non-Hindu people, Hinduism is a polytheistic religion consisting of a multitude of gods and goddesses. Estimates of the number of Hindu deities range from a few thousand to an extreme of thirty-three million gods. Yet from the Hindu viewpoint all are divine creatures who are different manifestations of the one divine spirit, the supreme lord.

Within man there is also a divine spirit or soul, called atman, the counterpart of the universal soul or Brahman. Since Brahman is an unseen and impersonal spirit, so is the atman in each person. Hinduism has as its primary goal the return of the personal soul to its original abode with the supreme lord, the Godhead. Man must free himself from maya, material substances, the world known through the five senses. To attain union with Brahman and to escape the evils caused by materialistic forces, such evils as lust, greed, and anger, are signified by the expression, the most holy of words, "That thou art." Hindu worshipers operate on two levels. One is at the level of the common person who has neither the will nor time to devote to religious exercises. This person is called a "devotee." The other is at the level of the person who through sacrifice and yoga practice has attained a state of highest perfection. This person is termed a "yogi." If one practices the required yogas and performs good action or karma according to the dictates of the supreme lord, that is *bhakti* action, and in like manner the fate of one's soul be determined. What number of rebirths or reincarnations the soul must endure and into what other forms may this soul be contained depends on one's measure of bhakti.

Hindus have little concept of heaven and hell, or a state of eternal bliss or torment. Each person has a soul, its source being the Godhead, and when the body dies, a happy event, the soul is released to return to its original source and made ready to enter another body, the process of reincarnation. The goal is to have the departed soul move to higher levels of existence until it attains perfection with Brahman, the first level of supreme perfection. However, the imperfect soul risks being reincarnated into lower forms of nonhuman life, such as animals and plants.

Since Brahman, a manifestation of the unseen, unknowable supreme lord, is an abstract being difficult for humans to know and understand, Hinduism has created a pantheon of divine beings to personify and humanize the Great Brahman. The chief deities after Brahman are a trinity, Vishnu, Shiva, and Brahma. If one reads the Bhagavad-Gita the conclusion is that there is only one supreme god, Lord Krishna, an incarnation of Vishnu. Krishna is everything, the creator, the source of all power, which becomes manifest in all things in nature, and he becomes incarnated in all other gods, demigods, animals, the Naga snake, the elephant, the cow, and others, plus the human being. In brief, Lord Krishna is the supreme lord. Whether all Hindus revere Lord Krishna above all other deities may depend upon the local interpretation of Hinduism. At least the other gods merit the adoration and service from the devotees. All of the deities bring blessings and comfort to the people. They mete out punishment for evil deeds committed, and they bestow rewards on the good people. Hindus seem to receive greater pleasure in serving the gods, performing their sacred duties, than in receiving from the gods their blessings and rewards.

Brahma, the creator of god, according to one legend, came from the navel of Vishnu. In turn, Brahma created the first king of India, Manu, a hermaphrodite who could bear children by himself. A few generations later a great flood threatened to destroy the world, but the tenth Manu, warned by Vishnu, saved his family, which then repopulated the earth, a story not unlike that of Noah and the Flood in the Old Testament. Brahma's lifespan is also a measure of cosmic time and the cycles of births and rebirths. When Brahma's days are over, the old world will die and a new one will begin. Since Brahma's lifespan is almost infinite, having lived almost eight hundred billion years already, the earth's demise is in no immediate danger.[1] Brahma has a wife, Sarasvata, who is the goddess of the arts, music, and speech. Brahma is depicted as having four heads and arms.

Vishnu is more popular than Brahma. He is the savior and protector of mankind. He is a benevolent deity, of a sun god origin like the Greek Apollo. He loves his human creatures, and is always present among them. He is also the ruler over the other immortal gods. A legend about the creation of the universe relates that Vishnu slept for eons of time in primeval waters upon the coils of a thousand-headed cobra before he was born. From his navel grew a lotus flower, from which came Brahma, who created the world. Vishnu was born as a man on earth to save the world from evil demons. Legend says that Buddha was born from the navel of Vishnu, as well as the lesser Hindu gods or "avatars," such as the fish god, Matsya, who saved Manu, an early Adam, from a flood. Vishnu is pictured as having four arms holding his attributes, a conch shell resting on the snake Ananta, and a lotus flower springing from his navel. He is pictured also as riding on a bird, Garuda. Legend says that he came to earth to save mankind disguised in many forms (avatars). Among these lesser gods were Krishna and Rama. Vishnu's popular wife, Lakshmi, is goddess of wealth and beauty.

Lord Krishna, probably the most favored God of all in the eyes of the common people, is a hero god who relates to his friend, Ajuna, that the road to salvation is by way of meditation and the avoidance of desire and action. Krishna offers three paths to salvation, knowledge, right action, and devotion. If a person meditates on Krishna, the soul's chances for union with Brahman are greatly enhanced. It is one's sacred duty to fight evil and to perform good deeds. In many respects Vishnu and Krishna resemble the mission of Jesus and his life on earth. One major difference would be that Jesus was a celibate, while the Hindu gods enjoy sexual pleasure.

Lord Krishna was born in a humble rural village, Mathura, where a small temple in his honor can be seen. The village is small, typical of thousands of Indian villages where the people are poor and the surroundings are primitive. Even the temple is a symbol of simplicity and humility. As a young man Krishna herded cows, played with the milkmaids, and drove snakes from the village. In fact, Krishna was so human that he did not know that he was a god. His birthday, in September, is a national holiday.

Rama, the hero of the epic Ramayana, wages war against all evil forces. As a warrior he is a model for the rulership of a strong monarch or a patriarchal husband and father. Sita, his wife, is the perfect wife and mother. At one time, Sita was rescued from the hands of the evil demon, Ravana, by a monkey god, Hanuman, and his army of monkeys. Hence monkeys come to have a place in the Hindu family of gods.

Shiva is the creator of life, the governor of the world, the destroyer of what has been created, and also the source for fertility, wealth, health, and protection of mankind from its enemies. Shiva is indeed a complex set of divine components. Shiva is recognized by three symbols: the phallic lingam, the trident, and the drum. He is pictured also as riding a white bull, Bandi, a symbol of both power and fertility. In Shiva there exists a dual nature, love and hate, creativity and destruction, eternal activity and eternal peace. Shiva is the source of all life, the god of health, the source of the Ganges river, and the master of the graveyards. His third eye, located in the forehead, represents destruction, yet Shiva is the protector of children. Shiva becomes a primary god in Hindu worship, being so powerful as first to create life and then cause death.

Shiva's wife, Shakti, has four female counterparts. First she is the mother goddess, then the goddess of fertility, the goddess of the Tantric sect that worships erotic sexuality, which is thought to have the power to free mankind from all evil. The union of Shiva and Shakti produces new life as well as sexual pleasure, hence sexuality has the blessing of the gods. Secondly, Shakti is also the goddess Durga, the slayer of the demon buffalo, Mahiska, so she becomes a savior of mankind. Shakti is pictured as carrying weapons that can destroy the demons. In another form Shakti becomes the goddess Kali, the patron saint of thugs and thieves who, in turn, can command that animals be sacrificed. It would seem that in this role Shakti is an evil force, yet in another form, that of Parvati, she is the bride of Shiva, a symbol of love and forgiveness. Pilgrims who climb Mount Kailsa bring offerings to Parvati.

A few other Hindu deities warrant a brief mention. Ganesha, the elephant-headed son of Shiva, is able to remove all obstacles for those who seek new adventures. He is also the god of good luck. The monkey-god, Hanuman, is the guardian spirit of the rural villages. Yama, the god of death, renders judgments on the souls of the dead. Only those bodies cremated on the banks of the Ganges can escape his judgment/and the trials of reincarnation. An accessory to Yama is Agni, a primeval fire god who carries the released souls after cremation to Brahman.

Hindu Philosophy and Ethics

One may ask of what value these gods are to mankind? If they have value how can mere mortal humans ever reach or communicate with them? As in all religions, man hopes to find peace and security while life on earth endures, and after that peace for his soul after death somewhere in heaven or in the abode of the gods.

The Hindu gods do offer mankind while living on earth the opportunity to find peace and security, and after that phase of life is over, even greater peace and security after death. Hinduism first holds out to mankind four goals or blessings for a life with and by the gods. First man is expected to prepare himself or herself for a useful everyday existence on Earth. Man and woman are expected to enter into marriage, bear children, and to find the material means by which to support the family. Women are expected to be the mothers and homemakers, while the men are expected to acquire those skills by which they can be employed and earn the means to support the family. He is expected to earn more than the minimum requirements to satisfy the family's needs. There should be a surplus of gain to assist in the support of the state and the religious establishments. But the gods also expect a surplus for the enjoyment of leisure time, especially during the years of retirement. It is proper that all humans have some time and money to enjoy the arts, the beauty of nature and the peace that comes with a day of rest. Needless to say, the majority of Indian Hindus fail to achieve these lofty goals when faced with the peril of bare subsistence and desperate poverty.

Secondly, mankind has a right to expect something more from life than mere existence and toil. There should be time and place to enjoy the sensual pleasures that the human being is designed to experience. Sensual pleasures are not evil in themselves, but, again, moderation is recommended by the gods. The right to enjoy pleasure is found in the concept of *kama,* a force that might be compared to that of the Greek goddess Aphrodite or Eros. Kama represents the force or goddess of love, especially sexual love. Love binds together family members, and as an emotional experience beyond the family, kama binds together larger social groups. But kama places a special favor upon sexual love and intercourse. For the family to bear children is a supreme blessing, but it is also good that man and woman in marriage can enjoy the pleasures to be found in sexual intimacy. The joys found in the daily life of humans on earth include also the joys received from the dance, the theater, and music.

Thirdly, the gods remind mankind that all of life is not the duty to work and to find good pleasure, but more of man is required. If man is to receive the full measure of favors from the gods, then men and women must live disciplined and moral lives as prescribed by the laws of the gods. The highest statement of the law of the gods is found in those commandments attributed to the first man, Manu. If man's pursuit of pleasure is permitted to run rampant, unchecked, the only ultimate result will be death to man and his society.

The moral laws are incorporated into the Hindu concept of morality, *dharma.* Dharma prescribes all of the dos and don'ts for right living. Scarcely any aspect of human activity escapes the laws of dharma. All aspects of marriage and family, all social relationships from family to state to caste system that determine a baby's destiny at birth are all a part of dharma.

Finally, the Hindu gods offer to mankind the possibility of attaining the highest virtue, the supreme goal of life, release of the soul from the trials and pains of earthly existence. Release or liberation of the soul is called *moksa.* Moksa is the ultimate goal of every Hindu, the return of his or her soul on death to its universal self, Brahman. In Hinduism the human soul or atman is an integral part of the universal soul, and the atman must return to its original source. Under certain conditions the soul may return to Brahman immediately after death, especially if the body can be cremated on the banks of the Ganges and the ashes returned to its sacred waters. Otherwise the soul must undergo endless cycles of birth and rebirth, or transmigration, before it can rejoin Brahman.

A basic tenet of belief in the Hindu religion is that things are in a state of constant and eternal change. The source of all things on earth and in the creation of the universe is some form of universal energy or force or a spiritual flux from which all things are fashioned. It is this divine force that is real, not the physical products created from and by this force.

In the Western concept of change life moves in a horizontal plane, from bad to good, from inferior to superior, from imperfection to perfection, but always moving in a straight line, not in cycles. But in Hinduism this endless change or movement rotates in cycles from a beginning or birth to a final completion in the act of death, whereupon the cycle of birth and death is repeated through eons of time or billions and billions of years. Man's soul in a similar way may be subjected to the almost endless cycles of change or transmigrations. When the soul has been cleansed of its human attributes, its physical illusions, or maya, then the soul may return to its original source in the Oversoul or Brahman.

The Hindu concept of time is measured in terms of how long it takes to complete a cycle. The universe begins with a birth in a state of perfection. As the cycle moves along its course, gradually decay and imperfection set in until finally at the end of the cycle all things end in death. The universal cycle requires a period of 4,520,000 years, a "Great Yuga." A single day of Brahma, the creator god, the supreme being as created by the god Visnu is one thousand Great Yugas or a *kalpa.*

The Hindu concept of the beginning of time may not conform to modern concepts of the age of the universe, but certainly it is a more realistic measure of the age of the universe than the one related in the Old Testament, which many fundamentalistic Christians state to be somewhat less than ten thousand years.

Hinduism proclaims that man is the master of his or her own fate. Each person is responsible for his or her redemption from sin. There is no merciful, compassionate God as in Christianity who can absolve man from sin by having faith that God has the power to do so.

In the Hindu religion man can accumulate a record of good and evil deeds during his or her lifetime. The record of these deeds, *karma,* is the sum total of all of the acts and thoughts of a human being during all of its previous re-incarnations, including the present life. Man's hope and goal is to earn more good karma than bad karma. Good karma gives the soul a chance to leave the cycle of births and rebirths, thus being able to ascend to a higher realm where the cycles no longer operate. Bad karma condemns the soul to endless cycles of reincarnations, sometimes being born into forms of lower animal life or even plant life. If sufficient merits or good karma have been earned during life on earth perhaps the gods will release the soul from its transmigratory destiny, after suffering torment in hell, ruled by Yama. One form of soul torment is to be eaten by reptiles or to be boiled in oil.

Man earns good karma by controlling his emotions, his ego, and controlling especially those sensual passions that long for the pleasures of the material world. An ideal life would be to live like an ascetic monk or nun, freed from the temptations of greed, self-esteem, and sexuality. Often older people, during the time of retirement, seek escape from the evil world by adopting an ascetic lifestyle or even living in a monastic community.

However, man's freedom to choose his or her own lifestyle is limited by predestination, that is the fact that one's future life is predetermined by god before birth. In a sense, one's marriage, station in life, occupation, even one's gender is all predetermined. Some students believe that Hinduism therefore produces a fatalistic view of life. Normally so pessimistic an outlook on life would create an abnormal rate of crime, drug use, sexuality, and suicide. However, there seems to be little evidence that this dire result has afflicted India. It is true that India tends to be reluctant to enter the modern world of science and industry, but whether Hinduism can be blamed for this is uncertain.

How then is man to control his passions, his desires, and his ego? The Hindu reply would be, "Follow the rules of Dharma, those god-given formulae for salvation." The divine rule says to practice the four paths to the ultimate truth. The first path is right conduct, that is to obey the commandments, harbor no evil thoughts and commit no evil acts, love your neighbors, and do no harm to other people. The five rules for right conduct or *niyana,* are: poverty, serenity, austerity, learn about the gods, and obey the law of the gods.

The second path is to accept one's birth station in life, that is, accept *artha.* This is one's duty to accept his or her caste. The birth position or caste determines one's marriage, social status, and lifetime occupation. The castes are beneficial. Highest is the Brahmans (the mouth), those people who represent the highest social order of scholars, philosophers, theologians, priests, teachers and artists. Next in order are the Kshatriyas (the arms of Brahman), who are destined to become the rulers and soldiers of the state. Then comes the Vai Shyas (the thighs of Brahman) who will be the producers of wealth, the farmers, the craftsmen, the merchants, the doctors, and the technicians. The lowest of the castes is the Sudras (Brahman's feet). They are doomed to do the poorest, most menial types of work, the unskilled jobs, the work that needs strong backs and little knowledge. Below all of the castes are the untouchables, the Sudrus or Harijans, some 15 percent of the total population. For the Harijans Gandhi sought freedom, gaining it with the passage of the Indian Constitution of 1947. The untouchables are for the most part rural people who are forced to do the most odious jobs, such as the collectors of garbage and the tenders of the dead. Despite constitutional freedom, this group's lowly status remains relatively unchanged. However, for the most part, they seem to accept their status while being comforted by the promise offered that if they live a good life their souls will be rewarded in some future reincarnation.

A third path as prescribed by karma is Kama-Sutra, an obligation to practice and to enjoy sexual relations abundantly, but within the prescribed marital relationship. However, severely forbidden are adultery, premarital sex, promiscuous relations, and homosexuality. Birth control legislation has been defeated regularly since 1975. Many children are expected, six or seven at least, and every mother has a duty to bear children. Since a male child is thought to be indispensable to the survival of the family tree, at least it is necessary to bear children until a son is produced.

The final path is moksha, the final union with Brahman. Union with Brahman is attained by the practice of a series of *yogas,* that is, by following a set of rigid disciplines for the control of life on earth. Those Hindus who practice the yogas are said to be doing *bhakti,* devotional services designed to rid the body and soul of all worldly and immoral acts and thoughts. Bhakti is a purification process, and those who practice it are called *bhaktas* or devotees. The highest level of spiritual achievement comes to those who are called *yogis.* Their souls may escape the penalty of reincarnation.

The first yoga, *raja yoga,* is the path of meditation or insight meditation, the methods by which one learns to control the physical senses to such an extent that all external sensation is excluded from the mind. The mind, or thought processes, include the body sensations, the conscious mind, the subconscious mind, and, at the highest level of activity, the soul knowledge. The object of meditation is to receive only transcendental, nonsensory, knowledge, something akin to intuition. One must learn to transfer his or her identity with his or her body, mind, and emotions to a higher level of eternal being, or Brahman.

Most intricate techniques have been derived to achieve this trancelike state of mind. Yoga means "yoke," or a link between god and man, and a union of physical and mental energies. One must learn to breathe properly, to control all aspects of the human body, including the processes of digestion and elimination. The preferred position of the body in meditation is to be seated on a floor in the lotus position. Some eighty-four positions have been prescribed. To accentuate the effect of proper body positions, hypnotic techniques such as gazing at a lighted candle or listening to a monotonous sound are useful. A commonly used sound is speaking a *mantra,* a repeated, seemingly meaningless sound, which in truth represents the voice of the gods speaking. The words are intended to produce a sleeplike state that will enhance the state of deep concentration. The most used mantra is *om,* pronounced "aum," which represents the trinity of Brahma (creator), Vishnu (intelligence), and Shiva (cosmic consciousness). *Om* also means "I Accept." Geometric symbols or *yantras* are used to assist the person to concentrate on divine things. The shapes of the figures often represent natural forms, such as plant leaves or flowers, which when dangled before the eyes of the devotee will help induce the state of meditation.

However, before meditation can begin the person must renounce all sensual pleasure—sex, wealth, food, and drink—and have the body made clean by bathing in water.

The second yoga is *karma yoga,* a command to do one's duty to God, to society, and to family. This divine path of action commands one to do work faithfully, to practice charity, to do good deeds to others, to go on pilgrimages to holy places, and to live a selfless life.

The third yoga is *bhakti yoga,* the path of love and devotion. This yoga requires a love for God that is best expressed as giving love to one's family, husband and wife, children, and the ancestors, alive and dead. Love of God is the highest karma, and probably there is no greater expression of divine love than love as found in the marital relationship. Sexual activity in marriage has no puritanical overtones in Hindu ideology. Sex is an act blessed by the gods. This yoga requires a tolerance for all other peoples and religions, for they are all a part of God's creation. The goal of peace and nonviolence, as Gandhi taught, is derived from this yoga. Likewise the command to be charitable and to use one's wealth to support schools, hospitals, temples, and to help the disabled, the children, and the poor comes from this yoga. The love yoga requires a duty to work and to be loyal to one's employer, a condition not conducive to the organization of labor unions.

The fourth yoga, *juana yoga,* is the pathway of knowledge by which we learn to distinguish between one's self, one's ego or physical self, from our true or real self, the self that is a part of the eternal Brahman. This yoga teaches that the visible, material world is an illusion or shadow called Maya. The true self must understand that it is destined to be united with Brahman in a series of births and rebirths.

Western religions view world history as moving in a horizontal continuum, always moving forward in a progressive, upward direction towards some ideal state of perfection. The Hindu world is one in which movements are cyclical, moving from one stage of birth to death, and then a new cycle of births and deaths begins. The world is now in a cycle that began in 3102 B.C., and is to last for 428,000 years. Finally the world will be destroyed in a catastrophic series of fires and floods. Out of this chaos will come a better world.

All religions confront mortal humans with a set of moral codes and spiritual aspirations that most people cannot achieve so long as they live in the everyday world of family responsibilities, work obligations, and temporal, material temptations. In the final analysis religion offers a system of beliefs and rituals, duties and commandments that can be achieved only if one lives as an ascetic who can devote all of his or her time and abilities to the business of living a religious life. Unless a person can live isolated in a monatic setting, living the life of a priest or guru, or a Hindu holy man, a *saddhu,* or a person at the age of retirement who is preparing the soul for death, the ideal may never be reached. Saddhus are identified by wearing a white horizontal stripe on the forehead, a sign of love for Shiva, or by wearing a trident, a sign of love for Vishnu. Hinduism does make provision for a monastic life for most holy men and women by permitting them to live in a community of religious activity, devotion, and labor, an ashram.

But for the average person, religion must be reduced to a series of simple acts and words that can be understood and practiced while living in a world of hardship, disappointments and pain. Worship for the average person, therefore, is reduced to saying prayers and mantras before the family altar, in temples, and before the shrines and images encountered on pilgrimages. Religious festivals and ceremonials pay homage and love to the Gods by the presentation of prayers, gifts, and love. Purification rites, initiation rites for newly born infants and the children who reach puberty, funeral rites, and other rites facilitate the passage of a person from one stage of life to another. Perhaps the highest mark of fulfilling one's duties to God, or karma, is the performance of the daily tasks of living according to the sacred laws. In other words caring for the family, helping the neighbors, refraining from acts of anger and violence, obeying the laws of the land, and protecting nature's environment from harm are some of the most sacred acts for a Hindu follower. Personal devotion to the gods, be they Krishna, Vishnu, Shiva, or the many other deities, plus the daily observance of the dietary restrictions such as eating no meat, fish or milk, and respecting the rights of sacred animals, especially the cow, will fulfill karma and bring to the soul a higher place near Brahman, the absolute. All Hindus, no matter to which sect or to what deity they pay homage, can unite in saying the following prayer: "O Lord, Progenitor, Creator of the Universe, source of all prosperity, self-illuminated, giver of all happiness, we pray Thee to wipe off all of our vices, evil propensities, and distress and confer upon us all the virtues, create the impulses for good deeds and righteous nature, and provide us with other resources that may bring bliss to us."

Marriage and the Family

As a final note on Hinduism it seems appropriate to sketch a few aspects of marriage and family life in India. No institution is more holy to a Hindu than the family. From time immemorial the family has been built on a patriarchal structure in which the male is predominant and the female assumes a submissive role, first to her father, then to her husband after marriage. Male children are given preference to the girls in terms of family love, allocation of work duties, opportunities for an education, and freedom to participate in political and civic activities. It is good to note that one of India's best known prime ministers was Indira Gandhi, the mother of a recent prime minister, Raji Gandhi. Traditionally, marriages have been arranged by the concerned parents, often contracted when the children are only eight or ten years of age. Dowries are provided by the parents of the bride, an old custom retained in the present to help seal the marriage and guarantee some monetary aid to the wife in case of divorce. In modern India, younger people are gradually moving away from traditional customs by marrying freely for love and abandoning the practice of a dowry. From birth the female child knows that her future career is to be a wife and mother. After marriage she leaves her home to become a member of her husband's home, where she may be a minor person, ruled by her mother-in-law and husband with little voice to assert her own rights and feelings.

Polygamy is permissible, but for the masses of people, one wife is all that one man can afford. Birth control is taboo, although abortions are committed. The practice of burning wives on the husband's funeral pyre is outlawed, although infanticide and wife beatings are acceptable, at least according to ancient traditions. Legislation today is attempting to bring India's family practices into the twentieth century, yet legislation cannot be expected to eradicate old traditions in only a generation or two.

Summary

In retrospect a Western observer with a modest knowledge of India gained by travel and study, might attempt a "nutshell" version of Hinduism. If so then his summary view of Hinduism would be as follows:

1. The gods have informed the devout Hindu that man's mission on earth is to prepare his soul, an integral part of the absolute soul, or Brahman, to join Brahman, its counterpart, after death, perhaps immediately or perhaps after eons of reincarnations, all depending on one's accumulation of good deeds, or Karma. The good deeds are not only the good deeds done by the person concerned, but also by all of those who possessed the soul in previous existences.

2. The gods have told the devout Hindu that mankind is bound by the sacred law of karma, that is, the law of cause and effect, which says that each person is responsible for his or her own salvation, that you reap what you sow. Good karma, the necessary good deeds for salvation, comes from our own free choice of good or evil.

3. The gods have placed the burden of salvation upon the home, the family, and especially the wife and mother. Prayers in temples and pilgrimages to sacred shrines all win merit or good karma, but it is at the family altar in the home, an altar dedicated to one or more gods, that the child learns the path to Brahman. Although the family is patriarchal, ruled by the male and particularly by the eldest male, it is the wife and mother who is truly the "master" of the home.

4. The gods have given to man the sacred law of dharma, the list of duties or commandments a good Hindu is expected to obey. Dharma is most inclusive, comprehensive, and demanding, so much so that the person has little room for free will or choice, except the choice to obey or not to obey. The sacred law covers every aspect of life, marriage, family, child rearing, work duties, social position, sex life, and all things possible in the daily life of a Hindu. Dharma prescribes the castes into which a child is born, and from which there is almost no escape. The four castes plus the noncaste untouchables determine one's future destiny. To follow another way of life would require strong will and heroic courage.

Within each caste Dharma defines the stages of life development, from birth until death. First the child is born, passes through the period of infancy and childhood, a period for learning the Hindu way of life. Then comes the adolescent stage, when the child becomes an adult. The young adult is initiated into manhood or womanhood by special rites. Now these persons are ready for marriage, parenthood, and the world of work. It is in this stage that Hindus are expected to fulfill the three obligations: of Dharma, doing one's duty; of artha, earning a living; and of rati, the enjoyment of the pleasures of sexual relations in marriage and the rearing of children. Then the adult reaches the age of retirement from worldly activities and responsibilities. Now the aging man and woman begins the preparation for death and reincarnation. Life becomes more ascetic, more given to devotional studies and meditation and seeking purification of the soul by putting behind the pursuit of sensual pleasures and devoting much time to acts of charity and love, *sannyana*. If the soul has been purified sufficiently, a state of being, moksha, has been attained. The purified soul is now ready for the final stage of death. Death is a happy event for now the soul is free to join its counterpart, Brahman. The union may come immediately after death or it may be delayed for eons of time, all depending on the record of karma and the number of reincarnations that may be required.*

---

*The author is fully aware that a Hindu Indian, reared in his or her traditional faith, may not always accept this interpretation of Hinduism as being the orthodox or correct interpretation.

8

Buddhism

A Western traveler to the Orient might receive a superficial introduction to Buddhism when visiting some of the Buddhist temples in Thailand, Burma, Indonesia, China, and Japan. In these temple areas will be found statues of Buddha, statues where Buddha is seated, standing, lying down, and always with a benevolent, kindly smile on the face. Bangkok is a photographer's delight, for here one sees a multitude of temples and statues, adorned in gold, blue, and most of the colors of the rainbow. Guarding the temple doors are grotesque figures of fierce-looking demons, and walking about the temple grounds are groups of young men, Buddhist monks, who are identified by their shaved heads and saffron-colored robes. In Nara, Japan is the world's largest Buddha statue, housed in a large, wooden temple. At Kamakura, Japan, one can see the largest Buddha image cast in bronze. But the Buddhist temple complex that leaves an everlasting impression on the viewer is the Shwedagon temple in Rangoon, Burma. Here is a group of smaller temples surrounding a large temple bearing a high, pointed spire, all decorated with gold leaf and innumerable decorative floral designs, in brief, a gorgeous display of color and eye-appealing designs. The temple area is on a hill and as you mount the stairs to the temple floors, souvenir booths offer trinkets and literature for sale. The Buddhist worshipers are offered small packets of gold leaf that they can donate to one of the shrines for the repair of a Buddha statue. The morning my wife and I visited the Shwedagon temple there had been a hard rain, so the brick pavement was covered with an inch or two of water. A visitor can find a friendly dog to escort him. Many mongrel dogs find a safe haven here, for good Buddhists would not harm an animal. But walking barefeet (no shoes are allowed in temples or on temple grounds) in water thickened by dog droppings caused me to wonder what feet-bathing facilities would be found at the end of the visit. It was a cold water tap, minus soap or towel.

Many Buddhist temples are found in Japan and China. In Japan Buddhist temples may be found beside a Shinto temple or shrine. From childhood I had read about Angkor Wat in a *National Geographic* magazine.[1] In 1960 it was my pleasure to visit this Hindu-Buddhist temple area in Cambodia, now Kampuchea. It is hoped that civil war in the country since 1970 has not damaged the temple ruins any more than tropical jungle growth has already done so in the past five hundred years. Angkor Wat is truly one of the wonders of the world's architectural achievements. But as a religious monument a visitor can see carved on walls and in statues a record of the political and religious life of the Khmer civilization from about A.D. 800 to 1500.

About 9 percent of the world's population is Buddhist, as compared with 42 percent who are Christian, 20 percent who are Hindu, and 28 percent who are Muslim. From the Western viewpoint Buddhism seems to be a philosophic, rational program of good living, more or less on the model of Plato or Confucius. Buddhism denies the existence of any god or supernatural power. There is no divine revelation to tell man how to win salvation for his soul. Buddha is no Jesus, no messiah with a divine message of salvation. There is no heaven or hell, or some form of eternal punishment for sins committed on earth, or rewards for good deeds performed.

Buddha discovered the ultimate truth through his own efforts; hence each person must seek to find salvation by his or her own efforts. Buddhism tends to be a tolerant religion, since there is no single canon or standard by which to measure any orthodox truth. Life is to be lived on earth, not in heaven. So Buddhism seems to be no more than a code of moral conduct, a correct lifestyle guided by proper control of the emotions and a regimen of right thinking. Man's mind is the center of the universe, and mind has infinite capacity for change and growth. Buddhism rejects the use of miracles, magical interventions, or any supernatural phenomena to facilitate man's relations with a divine power. Buddhist rejects also intolerance and autocratic government. Violence is not the Buddhist way. All life is sacred and deserves to enjoy life. In a sense, the last words Buddha is reputed to have spoken summarize his way of life: "Work out your own salvation with diligence. Be a lamp unto yourself."

In the United States today it is estimated that there are over four million Buddhists, with more than a thousand temples, study groups, or Buddhist associations. The largest number, 250,000, are found in southern California. One of the most successful Buddhist schools in the United States, the Naropa Institute, is located in Boulder, Colorado. Its leader is Guru Trunga Rinpoche (precious one), who claims to be a direct incarnation of Buddha. He came to the United States from Tibet in 1970. Robert Greenfield in his 1975 *The Spiritual Supermarket* describes some of the popular manifestations of Buddhism in the United States. For example, he describes a popular self-help movement that captured the interest and pocketbooks of many Americans during the 1960s and 1970s, a movement called "Transcendental Meditation." It was introduced to the United States in 1968 by Maharishi Makesh Yogi. In a brief period of time over a million Americans joined training centers to learn the art of meditation. No longer was meditation a technique that could only be mastered by professional students or gurus; now every person could learn how to meditate with the aid of a teacher or guru in a few lessons for pay. Additional lessons could be learned from tapes and books. "TM" was sold as a means for reducing stress induced by working and living in a highly competitive economic and social world. Meditation would reduce blood pressure and heart attacks, rescue one from addiction to drugs and alcohol, and, by all means, TM would prolong life. Any knowledge gained through TM about Buddha or nirvana was only incidental. Probably Buddha would not be pleased to have his teachings reduced to commercial enterprises.

According to Buddha the world from the beginning has been a place filled with pain and suffering, or *dukkha*. Life is always in a process of decay and death. In this world all creatures are born to live and to die, and to be reborn after death in an almost endless cycle of births and rebirths. The objective of Buddhism is to find some escape from this painful process of reincarnation or rebirths. The escape that Buddha provided is his "middle way," the way of knowledge.

The Life of Buddha

Buddhism, like many other religions, traces its origins to a gifted person, in this case Buddha. He was only a man, not a god, or even a prophet of god. The name Buddha comes from a Sanskrit word meaning "to know." Later Buddha's followers changed his nature from being merely human to one born of the gods, a divine creation.

As with the life of Jesus, it is difficult to separate fact from fiction. He was born about 540 B.C., or perhaps 567 B.C., on April 6, or perhaps May 17, in Lumbini, 155 miles west of Katmandu in Nepal. He was born a Hindu prince. His father was a lord or ruler of a Hindu tribe. He had a childhood and youth of luxury and pleasure. His father wanted him to be free of all want and pain. He was to be confined to the palace grounds with its beautiful gardens and fountains. Forty thousand dancing girls were brought in to give young Buddha great pleasure. He was never to learn how ugly and cruel the outside world was in reality.

Buddha's first name was Gautama, a name belonging to his caste position. Later the name Siddhartha was added, meaning "one who attained his aim." One night during his quest for peace of mind he sought rest and a place to meditate under a fig or "bo" tree in the town of Gaya, near Patna in northeast India. "Bo" is a shortened form of Buddha or Enlightenment.

Although Buddha denied that he was an immortal being, only a century later his followers had proclaimed him to be a god. A volume of myths was created to give proof of his supernatural being. Only a few of the myths can be related here. One legend says that Buddha came from the navel of the god Vishnu, a symbol of the fact that Buddhism did come from Hindu roots. Another legend says that Buddha had a miraculous birth, one like the birth of Jesus, by an immaculate conception. His mother dreamed one night that a white elephant, a good omen, had entered her body and she became pregnant. One day as she stopped to pick some flowers in the palace garden, the child was born. Immediately after birth, the infant rose up, took seven steps, raised his right hand to the sky, put his left hand down, and said, "Above heaven and below heaven, I alone am the world honored one." Then a sweet rain fell on the baby. Then four angels appeared and caught the baby in a golden net and bathed him in a heavenly spray of water.

Buddha, like Jesus, was blessed with several supernatural powers. The seven first steps represent the seven life stages to enlightenment or nirvana. The first six stages are possessed by all humans, but the seventh stage represents the seven life paths to enlightenment. Later when Buddha was tempted by Mara, the evil one, his aides threw stones at him, but the stones were turned into flowers. When Mara sent a stone to kill Buddha, he was saved by a king cobra, Mucalindia, lord of the earth. The cobra in oriental religions is regarded as a good spirit, not an evil one as depicted in the Adam and Eve myth. There is some evidence from Gnostic texts that some of the first Christians considered snakes to be good spirits.

The biography of Buddha after birth continues a mixture of fact and fiction. From birth the royal father of Buddha, following the advice of a soothsayer, was determined to keep him isolated from the painful realities of the cruel world outside of the palace. Before Buddha experienced the reality of life for most human mortals, he was married at the age of sixteen to a princess, his cousin, Yashadaia. She gave birth to a son, Rahula. One day Buddha asked his charioteer to take him on a tour of the streets outside of the palace. His eyes were opened and he saw an old, decrepit man hobbling along. Another day he saw a sick man, weak and lame, and on a third trip he saw death in the form of a corpse being carried to the grave.

Buddha began to wonder about the worldly condition of life. There must be a better way to secure human happiness, he thought. At this point Buddha did not know what the better way might be. Then, on another day, he saw a mendicant beggar who had left the real world of pain, desire, wealth, greed, and fear, after which the beggar found peace of mind and happiness. Buddha declared that now the formula for happiness had been found. The key to salvation or happiness was to escape into nirvana, not a place, but a state of mind in which one is released from fear and desire.

Then Buddha made the decision to find salvation in the same manner as the begging monk. At the age of twenty-nine he left the palace and his family to become a wandering beggar. He left secretly by taking his charioteer into a forest. There he changed clothes with the charioteer, who returned them to the palace. Buddha shaved his head, dressed in plain clothes, and began his search for enlightenment. For six years he studied with Hindu gurus to learn the art of meditation and yoga practice. But Buddha failed to find happiness by following the Hindu model. So Buddha joined a group of wandering ascetic monks who traveled across northern India and Nepal. While with them he lived a most demanding, sordid way of life. He dressed in rags, permitted his body to be covered with dirt and lice from a denial of all bathing, and practically died of starvation.

He tried to survive on one grain of rice per day. Occasionally a milkmaid would give him a bowl of curds to eat. However, this harsh denial of the physical needs of the body failed also to give Buddha the key to salvation. So Buddha left his begging companions to continue his wandering journey through northern India.

During these journeys in the forests of northern India, Buddha learned of his kinship with the creatures of nature. Like St. Francis of Assisi he claimed as his friends the sun and the moon, the birds and trees, and even all of nature's creation as his loving companions. All things, animate and inanimate, are endowed with the divine spirit of the Creator. In a grain of sand, in every cell of his mind and body, Buddha saw a part of the Creator. Hence Buddha condemned the taking of life in any form.

Out of Buddha's conviction that all of nature's creation is sacred and deserving of life and respect from all of humankind arose the central thesis of Buddhism that love and compassion must prevail as the way of life for all of mankind. In this respect Buddha is not unique, for all of the great teachers of the many religious faiths have taught that love must become the pattern by which humans mold their lives. Buddha's concept of love was a universal love for all of nature and for all of the human race. Not only should one love oneself and one's family, but all of the human species, no matter what race or place.

Buddha said that love comes with understanding, and understanding comes when one obeys the precepts or commandments, and practices long and diligently the acts of concentration and meditation. Buddha listed five precepts as being essential for right living: Do not kill, Do not steal, Do not lie, Do not consume alcohol, and Do not indulge in sexual excesses outside of marriage.[2]

Buddha went to live in Gaya, a place near Benares on the Ganges. In this holy setting he began to ponder the meaning of life and what could be done to improve it. Again like Jesus, while in his lonely isolation, the evil one, Mara, came to tempt him. Mara urged him to give up his search for truth and return home to his wife and child. But Buddha resisted this temptation. Then Mara tried to kill Buddha with storm and lightning, but Mara was frightened away when Buddha touched the earth, and cried, "I bear your witness." For seven weeks, a magic number, Buddha continued to meditate alone. Then Mara returned and told him that by meditation no mortal person could ever understand him. This remark caused Buddha to realize that meditation would be worthless if he were to leave the world before a meaningful program of belief could be forged. So Buddha came to Banares to meditate. For forty-nine days he meditated under a fig tree. While in a trance, under the tree, he found in a flash his way to enlightenment. He became Buddha, the enlightened one.

Buddha continued to meditate for forty-nine more days, during which time he formulated his way of life, the way of the four noble truths and the eightfold path to enlightenment. Thus began Buddha's ministry of forty-five years spent preaching, teaching, founding a monastery, a *sangha,* and winning to his cause a few disciples who would become the missionaries for Buddhism. Buddha's best friend and aide, the first administrator of the sangha, was Ananda. Buddha died at the age of eighty. According to legend he died of dysentery from eating poisoned mushrooms while visiting his friend, Cunda. Lest Cunda might think he was responsible for the poisonous mushrooms, Buddha told him not to feel guilty for this was one of the two best meals he had ever eaten. It opened the gates to nirvana for him. The other meal so blessed was the one he ate under the bo tree, for it had given him the strength to meditate and discover his truths. It was said that Buddha died in the arms of his friend Ananda. His body was cremated, and the remaining parts were distributed across India to become magical relics housed in special dome-covered memorial repositories called *stupas*. To have a hair from Buddha, or any part of his body, would be sufficient cause for his followers to build a beautiful temple in his memory. A visitor to Nepal, Buddha's birthplace, will see many temples and stupas built for the worship of Buddhism. Temples may be painted with Buddha eyes, blue eyes painted on a gold background, eyes looking in all four directions, signifying that all people are under the constant watch of Buddha. Around the temples will be found Buddhist monks dressed in red or saffron robes, with shaved heads, the right shoulder bare, walking clockwise around the temple carrying prayer flags, prayer wheels, or prayer beads, and all the time reciting scriptures or mantras. The odor of burning incense adds to the reverence with which one views the temple scene.

Ananda wrote down Buddha's thoughts and sermons, which became the Buddhist scriptures. In a few years after his death Buddhist disciples grew from five to over twenty thousand, with five hundred missionaries. Although Buddha denied that he was anything more than an ordinary mortal, soon, in the eyes of his followers, he became a divine being.

The Teachings of Buddha

Buddha's way to salvation has been called the "middle way." During his ascetic wanderings he had learned that life is all pain and death, not worth living. But he learned also that a person who gives all of his life to pleasure and sensual living does not find happiness either. The right or best way was, like Aristotle's golden mean, the middle way. If man pursued the middle way he would learn to deny his desires for power and pleasure, the causes for human suffering on earth and death. Thereby he would find enlightenment and eventually nirvana.

Buddha was reared in the Hindu tradition, and just as Jesus was reared in the Judaic tradition, both teachers sought to modify their inherited faiths by making the individual person and his or her relationship to God the central core of the religion. Jesus sought to soften the Judaic emphasis on obedience to law and Talmudic regulations. Buddha sought to remove much of the supernatural from Hinduism. Hindus worshiped too many gods and used too many relics, magic prayers, and superstitious beliefs. In the long run both teachers failed to protect their religions from acquiring later all of the supernatural attributes and magical rituals that they had deplored. Yet no one can deny that both Jesus and Buddha did leave religions that had more concern for the freedom and welfare of the individual person than their original faiths.

In all of his teachings Buddha followed the middle way, which taught that we ought to be tolerant of all other religions and to avoid life styles given to either the extreme of gluttony and pleasure or to excess asceticism, Buddha saw no need for a church institition or a group of priests. He saw no need to believe in miracles or supernatural agencies as means to reach nirvana. His doctrines, called *dhamma,* akin to Hindu *dharma,* was merely discovered by Buddha, not invented. These truths were always available to mankind, since they are inherent in the very nature of human beings.

Dhamma, Buddhist doctrine, is found in a collection of sermons called the Pali documents, and in the Tripitaka or "Three Baskets." The Pali language is a dialect of ancient Prakrit, a vernacular form of Sanskrit. Buddhists say that the best way to know Buddhism is not to read about it, but to practice it. One can sympathize with a remark attributed to a king of Paekche who sent an emissary to Japan in A.D. 552 to promote Buddhism. The king wrote, "This doctrine is amongst all doctrines the most excellent, but it is hard to explain and hard to comprehend. Even the Duke of Chou and Confucius could not attain knowledge of it."[3]

In the dhamma is found the teachings of Buddha. He believed that the human body is impermanent, subject to decay. All other aspects of the body, the mind, the personality, and the spiritual being or soul are also subject to decay and dissolution. Hence in each rebirth of the soul there would need to be an entirely new collection of psychic and spiritual elements, otherwise there would be no end to suffering, which would prevent any union with the oversoul or God. The essence of Buddhism is a belief that man and his or her soul must attain nirvana, a state of nothingness. Nirvana can be reached only by practicing dhamma. There is no afterlife in heaven or hell. There is no resurrection or transmigration of souls. There is no god of creation, no God to whom humans can turn for relief from pain and suffering. One might find God in Buddha's concept of enlightenment or truth, a condition that all humans can attain, but this God has no power or force outside of or beyond the human person.

Buddha announced that there are four noble truths to enlightenment: (1) suffering and pleasure are essential elements in all of human existence; (2) suffering and pain are caused by desire, or tanka; (3) escape from suffering comes by destroying all desire for wealth, pleasure, and all other ego drives; (4) escape from suffering will come if one follows an eightfold path to nirvana.

The first truth, or *dukkha,* states that suffering is found in all of life from birth until death. All forms of existence are impermanent states, be they mental or physical. All life is transistory, aimless, and painful, always subject to many births and rebirths.

The second truth, or *tanha,* says that suffering is caused by the desire for personal fulfillment or desire. Desire is made manifest in the form of human actions, called *karman.* Karman motivated by desire includes passions, ignorance, hatred, greed, pleasures of all kinds, delusions, accumulated wealth and all material possessions, desire for power and position in higher social orders, plus a host of other desires, including the belief that all ends with death. Buddhists have created a symbolic image to represent the principal desires, a symbol often seen in Buddhist architecture and religious art. It is a circle design in which there are three colored figures, a cock representing passion, a snake representing hatred, and a pig representing delusion or ignorance.

The third truth, or *nirodha,* is the cessation of desire. If all desire is eliminated, then the person has achieved nirvana, the supreme goal for every human to attain. No one can sense nirvana, for it is beyond the limits of space and time, or any form of earthly experience. Nirvana is supreme happiness found in the wisdom and peace of Buddha.

The fourth truth is the Buddha's Way. It is the guide to nirvana, the eightfold paths to nirvana, the equivalent of the Judeo-Christian Ten Commandments. In the eight right actions can be found the three basic elements for virtue in the Buddha's plan for action: wisdom, morality, and meditation. The eight paths, briefly stated are:

1. Right knowledge, that is, accept the four noble truths.
2. Right aspiration or thought.
3. Right speech, avoidance of obscenity and words that demean others. Avoid gossip and lies.
4. Right behavior, no stealing, sexual immorality, drunkenness, or murder.
5. Right effort, the necessary willpower to do right actions.
6. Right livelihood, the command to do honest work faithfully, never cheating, stealing, or loafing on the job. Refrain from prostitution, selling drugs, alcohol, meat, armaments, or engaging in slavery.
7. Right mindfulness, a statement that what we are and will become is determined by our thoughts.
8. Right concentration, or the practice of correct meditation and yogas. Concentration is the one essential element in the practice of meditation. It is a quality of mind control by which all external distractions, feelings, and sensations are divested from the mind. Meditation is the ability to cultivate this higher form of psychic power, which reveals to the person superknowledge and insights. In the meditational state one ceases to have contacts with family, friends, work, or any part of the external material world.

Buddha faced the problem of finding a religious system that mere mortal, ordinary people could practice. How could men and women, busy with the duties of family and work, find time to devote to meditation and yogas? These are most time-consuming and disciplined activities for the human mind to undertake. The most opportune place for the best acts of meditation to occur would be in a monastery, or a Buddhist sangha. In the Buddhist tradition three "jewels" were recognized. They were the acceptance of the dhamma, that is, the creed and prescribed duties, retirement to a sangha, and attainment of enlightenment.

The Buddhist Clergy

Life in a sangha is regulated by many rules of conduct, 220 for monks and between 290 and 355 for nuns. The basic rules require that the initiates take vows of chastity, poverty, and obedience. No one is permitted to use alcohol, milk, or sugar. Abstinence from all sexual activity is required. Married men may join a sangha, but after they do they must remain celibate. Food is eaten only in the morning, none after noon. A monk must earn his meal by taking a brass bowl and going begging in some residential area for his rice. Housewives expect the arrival of the monkish beggars, so they are prepared to greet the hungry visitors with buckets of rice. The families believe that they are privileged to serve the monks, for in this manner the family members receive merits for their own road to nirvana.

Anyone can join a sangha, male or female, old or young. The period of monastic life might be for a lifetime or for a few months. In Buddhist countries many young men enter a sangha during the "rainy" season, when farm work is impossible. After two or three months they go back home. Of course, the ideal initiate is one who is willing to make a lifetime commitment. Four types of memberships are recognized: monks, nuns, male laity, and female laity. Members must be twenty years or older, and they enter with the consent of parents and wife, with a clean record of having no criminal offenses charged against them. In Thailand it is estimated that 25 percent to 40 percent of the young men enter the sangha as temporary members.

The initiate takes the three vows mentioned above. The vow of poverty is expressed by wearing a simple dress, a saffron-colored robe, a shaved head, and owning only a few items, such as his bowl, a razor, and a towel or two. The sangha is supervised by an abbot, whose task is to train the new members. Student novices spend most of their time in study of Buddhist texts and learning the art of meditation. Daily life in a sangha begins by rising early, then meditating for an hour or so, followed by taking to the streets to beg for the breakfast meal. Before the meal is eaten, the feet must be washed. The afternoon is used for more study and meditation. Then certain hours are set aside for people who come for spiritual counseling and instruction.

Although most monks and nuns live in sanghas or *wats,* they have no permanent home. Some may spend most of their time wandering about, sleeping wherever nightfall finds them, in the open, in a forest, or on a street. Many spend time making pilgrimages to sacred shrines. Eventually the dedicated monks and nuns hope to attain some holy status, which, although it may not bring them to the door of nirvana when they die, may bring them near to nirvana, Buddha-like state, one called *bodhisattva.* These almost divine persons become saints or gods to whom the common people pray and offer gifts. There is no limit to the number of possible bodhisattvas, thus making it possible for a Buddhist to worship the Hindu gods, or even Jesus. The "near Buddhas" continue to live on earth, where they can serve mankind. A legend says there were other Buddhas before

Buddha, and in the same manner there are many bodhisattvas who continue to serve all on earth, man and beasts, thereby earning merits that can be used to secure for their souls a place in nirvana, and perhaps even earn surplus merits that can be transferred to other souls for their salvation, a concept similar to the Catholic concept of purgatory and the value of surplus merits earned by saints.

In summary, a devout monk and nun have learned to know the principles of Buddhism. They know that the soul is atman, and the "no soul'" or self is anatman. They know that suffering is *dukha,* and that all life is impermanent. Salvation is earned by doing good or karman. Karman is action with a moral purpose. The soul must endure *samsara* or the sequence of repeated births, until nirvana has been reached.

Ritual and Customs

If India were to become a land of Buddhist monks and nuns committed to the vows of chastity and poverty, in a century India would cease to be. Buddhist philosophers will need to find simpler, more practical interpretations of Buddha's middle way, a religion that could be understood and practiced by ordinary men and women. Ordinary Buddhists, like Christian worshipers, can strive to reach the ideal goals, but to achieve perfection is unreasonable to expect. But the common Buddhist can obey the commandments. They can practice to some degree the six virtues of generosity, morality, charity, patience, vigor, some meditation, and study of Buddhist doctrines. They can make sacrifices and present gifts to Buddha and his bodhisattvas and say prayers before their altars. They can be faithful to their marriage vows and they can limit their sexual urges to the marriage bed. They can train their children to honor parents and grandparents, and to worship Buddha.

Meditation for uneducated working people is difficult. Far easier is to worship Buddha and win *punya* or good merits by the sacrifical presentation of gifts (food, flowers, money) on the altar of Buddha. Prayers for good health and fortune are directed to Buddha and his associates. The goddess Tara is worshiped as the mother of Buddha, a virgin mother also. Some believe that Buddha still lives on earth. This makes it even easier for people to pray to him. The practice of meditation is simplified by reducing the act to the saying of a few magical sounds or words, the mantras. A Buddhist sect known as the Tantrics practice a form of meditation which includes wild bodily movements and some excess sexual activity.

A common object used in Buddhist worship is some form of a prayer wheel, which, when whirled, can spin prayer messages to Buddha. Symbol designs, *mandalas,* are also used. One mandala is a picture of a turning wheel, the wheel of life. The hub of the wheel has three animal figures, each one biting the tail of the animal next to it. The animals, as mentioned earlier, are the cock, the snake, and the pig, representing passion, hatred, and ignorance. A more elaborate mandala is another wheel of life, this time with six segments. The first represents the world of gods and saints, signifying the virtues of love and peace. A second segment has the antigods, the evil forces of violence and materialism. A third segment pictures ghosts, greedy people who cannot be satisfied. The ghosts have mouths so small that they cannot eat sufficient amounts of food to satisfy their greedy stomachs. A fourth segment pictures life in hell. A fifth segment pictures animals who represent people who cannot control their bodily desires. And the sixth part belongs to the realm of ordinary people who work, meditate, care for their family, study scripture, do the best they can each day, and then die.

In each segment Buddha is shown, meaning that whatever our state of being is, Buddha is there to help us. The outer rim of the wheel has twelve chains that bind humans to this life on earth.

One other common symbol is the lotus flower in the earth representing our physical body; the flower, above the earth, is our enlightened mind. The unfolding of the blossom is intended to represent the unfolding or development of spiritual awareness.

Sects

Buddhism, as with other religions, over time developed divisions. Theologians disagreed as to what Buddha had taught as the truth. Although several different sects arose, all probably adhered more closely to one doctrine than do Christian Catholics and Protestants to original Christianity. Three groups represent the more important Buddhist sects today: the Theravada, or "Lesser Vehicle"; the Mahayana, or "Greater Vehicle"; and Zen Buddhism in Japan.

Theravada or Hinayana Buddhism, the "Way of the Elders," is the most conservative group, since it holds most closely to Buddha's original message. This version prevails today in Thailand, Burma, Cambodia, Laos, and Sri Lanka. Theravadas practice the most rigid, demanding tenets of Buddhism. Their ideal of true Buddhism is found in the sanghas. The only certain path to nirvana is to live the life of an ascetic monk, where life is all meditation and denial of the pleasures of life. They hold strictly to the belief that no divine force will assist man in his search for salvation. Nirvana is to be won only by personal will and effort. The supernatural powers of words, relics, and sacrifices are only futile gestures. This form of Buddhism offers little hope of salvation for the masses.

The Mahayana is a more liberal version of Buddhism that developed in India sometime around the early Christian era (no precise date can be given) or about five hundred years after Buddha's death. It was an easier faith for the common people to accept and practice. Today Mahayana Buddhism prevails in Tibet, China, Japan, and Northern India. This is a form of religion that can be lived in the home and workplace. No longer do you need to live in a monastery to find peace and salvation. Good Buddhists are expected to strive for perfection, but if one never achieves the goal of nirvana, then some may be able to become saints or bodhisattvas. The Mahayana Buddhists are called also "middle way"

Buddhists, never completely denying absolute existence or nonexistence. Their principal goals include the practice of the six perfections: morality, patience, wisdom, vigor, charity, and meditation. These Buddhists are expected also to venerate the images of the gods and saints, use mantras as substitutes for meditation, and especially practice charity to all persons and practice nonviolence toward all of God's creatures on earth.

The Spread of Buddhism

Buddhism had its origins in India, but it was never able to supplant the native Hindu gods. However, Buddhism had devoted missionaries who carried Buddha's wisdom to all parts of Asia. No one did more to spread the faith than the Emperor Ashoka, 264–226 B.C. He regarded Buddhism as the expression of the universal law of God or dharma. Buddhism was a good guide for both the state and its citizens. Ashoka called a conference of Buddhist leaders to codify Buddhist doctrine. Saints were deemed worthy of reverence, heaven and hell were parts of the universal cosmology. The use of such spiritual aids as prayer beads, candles, and incense was approved.

Ashoka sent missionaries not only to Asian areas but also to Egypt, Syria, Macedonia, and Greece. His most important missionary enterprise was to Ceylon (today's Sri Lanka), where the Theravadan version of Buddhism was introduced. Theravadan Buddhism was one of several offshoots of the Hinyana division of Buddhism, the earliest and most conservative and disciplined of the various Buddhist faiths.

After the end of the Ashokan Dynasty in A.D. 320, when the Gupta Dynasty came to power, Buddhism lost its favored position, after which it was forced to compete with traditional Hinduism for the hearts and minds of the Indian people. By A.D. 900 most Indians had ceased to follow the Buddhist way and had returned to Hinduism. Today very vew Buddhists are found in India.

However, Buddhism found many secure homes in other parts of Asia. By the second century A.D. Buddhism had arrived in Burma, Thailand, Cambodia (Kampuchea), and Laos. By the fifth century A.D. Buddhism was being practiced in Indonesia (Java and Malaysia). In Indonesia Buddhism was to be replaced by Islam in the thirteenth century.

By the second century A.D. Buddhist missionaries from India had come to China. Legend tells that two monks came to Luoyang in Huan Province as the first of the Buddhist missionaries. In Luoyang there is a memorial grotto containing over a hundred thousand statues of Buddha. In the third century A.D. the Han Dynasty accepted Buddhism as the predominant state religion. The Sui Dynasty, A.D. 589–618, continued to give priority to the Buddhist faith. However, with the advent of the T'ang Dynasty, A.D. 627–907, Confucianism was restored as the official religion of China. At first this dynasty tolerated Buddhism, but in 845 all-out war was waged against Buddhists temples and monasteries, and the faith's devotees. Buddhist leaders were charged with being enemies of the state, since they had become too wealthy and hence too powerful. Temples were destroyed, monastic lands were confiscated, and monks and nuns were forced to do common labor.

A brief resurgence of Buddhism in China occurred when the Mongol Empire under Kublai Khan, and his successors, A.D. 1280–1365, gave their support to Buddhism. Kublai Khan had earlier conquered Tibet, but he in turn had been converted to Buddhism, so the Mongol regime restored Buddhism as the official religion of China. Tibetan Buddhism followed the Tantric version of Buddhism, which had become popular in Southeast Asia during the eleventh century. Tantric Buddhism became popular simply because it tolerated the native gods and beliefs of the conquered people. Many of its beliefs stemmed from Hinduism. Tantrism also appealed to the masses of people, who found more satisfaction in the practice of occultism, magic, mystery, charms, rituals and mantra incantations than in meditation and the practice of yoga disciplines. Tantrism also gave a more equal status to all people and especially to women. The caste system was denounced. In the fourteenth century Tibetan Buddhism experienced a new sect known as the "Yellow Hats." This reform movement sought to revive the old monastic, disciplined way of life for salvation. When its first leader, or "lama," died in 1475, a tradition began a belief that henceforth all future lamas were reincarnations of the first lama. Thus all ruling lamas of Tibet became known as Dalai (Ocean) Lama, the divinely appointed ruler of Tibet. When China conquered Tibet in 1950 the rule of the Dalai Lamas ended, and the current Dalai Lama sought refuge in India.

By A.D. 552 Buddhist monks had come to Japan from Korea. Buddhism had earlier been established in Korea as the state religion. In the thirteenth century Japanese Buddhism developed a new form of belief known as "Pure Land" or Amida Buddhism. Amida, the Buddhist prophet, declared that in the pure land it was possible for all people to attain salvation without the need to be confined to a monastery where a strenuous life of prayer, study, meditation and denial of all fleshly appetites was required. By repeating a series of mantras, including the name of Amida, plus practicing a few simple rituals, salvation could be secured. Japanese people have for centuries been able to accept Shintoism, Buddhism, and Confucianism in a harmonious blend of national religions.

Zen

In Japan another form of Buddhism developed, called Zen Buddhism. It is a religion with no scripture or ritual, but Zen does recognize the truths of Buddhism and the basic goal of attaining enlightenment, nirvana, or nothingness. The word *zen* means meditation or concentration. Zen Buddhists believe that meditation is the only way to find truth. One distinctive mark about Zen is the expression of love for all things in nature, especially the beauty that is to be found in nature.

In all things of nature there is a vital force or energy that unites all living creatures, human and nonhuman. Zen developed in Japan in the twelfth century A.D., although its roots can be discovered in earlier times.

The essence of Zen is that one must realize or understand that enlightenment, or *satori*, is to be found in the here and now, the everyday life of each person. When one discovers the truth, at that moment he or she loses all sense of self, or status, or success, or friends, or even being in the world of today. When one discovers truth for the first time it is as if one has experienced the world for the first time. Each person must discover the truth for himself or herself. It is of no value to use prayer or religious rituals and gestures to find the truth. Truth comes in a flash when one realizes that mind and body do not exist. The experience of satori or truth prepares us for a happy life here on earth.

Zen can be achieved best in a monastery, but this reclusive life is not essential. One can become a Zen devotee by learning the art of meditation. The study of scripture is a waste of time. Zen is a religion of action and of mental and bodily discipline. Each person has within his or her being the power to meditate and to receive in a spontaneous, immediate revelation the truth. However, self-instruction may be insufficient so a Zen initiate would be wise to use a guru or teacher to give instruction in how to meditate. Meditative sessions often use a question-and-answer form of instruction, called a *koan* session. The guru asks questions of the students to which they must give answers. Such questions usually have no apparently logical or rational answers. For example, the question may be, "What is the sound of two hands when put together?" The answer is "clapping." Then the question is, "What is the sound of one hand?" Only when the students realize that there is no sensible answer can they understand that life has no meaning, or no answers, so there is no point in trying to understand the mysteries of life. Only things experienced have any meaning. Even death has no meaning, since it is beyond experience. Death is only a part of life, no more important than going to sleep at night.

A Zen Buddhist initiate must spend much time in meditation, during which he must learn proper breathing techniques, proper body positions, how to gaze upon a rock in the midst of a garden of sand, or at a painting that catches the act of a moment, such as a fish leaping from the water, or a flower unfolding, or the reality that empty space is as much a part of life as the presence of a mountain or a beautiful girl. Zen is awareness, direct and immediate, of life as it is, in its being, separated from all ideas and feelings about life. Forget the past and avoid thoughts of the future. The arduous practice of meditation will discipline the entire person, both body and mind. Bodily actions become automatic, with no need for making mental decisions. Hence, the martial arts of karate and judo are good examples of how the body becomes the master over the mind.

Zen Buddhism in Japan has joined with Shintoism to cause Japanese people to be most aware of the beauty to be found in nature. The protection of the environment becomes a high priority among Japanese life values, almost a sacred duty to protect nature and wildlife. Zen Buddhism is expressed in the art of flower arranging, in painting nature scenes in light brush strokes and pastel shades, and in simple arrangements of sand, rocks, and a few shrubs to form an attractive landscape pattern. Zen is reflected in the controlled actions of the players in the *no* drama. In everyday contacts, Japanese Zen is shown by acts of courtesy, polite bows, and controlled emotions.

In recent years Zen Buddhism has appealed to a few Western minds. The works of such writers as Alan Watts and Jack Kerouac reflect Zen values that Americans can accept easily. Such values as self-knowedge, self-will, the free expression of personal beliefs, and each person's right to find his own God or set of ethical values are all in tune with Zen philosophy. Zen Buddhism is not easy to describe to a nonfollower. This brief summary from an old Zen teacher may be helpful.

> Clear-sighted masters of the Zen do not have a fixed doctrine which is to be held to at any time and all times. They offer whatever teaching occasion demands and preach as the spirit moves them, with no fixed course to guide them. If asked what Zen is, they may answer in the words of Confucius, Mencius, Lao Tzu or Chuang Tzu, or else in terms of the doctrines of the various sects and denominations, and also by using popular proverbs. Sometimes they draw attention to the immediate confronting us, or they swing their mace and shout out "katsu," or perhaps they just raise their fists or fingers. All of these methods used by the Zen master are known as the "vigorous treatment of the Zen Buddhist." They are incomprehensible to those who have not yet ventured into this realm.[4]

Buddhism has been a positive, civilizing influence wherever it is found. It is a good religion. It tends to be conservative, holding to the good old ways of life, reluctant to move into the modern world of science and materialism. Buddhists seem to be relatively tolerant of other people and their religions. They tend to be family-oriented, most respectful towards the elderly and the dead ancestors, and more willing to submit their individual needs and wills to the needs and will of the larger social group. Like the Hindus, Buddhists abhor violence and war, yet they have waged war when necessary to protect their gods and their faith, as might be witnessed today when Buddhist monks in Tibet attempt revolutionary action against Chinese domination.

Hindus and Buddhists view all of nature's creatures as one with them, hence hunting, killing animals, and eating flesh are all taboo acts. Sexual morality is prized highly, yet moderation, not abstinence, is the guiding principle, and then only in the marriage relationship. Death for a Buddhist is received with peace and confidence, as with a Christian, but with less fear and regret, even with a sense of relief that the soul is now free to wend its way to eternity or nirvana.

Two concepts that people from the West can accept are the beliefs that each person is responsible for his or her own acts, and that our personal problems arise not from sin, original or otherwise, but from ignorance. If mankind can overcome ignorance then humankind can find a better way to a good life here on earth. Man is a learning creature, one who wants to know the secrets of creation and how to relate properly to all of God's creation.

9

Sikhism

The Sikhs, another Hindu sect, live primarily in northern India, in the Punjab province. Here some 60 percent of all Sikhs in the world live, or a total of 15 million believers. About a quarter million live in the United States. Sandra Widener has told of the life in a Sikh ashram or colony in New Mexico, near Espanola and Santa Fe.[1] This ashram was started about 1970. A visit to this ashram could give a better understanding of the Sikh religion than reading any book about it. The Sikhs are disciples of ten gurus who lived from the fifteenth to the eighteenth centuries in India This sect began as a reform movement within the Hindu religion, especially as a reaction against the social caste system. The first Sikh guru was a Hindu mystic, Nanak, who lived in the Punjab. During his lifetime he visited Tibet, Sri Lanka, Mecca, and some other Arab cities. He became greatly interested in the Islamic religion, and there is some belief that he intended to unite Islam and Hinduism to form a new religion.

Holy wisdom was passed through a line of ten gurus after Nanak, but after Nanak no new revelations were to occur. Instead Nanak's ideas were written into a sacred book, Granth Sahib, or Adi Granth, "The Growth," about 1603. In 1699 Guru Gohm Singh ordered that henceforth this book would be a substitute symbol for a Sikh guru. The main headquarters for Sikhism is in Amritsar, Punjab, India. The name "Amritsar" means "pool of immortality," and takes its name from the fourth guru, Ram Dam.

Gobund Singh, the tenth guru, founded a strong military brotherhood to fight the invading Muslims from the north. This brotherhood has five distinguishing marks: *kes,* or long hair, *kanha,* or a comb, *hacha,* or short pants, *kara,* an iron bracelet, and *kirpan,* a sword. All members take the name of Singh, or "Lion." However, all Singhs are not Sikhs. I recall that our car driver in India was a large young man who wore a heavy beard with his head wrapped in a long-coiled turban. At first he seemed to be a dangerous person, fierce in appearance, but after a day in his company he proved to be a most friendly tour guide as well as a driver. He told how he had broken away from his family and his village to come to New Delhi to have a better life for his family. His decision to leave home had cost him the love of his parents and his community, but he was willing to take the risk so that his children might have a better chance for an education. In India most chauffeurs and many soldiers are Sikhs.

The identifying marks of Sikhs have special religious significance, in that all five marks are considered to provide protection to the person's body. By not cutting their hair Sikhs are not doing injury to any part of their body. The turban is a symbol of the unity of the brotherhood. The wooden comb symbolizes cleanliness, the short pants or underwear reminds the men that sex is confined to the marriage bed, the iron bracelet signifies devotion to the truth, and the small sword reminds them that they must protect the poor and the weak.

In the nineteenth century under Guru Singh, the Sikhs became the free state of the Punjab. However, it was soon taken over by the British in the 1840s and made a part of the Indian state. The Sikhs furnished British India with a number of its soldiers, a tradition that free India continues. But the Sikhs never forgot their longing for independence. They contend that when India accepted the independence of Pakistan and Bangdalesh, then the Sikhs should have been given their independence also. Sikh leaders claim that Indian officials had even made such a promise for independence.

Sikhism is a monotheistic religion, with one God, called Sat or "Truth." Their God has never been incarnated into a human form, therefore there is no human or earthly symbol for God. God is without form, is unknowable, and is eternal. God is represented by the number one ("1"), or the unity of God. Since God has the power to place his grace upon humans, he has, among other gifts, given man his revelations. God's revelations are made manifest in all forms and things in his creation of the universe. God is known to humans not by reason and intellect, but by seeing with the inner eye, the heart, by means of meditation and prayer.

Worship occurs both in the home and in the temple. In the home family members take turns reading from the Granth Sahib, which fulfills a part of the obligation to spend 10 percent of one's time in religious devotions. In the temple, no matter whether it is large or small, worship services may last for three hours, during which time prayers, scripture readings, meditations, and chants are all performed. In the New Mexico ashram guitar music is used to accompany the chants and old Indian folk tunes are also used. At the close of the service a meal is served using bread, butter and honey. The most-used chant is one that has the phrase, "There is one God, great is his name." Sikhs, like Hindus and Buddhists, use gurus to instruct the faithful in the art of meditation and prayer and the practice of the yoga techniques. Although the Sikhs do not stress the need for followers to retreat to a monastery, they do permit the more devout believers to live together in an isolated ashram. But in all forms of living, salvation depends upon the daily practice of right living, by which mind and body are brought into harmony with the divine universe. A good Sikh does his or her best to meditate, to chant the sacred mantras, and to abstain from the use of alcohol, tobacco, and meat, and to limit sex to the marriage bed. Sikhs are required to give 10 percent of their earnings to charity. In Sikhism both sexes are equal, all races and classes are equal, hence they reject the caste system. In the worship service all images, statues, relics, or other representations of God are rejected.

The final destination of the soul is union with God. This mystical union may occur if the soul and its body have lived a good life on earth as prescribed by the Granth Sahib. The penalty for disobedience is that the soul will be unable to join God, and forever after be doomed to an endless series of transmigrations, or, even worse, the most extreme penalty of being denied forever any reunion with God.

As for the future of the Sikhs, it is known that many of the young people are losing their devotion to the old traditions of Sikhism. Rural communities are losing their young people to the cities, where more secular interests prevail. Some of the young intermarry with Hindus, while others emigrate to the United States, England, and other Western nations to find better economic opportunities. However, the older people and the majority of the young cling to the Sikh traditions and the long-delayed hope for national independence. India remains reluctant to concede to Sikh demands for freedom, lest other minority groups demand the same. In the meantime relations between the Sikhs in the Punjab and the Indian government remain in a state of continual violence, somewhat similar to the conditions in Ireland where religious and political strife reigns between the Catholics and the Protestants in the British-ruled area of Northern Ireland.

10

Jainism

Mother India gave birth to Hinduism, from which arose three other religions: Buddhism, Sikhism, and Jainism. Jainism represents a small body of four million followers in India who are principally engaged in commerce, banking, and industry. The Jains owe their faith to an ascetic prophet, Vardhamana Mahavira, who lived approximately 599–527 B.C. "Mahavira" means "great hero," and the religion he founded comes from a Sanskrit word, *jina,* meaning "victorious." Jainism's religious symbol is a swastika, an ancient symbol for good luck.

The Life of Mahavira

Legend surrounds the birth of Mahavira, as it does the birth of Buddha and Jesus. Mahavira's conception was supposedly a matter of divine incarnation. It was said that, while in the embryo state, Mahavira was transplanted into his mother's womb. News of his impending birth was announced to the world by divine spirits or angels, and at the moment of his birth a bright star appeared in the sky. Since he was born as a supernatural being, Mahavira's followers declared him to be all-wise, all-knowing of the secrets of the universe. Being an omniscient person, Mahavira, one of the gods, no longer would have to suffer the evil forces of karma and endure the cycles of transmigration. Mahavira was a contemporary of Buddha, although there is no evidence that the two prophets ever met. Their life stories have much in common. Mahavira was the son of a tribal chief, Siddhartha, and, like Buddha, he lived a sheltered life during his youth. He married a princess, by whom he had one child, a daughter. Also like Buddha Mahavira became disenchanted with his palace life, so, at the age of twenty-eight, on the death of his parents, he left his family, gave away all of his possessions, and began the life of a wandering ascetic. After thirteen months he gave up wearing clothes so that in abject poverty he could spend all his time and energy in meditation and fasting. For thirteen years he continued this spartan life of denial of all worldly things in an attempt to achieve *Jina* the key to salvation. (To Jains the number thirteen is a magic number.) A legend relates that one day Mahavira sat down to rest under a saia tree on a river bank, somewhere in his homeland of Nepal. After two and half days, while meditating, *jina,* enlightenment, suddenly came to him. Henceforth, Mahavira would be called Jina or "the conqueror."

For thirty years Mahavira preached his message throughout northern India. He died at the age of seventy-two, near Patna, India. Some reporters say that he died deliberately, by fasting to death.

Jain Beliefs

Mahavira believed that all life is trapped in a cycle of births and rebirths. He sought to find an escape from these endless cycles. He refused to accept the Hindu belief in Brahman, that is, a state of nonexistence. Rather he believed that the universe was composed of two unrelated parts: jina, or soul, and *ajina,* or nonsoul. Ajina would be such elements as space, time, matter, movement, and stillness.

Although Jains do not honor any one god, they do honor seven divine teachers, called *tirthankaras,* a word meaning "ford crossers," or those who can cross the rivers of transmigration of souls. The universe has no beginning or end, but it does pass through cycles of rises and falls. In the same manner human civilization experiences rises and falls, a historical concept held by historians Arnold Toynbee, Arthur Schlessinger, and others. Since the beginning, twenty-four tirthankaras have lived and taught their plan for salvation. The last of the tirthankaras came in the sixth century and he was also called Mahavira, the last of the Jain teachers.

In Jainism the path to salvation is one that allows the soul to escape from the body, the nonsoul, the physical body which houses the soul. Until the soul can be released from the body it must suffer the cycles of births and rebirths. So long as the soul remains in the body it suffers pain. The Jain concept of soul finds the soul in all material things, earth, mountains, rivers, fire, air, wind, and in all living things, plants, animals, and humans. In fact there are an infinite number of souls in all of God's creation, a pantheistic belief. For example, Mt. Aby in central India is a most holy place for Jains.

Since the soul must escape from the material body, and since all matter is evil, then all matter is karma. Karma is created by people who do evil deeds. Good deeds create little, if any, karma. The problem arises, "How shall karma be removed from the body?" Five rules of conduct are prescribed: (1) destroy no life; (2) do not lie; (3) practice charity; (4) practice chastity; and (5) possess nothing, want nothing.

Jainism prohibits the killing of any living thing, a position on the taking of life that is more extreme than the view of the Hindus and Buddhists. Nonviolence is termed *ahisma.* It is said that Jains will wear masks over their mouths so as to not accidently swallow flies or other insects. Monks are even more extreme in protecting animals, in that they they will not take baths lest they kill body lice. They even refrain from walking in the dark for fear that they might step on a snake or some other animal. This respect for the sanctity of life carries over into politics. Jains refuse to engage in war or any kind of violent political action. Despite their abhorrence of violence and murder, Jains believe that starvation is the most sacred way to die.

Jains are forbidden to plow the fields or to smelt metal, for these acts would destroy or harm the sacred elements in earth or ore. So the Jains do not engage in farming, woodworking, metallurgy, chemistry, or any form of manufacturing. But, despite these prohibitions, the Jains have become most successful bankers and merchants. It is logical that Jains refrain from eating all forms of flesh. They are strict vegetarians.

Jains, like Buddhists, reject the Hindu caste system. In their scheme of life of all people are equal, men and women, all races and all social conditions. Jainism has most rigid restrictions on accumulating wealth and engaging in sexual activity, so strict that one must live in a monastery to be an ideal Jain. Accordingly, monasteries are an important aspect of Jainism. How wealthy Jains satisfy prohibitions against wealth is not explained.

At the age of eight children can join a monastic community. Monks and nuns devote most of their waking hours to prayer, meditation, and study. Monastics may leave the monastery to wander about and beg for food. While travelling, the monks always carry a small broom to sweep all forms of life from their path. Even the mouth must be covered. Although both men and women can become ascetics on an equal basis, the men in reality can escape karma more easily than women since men can roam about in the nude, a most holy state, while women must wear clothes. Members of a monastery are forbidden to speak to one another.

Salvation or "soul release" is strictly a personal decision and must be won by one's own acts. There is no God or intercessor with God who can prevent the soul from enduring the agony of transmigration. The rules for salvation are so difficult that the laity are not expected to meet them.

Undoubtedly this is the escape hole for rich men. Common people are expected to follow the rules of right conduct. The first rule or commandment is to control all passions, such as emotions, pride, anger, lying, greed and a host of other evil acts that build karma. One must practice charity, give freely of one's wealth to aid the poor, build hospitals, homes for the orphans, schools, and build temples for the Hindu gods. However, the Hindu gods are all inferior deities who are subordinate to Mahavira. In a sense the Hindu gods are not accepted as truly divine creatures.

All sexual activity is restricted to the marriage relationship. Jains must fast and meditate on specified occasions. Fasting is required twice a month and meditation is required daily, even for two or three hours for each session. The meditator must have a quiet retreat in his or her home where all external thoughts and concerns can be put aside. In meditation one must confess all sins committed, and ask forgiveness from all living creatures for any harm or injury that the person might have caused. Then follows peace of mind and a feeling of having done a holy deed. In some ways Jains resemble the Quakers, who also seek to find God and contentment in a quiet place, while meditating on things holy. Also like the Quakers, Jains refuse to engage in war and violence and they are committed to acts of charity in behalf of others, human and animal. A famous Jain saying is "A pious man eats little, sleeps, and drinks little."

Man's salvation while alive depends on his or her performance of good karma. After death this soul is beyond human or even divine intervention. The soul is at the mercy of the laws of the universe, which determine the number of births and rebirths. The souls of the most devout monastics may join the great soul in Nirvana immediately, never having to suffer the cyclical process of transmigration. However, even among the monks there are degrees of holiness that determine the fate of the souls.

The disposition of the dead body poses a special problem for Jains, who live today in a world concerned about the transmission of disease and the pollution of the environment. In India the traditional method of burial is to expose the corpse on a raised platform where wild birds and animals can cleanse the bones of the flesh. But for Jains who live in today's world, which requires that the corpse must be buried in the ground or cremated, there is a sacred dilemma. From the point of view of a Jain, to either bury or cremate the body pollutes that which is pure, the earth and the air. So the Jains have had to modify the religious prescription by accepting in most instances cremation as being preferred to burial.

11

Zoroastrianism

Zoroastrianism, was the dominant faith and the state religion of ancient Persia until the conquest by Alexander the Great in 330 B.C. However, Zoroastrianism was not completely replaced until the Muslims conquered Persia in the seventh century A.D. and forced the people to accept Islam. A minority of Zoroastrians fled to India, while a few remained in Persia to carry on the faith. Today they are scattered throughout the world. Only some 115,000 members remain, of whom seven thousand live in the United States.

Although Zorostrianism is a minor religion, it did have some impact on Christianity. Such Christian concepts as Satan, heaven and hell, the last judgment, resurrection, eternal life, and personal responsibility for one's salvation are basic beliefs that have come from Persia as well as from Israel.

Zarathustra

The prophet Zarathustra, the founder of Zorostrianism, is thought to have lived in the seventh century B.C. A traditional birthdate is 628. Details about his life are scant, hence myths provide most of Zarathustra's biography. It is said that he lived in heaven before his parents gave a miraculous birth to the child. His father was a priest of one of the old polytheistic religions of his day. The priesthood was hereditary then, as it is today, a condition that makes it very difficult for modern Zoroastrian churches to find priests. Like Buddha, Zarathustra left his wife and parents at a young age (twenty) to find spiritual answers to the many problems facing humans. He wandered for ten years seeking God. Seven of these years he spent alone in a cave until one day an angel, Vahu Mamah ("Good Thought") brought to him a divine revelation, which became the Zoroastrian Bible, the Avesta. A large part of this book is a collection of sacred hymns, the Gathas.

131

At first Zarathustra, like Jesus, found few disciples, but over many years his message did attract many followers. Just as the Roman Emperor Constantine embraced Christianity, the Persian king Vishtaspa, was converted to the new faith of Zoroastianism. Subsquently, all of his subjects were automatically required to become Zoroastrians. Zarathustra died in battle at the age of seventy-seven.

Zoroastrianism never developed a strong institutional form of religion. Basically it remained a family-based form of worship. Group worship took place in "fire temples," in which holy events and purification rituals, conducted by priests, would be held. One important celebration was the initiation of boys into adult manhood roles, a ritual very similar to the Jewish bar mitzvah for boys. The central focus of worship was the use of fire in a series of purification rituals, fire being a symbol for light and purity. Sandalwood brought to temples by the faithful would be burned and the ashes from the fire would be placed on the foreheads of the communicants, thus signifying that they had been blessed by God.

Zoroastrian Beliefs

One of the difficult problems in a monotheistic religion is how to explain how the one God could be responsible for both good and evil. Jews, Christians, and Muslims have had to construct an evil force, Satan, to explain the presence of evil among humans. Rational philosophers blame evil upon human will—man has the freedom to choose good and evil. A common man's simple explanation for his sins is that "the Devil made me do it."[1] All three of these major world religions derived this conception of the cause of evil from Zoroastrianism.

Zarathustra took an important step in the evolution of religious beliefs when he moved from polytheism to a concept of only two gods. The supreme god was Ahura Mazda, a god of light, purity, and goodness. He offers men and women salvation from sin in an eternal bliss if they choose his way of life. To solve the problem of evil in the world, Zarathustra created a lesser god, Angra Mainya, a god of darkness and evil. Since Ahura Mazda was the highest god, a precedent was set for future monotheistic religions. Lesser deities were accepted by Zarathustra, such as angels (God's messengers), who represent justice, good thoughts, power, and prosperity. The introduction of these lesser spiritual forces will later corrupt the religion's dualism, as followers begin to favor the lesser gods.

All existence is a struggle or war between good and evil. This conflict will continue for a period of twelve thousand years, the total era being divided into four periods of three thousand years each. Eventually the war will be won by goodness over evil. However, Zarathustra never believed that material things were in themselves bad or evil. It is the presence of evil within material things that seems to make them evil.

In Zoroastrianism each person is responsible for his or her own fate. Humans must choose the way of goodness or of sin. If one chooses the path of light, life, order, and rule, then he must practice all of the basic virtues, that is, he can not kill, cheat, lie, abuse sexuality, harm the family, and he must extend to others acts of charity and love. There is an obligation to have children, to protect one's health, to enjoy life and its pleasures in moderation, and to do an honest day's work. A good life is ruled by reason and moderation. Life must be freed from evil thoughts, angry emotions, greed, pride, and envy. An ascetic, monastic life was considered evil.

The life-after-death aspect of Zoroastrianism provided a major focus for its adherents. Within four days after death the soul of the deceased would be judged before Ahura Mazda. Since death is the work of the evil god, the corpse is an evil substance. Burial and cremation were forbidden, since in both practices the disposal of the body would contaminate the pure elements of nature, fire, air, water and earth. All of these basic elements are the central objects for worship. The traditional method for disposing of the body was to place the corpse upon an elevated platform so that the vultures coul pluck away the flesh, leaving only the bare bones exposed. This method of caring for the dead is generally forbidden in most societies of the world, so modern Zoroastrians are force to use cremation.

The final disposition of the soul follows a prescribed course of action. After the soul is judged, condemned souls are sent to the torments of hell, a state of pain similiar to the one portrayed by Dante in his description of hell. Good souls go to heaven for all of eternity, or until the final judgment, when the bodies are resurrected and a new world of light and order is created. Despite the terrors of hell, there remain opportunities for the soul to escape if it undergoes reform. After reformation the souls might join the good souls in the new world. Legend says that the good souls arise to heaven in the form of young, beautiful girls.

The final days on earth will be initiated by a savior who will be born of a seed of Zoroaster and a virgin, who would be impregnated by the holy semen from a lake. The savior will resurrect the dead, and the world will be destroyed by fire and flood, after which the earth will become a land of peace and plenty. One should note the similarity to the birth of Jesus and the Christian description of the last days.

Zoroastrianism in its initial stages was a religion relatively free from meaningless rituals, but a highly speculative, philosophical form of religion has little meaning for the common man. Hence, the religion eventually adopted magical rites, superstitious beliefs, and a body of priests to intervene with the gods. The priests were experts in the art of divination and magic. Much of the temple worship was reduced to repeating mantras, forecasting the future by astrology, and using symbolic rituals and ceremonies. As mentioned before, the fire rituals, symbols of purification, were most important. The celebration of the death of evil and the birth of a new world of purity through an act of miraculous resurrection occurs each New Year's Day. New clothes are exchanged to celebrate the death of the evil life and the beginning of a new pure life. Menstruating women undergo special purification rites at this time. Another ritual ceremony requires the drinking of a magic potion made from the juice of a native plant and mixed with milk and holy water. Such a drink induces a trancelike state of exhilaration, similar to the peyote trances of the Navaho Indians.

Despite the reliance on magic and superstition to honor and to know Ahura Mazda, Zoroastrianism does have several commendable beliefs that may have contributed to Christianity. There is the belief in a good, loving God and an evil force like Satan. Man is responsible for his own salvation. He must choose good over evil; he must live a loving, moral life and after death his soul will be judged in heaven. The final judgment by a merciful God promises eternal peace on earth.

12

Judaism, Mother of Monotheism

The Judaic religion cannot be separated from the city of Jerusalem, the central focus for most of the Judaic faith and history of the Jews. This city is also claimed by the Christians and the Muslims as their Holy City. Despite endless wars and crusades to secure the sole possession of Jerusalem for one faith or another, even today, despite the current occupation or possession of Jerusalem (according to the point of view of who is speaking) by the state of Israel, the future of Jerusalem remains in doubt. Perhaps it should be declared an international city under the jurisdiction of the United Nations.

Judaism can be called the mother of monotheism because no other earlier religion so boldly proclaimed that one god only, Jehovah, was the one and only true God. For a brief period of time a monotheistic religion had existed earlier in Egypt, but it was soon replaced by the old polytheistic faith of ancient Egypt. Whether this Egyptian experiment with monotheism could have influenced the Jews to adopt a one-god religion is a matter of academic debate.

Jews, Christians, and Persecution

From the beginning of the Christian era in history friction existed between the Jews and the followers of the Jewish Rabbi, Jesus. At first it seemed that the followers of Christ would be one more Jewish sect, but historical events determined that this was not to be the destiny of the Christians. The destruction of the Temple in Jerusalem by the Romans in A.D. 70 did much to undermine the power and prestige of Judaism. Moreover, the Jewish people were doomed to be scattered over far parts of the world, to become the people of the Diaspora who had only one bond to hold them together, the Torah and their God. In general the Romans were reasonably tolerant of both Jews and Christians in the first century A.D., but when the Christians multiplied in numbers and their influence spread, the Roman rulers became wary and oppressive. The Romans had always been fairly tolerant of the Jews so long as they paid their taxes to Rome and did not organize revolts against the Romans. When the Christians were thought to be just one more group of Jews, the Roman rulers more or less ignored them. By the second century the Christians were no longer to be ignored. But the relations between the Jews and the Christians ceased to be harmonious after the first century. The Jews wished to convert the Christians, and the followers of Christ wished to convert the Jews. If the Christians were to become another religion, then in the eyes of the Jews, Christians were heretics who ought to be persecuted and eradicated. Likewise the Christians, once they had some measure of political power, would declare Jews to be heretics and deserving of nothing better than death, or the status of slaves. Jewish historians have related in great detail how the followers of Judaism have been persecuted by Christian nations. Medieval Jews were forced to live in isolated ghettoes in Christian cities. In 1555, Pope Paul IV ordered that all Jews in Christendom were to live in ghettoes, and if they ever left the ghetto they must wear certain identification marks, such as a yellow hat or scarf. Pope Gregory XIII, 1572–85, ordered that all Jews in Rome must attend Christian church services so that the Jews might be converted. Christian segregation of the Jews continued until 1848, when it was officially ended by the Roman church.

In the fifteenth century the Jews of Spain experienced the torture of the Inquisition, by which they were driven from Spain to find refuge in Morocco, Tripoli, and Italy. During the eighteenth century rational philosophers like Voltaire, Rousseau, John Locke, and others began to advocate policies of religious toleration. The first signs of toleration for the Jews occurred in the Netherlands in the sixteenth century, and in England in the seventeenth century. With the Revolution in France came a major grant of toleration to the Jews, so that it seemed that the Christian world after the 1700s might be willing to accept the Jews as brothers under one God. But throughout the Christian world today, anti-Semetism remains as a potent force in national politics and in the social world of education and employment. However, the most offensive forms of anti-Semetism in the nineteenth century occurred in Czarist Russia. The Russian pogroms against the Jews were most grievous and cruel. Many Jews sought refuge in Western Europe and the United States. The cry for a national homeland for the Jews grew more and more vigorous after 1900. But how the Jews were treated in Russia before the Revolution of 1917 was mere blemish on the moral record of humanity when compared to what happened to the Jews of central Europe during the period of the Nazi terror and the tragedy of the Holocaust, when six million Jews were murdered.

Relations between the Muslims and Jews had been much more friendly and tolerant than between Jews and Christians until the establishment of the State of Israel in 1948. Since then Jewish-Muslim relations have become so hostile as to have caused wars in 1948, 1967, and 1973.

A Brief History of the Jewish People

The history of the Jews begins some four thousand years ago in ancient Meso-potamia, in the land of Ur, when a small band of sheepherders and merchants decided to move away in search of better pastures for their flocks. The history of the Jews, unlike the histories of other primitive people, has a written record, the Old Testament. No one can answer the question with certainty as to how much of the Old Testament is fact or myth. The early migrations of the Jewish people, the Hebrews, are recounted in the book of Genesis. Chapter 12 tells how Abraham, the son of Terah, who was a descendant of the first man, Adam, left Haran with his wife, Sarah, about 1750 B.C. (an uncertain date) to move northward from the fertile river valleys of the Tigris and Euphrates in to Syria, a distance of about seven hundred miles. This route was an old, well-traveled trade route by way of the Fertile Crescent, which, until modern times, was the principle route linking Europe with Asia Minor and the far Eastern countries of India and China. Genesis records that Abraham arrived in Canaan (Palestine) on the shores of the Mediterranean Sea near Schechem, or modern Nablus, a land that God bequeathed to the Hebrews. However, the Hebrews found Canaan quite inhospitable, so Abraham and his family departed to Egypt, a more wealthy and peaceful land.

In Canaan the people worshiped a number of fertility gods, the chief one being Baal, who was the creator of all living things. Baal was a storm god. Mot, an evil god of death, if he ever overpowered Baal, would bring famine and de-struction to the Canaanites. Baal's wife, Anath, was always in a condition of pregnancy, yet a virgin goddess. The Hebrew people had mixed feelings about Baal, but those who did accept Baal placed him as a second-rate god to Jehovah.

From Abraham and his family comes the Hebrew faith, Judaism. Abraham left an only son, Isaac, one whom God had commanded his father to sacrifice upon the altar, a stone in Jerusalem under the mosque, the Dome of the Rock. Although this cruel sacrifice was to test Abraham's faith and obedience to God, it also seemed to be a denial of the Hebrew abhorrence of paying homage to all kinds of idols and making sacrifices, which were characteristic of the pagan religions. Fortunately for Isaac, the sacrifice was countermanded by God at the last moment, and he was permitted to carry on the lineage of Abraham. Abraham's seed produced another son, Ishmael, perhaps an illegitimate child by his mistress Hagar, when it seemed certain that Sarah could no longer bear children. Later Sarah miraculously conceived and gave birth to Isaac. After the birth of Isaac, Sarah demanded that Abraham banish Hagar, and so she left to live in Mecca. A Muslim tradition says that Mohammed traced his religion back to the ancient Jewish prophets, and especially to Ishmael, the son of Hagar.

God gave to Abraham the Promised Land of Canaan over which land the Hebrews were ordained to be the rulers for all future time, a divine claim that some Jews in Israel use to reject all demands that the Palestinians should be given any part of ancient Israel and Judah. Abraham made a covenant with

God by which God promised to bless and protect the Hebrew people in return for their obedience to his law. God's blessing included the possession of Canaan, the birth of many children, and eventually the dominance of the seed of Abraham over most of the earth (Genesis 15: 18).

Later Abraham and his family left Egypt and returned to Canaan where Abraham purchased a burial site for himself and his family. At this site today in Hebron one can visit the Cave of Machpelah, now a Muslim mosque, but also where the tombs of Abraham and Sarah, Isaac and his wife, Rebecca, and grandson, Jacob, and his wife, Leah, are believed to be located. Outside the tomb area, in a garden, is the tomb of Joseph, the son of Jacob.

Abraham's lineage furnished the genealogical line of Hebrew patriarchs and leaders. The grandson, Jacob, was renamed Israel, meaning, one who wrestles with God. Jacob had twelve sons, who became the progenitors of the twelve tribes of Israel. In the Song of Deborah only ten tribes are mentioned. One of the sons, Yehudi, gives us the name "Jew."

The wanderings of the Hebrews took a portion of them to Egypt, the land of plenty. Other Hebrews remained in the land of Sechem. The later biblical story of Joseph (who is sold by his jealous brothers as slave to the Egyptian Pharaoh) may represent another voluntary migration to Egypt, or perhaps it reflects the capture of some Hebrew people by the Egyptian army when it invaded Palestine about 1500 B.C. There is no doubt that the Jews did live in Egypt for a period of time. Genesis 41:39 relates that the pharaoh told Joseph that "none is so discreet and wise as thou art." During the time of Joseph Egypt was ruled by Akhenaton, the pharaoh who tried to convert Egypt to a monotheistic religion.

Whatever the condition of the Hebrews was in Egypt, some biblical interpreters believe, based on the Book of Exodus, that around 1200 B.C. the Hebrews were suffering from being slaves, and that by the reign of Rameses II (1290–1223 B.C.) they were ready to revolt. Just as Abraham and Joseph had led their people along the God-ordained paths to freedom and prosperity, so another Hebrew hero appeared on the scene in Egypt. He was Moses. No other Hebrew prophet or leader did more to establish Judaism as a religion, one that has persisted to the present day and which has some fifteen million adherents. Moses is recognized by non-Jewish cultures as a world-renowned figure, as great man of prophecy, wisdom, and leadership.

The life of Moses is a familiar story known by most Jewish and many Christian children. His life story begins when his mother hides him as a baby, in the bullrushes along the Nile River, so that he would not be killed by an order of the Pharaoh that all Jewish male babies should be executed. Moses was saved when the pharaoh's daughter came to bathe in the river and found him. Moses was taken to the royal palace, where he was reared, grew to manhood, and eventually became a royal official.

Moses soon realized that the rule of the pharaoh had ceased to be beneficial to his people and that it was time for them to leave Egypt. Also Hebrew leaders were afraid that a long stay in Egypt might cause their people to desert Jehovah for the many gods of Egypt. Moses became dedicated to securing freedom for the Hebrews. The Bible relates that Moses fled to the desert after killing an Egyptian, and that while there he had a vision of a burning bush appearing before his eyes. From the bush, God ordered Moses to lead his people out of Egypt. The biblical story relates that Moses returned to Egypt from the desert of Midian and asked the pharaoh to free his people. But the pharaoh refused so God punished Egypt by sending plagues and locusts to bring famine and death to the Egyptians, a divine sign that God was now ready to free the Hebrews.

The flight of the Hebrews into the nearby desert of Sinai is told in the book of Exodus. By some miracle the fleeing Hebrews crossed the Red Sea safely when the waters parted for them, permitting them to cross, and then the suspended waves closed so as to engulf the pursuing Egyptian soldiers, drowning them. If there is any historical validity to the story of the Exodus, then it probably occurred about 1250 B.C. During their wanderings in the desert for forty years (forty being a magic number used in other religions also), Moses and his people arrived at the base of Mt. Sinai. Whether the biblical account of the life of Moses and the Exodus can stand the test of historical evidence is in doubt. William Stiebing[1] has concluded that the Exodus and the conquest of Canaan either did not occur in the late Bronze age, or that there is no historical evidence for these events. But another scholar, Charles R. Krahmalkov,[2] believes that Egyptian evidence does confirm the historical truth of the Exodus event.

The Exodus marks an important event in Jewish history, also for world history, since in the Jewish faith the seeds of personal freedom and the worth of a single human being, all so essential to the democractic way of life, were sown throughout the modern world.

Scientists have attempted to explain the miracle of the splitting of the Red Sea, and also to establish a more correct date for this event. Some scholars have suggested dates earlier than 1250 B.C., such as 1447 B.C., during the reign of Amennophis II. As for the parting of the waters, Hans Goodcjje of Johns Hopkins University suggested in 1981 that the correct date should be 1447 B.C., when a volcanic eruption occured on Thera, an island north of Crete. The eruption may have caused a tidal wave that could have caused the waters to separate. Other scholars have accepted this explanation, since the eruption of a volcano on Krakatoa in Indonesia in 1883 created giant tidal waves that reached areas hundreds of miles away. Another explanation of the Exodus miracle is that the "Red Sea" was a mistranslation of the words, "Sea of Reeds." Hence the Exodus route was across a marshy region north of the Red Sea, an area filled with reeds and easily crossed.

Once the Hebrews escaped into the desert, little is known as to how they survived. The location of Mt. Sinai is uncertain. At least five sites have been suggested, but among them Jebel Musa is the one most acceptable. The biblical record has Moses talking with God, in which conversation Moses is given the Ten Commandments, plus another covenant, the second one made between God and man. In this second covenant the Hebrews must accept Jehovah as the one and only true God, and all other Gods must be denied. God promised the Hebrews the land of Canaan for their homeland.

The idea of a covenant or contract between God and man marks an important step in the development of a humane religion. A contract implies some degree of equality between the parties to the contract, and in this case there seems to be a symbolic statement that not only is man made in the image of God, but that also man has some measure of divine personality if he is able to contract with the God of the universe. The covenant gave the Hebrews a special mission on Earth, namely to bring all nations to Jehovah's way of salvation. At first Jehovah was a storm god and a powerful war god. If need be God would permit the Israelites to use war as a means to defend their nation from its enemies. But the price the Hebrews had to pay for God's favors was that Israel was sworn to obedience to Jehovah and to him alone.

Moses gave Israel a moral code, a monotheistic faith, and a mission to fufill a God-given destiny in human history. The oriental religions view human history as a series of cycles without beginning or end, but for the Jews life on earth must move on a continuum to a better, higher plane of godly living, a view that the Christians would adopt. As for the Mosaic code, it was not completely the invention of Moses, for many of the moral precepts found in the Ten Commandments belong to the ancient Code of Hammurabi which was known as early as 1700 B.C. in Mesopotamia. The Ten Commandments are more than a set of moral obligations, for they also demand that man must give obedience to God and his law, and for the Jews the test of who is a Jew and who is not is the matter of obedience to the law.

Moses died before the Hebrews crossed the Jordan River into Canaan. Moses was succeeded by Joshua, a faithful friend of Moses. It was Joshua who led the Hebrews into the promised land of Canaan. They occupied the city of Jericho, which is reputed to be one of the oldest cities in the world and still in existence today. Scholars believe that Joshua and his army was only a small band of nomads and not the total body of Hebrew people. For two hundred years or more Hebrews would continue to migrate into the area of Palestine. The Israeli nation was destined to be formed by a process of conquest, peaceful immigration, and intermarriage with native Canaanites.

The final occupation of Palestine occurred between 1200 and 1000 B.C. Before 1000 B.C. the story of the Hebrews is one of constant tribal wars with the Canaanites, Bedouin tribes, and the Philistines who lived on the coast of the Mediterranean. As yet there was no kingdom of the Jews. The tribal chieftans of the Jews were called judges, and in the book of Judges is told the heroic deeds of such leaders as Ehud, Jepthal, Gideon, and Samuel. Not only did the Hebrew tribes fight the Canaanites, but they also waged war amongst themselves to determine what tribe would attain the dominant position. Finally Jewish leaders realized that the survival of their people depended upon securing unity under a single monarch. Judge Saul was chosen by his people to be a king who would create a strong government and army. Since some leaders objected to calling Saul a king, since only Jehovah could be called king, Saul was named *nagid,* or leader. However, before his death Saul was permitted to be called king, or at least so the lord told Samuel (I Samuel II:15).

Saul and his son, Jonathan, defeated the Philistines, but the victory was temporary, for the Philistines were victorious in a battle during which both Saul and Jonathan were killed.

After Saul's death in 1005 B.C., David was chosen to be king. He ruled 1005–961. For several years a son of David disputed the right of his father to be king but David proved his claim to the throne by defeating the enemies of the Hebrews as well as the contending tribes of Israel. He captured Jerusalem and made the city the capital of the kingdom. He created a theocratic state that united in one body religious institutions and the state; hence David was both king and high priest. His reign ended with Israel in a state of peace and prosperity.

Following David's death in 961 B.C., his son, Solomon, came to the throne. Solomon's mother, Bathsheba, was the woman after whom David had lusted and whose husband David plotted to have killed. Solomon was more a priest-king than a war-king, for he was to spend most of this time and money not in war but in turning Jerusalem into a beautiful city. He built the first grand temple of the Jews. He built fortress walls, palaces, and gardens. Like the Egyptian pharaohs, he conscripted slaves for construction. Solomon lived the life of an oriental potentate, with a harem of three hundred wives and six hundred concubines. Many marriages sealed treaty alliances with foreign states, such as his marriage to an Egyptian princess to guarantee an alliance with Egypt. Solomon courted the friendship of the queen of Sheba (Ethiopia).

When Solomon died, Israel commanded respect throughout the world of his day. Jerusalem and its holy temple, with its most sacred Ark of the Covenant, became the focal point of the Judaic faith for all times.

By the time of Solomon's death, 929, the unity of the Hebrew kingdom was in jeopardy. The northern Israelites resented the centrality of Judaism in Jerusalem, a southern city. Other Jewish sects objected to Solomon's definition of Judaism. The masses of the people resented the high taxes and forced labor Solomon had used to build Jerusalem. So when Solomon died the ten northern tribes were ready for revolt, which finally took place in 922. Now the nation of Israel was divided, the kingdom of Israel in the north, and the kingdom of Judah in the south, of which the son of Solomon, Rehoboam, was the king. Judah continued the lineage of King David. It was during this period of division, from about 800 to 600 B.C., that the prophet Elijah blamed Israel's troubles on the worship of pagan gods. The weakened Jewish kingdoms were easy prey for foreign powers eager to expand their territories. First the northern kingdom was conquered by the Assyrians under King Sennacherib in 700. In 587 the southern kingdom was taken by King Nebuchadnezzar of the Babylonian Empire. Many Jews were taken into Babylonian captivity, a period recounted in the book of Esther. A Jewish woman, the wife of King Ahasuerus of Persia, was persuaded to halt the execution of all of the Jews held in Babylon. This act of salvation is celebrated by the Jews through the observance of the holy day of Purim.

The Babylonian captivity of the Jews also prompted the writing of the book of Daniel. Daniel appears to be a sixth-century-B.C. attack against the cruel Babylonians. However, recent evidence proves that Daniel was written as a protest against the anti-Jewish ruler of Palestine, Antiochus IV, a Seleucid, Hellenistic ruler who was a descendant of one of the generals of Alexander the Great. Antiochus abolished worship in Judaism after he came to power in 175 B.C. Porphyry, A Roman critic of Christianity in the third century A.D., said that Daniel was written, not in the sixth century, but in the second century as an attack on Antiochus IV.³ Since the Jews were unable to overthrow oppressive rule, be it Babylonian or Seleucid, divine intervention became the last and only recourse for freedom for the Jews. Daniel brings down the wrath of God upon these evil rulers, as depicted in Daniel 3:17-20. Moreover, in a day when revolutionary utterance were treasonable offences, it was prudent for a critic to use an esoteric, symbolic style of expression.⁴

Many other Jewish prophets also warned the enemies of the Jews that their God would wreak vengence upon them. The threat of a pagan enemy coming to conquer Israel was also a mightyy weapon used by the Jewish hierarchy to command the loyality of the Jewish nation.

In 539 B.C. the Persians captured the Babylonian Empire. Cyrus, the Persian king, at first persecuted the Jews, but later permitted many of them to return to Jerusalem. During the period of the Babylonian captivity many of the Jewish worship practices came into use, such as the development of a synagogue to replace the central temple, then destroyed, as the place for worship. Other practices included the observance of the Sabbath on the seventh day, the writing of the sacred scripture—the Torah, and using teachers or rabbis to lead the people in worship services. The book of Ezekiel gives some information on these developments.

Even after the Jews returned to the Holy Land they remained Persian subjects until Persia was conquered by Alexander the Great in 330 B.C. After Alexander's death, his empire was divided into three parts. The Palestinian area was given to one of Alexander's generals, a Seleucid. In 198 the Greek ruler attempted to enforce upon the Jewish people a form of Greek religion and culture. The Jews resented the attempt and revolted against the king, Antiochus IV, under the leadership of the Jewish Maccabean family, or the Hasmonean Dynasty. From 164 to 63 B.C. the Jews had a brief period of national independence, a happy era celebrated in Judaism by the festival of Hannukah Lights, a holiday that usually falls about the same time as Christmas.

In 63 B.C. the Roman general Pompey captured Jerusalem and not until 1948 would the Jewish People once more have their own state. For the next two thousand years, the Jews would be scattered throughout Europe and many other parts of the world dreaming of the day when they would find a new homeland somewhere, preferably in Palestine.

After the Roman conquest the Jews became Roman subjects and some of them Roman citizens. The restless Jews continued their struggle for freedom, which caused the Romans to repress the Jews savagely in A.D. 70, burning the second temple, one built by the Maccabeans. A militant group of Jews, the Zealots, had engineered this revolt against the Emperor Vespasian, and its failure caused most Jewish leaders to lose faith in victory by military action. The Messiah becomes the prevailing hope for rescue. In the meantime, the Jews in the Roman Empire were accepted by the Romans as second-rate people, but were left quite free of persecution so long as they paid their taxes and did not attempt further revolts.

The only standing remnant of old Jerusalem today is a portion of the wall built by King Herod, which for modern Jews as become the "Wailing Wall," the sacred place for prayer.

The Jews did make one more final struggle for freedom when in A.D. 72 a small band of zealots, 961 in all, retreated to the desert near the Dead Sea, built a fortress at Masada, and awaited Roman assault. Finally the fortress fell to the Romans. All but two women and five children took their lives in a mass suicide. This was the end of Jewish armed struggle for freedom.

Before the state of Israel was created in 1948 an independent Jewish state was established in Khazan in A.D. 740. Persecuted Jews from Arabic and Byzantine lands fled to this area around the Crimea and the Caspian Sea, and set up the kingdom of Khazara. Here all religions were tolerated. Eventually Khazara would be incorporated into the Russian Empire.

The Sacred Books of Judaism

The end of the Jewish state did not destroy the faith. The faith lived on and grew as rabbis and theologians taught the Jewish religion and developed its theology. The Torah and the other sacred Books replaced the Temple as the center of the faith.

The Jewish people have in the Torah and other writings the history of their people and religion. It keeps them in touch with God. How much of the Old Testament record is fact and how much fiction is unknown, but more and more scholars and archaeologists who are doing extensive "digs" in Palestine tend to confirm that much of the Old Testament is fact and not mere myth.

The Jewish Bible, the Christian Old Testament, is divided into three subgroups: the Torah, the Prophets, and the Writings. Other sacred writings include the Talmud and the Mishnah. The Torah, or the Pentateuch, includes the first five books of the Christian Bible, beginning with Genesis. The earliest sources of these books date to about 1000 B.C., during the reigns of Kings David and Solomon. The original language of the Torah is Hebrew, but by the time of Jesus, a Greek edition was in general use. Some early manuscripts have been preserved that help scholars determine the original contents of these writings. One of the oldest texts is a fourth-century Greek collection of parts of the Old Testament, known as the Codex Sinaiticus, found in the monastery of St. Catherine at the foot of

Mt. Sinai. In the Vatican Library in Rome is another old edition, the Codex Vaticanus. This version is even older than the Codex Sinaiticus. In 1947, other old versions of the Bible were found in caves along the cliffs of the Dead Sea, the Dead Sea Scrolls. The scrolls do not contain all of the old Testament, but they do contain portions of all thirty-nine books of the Old Testament, except the book of Esther. A new translation of the Hebrew Old Testament was published by the Jewish Publishing Society under the editorship of Chaim Potok in 1982.

The Bible has been such an important aspect of Judaism that the Jews have been called the "people of the book." The Torah is the centerpiece of Jewish worship. According to orthodox beliefs, every word is sacred, the revealed word of God, and, therefore, no word can be changed. The Torah must be housed in a special cabinet in the synagogue, called the ark. At all costs the Torah must be protected from desecration. In ancient times it was believed that Moses was the author of the first five books of the Bible, the Torah or Pentateuch. The author of 2 Chronicles refers to a quote from Deuteronomy as being from "the book of Moses" (2 Chron. 25:4). However, modern scholarship refuses to accept the belief that the Torah is the work of Moses. As early as the seventeenth century, Baruch Spinoza observed that the books were full of repetitions and contradictions, and seemed to be written in several different styles. Many scholars took up this question, and in 1878 Julius Wellhausen published his *Prolegomena to the History of Israel,* in which he identifies four major authors, as well as several ancient passages, which have been incorporated into these books. Even in English translation the differences between the various authors is often obvious. The oldest major source is called J, because the author uses Yahweh (or Jehovah) for God from the beginning of his work. The creation story beginning at Genesis 2:4 is by J. In the Revised Standard Version, the word Yahweh is translated LORD (always written entirely in capitals). Another major source is E, so called because the author uses Elohim for God until after the name Yahweh is revealed to Moses from the burning bush. The third source is P, the priestly source. This source likes to include long genealogies like the one in Genesis 5, rituals and ceremonies, and has a distinctive style. His hymnlike story of creation is in Genesis 1. D, the Deuteronomist, wrote the book of Deuteronomy. The editing together of J, E, and P resulted on several occasions in having more than one account of the same thing, with inevitable contradictions. For instance, in J's flood myth, Noah takes onto the ark seven pairs of all clean animals and one pair of each unclean species (Gen. 7:2), but in P's version Noah takes on board two pairs of every kind, clean and unclean (Gen. 7:15). The final compilation of the "books of Moses" was accomplished by the P source (probably more than one person).

Once the Jewish kingdoms were destroyed, many Jews fled to far parts of the Roman Empire. The leaders of the Jews at that time were the judges, or priests, sometimes called the Kohanims. The two most important priestly groups were the Levites, a term often used to designate a priest, and the priests of Shiloh, of whom the best known judge or priest was Samuel.

Some Jewish historians refer to the Levites as one of the traditional Jewish tribes, but most prefer to regard the Levites as a special body of professional priests, and not as a social or ethnic group. If the Levites were a tribe, it would be a "thirteenth" tribe. The Shiloh priests stressed the need for a centralized religion in the hands of priests and kings. All religious sacrifices should be performed at some central altar and not be scattered throughout the empire.

The Torah

The contents of the Torah are beyond this study. A few observations are in order, however. Genesis relates the process of creation, human and nonhuman, by one God. This God is not a sun god or a nature god, but a human god who is deeply concerned about his progeny, the Jewish people, his Chosen People. God will help the Jews if they will remain obedient to his law and loyal to him. In Genesis 2, modern feminists are angered by what seems to be the inferior position of women as compared to men. John A. Phillips, in his *Eve, the History of an Idea,* analyzes how womankind became the inferior sex. Eve, like the Greek Pandora, was the source of mankind's evil, pain, and eternal damnation. Eve was weak when she yielded to the temptations offered by the serpent. So its was Eve who caused woman to be the evil sex temptress, and for her sin she must bear children in pain and be the servant to her husband. The Roman Catholic Church has redeemed Eve and womanhood from sin so long as they remain virgins before marriage and in marriage bear children and are obedient to their husbands.

Other chapters in Genesis relate the lineage of Abraham and his descendents, the story of Noah and the Flood, migrations to Egypt, the life of Moses, and how Joseph served both his master, the pharaoh, and the Jewish people who lived in Egypt.

Among the many generations listed in Genesis is Noah and his two sons, Sham and Ham. Noah was the first to make a covenant with God, and his sons became the fathers respectively of the Jewish people, (descended from Shem) and the Hamitic people (descended from Ham), i.e., the people of Egypt and Arabia. From the Noah story comes some basic Jewish symbols: the sacred relic of the ark, the dove as a messenger from God, and the promise found in the rainbow, which says that all will be well if the Jews keep their covenant with God. Exodus 19: 5–6 says, "If you will obey my voice and keep my covenant, then you shall be a peculiar treasure unto me above all people, for all the Earth is mine, and you shall be unto me a kingdom, and a holy nation."

All of the books in the Torah instruct the Jewish people on what they must do to earn God's blessings, the essence of which is to obey God's laws. Deuteronomy 28 makes clear the penalties for disobedience. Man will be cursed many times, even unto total destruction. The scourge of the Assyrians and the Babylonians will be interpreted by the prophets as just punishment from God for being disobedient.

The Prophets

The prophetic books form the second of the three divisions in the Old Testament. The earliest prophets, not counting Moses, were Elijah and Elisha, in the ninth century B.C. In the eighth century Amos and Hosea appeared, and in the seventh century there were Isaiah, Nehemiah, Jeremiah, and Ezekiel. The later prophets appeared on the scene after the destruction of Israel. After the seventh century the primary message of the prophets was no longer to refrain from worshiping pagan gods and idols, but to obey God and pray that God would send a messiah to save the Jewish people.

After the seventh century the prophets preached a new message, an urgent one, that if the Jewish people were to be saved, more than obedience to God would be required. In fact God could work miracles and send a deliverer, a messiah, to save the Jewish people from their enemies.

The word "prophet" comes from a Hebrew word *nab,* meaning "to be called." The later prophets did not rely upon performing miracles to instruct the people, as did Elijah, who brought fire down from heaven to destroy the allies of Baal, or Elisha, who raised the dead to life. The later prophets, as well as the earlier ones, were regarded as messengers from God, along with the seven archangels, Raphael, Uriel, Michael, Raquel, Sariel, Gabriel, and Jeremiel. Note the "el" endings, which signify that all come from God or Elohim. Other Jewish messengers were the angels, such as the one who told Sarah she was to bear a child, or the one who warned Lot that Sodom would be destroyed, or the one who told Abraham not to sacrifice his son, Isaac. Prophets warned individual persons as well as the entire nation to remain obedient to Jehovah only.

Prophetic messages ranged from the mystical visions of Ezekiel to the ethical admonitions of Micah or Hosea. The latest of the prophets were Isaiah and Jeremiah. One must read the books of prophecy to learn the messages of the several prophets. One constant message is the duty to obey God and his law. Ezra stressed the need for obedience to law. He told the Jews that more important than the restoration of the Temple or the reestablishment of the kingdom of the Jews was obedience to Moses' law.

In addition to the duty of obedience, the Prophets preached a vision of a new Jerusalem, when it would be restored to its former glory and power. Such visions of future hope are found in Ezekiel 37:7–10, Isaiah 6:3, 2 Isaiah 42:1–6, Zechariah 12–14, and many other places. The new Jerusalem was to be on earth, not in heaven. Ezekiel sees God waging war with Gog for the land of Magog (Satan), an idea borrowed from the Zoroastrians. Zechariah portrays an apocalyptic vision of death to Israel's enemies and the restoration of God's rule on earth centered in Jerusalem. He is the first to mention the resurrection of the body from the dead. It is not clear whether he means the fleshy body or the soul.

But it was Isaiah who did most to develop the idea of a "suffering servant" whom God would bring to earth to redeem man from his sins and to restore the kingdom of the Jews. This same idea of a suffering servant or a messiah is presented in the books of Daniel and Enoch. After the final days on earth, marked by the appearance of plagues, famines, and other catastrophes, the world will be destroyed. Then there will appear the messiah to restore the freedom of the Jews from the Romans and the Jewish nation will again have its kingdom to be ruled by one from the house of David. The Messiah was to be a military hero, not a Jewish saint who preached, "Turn the other cheek."

The Writings

The Writings might be better named the wisdom books. At least the wisdom concept prevails in most of these books, in which the authors were influenced by the Greek philosophy of wisdom or Logos. During the fourth and third centuries before Christ, after the Jewish kingdoms had been destroyed, Palestine became a part of the Alexandrian (Hellenistic) Empire. During this era the Greek language came into general use. Even Jewish intellectuals used the Greek language. With language came also Greek culture, the arts and sciences, the religious cults, and the philosophies of Plato and Aristotle. The Hellenistic contribution to the Jewish Bible is found in the introduction of the wisdom concept, a concept already familiar to Egyptian and Greek theologians. The writings of the prophets were concerned with the future destiny of Judaism, while the wisdom writers were more like senior sages who had important knowledge gained from years of experience to pass on to the younger generations. Wisdom or Logos represents the Greek concept of ultimate truth or ideal knowledge that existed before creation of the universe or of man. Jewish wisdom literature is found especially in the books of Job, Proverbs, Psalms, and Ecclesiastes. Some historians believe the book of Proverbs was borrowed from the Egyptian book, *The Wisdom of Amenope*. A more important collection of wisdom writings, not in the Old Testament but in the Apocrypha, is a book known as the Wisdom of Solomon.

The nine chapters of Proverbs are rich with wisdom pronouncements. Chapter 3:13 says, "Happy is the man that findeth wisdom, and the man that geteth understanding." Verse 19 reads, "The Lord by Wisdom hath formed the Earth, by understanding hath he established the Heavens." The same Platonic idea that wisdom existed before creation is found in chapter 8:23, which says, "I, Wisdom, was set up from everlasting, from the beginning, before even the Earth was." In brief, Proverbs conveys the message that virtuous men will prosper, that God looks with favor on good fortune achieved here on earth.

Ecclesiastes promises also a prosperous, happy life for man if he obeys God's commandments. Chapter 9:16 says, "Then said I, wisdom is better than strength; nevertheless the poor man's wisdom is despised, and his words are not heard." Yet the writer of Ecclesiastes offers a pessimistic picture of life, as it is related also in Job, that no matter how wise a man can be, or how obedient to God man is, much of human existence is beyond hman control. "To everything there is a season, and a time for every purpose under Heaven." So Job asked also the question, "Why must a good man suffer pain and defeat?" The answer is that it is not your time to prosper and to enjoy the blessings of life. It is your time to suffer pain, poverty, and death. All men are destined by fate to suffer evil or to enjoy goodness.

The Psalms are songs and prayers in praise of God's blessings that are intended to remind the people that no matter what happens they must have faith that God's goodness prevails over all things. Already by the time of the prophets and the wisdom writers the nature of Jehovah had become more benevolent and forgiving of human error.

Daniel strikes a new note in the course of Judaism when he announces in his book that a messiah will come from God to destroy the enemies of Israel and will bring freedom and peace to the nation of Israel in a new kingdom of the Jews. Daniel was written about 164 B.C., during the period of the Maccabean revolt against King Antiochus IV, who had tried to outlaw all Jewish worship. The book of Daniel is a prologue to the New Testament book of Revelation, which pictures a time when tyrants will be overcome, and a messiah will arrive to bring forth the dead in a bodily resurrection, after which the reign of the lord will prevail on earth, an era of peace, brotherhood, and world dominion for the Jewish nation.

Mishnah, Talmud, and Law Codes

As time passes all sacred scriptures need interpretation and emendation as new material is found or changing conditions require new interpretations. Jewish scholars first edited many legal interpretations of the Torah into a book called the Mishnah, meaning "to repeat and to study." This book was completed by the end of the second century A.D. However, as time passed, more interpretations of Scripture were required, and these were collected in the Talmud ("learning"), a process beginning in the fifth century A.D. and continuing to the present.

The Mishnah combines a textbook for students and a book on Jewish law. It is divided into six orders or chapters dealing with problems arising from the conduct of family life, sexual behavior, agriculture, the proper observance of festivals and sacrifices, civil law, regulation of the Temple, rites for purification, rule for sanitation, and the position of women.

The Talmud is a much larger collection of rules and interpretations. Two versions are used, a Jerusalem version and a Babylonian version. The Babylonian version is much larger than the Jerusalem one, containing over 2.5 million words. Neither version is read widely by the people as the text is too complex to be easily understood. There is no prohibition against lay use of the Talmud. It is read primarily by scholars and rabbis. Chaim Potok in *The Promise* describes how a rabbi studies the Talmud. The Talmud spells out the legal obligations required in the Torah. Many rules concern the observance of the Sabbath, such as to not get married, or ride a horse, or dance, or work. The Talmud includes the Mishnah plus the Gemara, which contains additional commentaries on the Mishnah.

During the Middle Ages so many interpretations and commentaries on the Torah were offered by so many rabbis that it became almost impossible to deduce from the many volumes what should be the true law. So there began a process of codification of this voluminous material into a more simple and organized form, namely, law codes. The first compiled code came during the fifteenth century by Rabbi Joseph Karo. But the most prominent codification was the work of Maimonides, a Spanish rabbi, A.D. 1135–1204 and the best of the Jewish scholars and philosophers. He was a rationalist philosopher in the mold of Aristotle. Like the Christian Aristotelian, St. Thomas Aquinas, he sought to reconcile reason and revelation. Maimonides in his *Guide to the Perplexed* sought to prove that God, his commandments, and his prophecies all could be explained by reason as well as by faith.

The Fundamental Tenets of Judaism

The Hebrew (meaning of "Hebrew" is a matter of much dispute among scholars) religion found its highest ideal and its most treasured value in one divine being, called Yahweh by the Jews and known to later Christians as Jehovah. Whereas the Greek philosopher Plato idealized man as he might be organized in a utopian state as descripted in his *Republic* and Neo-Platonists, like the Greek Jew, Philo, envision man to be the ideal, incarnate expression of the Logos, or the idea of good, for the Jews the ideal truth was one universal God, the creator of man and the universe. He promised the Jewish nation that they were the Chosen People, destined to be the lords of the earth, and, in due time, to bring onto earth a rule of order, law, and peace. This God, Yahweh, became the central object of worship. All other gods were to be denied any obedience.

The relationship between man and God was formulated in a contract or covenant agreement. The contract provides that mankind will enjoy freedom and salvation from his sins and for his nation's sins if obedience to God is given. The problem of evil in the world, that is, the original sin of Adam and Eve, will be redeemed by obedience to God's commandments. The welfare of the individual and the nation are bound together, the sin of one Jew will endanger the peace and salvation of all other Jews. Likewise the merits of a good Jew will enhance the virtue of the whole nation. In the covenant idea, a political scientist can find the roots of a democratic society, for if man can contract with God, then truly the individual person ranks high in God's esteem. Even kings are bound by the law of God, the same as the lowly peasant.

A second basic idea in Judaism is that sin and morality are both social and individual matters. Ezekiel (chapter 18) says that man has his own responsibility for his conduct in daily life, but he has also a responsibility for the guilt or innocence of the entire nation. According to Ezekial man did not inherit original sin from Adam and Eve, nor is God responsible for all of the evil in the world. Only man brings evil to the world, for God gave to man the freedom to choose between good and evil. Therefore, if man is to be redeemed from evil, then he must make the first move for salvation.

Then a third idea is the formula for redemption from sin. Since all men and women too are priests, then they must discover the way to salvation. Moses said, "You shall be unto me a kingdom of priests." The salvation way includes acts of atonement and suffering. Ezekiel believed that redemption could come by confessing one's sins, or by doing an act of penance. He believed also that man needs the support of his fellow men in prayer and in congregational worship. No priest is needed to intercede with God. Leviticus 24:22 reads, "You shall have one for the stranger and the native, for I am the Lord." All men are born free and equal.

Later prophets like Isaiah (chapter 13) will offer another solution to the problem of sin, in that God will send a messiah to bring goodness to mankind through a suffering servant who will bear the sins of mankind and elevate the poor and lowly to high positions.

A second theme stresses the belief that man is basically good, and all things on earth are to be enjoyed by man here and now, not later in heaven. The Hebrews saw hard work and education as God-given routes to a good life on earth. The accumulation of wealth was not evil so long as wealth was used wisely in the practice of moral living and charity. Sex and family life were among God's blessings so long as marriage and sexual activity were ordered in harmony with the commandments. Divorce was permissible, but sexual behavior outside of marriage, such as adultery, homosexuality, and premarital sex, was evil. The pleasures of life, dancing, drinking, sports, and festivals were all deemed good if not done in excess.

The goodness of life on earth was expressed also in the messianic hope for a new Jerusalem, which was to be established on earth and not in heaven. Life after death was small concern to most Jewish people. The most common belief was that the soul after death went to some shadowy place called Sheol, which was not a place for judgment or for punishment, but only a resting place for the departed souls (Isaiah 26:14).

Another aspect of Judaism that has attracted the attention of non-Jewish people is the emphasis on obedience to law. Judaism, like Islam, is a social religion in which all aspects of life are to be regulated by sacred law. The basic law is found in the Ten Commandments, especially in Deuteronomy, where many detailed instructions for moral behavior are given. As mentioned above, further rules are given in the Mishnah and the Talmud, even to the number of 613 rules.

Moreover, good Jewish followers are commanded to search for the truth and knowledge by study and the use of reason. Seeking the truth means that the Jewish people must have access to libraries, schools, colleges, and seminaries. For a Jewish family, no financial burden is too great if it allows the children a full and complete education. Every family is obligated to teach the children knowledge of God and truth. Truth means also the practice of honesty in all transactions (Psalm 31:19 and Proverbs 12:19). Good men do not lie, or violate their sworn oaths, or plagiarize the words of others. Micah 6:18 has a succinct statement of Judaic virtues: "And what doth the Lord require of thee, but to do justly, and to love mercy, and to walk humbly with thy God?"

To do justice is another commandment (Isaiah 58:18). Justice is the foundation of civil law, the government, and social ethics. Psalms 145:17 says, "Thy justice is everlasting justice." Justice means moderation as it is applied to the punishment of criminals, not the vengeful justice of Hammurabi's code.

The highest moral virtue is to express love and to act peacefully in all human relationships. Redemption of the soul means peace, "for he who loves peace cannot fear death." The Hebrew word for peace means that the peace of death brings the soul to a house of eternity, for eternity is viewed as a continuation of earthly life.

It is true that all human religions provide some disposition of the soul after death. Soul represents the inner vital aspect of life, separate from the physical body, something immortal that is destined to return to God after death. Soul also represents the sum total of all good merits earned by each person, if not by all of the previous generations of man. In the covenant with God, Judaism holds that the souls of past generations contain merits that are to be used for the benefit of future generations. The soul concept is not just the soul of a person but the collective souls of all Jewish people, past, present, and future. In a sense Jewish people venerate family ancestors since they continue to belong to the living present. For the Jews heaven and hell are only symbols, so no one knows what they are. If there is a hell, then punishment for the soul in hell is only temporary. Moreover if there is a heaven and hell, how can God rule both places, since there is only one God to rule over all. When Jesus as a Jew formulated the Lord's prayer, by "Thy kingdom come" he meant not only a heavenly paradise, but even more a place on earth where peace and morality reigns.

Customs, Rituals, and Holidays

Each religion has its own set of scriptures and tradition that describe man's relations to God and how man is to live on earth in harmony with the laws of God. Each religion prescribes the daily schedule of words and acts by which God is to be honored. Oriental religions place the altar before which people worship their deities in the home more often than in a temple, whereas the Jews require the practice of devotions in both the home and the synagogue (the Greek word for a meeting place). The synagogue is designated also as a house of prayer and a house of study. Worship is held on a special day, the Sabbath, a day beginning at sundown Friday evening and ending Saturday evening. The most traditional Jews on the Sabbath refuse to cook meals, to travel, or make any purchases or business transactions.

The synagogue houses the sacred ark, in which the Torah is kept. The sexes are usually separated in the synagogue. The rabbi or any person who leads the service does so from a raised platform or pulpit, as in Protestant churches. The typical Jewish service features scriptural readings, prayers, the chanting of hymns, often from the Psalms, by a cantor, and the giving of a sermon or lesson by the rabbi, and concludes with the "alenu" prayer, a prayer for doing one's duty to God. One basic prayer, Shema, is the first to be learned by children and the last to be said to the dying person (Deuteronomy 6:4-9). Tradition holds that at least ten men must be present before a public prayer can be offered. During the service men wear a prayer shawl *(Tallit)* and a head covering *(yarmulke)*, although these requirements do not apply to the reform synagogues.

For many Jewish Americans synagogue attendance occurs only on the occasion of high holy days. Hence prayers and scriptural reading are done in the home, an indication that home worship may be more important than congregational worship. In the home and in the synagogue are found sacred symbols such as the seven-armed menorah or candlestick, a symbol of God's light, and the six-pointed star of David. Synagogues, like Baptist churches, are governed in a democratic manner by congregational decision. The rabbi, the leader or teacher, is endowed with no special powers, such as Catholic priests enjoy.

From life to death special rituals are observed to commemorate the passages of life. The male infant is circumcised on the eighth day after birth, a painful introduction into the Jewish community. Circumcision was commanded by Abraham as a condition for membership in the Jewish nation. Tradition alleges that circumcision gives the person power to control his body. Bruno Bettelheim calls circumcism a symbolic wound, which many primitive tribes practice. In some cultures the female is circumcized also by removing the clitoris. The medical profession in the United States finds no health reasons for the practice. Its only purpose is to fulfill a religious obligation.[5]

At the age of thirteen the Jewish boy is initiated into adulthood by the celebration of bar mitzvah. For girls the service is called bat mitzvah. The initiation requires that the boy prove his adulthood by reading from the Torah in the Hebrew language.

The education of the children is a prime obligation for the parents. Children must learn their religious heritage as well as the contents of the Torah. Marriage is the fulfillment of the commandment "to be fruitful and multiply." Marriage is an act entered into freely by both male and female, a contractual arrangement in which the woman will receive certain property rights in case of divorce. Divorce is recognized, but in a patriarchal society, the man enjoys more rights in marriage and divorce than the woman. In earlier days marriages were usually arranged by the parents of both parties to the marriage, and often negotiated with the assistance of a profesional matchmaker. Today, in the Western world, matchmakers are frowned upon, as well as marriages outside the Jewish faith. In other words, couples are free to make their marriage decisions without parental approval, but with the hope that parental blessings will occur. Weddings are performed by a rabbi, a ring is given to the bride, a cup of wine is shared by both persons, after which the groom smashes the cup or glass to symbolize the destruction of the Temple. The wedding takes place under a canopy (*chuppah*), a symbol of their home to be and under God's blessing and protection.

Based on teaching Jewish college students for ten years, during which time I attended Jewish weddings and funerals, counseled parents and students, and had in my classes many students who were training to be rabbis in a nearby seminary, I can only conclude that the Jewish family is the center, the lifeblood of Judaism, not the synagogue or the wearing the star of David. In pre-Christian days the wife and mother had a most inferior position to the father and husband. Wives and children were legally no more than chattel, pieces of property that the father could dispose of as he chose. Children could be sold into slavery, or even killed, and the wife could be divorced at the will of the husband. However, in reality the Jewish wife and mother more than the father is the one who rules the family, directs the education of the children, and controls the family purse. The Old Testament records the deeds of several strong women such as Esther and Ruth. Christianity inherits from Judaism a measure of respect for women, even a position of near equality to the male, a position better than most other religions have accorded to women.

It is in the home that the Sabbath is best observed. On Friday evenings special blessings are observed, candles are lit, special food is served, and the children are blessed. It is in the home where the dietary laws are enforced, and the use of kosher foods (that is foods chosen and prepared according to biblical dictates) are served. Meat animals, other than the pig, whose flesh is forbidden, must be slaughtered and bled by a special person, a *shochet,* one who is supervised by a rabbi. Special tools are used to prepare the meat. The blood must be drained completely, for to consume blood is to consume the soul. The sale of kosher foods must have the approval of a rabbi, no matter what the rules provided by the local governments may be. Pork and shellfish are taboo, as is the eating of milk and meat at the same time (Exodus 23:19). Most nongame fowl is kosher food, as well as all animals that chew the cud and have cloven hooves and fish with fins and scales.

Jewish funeral rites add to the significance of the Jewish faith. The rites of mourning are prescribed by law. After the body is prepared for burial, normally within a day after death, it is to buried, not cremated. After the funeral a period of mourning in the home continues for seven days, and special prayers, the Kaddish, are said. Each year the death is remembered by a special rite and the graves are visited during the high holy days.

Judaism requires the purification of the soul before death. "Before God you should be purified." Sacrifical living is the process for receiving purification. Old Testament Jews practiced animal sacrifices to atone for their sins, a practice that continued until the destruction of the Temple by the Romans in A.D. 70. After this event animal sacrifices were replaced by offering prayers, confessions, and doing acts of penance. Special purification rites were required, such as the observance of the holy days, especially the days at the end of the Jewish year, the days between Passover and the Feast of the Tabernacle, days deemed to be fasting days. Acts of purification include the observance of the dietary rules, and purification baths for women. Women must observe the purification baths, the mikvas, after menstruation and childbirth.

Significant holy days for worship and atonement include:

1. The Passover Feast of the Unleavened Bread, a spring festival found among many primitive people in the northern hemisphere (the Christian Easter festival is another one), which celebrates the springtime renewal of life. For the Jews it celebrates the night of the tenth and last plague which God sent against the Egyptians: "It is the LORD's passover, for I will pass through the land of Egypt that night, and I will smite all the first-born in the land, both man and beast, . . . but I will pass over you. . . . This day shall be for you a memorial day, and you shall keep it as a feast to the Lord" (Exodus 12:11-12, 14). Thus the Passover became the great national feast of Israel, celebrating its establishment as the people of Yahweh. Passover is celebrated by a seder meal on the first night. The seder dinner requires two to three hours, during which the family eats samples of the scarce desert food that Moses and the wandering Jews were supposed to have eaten, such as the unleavened bread and bitter herbs. Kosher meat dishes are cooked without butter and cream. Wine is served also. Between the dinner courses passages from the Torah are read.

2. Shavuoth, or Pentecost, a harvest festival held seven weeks after Passover, marks the beginning of summer. It is dedicated to the sacred Law.

3. Ten Days of Penitence or the Days of Awe, a festival held on the first ten days of Tishri, which include the first two days of the New Year, or Rosh ha-Shanah, and the last day, or the Day of Atonement, Yom Kippur. Rosh ha-Shanah is known also as the Feast of Trumpet, occasion when the *shofar*, a ram's horn, is blown to mark the day of creation and the Day of Judgment. The Day of Judgment is Judaism's highest holy day, the one day for the repentance of sins. Yom Kippur is a day of fasting and a day when any vow made under compulsion can be disowned. It is also a day when all people can ask for the forgiveness of sins and make repentance for sins committed. The book of Jonah is read during the service on this holy day.

4. Hannukah, or the Feast of Lights, is a celebration of the Maccabean victory over the Seleucid rulers who sought to destroy Judaism. This festival is celebrated for eight days, with one candle being lighted for each night. The festival is a happy occasion in which gifts are exchanged. Since it occurs at approximately the same time of the year as Christmas, in the United States both events are often celebrated together as a symbol that Christians and Jews share a common religious heritage.

5. Sukkoth, or the Feast of the Booths, is a fall festival of thanksgiving for the harvests. Meals are eaten outdoors in booth or *sukkoths*.

6. Purim is the celebration of Queen Esther's role as the savior of the Jewish people, who were being held captive by the Persian king and who were sentenced

to death on the order of the king's minister, Haman. Esther persuaded the king to let her people go free, which for many Jews did result in freedom to return to Jerusalem. The event is told in the book of Esther. This happy outcome for the Jews is celebrated with great merriment and the exchange of gifts.

Sects of Judaism

Although the people of the book exemplify a high degree of tenacity, survival, and success, created by a faith that inspires obedience and loyalty, still Judaism has experienced internal dissenting sects or divisions. However, the differences are never so great as to cause a major rift in the unity of Judaism. At the time of Jesus, Judaism was divided among four sects or parties: the Sadducees, the Pharisees, the Zealots, and the Essenes. The Sadducees represented the most conservative element of Palestinian Jews, the rich, the priests, the political bureaucracy, or those Jews who wished to work cooperatively with the Roman rulers and avoid a civil war. They sought also to live in peace with the Greeks and their heritage. The Sadducees lived by the Law and only the Law. They ruled out any possibility of a messiah to come to deliver them from their captors. They rejected any belief in the power of angels, demons, miracles, or in the possiblity of a bodily resurrection and the end of the world. Only the Torah was accepted as the sacred scripture. Among the Sadducees two groups differed over the interpretation of the Torah. The Shammai believed that the righteous would enjoy eternal life and wicked would suffer eternal damnation. The Hillel was more liberal in believing that God was merciful and that would permit the souls of the wicked to return to eternal life after having been purged by fire in hell.

The Pharisees, the "separated ones," were a more liberal group that accepted the Torah and also the oral traditions found in the Mishnah. They represented the rabbis and the scribes. They believed in the messianic redemption of Israel, in the Last Judgment, angels, and the bodily resurrection. They also supported congregational worship in the synagogue. After the destruction of the Temple in A.D. 70 the Pharisees became the principal leaders of Judaism.

The Zealots were the extreme militants, the heirs of the Maccabean rebels, who sought to destroy the Roman rule by force of arms. The name comes from a character in the book of Numbers, by the name of Phinias, who had a reputation for killing evil persons and was said to be "zealous for his God."

The Essenes were a small minority group who deemed life on earth to be evil and painful, and not worth the fight to survive. So they retreated to the desert around the Dead Sea to live a communal, almost monastic, life of isolation and asceticism. Although men and women lived together as one family, sexual relations were taboo. The Essenes lived with the hope that a messiah would come to save them from the Romans. Some members even went so far as to draw up battle plans against the Romans in a document called, "The War of the Children of Light against the Children of Darkness." Probably the best known Essene was John the Baptist, although there is some question as to whether he was a bona fide member or just a sympathizer with their cause. John the Baptist baptized Jesus in the Jordan River and declared him to be the Son of Man. Essenes are also known as the people who kept ancient copies of the Old Testament, now known as the Dead Sea Scrolls, written on metal scrolls and parchment hidden in desert caves. They were discovered first in 1947–48.

The Samaritan sect dated back to the time of the Assyrian conquest of the northern kingdom of Israel; a small band of Jewish peasants remained in Samaria and became a part of the Assyrian Empire. This group, the Samaritans, survive in Israel today in and around the city of Nablus. Being separated from the mainstream of Judaism, the Samaritans over time have developed some non-orthodox beliefs that have caused them to be rejected by the majority of Jews. It is interesting that although the later Christian and Muslim rulers of Palestine tried to destroy this small community, it did survive.

Samaritans reject Jerusalem as the center for worship. Instead the sacred home for the Samaritans, the place to which prayers are to be directed, is Mount Gerizim. Samaritans claim to be the true descendents of Abraham through a lineage descending from Joseph and the priests who belonged to the house of Levi. In brief, the Samaritans are a most conservative wing of Judaism that accepts only the Torah as the guide to faith, that is, the faith as it was known at the time of King David. The Samaritans see themselves as the only true children of Israel, as Jews who have remained faithful to the Law of Moses, the Torah, without change or error.

Another sect that split off from Judaism, in the eighth century in Persia, was the Karaites. From Persia this group moved to Spain and Lithuania. In Lithuania the majority were liquidated by the Nazis during World War II. Karaites are a most fundamentalist sect, like the Samaritans, in that they accept only the Torah, denying the validity of oral traditions. They observe rigidly all of the dietary restrictions, the marriage obligations, and the strict observance of the Sabbath. All of the holy days are accepted excepting the happy festival of Hannukah.

Another Jewish sect found in Ethiopia is the Falasha Jews or Beta Israel Jews. They adhere to the conservative Jewish traditions, which recognize the Torah as the only sacred scripture. In recent years they have begun to accept also the oral traditions. They use the Ethiopian language. In 1984 some hundred thousand Falasha Jews moved to Israel.

Modern Judaism, certainly as Judaism is practiced in Western Europe and the United States, has at least three major divisions—Orthodox, Conservative, and Reform. If one is a member of the Orthodox tradition, the Law or Torah is cherished, all of the 613 commandments in the Halakah are observed, and all Scripture is held to be inerrent and unchanging. A Jew's mission on earth is to do God's will, no matter how difficult this may be to do in a modern world more secular than religious. A good Jew is expected to pray three times a day, eat only kosher food, observe the Sabbath, refrain from sexual intercourse for two weeks of each month, avoid interracial or interreligious marriages, and devote much time to the study of Scripture. In a sense the Orthodox Jew prefers to remain isolated from all human contacts lest he or she be contaminated by the materialistic outside world. Women are expected to respect their fathers and husbands. They are excluded from the rabbinate, from studying the Torah and from reading from the Torah in the synagogue. A woman does not count in the required quorum of ten persons required to hold a prayer meeting.

In the United States, Orthodox Jews constitute about 40 percent of all Jews, and, like fundamentalist Protestants, they expect the arrival of the Messiah sometime in the future. Herman Wouk in his *This Is My God* has written about the life of the Orthodox Jews.

A less conservative body of Jews is the Conservative group, about 30 percent of the Jewish population in the United States. The conservative wing was formed in the United States by a distinguished scholar, Solomon Schechter. In general the Conservatives hold true to the Torah and the traditional rites and ceremonies, but they tend to be more tolerant of other groups, Jewish or non-Jewish. They no longer place emphasis on the coming of the Messiah. Women are given an equal place in the synagogue. The vernacular language may also be used in the services and prayers along with Hebrew.

The most liberal wing of Judaism can be found in Western Europe and the United States, a group that in many ways resembles the Protestant church in its form of worship. About 30 percent of American Jews belong to the liberal or Reform branch of Judaism. The Reform movement began in Germany about 1810. It came in response to a desire on the part of some Jews to accommodate themselves to the modern, scientific, democratic societies in which they lived. In the United States Rabbi Stephen Wise is credited with being the first leader of the Reform branch of Judaism. In 1885 Rabbi Wise said, "We recognize in the modern era of universal culture of heart and intellect, the approaching of the realization of Israel's great messianic hope for the establishment of the kingdom of Truth, Justice, and Peace among man."[6] Reform Judaism represents a scientific, humanistic, evolutionary approach to religion. It rejects strict interpretations of Scripture or strict observance of the dietary laws, dress codes, or rituals. Although Reform Jews believe the soul is immortal, they do not believe in a bodily resurrection or eternal punishment in hell. Like liberal Protestants, Reform Jews devote much time and money to the improvement of social and political conditions. They would like to rid religion of all supernatural phenomena. They favor the equality of the sexes, even to holding official positions in the synagogue. In the United States the most significant reform seminary is Hebrew Union College in Cincinnati, Ohio, founded by Rabbi Wise in 1875. In Israel it is the Reform group, the Ashkenazi group, that is most willing to make concessions to the demands of the Palestinians.

In the United States there is a more extreme reform group, the Reconstructionist, led by Mordecai K. Kaplan. This group hopes that a more liberal form of Judaism will enable them to be more acceptable to the Gentile world. However, these liberal trends within Judaism meet resistance from the Orthodox Jews. Rabbi

Pinchas Stolper of the Union of Orthodox Jewish Congregations warns the Jewish people that too much liberalism will be the death of Judaism. Already too many Jews are leaving their faith and becoming lost to the Jewish nation. Stolper claims that only some 20 percent of the Jews ever attend regular worship services in the synagogue.[7]

A group of highly charged mystics or zealots is the Hasidim sect. In many ways Hasidism represents the most extreme proponents of Jewish orthodoxy. The name of the group refers to a man of piety. A person is to judge not by his knowledge but by how he lives his daily life. The ideal Hasidic is a righteous person as mentioned in Genesis 6:9, one who is a teacher, a counselor, or anyone who is willing to help his fellow man. He is not a rabbi or priest who holds some office to which he is appointed or ordained.[8]

The Hasidim today number only about 250,000 in the world, of which about 200,000 live in the United States, most of them in the New York City area. There are some forty communities or courts in the United States; the largest is the Lubavitch court in Brooklyn.

The Hasidic movement has its origins in thirteenth-century Poland, when Prince Balesow invited persecuted Jews to come to Poland in 1264. By 1500 some three hundred thousand Jews had sought refuge in Poland. The Jews were granted much autonomy and freedom to have control of their local communities, schools, and synagogues. A few Jews even became civil governors over their local provinces. This happy state of affairs was short-lived, for in 1648 Poland was conquered by the Russians. Then Jews were massacred by the thousands. One estimate is that five hundred thousand were killed in Poland. Only a tenth of the Jews survived. Many of those who did fled to England, the Netherlands, Turkey, Italy, and Egypt.

During the liberal period of the French Revolution the Jews had the freedom to regroup and enlarge the scope of their activities. The founder of the modern Hasidic movement is said to be Rabbi Israel ben Eliezer, or Besht, as he is commonly known. Besht is an acronym for Bael Shem Tov, or "Master of the Good Name." Besht was a poor mystical prophet who claimed to have inherited secret knowledge or "gnosis" from a legendary writer and prophet, Shimon ben Yabai, who wrote a book, *Zohar,* in which the secrets of a second-century-B.C. Jewish sect, the Kabbalists, were recorded. This book was said to have been used by the Maccabeans in their war against the Seleucid rulers.

Hasidic Jews are mystical visionaries, filled with the joy of God's spirit. For them magic and the supernatural are as real as the rising sun, and chapter 2 of 2 Kings, which tells of Elijah ascending to heaven in a chariot, is no myth. It is the truth.

Hasidism takes its beliefs from the Kabbalist tradition of mysticism. The Kabbalists united Hebrew beliefs with Greek Neo-Platonism, as taught by Philo (20–50 B.C.). They held that Plato's Logos could unite man and God by following a rigid discipline of prayer and meditation. Hasidim are to perform four duties: read the Torah, visit the rabbi regularly to offer confessions and receive instruction, attend worship services, and contribute faithfully to charity. Living as an ascetic and doing good deeds mark a Hasidic Jew, but even more distinctive is their enjoyment in expressing the God feeling that is in their person. Hasidim love music, song, and dance. Like all other sects of Judaism, the Hasidim celebrate the Simchat Torah, "Rejoicing of the Torah," a holy day when the last portion of the Torah is read, after which the men, (women are excluded) have a festival of song, dance, and merrymaking.

Prayers and meditation are also important, for they are believed to possess magical properties. By reciting one prayer, a *shima* of 258 words, miracles can be made to happen. Rabbis are all supposed to be miracle workers. The cantor, the leader of songs, is even more important to Hasidic worship than to other Jewish groups.

The woman's place is in the home, rearing children and serving her husband, yet her positon is not so inferior as it might seem, for the central place of worship is in the home; hence the mother places a major role in the education of the children. Hasidic men are the ruling element in their society. They are recognized by their devotion to the Law, by their semi-ascetic lifestyle, their practice of sex restricted to procreation, and by their dress—the men wear a yarmulke, sometimes with a fur hat, a girdle, no collar or tie, and a trimmed beard with sidelocks.

Hasidic Jews accept a pantheistic concept of nature in that God is to be found in all of nature. A child may be scolded for pulling off a tree leaf carelessly because the child has harmed God in the leaf.

In brief, Hasidic Jews find God in their souls, a power not subject to the laws of time and space. Salvation is to be theirs if the rules are observed: to lead a good life, pray, visit the rabbi, call upon the angels when needed, and enjoy God through dance, music, and song. In Israel the Hasidim are the most conservative of the Orthodox Jews. They dream of the day when the Temple can be restored in Jerusalem, when Israel will become the Kingdom of the Jews, when King David's theocracy will be recreated, when only the people who were born in the faith can be citizens of Israel, and when the state of Israel can encompass the God-given biblical lands of Judah and Israel.

The Jews of Israel

Israel today has two groups, the Sephardim, a Spanish name for a Jew, and the Ashkenazis. The Sephardic Jews come largely from North African countries, and since the Six-Day War in 1967 many Tunisiam and Moroccan Jews have emigrated to Israel. This group is now the dominant religious and perhaps political group, in Israel. Members of this group are the most likely to oppose land concessions to the Palestinians. They also seek to pass legislation that would require all Jews to observe the traditional rules on marriage, dietary practices, worship rituals, and the definition of who is a Jew. Sephardim generally seek religious control of the schools. They want to eliminate from the curriculum the corroding influence of modern science and humanism. The Sephardim dream of the day when Israel might have a theocratic state in the manner of the time of King Solomon, or like the modern states under Islamic control. They would prefer that only natural-born Jews become citizens of Israel, and they would forbid all marriages to non-Jews. Probably 60 percent of the Jews in Israel are Sephardic. Probably only one-fourth of all world Jewry are Sephardic, however.

The Ashkenazi Jews represent the liberal, Reform Jews in Israel. They came from Europe, especially from Germany, and they are more educated and wealthy on the whole. This group, like the Reform Jews in the United States, accepts changes in theology, and is more receptive to intermarriage and concessions to the Palestinians.

Zionism

The movement to secure a homeland in Palestine for the Jews and to support the new Israel in its struggles to survive amidst the Arab Islamic world is known as Zionism. The Zionist movement was founded by Theodore Herzl in 1887. He had a vision that a Jewish homeland could be established in Palestine. With the support of other Jewish leaders, especially a British scientist, Chaim Weizmann, the Zionists were able during World War I to convince the British government, which had control over Palestine, to recognize the right of the Jews to have a homeland, a place of refuge, in Palestine. In exchange for Jewish support of England's war efforts, in 1917 the British government issued the Balfour Declaration, in which Jewish emigration to Palestine was approved and the intention declared that later a homeland would be established. As a result of World War II and the Nazi Holocaust, the Allied powers and the United States recognized the founding of the state of Israel in 1948.

The Zionist movement came out of a series of anti-Semitc movements in Russia and eastern Europe in the late nineteenth and early twentieth centuries. Anti-Semitic oppression and discrimination had been a constant aspect of life in Europe since the beginning of the Christian era. In 1555 Pope Paul IV had ordered that all Jews must live in segregated ghettoes. Ivan the Terrible, a Russian Czar (1530–84), ordered that all Jews who refused to convert to Christianity be drowned. In the late nineteenth century the Russian government promoted wars against Jewish communities, called pogroms. The first one occurred in Odessa in 1871. In 1882 Russia forbade Jews from living in rural villages, hence they were force to live in urban ghettoes. The Nazi Holocaust, however, was the most obscene, cruel, and destructive of all anti-Semitic moves against the Jewish people in all of world history. In the previous history of the persecution of Jews, the Catholic nations of Spain and eastern Europe took the record for the most cruel and persistent campaigns against the Jews. The papacy has been severely criticized for the unwillingness of the Roman Catholic Church to speak out against the murderous policies of Nazi Germany, but history does not exonerate the

Protestants either. Martin Luther damned the Jews as "Christ killers," claiming that they drank the blood of Christians, and that they were a scourge on humanity and should be eradicated.

The Cycle of Toleration and Persecution

By the 1700s a few signs of tolerations for the Jews began to appear in Western Europe. Movements for religious toleration did not come from the Christian Church so much as from a group of enlightened scholars and writers who saw that man might be better redeemed from sin by the use of science and rational thought than by the worship of Christ. This is not to say that individual Christians were not in the vanguard of the fight for religious freedom and tolerance of other religions. However, it was humanists such as Voltaire, Diderot, Locke, Rousseau, the Jewish philosopher Spinoza, the German poet Gotthold Lessing, and a host of other enlightened thinkers who laid the groundwork for the acceptance of the ideal of freedom and tolerance.

Religious freedom and toleration found a fertile, acceptable environment in the commercial cities of Western Europe. Early signs of tolerance of the Jews could be found in Venice and Florence in Italy by 1700. Also in the Netherlands and in England were signs of toleration of the Jews. In England the Jews were given the right to become citizens by Cromwell (1648–89). In 1683 England passed the Act of Toleration, which gave all religions the right to worship, although members of the Church of England retained a preferred legal status. In the American colonies, Jews were permitted to worship in Rhode Island in 1644, and in the New York colony Jews were granted the same privilege in 1655. By 1763 all colonies had granted the Jews freedom to worship their faith.

The Netherlands granted toleration to the Jews during the reign of William of Orange, who later became the English King William III (1672–1702). Religious toleration for the Jews often came as the result of a financial deal between wealthy Jews and financially strapped monarchs who needed Jewish money to fight a war. So it was with William of Orange, and so it was when some German states and Austria needed money to fight the Protestants during the Thirty Years' War (1618–48).

The French Revolution and the Napoleonic era in France gave to the Jews the same benefits of citizenship and religious freedom as were given to all French people. Wherever Napoleon's armies conquered and set up revolutionary governments, the Jews were granted their freedom. Thus by 1870 most Westen states had recognized the Jews as being worthy of free and equal rights as citizens of the state. Yet official freedom did not bring to an end the long, persistent Christian hatred of the Jews. France had a notable example of anti-Semitism in the Dreyfus Affair in 1895. During the 1920s Jews in the United States were subjected to a barrage of anti-Semitic statements and acts, some of which were sponsored by automaker Henry Ford in his *Dearborn Independent* paper. He published and circulated for public consumption the infamous *Protocols of the Elders of Zion,* originally forged by the czarist Russian secret police. The *Protocol* charged the Jewish bankers were conspiring to destroy the Christian world by foisting upon them the evils of communism, Darwinism, depression, and war. Unfortunately, a number of American hate groups, the Ku Klux Klan, the Aryan Nation group, the John Birch Society, Father Coughlin, and too many fundamentalist Protestant Churches have kept alive these old myths and fears of the Jewish people.

Today liberal Catholics and Protestants seek to reach accommodation with the several Jewish groups in the United States. Ecumenical meetings are held among Catholic priests, Protestant ministers, and rabbis. Intermarriages are becoming more common and accepted by Christians and Jews. Universities and colleges have removed discriminatory admission practices against Jewish students. Some Jews might question this statement. In its foreign policy America has given to Israel the promise of almost unconditional support in any war that might involve Israel in the future. Since 1948 the United States has given Israel over $30 billion. In the past fundamentalistic Protestants have been reluctant to accept Jews on an equal basis, but in recent years these groups have had a change of heart. Since the 1970s many of these churches have been giving support to the Israeli state, perhaps less for any love for Jews than because these apocalyptic Protestants see Jerusalem as the place where Christ is destined to return to earth.[9]

13

The Advent of Christianity

Of all world religions Christianity has the largest membership, about one billion adherents, of whom almost 60 percent are Roman Catholics, 35 percent are Protestants, and the remaining 15 percent are Greek Orthodox, Egyptian Coptic, and other Christian sects. In the eyes of Christians, most of whom live in the Western World, Christianity is the one and only true religion. Christians today identify themselves with those societies that represent anti-Communist values and prodemocratic, procapitalistic systems, which they believe will, in the long run, produce the most beneficent and enlightened communities for human habitation. However, Christianity is no guarantee that tyranny and dictatorships will not prevail. Witness the Christian states of Latin America and Nazi Germany, where autocratic, oppressive regimes have been in control.

Scholars may debate the issue of whether Christianity produced the Western form of civilization, democratic and capitalistic, or whether these lifestyles developed independently of the Christian church. Max Weber in his study of the rise of Protestantism and capitalism in the sixteenth century concluded that Protestantism was a prime mover in the growth of free capitalism.

Since 1600 Christian nations have played the dominant role in world politics, economic developments, and unfortunately also in the conduct of the major part of world imperialism and wars. But Christians believe they have also been a primary factor in the development of science, medicine, social-welfare reform, the abolition of slavery, and the promotion of international peace and goodwill among nations.

What factors have enabled Christian nations to have been so successful in the past two hundred years, if success is measured in terms of wealth and political power? A devout Christian might reply that it is God's blessing upon his people for their faithful service and devotion to his Christ. Or a Christian might say that it was in God's plan for the universe that Christian nations would become the models for heaven on earth, societies marked by love for justice and charity to others. The Christian religion projects a future for mankind that must always move upward in a steady progression from a state of less than perfect toward one of ideal perfection, the city of God.

The Spread of Christianity—Conversion and Syncretism

In the history of Christianity many devoted Christians believed that their faith was the best of all, the faith that God had chosen for all peoples of the world. They believed that God had commanded that this faith be brought to all nations of the world. Much credit must be given to the many devoted and zealous missionaries throughout the ages who have given their lives for the sake of the Christian gospel. Many were truly soldiers of the cross who sacrificed their lives to become the martyrs of the faith, those heroes in heaven who are the saints. Christian missionaries begin with the Apostle Paul and his associates. Other noted Christian missionaries include Boniface, who brought the faith to the Germans and the Franks; Augustine (not to be confused with Augustine of Hippo), who brought the faith to the Celts of Britain; Patrick, who introduced Christianity in Ireland; the Dominicans and Franciscans of the fourteenth century; the Jesuits of the sixteenth century; and the many Protestant missionaries now active in all parts of the world.

One most important factor in the growth of the Christian church is that in the fourth century A.D. one Christian sect among several became the accepted state church of the Roman Empire. After the Emperor Constantine had given this Christian church his blessing and it became endowed with the power of the imperial state, rival Christian sects or non-Christian religions were suppressed as being heretical or pagan. But in turn the early Christian fathers pursued a policy of compromise and conciliation with the non-Christian people of the Roman Empire. It is true that the Christianized Roman government used its power to suppress rival sects, no matter what brand of faith, but it is also true that the Christian leaders practiced a syncretic, pragmatic policy of adopting many pagan worship practices and beliefs as compatible with Christian worship and worthy of being accepted as good Christian belief and practice. For example, in Latin America in working among the native peoples the Roman Catholic Church accepted into the body of its saints many of the former native gods and goddesses, some identified with Christ, the Virgin Mary, or even Jehovah. This policy of syncretism is expressed in a letter Pope Gregory I wrote to St. Augustine, the missionary in Britain, around A.D. 596, cautioning him to be respectful of the beliefs of the native Celts:

> Destroy the idols, but the temples themselves are to be sanctified with holy water, altars set up, and relics enclosed in them. In this way, we hope the people, seeing that their temples are not destroyed, may abandon idolatry and resort to these places as before, and may come to know and adore the true God. They are no longer to sacrifice beasts to the devil, but they may kill them for feasting

to the praise of God. If the people are allowed some worldly pleasures in this way they will more readily come to desire the joys of the spirit. For it is certainly impossible to eradicate all errors from obstinate minds at one stroke.

So early in the history of the Christian Church signs of syncretism were visible as the church borrowed elements of belief and worship, not only from Judaism, but also from the other religious traditions found in Greek Hellenism and prevailing cults in the Roman Empire.

Several of the Christian holy days had their origins in non-Christian faiths. Two universal festive days in the northern hemisphere are the spring equinox (corresponding to the Easter–Passover season) and the winter solstice (the Christmas season). Easter reminds us of the celebration of the return of spring with its resurrection of life among both animals and plants. Eggs and rabbits have long been traditions signifying fertility and birth. Easter derives its name from a Persian Mithraic goddess, Eastre, a fertility goddess comparable to the Greek goddess Demeter and a host of other mother goddesses found among the many cosmic religions.

Most pagan religions celebrate the beginning of the return of the sun to its full glory after the winter solstice about December 21. The warming sun means the return of fertility and growth to the earth, upon which the people depend for their food and survival. Pagan people celebrated by burning fires and lighting candles, all symbols of the returning source of light, the sun. The Jewish Hanukkah celebration is a recognition of the returning source of light, as it is called also the Feast of Lights. Christians have linked the birth of Jesus with the winter solstice, though probably Jesus was in fact born in a spring month. No one knows for certain when Jesus was born, either the day, the month, or the year. At first the birthday of Jesus was celebrated on January 6, but in the third century it was changed to December 25.

Most of the ritual and ceremonies associated with Christmas have come from pagan sources. The burning of yule logs and the decoration of Christmas trees come from pagan Germanic beliefs; the eating of the plum pudding celebrates the bounty of a Celtic goddess, Daga; the eating of roast pig comes from a Norse goddess of fertility, Freya; to be kissed under the mistletoe is a Celtic tradition that promises good luck to those who kiss under the mistletoe; and the drinking of the wassail comes from an Anglo-Saxon toast, the words of which were, "Was nai," "Be hale and hearty." Other Christmas traditions go back to early Christian beliefs and customs: Santa Claus comes from the patron saint of the Germans, St. Nicholas; and the use of holly as a decoration comes from an early Christian practice of using the red berries as symbols of Christ's blood.

In Sweden the winter solstice is ushered in by remembrance of Santa Lucia, a Sicilian girl condemned to burn at the stake in A.D. 304. Her funeral pyre did not burn, so she had to be stabbed to death. Many years later she supposedly returned to Sweden bearing gifts of food and wearing a crown of lights. She became a symbol of fertility who would bring prosperity and plenty to the Swedish people. Her day is celebrated on December 13 in a family celebration in which the eldest daughter is dressed in white and, wearing a crown, brings food to her parents' bedroom. The celebration of the winter solstice is almost universal among all people who live in the northern hemisphere.

Christians borrowed other practices from non-Christian religions. When Pope John Paul II visited Kenya in 1985 he saw firsthand how the church had absorbed many of the native African animistic beliefs. For example, the Kenyan church was using animal sacrifices, which the church could approve since it was a common practice among the Jews as related in the Old Testament. The church has tried vigorously to forbid plural marriages and the continuing worship of the native gods.

Did certain Christian beliefs come from earlier religions? The ancient Egyptians had beliefs in a virgin mother of God and in the resurrection of the body of gods. Egyptians conceived of an afterlife in which the gods judged the good and the wicked, condemning the souls of the evil ones to eternal torment; from the Sumerian-Babylonian cultures come the Old Testament accounts of creation, the Flood, Noah and the Ark, and even many of Moses' Ten Commandments. The Babylonian mother goddess, Ishtar, a spring fertility goddess, experienced a resurrection from death each spring.

The Persian Zoroastrians conceived of a world in which battles rages between the forces of good and evil, or light and darkness, a state of conflict found in the Judeo-Christian faith as Jehovah wages war against the evil Satan. The Zoroastrians also believed that the souls of men would be judged in the afterlife to determine which would live forever in the land of light or in the land of darkness.

The Christian theologian Origen accepted the divinity of the planets, for he said that the sun, the moon, and the stars worshiped Christ when he ascended to heaven. The Christian Eucharist or Lord's Supper may have found its inspiration, in part, from a Mithraic sacrament existing at the time fo Jesus in which the people drank the blood of a slain bull, a sacred animal in which the power of God resided. The blood-consuming act symbolized that the power and love of God had entered the human soul. Moreover, the sacrament was a bond of union among the believers. Mithraism also foresaw the day when the world would be consumed by fire for its sins, that the human body would be resurrected, after which the soul would enjoy eternal life if it were judged to be good. During Mithraic worship services, candles were lighted, incense burned, and censers swung. The people atoned for their sins by confessions to their priests and in turn the priests gave absolution for the sins by laying on of hands.

The Greeks had the idea of the resurrection of bodies and souls, at least for the gods. Adonis and Aprhodite return to earth each spring after the winter's death, and Dionysius died and lived again. Both the Egyptians and the Greeks limited resurrections to the divine persons, mortal humans could not be resurrected.

The Greeks of the era of enlightenment and the philosophers Aristotle and Plato did not believe that the human body could be resurrected, only the human soul. Body and soul were separate entities. The things of the spirit were of a higher order than things of the flesh. Reality was in the unseen aspects of life, the Logos or the eternal Ideas, from which both the Gods and Man were derived. The gods were preordained spirits sent to earth to deliver mankind from evil. The Christians, as in the gospel of John, will accept the concept of the Logos or the Word as becoming incarnate in the form of the human person, Jesus, also the son of God. This concept of the nature of Jesus is distinctly of Greek origin and not from the Jewish heritage. The Jews saw the expected Messiah as a human person and not as a spiritual being. The use of the word "Christ" for Jesus is from the Greek meaning "anointed one." It is a translation of the Hebrew *messiah,* meaning the same thing.

The later Hellenistic religions or cults sought to find a god who could be a compassionate, understanding companion for humans to worship, a god to whom people could tell their woes and troubles, and from whom they could receive a comforting word of hope and help, a god, like Jesus, who could be called our friend and teacher. The Hellenes found in their mystery and gnostic cults more satisfaction from a religion filled with mystery and emotion than one based on too much rational speculation. So the Apostle Paul found more wisdom in feeling and faith, that is, to know God from the heart and not the mind, than in theological analysis and reason. Moreover, the captive subjects of Rome who lived in Palestine, Asia Minor, Egypt, and Greece, were seeking some escape from Roman rule. Since armed rebellion seemed to be a futile means of escape, the people were ready for a miracle-working savior who could redeem them from Roman bonds.

However, even though the Roman Empire before the fourth century A.D. discouraged the proliferation of many cults and religions antagonistic to the worship of the Roman gods, the empire, perhaps unwittingly, offered several opportunities for the spread of the Christian faith. First the empire maintained a high degree of peace and order with some measure of toleration for the non-Roman cults so long as they were not a source of rebellion. A stable political climate was conducive to trade and travel, and along with merchants and travelers also went the Christian missionaries. Secondly, communication among the diverse people of the Roman Empire was enhanced by the use of common languages, Latin in the West and Greek in the East. Even in the days of Jesus, although Aramaic was the people's language, the learned people communicated in either Greek or Latin. Finally, the spread of Christianity, or even its survival, must be credited in part to the fact that despite the persecutions of Roman authorities during the first to third centuries, Roman rule never sought to destroy totally and for all time any of the nonorthodox religions—Judaism, Christianity, Mithraism, Gnosticism, or any of the others. Roman religion had degenerated into emperor worship and so long as the people gave homage to the emperor, it mattered little to the authorities what other gods were worshiped.

At the time of Jesus people were searching for new gods and religions. Judaism was in disarray, having divided into several hostile sects, each striving for power, and most of them were seeking some escape from Roman rule so that the old kingdom of the Jews could be restored. The Greek people longed for the days of national freedom before the Roman conquests of the first century B.C. Syrians, Persians, and Egyptians were all eager to restore their ancient kingdoms and empires. Many of the non-Latin people in the Empire craved to speak their own native languages as well as to have their own free nationhood. Perhaps many people in the first three hundred years of Christendom believed that worship of Christ would bring them freedom both on earth and in heaven.

Christian leaders discovered early that converts could be won by war and conquest as well as by the sermons of the missionaries. If a pagan chief or king could be conquered and converted, then automatically all of his subjects would become Christians. Before the pagan Roman emperor Constantine won a victory over his rival for the imperial throne in A.D. 312 he is reported to have seen a cross in the sky, a sign that Christ would be on his side in the war, and that victory belonged to Christ. So Constantine declared that Christ was his lord. It should be noted that perhaps his mother, Helena, a Christian, may have had more to do with her son's conversion than any miracle in a battle.

The conversion of the northern Germanic tribes to Christianity is also a story of how a king was converted, thereby converting his people. King Clovis of the Franks converted his people to Christianity in A.D. 496. When the emperor Theodosius declared Christianity to be the state religion in A.D. 380 he set out to destroy the Aryan heresy among the German tribes. All heresies were outlawed, and a precedent was set that the power of the state should be used to destroy all heretical Christian sects as well as non-Christian faiths. In the sixth and seventh centuries the Celts and Anglo-Saxons in the British Isles were converted by force. At the Synod of Whitby, 664, the Anglo-Saxon kings adopted the Roman Catholic form of Christianity, and so the people of Britain became Roman Catholics. When converted, the kings were accepted by their people as gods, and if they wished to have salvation for their souls they had to obey the king and worship him. From these pagan heritages Christian kings became anointed as being divine, bearing titles such as "The Lord's Anointed" or "Christus Domini." In this manner, Charlemagne, king of the Franks, was crowned by Pope Leo III in A.D. 800 as emperor of the Holy Roman Empire, ordained by God to be the ruler of the Franks and Germans, and whose subjects must become Christians.

A classic example of mass conversion on the conversion of a king is the case related in chapter 1 about Russia—Czar Vladamir in 987 decided to search for a new religion for his country by sending emissaries to various religious groups to find the best religion for Russia. His choice, finally, was the Greek Orthodox Church, a decision which the czar sealed by marrying a Byzantine princess.

By 1100 most of Europe had become Christian. In the West the Roman Catholic Church was predominant, while in the East it was the Greek Orthodox Church. Islam had a small foothold in Europe, mostly in Spain and the Balkan countries. From a new religion preached by one Jewish teacher, Jesus of Nazareth, Christianity had become a major world religion. Jesus in his lifetime had only a handful of followers, yet by the year of the millennium, his faith had become the Church of the Western world. If ever a miracle had occurred in the history of Christianity it was first its survival in the first three hundred years and then the remarkable rise to power that followed.

The Life of Jesus: Fact and Legend

Who was the man Jesus? Was he god or man, or both? His contemporaries called him the Christ or the Messiah. One time Jesus asked his disciples, "Who do they say I am?" (Matthew 16:13) Some replied that he was John the Baptist or Elijah, then Peter answered, "Thou art the Christ." Mark refers to Jesus as the Son of Man. However, nowhere in the Scriptures does Jesus refer to himself as the son of God or even the Messiah. He does call himself the Son of Man some seventy times. It is probable that the Son of Man reference means that Jesus was only a human being.

For the first three hundred years after Jesus, or until the Council of Nicea in 325 established an official definition of the nature of Jesus, the Christ, Christian theologians debated the question of who Jesus was. Christian churches were even organized on the basis of competing definitions. One group said that Jesus was only a man, a teacher. Another group said that he was pure spirit, never lived in the flesh, and that he existed before he was born. A third group said that he was both human and divine. This was the position adopted by the Council of Nicea, and the one that all Catholic and most Protestant churches continue to believe. But the public image of Jesus remains murky even today. A recent Gallup poll reported that 42 percent of the respondents said that Jesus was God in the form of man. And 62 percent believed that he will return to earth someday. Two-thirds believed that one must accept Jesus as their lord if they are to have eternal life.

Except for the biographical sketches in the first three gospels, precious little is known about the life of Jesus. A Jewish historian of the second century, Josephus, does mention the existence of Jesus and that he was crucified. The Roman historians Tacitus, Suetonius, and Pliny the Younger do make mention of Jesus as having preached in Palestine and being crucified. However, all of the passages that mention Jesus are controversial, and some are considered by scholars to be later interpolations by Christians. Taken altogether, the evidence suggests that there once lived a man in Palestine by the name of Jesus. But it is also recorded that some of the early Christians denied that Jesus ever lived. He was only pure spirit.

The traditional account of the birth of Jesus relates that he was born of Jewish parents whose lineage can be traced through his father, Joseph, to the family of Jesse, who were the descendants of King David. His mother was Miriam or Mary, who, centuries later, would be proclaimed by the Catholic Church to be the virgin mother of God and that the conception of Jesus came from the Holy Spirit as a miracle from God. The name Jesus is the Greek version of the Hebrew name Joshua, which means "Yahweh helps." Jesus was born in Bethlehem, a few miles south of Jerusalem. His parents had gone there from their home in Nazareth to be counted in a census ordered by King Herod. While in Bethlehem the baby Jesus was born in a cave stable, a place now enclosed by the Church of the Nativity. The place of birth is marked by a silver star and jeweled ornaments and lanterns, a far cry from the primitive birthplace stable.

As with the birth of most divine beings in many religions, so the birth of Jesus has been adorned with a number of mythical events. In the nativity story there is the mystery of the star of Bethlehem. Was it a miracle or the natural event of two planets, Jupiter and Saturn, coming together at a moment in time? How did the traveling magi, who brought gifts to the infant Jesus, receive information that the Messiah was about to be born in Bethlehem? Angels must have conveyed the good news of the impending birth. Then there is the story of the flight of Jesus and his parents to Egypt. Among the Gospels only Matthew relates this story, that King Herod ordered the massacre of all male children under two years of age, and that an angel told Joseph to flee to Egypt. That King Herod was a brutal tyrant no one denies. Josephus, the historian, relates that each day of his reign some of his enemies were put to death. He caused his own son, Antipater, to be murdered as well as two of his sisters' husbands, his mother-in-law, and his wife, Mariamne. But did the birth of Jesus, an obscure Jewish boy, cause Herod to execute masses of children out of fear that the proclaimed king of the Jews, the Messiah, might usurp his power and threaten the supremacy of the Roman Empire? Whether the flight to Egypt is true or false, it does connect the life of Jesus to the patriarch Moses, who led his people from Egyptian oppression to freedom in the Sinai Desert. Thus Jesus inherited the noble line of David and the sacred traditions of Moses and his covenant with God.[1]

The father of Jesus, Joseph, was said to be a carpenter. But was Joseph the real father of Jesus? The Gospels report both the miracle conception of Jesus and his natural conception by some human male. If the father was not Joseph then it must have been some other Palestinian male. At the time some critics said Jesus was the bastard son of a Roman soldier. Stephen Mitchell in his book, *The Gospel According to Jesus,* accepts the view that Jesus was an illegitimate child and that he was scorned by his neighbors as a bastard.

Whatever may be the truth about the birth of Jesus, the Gospels do report that Joseph and Mary had other children, four brothers, Judah, Simon, Joses, and James, and at least two sisters. Jesus' brother James would become the leader of the Jerusalem Christians after Jesus' death.

Prior to the nineteenth century, little historical research was done to discover the real Jesus. For someone before that time to have questioned the orthodox view that Jesus was both human and divine would have been to risk excommunication or even death. By the time of the nineteenth century historians were beginning to have the freedom to find the truth about Jesus and his origins. Thomas Jefferson had prepared a version of the New Testament in which he sought to eliminate all mystical aspects from the message Jesus preached. But more scientific historians also began to research the life of Jesus. Among the first to do so were Albert Schweitzer, in his *The Quest for the Historical Jesus,* and Ernst Renan, in his *Life of Jesus.*

Historical documents and archaeological findings provide some information on the life of Jesus and the early Christians. Today a large number of historians have written their accounts on who Jesus was. A. N. Wilson, an English historical biographer, has written one of the most interesting accounts, *Jesus, a Life,* a 1992 book in which he incorporates the most recent historical evidence and interpretations. Jesus is pictured as a genuine human being, a Jew who in many aspects does not represent the mythical Jesus portrayed to many young Christians in their religion classes. Wilson believes that Jesus was a Jewish *hasid,* a characterization first made by Geza Vernes in his book *Jesus the Jew.* A hasid was a common Jewish teacher of the first century who went about "healing the sick, casting out devils, controlling the weather, and quarreling with the religious leaders in Jerusalem."[2]

James Charlesworth, an eminent scholar of the Dead Sea Scrolls, has edited and written certain chapters in a book entitled *Jesus and the Dead Sea Scrolls.* From this source, contemporary with the life of Jesus, Charlesworth depicts Jesus as a down-to-earth human being who found his friends among the lower classes of Galilee, the fishermen, the peasants, the outcasts such as whores and lepers, and even tax collectors. Jesus was no ascetic who deemed sensual pleasures of life evil, as did the Essenes, the authors of the Dead Sea Scrolls. Jesus did not brand sexual behavior as evil. He accepted into his circle of friends several women, even though he did not choose a woman to be one of his disciples. Jesus was not a member of the Essene community, nor were his teachings adopted from the Essene teachings, even though in many aspects there were common threads of love and compassion expressed by both Jesus and the Essenes. Jesus preferred to love and work in the everyday world, not like the Essenes, who shunned the evil world of conflict and sin.

John Meier, a Catholic biblical historian and author of a life of Jesus entitled *The Marginal Jew,* concludes as do many biblical historians that the Gospels contain more myth and legend than historical fact. Most Christians' image of Jesus is based more on myth than fact. Meier presents Jesus as a typical Jewish layman of his time, neither a priest nor a rabbi.

In his recent book, *The Historical Jesus, the Life of a Mediterranean Peasant,* John Crossan views Jesus as belonging to a Gallilean peasant family who tended to be dissident, rebellious, and critical of both the prevailing political and religious institutions of the first century. However, these peasant people lived within the Hellenistic cultural environment of various urban areas. It was this rural background that causes Jesus to want freedom for his people, but not a freedom that had to be won by violence or rebellion. The peasant culture also longed for a time when all, both men and women, might enjoy a state of social equality while living, like the Essenes, in a communal, egalitarian society that would be brought to earth by divine intervention.

A most disturbing conclusion that most if not all contemporary historians have of the New Testament and the life of Jesus is that the gospel record of the birth of Jesus is a pure myth invented by the early authors of the Gospels to prove that Jesus was the divine messiah who had been prophesized by Isaiah. So that the prophecy could be fulfilled, Jesus has to be born in Bethlehem, the city of David, and into the family of David.

Contemporary historians who proclaim that the traditional version of the birth of Jesus is for the most part pure myth are too numerous to mention.[3] However, one should not conclude that since certain parts of Scripture are more myth than fact that the mythical accounts are of no value. When the record of human achievement is weighed in the balance of fact and myth, it may well be found that myth rather than truth has been the major force in human society for motivating, inspiring, and unifying all human social groups, be it family, church, tribe, or nation.

That Jesus was born a Jew there seems to be no doubt. No one knows his exact birth date, but historians guess that it was between 10 B.C. and A.D. 4. As to the time of the year, no one knows. Certainly it was not on December 25, a birthdate assigned to Jesus many years later and a day the Romans celebrated as the Saturnalia, the beginning of the winter solstice. Jesus was born in Nazareth of a poor peasant family.

It is assumed that Jesus was taught the Hebrew scriptures, the Hebrew language, although the common dialect of his community was Aramic. He probably observed the Jewish rituals and holy days, obeyed the Jewish law, and his friends were most likely Jewish. Jesus was a most intelligent boy, but what formal education he had is unknown. There is evidence that he went to Jerusalem for a brief period to study with a famous rabbi, Hillel the Elder. Rabbi Hillel was known to be a liberal Jew who taught that it was more important to love your neighbors and to love your enemies than to follow a strict observance of Jewish law. When Jesus was twelve, the Gospels say, he confounded the rabbis in the Jerusalem Temple by his intelligent and complex questions. The gospel record really begins with the life of Jesus when he was about thirty years of age. By then his father, Joseph, was dead. Jesus' ministry was said to have begun on the occasion when he was baptized in the Jordan River by John the Baptist A.D. 28–29.

Following his baptism Jesus left home and began to preach to the people in his home area near the Sea of Galilee. Probably Jesus never went more than a hundred miles distance from Nazareth preaching his message of love. The one underlying theme spoken by Jesus was that he foresaw that sometime the kingdom of God would prevail on earth. Jesus never promised that the kingdom would arrive today or at any specific time. He said that no one knows the time, but it will come. The advent of the kingdom might come through the intervention of God's agent, the Messiah, in fulfillment of Jewish prophecy, in an apocalyptic, miraculous destruction of the evil world, or what is termed the Parousia. Or the kingdom of God might come to earth by way of baptism, upon which act mankind would experience a new birth, a revolutionary change in the behavior of men and women. For, Jesus said many times, the kingdom of God is within you. Human sin, jealousy, greed, violence and selfishness would be replaced by thoughts and acts of forgiveness, compassion, and love. However, for the first century A.D. many Christians believed that the end of time, the kingdom of God, had arrived already, or if not already then it would come soon.

Before any further exposition of the Jesus message it should be noted that Jesus was no revolutionary figure. He had no plans, or even any desire, to overthrow the established political order, be it the local governments of Jewish-Roman governors or the mighty Roman Empire. When he told his disciples to render unto Caesar those things that belong to Caesar he was telling them to obey the existing authorities. Nor did Jesus wish to establish a new religious group to replace his father's Judaism. Jesus was born a Jew and at the time of his death he remained a Jew, even though many Jews had rejected him and denounced him as a false messiah. He preached his message to his Jewish brethren. Jesus said, "Don't think my purpose is to destroy the Law; but to fulfill it." If Jesus had any plans in reference to his own faith it was merely to reform and revitalize Judaism. Jesus wanted to free Judaism from its legalistic chains, wrought by the hundreds of commandments and rules that the Jewish people were expected to obey. Judaism should be reformed, liberalized, so as to make it more in harmony with the needs of the day. Religion, like any human institution, must remain a viable one by changing as society changes. Otherwise it fails to meet the needs of its followers. Jesus was witness to a critical period in the lives of the Jewish nation, which was struggling for release from the yoke of Rome. There is speculation that Jesus was a member of the Hakamin sect of pious Jews, a group related to the Pharisees. This sect had two basic beliefs. First, Judaism was in need of a spiritual revival. Second, the Jews should be liberated from excess obedience to the Law. "The essence of the Law was its spirit, not its literal enforcement" said the Rabbi Hillel. The Hakamin sect opposed the most orthodox Sadducees, who placed the center of Judaism as residing in the Temple, which to some Jews had become a disgraceful place of cheap and evil business transactions. The charge was made that the Temple had replaced the faithful as the proper center for worship. The Hakamins believed that Judaism should become a universal religion, appealing to all people, and that it should not be confined to the Temple in Jerusalem. Whether the Hakamins would embrace the Gentiles is unknown.

Jesus had a simple message of love, forgiveness and peace for a world filled with anger, distrust, and hostility. Jesus would have his followers obey the Judaic Law, all of the moral codes, but he said there is a higher law, a new commandment, "To love your neighbor as yourself." The most worthy human mission on earth is to love all of mankind, to have compassion for the sick, the poor, the oppressed, and to render acts of love and mercy to all in need regardless of their station in life. Jesus' message of love is most beautifully expressed in the Sermon on the Mount, when he offered guides for Christian behavior (Matthew 5–7). In the Lord's Prayer can be found the same message of love and peace (Matthew 6:9–13). However, Jesus was not the first to utter these words of compassion and love for humankind. Similar messages of love were found among the Zoroastrian scriptures, which were written six centuries before Jesus. The Essene "Teacher of Righteousness" found in the Dead Sea Scrolls taught the same message of love. "Blessed is he who clothes the naked with his own robe and gives his own bread to the hungry. Blessed is he who renders a just judgment, not for remuneration, but for the sake of justice, and does not wait around for something in return. Blessed is he on whose lips are both truth and righteousness." Buddha also taught a love message, and in the statements of the Jewish prophets Hosea, Micah, and Isaiah one finds early statements of the love commandment.

Hans Küng has summarized Jesus' message of love as follows:

> Jesus' life and work make it clear that this God is a philo-anthropic (loving humanity) and a sympathetic (co-suffering) God, down here with us. The God who manifests himself in Jesus is not the all too masculine often arbitrary God we can still find in the Old Testament and the Koran as well. Rather, this is a God who not only demands love, but gives it, even to failures; and who thus may be called "Father" (and surely "Mother") also. This is why Christians share with the New Testament . . . the conviction that God has love, still more that God is love."[4]

Not only did Jesus bring the message that God is love, universal love for all people, but that this God of love requires that all people in turn must love one another. Jesus brought a message of hope for the poor and oppressed people of his time, and in our time as well. He promised that no matter how harsh the conditions on earth may be, in heaven human beings can find relief from pain and suffering. The concept of a messiah or deliverer who will come to save mankind had been spoken many times by the Hebrew prophets Isaiah, Enoch, and Daniel. In the book of Daniel, written about 165 B.C. as a diatribe against Babylon, there is the prophecy that God will send a messiah to save Israel from its enemies. However, before the messiah arrives the world will be destroyed by a series of catastrophic, apocalyptic events, after which a restored world of resurrected souls will rule the earth in peace.

Jesus accepted the idea of a messiah who would bring the kingdom of God to earth. In this belief, Jesus must have been influenced by John the Baptist, who also preached that a messiah would come to deliver Israel from the Roman rule. When Jesus was asked by Peter if he was the Messiah, Jesus did not reply, nor did he deny it. Certainly Jesus expected the Messiah to come someday, but whether Jesus was this instrument of God to bring a reign of peace and love to earth remains in doubt.

While Christians awaited the day of ascension to heaven, there also was need to live in this world. To offer some practical guidelines for daily living Jesus outlined an everyday program of Christian living. He said to repent of your sins, be baptized, seek salvation for your soul and do those things that are required of you. He said to his disciples to sell their worldly goods, leave their families, and follow him (Mark 3:33–35). But for the masses of common people this was not a realistic commandment. So as you do your daily tasks, Jesus said, care for your family, obey the commandments, love your neighbors as yourself, and be a good Jewish person, a credit to your God, Jehovah.

Jesus blessed the institution of marriage and denounced divorce (Matthew 19:4–6) by saying, "What God has joined together, let no man put asunder." As a good Jew he found that sex was good, blessed by God, so long as all sexual activity was confined to the marital relationship. He would have condemned adultery, premarital relations, homosexuality, prostitution, abortions, infanticide, and probably contraception. However Jesus was no ascetic celibate, certainly no role model for future monks and nuns.

Although Jesus did not marry, many of his disciples were married, for example, Peter. Some of his best friends were women, Mary and Martha, even a fallen woman such as Mary Magdalene. On one occasion Jesus blessed a barren woman (Luke 20:34–36), and on another he suggested it might be better to not marry (Matthew 19:12), but as a rule, Jesus, like other Jews, believed that large families were desirable, that the father should be the dominant force in the family, but the wife and mother should play a prominent role in the education of the children and making decisions concerning the home and family. Jesus loved children, for he said, "Let them come unto me." His compassion for children set a precedent that children should not be sold into slavery, or regarded as property, or subjected to inhumane abuse and deprivation. The innocence of childhood becomes a symbol for the meek and humble Christian.

Jesus did not condemn slavery outright, for slavery in his day was a universal and accepted practice. But his central thesis of love could never condone the practice of slavery as good and moral. In the years before the nineteenth century and the invention of steam power and the coming of the Industrial Revolution, not even God could have abolished slavery, for it was the lifeblood of every nation's economy.

During his ministry, about three years, Jesus preached to thousands of people, but few chose to sell their goods and to follow him. Probably fewer than three hundred persons became his followers in his lifetime. He did enlist the support of twelve men, his apostles, Peter, Andrew, Matthew, James of Zebedee and his brother John, Philip, Bartholomew, Thomas, Thaddaeus, Simon the Zealot, James of Alphaeus, and Judas Iscariot.

His followers, mostly poor, working class people, knew him to be a good rabbi, a friend of the poor and outcasts, one who had some superhuman power, but they never thought he was the son of God.

In A.D. 30 or 33 Jesus went to Jerusalem to celebrate the Passover holy day. He was welcomed into the city by his friends and followers, but soon when Jesus called for the destruction of the Temple, the heart of Judaism, for harboring sinful men and evil transactions of business deals, his friends turned against him. The Pharisees became alarmed and accused Jesus of wanting to destroy Judaism. They went before the Roman authorities and denounced Jesus as a dangerous rebel, a threat to the security of the Roman state. They said Jesus should be condemned for treason and executed.

Did Jesus know that his life might be in danger when he went to Jerusalem? The hindsight of the writers of the Gospels would say that he did know, that the prophecy of Isaiah had been told to him, that he was destined to die for the salvation of his people, that he was the "suffering servant" and that to die for his beliefs was his divine duty. Anyway, the story is that Jesus was arrested by the Roman guards when his presence in the Garden of Gethsemane, where he and his disciples had retired to escape the wrath of the Pharisees, was made known to the police by Judas. The soldiers came and arrested him and took him into the city to be tried. Different versions of the trial exist. One version says that Jesus was tried by the Sanhedrin, a body composed of seventy-one scholars, high priests, and Orthodox Pharisees, presided over by the judge, Caiphas, who charged Jesus with violation of the laws, performing miracles, and criticizing the priests. When asked if he was Christ, Jesus admitted that he was.

No Orthodox Jew could ever admit or accept that Jesus was the Messiah, the Christ. Although Judas offered to repent of his betrayal and return the bribe money to its donors, the Jewish leaders refused to accept the return of the money. Jesus was turned over to the Roman governor, Pilate, for judgment and execution. The Sanhedrin had no power to execute criminals. Before Pilate Jesus was charged with being a "King of the Jews." No Roman could tolerate a rival for the control of Palestine or one who, like the earlier Maccabeans, might organize a revolt against Rome. However, Pilate was reluctant to make any decision so he turned Jesus over to King Herod, a lackey ruler of Palestine under Roman control. Herod refused also to render a decision and Jesus was returned to Pilate for a final judgment. The Sanhedrin pressured King Herod to make the decision instead of Pilate and so Herod did make the final decision.

The gospel of Luke says the Sanhedrin trial took place in the morning, but Mark and Matthew say that the trial was at night. The Gospel of John says there was no trial, only a hearing before the High Priest, Ananias. Hyman Maccoby in his 1983 *The Sacred Executioner,* thinks there was only a Roman trial before King Herod and that Herod was not pressured by the Sanhedrin and the high priests. Maccoby believes that Jesus died as a political sacrifice to avoid another Jewish revolt against Roman rule. John 2:50 offers this conclusion to the trial and death of Jesus. "It is better for one man to die for the people than for a whole nation to be destroyed." Certainly a myth circulated for many ages by the Christians that the Jews were "Christ killers" has little validity. The blame for the death of Jesus should not be placed on all of the Jewish people. If someone has to be declared guilty of a wrongful execution, the blame must be placed on a few fearful Jewish aristocrats and the Roman officials who feared that this itinerant, poor preacher from Galilee was about to overthrow the established Roman rule in Palestine.

Jesus was crucified on a hill outside of the city called Golgotha ("Skull") or Calvary, the site now for the Church of the Holy Sepulchre. The execution took place on a Friday after Passover. Jesus was buried in a cave tomb borrowed from a friend, Joseph of Arimathea. Another tomb site, Gordon's tomb, has been given as the correct burial place. This tomb is in East Jerusalem, near the valley of Kidron. Three days after the burial on a Sunday, Mary, mother of James, Mary Magdalene, and Joanna came to the tomb and found that it was empty. Where was the body of Jesus? Had it been stolen? Later the same day two of Jesus' disciples, on their way to the village of Emmaus, saw a man they did not recognize. But Jesus identified himself and told them that he had fulfilled his mission to become the suffering servant. Jesus was persuaded to remain with them in their home in Emmaus and stay overnight. During the evening meal Jesus took the bread and broke it, and gave it to his friends who, like a miracle, saw that he was Jesus. They rushed to Jerusalem to tell the other disciples and friends that they had met with Jesus and that he was truly the risen Christ. The Resurrection had occurred.

> The life of Jesus did not end with the crucifixion event. Perhaps the most central tenet in the Christian faith is the acceptance of the resurrection of the Christ, be it fact or myth. For Christians of the first century or the twentieth there was no doubt that Jesus rose from the dead on the third day and ascended to Heaven where he and all Christians wait for the day when he returns to earth to preside over the Final Judgment, after which all good Christian souls, and perhaps bodies, will enjoy eternal salvation.

The Resurrection may be the date to mark the birth of the Christian Church, but the traditional date is the Pentecostal celebration, forty days after the Resurrection. On Pentecost a group of the followers of Jesus under the leadership of Peter experienced, so they said, the spirit of Jesus descending from heaven upon them. Acts 2:2–3 relates this event as follows: "And suddenly there came a sound from Heaven as of a mighty rushing wind, and it filled all the house where they were sitting. And there appeared unto them cloven tongues like as of fire, and it sat upon each of them." This gift of speaking in many strange tongues was said to have given the apostles the ability to speak to the people in many languages. This spiritual experience would also permit the Church later to admit the Holy Spirit to membership in the Holy Trinity, along with the Father and the Son.

Albert Schweitzer in his *Quest for the Historical Jesus* reminds the liberal, scientifically oriented Christians of today that we must view Jesus in the light of his day. For Jesus and his neighbors to believe in miracles, angels, demons, and spirits was as natural as drinking water from a spring. If Jesus was the son of God, then he must be able to perform miracles, or how else would the people believe that he was divine? The Old Testament contains many references to the existence of spirits, angels, demons, witches, and all kinds of supernatural happenings. Lucifer was a fallen angel. Humans could communicate with spirits (Deuteronomy 16:10–12, Isaiah 14:1, and Samuel 28:7).

Even today many people believe in the existence of angels and demons. Spiritualists hold séances in their homes and claim to be able to communicate with the dead. Haunted houses and evil spirits are not necessarily confined to Halloween, for many people have such weird experiences every day of the year. Yet there is no scientific evidence that any of the supernatural forces exist, or that the spirits of the dead ever communicate with the living.

The greatest possible miracle, however, is the resurrection of the human body from the dead. Most religions have had a belief that it was possible for a dead body to be resurrected to life, probably less so among the Jews than with other religions. Since Christianity has placed so much emphasis on the Resurrection, it is likely that this belief came from non-Jewish sources. It is true that the later Jewish prophets had the idea of a messiah coming to earth and that the souls of the dead would be raised, but most Jews, like the Sadducees, rejected the resurrection idea. It may be that Jesus and the Christians adopted from Isaiah the resurrection thesis that the souls of the dead would be raised (Isaiah 2, 9, and 48–60). Psalms 16:8–9 also speaks of souls being delivered from death.

Whether the Resurrection event, so central and vital to those who profess a belief in the godhead of Jesus, came from Jewish traditions or arose from the reports of the Crucifixion as told by those disciples and friends of Jesus who had witnessed it is uncertain. Resurrection experiences are a part of many religions, for there is no better way to convince the followers of the faith that their prophets and leaders come from God or are in themselves truly God.

Although the majority of Christian theologians and believers accept as truth the bodily resurrection of Jesus, some Christian scholars today refuse to accept the concept of a physical resurrection. Even Paul thought the Resurrection was a spiritual one, not a physical one. The question arises, "When did the idea of a bodily resurrection become an integral part of the Christian canon? James Bentley in his study of the oldest extant copy of the New Testament, the Codex Sinaiticus, found that the gospel of Mark, the gospel generally accepted by scholars as being the oldest of the Gospels, ends with Chapter 16, verse 8.[5] Chapter 16:1–8 only relate the story of the crucifixon, ending with three women, Mary, the mother of James, Mary Magdalene, and Simone entering the tomb only to find a young man in white, but not the body of Jesus. Versus 9 to 20, which tell of the Ascension, were added at a later date, perhaps a century later. Only after some four hundred years did Christians universally accept the belief in a bodily resurrection. The Christian Gnostic Gospels, written in first and second centuries, repudiate the idea of any bodily resurrection.

Centuries of Interpretation and Debate

The question of who Jesus was or what is the real Christ has challenged each generation of Christian thinkers. Orthodox Christians may assert that since God is eternal and unchanging so God's truth must never change. In the first four hundred years of Christianity many versions of the nature of Jesus Christ were offered. Only when the Christian Church became the state church of the Roman

Empire was debate suppressed and everyone who deviated from the approved Orthodox version of the Truth declared a heretic. In the fourteenth and fifteenth centuries a few daring voices dissented from orthodoxy, but it was not until Martin Luther in the sixteenth century that the dissenters were able to speak without fearing for their lives.

By 1800 new cultural forces were arising to create a new climate for dissent and free discussion of issues, even religious issues. Materialism, capitalism, and science were all to impact heavily on how people were to think and believe. More and more science was being accepted as a better avenue to truth than faith, for too often faith was associated with magic and miracles. Before the 1800s scientific treatment of the nature of Jesus Christ was unthinkable. But during the nineteenth century a few daring historians and theologians began to research and study the nature of Jesus Christ and the history of the Christian Church.

One of the first attempts to analyze the Christian faith objectively was made by Thomas Jefferson. He sought to edit from the New Testament all references to miracles and supernatural elements. The first serious reevaluation of the life of Jesus was made by a German theologian, Friedrich Schleiermacher, who in 1819 gave a public lecture on the life of Jesus. Both in lectures and writings he downplayed the role of miracles, but retained belief in the divinity of the Christ since this represented the human essence of God. For Schleiermacher Jesus was more the Christ than the human Jesus. In 1863 a French historian, Ernest Renan, wrote his *Life of Jesus,* in which he accepted that Jesus was a sublime, divine person who was an unprecedented role model for the conduct of human behavior. In 1910 the famous German theologian, organist, and African missionary, Albert Schweitzer, wrote his *The Quest of the Historical Jesus.* Schweitzer sought to demythologize the life of Jesus yet he found that the real Jesus could not be discovered from a historical treatment of his life. "In proportion as we have the spirit of Jesus we have the true knowledge of Jesus" (p. 339).

A typical exponent of the liberal, scientific approach to a study of the life of Jesus is the German theologian Rudolf Bultman. In his 1958 *Jesus Christ and Mythology,* Bultman declares that if the Bible stories were read symbolically, like allegories or fables, or parables, considerable value could be learned on how to improve human relations. Even those who denigrate the value of myths concede that they do have value for human behavior. Bultman states,

> For the world view of scripture is mythological and is therefore unacceptable to the modern man whose thinking has been shaped by science and therefore cannot be mythologized. Modern man can accept as Truth only that which can be conceived in terms of reason and science. Miracles do not fit into a universe which operates on the basis of predictable regularity and causality (p. 36).

> Freedom is obedience to a law of which the validity is recognized and accepted as the law of his own being . . . We may call it the law of the Spirit or in the Christian language, the law of God (p. 41).

Now it is the word of God which calls man into genuine freedom, into free obedience, and the task of demythologizing has no other purpose but to make clear the call of the Word of God from a by-gone world view (p. 47).

Scripture must have relevance to the modern world. . . . The Word of God is only the Word of God as it happens here and now. And since the Word of God and the Church are bound together, it follows that the relevant Church must be in tune with today's needs and concepts of reality (p. 82).

Bultman's concept of God is beautifully expressed by Albert Einstein's definition of God as that which is found in law, beauty, and reason.

Another modern theologian who has had great influence on the interpretation of Jesus and the Christian Church is Karl Barth, a Swiss pastor who came from a Catholic background. Yet Barth is considered by many critics to be an enemy of the Catholic Church, since he sought to prove that the Bible stood supreme over the Church and its sacraments. In his several writings, including *The Knowledge of God and the Service of God* (1943), *The Protestant Theology in the 19th Century* (1947), and the massive, multivolume work *Church Dogmatics,* Barth came to the conclusion after an intensive study of Paul's epistle to the Romans that the foundation of Christianity must be based on the Bible. However, Barth never accepts the Bible as an inerrant revelation from God. The value of the Bible is found in its message that God loves all of his people, regardless of race or class or creed, and that all are destined to inherit a world of peace and freedom. The Bible is not what man thinks about God, but what God thinks about mankind (Dielenberger and Welch, p. 256).

However, Barth, as Hans Küng points out in his *Theology for the Third Millennium,* warns modern historians and theologians who seek to humanize the Christ not to destroy the transcendental Christ. Barth wants to bring Christianity into the modern world without sacrificing the centrality of Christ. "Jesus Christ is the decisive criterion for all discourse about God and man. Jesus Christ is the one, the only light of life" (Küng, p. 275). What matters is not the physical life of Jesus, or even his resurrection, but that indescribable quality of spirit that transcends description and analysis.

Reinhold Niebuhr, an American pastor who served an inner-city church in Detroit from 1915 to 1928, and who saw firsthand the poverty and social injustices forced upon the people who lived there, became a critic of twentieth-century capitalism and war. In his *Man and Immoral Society* (1935) and *Destiny of Man* (1949) he said that the salvation of humankind from social injustice and poverty will not come from some miraculous act of God. Salvation from the social abuses depends upon the recognition of Jesus as the revelation of God. The Church must give witness to the presence of God and the Christ. God is supreme and above all things, the Church, theology, science, and society in general. The Church must proclaim the primacy of God in all of human activity. Niebuhr asserts that God's love comes freely for all people, that it does not depend upon one's personal merits or works. Revelation is the source of knowledge about God, but Niebuhr disclaims that the Bible is inerrant and that all of the myths and miracles recorded therin should be taken literally.

Niebuhr was above all else a pragmatic proponent of such social legislation as exemplified by Roosevelt's New Deal program of the 1930s. Until the Christian message of love and social justice could be implemented into the daily lives of the nation's citizens the Christian Church had failed its mission. Niebuhr was no friend of American imperialism, nor of world communism. He gave active support to the formation of the United Nations and the cause of world peace. Niebuhr viewed God as an unknowable, mysterious force that could be brought to human understanding as a symbol of God's power and love as it was manifested into a more just, moral, and benevolent society of people.

Paul Tillich was another twentieth-century theologian who sought to effect a compromise between this modern scientifically oriented world, a world more concerned with matters of the flesh and material than the spirit, and a religion that remains bound by stultifying dogmas and meaningless rituals. Tillich came to the United States in 1933 from Germany, where he had been expelled from his teaching post because of his refusal to support Hitler and his Nazi tyranny. While in the United States until his death in 1965 he lectured at various universities, notably the University of Chicago, and wrote a number of books and essays in which he developed his ideas about the nature and functions of religion. Tillich is best known for hys *Systematic Theology* (1951-1963) and *Dynamics of Faith* (1957).

Tillich has great faith in the power of religion to change the condition of human existence for the better, but before the Christian Church can succeed in this effort it must also accept the reality of change. The true spirit of Christ must be discovered and brought into action. The Christian Church must shake off its shackles of superstitions, outworn dogmas and rituals, and believing in the reality of myths and miracles. The Church must accept the reality of change by accepting new modes of belief and action. Otherwise the traditional Church will become irrelevant to modern society and cease to be a force for the betterment of the human world. To say that God is dead and the Church has become meaningless is nonsense. However, the Church must accept the reality of scientific truths. Ancient concepts of the nature of man and the universe are no longer useful for human understanding of God. The Bible must be interpreted not as a body of fact, but as a collection of symbols that reveal God to mankind. "My whole theological work has been directed to the interpretation of religious symbols in such a way that the secular man, and we are all secular, can understand and be moved by them," Tillich wrote in *The Future of Religions* (p. 29).

Tillich's writings are abstract and not easy to understand. Certain ideas, however, are most understandable. He cites the book of Revelation as being symbolic of the human destiny to progress or develop over periods of time into a better world on earth. However, the course of development has no guarantee that it will be free of reverses and pain. Tillich saw Jesus as only a symbol of

God, for if he had been God he would not have been crucified. Truth in the spiritual realm is revealed by acts of faith and not by rational research and study, yet Christians are obligated to accept the truths revealed by science. Our knowledge of God comes through the Christ, the symbol of God.

Tillich proposed a new religion, perhaps a new version of Christianity, called the "Religion of the Concrete Spirit." This religion would embrace the Apostle Paul's doctrine of the Holy Spirit. It is this spirit that motivates the Christian to embrace the spiritual values of love, beauty, and justice. The new religion would retain the mystical elements of the sacraments without endowing them with concrete forms that would cause them to be objects of worship. Religion is revealed by its symbols.

> Religious symbols are not stones falling from heaven. They have their roots in the totality of human experience including local surroundings, in all their ramifications, both political and economic. . . . The religious symbols say something to us about the way in which men have understood themselves in their very nature. . . . The universality of a religious statement does not lie in an all-embracing abstraction which would destroy religion as such, but it lies in the depths of every concrete religion.[6]

Although Tillich was loyal to the Christian faith, he saw the possibilities by which Christians could profit from an understanding of other world religions. Each generation needs to discover God, the infinite Holy Spirit, in its changing world of science and social conditions.

In his *Jesus Through the Centuries* Jaroslav Pelikan says, "Regardless of what anyone may personally think or believe about him, Jesus of Nazareth has been the dominant figure in the history of western culture for almost twenty centuries." Pelikan's analysis of Jesus Christ through the centuries is an interesting study of how the personality of Jesus and his teachings have permeated every aspect of Western culture, art, literature, social reforms, democracy, world peace, and ethical conduct. Jesus represents the incarnation of God, that which is love and compassion for all of mankind.

In his 1964 *The Humor of Christ* Elton Trueblood pictures Jesus as an intelligent, gifted human being who had a talent for hyperbole, ironic criticism of his opponents, and the use of simple parables that the common people could understand. He ridiculed the Pharisees for their false pride and pomposity. He called kings the benefactors of mankind which, of course, they were not. In the parable of the talents (Matthew 25:14–30) Jesus gave a reverse twist to the meaning of who was the master—not God, but the devil. In the parable of the unjust steward, related only by Luke, Jesus must have been joking, for it contradicted his moral values.

The twentieth century gave rise to "process theology," a new Protestant theology compatible with science. This theology asserts that there is only one constant in human experience—change, and that religion is not exempted from this fact.

Unless the Church conforms to new standards for the search for truth and unless the Church adjusts itself to the social pressures and needs of the modern world, it will no longer be a significant force in the life of modern people. Some of the leading exponents of process theology are Alfred North Whitehead, Rudolf Bultman, Thomas Sheen (*First Coming*), Harvey Pothoff (*God and the Celebration of Life*), and others.

Process theology views the human race in a cosmic perspective, that people are only one part of God's creation, as being sacred and needing protection. God did not intend that man should so dominate all of the earth as to destroy it, its creations, and its environment. Moreover, God's truth is in an everchanging, developing process—the final word has not been written. The search for truth must use the tools of science and reason and if myths and supernatural phenomena must be discarded, then so be it.

The question of whether Jesus was human or divine or both may never be resolved. Those who believe that he rose from the dead and thereby promised a similar resurrection for his followers cannot be convinced by science and reason that the Resurrection was not a historical fact. For these persons truth is found by faith and faith alone. But for those Christians who will be convinced by the evidence of science, not faith, the supernatural aspects of Jesus cannot be accepted. However, even an atheist must admit that the success of the Christian Church in preaching Jesus' message to millions of people might be termed a "miracle." Christians must admit that the love message for human conduct must be shared with the Buddhists, the Hindus, the Muslims, and other teachers of peace and love among all people.

But not all historians of the first century A.D. are convinced that Jesus during his lifetime was truly an apostle of love and peace. Anthropologist Marvin Harris in his book *Cows, Pigs, Wars and Witches* cites evidence that Jesus, along with John the Baptist, the Essenes and other messianic Jewish groups, was a revolutionary Jew who sought the overthrow of Roman domination through the intervention of a messiah from the lineage of King David. The gospel record that Jesus was the son of God who came to redeem mankind from the sins of Adam and Eve was devised by the gospel writers long after the death of Jesus and only after Jerusalem had been destroyed by Titus, son of the emperor Vespasian, in A.D. 70.

Jesus was executed by by Roman authorities, not for any teachings that might have been in conflict with traditional Jewish beliefs, but for his role as a leader of anti-Roman acts.

14

The Pauline Church of the
First Two Centuries

The death of Jesus left a small band of Jewish disciples and followers in Jerusalem to carry on his mission of promulgating love and brotherhood. Only a few thousand had taken up the cross to follow him. In his *History of Christianity* Paul Johnson estimates that Jesus had some eight-thousand followers. Acts 2:5 mentions 120 persons. Whatever the number was, it was small. After the Crucifixion the Christians were discouraged and frightened, but later, when they learned that Jesus had risen from the dead, their courage and strength were renewed. Now the Jewish Christians were confident that the Parousia, the Second Coming of Christ, would be realized. On the day of Pentecost, when the Holy Spirit descended upon the Christians, some three thousand persons were baptized and received into Christian fellowship.

For the next three hundred years the Christians grew in number and influence so that by the fourth century the Christian Church was established as the state church of the Roman Empire. But growth in members and power did not come easily, for within the Christian body there were several competing sects, and without there was the constant threat of oppression from Roman authorities. Many Christians before A.D. 300 were persecuted and killed, but hindsight suggests that the more the Christians were oppressed the faster and greater was the growth of their movement.

At the time of Christ's death the Roman Empire, especially in the regions of the East and Africa, was rife with dissent, even rebellion, against the domination of Rome. This division even occurred within Christian ranks. The unhappy subjects of Rome realized that rebellion was a risky, probably impossible, venture, so many were seeking freedom and escape through some form of religious expression. The people were seeking a religion that put its trust in one God, a God with whom people could communicate and one who would respond with love and compassion to the needs of the people. A fatherlike God was in demand. If God was to love the people, then the people had to respond with love. The love relationship with God was not one of the mind and reason, but a more satisfying one of emotion and mysticism. In some of the Jewish sects these needs could have been met. Even in the Greek mystery cults and in the Zoroastrian magi there could be found the promise of a loving God, that a better world would surely come to relieve the oppressed of their oppressor, Rome. But it was the destiny of the Christian message that it could be the one religion that would best meet contemporary needs for spiritual satisfaction.

The Essenes

Since the discovery of the Dead Sea Scrolls in 1947 new facts have come to light about a small Jewish sect, the Essenes, who wrote on the scrolls their version of the Torah, plus other writings that describe their worship practices and beliefs. Reading excerpts from the Scrolls one is struck by the similarities between the teachings of Jesus and the beliefs of the Essenes. In his *Dead Sea Scrolls, 1947–1969* Edmund Wilson points out several such instances. No one knows whether Jesus and the first Christians borrowed ideas and beliefs from the Essenes, but a case could be made that there were close contacts between the Essenes and the followers of Jesus.[1] It is known that John the Baptist was closely related to the Essene commuity, either as a member or one who had lived in an Essene monastery for a time, and it is known that John the Baptist was a close friend and teacher of Jesus.

The Essenes preferred to escape Roman oppression by fleeing into the desert near the Dead Sea rather than to try to fight the Roman soldiers. In fact the Essenes arose in the third century B.C. in protest against the anti-Jewish rule of the Seleucid monarchy. The Essenes organized a monastic, communal style of living in a remote region where they thought they would be safe from oppressive rulers and a sin-ridden world. The Essene community was male-dominated, women were regarded as evil temptresses. All male members had to remain chaste, and new members were recruited by adopting male children. Marriage and sex were not for the Essenes. The prophetlike leader was called the "Teacher of Righteousness," of whom there were probably several. Life in the monastery was harsh. Time was spent in prayer, sheepherding, and hard work. Pleasure of all kinds was taboo. Purification by water was used to initiate new members, hence the sacrament of baptism. Like Jesus, the teacher of righteousness preached a message of love for all people, that all people were of equal worth, and that God was a loving, forgiving God. The Essenes accepted Judaic law and used the Jewish Sabbath, but, more than other Jewish sects, they placed great hope in the belief that a messiah would come to deliver them from their enemies and a sinful world. They were confident that the promised suffering servant as described by Isaiah was to be the promised messiah. Unlike other Jews but like the Greeks, they believed that the body and the soul were separate entities, and that the soul after death was released to return to its original source, God. They accepted also the Zoroastrian concept of a dual universe in which there was a god of light or goodness and a god of darkness, or Beliar or Satan. The god of light will be the judge of the souls after death.

It is likely that the two sacraments used in the early church came from the Essenes. As mentioned earlier the Essenes practiced baptism, and the Eucharist or Lord's Supper may also have been in imitation of the Essenes, who shared both a noon and evening meal, not only as a source of food for the body, but as a spiritual experience that bound the group together in fellowship with God. Some scholars have suggested that the gospel of John was borrowed from the Essenes, who, in turn, had borrowed the mystical concept of the word or Logos from Greek Neo-Platonic sources.

The Beginnings of the Christian Church

The first-century Christian Church was called an *Ecclesia,* meaning a community in the Greek language. The Jerusalem Christians worshiped basically in the same manner as the Jews. The worship place was the Jewish synagogue, whether shared with the Jews or in a separate building. The Jewish worship service was used, the Torah was read, the Psalms were chanted, and the Jewish holy days were observed. They even circumcised the male infants and ate kosher food. Perhaps the most significant break with Jewish worship practices was that the Christian Sabbath was on Sunday, in commemoration of the Resurrection day.

The early Christians also introduced what for mainstream Jews were two new sacraments, baptism and the Lord's Supper or the Eucharist. The Lord's Supper may have been instituted as a memorial of the last meal the resurrected Jesus had with his disciples in the house in Emmaus, or, more likely, it was the occasion in the upper room on the eve of Jesus' arrest and trial, when he broke bread with his disciples for the last time, as reported in Luke 22:19. The use of bread and wine in a religious service was a common practice among the Greek mystery cults and in Persian Mithraism. In addition to a memorial meal the Christians shared a common meal of fellowship and love, known as *Agape,* the Greek word for love. The spiritual leaders in the Jerusalem church were rabbis or teachers with certain assistants known as elders or presbyters, who assisted in the worship service, and a group of deacons, who collected the tithes and administered to the sick and the poor. When Paul visited Jerusalem he was received by its chief elder, James, the brother of Jesus, and leader of the Jerusalem church (Acts 21:8).

That the small Christian church in Jerusalem ever survived or did not become reabsorbed into the Jewish faith is almost a miracle. These rebel Jews were hated by the orthodox Sadducees and Pharisees out of fear that they might disrupt further the unity of the Jews, or even provoke retaliation from the Roman authorities. In A.D. 36–37 a mob attacked the Jerusalem Christians for having said that the Temple was not the dwelling place of God. One of the Christians, Stephen, was stoned to death. Peter and John were both arrested for preaching in the Temple. Eventually they were released and left Jerusalem. Later Peter was found in Antioch. After the Romans destroyed Jerusalem in A.D. 70 both Jews and Christians left Jerusalem for safer homes in Asia Minor and Syria. As the Jews and Christians began to mingle with the Gentile people who used the Greek language, these Jewish groups also began to speak Greek and adopt some of the Gentile customs.

Thus Jerusalem was not destined to be the birthplace of a new Christian church. The Jews declared that Jesus was a false prophet, a blasphemer of the truth. Not only did the infant Christian church suffer opposition from the Jews but by 100 the Roman state began a serious campaign of oppression against the Christians. So the early Christian people found the best haven for safety and growth among the Gentile people of Asia Minor, in the cities of Tarsus, Ephesus, and Antioch, as on the isle of Cyprus. Christians would also find converts in Greek Macedonia. Much of the success of the new Christian movement in Asia Minor must be attibuted to the dedicated missionary work of the Apostle Paul and his friends. Paul made three missionary journeys throughout the eastern Mediterranean region: the first in 46, the second in 49–52, and the third in 53–56. His principal friends were Barnabas, Timothy, and Silas.

The first Christian church was founded in Antioch, or, at least it was here that the Christians were first called "Christian" (Acts II:26). From Antioch the gospel or the"good news" was to be carried to all parts of the Roman Empire. The Church would find its most success winning converts in the eastern regions of Asia Minor and Egypt among the Gentiles and the Hellenized Jews. The language used in the Church was not to be Hebrew or Aramaic, but Greek. Jesus was to be called the son of God, the Greek version of his nature, not the son of man, the Hebrew. The Jewish term messiah would be replaced by the Greek equivalent term, Christos.

Paul of Tarsus

The first-century Christian church is dominated by the presence of the greatest Christian missionary, the dynamic Paul of Tarsus. He was the guiding spirit, the inspiration for a group of Christians who were anxious to seek a rebirth by breaking loose from the chains of Judaism and making their appeal to the non-Jewish people, the people who lived in the Gentile world. Under Paul's leadership the Christian Church began to develop its own theology, services, and organizational structure.

Paul, like Jesus, left a meager biography. Very little is known about his youth and his early education. He was born in Tarsus, a thriving commercial city in Asia Minor, of modern Turkey. Tarsus had become a center of education and culture in which the Greek philosophies and religious cults were known. Undoubtedly young Saul had become familiar with the intellectual aspects of his city. The fact that Paul is known also as Saul may be confusing to us, but to the people of his day it was common practice to use a Latin name, Paul, since his father was a Roman citizen, and also his Hebrew name, Saul. Paul's family was well educated and a reasonably wealthy one since his father was a successful tent maker who made tents from both leather and fabric. Paul was born sometime between A.D. 5 and 14. As a good Jewish infant he was circumcised on the eighth day after birth. In the Jewish tradition his parents taught him the Hebrew Scriptures and traditions. Living in a Greek-speaking area, Paul learned to read from the Torah in both the Hebrew and Greek languages. He also read some of the Latin classics. His parents were a part of the Jewish diaspora who had left Jerusalem for a better and safer life in the Gentile world of Asia Minor. Thus Paul had become acquainted with the Greek Gentile people among whom he would find most of his Christian followers.

As a young man he had been sent to Jerusalem by his father to study Judaism. Here he joined the Pharisee sect, the one to which his father belonged. Other sources say that he joined the Sadducees, but in either case he became associated with Jewish groups that were zealous defenders of their faith. Certainly they would regard as heretics the young Nazarene Christians led by Peter and James, the brother of Jesus. At this time Paul or Saul was no friend of the Christians.

Paul may have studied with Gamaliel the Elder, a famous Pharisee rabbi who preached that world would end in a apcalyptic disaster after which a divine savior would come to redeem the world from sin, a prophecy that could be found in both Hebrew Scripture and in the teachings of several of the Hellenistic cults. It may be that Paul had received from Gamaliel his later conviction that in the death of Christ upon the cross the old world of sin would be destroyed and a new age of perfection would come with the return of Christ to earth at some future time.

While in Jerusalem Paul joined in the persecution of the small band of Nazarenes. Among other deaths, the persecution caused the death of Stephen, a Christian disciple who was stoned by an angry mob. Jewish hostility to the Christians caused Peter and James to be arrested and later banished from Jerusalem. Even after Paul left Jerusalem he continued his attacks on the Christians who lived in small communities along the coast of Palestine. Later Paul returned to Jerusalem to prepare for further attacks against Christian groups in Syria, Cilicia, and Asia Minor.

Every Christian child in Sunday School has learned about the miraculous conversion of Saul on his way to Damascus. Acts 9 relates how Saul was blinded suddenly by the sun, and as he fell to earth he heard a voice saying,"Saul, Saul, why persecutest thou me?" When Saul or Paul asked who was speaking, the voice replied, "I am Jesus who thou persecutest." Paul had seen the risen Christ, and, henceforth, he vowed that he would be an apostle for him. (Jesus called his disciples *apostles,* those who could speak for him. Paul never saw or knew Jesus in the flesh.

Blinded after the Damascus road experience, Paul was taken to Damascus to be sheltered in the home of Judas. Here a Christian by the name of Ananias came to visit Paul, during which he cured Paul's blindness. This house in Damascus is now a tourist stop in which there is a small basement chapel for worship. It is said that Ananias baptized Paul in the Christian faith and then told him that he had been chosen by God to bring the Christian gospel to all peoples, Jews, Gentiles, and all others, even to kings (Acts 9:15–16). In the meantime Paul's former Jewish friends sought to have Paul arrested for being a traitor to their faith. Legend says that Paul's new Christian friends enabled him to escape from Damascus by freeing him from prison, letting him down from a prison window in a basket (2 Corinthians 11:33). Tourists are shown the very window from which Paul escaped.

For a few years Paul seemed to have disappeared from public view. Perhaps he spent sometime with a Nabatean Jewish sect in Petra. He appeared again in Jerusalem to help the Christians there, but his life was threatened again so he left for Tarsus. Tradition dates the beginning of his missionary enterprise from when Barnabas took him to Antioch to preach in the Christian church there. Antioch was the largest city along the Mediteranean coast.

For the next ten years Paul became the foremost Christian missionary in the history of the Church. His first journey, A.D. 45–49, took him to the Jewish communities of Cyprus, Asia Minor, and to portions of Greece. The Jews refused to listen to him, however, so he and Barnabas were forced to flee to Iconium in Turkey. Everywhere Paul was rejected by the Jews. Paul and Barnabas then returned to Antioch, were they made plans to go on a second journey, A.D. 49–52, to Tarsus, a mountainous region. Paul had as his aide another friend, Silas, and later, when they entered Troas on the shores of the Aegean Sea, they were joined by Luke, a physician, and Timothy. The missionary party left Asia Minor to enter Greece, where they visited towns in Macedonia and other Greek people in Athens, Corinth, Philippi, and Thessalonica. In Athens the Christians were mocked and scorned but in Corinth they received a warm welcome. The church at Corinth would become one of Paul's favorites.

Paul had learned in Greece that the most promising recruits for the army of Christ were to be found among the Greek Gentiles and not the Jews. Paul's third and last journey, A.D. 53–58, took him and his friends to Ephesus, Macedonia, and then along the eastern coast of the Aegean, and eventually back to Jerusalem. In Jerusalem Paul sought to effect a reconciliation with the Jews, but instead he was arrested by the Jewish leaders for failing to give honor to the Temple and the Judaic faith. Paul was sent to Caesaria for imprisonment, but since he was a Roman citizen he appealed to have a trial in Rome. On the way to Rome he experienced a shipwreck and almost drowned. Eventually he and his guards reached Naples (Acts 27:22–26). From Naples Paul went to Rome on foot, where he was placed under house arrest for two years. During this time Paul was free to preach and meet with the Christians in Rome. Tradition attributes his death in Rome, and the death of Peter also, to a mad act of the Emperor Nero, who falsely charged the Christians with having caused the burning of Rome in A.D. 64. Whatever the truth might be, Paul and Peter were put to death by the Roman authorities. Over the grave of Paul in Rome is now the Church of St. Paul Without the Walls, and over Peter's burial place stands the magnificent Church of St. Peters and the Vatican.

The question of whether Paul wished to destroy Judaism and convert all Jews to Christianity is moot. It is true that in many respects he did depart from Judaism, but in most respects the Christian church retained its Jewish heritage. Paul did give Judaism a new interpretation and a new direction. He did reject the necessity of the rite of circumcision for admission into membership in the Church. The highest virtue for Paul was not the Judaic passion for obedience to the Law, but the Christian commandment to "love thy neighbor as thyself." Paul's view on sex is certainly not the more liberated view of the Jews, but Paul never desired to escape from his Jewish roots, for in Romans 9:1–5, Paul admits his debt to Judaism.

But Paul also had inherited from his home environment some elements of Greek and Hellenistic religious concepts. When Paul lists his concept of virtues and sins he is more Greek than Jew (Galatians 5:19–33). He accepted the Greek belief that the body and soul are separate entities, quite unlike the Jewish belief that body and soul were united in one body and, hence, inseparable.

Tenets of Pauline Theology

Paul's theology became the foundation stone on which the Christian church would be built. It is in Paul's several epistles to his Christian churches that his theology can be found. But theology, as with other aspects of human endeavor, does change over the years. When a comparison is made of Christian theology and practice during the Pauline era and the church at its height during the Middle Ages under Pope Innocent II, one may well wonder if it is the same Christian Church.

Paul's theology is found in his letters, which make up about half of the New Testament. Scholars are not certain that Paul actually wrote all of the epistles credited to him. Scholars seem to agree that he wrote 1 and 2 Corinthians, Galatians, Philippians, Philemon, 1 and 2 Thessalonians, and Romans. Questions have been raised as to the authorship of 1 and 2 Timothy and Titus; Paul may have written parts of them. However, none of Paul's letters were written into their present form until a half century after Paul's death.

Paul had one basic goal in his mission to serve Christ—to heal the breach between the Gentiles and the Jews. He hoped to find some formula by which the two groups could be reconciled and worship together. The challenge before Paul was the problem of creating a new religion that would join together the Jewish Jehovah and the commandments with the Hellenistic concept of Christ and the Messiah, the fact of the resurrected Christ, and the eternal soul that would survive the death of the body.

In the Christian Church as conceived by Paul, all persons were invited to enter if they would accept baptism and acknowledge Christ as their savior and redeemer, be they Greek or Jew, rich or poor, master or slave. No longer would circumcision be necessary for church membership. Paul believed that the salvation of the soul did not come from a strict observance of the Jewish Law, but instead salvation came by way of the cross, that is, one must accept on faith that Christ had died on the cross for our sins. In Romans 5:16 Paul said, "For if through the offense of one many be dead, much more by the Grace of God, and the gift of Grace, which is by one man, Jesus Christ, hath abounded unto many." In Romans 7 and 8 Paul concludes that man is justified by faith alone or by a higher law, the law of the spirit.

The central theme of Paul's theology is that souls are saved by faith, that it is God's mercy that saves all souls, and that the proof for God's Grace is that He sacrificed his son, Jesus Christ, on the cross for the redemption of man's sins.

Next Paul needed to prove the divinity of Jesus, that he was the son of God. What better proof could be found than that Jesus rose from the dead on the third day after the crucifixion? The Resurrection experience became the foundation stone on which Paul would build his Church, for now there was no doubt that Christ is divine. For Paul the Resurrection was a historical fact. Paul was certain that the Christ was the Messiah, the suffering servant, the second Adam, and the last Adam, as had been prophesied by the ancient Jewish prophets.

Paul's concept of the nature of the Resurrection is unclear. Did he accept the Judaic version of a bodily resurrection? It should be said that Judaism gave only slight attention to life after death, or to the matter of resurrection in any form. Paul was familiar with the Gnostic Christians who rejected the idea of a bodily resurrection, believing that only the spirit or soul could be resurrected. If there is doubt about Paul's form of resurrection, the weight of the evidence is that he believed that only the soul would be resurrected. In 1 Corinthians 15:44 Paul says, "There is a natural body, and there is a spiritual body, and the spiritual body is the risen one, the natural body dies in corruption." If Paul did accept the idea that the body and the spirit were separate entities, then he had adopted the Greek or Gnostic interpretation and not the Jewish one.

If Christ was risen from the dead, then logically all Christians may be raised from the dead at some future time. Paul made the Resurrection thesis the core of his letters to the several Christian churches. The entirety of 1 Corinthians 15 is devoted to the resurrection experience. The promise of the resurrection is repeated many times in the New Testament, for example, Romans 1:4 and 10:9 and 1 Thessalonians 4:13–18. Just how and when the Resurrection would occur is not detailed. Paul makes clear that his concept of the bodily resurrection is not of the physical body but of the spiritual body (1 Corinthians 15:1–38 and 44). Paul's version of resurrection is distinctly Greek and not Jewish sources. The Greeks believed in only a resurrection of the soul or spirit. The body and the soul were separate entities, and after death the soul joined its counterpart, God, in heaven.

Paul made the Resurrection event the crucial element in Christian theology. He said, "If the dead are not raised, then Christ is not raised." The truth that states Christ was risen guarantees to all Christians that the Resurrection is the fulfillment of scriptural prophecy and this reward in heaven is yours when you accept the Christ as your savior.

Skeptics and scientists have many doubts about the miracle of the Resurrection. It defies both logic and science, but a Jewish scholar, Pinchas Lapides, a professor at Göttingen Unviersity in Germany, thinks the Resurrection of Christ must have been a real experience since it is the only explanation for the fact that a small band of terrified disciples fled from the scene of the crucifixion only to soon go forth into the world confident of their mission to preach the gospel of Christ.

Even today the majority of Christians accept the reality of miracles, mystery, and resurrection from the dead. Probably the very essence of religion is the ability or willingness of its adherents to accept the reality of the supernatural, not on the evidence of science, but on a deeper source of truth from one's heart, on faith rather than reason. Among Protestant Christians in the United States there has recently occurred a revival of belief in the supernatural aspects of Christianity among the fundamentalist and evangelical churches. As far as they are concerned, if the sacred Scripture records these mystical events, and Scripture cannot be in error, then these strange events are true. Writing in the *New York Times Magazine,* Fran Schumer reports that many Christians are returning to a mystical form of worship, one typical of Christianity in earlier ages. Even intellectuals are joining the back-to-God movement. "Tradition is back on the agenda with a positive force." People are reacting to science, which has brought to the world the nuclear terror and the Holocaust. Science is no longer a safe guide for human morality and behavior. "What most intellectuals do agree on is that the essence of religion, the concern with transcendence, the interest in ethics, morality, and a desire for roots will continue to seek expression in the culture."[2]

Paul accepted the messianic concept preached by the Jewish prophets Isaiah and Daniel and by the Essenes and by John the Baptist. Paul believed that the fulfillment of the prophecy came with the birth of Jesus and his Resurrection. Jesus was the legitimate heir of King David. Paul never doubted that Christ would soon return to earth to judge the souls of men. Paul believed that the Parousia, the Second Coming of Christ, was imminent, or even that the event had occurred already and that contemporary Christians were living in the days of the Last Judgment. The Pauline Church rested on two basic principles: the certainty that salvation comes by faith and not by good works, and the conviction that Christ will come again to judge and redeem mankind from its sins. No man knows when the Christ will appear, but that he will no man should ever doubt.

Paul accepted the Judaic Jehovah as the one, true God, and that Jesus was his son, the Messiah, the suffering servant, the one ordained by God to redeem mankind from original sin. Paul accepted the reality of the Holy Spirit, the incarnate spirit of God in the body of Jesus. There is no doubt that Paul saw God as one, and by no means could he be divided into three parts. Hence the idea of the holy Trinity came into Christian theology at some later date. In his 1986 *The Mythmaker: Paul and the Invention of Christianity,* Hyman Maccoby offers a radical view that Paul accepted a Hellenistic, Gnostic concept of God. This view holds that the world is composed to two forces, good and evil and that they are represented by one god of light and another god of darkness. Mankind can be saved only by the god of light or goodness. Maccoby says that it was this god that Paul accepted as his God. Gnostics had branded the Judaic God, Jehovah, as the creator of darkness, or evil.

Paul makes frequent use of the term "freedom", but his freedom was not the current concept of personal freedom in a democratic society. His concept of freedom was freedom from the burden of original sin and freedom from the excess and narrow application of Jewish Law (see Romans 6 and 7). But Paul seems to hedge his concept of freedom even more, for there is evidence that he accepted to some degree the doctrine of predestination. He acknowledged that mankind has the gift of free will, that is, that humans can choose the way of righteousness or evil, but then he seemed to think that God ordains one's future destiny even before birth, just as he did in the case of Jesus. There is evidence for Paul's belief in predestination in Romans 8:29-30 and Ephesians 1:3-14. In Ephesians 1:5 Paul says, "Having predestinated unto us the adoption of children by Jesus Christ to himself, according to the good pleasure of his will." Later Christians, especially St. Augustine and John Calvin, will give the idea of predestination a prominent place in their theological system of Christianity.

Paul never meant that humans would be free to pursue the pleasures of the world without suffering some inhibitions and penalities. Bacchian orgies were not in Paul's list of virtues. In fact Paul may have been the original Puritan father, for he went far beyond the Judaic restraints on the freedom to enjoy sexual pleasure and other sensuous activities. The Jews employed the Aristotelian concept of moderation in all human activites. The ideal life pattern was to be found in avoiding excess in either the pursuit of good or evil. Paul's standard of ethical behavior was more akin to that of Greek Stoics than to that of the Jews. Paul would have preferred that humans follow an ascetic life in denial, poverty, and sacrifice, much like life in a monastery.

Justification by faith did not exempt a Christian from living an upright moral life. This meant that one must obey all of the commandments and practice love toward others. If a person was truly reborn as a Christian, he could not help but live the Christian life in service to others and with heartfelt love for God, Christ, and all mortal humans.

Structure, Rites, and Mores of the Early Pauline Church

Paul may have been a visionary prophet, but he was also a rational, practical leader who had considerable organizational skills for constructing a new church.

He saw the need for a form of church organization and government by which the Christian community could be given direction for mutual cooperation and spiritual reinforcement. There was need for a statement of beliefs and a set of rituals and worship practices. Paul conceived the Church to be a body of believers bound together in a state of holy communion. In Romans 12:4–5, Paul refers to the Church as the body of Christ. The Church is also the bride of Christ, bound to Christ in a state of holy matrimony. The Church was to be open to all persons regardless of class, race, or previous religious affiliations. "In Christ there is no east nor west, no Jew nor Gentile, no bond nor free, no male nor female" (Galatians 3:26–29).

The mark of a Christian was no longer circumcision but only the sign of the cross. The church used two sacraments, baptism and the Lord's Supper or Eucharist, to signify first admission to the body of Christ and second confirmation of membership in the group. Baptism signified that the new-born Christian had experienced a resurrection, with the old body of sin washed away to present a new, purified body of God. The new Christian must acknowledge Christ as his or her savior, the one ordained by God even before his birth to come to earth to save mankind from its sins. The ritual of the Lord's Supper or Eucharist was in commemoration of the last meal Jesus had with his disciples in the upper room before is death. But the Last Supper was also a feast among friends to express their thanks to God for all the blessings that had been granted them. The Essenes ate together in a love feast. So did the early Christians share a common meal in an act of love. The Greek mysteries used a sacred meal to express their love for God and unity with God by believing that the bread and wine consumed was a symbolical representation of the body and blood of their gods.

The early Christians worshiped in the manner of the Jews in a synagogue, but on Sunday rather than the Sabbath, in recognition of the Resurrection day. A rabbi, teacher, or priest presided over the services. The sexes were separated in such a manner that the women were placed in an inferior place in the building, probably in a balcony. The worship services included the reading from the Torah, singing or chanting the psalms and hymns, the offering of prayers, and a sermon exhorting the congregation to be loyal to Christ and obedient to the commandments. In 1 Timothy 2 and 5 one can find some insights on the conduct of the services in a Pauline church. The best account of the early church is found in Acts.

Church government was simple and democratic. Christians were few in number, living apart in separated towns and communities. Many Christians lived in communal groups, like the Essenes, where all property and work were shared. Hence there was little need for any sophisticated bureaucracy or system of laws and government. There was no centralized authority to coordinate and supervise the several Christian churches. Church government consisted of committees elected by the male members of the congregation, called the presbytery or synod. Its members were called presbyters or elders. The chairman of the presbytery was an *episcopus* or bishop. A few men, three or four, were chosen to aid the presbyters or elders by collecting the taxes or tithes and administering to the sick, poor, widows, and orphans, and maintaining church property. These aides were called deacons.

Pauline theology contained messages for people's everyday living. Guiding principles for marriage and family, the marketplace, and even politics were announced by Paul. In 1 Corinthians 7 Paul outlines the conditions for a good marriage and family. The Jews saw no reason to be celibate, for Genesis 2 relates that God admonishes his people to be "fruitful and multiply." Sex in the marital relationship was a high virtue. But Paul said it was better to marry than to burn, but it was better still to not marry. Paul's ideal life was to live in a celibate, monastic community freed from the contamination caused when Eve tempted Adam. Paul's abhorrence of sex may have been derived from his associations with the Greek Stoics and the Jewish Essenes. Perhaps the dogma of the Virgin Mary, although it was adopted officially by the church much later, may have been inspired by Paul.

Paul, like Jesus, loved children, but he preferred not to be a parent. In his day wives and children were legally the property of the husband and father. Children could be sold into slavery, a legal condition that prevailed even in England until the fourteenth century. Under Roman law it was legal to practice infanticide as a birth control measure, but both Judaism and Paul rejected this cruel practice. Paul would agree with the Jews that certain sexual practices outside of marriage that might interfere with maximum procreation were immoral and should be made illegal. Therefore abortions, contraception, homosexuality, and masturbation were deemed ungodly acts.

In Ephesians 5 wives are advised to submit themselves to their husbands. This is repeated in 1 Timothy 2:11-16. In 1 Corinthians 7:32-33 women are adminished to remain silent. Paul, however, only reflects the traditional attitude toward women in the society of his day. Since the beginning of time in most human societies the male had been honored with a position of supremacy over both the female and the children. In the church men were told to leave their heads uncovered for they were the image and glory of God. but women were to cover their heads in church as a sign of feminine submission. In one sense Paul had declared that in the church men and women were equal, but in the everyday world women were second-rate persons. Paul did accept women as coworkers in the church, as, for example in 1 Corinthians 16:19 Paul salutes two women, Aquila and Priscilla, as being Christian brethren. However, Paul did accept the prevailing position of women. Was Paul a woman hater? Did he truly believe the women were inherently temptresses who would lead men into sexual immoralities? Did he believe that sex was included in God's plan for a paradise on earth? Although the Roman culture was prone to sexual excesses, there were a number of religious groups who took issue with the Roman tolerance for free sexual expression. Not only Pauline Christians, but also Zoroastrians, Gnostics, and Stoics deemed sex evil and unclean.

In Ephesians 6 children are advised to obey their parents. The advise is repeated in Colossians 3:20, but with the caution that fathers should not provoke and discourage their children.

Although marriage was not a sacrament in the Pauline church, Paul, like Jesus, disapproved of divorce, as well as such extramarital sexual behavior as adultery and fornication. Paul did compare the marriage relationship of husband and wife to the relationship of Christ and the church. As Christ was the head of the church, so the husband should be the head of the family. Paul warned Christians not to marry pagans.

As a rule, Paul did not question the prevailing social, economic, or politcal institutions of the Roman world. He did not denounce the Roman imperial system of government. His concept of liberty did not suggest a democratic form of government. Christians were expected to obey Roman law and render unto Caesar those things that belonged to Caesar, namely, obedience, payment of taxes, and refraining from all treasonable acts. Paul did not seek to establish a theocratic state on earth. Perhaps Paul's willingness to accept the prevailing status quo was due to thinking that worldly matters were of little consequence since life on earth would soon be replaced by the Parousia, Christ's return to earth and the imposition of a new order of justice and peace. Paul was also sufficiently wise to realize that a small band of Christians was in no position to challenge the might of the Roman Empire. The most that Paul could expect was that the Romans would accept the Christians on an equal basis with the Jews and permit them a small degree of autonomy. Paul said that to disobey Rome was to disobey God.

Paul accepted the institution of slavery, without which no civilization could have survived economically. No nation or religion dared challenged the justice of owning slaves before the introduction of steam power in the eighteenth century. Slaves were freed in the United States in 1863 and in England in 1833. Before then slave traders and slave owners were Christian, Jewish, Muslim, Hindu, and members of innumerable other religious groups. Paul in his letter to Philemon urges the slave master to be kind to his slave (see also Ephesians 6:5 and Titus 2:9).

As for the ownership of property and the accumulation of wealth, Paul was a good Jew who believed that all property belonged to God, but that man was free to use his property for his personal benefit so long as he exercised care in its use and returned a goodly portion to the service of God's mission on earth (see Psalms 24 and Leviticus 9). Although Paul had an abhorence of material things such as greed and riches, he allowed the possiblity of salvation to a wealthy man if he were to use his wealth for God's work. In 1 Timothy 6:17–21 Paul says wealth is not evil, only the love of wealth. Paul frequently urged his church members to donate to the church often and abundantly (see 2 Corinthians 8:1–9 and 9:6–15). Since life on earth was to be temporary, Paul said not to worry about the temporal conditions of mortal man on earth. Since man cannot serve two masters, God and mammon (Matthew 6:19–24), then man had better tend to God's business and prepare for the Second Coming.

Paul was a man of virtue wholly dedicated to spreading the gospel of the Christ, which was that man could be saved from original sin only by faith that God's grace had permitted the Christ to be sacrificed on the cross for the redemption of mortal sins. In Galatians 5:15–26 Paul offers a long list of virtues and vices. The vices included such acts as heresy, sedition, strife, hatred, drunkenness, and witchcraft. But of all of the mortal sins Paul listed pride was the greatest.

Although he condemned witchcraft, Paul did not take issue with other supernatural phenomena such as the performance of miracles in healing the sick or raising the dead from the grave. Nor did he condemn *glossalalia,* the miracle of people filled with the Holy Spirit being able to speak in unknown tongues. In 1 Corinthians 12:4–14 Paul says that Christians have many special gifts, including glossalalia, that can be used in the service of the church.

15

The Formation of the Christian Church— A.D. 100 to 400

After the death of Paul, the Christians had lost their charismatic leader and perhaps any certain direction for the future. For the next two centuries the church would fight to survive. Prospects for growth seemed dim and the future was beyond prediction. Christians risked being destroyed by the Roman government, which engaged in a program of persecution including even the execution of Christian leaders. Christians risked being outbid for the support of the people in the empire by rival religious sects such as Gnosticism and Mithraism. The Christian Church might even self-destruct as competing sects within sought to prove that their brand of Christianity was the only true gospel preached by Christ.

Although Christian churches had been founded in most of larger cities of the Roman Empire by the year 100, the total membership was small and by no means were the Christians any threat to the power of the empire. The Church found its greatest appeal among the lower classes, the tenant farmers, the craftsmen of the cities, and the numerous slaves. The heaviest concentrations of Christians were found in Greece, Palestine, Egypt, and Asia Minor (Syria and Bythinia). Statistics on membership in the Church are vague, but certainly by 100 no more than 20 percent of the people were Christians. A more likely figure would be 10 percent.

Paul had left a number of independent churches with no central authority to provide a common creed or system of government.

John Romer summarizes as follows: "There was a multiplicity of churches, of teachings, of holy books; it was a world with no clear Christian creed, no single body of accepted truth and no new Testament."[1] Despite the many obstacles to its survival, the Church did survive internal dissension, external competition, and persecution so that by the fourth century one brand of Christianity became the state church of the Roman Empire, endowed with such power that it could suppress rival sects and religions.[2]

By 200 many Christians had concluded that the Second Coming was not so imminent as believed in the first century. By now many Christians began to accept the fact that the millennium might not arrive before the millennium year, 1000. That Christ would eventually return to earth was never in doubt. The Second Coming was a basic tenet of Christian belief. Now the Christians were faced with the problems of survival and growth in a hostile world. Brave and intelligent leaders had to be found to guide the Church and retain the loyalty of its small membership. The state religion of Rome was still the Greek pantheon of gods with Roman names, but in reality religious worship had become the observance of routine rituals, primarily in the home, and the worship of the emperor as both the god Jupiter, father of the gods, and as a divine emperor bearing the title "Pontifex Maximus." In general, Roman rule was reasonably tolerant of other religions so long as they did not threaten the power of the state or undermine faith in the value of the pagan gods. By 200 most citizens of the empire paid their respect and devotion to the ancient gods by bringing their prayers and gifts to the altars of Zeus, Apollo, and Demeter in Greece; to Osiris and Isis in Egypt; and to Zoroaster and Mithra in Persia. The Jews, though dispersed, retained their loyalty to Jehovah. The Hellenistic cults, the Stoics and the Epicureans, were active in the eastern provinces.

Nonetheless, the Church was destined to survive and grow. By 250 the Church of the poor brethren had attracted to its membership people of wealth and status. The Church became a haven by which people of wealth could protect their holdings from Roman taxation. Wealthy people would bequeath their property to the Church. Widows with property were encouraged to forgo remarriage and join the Church, donating their property to it. In fact, the membership of the Church had a predominance of female members. Not only were widows recruited, but the Church was happy to receive young, virgin girls into its membership. Since girls were often married at the age of thirteen to men many years older, a large number of young widows became candidates for church membership. As the Church accumulated wealth there arose a need for skilled bureaucrats to manage and invest it. As a result the Church could offer attractive offices or benefices to ambitious men with talent and capacity for leadership.

But before the Church could celebrate its victory over all other competing religious groups, many dangerous obstacles had to be met and overcome. First there was the problem of how to survive Roman persecution. In the first two hundred years of Christianity, Christians were always in danger of being suppressed. One serious and early act of persecution occurred in 64, when the Emperor Nero falsely accused the Christians of setting fire to Rome. At this time the Apostles Peter and Paul were arrested and soon after executed, thereby making them early Christian martyrs. Emperors Domitian and Marcus Aurelius in the second and third centuries continued to persecute the Christians, adding to the list of martyrs destined to become saints and persons gifted with miraculous spiritual powers. Ironically, the more the government persecuted and killed Christians, the greater their numbers seemed to be, and they continued to increase their influence in the governing of the empire. In 249 Emperor Decius attempted to restore the worship of the Roman gods as a mark of respect for the one thousandth anniversary of the founding of Rome. All citizens were ordered to make sacrifices to the Roman gods. The Jews and Christians refused to obey the order. For the next two years severe persecutions of both groups followed. Emperor Diocletian, 284–305, attempted to destroy all vestiges of Christianity, the clergy, the Scriptures, and the entire Christian population.

But by now the Christian Church had become too powerful, too wealthy, and with too much political clout to be destroyed. Finally, the Roman rulers reversed their policy toward the Christians.

Constantine and the Council of Nicea

In 321 Emperor Constantine issued an edict of toleration by which Christianity was given recognition as one of the approved state religions. In 380 the Emperor Theodosius I declared Christianity the official state religion of the empire. Now the Church was in a position to turn the tables on its rivals and declare them to be heretics who must be destroyed. An orthodox creed was adopted and all persons who did not accept it could be declared heretics.

The process had already begun. In 325 when Constantine called together the Christian bishops from all over Christendom to meet in Nicea, a town near Ismik in modern Turkey, to debate the nature of Christ, and then to arrive at a final statement of Christian belief. A principal Christian heresy of the time was Arianism, which held that Christ was not divine, or at least not on the same level of divinity as God. A consensus of belief rejecting this position was adopted at Nicea, resulting in the well-known Nicene Creed, which is recited in all Christian churches. Arianism was ordered destroyed.

The Nicene Creed had first been drafted by the early Church historian Eusebius of Caesarea in Palestine. The creed declared that God was found in three parts, the Trinity: God the father, Christ the son, and the Holy Spirit, all parts of equal divinity. But the issue of the nature of Christ did not disappear from Christianity. How could a monotheistic religion have three Gods? If Jesus was God, and if Jesus was a man, does that mean that all men have within them the divine element? If that is true could not some ambitious monarch in the future claim that he is God and rule by divine right as absolute monarch over his people?

The Council of Nicea also drafted rules on worship practices, usury (the taking of interest on loans was declared immoral and illegal), and clerical celibacy as a practice not accepted in the Eastern church. In 381 the Council of Constantinople reaffirmed the Nicene Creed.

Interesting legends have appeared to explain why the pagan emperor Constantine converted to Christianity and made it possible for the Christian Church to become the state church of Rome. The traditional legend says that Constantine had a battle at Milvian Bridge in 312 with a rival for the throne, Licinius who was eventually defeated and killed by Constantine's forces. The victory came to

Constantine because he had a dream on the eve of the battle in which he saw a cross, which he interpreted as being a message from God that if his soldiers carried into battle banners bearing the sign of the cross then he would win the battle. A more likely explanation comes from the fact that Constantine's mother, Helene, was a Christian, and that is second wife was also a Christian. Perhaps Constantine was influenced by Christian teachers. The important thing is that Constantine became a Christian.

Much wealth was given to the Church, with which new church buildings, schools, and monasteries could be financed. The clergy became exempt from rendering public services to the state. Church properties that had been taken by the state were returned, and henceforth all church property became inviolate and beyond the control of the state. Since the church lands escaped taxation, land was increasingly given to the church. By the end of the Middle Ages, the Christian Church had become the principal landowner in Western Europe, oftentimes rivaling kings in terms of worldly possessions. Church wealth would become a source of misuse and scandal, and an important factor in the rise of the Protestant revolt against the Roman Catholic Church.

The Christian church was now in a position to create a system of government, to establish an offical canon of belief, to define the orthodox Scripture by deciding the makeup of the New Testament, and to draft a set of rules by which to administer the sacraments, regulate the clergy and the monastic orders, and centralize the control of the church in the hands of the bishop of Rome, the Pope. The Church would have the power to eliminate its competitors, the rival heresies and religious groups. It would begin an effort to exercise control over all aspects of human life, the family, the social conditions, the economic world, and the political systems of government.

Heresies

The question of what to do about rival Christian heresies and "pagan" religions was a major focus of concern for the early church. The Emperor Theodosius enacted over a hundred statutes against heretics. The most serious heresy, one that seriously threatened to divide Christendom, was *Ariansim*. In the fourth century a Christian teacher, Arius of Alexander, refused to accept the definition of God as stated in the Nicene Creed, that is, the idea of the Trinity. Arius could not accept that Jesus was the son of God. He saw Jesus as a great moral human being, a successful teacher of ethics, and a humanitarian who preached the message of love for all of mankind. But, after all, Jesus was a man, born of a natural mother, one who could not have existed before his birth. Arius could not accept a belief in a virgin birth, nor that there was a time when Jesus existed as the word in God before his natural birth. In brief, Jesus, the Christ, was not God and could not be equal to God.

The Arian heresy had its greatest acceptance among the northern tribes of

Germanic people after the missionary Ulfilas had brought Christianity to them in the fourth century. It was some of these Christian tribes who would invade Italy and sack Rome in the fourth and fifth centuries. one of the landmarks of Arianism today can be found in Ravenna, Italy, where an Arian church, St. Apollinare in Classe, is located. On the walls of this church are found some of the best examples of Byzantine-style murals depicting the Christian story and its principal characters. The church was built by the Arian king Theodoric in the sixth century. Although the Arians practiced a fairly tolerant attitude towards other Christians, orthodox Christians responded only in persecution and death sentences during the fourth to seventh centuries, when Arianism was finally destroyed.

Another heresy that threatened the authority of the state church was *Nestorianism*. Nestorius was a monk who became the patriarch of Constantinople (412–444). The patriarch of Constantinople was the prime contender with the bishop of Rome for the position of supreme leadership among the Christians. Nestorius denied that Mary, the mother of Jesus, was the mother of God. Mary was only the mother of another human being, named Jesus. If one were to accept the idea of the virgin birth, that would make Mary a goddess, which was theologically unacceptable. Nestorius was eventually condemned as a heretic and exiled to the desert in Egypt in 435. A few of his followers fled to India and China, but the largest portion of Nestorians remain today in Africa as the Ethiopian Christian Church.

Another fourth-century Christian heretic was the teacher *Apollinaris,* bishop of Laodicea. Apollinaris denounced the Arian position that Christ was only a human person, believing that Jesus was more divine than human. Nonetheless he thought that Jesus was not all God. Neither was Jesus a perfect human being, for he lacked the element of reason. Jesus had only two elements, body and soul. The views of Apollinaris were condemned by the Council of Constantinople in 381.

One more heresy that arose over the true nature of Jesus was *Monophysitism,* a heresy stating that Jesus had only one nature, a divine nature that occurred after his incarnation. The Monophysites had the support of the wife of the Emperor Justinian, Theodora. Although the heresy was banned by the Council of Chalcedon in 451, it continued to have the support of Theodora, enabling it to survive in Syria, Egypt, Ethiopia, Iraq, and Armenia. Today the Monophysites bear the name of the Jacobites, a name taken from an early Syrian leader, Jacob Baradi. The Jacobite Church recognizes the leadership of the patriarch of Antioch.

The bishop of Brescia in 390 claimed that there were 156 distinct heresies. Whether that number is correct or not, the fact is that the Christian Church was split many ways before the papacy and its support from the temporal power of the Roman Empire created a state of unity within Christendom during the period before the tenth century. Only a few more of more troublesome heresies need to be mentioned.

The *Donatists,* a group of Christians who resembled the Jewish Essenes had their base of operation in Carthage, North Africa. The Donatists stressed the importance of moral righteousness and puritanical standards of conduct. The clergy must remain pure and celibate, insulated from the evil outside world, and follow an ascetic lifestyle. An impure clergy could not administer the sacraments, for they would defile the sacred rites. The clergy must avoid all connections with business and politics. What was good for the clergy should also be practiced by the laity. Donatism was a movement to free the slaves and aid the poor peasants in their struggle for freedom from their wealthy landlord masters. The Donatists denounced the Roman government for its evil and corrupt emperors and bureaucrats. The Donatists hoped to secure an independent nation in which they would have self-rule and the use of their native Punic language. Until that time the Donatists demanded the separation of the church from the state. The Donatists were outlawed, persecuted, and destroyed.

Another heretical sect was *Montanism,* a second-century faith centered in Asia Minor. Montanus, its founder, was a charismatic prophet who took seriously the pentecostal experience, where the people are filled with the Holy Spirit and speak to God in strange tongues. Modern Pentecostals derive from these forefathers the idea that a church clergy and ritual are irrelevant to salvation. If one is filled with the Holy Spirit in his or her heart then communication with God can be direct and personal. Unlike the orthodox Church, the Montanists elevated women to a high status in their church. Women could also be gifted prophets and bearers of God's Truth, truly a heretical belief in the second century. Eve was pronounced the source of wisdom, and Moses' prophetic sister was given high recognition. Like the Donatists they stressed the need for a celibate, ascetic lifestyle for their members. Life on earth was only a brief interlude before Christ would come to earth again. While on earth the Montanists hoped to be free of all imperial control so that they might have the privilege of self-government and the use of their native language. The three hallmarks of Montanism were that the era of prophecy was still with us, that martyrdom for both men and women was a sacred experience, and that the Second Coming was imminent, and all persons should make ready for the event by living in chastity and poverty. Montanists welcomed persecution for this was a sign that the Second Coming was near. Moreover, life on earth was not worth the living, so filled was it with sin and pain. Hence all good Montanists anticipated the Parousia with joy.

During the fourth and fifth centuries a most challenging group of heretics followed a British monk, *Pelagius,* who was destined to engage in debate with St. Augustine over the issue of original sin. In 412 Augustine took issue with the contention by Pelagius that children were born free of sin and that they could not inherit sin from their parents. Pelagius concluded that if infants were born sinless there was no need for the sacrament of infant baptism. Pelagius also denied the doctrine of predestination. By virtue of the God-given gift of free will human beings always have the freedom to choose between good and evil. Augustine, of course disagreed. In his view, Adam and Eve were born free of sin, disobeyed God and as a result were destined to live in sin and pain, a condition that would be transmitted to all of the human race. In the eyes of Augustine mankind could be redeemed from original sin only by Grace of God. Even man's freedom to choose between good and evil was severely limited since God had preordained even before birth that some humans had no choice in the matter of salvation. Pelagius could not accept this rebuttal and was condemned in 418 by the Synod of Carthage, after which he disappeared from the Christian scene.

Gnosticism

During the first four centuries of Christendom the orthodox state church had to contend not only with internal heresies but also with several non-Christian religious groups. One the of the most popular of the "pagan" movements was Gnosticism. Some scholars think that the Gnostics might have won the contest for the souls of the Roman people if Emperor Constantine had not given his support to what became the dominant wing of Christianity. Elaine Pagels in her book *The Gnostic Gospels* offers a definitive account of the Gnostic movement.[3]

Before 300 several varieties of Gnosticism were being preached, most successfully in Asia Minor and North Africa. New light on the Gnostic religion was made available when the Nag Hammadi documents on Gnostic teachings were discovered in Egypt in 1945. Although there were several different Gnostic teachers, all had some basic teachings in common. The Gnostics borrowed freely from Greek Neo-Platonic and mystery cults, as well as from Judaism, Christianity, and Zoroastrianism.

The principal Gnostic teaching was the belief that knowledge about God was a form of special or secret knowledge, called gnosis. Gnosticism's best-known teacher was Valentius, an Alexandrian mystic and theologian of the second century.

Gnosticism was a special form of knowledge or wisdom that could be transmitted to others only by a process of intuition or meditation. Gnosis could not be learned by any rational or logical process of study. Gnostics denied the Jewish-Christian belief that Jehovah was the one, true God. Gnostics had a dual system of divinity in which there were two gods, the high god or the first principle god, and a low god of creation who created the world and all that is in it. The highest god is invisible and incomprehensive to mortal minds. When he joined with Thought or Logos the realm of the Spirit was created. From Logos was created two new deities, Christ and a female Holy Spirit. From this creation there arose Jesus, the Savior. The Savior then joined with a lower form of wisdom, called Sophia. Out of this creation came the lower God of creation, the God who is called by the Jews Jehovah, and by Plato the Demiurge. Jesus, the Logos, was never a real human person, for he was always pure spirit. His physical body was only an illusion.

The lesser god created male and female humans equal, a revolutionary concept for second-century mankind. In the Gnostic church women played a prominent role, an idea that did not endear Gnostics to the then male-dominated world. Since Jesus had never been born or died there could not have been a Resurrection.

Without a Resurrection experience there was no foundation for the Christian Church. Gnostics saw no need for a church organization, priests, or creeds. Gnosis is within the souls of all persons. In the manner of Buddha, the sacred truth, gnosis, is learned by a process of meditation. That is, the kingdom of God is within you, waiting for you to discover God for yourself. Gnosticism also solved the puzzling problem of how one god could create both good and evil, by creating a dualism of two gods, one for goodness and another, Jehovah, for evil, an idea rejected by both Jews and Christians. Gnosis would give to man freedom from sin and the promise of immortality, although immortality was for the soul alone. Life on earth was evil, but since mankind must exist on earth then human life must be lived in an ascetic, purified manner.

Gnosticism was not a popular religion, neither to understand nor to practice, and this fact may have contributed to its failure to win the competition with the more orthodox forms of Christianity. There was also no clergy or organization to maintain a measure of order and direction to the group. Members were initiated into Gnostic groups by an act of baptism in which the secret knowledge of gnosis would be imparted to them. The question remains: "Were the Gnostics Christians?" since they were persecuted by the state church as heretics and successfully so, there seems to be little doubt that they were Christians.

Marcionism

Marcionism, another competing sect, never claimed to be Christian. During the second and third centuries Marcion, a Mesopotamian ascetic and visionary, taught a form of Persian Zoroastrianism in which dual gods, one of light or goodness and one of darkness and evil, ruled the universe. The good god was so pure that no man could approach him. This god, the god of love also, did not belong to the earth world of evil matter. This supreme god later created a lower god, Jehovah, who then created the material world of earth and man. This lower god was deemed to be unworthy of worship. But to redeem the world the god of love did send Jesus to earth. Jesus was not the messiah of the Jews. He appeared to be human, but that was an illusion, for Jesus was only pure spirit. Being pure spirit there could have been no Resurrection for there was no body to resurrect. Marcion rejected all the Old Testament and most of the New Testament. He accepted only the gospel of Luke and Paul's epistles. Paul was the only one of the apostles accepted by Marcian. Jesus could never have found his origins in the Jewish lineage, for he would have been contaminated by the evil Jehovah. Marcionistes resembled the Gnostics in that they rejected the sensual, material nature of man for a life lived in a monastic setting in chastity and poverty. No member was to eat meat, consume alcohol, or enjoy any of the pleasures of human mortals. Sex was a special taboo. Marriage was tolerated as a necessary evil for procreation only. The ideal life was the monastic one, without wife and children, and isolated from the temptations of the world.

Marcion died in 160, after having established ascetic communities in Syria, Carthage, Antioch, Smyrna, and Egypt. Although Marcion in most respects found his concept of the god of love in the letters of Paul, his ideas were condemned as a heresy.

Manicheism

Manicheism was another dualitic religion. The founder was Manes, a Persian prince A.D. 216–274, who sought to unite several contemporary religions into one, new religion.[4] Manes hoped to discover a common thread in Buddhism, Zoroastrianism, and Christianity by which this new faith could be formed. Manes regarded himself as a prophet of all three of these religions. At first his friends applauded him for his grand design, but soon the people of Persia rejected the idea of only one, universal religion. Even in the twentieth century mankind is not ready for a universal religion, as demonstrated by the meager success of the Bahai faith to win converts anywhere in the world. Manes was imprisoned for heresy and later died in prison. Manicheism did survive in India and China, but in the fifth century it was branded a heresy in the Christian world and destroyed.

For a brief time Manicheism did offer a threat to orthodox Christianity. Even Augustine flirted with Manicheism in his youth. Some scholars believe that Manicheism did resurface in the Christian world during the thirteenth century, when similar beliefs were held by a small group of dissenters in southern France known as the Cathari or the Albigensians.

Manicheism shared many beliefs with the Gnostics and the Marcionites. Two god forces ruled the Manicheism world, one light and goodness, the other of darkness and evil. In the creation process there was first the god of light, the father of greatness. The the god of darkness, Jehovah, was created, and he became the evil one, the prince of darkness, or Satan. Hence Manes rejected totally the Old Testament. But to save mankind from the evil world the god of light creates from himself the Mother of Life. Adam, the primordial man, is saved from sin by the Mother of Life, who will send to earth a savior, the son of God, or Jesus. The spirit of light, Jesus, is found in all things on earth, for the spirit of light in the form of light particles lives in all things. After death it is these light particles, the souls of the dead, that are carried to paradise.

Procreation is discouraged, for the particles of Light are in the sperm, and so long as sex and babies exist these divine particles cannot be released. Finally the world will end and all things will be destroyed. Then Christ and all particles will ascend to paradise, where Christ will judge them as being good or evil. After 1468 years the world will be consumed by fire. The purified ashes will be gathered and brought to paradise. The evil ashes will be thrown into a pit and buried forever. Never again will the god of light need to do battle with the evil prince of darkness.

Manicheism was a religion best suited for philosophers and saints, not for the common people. An esoteric theology was beyond comprehension by the unschooled, and the requirements for salvation could be met only in a monastery, if even there. Manes realized that only a few person could meet his rigid standards of morality. Only the elect, a small group, could be expected to live the perfect life. As for the masses, their predestined mission on earth was to served the elect with food and shelter. Upon death the souls of the elect ascend at once to paradise, but the soul of the common man must endure an endless cycle of births and rebirths, as in the Hindu faith. When the world comes to an end, all bodies of the dead will arise to join their souls in paradise.

Manichean services had many Christian features. Most of the New Testament was read, especially the letters of Paul. Hymns were sung in praise of the planets, the sources of light on earth, and in honor of the four elements of fire, air, water, and wind. Christmas was observed in honor of the sun. Each year one month of fasting and seven days of atonement were observed. The faith accepted miracles, angels, and magic as natural properties of the divine spirit. Salvation came by way of Jesus, who holds the key to the true knowledge of self. However, the Manicheans had little in the way of a clergy or church government. They were antigovernment, antipapal, and opposed to everything associated with the Roman Empire. It was no wonder that the movement was branded heretical and suppressed by the Persian government. Manes was executed in 276.

Mithraism

One more challenge to orthodox Christianity was a surviving remnant of the ancient Persian worship of the bull, Mithraism. Mithra was the Persian god allied to the dominant god of light, Ahura Mazda. When Mithraism was revived in the second and third centuries it found its greatest appeal among the Roman soldiers and "macho" men who prized the value of brute strength, like that of the bull. Mithra was a warrior god dedicated to fighting evil. He was symbolized by a bull figure that portrayed courage, militancy, and manhood. Worship centered on the sacrifice of a bull, after which its blood would be drunk. Thus the spiritual properties of Mithra could be assimilated into the human body. Salvation of the soul was gained by pursuing a disciplined life, a life given to a Stoical pattern of chastity and control of the passions of anger, greed, and gluttony. The virtue of fighting evil also became a potent force for stimulating the soldier in battle against enemies on earth. The war against the Devil will finally end in victory for the army of Light, the army of Ahura Mazda and Mithra. Since the communion meal or the Eucharist in the Christian church consumes the bread and wine, symbolical of the blood and body of Christ, one cannot but speculate that the Christian rite may have influenced by the Mithraic practice of consuming the blood of the bull. By the fourth century the orthodox Christian church had become the state church of the Roman Empire. Allied with the power of the state, by the sixth century most of the heresies and competing cults had been suppressed.

The one Christian Church, henceforth, was to expand, grow in numbers and power until it becomes the dominant force of medieval society. Now the Church could turn its attention to the organization of highly structured system of government and the establishment of a universally practiced system of worship and sacred rites. It would be a system of religion few persons would dare to question or challenge until the sixteenth century.

16

Islam

One of the great world religions is Islam which, like Christianity, has its roots in Judaism. One fifth of the world's religious population belongs to the Islamic faith, far more than those who are Jewish, and about half the world membership of Christianity.

Travelers in the United States or Western Europe know that when they see a building with a cross on top of it or a tall spire reaching toward heaven from the roof top they are probably in a Christian country. In Islamic lands the dominant faith is more easily identified by a large building, often with a domed roof, and adjoining it a tall tower, or minaret. This is probably an Islamic mosque, or place of worship. In Christian lands some of the older churches might have a similar tower near the church that houses a bell to call the faithful to worship. The Muslim minaret serves the same purpose, to call the faithful to prayer or to worship. The call to prayer is usually given by a person, a *muezzin,* who chants a call in the form of a prayer to awaken his fellow Muslims. Sometimes today this call comes in a form of a mechanical recording, sometimes lacking in acceptable recording standards. On the streets in an Islamic city, a Western visitor notices that most of the women are dressed in black, flowing robes, or a *chador.* This dress covers all of the body. The face sometimes is almost completely covered by a black veil, with only slits provided for the eyes. Occasionally the robes may come in green, purple, white, and other colors.

A Muslim mosque bears resemblance to a Christian church. The building contains a large auditorium for congregational prayer and worship. At one end of the room there is an altar or pulpit, facing toward Mecca, from which an imam or priest will read the Koran, offer prayers, and give an instructive message or sermon. There are no pews or seats, so the communicants stand or kneel on richly carpeted floors. Both Muslims and non-Muslims who come into the mosque must remove their shoes at the entrance and enter in bare feet. Visitors are provided with felt slippers to replace their shoes. Many Christian cathedrals also have no pews or seats for the people.

Mosques are adorned with beautiful stained-glass windows that admit an abundance of light. However, unlike Christian windows, the patterns contain no human or animal figures, only geometric symbols or abstract pictures. Since human forms cannot be depicted in Islam, there are no statues of Muhammad or other Islamic prophets. Islamic worship stresses the need for body purifications, so outside of the mosque there are water basins in which the people can their wash their hands, faces, and even their feet.

A Christian or a Jew would find many familiar passages and commandments in the Koran, the Muslim holy book. Muhammad, the founder of Islam, borrowed freely from the Hebrew Old Testament. Both Christians and Muslims acknowledge their spiritual debt to Judaism, the Hebrew prophets, and the holy city of Jerusalem.

In the Christian world many misconceptions about Islam prevail. Too often the people of Islam are pictured as being wild, nomadic Arabs living in the desert with their camels and goats, the men enjoying the pleasures of many wives, the women treated no better than the animals. Islamic people are often portrayed as uncivilized zealots like Ayatollah Khomeini in Iran, thriving on hatred, the execution of enemies at home, and the waging of war against enemies abroad.

Unfortunately too few Americans are students of medieval history, a time when Europe was in the Dark Ages and German barbarians from northern Europe had invaded and conquered the Roman Empire without sufficient time to absorb Roman civilization. During this period, 500–1100, a traveler in the Muslim world of the Middle East, North Africa, and Spain would have been astonished to find cities in which people lived in luxury and were steeped in the sciences and philosophy. It was the Muslim, Arabic scholars who did the most to preserve Greco-Roman culture during this time, eventually transmitting it to the Christian world. It was this Arabic heritage on which the European Renaissance was to be built after the fourteenth century.

But the Islamic Arabs were not content to use the Greco-Roman heritage. For four centuries they enlarged the scope of scientific and mathematical knowledge far beyond what they had inherited. Muhammad commanded his people to study and create learning in all fields of science, philosophy, literature, and art. Muslim scientists knew how blood circulates in the body, how the planets revolve about the sun, and how mathematics could use the concept of zero advantageously. The works of the famous Jewish philosopher, Maimonides, were translated into Arabic so that his wisdom might be used by Islamic theologians. If Christians visit Spain today and enter the massive Mosque of Cordova, a part of which is now a Catholic cathedral, or visit the Alahambra in Granada, all doubts will be put to rest concerning the value of the world's Islamic heritage.

The Life of Muhammad

Just like Christianity Islam can locate its birth at a specific place and date. Islam was born in Saudi Arabia, in a town called Mecca, in 623. Muhammad ("the Highly Praised One"), Islam's prophet, was born in Mecca in 571. His father died before Muhammad's birth and his mother died when he was six years old so he was reared by a good, intelligent uncle. Legends about Muhammad's birth say that his mother was told by angels that her son would become a prophet and a ruler. It is said that on the night of his birth a star shone so brightly that his mother could see for miles. As soon as the baby Muhammad was born he picked up a handful of earth and he also saw this bright star.

Muhammad's uncle was a trader who often traveled along the trade routes that traversed the Fertile Crescent area from Egypt, Palestine, Syria, Persia, and on to India. As a young man Muhammad traveled the same routes, first with his uncle, later as an employee of a wealthy widow who engaged in trading with Eastern countries. At the age of twenty-three, Muhammad married his employer, Khadija. Although he had little formal education, he was a most intelligent observer of the customs and religions of the countries through which he traveled. He learned about the religions of the Jews, the Persian Zoroastrians, the Indian Hindus, and the Christians of Palestine and Greece.

About 613 Muhammad, then age forty, began to experience visions in which the angel Gabriel would come to him while he was living like a hermit in a cave. Gabriel told Muhammad to go into the world and preach a new revelation from Allah, his God. Muhammad began to preach to his neighbors a message that first condemned the old polytheistic beliefs and then proclaimed himself the prophet of a new monotheistic religion. As with Jesus, who preached a new revelation, Muhammad incurred the wrath of his fellow Arabs. His life was in such great danger that he and his few followers were forced to leave Mecca and seek refuge in a nearby town of Medina in 622. The event, known as the Hegira, became the date to mark the birth of Islam. In Medina, Muhammad organized a small army to return to Mecca and fight his enemies, which occurred in 630. His conquest of Mecca in 630 established that city as the most holy of all Islamic cities.

For centuries, Mecca had been the most sacred of places for the primitive religion of the Arabs because in the city there is a sacred stone, the Kaaba, around which the people made their prayers and offerings. So Mecca, like Jerusalem, became the only place above all other places for the devout to visit. Islam requires that once in a lifetime a good Muslim must visit Mecca in the form of a relgious pilgrimage. It is said that a visit to Mecca and the Kaaba will assure one's soul a place in paradise.

At first Muhammad hoped that his new revelations from Allah would appeal to both Christians and Jews and convert them to Islam. Although Muhammad accepted the holy status of Abraham, Moses, most of the Jewish prophets, and Jesus Christ, neither Christians nor Jews became converts to Islam in any significant numbers. Rejection of Allah meant that in the future those Jews and Christians who lived in Islamic countries would be classified as second-class citizens but usually allowed to practice their religions so long as they paid special taxes. Muslims did persecute their Christian and Jewish subjects, but historians agree in general that if these persecutions are compared to those committed by Christians against Muslims, as during the Crusades and the Spanish Inquisition, Muslim treatment of minority groups was much more tolerant.

Muhammad traced his lineage to the Jewish patriarch Abraham. He came from a line of ancestors that claimed ten generations from Adam to Noah, and ten generations from Noah to Abraham. With Abraham Islam, like Judaism, began its life on earth.

The Arabs as a race trace their ancestry from Abraham's illegitimate son, Ishmael, whose mother was Hagar, the handmaiden of Abraham's wife, Sarah. Islam teaches also that the holy stone in Mecca, the Kaaba, was built by Abraham and Ishmael. The Koran teaches that at another stone, Al-agra in Jerusalem, God ordered Ishmael to be sacrificed by Abraham, not the other son, Isaac as related in the Old Testament. Isaac and Ishmael buried their father, Abraham, in the Cave of Machpelah near Hebron. The twelve sons of Ishmael founded the several Arabic tribes (see Genesis 25:13-16). Ishmael married an Egyptian woman, Fatima. The same angel Gabriel who was God's messenger to Daniel (Daniel 8:15ff) revealed the Koran to Muhammad. Tradition says that Muhammad traveled to Jerusalem on his white horse, El-Burak, where he prayed with Gabriel to all of the Jewish prophets and then ascended to heaven from the al-agra stone. It is this stone that is housed in the mosque, the Dome of the Rock, in Jerusalem, which is Islam's third most holy city after Mecca and Medina. Legends say that Muhammad returned finally to Medina after passing through seven heavens to God.

After Muhammad had won a victory over his enemies in Medina, he was in a position to consolidate his position as the prophet of a new faith. He claimed to be the last of a long line of patriarchs and prophets, preceded only by Jesus Christ. He lived out the rest of his life in Medina with his wives (ten) and his daughter and heir, Fatima. He lived a simple life in humility and poverty, but dedicated to the propagation of his faith. By the time of his death in 632 he had gained the support of the many tribes in Arabia. Possibly his several marriages were to bind the leadership of some of the tribes to himself and his religion. Muhammad never foresaw the day when Islamic rule would extend beyond the boundaries of Arabia to the furthermost parts of the world, India and China.

Muhammad did not claim to be anything more than a devout prophet or messenger of Allah. He denied that he had any supernatural or divine powers. Although Muslims never worship Muhammad as a god nor award to him a greater measure of honor than the Koran, still many legends would arise to credit Muhammad with powers to work miracles. Soon Muhammad's followers ascribed to him the power to act as an intercessor with God to plead for mercy for the sinners in the last days of judgment. It was claimed that Muhammad could control the movement of the planets, that he was born without sin and lived a sinless life, and that the Muslim mystics saw in Muhammad an expression of God himself, the very same divine light that emanated from God and through which all creation occurred.

Muhammad left as his heir a daughter, Fatima, who married Ali Talib, a cousin. Other of his followers thought that a friend of Muhammad's, Abu-Bakr, a tribal chieftan or caliph, should be his successor. This dispute over who was the rightful heir would create the two most prominent sects within Islam, the Shiites and the Sunnis. Abu-Bakr declared that if Muhammad was dead, he still lived among those who would venerate him as God. Among the common people it was easy to worship Muhammad as god and still living.

The Spread of Islam

The story of the rapid expansion of Islam throughout the Eastern and the Mediterranean worlds is a record that even a skeptic must admit might have been inspired and engineered by the mighty God, Allah. Within a generation Islam had conquered and united all of the Arabic tribes under the leadership of Muhammad's successors. Caliph Oman subdued the Sassanian Empire by 634. In just twenty more years Islam had conquered Syria, Palestine, all of Mesopotamia, which includes modern Iran and Iraq, and Egypt. By 715 Muslim rule had been extended from Spain in the West, to India in the East, and all across the Mediterranean shores of North Africa. The defeat of Muslim expansion into northern Europe came when the Frankish King, Charles Martel, in 735 checked the Muslim advance at the battle of Tours in southern France. Thus until the fifteenth century, Islam's Western European expansion was confined to the Iberian peninsula, Spain and Portugal.

However, Christian Europe remained fearful of Muslim invasion, especially from the East through the Balkans by the Ottoman Turks, until the Muslims were decisively defeated in the seventeenth century. First came the Seljuk Turks into Byzantine territory in 1074, then the Mongols under Genghis Khan, 1206–27, into Russia and the Balkan countries, and later the Ottoman Turks, who finally conquered the eastern lands of Christianity by 1284. The frightened Christian countries in Western Europe, under the leadership of the Roman Catholic popes, began to wage war against Islamic states, beginning in 1047 with the First Crusade. The Crusades enlisted the support of popes, Christian monarchs, feudal nobility, merchants, freebooters and adventurers, all for fame and fortune as well as to protect the Christian world from the Muslim infidel. Altogether eight Crusades, 1096 to 1270, brought Christian soldiers and adventurers to Constantinople and Jerusalem. Wherever the Crusaders went, cities and countryside were sacked and looted, while the Christian monarchs fought one another for control of the spoils. The First Crusade did manage a Christian state, governed on a French model, until the Muslim forces under Saladin recaptured the area in 1187. Five later crusades were abject failures. By 1270 the Christians had been driven from the Holy Land, marking the end of the Crusades.

Although the Crusades did little to enhance the image of a peace-loving Christ, they did introduce Western Europe to the rich heritage of science, literature, and art that the Islamic world had borrowed from Greco-Roman cultures. The Crusades were one instrumental factor in the development of a new age of learning and science in Western Europe, the Renaissance. For the bankers and merchants of Venice and Florence the Crusades opened new trade routes to the East, sowing the seeds of capitalism, from which profits the Renaissance achievements would be financed. Feudal nobility received a boost with the formation of three knightly Christian orders, the Knights of St. John or Hospitalers (today known as the Knights of Malta), the Teutonic Knights, and the Knight Templars. These orders of feudal nobility were given special tax and religious privileges by their kings and popes in exchange for rendering military and medical services to the marching crusaders.

The final Islamic threat to Europe was removed when Christian forces defeated the Ottoman Turks in Austria in 1697. The defeat was recognized by the treaty of Carlowitz in 1699. India remained under Muslim (Mogul) rule until the Mogul rulers were defeated by the British trading companies and empire builders of the eighteenth century. India became an offical part of the Britsh Empire in 1858, following the defeat of the native Indians in the Sepoy Rebellion of 1857.

The Koran and the Sacred Traditions of Islam

Knowledge about Islamic beliefs is found primarily in the Islamic holy book, the Koran, or "Recitations." The Koran is composed of the sayings of Muhammad, which were written sometime after his death. The wisdom of Muhammad is, according to Islamic belief, the revealed truth of Allah, and so the Koran is regarded as a collection of sacred, infallible truths. Muhammad is proclaimed by his followers to be a prophet who was promised by God to reform Judaism, in the same manner that Christ was sent to reform it. However, Islam, while accepting Christ as one of the prophets, does place him below Muhammad in terms of spiritual rank. Only Muhammad is the true prophet of God.

The Koran contains 114 *suras*, or chapters. With the exception of the first chapter they are arranged roughly in the order of length from the longest to the shortest. Hence there is no logical order for the sayings of Muhammad, an illiterate man who believed he had received them from the angel Gabriel. The Koran is based on the Old Testament, with a few parts taken from the New Testament. Since Islam accepts the validity of all of the Jewish patriarchs from Abraham to Moses, the Jewish prophets, and the Christian Christ, both Jews and Christians might claim that the Koran is only a modification of Torah and the Christian Gospels. Allah's name appears in the Koran ninety-nine times.

The Koran contains rules on all aspects of life, government, family, sex, children, slaves, charity, economics, war, and peace, in brief the entire gamut of human activity. A Muslim is born into the faith and dies in the faith, a condition most similar to the Jewish faith. In addition to the Koran, the Islamic sacred literature includes the Hadiths, a collection of six books prepared in the ninth century. Shortly after the death of Muhammad, his followers found that the Koran was inadequate to explain all of the guiding rules by which Muslims were expected to live.

Within two hundred years after Muhammad many *sunnahs,* or oral traditions developed, designed to explain what Muhammad said, what his life was like, and what practices had developed according to the rules laid down in the Koran. The Hadiths were an attempt to codify and organize these oral traditions into some useful and acceptable form. The most orthodox Muslims reject the legitimacy of the Hadiths. Like some fundamentalistic Christians, they accept only the true word of God, in this case the Koran, as sacred scripture.

The Islamic faith places the duty to obey the law as God's commands as the highest of all commandments. Islam, like Judaism, might be called a religion of law. Islamic law is the application of the guiding principles found in the Koran to the everyday life of all Muslims. Islamic law takes two forms. One is the *sharia,* judicial pronouncements of the highest importance because they are believed to represent the will of God, not of man. All aspects of life on earth are covered in the sharia. The other branch of law, the *fiqh,* is the manmade interpretations of how God's law is to be applied in judicial courts. In the law schools, students preparing for the legal profession would use the fiqh books as their texts.

In Christianity professional religious scholars, or theologians, have played an important role in defining the true meaning of Christ's message. The several Christian denominations have had their origins in the theological thoughts of such men as St. Augustine, St. Thomas Aquinas, Martin Luther, John Calvin, or John Wesley. In Islam theologians play a most minor role. No matter what the difference are among the Muslims, all tend to adhere closely to the fundamental statement of principles given in the Koran.

Two schools of theology that are important in clarifying Islamic principles and that were influenced by contacts with Greek philosophy and its use of reason to solve human problems were the Mu'tazilite school and the followers of Al-Ash'ari, both of which developed in the ninth and tenth centuries A.D.

The Mu'tazilite school applied rational interpretation to the study of the Koran to discover certain common beliefs that undergird all of the Islamic faith. First proclaimed was the all-importance of God, the one and only God, Allah. Any form of dualism or polytheism was rejected. The goal of finding unity of belief was affirmed also by the rejection of any form of belief in predestination. God, this group asserted, gave to mankind the gift of free will by which it could choose good or evil. This more liberal school of thought is accepted today by the Shiite branch of Muslims.

A more conservative school of theology follows the ideas of another teacher, Al-Ash'ari, who accepted Greek rationalism as a convenient tool to be used as a dialectical weapon to convince the non-Islamic subjects of Islamic states that they should convert to a better form of religion, that is, to Islam. Reason was not the way to truth. Truth had already been found and expressed by Muhammad in the Koran.

The Basic Tenets of Islam

What message did Muhammad preach? It was a simple, nontechnical message that the common, illiterate masses could understand. There is only one God, Allah. He has no human attributes, nor is he to be depicted in any human form in art or statue. Allah is the creator of life and death, the guide to a righteous life, the friend and protector of the sick and the poor. In the Final Judgment after death Allah will judge the souls to be condemned to hell or to be rewarded with a life of joy in a heaven abounding with beautiful maidens, lush gardens, and cool rivers. As it is recorded in the Koran, sura 2.

> True piety is this: To believe in God, and the Last Day, the angels and the Book, and the prophets, to give one's substance however cherished to kinsmen and orphans, the needy, the traveler, the beggars, and to ransom the slave, to perform prayers, and to pay the alms, and they who fulfill the covenant and endure with fortitude, misfortune, hardships and peril, these are they who are true in their faith, these are the truly God-fearing.

The core tenets of Islam are recorded in the five pillars of faith, the duties owed to God:

1. First there is the confession of faith, the *shahadah,* always said in the form of a prayer, as follows: "There is no God but the one God, and Muhammad is his prophet." The prayer also asserts the belief in the Koran, the angels, and the last judgment.

2. To perform the *salat,* or daily prayers, five times a day, always facing toward Mecca. The person in prayer bows first from the waist and then kneels in a prostrate position with the forehead touching the ground. The most essential prayer offered in both public and private worship is in the Koran, sura 1, "The Opening":

> In the name of Allah, the Beneficent, the Merciful, praise be to Allah, Lord of the World, the Beneficent, the Merciful, owner of the Day of Judgment. Thee alone we worship. Thee alone we ask for help. Show us the straight path, the path of those whom Thou hast favored; not the path of those who earn Thine anger nor of those who go astray.

Before prayer the body must be purified by water, or sand if water is not available. The hand, feet, face, and genitals are all to be washed. Even the bathrooms are so arranged that the occupant will face in the direction of Mecca. The summons to prayer is announced by a caller or muezzin, who chants a prayer from atop a tall tower or minaret. Today mechanical recordings are often used.

3. The third pillar, or *zakat,* makes compulsory the giving of alms, or a contibution to charity based on a certain percentage of one's wealth, commonly an amount equal to one-fifth of one's income.

4. The fourth pillar requires the observance of Ramadan, a month-long period of fasting from dawn to dusk during the month of Ramadan, the ninth month of the year. This observance is based on the Jewish period of atonement. In Islamic terms, Ramadan honors the time when God revealed his word to Muhammad in 614. All people over fourteen years old are required to take no food or drink, nor engage in sexual intercourse, during the daylight of the period of denial. The end of Ramadan is celebrated with a two-day festival called Id-al-Fitr.

5. The fifth pillar requires that each Muslim make a *haj,* a pilgrimage to Mecca, once in his or her lifetime. Pilgrims go to Mecca with shaved heads dressed in a special ritual gown. In Mecca the prescribed routine is to circle the Kaaba seven times and then kiss the Kaaba. Next to entering paradise, the haj is a Muslim's supreme experience of spiritual achievement.

Since Islam is so vital a part of the everyday life of a Muslim, volumes would be required to detail how religion enters into every aspect of public and private life. The enforcement of Allah's guidelines for a righteous life on earth requires more than the moral impulses from a person's conscience and voluntary compliance. It requires the strong arm of government and law. As a rule, the government of a typical Muslim state is a theocratic monarchy in which the ruler is the head of both state and church. In Islam each Muslim is free to read the Koran and to act as his or her own priest, as within the Christian Protestant churches. There is no hierarchy of priests and bishops. There are religious officials, the imams, who preside over the worship services in the mosques, and who instruct the members in their faith and obligations. Mosques and their religious bodies conduct schools for the training of children in the faith. At a higher level of education, Islam has provided universities, theological seminaries, and law schools for training professional religious leaders. The trained legal experts are the mullahs or ulemas, who serve as religious teachers and as judges in the courts. The University of Al-Azar in Cairo, Egypt, is considered to be the best institution for religious instruction and legal interpretation. In a sense, Al-Azar might be compared to the Vatican in Rome as being the single most authoritative source for the determination of Islamic truths, that is, God's law, the Shariah.

Is there a moral and judicial dilemma posed by the Islamic doctrine of free will and the belief that Allah rules all acts and thoughts of man, as if life for each person must have been predetermined before birth? Yet the Koran makes man the master of his own fate also. There is no intercessor to plead man's future destiny on earth or after death. However, Islam is divided on the issue of predestination. Those who follow the policies of the Ummayad dynasty accept a belief in predestination, while those who follow the policies laid down by the Abbasid dynasty hold to the doctrine of free will. One theologian of today, Al Askari, has offered a solution to the dilemma. All of man's acts are predetermined by God, but man has the responsibility for his acts because he wills to do them. He concludes that man's freedom to act is only a delusion; he only thinks he has a free choice, for in the final judgment God decides man's fate by his own standards.

An Islamic saying declares that marriage and family are one half of the good life. The other half is obedience to the Koran and its duties. Family rules seem to closely follow Jewish practices, as stated in the Torah. Marriage is an important step on the road to Paradise. It is a religious institution. In practice today marriages are still arranged by the parents of the bride and bridegroom. Polygamy is allowed but the husband is limited to four wives, although Muhammad had as many as ten wives. King Abdul Aziz, founder of the kingdom of Saudi Arabia, in the early 1900s had over three hundred wives, giving rise to forty-two sons by twenty-two mothers. Most of the marriages were entered into for politcal reasons. The king could consolidate the many Arabic tribes into his realm by marriage with the daughters of tribal chieftans. In practice very few Muslim men have more than one wife, since the husband is financially responsible for the full support of his family, and each wife must be financed equally on an acceptable standard of living. Probably fewer than 20 percent of Arab men have multiple wives. Husbands and wives are permitted to have equal rights of inheritance. Strict segregation of the sexes is required outside of the home, both in the mosques and the streets.

Women in Islamic Society

Muhammad said, "If a man and a woman are alone in one place, the third person is Satan." Women, being desirable sex objects for men, must be secluded, properly robed, and protected from male advances. From the Western point of view women in the Muslim world seem to be captives in a male-dominated society with no rights or positions of respect and worth. If one compares the position of women in the pre-Islamic world of primitive religions, Muhammad did advance the position of women. But by modern feminist standards Muslim women are still living in the Dark Ages.[1]

Muhammad's concept of the proper role for women might be compared with the Judaic concept of a good wife, as told in Proverbs 31:10–31, where the good wife, one deserving of great praise, is the wife who serves her husband, is virtuous, works diligently to care for the children and the home, and fears the Lord. Since much of the Koran was borrowed from the Jewish Old Testament, Muhammad would probably have accepted the Jewish version of a good wife.

Women played an important part in Muhammad's life. Muhammad's first wife, Khadija, was his former employer in her trading business. She bore him six children, and she was the source of money for his religious missions. Although he married as many as ten women, he ordered that no Muslim man should have more than four wives, and that each wife was to be treated equally. Women were given legal rights in the courts, and even the seclusion of women in the home was designed to protect them from rape and male violence. Women were allowed to be doctors, since male doctors were forbidden to examine and to treat female patients. Even though male children were always preferred to female children, girls could inherit a third of their father's wealth.

A Muslim woman in public is recognized by her veil and chador, a robe covering the entire body. The chador may be more a traditional custom than a religious requirement. In most Islamic countries today, especially in the modern, Westernized countries of Egypt and Morocco, young women and girls customarily wear western dress in public, usually dresses, for pants are taboo. Shorts are totally forbidden. Among the more fundamentalist Muslims, such as those in Iran today and among the puritanical Wahhabic sect of Muslims, even the girls must wear the veil and chador. In Iran women are not permitted to go shopping. The police watch for women who leave the seclusion of their home and will arrest those who do. Bedouin women and women in the rural villages seem to have more freedom of movement outside of the home, but they too wear the veil and chador.

In Egypt Muslim women have the greatest amount of freedom in the Islamic world. Women are beginning to enter the business world and the professions. Almost half the college students in Egypt are women. Even in conservative Saudi Arabia a third of the approximately two million students in all grades are female. In Egyptian universities, as elsewhere in the Muslim world, the sexes are carefully segregated—as a result female students cannot attend classes taught by male professors, a potentially severe handicap to their education. So television is used to pipe lectures by men into the classrooms of women. In Egypt the wives of former president Anwar Sadat and the current president Hosni Mubarak are providing leadership and role models for the feminist movement. Yet Nawal El Saadam, a fifty-year-old doctor and feminist leader writes that in modern Egypt women can be married without their consent, women cannot petition for divorce, women have no right of child custody in case of divorce, husbands can forbid their wives from traveling or working outside the home, baby girls are frequently subject to female circumcision, that is, removal of the clitoris, women have no right to alimony if they are divorced due to their refusal to have sexual relations, and women have no right to use contraceptives. In the judicial courts it takes two women to equal one man as a witness before a court.

Sandra Mackey describes the role of a Muslim woman:

> Women survive by placing themselves in the hands of men. It is in this basic relationship of master and servant that a woman's physical needs are met. Emotionally she draws her strength from other women, from her place in the family, from her image of herself as a prized possession, and, after marriage, from her role as a mother. . . .
>
> For like most Saudi women, they had little to do but wait. A woman waits to be married, then she waits for the next time she will have a sexual reunion with her husband, then she waits for the next child to be born, and finally she

waits for old age, when, relieved of her child-bearing duties, she assumes a place of honor within her family.[2]

Modern Business in the Islamic World

The Koran prescribes the basic rules by which all nonfamily affairs are to be governed. In the areas of business and economics all transactions are governed by the laws of both church and state, for there is no separation of the two. In general, commerce and business, as well as agriculture, are blessed by the Koran. Even Muhammad was a trader. He knew the value of trade and banking. But the Koran never went so far as to approve the capitalistic system of free enterprise in which the marketplace, not the government, would determine the value of goods and labor. As among the early Jews, it was believed that God approved of the private ownership of land and other assets. It was good to make a profit in business and banking, but to gain wealth for its own sake, without any limits on the amount, was evil. The production of wealth was good since the owners could give larger amounts of money to the charities sponsored by religious organizations. But charging interest on loans was condemned as a sinful transaction. Since wealth tends to corrupt man, then it is the duty of the church and the state to save man from his evil instincts to profit at another's expense. In the modern world, Islam may be nominally anticapitalist, but the twentieth-century development of oil resources in Saudi Arabia, the Persian Gulf states, Iran, and Iraq, all Muslim states, suggests that the Islamic faith can embrace capitalistic enterprise with enthusiasm and confidence.

In her book *Islam and Capitalism* Maxine Robinson provides a good study of the economic aspects of Islam. Islamic states have been slow to adopt capitalist systems, but gradually today they are accepting Western-style systems of free enterprise. The ownership of private property has always been approved by the Koran. Now interest charges are being legalized on the grounds that a lender should be paid for the use of his money. So instead of interest being paid on the loan, the loan as acutally granted is smaller than the amount required as repayment, so that the interest fee is hidden. New businesses are usually initiated and controlled by the state. Labor unions and laws restricting the use of women and children in the labor market remain in the eighteenth-century style of little or no effectiveness. Egypt in 1942 was the first Islamic nation to permit the organization of labor unions. In brief, the Islamic states are only beginning to adopt western capitalistic enterprise, technology, and science. More than anything else it has been oil that has brought an industrial revolution to twentieth-century Islamic countries. But, as is the case in Iran today, Western capitalism and technology have provoked violent reactions from those who wish to keep Islam in a noncapitalist, non-Western state.

Islamic Concepts of Justice and Rules Governing Daily Life

The Koran accepts the ideal of the brotherhood of man and the pursuit of peace among nations. Yet Islam blesses the use of holy war, a *jihad,* if it is necessary to defend Islam or to promote its extension into other lands. Those soldiers who die for Allah in religious crusades are assured of immediate entry into paradise and enjoyment of the highest level of happiness that Allah can provide there.

That the faithful on earth may be free from sin, Islam prescribes strict rules for daily living, in the same manner that biblical Jews had their daily lives regulated by church and state. The Koran provides for the establishment of theocratic states where church and state are united as one governing body. Kings are heads of both the state and the church, but in a sense the real power of government may rest more in the hands of ruling forces in the church, the mullahs or religious judges who preside over the courts. A Muslim's first duty, however, is to obey God, not the state.

The mullahs interpret and apply Koranic law, a system of law based on the ancient principle of an eye for an eye, a tooth for a tooth. Penalties for infractions of the law are severe. A thief might have his arms cut off, or, in the case of a second theft, his legs cut off. For a third theft he could be executed. A woman caught in adultery might be beheaded in a public execution. Her male companion might expect the same deadly fate. Islam holds sacred the ideal of a patriarchal society in which the woman is believed to have been created from Adam's rib, and so, based on her origin, an inferior being. Islam holds that God's laws are best executed by an autocratic system of rulers. Democracy, parliaments, and voting rights are not preeminent elements in any Islamic nation.

Non-Muslim residents in Islamic countries are given a second-place status. Normally they would retain the right to worship their faith, at least in private, so long as they pay their taxes, obey the laws of the land, and do not proselytize Muslims to convert to their faiths. Islam, as does Judaism, forbids the eating of pork, the use of alcohol, and gambling. Slavery was permitted on the condition that the slave be treated humanely, a condition not unlike that of Judaism and early Christianity.

Finally, at life's end, a Muslim knows that his or her soul is to be judged in the hereafter. Every act committed during one's lifetime is under the scrutiny of God, and man must take responsibility for the decision rendered by God in the final judgment. Man may think that he has the gift of free will, but probably Allah will rule his or her destiny after death. Islam accepts the resurrection of both the body and the soul. For those souls to be chosen to enter paradise there will be awaiting an Eden of cool waters and beautiful maidens. Those souls destined for paradise are the heroes fallen in battle for their God, for jihad fought for the faith. For the lost souls damned to hell the torments are terrible, such as having to drink molten lead until the skin is burned away. It is said that Dante's legendary description of hell was borrowed from the Koran.

Islam, as many other religions, accepts the presence of supernatural phenomena such as angels, evil spirits (*jinns*), astrology, magic, miracles, and saints. Albert Hourani has described the role of saints for Muslims as follows:

> The friend of God was the one who always stood near Him, whose thoughts were always upon Him, and who had mastered the human passions which took man away from Him. A woman as well as a man could be a saint. There had always been saints in the world and always would be, to keep the world on its axis. . . . The friends of God could intercede with Him on behalf of others, and their intercession could have visible results in the world. It could lead to cures for sickness or sterility, relief of misfortune, and these signs of grace were also proofs of the sanctity of the friend of God.[3]

Islamic Sects

Like other religions, Islam over time developed divisions within the original body of believers, yet despite the differences in detail, the various sects do accept the basic tenets laid down in the Koran. The two most important Islamic sects are the Shiites and the Sunnis. In general the Sunnis are more liberal in their interpretation of the Koran and its laws, while the Shiites are more orthodox. This division within the ranks of Islam first occurred over the issue of who was to be the rightful heir to Muhammad. The Sunni, a word taken from the word *sunna,* or the oral traditions of the prophet, trace their lineage to Muhammad's friend and chief general, Abu Bakr. He was elected caliph, or head of Islam, after Muhammad's death. The Sunni claim that they are the only true followers of the faith and until 1959 they refused to recognize the Shiites as true Muslims. Today there are about seven hundred million Sunnis compared to about ninety million Shiites. The Muslim world extends from Indonesia on the east to Morocco and North Africa on the west.

The name of the Sunni sect comes from their willingness to accept the oral traditions and interpretations of the Koran after Muhammad's death, which collectively were called the *sunnas,* and later the Hadiths. The Sunnis believe that the caliph or leader of Islam should always be elected, not conferred by heredity. Since in Islam there is no hierarchy of priests to establish a final, orthodox version of Islam, no one can claim that his version is the true one, the one Allah and Muhammad would have declared to be the truth.

The Shiites (meaning "partisans") claim that the legitimate heir of Muhammad was his daughter's husband, Ali. In 656 A.D. Ali and Fatima's son Hussein led a fight against the Sunnis in which, five years later, his army was defeated. Hussein was tortured and beheaded. Today the Shiites of Iran honor the memory of Hussein's death with an annual procession in which marchers in a frenzied demonstration of their faith beat and whip themselves with chains and branches. This is done in the belief that their souls will be purified by suffering physical pain. Shiites claim that since Muhammad's death there have lived twelve *imams,* or prayer leaders. The last imam, the twelfth one, went into hiding in 939. Shiites believe that he will emerge later to rule the world as Mahdi, the messiah. Imams are considered to be intercessors between Allah and man. Ayatollah Khomeini claimed that he was a descendant of the seventh imam, and hence the rightful ruler of the Shiites. Shiites have become the largest Islamic group in the countries of Iran, Iraq, Bahrain, and Palestine.

The doctrinal differences between Sunnis and Shiites are minor, for all Islamic groups agree on the basic tenets of Islam. Between the Shiites and the Sunnis these differences do appear: the Sunnis are willing to accept both the Koran and the traditions, the Hadiths, as truth. The Sunnis are willing to accept into membership of the body of Islam all persons who profess a belief in Allah and his prophet, Muhammad, even though later in their daily lives these people may seem to violate the duties of Islam. Sunnis say, "Give these possible sinners the benefit of the doubt, and let God be the judge of their sins on the Day of the Last Judgment." Another point of difference is that the Sunnis tend to accept a belief in predestination. The Shiites stress more the idea of free will, that each person has a God-given power to direct his or her own destiny, and that each person must be held accountable for all evil deeds committed. When a final judgment is made about the differences between Shiites and Sunnis, it may be far more a political difference over what dynasty or form of rulership shall prevail than basic differences over religious beliefs.

In the eighth century a minority group of Shiites, the Ismailis, created one more division in the Islamic community. The primary cause for the split was a conflict over who should be the seventh imam, that is, who would be the legitimate heir of the Prophet Muhammad and the spiritual and political leader of Islam. Upon the death of the sixth imam, Jafar al-Sadiq (765), two sons were left to claim the office of imam, Muhammad ibn Isma'il and Musa al-Kazem, the younger son. The Ismailis recognized Musa al-Kazem as the seventh and last of the imamate succession; hence they are called the Seveners.

The majority of Shiites selected the older brother, Muhammad ibn Isma'il as the legitimate imam, the one who continued the succession of imams until the twelfth imam, the child Muhammad al-Mahdi. He disappeared mysteriously in 939. With the disappearance the Shiites believe that he was the last of the imams, but that in due time he will return, like Christ, to earth. Upon his return as the incarnation of God, earth will enjoy a long period of peace, justice, and brotherhood. The acceptance of the twelfth imam has given the Shiites the name of the Twelvers.

Ismailite groups, motivated by a missionary spirit and a belief that violence to achieve one's goals was a divine blessing, had won by the tenth century control over a large portion of the area between India and Egypt. Ismailites became rulers in Syria, Palestine, Mesopotamia, Bahrain, and Egypt. In 969 the Fatimid Ismailites conquered Egypt, claiming that its ruling family was the direct descendant of Fatima, the daughter of Muhammad.

Since the Ismailites believe that incarnations of God in the form of new imams will continue throughout time, they continue to expect the arrival of new imams, even that a twelfth imam may appear someday. The majority of Shiites have rejected these radical ideas. Today the Ismailites are represented by the Druze Muslims, who are found in Lebanon, Syria, and Israel, totaling about seven hundred thousand members. The Druze in Lebanon have become a principal Muslim group seeking to oust the Christian Maronites and make Lebanon a truly Islamic state. The Druze in Israel have full rights as citizens, with the same rights as other Muslim groups and Christians. The Israeli Druze, however, seek to have an independent state someday, so they are divided between those who would remain loyal to Israel and those who wish to join with the Palestinians to have an independent Palestinian state, but who desire to recognize Israel's right to keep its national sovereignity.

The Islamic Druze proclaim Allah as the one, true God, but his prophet is not Muhammad, but Al-Hakim, a Fatimid Caliph who ruled in Egypt from 996 to 1021. They recognize the equality of the sexes, which other Muslim groups do not. In place of the five pillars of Muhammad they have substituted seven commandments that declare Allah to be the one God, reject associations with any other religious groups, and mandate defense of their faith wherever and however it may be necessary, even if it means the use of arms. During the nineteenth century and especially since 1975 the Druze have fought frequent battles against the Christian Maronites in Lebanon.

The Druze believe that God continues to reveal his truths in revelations to his prophets, so new interpretations of Islam can be expected. Along with Muhammad and Jesus, the Druze accept the father of Moses, Jethro, as another legitimate prophet. The Druze accept no converts to their faith, nor are they permitted to marry non-Druze persons. Neither do they make pilgrimages to Mecca. At all costs the Druze believe that they must retain their own religious identity. They are taught to live apart from the rest of the world, and to be happy with whatever fate Allah deals out to his people.

Another offshoot of the Ismailis is a group of religious terrorists called the Assassins, a term derived from the use of hashish to stimulate their religious emotions to a point of frenzied madness. This twelfth-century Muslim groups believed that it was a duty to kill in the name of Allah. Fortunately for the world today, only the name "assassin" remains of this terroristic sect.

Another Islamic sect that arose in the eighth century as a reaction to the materialistic and imperialistic goals of the ruling Umayyad dynasty, the champion of the Sunnis, was the Sufi group. The Sufis expressed their displeasure with the wealth and worldliness of many Muslims by retreating to the desert, where they lived as wandering ascetics, abstaining from all worldly pleasures and dressing themselves in woolen robes, called *sufis,* an Arabic word for wool. The Sufis claim that their dogmas and practics are the most pure of all Muslims. Their primary goal is to rid the souls of mankind of self-love and replace it with God-love. The ego aspect of human nature must be eradicated if the path to salvation is to be achieved. The Sufi Way has seven stages: repentance, abstinence from worldly pleasures, detachment or isolation from the world, solitude, poverty, patience, and self-surrender to God. The seven-path program is completed when ego leaves and divine love enters the human soul.

The founder of Sufism was a mystic, Ahmad al-Qadiana, who lived in Cairo. He proclaimed himself to be a prophet who had come to earth as an incarnation of Allah to revitalize Islam and to cast out all of the evil influences of the material world. Sufism became an expression of a mystical element, a form of religious expression found in most religions by a minority of most devoted adherents, and found most often in cosmic and oriental religious systems. Mystics find God in many ways and forms; each form is of equal value and acceptable to God. Mystics have deep faith that supernatural forces do operate on earth, hence angels, spirits, demons, and magicians are all divine forces to be praised and accepted as God's messengers. The love of God may be found in obedience to God's law, as in Judaism, or in meditation, as in Buddhism, or in following a prescribed set of prayers and rituals, or in doing acts of charity and service to the downtrodden and the oppressed. But of equal value in God's eyes are ecstatic emotional responses stimulated by love for God and expressed so that the world can share the devotion to God. Typical mystical worship practices are songs and dances, gyrating movements of the body, even flagellations or tortures of the physical body, plus the experience of visions, dreams, and other hallucinatory mental images, often excited by the use of drugs. All these things are pleasing to God. God is not some external being, for God is within oneself. Sufis go further and find God in all things of nature, the planets, the sky, plants, animals, humans, and nonhuman beings such as angels.

Mystics seek to know God by way of meditation, for the knowledge of God is planted within the mind and soul before birth. By meditating the inspired human will learn the secret knowledge of God, and this knowledge will be revealed in a mystical experience of sudden or instant illumination, an intuitive response. Before one can succeed in the discovery of divine knowledge the physical body must be purified and prepared for meditation. The ideal place for gnosis to occur is in an isolated monastery where one must live a disciplined, ascetic life. A devout Sufi needs also the guidance of a master to teach the art of meditation, which will produce intense concentration and mystical trances. Some of the mystical practices include the repeating of the ninety-nine names for God while fingering prayer beads, and using special breathing exercises. Listening to music or dancing may enhance the act of illumination. For some Sufis the highest form of illumination comes in the form of ecstatic dancing, as might be practiced by the "whirling dervishes." The wild dancing represents the movements of the planets. Their movements are a secret, and when the dancing reaches a climax the dervishes collapse in a trance. As they fall they enter into God. Thus the dervish becomes a part of the total universe or God. Eventually the dervish becomes a perfect human who can teach others God's truth. Among the Sufis the most holy men become saints and their tombs become shrines to which pilgrims go to receive divine blessings. After death the dervish saints become the guides who will accompany the souls to their everlasting abode.

Sufis have made a fine art of meditation in that they prescribe the proper method of concentration. First the meditator must touch five centers of the body, beginning with the heart, then the spirit center found in the heart, then the secret center between the heart and the spirit center, then the forehead, seat of the mysteries, and finally the brain, the deeply hidden source of mystery.

Other Islamic sects are active in various parts of the world. One small group in North Africa, Oman, and Zanzibar is the Kharizites. They preach a puritanical way of life, including a belief that some sins are so grievous that God cannot forgive them. Most Muslims believe that the only unforgiveable sin is to not worship Allah as the only true God. The Kharizite list of the unforgivable sins includes desertion in battle, unlawful killing, and the practice of magic.

Another small sect was the Wahhabi sect. This group was founded by Muhammad ibn Abd al-Wahhab (1703-1792). The Wahhabis were a most puritanical group that deplored the lax morals of too many Muslims. In many respects the Wahhabis resembled the Protestant Puritans in adhering to a most strict, severely enforced moral standard of conduct. They also were like the Protestant fundamentalists in that they regarded their scripture as the inerrant, revealed knowledge of God. They wished to return to the first days of Islam before any traditions had developed. Their concept of the truth was the only truth; all other beliefs were in error. For Wahhabis Muhammad is God, a divine being. Muhammad never claimed this, however. The Wahhabi sect was a primary force in the rise of the Saudi tribe of Arabs to power over other tribes, and in instigating the creation of an Arabian state, Saudi Arabia, in 1932.

A more recent outgrowth of Islam is the Bahai movement, founded by an Islamic teacher, Bahi Ullah in 1848. It is the largest minority sect in Iran, numbering about three hundred thousand followers. Today the Bahais are being persecuted in Iran. Bahai is an idealist effort to unify all of the major religions into one universal set of beliefs. Bahais believe that all religions are equally valid, and that all have common, basic goals, namely the improvement of human conditions on earth for a more peaceful, tolerant world in which all people, regardless of class, race, or religion can live together in harmony.

The Rise of Islamic Fundamentalism

Since World War II most religions have witnessed an increase in the influence and membership of those segments in the major religious bodies that wish to return to the original roots of their faith, while casting off the erroneous barnacles of tradition and human interpretations that have encrusted them over the centuries since the religion was first established. Fundamentalist reactions to this trend have become a major force among Christians, Jews, and Muslims in recent years. These groups, which claim that they are the orthodox, correct interpreters of God's will, not only disrupt the unity of the totaly religious body, but often become zealous political foes of the more liberal, modern wings of their religions. In general these conservative elements wish to eradicate all traces of Western capitalism, science, technology, and the wicked, depraved moral standards that corrupt youth by making available easy sex, drugs, and alcohol, and, worst of all, a social climate in which children and young people feel free to disobey their parents and question the wisdom of the rules made by church and state. If somehow people can return to an older, simpler way of life, the force of divine guidance will again restore mankind to its God-fearing state. Democracy is a dangerous political system. Too much freedom is given the citizen, who does not know how to rule himself. Children are running amok. Women are defying God's place for them when they claim equality with men and deny that men should rule home and govenment. If the modern world does not cease to practice these wicked ways, God will wreak vengeance upon us, and the world will be destroyed for our human sins.

Throughout the Islamic world today fundamentalism is on the rise. The American way of life has become a symbol of the devil's work. Technology, science, and material wealth are in ill repute. Western democracy, dress, and music are all evil and must be excluded from the Arab world.

Fundamentalist reactions against Western incursions into traditional Arab society have taken violent forms. In 1981 President Anwar Sadat was assassinated by a fundamentalist group of Muslims, the Muslim Brotherhood, in Cairo. This group was founded in Cairo in 1928. It was banned by President Nasser in 1950 and later by Sadat who believed that church and state should remain separate institutions. The militant brotherhood gained momentum following the 1967 Seven Days' War, during which Israel defeated the Egyptian forces.

The most successful of the fundamentalist Muslim victories has occurred in Iran, when the radical revolutionary movement led by Ayatollah Khomeini over-threw the American-sponsored regime of the shah of Iran in 1979. The ascent to power of the Kohmeini Shiites turned Iran away from becoming a Western industrial state modeled after American forms of education, dress, and cultural values, back to a pre-sixteenth-century Islamic state.[4]

Women must again wear the veil and the chador and retire from the work world and colleges. Strict enforcement of the traditional marriage arrangements, separation of the sexes, the prohibition of the use of alcohol and the exclusion of all American-style cultural activities are again in effect. No longer is Iran to be ruled by a secular monarch and an elected parliament, but by a theocratic body of Muslim mullahs or judges, headed by an ayatollah. The reactionary rule in Iran seeks to extend its power over its neighboring Islamic states, Saudi Arabia, Egypt, the Persian Gulf emirates, Lebanon, and Iraq. In Lebanon since 1980 civil war has raged incessantly as Christians fight Muslims, and Muslims fight each other. The current terrorism in Lebanon can be attributed in large measure to an Iranian-sponsored terrorist group, Hezbollah, the "Party of God."

The Future of Islam

Even though the Islamic fellowship has its internal differences and feuds there is little danger that Islam will commit suicide, any more than centuries-old conflicts between Christian Catholics and Protestants destroyed Christianity. For when the battles are over, no matter which side has won or lost, all true Muslims can find unity in the basic tenets of their faith. All Muslims, regardless of the particular sect to which they belong, can join each day in reciting this prayer to Allah: "God is most great; God is most great. I testify that there is no God but Allah. I testify that Muhammad is the prophet of Allah. Arise and pray, arise and pray. There is no God but Allah."

And all good Muslims, at least most of them, can take time out of their daily work schedules to celebrate the glory of Allah on the occasion of the Islamic holy days. The three most important are: Ramadan, the holiest period in the Muslim calendar, when Muslims remember the time when Muhammad received his revelations from Allah; 'id-al-Fitar, the spring festival when Muslims celebrate for three days the end of Ramadan, an occasion, like Christmas, when children receive gifts and the entire population eats and dresses and plays in a spirit of great joy; and 'id al-Kaha, a fall celebration of the biblical story of Abraham's willingness to sacrifice (as the Muslims tell it) his son Ishmael (but God intervened and instead a sheep was sacrificed). At this time Muslims attend prayer services in the mosques and afterward celebrate with a feast of meat from sheep that have been sacrificed. Other high festival days occur on the birthday of Muhammad and the Islamic New Year. Islamic holidays do not happen on the same day and month each year, since the Muslim calendar uses a lunar month of twenty-eight days instead of the Gregorian calendar used in the West.

Islam has a noble ancestry, having roots in the religions of both the Jews and the Christians. Perhaps the time has arrived when brothers and sisters of the Book and of the God Jehovah (Allah) can find a common bond in mutual brotherhood and peace.

17

Roman Catholic Orthodoxy, 400–1200

The Fall of the Roman Empire

A Christian in Rome about A.D. 500 must have wondered about the future of the Church. Would it survive while the Roman Empire in the West was in a state of siege from northern barbarians because it was suffering from internal decay and dissolution? The center of the Roman Empire had been removed from Rome to Constantinople, the Greek city of Byzantium, which the emperor Constantine renamed. Not only did the government move east, but also Rome was no longer to be the cultural center of the empire. Western Europe was to regress into a five-hundred-year era of poverty, political disunity, and cultural stagnation, an era to which historians refer as the Dark Ages. What would be the fate of the church in the West? It had lost its strong arm of defense from religious and political enemies. It had lost its support from men of wealth and learning. Although the empire in the East remained wealthy and powerful, could the Western church count on it for protection? Or would the Western church be forced to depend on its own resources and leadership for survival?

The decline and fall of the Roman Empire in the West has been analyzed abundantly, most famously by an English historian, Edward Gibbon, in *The Decline and Fall of the Roman Empire*. The traditional date for the fall of the empire is 476, when the Germanic chieftain Odoacer forced the last emperor to abdicate. Gibbon has blamed the Christian Church as one of the factors causing the fall of Rome, since Christians placed loyalty to God ahead of loyalty to the emperor. The Roman religion had made the emperor a god and his rulership a divine institution, but in the eyes of a Christian the emperor was merely another human being who deserved no honor beyond that of any mortal king or governor. Yet Christians must have realized that their existence depended upon the support of the imperial government and that to destroy or undermine the empire would not be to their advantage.

The Formation of Feudal Society
and the Survival of Christianity

As Western Europe entered the Dark Ages after the fall of Rome, the Christian Church had to learn to adapt to a new lifestyle on earth. New political systems and new economic systems began to evolve, creating new societies and a new social order. Northern and western Europe found that Roman society and control had been replaced by the rule of the several Germanic tribes. In France there would be the Franks, in Britain the native Celts would be ruled by the Anglo.-Saxons and Normans, and in Scandanavia the Vikings and Danes would form new states. The Ostrogoths would rule Italy, the Visigoths became the dominant force in Northern Spain, and in the German areas the Goths and other tribes would be Christianized and become founders of numerous political entities, duchies, counties, and kingdoms.

The Germanic nations would be forced to develop a new economic system to replace the Roman system of large estates or villas. The new system would be feudalism, a political-economic system by which the masses of people, living in a nonmonetary age, exchange their labor for protection. A few people, kings, lords, and lesser noblemen who possess armies and arms, many of whom were tribal chieftains, would control the land. Some of the lesser people would exchange their prowess for fighting and become soldier knights for food and keep. The greater number of people offered their services as farmers and craftsmen in exchange for the privilege of food and a minimum subsistence standard of living. These persons would become the serfs, semi-slaves bound to the manor on which they live and to work in perpetuity. The Church would be forced to become a part of the feudal society. Bishops would become feudal landowners with serfs. A few of the brighter sons of serfs might become priests to serve their local parishes. For five centuries Western Europe lived in a world of poverty, ignorance and superstition, periodic famines and plagues, but worst of all, all people, rich and poor, powerful and powerless, lived in a veritable state of anarchy, where war between the noble factions raged constantly. The poor unarmed peasants were often the innocent victims of these feudal wars. It was not an era of which Christians could be proud. The best that can be said of the feudal era was that human life did survive, despite the devastating losses from disease, war, and poverty.

There was some semblance of order and peace, and much of the credit must go to the Church. For a few centuries remnants of Roman culture were preserved, again because of the Church. By 1000 Western Europe began to receive some of the lost heritage of the Greek and Roman cultures. Christian monks and scholars began classical studies and translations. Christian theologians introduced Greek philosophy and the concept of reason into the study of theology.

In this recovery of the ancient cultures and works of wisdom, Muslim civilization must be given a large measure of credit. It is true that Islam became a threat to the peace of the Byzantine remnant of the empire after the eighth century. But Islam was also a threat to Western Europe as it dominated North Africa and Spain, and threatened to invade France and Italy until Muslim forces were defeated by the Frankish king, Charles Martel, in 732. Even though Muslim Arabs were to conquer most of the Byzantine Empire, and eventually all of it by 1453, and they were always a perceived enemy of Christianity, Christians must recognize that if it had not been for the Muslim scholars and some wise Muslim rulers who appreciated beauty and learning, the Christian world might never have received the blessings of its own ancient cultures.

Despite the hazards and obstacles for survival during the Dark Ages, the Church did survive. The Church had become the state church of Rome in the fourth century. It had survived a last-ditch effort by the emperor Julian, who in 361 tried to restore the old Roman pagan gods to their former position of power and to destroy the Christian Church, but Julian's effort was doomed to failure when he was killed in a war against Persia in 363. Julian had tried to enlist the support of the Jews in his campaign against the Christians by offering to rebuild the Temple in Jerusalem, but the Jews spurned his offer. Even Julian's friends offered no support in his war against the Christians.

Despite the competition from the several heretical groups, by 500 Christian churches were established throughout the empire. In Egypt the gods Isis and Horus had become the Virgin Mary and her son, Jesus. The Third Council of Ephesus in 401 declared Mary to have been the Virgin Mother. Diana, the Greek goddess of Ephesus, was now replaced by the Virgin Mary. Apollo, the Greek sun god, had become the Christ. The Roman worship of the winter solstice, a part of the sun god worship, had become the celebration of the birthday of Jesus. The oracles of Delphi and Sybil were incorporated into Christian worship. As the Germanic tribes were converted first to Arian Christianity and later to orthodox Christianity, Church fathers made the wise decision to introduce into Christian worship many of thier pagan practices and holy days.

By 500 it was quite evident that the body of Christ, the one Church indivisible, was not to be, despite the adoption of the Nicene Creed and an almost successful elimination of the heretical sects. On the frontier, some of the heresies and dissident churches survived. Many of these groups were motivated more by national interests for an independent state in which their own language and culture would prevail than by any serious theological differences with the orthodox position. The first Christians to form their own independent, national church were in Armenia in 301. At this time the Armenian state had a large empire between the Black and Caspian seas, where Armenians remain today as a part of the former Soviet Union. The Armenian Apostolic Church is still alive, and dreaming of the day when national independence may be restored. The Armenian church follows the Orthodox Eastern Church in its theology, and has as its symbol Noah's Ark.

Other heretical Christian churches that have survived to the present are the Monophysite Church in Syria and the Jacobin and Coptic Churches in Egypt and Ethiopia. The Nestorian heresy survived for a few centuries in China, but it was replaced by the Buddhist faith.

However, the orthodox church retained the loyalty of the Christians who lived in Europe, even in the Slavic countries of eastern Europe. In 1054 the orthodox church was divided, an event to be related later. For many centuries the Byzantine or eastern part of the empire continued to be prosperous and a strong bulwark for the West against the inroads of Asiatic Tartars, later the Seljuk and Ottoman Turks, and also the frequent attacks from the Arabic Muslims. The eastern empire, as with the Islamic nations, created centers of learning where the ancient classics and philosophies were studied, and advances in science and architecture were made.

The Christian resident of Rome in the year 1000 had reason to be confident of the future of his church. It not only had survived, but had become the dominant spiritual force in Europe. In fact the Church was well on its way to becoming a dominant force in the direction and control of politics throughout Western Europe. By now the papacy and the Church based in Rome was beginning to exercise control over the new Germanic states and principalities. By 1200 the Roman Catholic Church would be the most powerful and wealthy single entity in Western Europe. A most important step on the road to power occurred on Christmas Day, 800, when Pope Leo III crowned Charles the Great (Charlemagne), king of the Franks, the Holy Roman emperor. The Holy Roman Empire was a paper state which, in theory, was to rule all of Central Europe, but which in reality had little power. This act of coronation signalled a joint alliance between temporal and spiritual powers, the powers of a monarch and of a pope. This alliance of pope and kings became a mighty force to fight heresies and pagan enemies, to organize and promote crusades against the infidel Muslims, and to secure the internal peace of the European states from the ravages of feudal war. Together pope and kings could restore political unity and power to Europe, and be instrumental in the promotion of commerce, wealth, production, and the restoration of learning and culture after the Dark Ages.

In 733, a Frankish king, Charles Martel, had stopped the advance of the Muslims at the Battle of Tours in southern France. On the eastern front, the Byzantine Empire held back the invaders from Asia and Africa, most of whom were Muslims. By 1000 the Muslims had occupied almost half of the areas that at one time had been under Christian control—southern Spain, Egypt and North Africa, Syria, and Persia. The remainder of Christian territory had become relatively stable and was now on the road to recovering some degree of economic production and intellectual activity. Moreover, the year 1000 was the year of the millennium, when Christians believed that, according to the book of Revelation, Christ was due to reappear on earth. This was a time of great expectation and hope for the Christian Church.

Although the Parousia, or the second coming of Christ, did not occur as some Christians expected, the Church under the guidance of a series of able popes continued to grow in numbers and power. By the thirteenth century the papacy became the undisputed head of Christians in the West, and under Pope Innocent III, 1198-1216, the church and the papacy exercised a dominant position in the political and economic affairs of the Western European states.

If Christianity had continued to follow the pattern of the first-century Church it would have remained another branch of Judaism with certain modifications such as the relaxation of strict observance of the Mosaic codes and the acceptance of Jesus as one of the prophets and the Messiah prophesized by Isaiah. The Pauline churches, as described in the book of Acts, continued to use the Judaic worship services, such as reading from the Torah, separating the sexes in the synagogues, singing the psalms, and teaching a sermon delivered by a rabbi. Later the Pauline churches admitted Gentiles to their membership and substituted the rite of baptism for circumcision of the male as the hallmark of membership.

But by the fourth century the Christian Church had shed most of its Jewish heritage, and taken on a new image. For the next one thousand years it was this new Christian Church that spread the gospel to all parts of Europe and eventually caused Europe to become the center of world Christianity. The most powerful monarchs to the most humble peasants, and all social classes in between, became equals, nominally at least, before the throne of God, at whose side sat the Christ. And all persons, of both sexes and all races, were in the membership of the Church, and sworn to obedience to God and his Church.

Development of Basic Dogma and the Canon

As the Church became a controlling force in European society, it had to define what a Christian believes and accepts as the true faith. A definitive statement of belief was needed, and this statement had to have the blessing of God if it was to be accepted as authoritative. Scripture and all other statements of beliefs would have the greatest authority if they were declared to have come to man by way of direct revelation to inspired prophets or men of wisdom. Revealed wisdom would be given even greater authority when it was confirmed as God's truth by leading Church officials such as theologians, bishops and popes, Church councils, and inspired writers and preachers, who, in the eyes of the Church, were honored as saints. Holy Scripture, the declarations of Church councils such as the Nicene Creed, the dogmas as issued by the ruling papacy, and the accumulated practices of the Church known as the Traditions took on the air of unquestioned authority. All of the above constituted the official standards of belief by which a Christian was to be measured for membership in the Church.

The first official statement of Christian belief was expressed in the Nicene Creed of 325. This creed was probably drafted by the church historian Eusebius and adopted by the Council of Nicea called by emperor Constantine. Five basic tenets of belief were stated: (1) the concept of the Holy Trinity, the idea that God the Father, Jesus the Son, and the Holy Spirit are all of one substance; (2) Christ came to earth to save the souls of mankind; (3) the Resurrection of Christ gave all mankind the promise of eternal life; (4) the promise that Christ will return to earth gave hope that all Christians will enjoy eternal life; (5) there is only one Catholic and Apostolic Church into which one can be baptized to secure remission of sins.

The Nicene Creed, as well as other brief statements of belief, were convenient and easy summaries of the basic tenets of Christianity, but more detailed expositions and proofs were needed to convince the doubters that the one Church contained the ordained road to salvation. In other words, the Church had to have a Bible, a detailed historical record that detailed how divine will came to be made manifest in a human institution, the Church.

The Christian Scriptures have two parts, the Old and the New Testaments. Before 100 the only Scripture available was the old Hebrew Bible, then written in the Greek language. Probably by 100 the early Christian churches used bits and pieces of the messages spoken by Jesus and some of the letters of the Apostle Paul. The New Testament as an organized and canonized or legitimized book of guidance for the Church did not become available until the fourth century.

One of the first collections of books that formed the New Testament was made by Marcion, a heretic, about 150. This collection contained only the book of Luke and a few of the Pauline letters. Another collection, the Muratorian Canon, made about 170, contained all four of the gospels and most of Paul's letters. About 180, Ireneaeus, an associate of the bishop of Lyons, was known to have used the gospels to combat heresy, and he is credited with using the name, New Testament, for his collection of books. Emperor Constantine encouraged his aide and historian, Eusebius, to prepare a collection of books for a New Testament, a collection that is basically the same as that of the New Testament of today. The Jerome Vulgate edition of the Bible was a translation into Latin (Vulgate meaning the popular language of the time) of the Hebrew Old Testament and the Greek New Testament. Jerome was an Italian secretary to Pope Damascus and a noted scholar of his day. Later he was to be canonized by the Church as a saint. The Vulgate Bible remains the accepted Bible for use in the Roman Catholic Church.

The New Testament

Although some biblical students credit the gospel of Luke as being the first gospel to be written, most scholars believe that the weight of evidence gives first place to the gospel of Mark. Probably Matthew and Luke borrowed much of their material from Mark. Matthew contains mostly material found in Mark, that is, 600 of 661 verses are identical. Mark was probably written in Rome for Gentile readers. It is thought that Mark, who never saw Jesus, nor did any of the writers of the first four gospels, received his information about Jesus from Peter. Mark was Peter's secretary. Matthew was probably related to the church at Antioch and wrote his gospel for that church. Luke was one of the missionary aides of Paul, so he had first-hand information about the Pauline churches. Luke is credited also with being the author of the book of Acts, the first history of the Christian church. Both Matthew and Luke had access to sources other than Mark. Not always do the writers of the gospels relate the same event in the same manner.

Only Matthew and Luke relate the Nativity event. Luke says that the disciples witnessed the Crucifixion of Jesus, while Mark and Matthew said they fled from the scene before the Crucifixion. However, the differences are so minor that some scholars say they may have been errors in translation rather than errors in relating the truth about a particular event.

A more serious criticism of the gospels is that the real authors may not have been the men whose names are given to the gospels. It is thought that the book of Mark originally ended with chapter 16, verse 8, and that verses 9 to 20 were added later by a church council, probably the Council of Chalcedon in 451. The Codex Sinaiticus, one of the earliest Bibles, which was found in 1859 in the monastery of St. Catherine at the base of Mt. Sinai, did not contain verses 8 to 20 in the book of Mark. Another early edition of the Bible found in Egypt in 1947, the Nag Hammadi Papyrus, makes no mention of a bodily resurrection, only a spiritual resurrection.

The first three gospels (Mark, Matthew, and Luke) contain a common theme or message; hence they are collectively called the "synoptic" gospels. The fourth gospel, the book of John, introduces a new message about the nature of the Christ. John was said to be a disciple of John of Zebedee. John was more Greek than Jew in his approach to theology. He was quite familiar with Greek philosophy, especially the Hellenized version found in Neo-Platonism. With the opening sentence in his gospel there is revealed John's Platonic origins. "In the beginning was the Word, and the Word was with God." That sentence reflects Plato's concept of reality, or God. The Logos, or the Word is very similar to Plato's Ideas or Forms—invisible, ever-present ideas that preceded all of creation, forms by which all things were created, and one of which dwells in the human being as the soul. By this philosophy, the physical world does not exist. It is only an illusion of the mind. When John interprets the human man, Jesus, and seeks to find his true nature, it is not the physical Jesus who is real, it is his spirit or Word that is real. The Apostle Paul agreed that the Logos concept of Christ is correct, and that it was only the spirit or Logos of Christ that was resurrected. John viewed Christ as the Messiah who was created even before the beginning of time to become the Messiah and who will come to earth to save mankind from original sin and to prepare the world for the Second Coming and the Final Judgment (John 3:15-17).

The epistles of Paul are, for the most part, identified as having been written by a known person, Paul of Tarsus. The earliest known Christian document is Paul's first epistle to the Thessalonians, written about 51. Of all the books of the New Testament, the letters of Paul are nearest in time to the life of Jesus, written about twenty-five years after his death. Scholars generally agree that Paul wrote the book of Romans (perhaps chapter 16 was added later), 1 and 2 Corinthians, 1 Thessalonians, Galatians, Philippians, and Philemon. The authorship of the other letters that bear Paul's name is uncertain. It is interesting that Paul never mentions the four gospels, nor do they mention any of Paul's letters. Moreover, Paul never saw the man Jesus but he never doubted that Jesus lived and preached, and that he had been commissioned by God to save the world from sin (Galatians 1).

The most controversial of all of the books in the New Testament is the last, the book of Revelation. This book was written about 95 as a diatribe against the Roman Empire and its persecution of Christians.[1] The author, John, is thought to be John of Ephesus, who lived on the Island of Patmos in the Aegean Sea. Tradition says that John was the brother of the Apostle James, who, with other Christians in Jerusalem, fled to escape the persecutions carried out by the emperor Diocletian during the first century. John sought refuge in Patmos, where he lived in a cave for eighteen years. The cave is now covered with sacred icons of John that the natives believe can work miracles for them. In fact no one knows who the author of Revelation was.

John wrote the book of Revelation as a veiled attack on the Roman Empire. He realized that a small band of Christians was no match in military strength for the Roman army. John sought to find another way of escape for the persecuted Christians. His plan for deliverance form the Romans was inspired by the messianic message found in the book of Daniel. Daniel promised the oppressed Jews that an apocalyptic event sent by God would destroy the evil oppressor, after which the Jewish people would enjoy an era of peace and happiness. In the same miraculous manner the Christians would be saved by God from the Romans. The evil Roman Empire is depicted as a satanic power that will be destroyed by the God-sent four horsemen of the Apocalypse. Each horseman becomes a symbol for the destructive powers of plagues, famines, cruel beasts, and war. Other symbolic death-inflicting forces include the four beasts and a red dragon or serpent, which represents Satan. Mankind will be saved by angels form heaven, who will bind Satan and destroy the enemies of the Christians. Then God will send to earth a savior in the form of a lamb, Jesus, the Messiah. After Jesus arrives on earth a new Jerusalem will be born to rule over the earth for a thousand years. The new Jerusalem will be ruled by the king, the Christ, and all of the faithful devotees of the Christ will inherit eternal life in heaven.[2]

Revelation was not readily accepted by early Christian theologians as a book that should be placed among the other sacred books of the New Testament. Revelation was first included among the twenty-seven books of the New Testament by the patriarch of Alexandria about 367, but among the Eastern Christians it was not accepted officially until the eighteenth century.

Traditionally Christians read Revelation as a blueprint for the future of the world. In due time God will destroy the evil world and its lost inhabitants, and a few saints will live in blissful heaven for all of eternity. Today liberal Christians are reluctant to place much credence in the promises of John in Revelation.

Jesus the Man

In reply to the question, "Who was Jesus?" the three synoptic gospels present slightly different interpretations of the nature and personality of Jesus. The first gospel, Mark, pictures Jesus as a good Jewish humanitarian who went about Palestine preaching a message of love and future eternal salvation in heaven. Jesus made no claim to be a king or a messiah, or the son of God. He was a humble Jewish rabbi who wanted to reform and revitalize his Jewish faith. He was not destined to be the founder of a new religion, nor was he to be the divine savior of mankind. Yet in chapter 8 Mark relates that Jesus asked his disciples, "Who do they say I am?" Peter replies, "You are the Messiah." Jesus did not reply "yes" or "no," but warned his disciples not to "tell anyone about him." Jesus did not seem ready at this time to proclaim himself to be either the Messiah or the son of God.

Matthew and Luke, building on Mark's biography of Jesus, offer two other versions of the nature of Jesus. Matthew, written about 80, presents Jesus as the Messiah, the heir to the Jewish lineage that can be traced from Abraham to Judah to Jesus. In this manner Jesus became the fulfillment of the prophecies of Isaiah and other Jewish prophets that a messiah would be sent by God to save his people from their enemies. Matthew offers another line of descent for Jesus, that is, one directly from God. Since Jesus was born of a miraculous conception through the intervention of the Holy Spirit, he was destined to be the son of God as well as the son of man.

Matthew makes clear that Jesus is more than a Jewish rabbi or a reformer of Judaism. He is ordained to be the founder of a new church, for when Jesus told Peter he was the rock on which a new church was to be built and that Peter was to be the keeper to the keys to the kingdom of heaven, Matthew implies that it is time to break the ties with Judaism, and to make a new covenant with God, a new Torah in which the primary law is love. Matthew also derides those scoffers and critics who deny the resurrection of the dead Jesus, and who claim that his body was stolen from the tomb. For Matthew the Resurrection was a historical event. Yet Matthew never claimed that Jesus was resurrected in the flesh. The risen Christ signified that his spirit was to be found in the resurrected body of a small band of dispirited followers who were commanded to go forth and build the church of Christ, the resurrected body of the Christ. Matthew saw the Christ as a royal, majestic person, a king, the son of God, who would bring to earth peace and eternal salvation for all men in heaven.

The gospel of Luke gives another dimension to the personality of Jesus. Luke makes Jesus out to be a more humble, less royal personage, one who can mingle and sit with the common people. He became a more lovable person, one who could give hope and inspiration to the lowly, powerless classes. Jesus found friends among tax collectors, the outcasts, and the sinners. "But I eat my food and drink my wine and you say, 'What a glutton Jesus is, and he drinks, and he has the lowest sort of friends' " (Luke 7:34).

Jesus saw his mission to be one to save the sinners, for they needed his love and care, not the righteous, who were saved already. When the tax collector said to Jesus that he was a sinner, Jesus replied, "I tell you, This sinner, not the Pharisee, returned home forgiven. For the proud shall be humbled, but the humble shall be honored" (Luke 18:14).

The Protestant Revolt and New Bible Translations

From the beginning of the Christian Church the Bible was declared to be sacred literature which, although written by men, came to the authors by way of divine revelation. That the Bible, however, was so divine as to be inerrant and free from criticism and change was not considered the case in the early centuries of church history. The concept of an inerrant Scripture began to be seriously promulgated only during the nineteenth century, when certain scientifically oriented scholars began to question some of the biblical statements.

When the Protestant Christians declared their independence of the Roman papacy in the sixteenth century a new Bible was needed. The Latin Vulgate Bible could not serve the needs of these new churches. The Bible took on a new value. It became the supreme authority for determining the correct doctrinal positions of the church. No longer was the Roman pope, the vicar of Christ, the supreme arbiter of religious doctrine. Moreover, Protestants believe that every person is his or her own priest; hence every person must be sufficiently literate to read the Bible in his or her native language. Thus, the new Protestant Bible had to reflect the religious perspectives of Protestant theologians. For example, the word "church" became the word "congregation" in the Protestant Bible. Other changes had to be made in the biblical text. Priests become elders, penance became repentance, and charity became love.[3]

Even the Roman Catholics prepared an English version of the Vulgate Bible, known as the Douai Bible. This Catholic Bible was edited by English Catholics who fled from England to escape persecution during the reign of Queen Elizabeth. These Catholics found refuge in Douai, Belgium, where their Bible was published.

The Dutch scholar Erasmus made one of the first translations of the New Testament from earlier Greek editions in 1507, and it was this text that Martin Luther used for his translation of the New Testament into the German language in 1521. In 1524 William Tyndale used both the Erasmus and Luther translations to prepare the first Bible to be written in English. Tyndale was condemned by good King Henry VIII to be burned at the stake. However, he was able to escape to Belgium and Germany, only to be imprisoned in Brussels and burned in 1536. In 1538 Henry VIII, now a Protestant, ordered a new English Bible to be printed. Henry's Bible was edited by Miles Coverdale, an aide to Tyndale, hence this Bible, called the Great Bible or the Cranmer Bible, was basically a copy of the Tyndale Bible. In Geneva, Switzerland, a Protestant Bible was written for the Calvinists by Theodore Beza. Later this Geneva Bible would be used in England during the reign of Queen Elizabeth, where it was know as the Bishop's Bible. Later, when King James I ruled England, he ordered that a new version be published. The King James Version of 1611 was the most authoritative English-language Bible for more than three hundred years, and is still the translation of choice for many Protestants.

The Protestant revolt against Rome prompted the Roman Church to reaffirm the validity of the Vulgate Bible at the Council of Trent in 1546. In 1904 Pope Pius X ordered a revision of the Vulgate Bible currently used in Catholic churches. The Vulgate Bible differs slightly from the Protestant versions in that it includes a few books, called the Apocrypha, that Protestants reject as being of dubious revelation.

Today Protestants are deeply divided over the issue of whether the Bible, every word of the Bible, is God's word, and therefore must be read as the truth and only the truth. Modern liberal critics of those who contend that the Bible is inerrant ask the question, "Is man made in the image of God, or is God made in the image of man?" Bible historians often equate the biblical record as being a combination of true historical fact and traditional myths, such as the myths told in the Greek legends or the Sumerian and Egyptian myths. The fact that some aspects of the Bible may not stand the test of scientific investigation or that certain contradictions of statement occur has caused great dissension among Christians in recent years. However, whether the Bible is historically accurate in all aspects or is only a record of what ancient people believed to be true should not overshadow the basic message of love and human coexistence in peace found in the Bible.

The Church Fathers and the Development of Christian Theology

Early in the history of the Church it was realized that there was a need for a rational, philosophical defense of Christian tenets of faith. Faith might suffice for the masses of Christians, but for the more sophisticated intellectuals something more than faith was required. The Church needed a professional group of educated scholars who could provide rational, logical answers to the many questions posed by Christian beliefs. There was also a need for someone to translate abstract Christian doctrines into everyday, practical rules and practices, or church law and rituals.

In the second century certain bishops began to draw upon Greek philosophy as a resource for finding rational answers to religious questions. Examples of questions posed were: What is the real nature of the Christ? What is the role of the clergy? Is the Church necessary for salvation? What is the real truth in the message of Jesus? Answering such questions was the job of theologians.

JUSTIN MARTYR

One of the first theologians was Justin Martyr, who in the second century used Neo-Platonic philosophy to argue that Jesus was divine. He declared that Jesus was the Logos or the Word, or that which preceded creation and from which pattern God created all things. Jesus, being the Logos, is by nature divine, according to Justin, a part of God but not created by God. This quality of innate divinity in Jesus is found also in all humans, and it is this God quality in mankind that permits all of us to love, to reason, and to be moral. The Logos in Jesus, the Christ element, has the power to free mankind from sin and ignorance. Only through the Christian Church can Christ free mankind from sin and secure for him eternal salvation.

THE ALEXANDRIAN SCHOOL: CLEMENT, ORIGEN, AND CYPRIAN

In Alexandria, Egypt, a school of philosophers or theologians developed that would have profound influence on the evolution of Christian theology. One of the earliest of this school of theologians was Clement, who is better known for his illustrious student, Origen, and for Origen's student, Cyprian. Origen (185–251) was first a follower of Gnosticism. Like Justin, he used Platonic philosophy to interpret the Christian message. The Logos was Christ, and Christ was never created. Christ was always a part of God. Both God and the Logos are equally divine. Origen's theological conclusions can be found in his work *First Principles*. God is wisdom and love incorporated into the Logos, or the Christ. Another God was responsible for creation, and that God was Jehovah. Hence Origen downplays the role of the Old Testament in the Christian Church. The only authentic Scripture is the New Testament. The source of all creation, physical and spiritual, comes from the Logos. In the beginning all spirits were created pure, but all spirits except Jesus rejected God. The rejecting spirits become the fallen spirits, which have bodies that became humans, angels, and demons. Origen believed that the fallen spirits could return to God if they so chose. Salvation comes from a process of free choice, not from an act of predestination. The fallen spirits can be resurrected to their original state of purity; even the Devil can be saved, through the grace of God and the power of the Christian Church.

Salvation comes only by way of the Church. The Church is the bride of Christ, one undivided, universal Church. The Church, which in many ways resembled the Roman state, was superior to the state. The hierarchy of bishops was chosen by the bishops, and the bishops ruled the Church and its members. The power of the bishops comes from God through the Holy Spirit, when an ordained bishop lays his hands on a clerical initiate. Salvation is given by Christ through the agency of the Church, observance of its rules and sacraments and accepting Scripture as holy truth. Since Christ unites in one body the human and divine elements it is certain that man has also a spiritual aspect that will enable him to attain to glory in heaven. Origen denied a belief in any physical heaven or hell, or that the soul was destined to suffer torment in hell.

Origen included in the Christian Church all people, regardless of race or class, but not heretics. He was a vigorous opponent of heretics, especially the Gnostics, of which he had been one in his youth.

Cyprian had been a provincial governor, so he knew about the daily problems of government and the organization of social institutions. He accepted Origen's definition of the power of the bishops and the policy that the laity and the clergy should be separated in the administration of the sacraments and the governance of the church. Salvation came only through the Church. He defined more clearly the status of a bishop. All bishops were equal members of a "college," with the bishop of Rome being first among equals. However, Cyprian believed that the supreme ruling voice for the Church was the Church council, not the bishop of Rome (the pope).

AMBROSE

A third theologian who influenced greatly the evolution of Christian practice and belief was Ambrose (339–397), bishop of Milan for twenty-four years. Ambrose's father had been a Roman prefect, or governor. Thus Ambrose came from an aristocratic, wealthy family that gave him a sound education in Greek philosophy and Christian theology. He was instrumental in expanding the temporal powers of the Church over the civil governments of the area. For example, Ambrose forced the emperor Theodosius to do public penance for the murder of thousands of people in Thessalonia. Ambrose fought the Arian heretics in Northern Europe and denounced the worship of the Roman gods. He asserted that the bishops were the supreme rulers over both the church and the state. He encouraged the practice of congregational singing of hymns and reading the liturgy. He supported belief in the power of relics and other magical forces. His concept of the universe was typically medieval in that the universe had seven heavens, a purgatory, and a hell of three levels of torment, in which souls were to await the Final Judgment. Ambrose also contributed to the use of the basilica style of church architecture in the early Middle Ages.

AUGUSTINE OF HIPPO

The most important of the early church theologians was Augustine, who was born in North Africa, near Carthage, and lived 354 to 430. Augustine's mother was a Christian. Young Augustine, according to his autobiography, *Confessions,* was a restless and wild young man who probably caused his mother some sleepless nights. Yet he was intelligent and gave serious thought to the problem of sin and how one could overcome the evil of sexual temptation and immorality. Early he began a search for some religion that might give him the answers to how one can save his soul from evil. First he turned to a prevailing heresy in his homeland, Donatism, but since Donatists advocated a most severe form of puritanical asceticism, a completely nonsexual life, Donatism was not for young

Augustine. So he joined another heresy, Manicheism, which he followed for nine years (373–381). Manicheans were strict vegetarians who spent much of their life fasting, praying, avoiding evil pleasures and sex, and, where possible, avoiding daily work. Needless to say, some Manicheans had to work lest the entire body of the church starve. A basic belief of the Manicheans was that in the universe a war was being waged between the forces of light or goodness and darkness or evil. Since the Gnostic Christians and the Manicheans held similar beliefs, Augustine was well acquainted with this dominant heresy of his time.

In 382 Augustine went to Rome, where he met Bishop Ambrose and became acquainted with his Neo-Platonic views. But Neo-Platonism was also not the answer to Augustine's search for the road to salvation. In 387, after a dramatic conversion experience, he was baptized as a Christian in the city of Milan. Soon he joined the battle against the Donatist heresy, a campaign that lasted for twelve years. At the same time he participated in the war against the Arian heretics.

Augustine was destined to become a preeminant Catholic theologian, for which he would be canonized as a saint. Augustine's most important writing, other than his *Confessions,* was *The City of God.* His goal in this book was to provide a rationale for the theological and dogmatic beliefs of the Church, primarily his conviction that the Roman Catholic Church was the only true, universal Church and that all other Christian churches were heresies doomed for extinction. He agreed with the Neo-Platonists that God cannot be described, for God was created from Mind, the Mind of God. From Mind came the Soul, which created all things on earth. Hence, man and the stars are related in the same manner as man is related to God. All things on earth are related, and all are a part of the divine. When the soul enters the human body at conception it suffers a temporary death, in its tomb, the human body. From this tomb the soul is to arise to heaven when the body dies. Man is immortal only because the Soul, the real person, is immortal. The human body, the material one, is evil. Heaven is for the purified souls made pure by a human body who lives the good life on earth and obeys the Church. Between God and earth is a chain of divine intermediaries or agents ranging from the evil demons to the good demons or angels and the saints. The intercession of the good angels was necessary for salvation. Augustine placed faith in the power of magic and miracles, in relics and ritual to effect a purification of the soul.

Only through the Church can man be saved, preached Augustine. Man is sanctified by the Church and its sacraments and rules. Augustine saw history moving through six stages. In his day, the world was in its final stage, the stage between the First and Second Coming of Christ. When Rome fell to the barbarians in 410 it was God's plan that the Church would inherit the power and glory of Rome. The universal Church of the elect would bring to earth the rule of the City of God, a perfect world of peace, justice, and freedom from evil. The final stage of history means the victory of the City of God. In the meantime, until Christ arrives, man must be content to suffer the world as it is, to remain loyal to the Church, to obey its laws, to eradicate heresy, and to elevate the power of the Church over that of the state.

Augustine introduced into Christian theology the concept of predestination, an idea that limited severely the action of free will in man's progress toward salvation. Predestination applies to both the human soul and the destiny of society. All things are determined before creation, and human choice or direction have no power to alter the divine plan. Theologians are hard pressed to find any biblical justification for a belief in predestination. The only scriptural text which might seem to link predestination to Christ's formula for salvation is found in Romans 8:28–30 and Matthew 20:23 and 22:4. In Romans the citation reads, "For whom he did foreknow, he also did predestinate to be conformed to the image of His Son, that he might be the firstborn among many brethren. Moreover whom he did predestinate, them he also called and whom he called, then he also justified, and whom he justified, then he also glorified."

Augustine reasoned that man was created good, free of sin, but the act of disobedience to God by Adam and Eve brought a curse upon all of mankind, a curse transmitted from Adam to all of his sons, and to all future generations of humans. Only by the grace of God and faith in God's grace, as Paul believed, can any human soul be saved. Augustine seemed to have retained some faith in the value of free will or choice. During the time of Augustine, the Pelagian heresy was active. This heresy preached that man was free of original sin and that man could save his soul without benefit of the Church. Neither Augustine nor the Church could accept such a heretical belief, so Pelagius was condemned as a heretic by the Council of Rome in 418. However, the issue of predestination did not disappear with the death of Pelagius. After Augustine, the most ardent exponent of predestination was John Calvin, the founder of the Protestant sect Calvinism in Geneva, Switzerland.

Augustine contributed greatly to the structure and theology of the Roman Catholic Church. He gave his blessing to the Nicene Creed, the doctrine of the Holy Trinity, the belief in original sin, and the belief that salvation requires both faith and good works, the good works of being faithful to the Church, obeying its laws, attending confession and doing penances, and practicing charity to help the poor and the oppressed. Augustine held that just wars against infidels and heretics did not violate the commandment, "Thou shall not kill."

Augustine, like Paul, abhorred almost all sexual activity as being among the most vile of sins. Sexual sin was a major aspect of original sin, and Eve, the female, was the worse transgressor. Sex is the devil, and this sin is transmitted through the female, the direct heir of Eve's sin (Romans 5:12). Women were not to be trusted, for they had brought sexual sin into the world. Therefore, women must be made subject to their husbands and fathers, and to the male clergy of the Church. The only justification for any sexual activity was for the procreation of children in marriage, and then only for the rare occasions when conception might occur. All other sexual activity of any kind after or before marriage was forbidden.

In fact Augustine believed that all of the human race was so depraved by original sin that it was man's lot to suffer the life of virtual slavery until the day of his or her death. Man must obey without question the laws of the state, but both man and the state must obey the laws of the Church. When Rome fell it was God's destiny that the Church in Rome and the papacy were to inherit the power of the Roman Empire. The clergy was ordained to order the affairs of both the church and the state. Only the ordained clergy could administer the sacraments, and, contrary to the belief of the Donatists, the moral character of a bishop or priest in no way invalidated his right to administer the sacraments. The union of church and state had been ordered by God and it is the duty of the state to enforce the rules and decisions of the Church. The mission of the Church was to secure for all people the blessings of justice and peace, and in the final days to bring to fruition the City of God on earth. As Augustine wrote in *City of God*,

> This heavenly city, then, while it sojourns on Earth, calls citizens out of all nations, and gathers together a society of pilgrims of all languages, not scrupling about diversities in the manners, laws, and institutions whereby Earthly peace is secured and maintained, but recognizing that, however various they are, they all tend to one and the same end of Earthly peace.[4]

Augustine declared that the observance of the sacraments was indispensable for the salvation of souls. He instituted the practice of infant baptism and the adoration of saints. The first saints were the martyred Christians. Saints could serve man as intercessors with God in the reception of prayers and the awarding of blessings to the faithful. The bones and relics of the sanctified martyrs were endowed with magical powers by which human illnesses could be cured and future events could be predicted. Miraculous results could be achieved by making pilgrimages to sacred shrines, and even in the Eucharist a miracle occurred when the bread and wine were transformed into the blood and body of Christ.

Augustine's endorsement of saints was challenged by other theologians on the grounds that veneration of saints might be interpreted as worshiping other gods than the Christian God. But for the people the adoration of saints and the use of relics provided a realistic bond between God and man. In a sense the images of Christ, the Virgin Mary, and the saints brought into the Christian home the living presence of God.

Augustine lived a busy and constructive Christian life as a teacher, author of over one hundred books, preacher of hundreds of sermons during a ministry of thirty-five years, preeminent scholar and theologian, and bishop of Hippo, making him an experienced administrator. In his *Confessions,* Augustine describes his conversion to Christianity: one day he heard a childlike voice singing, "Take up and read [the Bible.]" His first Bible reading came from Paul's letters to the Romans, chapter 13, where he read Paul's admonition to take up the cross, abandon evil ways, and follow the Christ. No one person after Jesus and the Apostle Paul did more than Augustine to give direction to the future development of the Roman Catholic Church. Later theologians Anselm, Thomas Aquinas, and others would make their contribution to the progress of the Church, but none would be more Catholic than Augustine. The course of development for the Church for the next thousand years would follow the blueprint drafted by Augustine.

JOHN CHRYSOSTOM

Although Augustine was among the most honored of all Church Fathers, he was not without his critics. A contemporary theologian, John Chrysostom, the bishop of Antioch, took issue with Augustine's belief that a strong, autocratic government for both the sate and the church was necessary. He said that no single person could lay claim to having divine power. The divine element is in all humans equally. Chrysostom granted that at times evil men would need to be ruled by a strong government, but declared that all too often dictatorships create more evil than good. Tyrants will legalize slavery, the exploitation of women and children, and conduct massacres and war against other humans. Moreover, the use of force is contrary to the Christian gospel, and in the end force will destroy both the church and the state. The only salvation for man is to be free to solve his own problems. Human bondage is not the way to salvation. Man earns his right to be free to solve his own problems through the rite of baptism.

The Muslim Contribution to Christian Theology

By the eleventh century church scholars were becoming acquainted with ancient Greek culture. Much of the recovery of Greek science and philosophy came to Western Europe by way of the Arab Muslim world. Muslim philosophers such as Averroës (Ibn Rushd, 1126–1198) and Avicenna (Ibn Sina, 980–1037) were disciples of the Greek philosophers, Plato and Aristotle, who had brought to the scholarly world knowledge of how to use rational processes to find reality and truth. The Jewish philosopher Maimonides (Moses ben Maimon, 1135–1204), trained in the Muslim school of philosophy, also contributed to Western learning at this time. Thus by the eleventh century Western theologians are ready to build new theological systems on the foundations of Greek rationalism and the wisdom of the earlier Christian theologians, Augustine and others.

Theologians of the Late Middle Ages

The theologians of the late Middle Ages used both faith and reason to gain knowledge about the divine elements of the universe. One of these scholars was Anselm (1034–1109), an Italian scholar who went to England and eventually became the archbishop of Canterbury. He proclaimed the doctrine that kings could not rule the church, rather it was the church that should rule the kings. In this respect he followed the advice of Augustine. But he went beyond Augustine by believing that reason and logic in the form of deduction provided better avenues to divine knowledge than faith alone. Anselm reasoned that if one can think of God, who is the highest of all ideas or thoughts, then God must exist. He said, "I believe so that I may understand." Anselm became a foremost exponent of the idea that in no manner should the state be permitted to restrict the freedom of the Church to operate.

A younger contemporary of Anselm, and also a great theologian, was Peter Abelard (1074–1142). He was French born, educated in a cathedral school in Paris, and later taught theology. His life contained elements of both romance and tragedy. While at the cathedral school he fell in love with a niece of a canon of the school, Heloise. Being a cleric he could not marry, yet he fell in love with the girl. But when the romance produced an illegitimate child the penalty was severe. The uncle had Abelard castrated and both of the lovers were ostracized to live a monastic life.

Later both formed a new monastery, the Community of the Paraclete. Although Abelard and Heloise were never permitted to live together, they did write many letters, which have become prized by romantic lovers. Even in death the couple, buried in a cemetery in Paris, continue to furnish a sense of commitment for lovers who still pledge vows of love over their graves.

As a theologian Abelard sought to weed out the contradictions and discrepancies in Christian theology by using the Socratic or dialectic system of deductive reasoning. His best-known work *Sic et Non* ("Yes and No"), poses 158 questions currently in dispute. Abelard believed that by asking many questions, debating the issues, and using many citations from various sources, finally the truth, the one truth, would be found. He took issue with the Augustinian belief in predestination. Salvation came from the exercise of free will. He denied that man should be penalized for his sins, for salvation comes from God's grace, a gift of free love from God. Abelard's generous interpretation of God's forgiving love caused him to be excommunicated for a few years, after which he was to be reconciled to the Church.

A disciple of Abelard was Peter Lombard (1100–1160). He became an archbishop of Paris. In imitation of Abelard's *Sic et Non* he wrote *The Four Books of Sentences*. Like Anselm he used the Socratic dialectic to analyze the dogmas of the Church. What was the nature of Christ, the sacraments, the Resurrection, the Virgin Mary, and the many other aspects of Church beliefs? What Lombard attempted to do in his book was to synthesize and simplify the entire body of Christian theology so that students would no longer be confused about the truth. For many years his book was used as a standard text on theology in church seminaries.

The use of rational analysis in the study of church doctrine is given the name scholasticism. Another scholastic scholar in the line of Abelard and Lombard was Albertus Magnus (1193–1280). A German, he studied in Italy and later taught at the cathedral school in Paris. He became a bishop of Paris, but he is best known as the teacher of Catholicism's most famous theologian, Thomas Aquinas

(1225–1274), whose best-known work, *Summa Theologica,* is a grand effort to reconcile faith and reason in the search for divine truth. From Albertus Magnus, Aquinas learned that the Aristotelian method of reasoning was the best way to truth. In fact, reason could stand alone, even without faith, as the best source for truth. However, Aquinas never discarded the value of faith, for he taught that there was no conflict between faith in revealed truth and truth found by the way of reason. He sought to take all known knowledge of his time and bring it into harmony with Christian doctrines.

In *Summa Theologica* Aquinas asks 631 questions that he seeks to answer by using logical deduction and analysis of many citations from both Christian and pagan sources. An example of his methodology is found in his answer to the question, "Does God exist?" Aquinas first refutes the objections to God's existence, then follows with proofs from authoritative sources. Aquinas gives five proofs for God's existence: (1) Since motion is universal there must have been a prime mover, namely God; (2) Nothing happens unless there is a cause for action. Therefore, God is the first efficient cause; (3) The very existence of all things can be attributed to the fact that nothing can exist from nothing; (4) In nature there are gradations of goodness or perfection from imperfection to perfection. For one to attain the state of perfection is the highest mark of perfection, God; (5) All action must have direction or purpose. There must be some intelligent being to give purpose to one's life, and that intelligent source is God.

Thomas Aquinas became the most exalted of all Christian theologians, for which he was canonized as a saint. He gave final authority to the doctrines and practices of the Roman Catholic Church. As Mircea Eliade says in his *History of Religious Ideas:*

> The Thomist reform affected the entire field of philosophy and theology; there is thus not a single question relating to these domains in which history cannot note its influence and follow its traces. . . . But the importance of Thomism results from its having been proclaimed in the nineteenth century as the official theology of the Roman Church.[5]

As praised as Thomas Aquinas was he was not without his critics. Two of his most known critics were Bonaventura and John Duns Scotus. Bonaventura (Giovanni of Fedanza, 1217–1274) was an Italian Franciscan who taught at the University of Paris and became head of the Franciscan Order of Brothers Minor. As a mystic he rejected the rational approach to knowledge, but he did accept the mystical idealism of Plato, since Plato believed that the truest knowledge came through meditation and prayer. St. Francis of Assisi had great influence on the life of Bonaventura. Francis found God in all things, almost in the image of a pantheist. Bonaventura made Christ the focal point of his religious thinking. The mystery of Christ and the message of love were the primary concerns of the Church. God is love, and God is known best by way of meditation and revelation. However, Bonaventura never discarded completely the value of reason.

In his *Commentaries,* based on Lombard's *Sic et Non,* Bonaventura claims that God created the universe for one purpose only and that was to give the human soul the freedom to escape from the world of sin and to begin its destined journey upward to God. The sole purpose of the Church was to provide the vehicle for this journey.

The other critic of Aquinas was John Duns Scotus (1265–1308). A Scottish theologian and a member of the Franciscan Order, he also doubted the value of reason as a theological tool. The essence of Christianity is God's love for all things created. His love is preeminent, and Duns Scotus therefore questioned the doctrines of original sin and predestination. He granted that reason had some value, but the highest of God's truths can be discovered only by the use of meditation and mystical intuition. After all study and thought, the Christian must accept God's truth on faith, and not by reason. Duns Scotus supported the validity of the dogma of the Immaculate Conception.

The word *dunce* is derived from John Duns Scotus. John Duns Scotus and his allies were called "Dunces." Since they were opposed to the revival of classical learning, and were critical of the rationalist theologians like Thomas Aquinas, the term took on a derogatory meaning.

18

The City of God on Earth: Temporal Church Power

If the Christian Church was ever to fulfill its destiny as projected by Augustine in his *City of God* it would need to acquire some measure of political as well as spiritual power. Theologians, authors of Scripture, teachers and missionaries, and the clergy are all essential ingredients, along with the communicants, in the building of a permanent, powerful Church institution. But somehow the Church had to organize a centralized body of authority, armed with sufficient power so as to command obedience and loyalty from its membership. If Jesus was said to have had two bodies, spiritual and physical, then the Church likewise needed two bodies, spiritual and temporal. The temporal or physical component of the Church body was formed when the authority of the Church began to legislate the conduct of almost all aspects of the Christian's everyday life, from the management of marriage and the family to the operation of the state and the economic affairs of the people. When the principles of the Christian gospel were translated into the rules for daily living, they were expressed as canons, laws, dogmas, doctrines, and traditions, which were decreed or formulated by the agencies of power, church councils, bishops, and the first of all bishops, the pope. It has been said that the history of the Roman Catholic Church can be written from the biographies of several notable popes, some of whom will be noted in the following paragraphs.

By 400 the Church was on the road to becoming a major power in Europe. The Second Coming of Christ had not arrived, and no one knew at what date the Christ would appear. Since the end of the world was not imminent, Christian people had to plan for building a Christian world here on earth. The simple, democratically organized church of the Pauline era, with church units scattered throughout the Roman Empire, would no longer suffice. The Christian Church required a centralized power center if it was to become the universal Catholic Church. When the Church was recognized as the state church of the Roman

Empire in the fourth century, the foundation for a strong church structure had been laid. Now the Church had the strong arm of the imperial government to command obedience to its rules. Penalties for disobedience could be assessed. All heresies and competing religious groups could be suppressed. The orthodox Church could claim to be the sole representative of God on earth.

By the eleventh century the Church had become a major ruling force in Western Europe, although the division of the Church in 1054 would prevent the Roman Catholic Church from exercising control over eastern Europe. When the Roman Empire in the West succumbed to internal forces of decay and external attacks from Germanic and Asiatic barbarians in the fourth and fifth centuries, the bishop of Rome and the Roman Church were destined to inherit some of the power and prestige of the imperial government. The papacy would adopt the manners and powers of the Roman emperor, and the Church would adopt the imperial forms of government and law, even down to the local provinces and parishes. As the Roman emperor claimed to be the agent of God on earth so the pope could claim legitimately to be the vicar of Christ, the chosen agent of God on earth. By the thirteenth century the church and the papacy had effectively made good their claims to supreme power by ruling over both the Christian people and the Christian monarchs.

The Rise of the Papacy

During the second and third centuries a tradition had arisen by which the ruling body of church elders in the early Church had become subjected to the dictates of the presiding elder or bishop. No longer was the bishop elected by the congregation, but now he was elected by the other elders or bishops. Origen had declared that only bishops could administer the sacraments since they were the descendents of the original apostles. Laity and clergy had become separate parts of the Church. Pope Leo I (r. 440–461) claimed that he was supreme among all bishops, although the tradition at that time was that all bishops were equal. The four other ranking bishops, in Alexandria, Antioch, Jerusalem, and Constantinople, rejected Leo's claim to power. Pope Gregory I (r. 590–609) has been credited with being the founder of the Roman papacy.

How did the bishop of Rome become first among equals? First the Roman bishops claimed that they were the legitimate heirs of the Christ by virtue of the claim that the disciple Peter, who was left to shepherd the Christian flock, had been given the keys to heaven by Christ. Since Peter had been martyred in Rome, the bishop of Rome could claim that Peter on his death had given these special keys to him. As early as 100 Pope Clement asserted that he had inherited Peter's power. However, before the Christian Church was acknowledged as the state church, no bishop had any real power to govern.

About 800 some forged documents began to surface that were used to prove that the pope was truly Peter's successor. These documents, the Pseudo-Isidorian

Decretals and the Donation of Constantine, although forged, became potent proof for the papal claim of supremacy. The Pseudo-Isidorian Decretals were a mixture of genuine Church Council decrees and forged documents. They were first brought to light by Pope Nicholas I (r. 858–867). They were alleged to have been written by a seventh-century Spanish bishop, Isadore of Seville. Pope Sylvester (r. 314–335) has been credited also as being the author of another forged document, the "Donation of Constantine," which claimed that the popes were supreme heads of the Church and were temporal rulers over the Roman Empire in the west as well. This gift of power was allegedly given by the emperor Constantine. In 494, Pope Gelasius I claimed these same supreme powers in a letter to the Byzantine emperor Anastasius. The Synod of Whitby in England in 664 and the king of Northumbria recognized these claims to papal power as having been granted by Peter to the Roman bishop.

Pope Gregory VII (r. 1073–1085) wrote a "Dictate of the Pope," in which he claimed to be the superior, universal source of power over all of Christendom, including all princes and kings. He wrote, "The Roman Church has never erred. . . . All princes shall kiss the feet of the Pope alone. . . . He may depose Emperors."[1]

Whether papal power owed anything to these forged documents may be questioned, but that the Roman popes were the supreme head of the church with powers to rule over both the spiritual and political life of Western Europe had become a well-established fact of life by 1200. Only the church councils might contest the popes' claims to such sovereign power. The pope assumed the title "Pontifex Maximus," a title used by the Roman emperors. However, in eastern Europe, the patriarch of Constantinople and the Byzantine emperors refused to recognize the popes' claimed superior powers. This issue of papal powers became a major factor in causing the division of the Christian Church in 1054.

In assessing the reasons for the power of the Roman papacy it must be recalled that the city of Rome, even after it fell, remained an important city as a center of commerce and of historical and religious importance. Pilgrims went to Rome to pay their respects to God and Rome's glorious past. Only Alexandria and Constantinople could rival Rome as important cities in the year 1000.

Pope Leo I was among the first great popes to give direction to the Church. He called the Council of Chalcedon in 451, which reiterated the Nicene Creed and recognized the mother of Jesus as the Virgin Mary. The Chalcedonian Creed became the official creed of the Catholic Church. Leo claimed also that the bishop of Rome was superior to all other bishops.

The next great pope was Gregory I. His claim to supreme power has been noted earlier. Gregory was a practical administrator who did much to set the traditions by which all later popes would govern the Church. He became the governor of Italy, thereby replacing the imperial governor. He defended Rome against the invading German Lombards. On Christmas Day 597 his missionary Augustine in England converted more than ten thousand Anglo-Saxon subjects of King Ethelbert. Gregory organized monasteries. He administered large church lands and papal estates. In brief, Gregory was a successful monarch, even a warrior. But he was also a dedicated spiritual leader who enhanced the power of the papacy. He blessed the doctrines of penance and purgatory, church beliefs that the burden of original sin could be lifted from the souls of sinners by transferring to these souls in purgatory some of the surplus merits or good works that had been earned by Christian saints while on earth. The concept of purgatory was not an invention of the Catholic Church, for long before this belief was held by some of the Jewish prophets, as well as by the Buddhists. The Gregorian chants used in church services today are attributed to Pope Gregory.

The power of the papacy continued to increase under later popes. Popes Stephen III (r. 768–733) and Leo III (r. 795–816) made alliances with the Frankish kings to wage war against German heretics and convert them to Christianity. Thus a precedent had been set by which it was proper for popes and kings to join hands against common enemies, pagan, Muslim, or rival Christian powers. An undetermined issue in the ninth century was which power body, king or pope, would become the victor if ever a contest for power was waged between kings and popes.

The alliances with the Frankish kings did enable the popes to control Italy, but the popes had to concede that the Frankish kings were the supreme temporal rulers in Western Europe, a condition recognized when Pope Leo III crowned Charles the Great (Charlemagne) emperor of the Holy Roman Empire on Christmas Day 800.

Pope Nicholas I (r. 858–867) used the forged Decretals as his justification for removing the archbishops of Cologne and Trier from their offices and for preventing the marriage of Lothair II, a Frankish king. By the end of his term, Nicholas had succeeded in establishing his rule over the bishops and churches of Western Europe.

Between 870 and 950 the papacy was in a period of decline, because a series of weak and often corrupt popes were in power. Henry III (1017–1056), a German king and emperor of the Holy Roman Empire, took the initiative to effect some papal reforms. He installed a line of German popes who engineered some reform measures. Pope Nicholas II, in 1052, with the aid of a wise colleague, reformed the method of appointing the pope by creating the system of cardinals to elect all future popes and to prevent national monarchs from putting their own popes in power. His eventual successor, his former aide, Hildebrande, came to power as Pope Gregory VII (r. 1073–1085). Gregory became one of the greatest of all Roman popes. He proclaimed the dogma of the infallibility of the pope, a doctrine finally accepted by the Vatican Council of 1869 as official church dogma. Infallibility was referred to those papal pronouncements on matters of faith that were declared to be free of error. Gregory also proclaimed the doctrine of the immaculate conception, a belief adopted officially by the church in 1854, that holds that the mother of Jesus was born without sin. Gregory appointed and deposed bishops at will. He made his legates or personal agents to various nations superior to all local bishops. He excommunicated Holy Roman Emperor Henry IV and compelled Henry to come to Canossa, a papal residence, on bended knee in 1078. Henry had been excommunicated earlier in 1076 for his refusal to give up his right to invest the clergy with their offices. However, Gregory failed to establish his right to rule over all monarchs when his army was defeated by the army of Henry IV. Gregory did pave the way for the accession to power of the church's most powerful pople, Pope Innocent III (r. 1198–1216).

Innocent III became a pope who exercised control over both the church and the nations of Western Europe. For a brief time he brought eastern Europe under his control when during the Fourth Crusade in 1204 his armies entered Constantinople and caused a Latin kingdom to be created there. For some fifty years, it seemed that Christendom had been reunited under the Roman church. Eventually the Turkish Muslim forces forced the Christian crusaders to lose control of the Byzantine Empire.

Innocent prosecuted heretics wherever they were to be found, thus giving him opportunities to interfere in the affairs of the national monarchs. He ruled as a prince over most of Italy, a right he had won from Holy Roman emperor Otto IV. He installed two German emperors as rulers of the Holy Roman Empire, made England under King John a papal fief, and forced the king of France to take back his divorced wife. Moreover, Spain and Portugal came under Innocent's rule. As a ruler of Italian provinces, he needed the support of other nations to secure protection for his papal states. Hence, he made alliances with Spain and England to wage war against France. By the time of his death (1216) Innocent III had made good on his claim to be sovereign over both the spiritual and temporal affairs of Western Europe. Papal canons or laws had become binding on all people in Western Europe. Every aspect of church organization, doctrine, law, or practice was the pope's will to order. He alone could grant dispensations from church penalties. He was deemed infallible in all matters of faith. The papal court was the final court of appeal. The pope could grant justice to all offenders and also provide absolution from all penalties applied. He granted indulgences or pardons to those who had committed mortal sins. He could nominate and depose bishops at will. He levied papal taxes on church property without the consent of the local clergy or laity. He sent his legates to Western monarchs and princes who became subject to the orders of the legates. He excommunicated kings and lay persons, and he placed obstinate nations under papal interdiction, thereby closing down all religious services in the offending nation.

For a time Innocent placed England under his control. No one dared to question his authority to rule over all matters affecting the Church, the monasteries, and matters of civil justice. The only restraint on the powers of the papal court was that it could not condemn a person to death. A convicted criminal had to be turned over to state authorities for execution. King John grudgingly acknowledged the pope as his overlord and England as a papal fief when he was forced to pay an annual tribute of 1000 marks to the papacy.

Although the English people resented papal taxation, the appointment of too many Italian clerics to church offices, and the subjugation of King John to a role as a papal puppet, the pope did find support from the disgruntled nobles, who wished to strip the king of his absolute power. In 1215 an alliance between the papal forces and the nobles forced the king to sign the Magna Carta, the first constitutional limitation on the power of an absolute monarch in England, and the beginning of a parliamentary system of government.

After the deaths of King John and Innocent III in 1216, papal rule over England continued until King Henry III and Pope Honorius reached an agreement that England would no longer need to send tribute to Rome and that the local bishops would be free to make their own church appointments. The relaxation of papal power came when both the king and the pope needed money to wage war against France, and the pope wished to promote another crusade to the Holy Land. On this occasion the nobles agreed to being taxed so that the pope might be supported.

Pope Honorius died in 1227, after which he was succeeded by Gregory IX (r. 1227–1246). Pope Gregory resumed the policies of Innocent III, that is, exercising all papal powers to the limit. He created the Office of the Inquisition in 1233, an office designed as a special court to try and punish heretics. In 1239 Gregory excommunicated emperor Frederick II. So that the public might be shown the extent of papal power, Gregory ordered that the relics of Peter and Paul, their skulls, be paraded through the streets of Rome. After the parade Gregory placed his tiara on the skull of Peter, thereby demonstrating that it was Peter who gave the keys to heaven to the Roman popes.

By 1241, with the death of Gregory, papal power went into a period of decline. Across Western Europe both feudal nobles and the local clergy began to resist papal taxation. The papacy slipped into an era of moral and spiritual decline. The waning power of the papacy permitted local nobles and clergy to campaign for a greater measure of freedom to conduct their affairs from papal control. The popes of the later Middle Ages, from the thirteenth century on, seemed to be more concerned with waging wars against heretics and recalcitrant kings than fighting the battle for Christian justice and charity. Popes needed more money for their wars, for their extravagant courts, and for their building programs in Rome. Popes lived in the manner of royal princes with mistresses and illegitimate children. Great wealth had come to the papacy, likewise to many of the bishoprics and monasteries, as wealthy Christians bequeathed their estates to the church, or while living gave their lands to the church as a means of escaping taxation by the state. New revenue measures included the sale of church offices, a practice called simony, the sale of indulgences, and even the acceptance of payments for administering the sacraments.

Ecumenical Councils

Prior to the tenth century and before the papacy had established its position as the supreme authority for making decisions on all issues concerning the Church, the Church councils had been the final authority for declaring the official positions on belief and church practices. Councils were called into session either by the Roman emperor or a chief bishop from a principal city. Delegates to the councils were the bishops and abbots from the many areas of the Empire, and for this reason they were called ecumenical councils. Throughout the history of the Roman Catholic Church twenty-six council meetings were held, the last one being Vatican II in 1962.

The first council was called by the emperor Constantine to meet in Nicea in 325 for the purpose of resolving the theological differences between orthodox and Arian Christians. Arius taught that Jesus was not of the same substance as God, but only the best of created beings. The Council of Nicea adopted the concept of the Holy Trinity as the correct interpretation of the nature of Christ. Christ was the son of God, of the same substance, divine but also human, in one body. The second council met in Constantinople in 381. This council was called by the emperor Theodosius I for the purpose of settling the Apolinarian heresy, which held that Christ must be wholly divine, not human, one with God, if he was to be able to save souls. This council accepted Mary as being the virgin mother of God.

The third council met at Ephesus in 431, called by the archbishop of Alexandria, Cyril, for the purpose of eradicating the Nestorian heresy. Nestorians believed that the Christ was both human and divine, both elements existing independently and not unified within one body. The Nestorians also rejected the belief that Mary was the mother of God—she was only the mother of Jesus.

The fourth council met at Chalcedon in 451, and was called by emperor Marcian to redefine the Nicene Creed. This council reaffirmed the Nicene Creed, which had proclaimed the doctrine of the Holy Trinity, and it also reaffirmed that Mary was the mother of God. Furthermore, the council stated that the papacy under Pope Leo I was superior to all other bishops, including the patriarchs in Constantinople, Alexandria, Jerusalem, and Antioch.

The fifth council in Constantinople in 553 reaffirmed the Chalcedon decrees.

The sixth council, also held in Constantinople in 681, sought to combat the Monophysite heresy, which held that Christ was wholly divine with no human elements. The council rejected this belief by asserting the orthodox position that Christ had two natures in one body.

The seventh and last of the ecumenical councils was held in Nicea in 787 to reaffirm the acceptance of the belief in the veneration of images or icons. This issue over the use of human images in church worship and architecture had become a major point of difference between the Roman and eastern branches of Christianity. The Synod of Constantinople in 754 had outlawed the use of images, a decision that displeased many elements of the eastern church, which believed that images of Christ not only gave reality to the person of Christ, but also symbolized the accepted fact that the emperor was the embodiment of Christ on earth.

During the period from the sixth to the eighth centuries Church councils established many current Catholic beliefs and practices—the Holy Trinity, the Virgin Birth, the veneration of relics and saints, the celibacy of the clergy, that priests must wear dark robes and tonsured haircuts, the nature of the Eucharist, and many other orthodox beliefs. Until the meeting of the tenth council or the Third Lateran Council, which met in Rome in 1179, no other important church councils met. The tenth council took action against the Cathari, or Albigensian, and the Waldensian heresies in southern France. Some historians believe that these heresies were forerunners of the later Protestant movements.

The sixteenth council met in Constance, 1414–1418, to take action against a disgraceful internal feud within the papacy. At one time, during the Great Schism, three popes vied for power. This council deposed two popes and forced a third one to resign, after which a reform pope was elected. So that future papal scandals might be avoided, the council ordered that annual councils be called to supervise and regulate the conduct of the papacy. Another reform council was called to meet in Basil in 1431, but it suffices to say that reform efforts were doomed to failure.

No further church council was called into session until a crisis within the Christian body was created by the Protestant Reformation. The Council of Trent took place from 1545–1563; it was actually a series of intermittent sessions that were held to heal the breach within Christian ranks, and if that was not possible then to minimize the spread of the Protestant rebellion. Needless to say the division within the church remained, so the council did the next best thing, that is, to effect reforms within the Catholic church that might preserve what was left of it. In brief the council reaffirmed the traditional doctrines of belief, the primacy of the Roman bishop, who was declared to be "The Vicar of Christ, of God and Jesus Christ," and the mandate that all of the clergy must be obedient to him. Certain reform measures were enacted to secure a better educated clergy, and a clergy once more dedicated to the service of the church. Past clerical and papal abuses, such as simony and the sale of indulgences, were forbidden. Bishops were ordered to be more alert in supervising the conduct of the priests in their local parishes. The decrees of the Council of Trent would remain as the blueprint of action for the Roman Catholic Church up to the present time.

The last church council to be held was Vatican II, called into session by Pope John XXIII in 1962. Pope John sought to modernize the Roman church by providing for more congregational participation in the church service, including the use of the vernacular language for the conduct of the Mass and congregational hymn singing. Pope John sought also to reduce the power of the papacy in favor of granting more power to church councils.

Not only did Pople John seek to light a new spark of democracy in the Catholic church, he gave support to other democratic movements current in his day. He spoke in favor of democratic governments for all nations and stated that third world countries in Africa and South America should be emancipated from their colonial overlords. In matters of faith, he spoke a revolutionary doctrine that all people should have freedom of belief, a position that might compromise the position of his church as the one, universal Church and the notion that the pope was infallible in certain matters of faith. Pope John encouraged ecumenical meetings in which representatives of all religious faiths might come together and seek to find mutually satisfying positions in matters of religious belief. He invited representatives from the several Protestant and Eastern Orthodox churches, as well as representatives from the other world religions to meet in Rome. He sought to reach some measure of accommodation with Communist countries and doctrines. He saw the need for protective legislation for the working people of the world, and a legitimate place for labor unions in the economic system. He encouraged the enactment of all forms of social welfare legislation, such as socialized medicine. Although Pople John was one of the oldest men to have ever held his office, no other pope was more revolutionary and democratic. His successors tended to be more conservative and younger in years.

Structure and Internal Workings of the Church

By the end of the first millennium, the Roman Catholic church had a sacred scripture, official creeds and doctrines, and an institution believed to be blessed by both God and the state as the one and only Christian church. Unfortunately human institutions are not always able to command loyalty and obedience simply by declaring that obedience and loyalty are commanded by God and his agents on earth. Human institutions require the existence of forms of government and laws, and a set of routine, regularized acts of worship that become habitual, signifying compliance and obeisance. Without these social controls, institutions are doomed to wither away and die. So long as the Christian Church had the strong arm of the Roman emperor to enforce its rules, to discipline the dissidents and the heretics, to punish the sinners, and to command the payment of tithes and perform acts of charity, the Church did not need an elaborate system of government. After the fall of Rome, however, imperial power was doomed to weaken and become impotent. Church leaders had to devise a substitute government for the Church.

Pope Gregory I has been credited with giving the Church its initial forms of government. The most natural plan for government was to use the model provided by the Roman Empire. The Church used the hierarchial system of authoritarian government in which power would descend from the top, the bishop of Rome or the pope, who inherited the prestige and power of the Roman emperor and in the eyes of the people was both god and king. So in a sense the pope aspire to the same titles and power that had formerly belonged to the Roman emperor.

From the pope power descended to the next layer of government, the archbishops; and then to the bishops who were to rule over perfectures, provinces, and dioceses; finally papal authority reached down to the lowest level of church government, the level of the parish priest. By virtue of the sacrament of ordination all members of the clergy were endowed with the sacred spirit and power of Christ. In the local parishes, the priests had assistants, the deacons, to help administer church property, care for the sick and orphans, supervise the collection of the tithes, and oversee the behavior of the communicants. As the Church acquired more and more wealth through bequests and donations, the church government at all levels needed the assistance of professional bureaucrats and skilled craftsmen. In all of the Church governments the laity was carefully separated from the clergy, which meant that the laity had little or no voice in the determination of church policy and its actions.

The Roman system of law became the canon law of the Church. Roman courts became ecclesiastical courts, with the Papal Curia becoming the supreme court of Christendom. The Church employed professional lawyers to codify and interpret the law. One of the first codes of church law was issued by the emperor Theodosius in 383. By the thirteenth century scarcely any aspect of human life escaped the purview of the law and the jurisdiction of the ecclesiastical courts.

All governments must apply penalties when offenders are caught in violation of the law. Oftentimes conformity to the law is best secured by the promise of rewards for good behavior and obedience. In an age of ignorance and belief in the power of the supernatural, a potent reward was the promise of eternal life for the soul in heaven. Moreover, to be called a Christian carried great weight in medieval society. A Christian had all of the preferred advantages for employment and protection by the Church and the state. By the same token, a Jew was no better off in Medieval Christian society than a leper, confined to restricted urban areas in a ghetto, and denied opportunities for employment and the enjoyment of equal protection under the law.

The Church offered rewards of good employment for many young men who happened to be the younger sons of the feudal nobility. In the Middle Ages the prevailing law of inheritance was primogeniture, a rule that gave a person's inheritance to the eldest son. The younger sons were to find employment as soldier-knights in the armies of the more important nobles, or in the bureaucracy of the Church, to be trained as priests and other administrators. The sons of the poor peasants were normally bound to the soil or the manor of a feudal lord, but occasionally the poor man's son, if intellectually inclined, might be taken by the Church, educated, and prepared for service as a priest or a monk.

Sermons on morality, Christian love and forgiveness, and the torture of torment in hell, caused many good Christians to obey the laws of the Church. If the promise of rewards in heaven were insufficient to command obedience, then fiery sermons on the works of the devil in hell might provide the required incentive to be a good Christian. But if exhortation from the priests and a sense of Christian dedication were inadequate to secure loyalty and conformity from the member-ship, then the Church could exercise its right to apply more effective penalties. The mildest of penalties for disobedience or a sinful act would be to make a confession of one's error before a priest, the sacrament of confession, upon which the priest might admonish the sinner to mend his or her ways, and then order the payment of a penance such as saying certain prayers or rosaries, or making a pilgrimage to a shrine, or paying a money fine or some form of work service. However, a perverse sinner, a heretic, a murderer, or an adulterer might be given a maximum penalty of excommunication, which excluded the person from all church services and relationships. An excommunicated person was literally a man without a country, an abandoned dog to be shunned and treated as if he or she were rabid. If the king and the nation were guilty of violating Church commandments, then the entire nation could be placed under an interdict by which all church services and actions were suspended.

Later the Church would institute a special court to try and punish the most evil of all offenders, the heretics. Pope Gregory IX in 1233 founded a special court, the Court of Inquisition, which had as its objective the extirpation of two prominent heresies, the Waldensians and the Albigensians in France. The Inquisition permitted confessions to be obtained from the accused sinners by torture, and convictions for heresy were always punishable by being burned to death at the stake. The Inquisition became a shameful practice that brought much criticism to the Church, especially when its courts used excessively cruel tortures against the Jews and the Muslims in Spain during the sixteenth century.

The reform Council of Trent took one more step to curb dissent and heresy when it issued a list of books forbidden to be read by Christians, the Index of Prohibited Books. As a last resort the Church could use military action to punish its enemies. Holy wars or crusades became a medieval way of life. Crusades were preached against the Muslim infidels who occupied the Holy Land and often threatened the security of Europe. Crusades were waged against heretics wherever they might emerge. Even the sixteenth-century Catholic wars against the Lutheran Protestants could be called crusades.

For most of the medieval Catholic Christians the Church offered many positive benefits for those who were faithful, disciplined communicants. The fear of punishment here on earth or in hell after death was undoubtedly a powerful incentive to be obedient Christians. But there were rewards promised by the Church, eternal salvation for the soul, the promise that Christ would return eventually to bring Paradise to Earth, and that even before the Advent of Christ the Church might be able to fashion on earth the "City of God." The Church by the eleventh century was beginning to lay the foundations for a number of social services, schools, universities, hospitals, orphanages, and other measures to aid the poor. The Church had taken measures to reduce the prevailing abundance of personal violence so characteristic of the feudal age.

The Principle Doctrines of the Catholic Faith

Before a person could enjoy the benefits of the Church, one had to be accepted into the membership of the Church. For most people of the Middle Ages, membership came with birth into a Christian family. For non-Christians, pagans, infidels,

Jews, and Muslims, conversion to Christianity occurred through the persuasive powers of missionaries or by a process of compulsory mass conversion when a tribal chief or a king was converted and automatically all of his subjects became Christians.

Membership in the Roman Catholic Church was conditional upon the acceptance of the basic doctrines and spiritual obligations as they were defined by the Church. The orthodox or correct formula for salvation was to accept the belief that through God's grace and mercy man could be freed of original sin if the initiate would accept this belief on faith. Justification by faith follows the system of salvation as conceived by the Apostle Paul. The Augustinian limitation on the freedom of man to choose to accept salvation on faith, that is, the doctrine of predestination, never became a widely accepted belief in Catholic theology. By the fourth century, theologians had added a second condition for salvation, that is, the need to do "good works," those acts that over time tradition has deemed to have value in the process of salvation. By doing good works, a Christian accumulates good merits which in the Final Judgment will direct his soul to heaven.

Good works include the total gamut of those Christian obligations that God and the Church expect each member to accept and perform. By the thirteenth century the Catholic church had achieved a position of such extensive power over the total society—the social, political, and economic aspects of medieval world—that it might be said that to be a good citizen, a devoted parent, and an honest laborer were all acts within the definition of good works. However, the church would limit the range of good works to those duties and obligations which the church prescribed specifically for spiritual perfection and purification. Good Christians were expected to obey the Ten Commandments, especially the commandment to "Love thy neighbor," and refrain from committing any of the mortal sins that the Church pronounced to be evil acts. The list of mortal sins ranged from murder, adultery, and theft, to the even more serious sins of heresy, blasphemy, and disobedience to the Church. Good works required faithfulness in church attendance, the observance of the seven sacraments, the practice of periodic confession of sins, the observance of the holy days, and making a pilgrimage to some sacred shrine at least once in a lifetime. Faithful Christians must pay their tithes to support the church and its activities, and at all times seek wisdom from the parish priest, whose wisdom is ordained to have come from God by way of Christ and his agent on earth, the Holy Father, the pope. No greater sin could man commit than to question the truth as found in the doctrines and dogmas of the Church as they had been defined by councils and popes.

A good Christian accepts the truth as found in the Nicene Creed and other statements of belief. The God of the Old Testament is the Christian God, and the words of God are written in the Bible. The doctrine of the Holy Trinity, that God, the Father; Christ, the Son; and the Holy Spirit are all of one substance, all divine. Yet the Christ has a dual person, a person in whom the human body and the divine element remain separate identities. The doctrine of the Holy Trinity is not found in either the Old or the New Testaments. Perhaps germs for the idea might be found in the first-century gospels, but the definition of the Trinity originated with fourth-century theologians and Church councils. Tertullian, in the third century, had defended the proposition that Christ had a dual nature, but it was the fourth-century theologians Basil of Caesaria, Gregory of Nyssa, and Augustine who developed the concept of the Trinity, which the Council of Nicea in 325 declared to be church doctrine.

For many years the mother of Jesus, Mary, was given no special spiritual status. In the New Testament she is depicted as a natural, human mother with no divine elements. In the twenty-one letters of the apostles in the New Testament, Mary's name is not mentioned. The early Christian theologians, Origen, Jerome, and Ambrose, viewed Mary as a human mother who had given birth to five sons and at least two daughters.

Augustine said that if Jesus was born of a virgin birth, then logically Mary must have been conceived immaculately, that is without the taint of original sin. Neither Thomas Aquinas nor Pope Innocent III accepted the immaculate conception doctrine. Pope Sixtus IV in the fifteenth century accepted the doctrine of the immaculate conception, and it was finalized in 1858 when Pope Pius IX published a papal bull announcing it. In 1950 Pope Pius XII went a step further by declaring that Mary's body had been transmitted directly to heaven by a miracle.

In the fifth century Christians began to worship Mary as the mother of God. Female goddesses were a common feature of most early religions, so if Mary became a goddess it would be in conformity with other religions. By the sixteenth century, the cult of the Virgin Mary had reached a place where she became a spiritual person equal to her son in heaven. Both Bonaventura and Ignatius Loyola honored Mary as the mother of God and one who intercedes with God to secure for man remission of sins. Of 433 churches and chapels in Rome, 121 are dedicated to the Virgin Mary while only fifteen honor Jesus Christ.[2] In the Eastern Orthodox Church, Mary is proclaimed to be celestial wisdom, or Saint Sophia.

The Seven Sacraments

Among the most important duties of the clergy and laity was the observance of the seven sacraments, those religious acts symbolizing the divine presence of God acting within the human person. They represent the outward signs of inward grace. For several centuries the number and the nature of the sacraments were in dispute. Except for baptism and the Lord's Supper or Eucharist, all others were matters for debate among the early theologians. Peter Lombard in his *Book of Sentences,* written during the twelfth century, was among the first to define all seven sacraments. At the Council of Florence in 1439 the seven sacraments were defined and accepted by the Roman Church. As defined by the decree for the Armenians, the seven sacraments are baptism, confirmation, the Eucharist, penance, extreme unction, matrimony, and ordination of the clergy. The first five were designed to enhance the spiritual perfection of all Christians, while the last two were directed to the control of the family and the clergy. Protestant denominations acknowledge only two sacraments, baptism and the Lord's Supper. The other five are celebrated only by Catholics.

The sacrament of baptism, by which a person becomes a member of the Christian fellowship and joins in union with Christ is an act performed with water, a symbol of purification for both body and the spirit. The application of water to the body or merely to the head, depending on the particular Christian sect, signifies that the stains of original sin have been removed and man's relation to God has been restored in love and acceptance. The old way of living has died and the baptized person is "born anew," a bodily and a spiritual resurrection. Baptism commits both the child and the parents to a vow that they will be faithful parents who will rear the child in the image of Christ. Catholics baptize the infant child by sprinkling the head soon after birth lest the child should die still bearing the burden of original sin. The more radical Protestant churches usually baptize by immersion, that is placing the total body under water, although some of the more moderate Protestant groups continue to use the sprinkling method of baptism. In the Baptist church traditional baptism occurs only at the age of adolescence or adulthood, about thirteen or fourteen years of age. Normally a baptismal service is conducted by an ordained person, a priest, bishop, or minister, but in the case of an emergency, such as impending death, a lay person may perform the baptism ritual if the proper words and acts are used.

The sacrament of confirmation symbolizes the time when the Holy Spirit descended upon Jesus when he was baptized by John the Baptist in the River Jordan. Confirmation is given to a child when he or she is approaching adulthood and the age of understanding. When the priest or bishop anoints the child's forehead with the sign of the cross, a second baptism is enacted in which the child is instructed to be faithful to his or her faith, to defend it against all enemies.

A third sacrament is the Eucharist (Greek for "thanksgiving"), or the Lord's Supper, or the Last Supper, in many of the Protestant churches. The sacrament is intended to strengthen the bond between God and man. It commemorates the last supper Jesus had with his disciples. In the time of Jesus it was a celebration of the Jewish Passover, which has been retained in the Christian church as a memorial to the final sacrifice Jesus made to redeem mankind from his sins. In the Catholic tradition, the Eucharist symbolizes a mystical union of the communicant with God through the body of Christ. The Catholic tradition believes that during the service of the Mass or Eucharist a miracle has transpired by which the elements of bread and wine are transformed or transubstantiated into the real blood and body of Christ. The bread used in the service presents the body of Christ while the wine (grape juice is used in many of the Protestant churches) represents the blood of Christ. As a rule Protestants reject the miracle of transubstantiation. However, the Eastern Orthodox Church does retain the belief in the miracle of transubstantiation. Until recently, since Vatican II in 1962, the laity was given only the bread, the presiding priest alone consumed the wine, lest some of the precious wine or blood be spilled accidentally. Since Vatican II members of the congregation also consume the wine from a common cup or chalice held by the priest. The bread or wafer is placed on the communicant's tongue by his or her own hand when handed it by the priest. Formerly the priest placed the wafer on the tongue. It was thought that the Methodist church was the first to substitute grape juice for the wine. In the Greek Orthodox Church only leavened bread is used, not the unleavened bread used in the Roman Catholic Church. This issue was one more factor in causing the split in the Church in 1054. In the Seventh-Day Adventist Church, the Lord's Supper is observed quarterly with an added ritual observance, the washing of feet, as the disciples did for Jesus.

The fourth sacrament, penance, was instituted by Christ as a means of enhancing the remission of sins that separate man from God. Penance becomes a means by which a sinful, but contrite person can confess his or her sins to a priest or confessor, and thereby be absolved of them. It is not the priest who absolves the sin, but Christ through him. The priest is only a vehicle by which the sinner and Christ are brought together. The confessor must never reveal the confessed sin to others. Penance is given only after the penitent sinner shows signs of contrition or sorrow for his or her sins. The word *contrition* means "to grind," or to be sorry for sins committed. After confession comes "satisfaction" for sins, or penance, the penalties for sins. The acts of penance include saying prayers, fasting, giving alms, or doing other acts of charity. The theological basis for penance is found in the gospel of John 20:23, where it is said, "Whosesoever sins ye remit, they are remitted unto them, and whosesoever sins ye retain, they are retained." Catholic theology explains penance as being possible when the stored up, accumulated merits of the good works of saints, martyrs, and other Christian heroes can be transferred to sinners so that their burden of sin may be relieved. Thus the souls of sinners may be cleansed of their sins before death.

Closely related to the sacrament of penance is the Catholic belief that through the clergy God can grant a dispensation or pardon from any penalties that might have been assessed for sins committed by an act of indulgence: Thus the sins of the living and the souls of the dead in purgatory could be granted freedom from all or much of the penalties for the sins committed during one's lifetime. It was the sale of indulgences by some unscrupulous priests, bishops, and even the pope that caused Martin Luther to become disenchanted with some of his fellow clergymen. The belief in purgatory was defined first by the papacy in 1259, although it was a long-established belief that the soul's journey to heaven might be interrepted for a period of time by remaining temporarily in a state of purgatory while the soul was cleansed of its sins. The soul in purgatory might be spared a final condemnation to hell if sufficient prayers and masses could be offered in behalf of the soul at risk.

A fifth sacrament, extreme unction, is administered to a person who is near death or who has died. A priest anoints certain parts of the body with oil and a prayer, not for the dead, but for the restoration of health to the person. Such a healing prayer is noted in James 5:14–15. A special form of the Eucharist, the Viaticum, is offered also. This sacrament becomes the person's last communion before the priest commends the soul to God.

The sixth sacrament, that of ordination, is an act by which the bishop confers the spiritual power of a cleric's office to anyone who is about to become an administrator of God's services and sacraments to his fellow Christians. The Biblical sanction for the sacrament of ordination is found in Hebrews 5:11 and 1 Corinthians 4:1–2. Prior to ordination, the priest-to-be has had six years of theological training and has taken the vow of celibacy, a vow that admits that he has severed his future life from marriage and family, and that he has committed himself to do God's work for the remainder of his life. Also the initiate has become a deacon before ordination, which means that he had some clerical experience before priesthood. As the bishop lays his hands on the candidate the initiate then becomes invested with the powers of the priesthood. The service concludes with the bishop anointing the candidate with oil, after which he hands to the candidate the symbols of his office, a shepherd's staff, a chalice for use in the Mass, and a paten, a container for holding the chalice. The bishop alone has the power to ordain a priest, for he represents the power of the papacy in his diocese, a degree of power superior to all other clerics in the diocese.

The final sacrament, that of marriage, symbolizes the union of the Christ and the Church. Marriage vows are for life. No divorce is permitted, although the marriage might be dissolved if there is evidence of an illegal marriage or that some vile sin had been committed by one of the spouses, such as adultery.

The Church for the medieval Christian was much more than weekly attendance at worship services, or confessions to the priest, or the baptism of a new baby, or a marriage, or a funeral service. The Church in reality was almost the totality of one's everyday life. Civil marriages did not exist. Only the Church sanctified marriage. In the Church office were kept the records of births, marriages, and deaths. Census and tax records were taken from parish records. The dead had to be buried in consecrated ground, usually within the church yard. Hence the living were kept in close communion with the dead. Cremation was forbidden since the body ought to be preserved to await the final resurrection.

Christian Architecture

The Church set the pattern for the architecture and art of the times. Each community, rural or urban, large or small, had some form of a church building. Rural churches were no more than crude log huts or small stone buildings. But in the larger towns and cities, where the church members had both the wealth and the skill to build grander things, Church architects designed majestic and beautiful monuments to the memory of Christ and the glory of God. The earlier Middle Ages adopted the Roman style of architecture, using heavy walls and the Roman arch and dome, a style named the basilica style. After the thirteenth century in Western Europe, especially in northern Europe, where the days were darker, architects designed church edifices with thin walls and large wall openings for stained glass windows, and with walls of great height, topped by a spire like a finger pointing to heaven.

The glory of all Church buildings was the Gothic churches of France, Germany, and England, the cathedrals of Rheims, Notre Dame, Cologne, Canterbury, and York. The floorplans used the symbol of the cross. The Gothic cross is typical in the West, where the leg of the cross is longer than the arm, and in the East the Latin cross, one where the leg and the arm are of equal length. The church's interior provided space for the altar, from which the priest conducted the Mass and other services. By the later Middle Ages churches began to have spaces for a choir and an organ. Normally the congregation remained standing during the service, which might last for two or three hours. Can one imagine the agony of the faithful during the service? Pews or seats were not customary. The interior also provided spaces for lighted candles, and numerous statues or pictures of the Christ, the Virgin Mary, and a host of saints. The walls might be decorated with paintings and most often with scenes and words depicting the stations of the Cross, the story of Jesus on his way to the Crucifixion. Stained glass windows permitted children to learn about the Bible and the biblical characters and the events associated with these biblical heroes.

The Magical Medieval Universe

Medieval minds were more attuned to a world of magic and supernatural power than modern Christians, who are often torn between the truths of the Bible and the truths of modern science. So it was relatively easy for the early Christians to believe in the miracles of Jesus, or the Virgin Birth, or the Second Coming, or that the priests and popes could bring the punishment of hell to mankind on earth for disobedience to the Church. The mystery of the Eucharist, the visions of saints, the protective wings of angels, and the destructive forces of evil spirits and ghosts were as real to the medieval mind as the rising of the sun in the east. No man or woman, alive or dead, could hope to escape the blessings of the divine creatures or the terrible pain and destruction that could be inflicted on all by those evil demons, Satan and his armies of evil spirits in hell.

The existence of angels was confirmed by the Lateran Council of 1215. Angels were creatures without bodies. They were pure spiritual beings and so numerous that they were beyond calculation. The word *angel* comes from the Greek, meaning a messenger to God who was created before the world was created. The Jews had their angels also. Jesus asked the angels to bless the Sabbath as the time for worship. In the Bible the archangels Michael, Gabriel, and Raphael appear to assist the Hebrew prophets, as Gabriel did Daniel and Michael Moses. Archangels are said to be messengers who bring the prayers of the faithful to God and can also heal the sins and the ills of mankind. Many Christians believe that they are blessed by having a special guardian angel who will offer protection from the wiles of the Devil.

The Devil was everywhere. He ruled hell with vengeance and woe be to those poor sinners whose souls were destined to hell. The torments of hell are graphically protrayed by Dante in his *Divine Comedy*. People believed sincerely that certain magical charms and signs could protect them from the Devil. Wearing of a cross, or sprinkling with holy water, or a special magical prayer are a few of the means by which one could escape the evil works of the Devil.

In the eyes of the typical parishioner the numerous saints of the Church ranked among the highest of the spiritual heroes, along with Jesus Christ and his mother, Mary. James Bentley in his *A Calendar of Saints* lists month by month the lives of over 450 principal saints, many of whom had been popes, bishops, monks, nuns, missionaries, teachers, and apostles. Saints were those persons who had given their lives in sacrificial service to the Church. Canonization as a saint was an act of recognition of their services to the Church. Recognition of sainthood begins with a thorough investigation by papal authorities of the life and achievements of the candidate for sainthood. The crucial test for sainthood is that there is proof that the candidate had performed at least two miracles during his or her period of service. After being canonized by the pope as a saint, the person becomes an object of veneration to whom the people can pray for help in solving many of their spiritual and worldly problems. The bones and material possession of the saints become prized relics before which the faithful can come and pray for recovery from illness, or more children, or bountiful crops, or mercy for the souls of deceased relatives in purgatory, or a thousand other pressing needs they may have.

The relics of the saints were so valuable that Christians have gone to war to secure the bones of their favorite or national saint. A church or cathedral so fortunate as to possess the body of a saint, or even a finger, or a hair, or even a portion of any of the saint's garments, becomes a shrine to which pilgrims come from many parts of Christendom to pray. Relics are said to include the nipples of St. Elizabeth of Hungary, the foreskin of Christ, the chemise of St. Margaret, the cross from St. Thomas, skulls of Peter and John the Baptist. The list goes on ad infinitum.[3] The Roman Catholic Church celebrates the validity of veneration of the saints by observing All Saints Day on November 1, and by the recognition of individual saints on their birthdays or anniversary of their canonization. The existence of angels is recognized by the church when it celebrates the Feast of Guardian Angels in October.

Good Christians are expected to make pilgrimages whenever possible, or at least once in a lifetime. Pilgrimages are most often made to the shrines of holy persons and saints, places where saints are buried, or where saints have lived, caused the place to become endowed with sacred powers that may be able to bestow on the penitent the answer to his or her prayers. The most sacred pilgrimage would be to go to the Holy Land and Jerusalem. In some respects the Crusades were pilgrimages to the many sacred places in the region, Bethlehem, Gethsemane, Calvary, Galilee, and the River Jordan. One of the most famous pilgrimages in literature is the one described by Chaucer in his *Canterbury Tales,* where pilgrims are on their way to visit the tomb of the martyred Saint Thomas a Becket. Other famous places for pilgrims to go are the healing shrines of Fatima in Spain, and Lourdes in France. MacDonald Harris in his *The Treasures of Sainte Fay* tells about a church in southern France at Languedoc that houses relics of the martyred St. Faye. Pilgrimages are often made to satisfy the penalties assessed by penances, but probably more are made out of genuine love for Christ. For medieval Christians, when medical science did not exist, the normal recourse for a sick person was to seek help from a priest who might be able to effect a cure by a prayer or some other magical rite that could bring God's healing power to the patient. That some ills are cured by spiritual intervention need not be doubted, provided the illness has a psychosomatic origin. It is interesting to note that many professional groups retain even today certain patron saints venerated in medieval times. For example, St. Jude is the saint of physicians, St. Francis the saint for the ecologists, St. Genesus the saint for the actors, and so on.

19

Daily Life in Medieval Christian Europe

By the thirteenth century the Roman Catholic church had become the one church in the life of the people of Western Europe. Its monopolistic position in the realm of things spiritual was not challenged by any other religious body. The church seemed to be well on its way to bringing forth on earth the vision of a City of God. Theologians viewed mankind as having been corrupted by original sin, and so this creature of God's making, man, was by his nature an evil person, or, in the view of the English philosopher Thomas Hobbes, a brutual, nasty, vicious creature that needed to be made subject to the control of some dictatorial form of government. The church had a blueprint for refashioning human nature, a blueprint drawn by Jesus, detailed by Paul and the Apostles, and put into operation by the Fathers of the Church in its first thousand years.

But also the Catholic church had become the prime mover in directing and controling the economic, the political, and the social life of the people of Western Europe. By 1300 Western Europe was emerging from the poverty and illiteracy of the Dark Ages. Signs of progress could be found in a few isolated areas of Western Europe, areas located near the sea and where more peaceful political conditions might be found. Towns and commerce existed in northern Italy (Venice and Florence), the Hanseatic towns along the Baltic sea, the Netherlands, the British Isles, and coastal areas of northern France. The rest of Western Europe remained in a state of feudal violence and war, poverty, mass illiteracy, and subsistence-level living, each day facing the hazards of death from pestilence (plague) and famine. The population remained static even though the birth rate was at its maximum. Most infants were doomed to die before age five, and even the parents, especially the mothers, had a brief life expectancy, probably less than forty years. Most of Western Europe remained rural and populated by poor, illiterate peasants, most of them bound to manors as serfs for life. Very few people possessed any degree of power or freedom. The common people were destined to be ruled by the church and their overlord in the feudal system. Probably 90 percent of the people lived on a subsistence level, tilling the soil or performing simple tasks as weavers, shoemakers, or stone masons. Human labor provided the power for farming and manufacturing. Scientific agriculture and the age of steam power were centuries away. Hence the economy was unable to provide even a small surplus that could provide the capital investment for increasing commerce, agriculture, and manufacturing. The finer things of life—education, hospitals, the arts, and architecture—or even such essentials as good water and sanitation, or a heated castle or hut during the winter were absent.

The one institution that was able to provide some of the better things of the good life was the church. It was the church that had the funds to spend for some measure of education, colleges, orphanages, and the support of artists, scholars, librarians, and architects. The Catholic church had the means, the power, and the leadership to bring to Western society of the Middle Ages some semblance of civilization. A much richer way of life could be found on the southern shores of the Mediterranean, the southern parts of Spain, North Africa, and the Byzantine Empire, areas where either the Muslims or the Byzantine Christians were heirs to ancient Greek culture and learning, and where commerce and wealth were relatively abundant. But in Western Europe, at a time when the feudal system offered neither peace nor adequate production of the necessities of life, society was fortunate to have the wealth and the leadership of the Roman Catholic Church.

From birth to death, and every day in between, medieval Christians felt the presence of the church. The church in its efforts to build a Christian society encountered some difficult obstacles to overcome. The people of Western Europe of that time, as today, consisted of many different ethnic and language groups, descendants of primitive Celtic and Germanic tribes. The Roman heritage had left the Latin language, many of its laws, its roads, buildings, and many pagan traditions. Hence the Christian Church had to absorb these pagan and Roman cultural heritages, and cover them with at least a veil of Christianity. By conquering the souls and minds of medieval men and women, and to a large extent also their economic and political systems, the Catholic church was able to bequeath to modern Europeans the fundamental ingredients for modern Western civilization.

Marriage, Divorce, Family, and Sexuality

As mentioned earlier the church baptized the infants, sanctified the marriages, set the patterns for family life, and eventually administered extreme unction to the dying and buried the dead. In marriage the church retained the Judaic and Roman practices of arranged marriages in which the parents of the prospective bride and groom made the decisions about who would be marriage partners. Marriages were not matters of love and free choice, but matters of parental rights and property arrangements. Marriage contracts defined the legal and property relationships between the families of the married couple as well as the rights of husband and wife. Two essential elements in the marriage contract were the primacy of the husband in the marriage and the disposition of the dowry or gift of property furnished by the bride's parents. The dowry served as a guarantee that the marriage would last, for in case of separation or divorce the dowry would be returned to the wife.

Marriages occured usually at an early age, such as fourteen for the girl and eighteen for the boy. Since the only occupational future for the girl was marriage and motherhood, it was normal for the girl to be married soon after puberty. Also since the future of most boys was destined to be that of a farm laborer (a few might become soldier knights, town craftsmen, or priests), there was no need to delay marriage. The matter of premarital sex posed few problems, since young people were married near the onset of sexual activity.

Although divorce was strictly forbidden by church and state, men were not punished severely for keeping concubines and mistresses, if they could afford them. Although the church condemned prostitution, men found abundant opportunities for extramarital sex. The wife's freedom of action was severely restricted. Adultery for the woman was punishable by death. The presence of illegitimate children posed no serious problem for families. In wills and the transfer of property illegitimate sons were usually given the same benefits as legitimate sons. The first homes for illegitimate children were built in Italy in the fifteenth century. Before homes were built, the families cared for their own "bastard" children. In a few instances unwanted children could be sold into slavery or killed, a practice inherited from Roman times, and one that the church sought to destroy. The emperor Constantine had outlawed the Roman practice of infanticide in 318, but old customs linger on for centuries.

Marriage was sanctified by the church and blessed by God for the purpose of procreation. Sexual pleasure in the marriage relationship was frowned upon by the church. Large families were encouraged, annual births were the rule. A mother might give birth to fifteen children before she died of exhaustion. Not only did large families fulfill the biblical injunction to "be fruitful and multiply," but they were necessary to maintain a stable population. All nonprocreative aspects of sex, such as masturbation, homosexuality, contraception, abortions, and all forms of extramarital sexual activity, were forbidden.

Jesus had denounced divorce as an evil and the Roman church accepted that it was a sin. Wealthy persons, lords and rich merchants, often could arrange to seek from the church an annulment of their marriages on the grounds of adultery, incest, bigamy, or nonconsummation of the marriage.[1] Poor families could seldom afford the costs of an annulment.

Traditionally among both the Judaic and Roman societies the family structure was a patriarchal one in which the husband and father were legally the owners of their wives and children. The male voice of authority was not to be challenged. Family members were property, like the cows and sheep, and the father could dispose of them as he chose. It was no crime to beat wife and children, or to abuse them sexually. The wife was bound to submit herself to the sexual desires of her husband and refusal could be grounds for annulment of the marriage.

Yet one must assume that for most families there must have been some signs of love between husband and wife and between parents and children. No matter how oppressed women and children were in the Middle Ages, it is safe to say that the Christian church had elevated the status of wives and children when compared to family conditions during the Roman times.

The church discouraged the remarriage of widows, but many widows, many still young women, did remarry to secure some economic security and companionship. Young widows often become the subject of scurrilous gossip if they did not remarry. But for most widows remarriage did not occur; hence they were left to be supported by their families or to engage in the sin of illegal prostitution.

The Christian church introduced into medieval society an abhorrence of sex. It was noted earlier that the Apostle Paul and some of the early Church Fathers, notably Augustine, had placed upon almost all sexual activities the curse of God. They taught that it was better to abstain from sex, but since children were necessary, then sex for procreation was tolerable.

Earlier Greek, Roman, and Judaic societies, by contrast, had taken a mostly liberal attitude toward sex, both in marriage and outside of marriage. The Greek physician Galen, for example, said sex was good for one's health. Homosexuality was accepted as normal in Greek and Roman societies, though not by the Jews.

But liberated views on sex were not for the Christians. The best Christians were those who remained celibate, like the angels—priests, monks, and nuns. The Church required that all Christians practice abstinence during Lent and on other holy days. The Lateran Councils of 1123 and 1129 ruled that all clergy must take the vow of celibacy. How many of the poor parish priests remained celibate will never be known. In the eastern church the priests were permitted to marry.

Property, Economics, and Attitudes toward Wealth

Not only did all affairs of the family come under the jurisdiction of the Church and its laws, but the church exercised control, or at least tried to, over all other aspects of human activity. In the economic world the church legislated the rules for the conduct of business and the ownership of property. In general the church accepted the prevailing Roman system of law governing the sale of property and the transmission of property to heirs. The church recognized the feudal principle that property upon the death of the father should pass exclusively to the eldest son. Younger sons had to find employment elsewhere in the service of some lord's army or in the church as a priest or monk. This matter of inheritance was one that concerned property owners only, of which there were few in the total population. The great masses of poor people were landless workers and serfs.

Perhaps the Christian leaders found some guidance from the Old Testament on how to organize and regulate a theocratic, church-ruled society in the manner of the kingdoms of the Jews. Judaism had accepted the value of property, money, and wealth as being good; poverty was no road to salvation. The only restriction Judaic law placed upon hard work, getting rich, and owning great sums of wealth was that a certain part of God's bounty should be returned to God in the form of tithes or donations to the church or synagogue. For Christians of the first century, or even until the Christians were recognized by the Roman state, the accumulation of wealth was viewed as sinful. Poverty was the ideal lifestyle for a Christian. So long as the Christians believed the Second Coming of Christ was imminent there was no incentive to pile up treasures on earth. Only treasures in heaven were worthy of possession. However, by 500 it was evident that Christ was not about to return soon, so the faithful were more interested in learning how to live as a Christian on earth.

So the church and Christian monarchs legislated rules to govern the transactions in business and banking, the enactment of fair or "just price" laws and fair labor practices. Both wages and prices were fixed so as to be just. Charging a fee for the use of one's money—usury—was immoral and illegal. Since most loans of the day were for consumption purposes rather than for capital investments the Church was attempting to protect the poor people from greedy loan sharks, many of whom were despised Jews who, in the eyes of the Christian majority, deserved to be deprived of immoral gain. Banking was one occupation that Christians permitted the Jews to practice in their isolated urban ghettoes. Christians found that Jewish "Shylocks" were a necessary evil in the economic life of both church and state. The Jewish bankers were most often the source of funds to finance papal Crusades and the building of church schools and cathedrals. Likewise kings and merchants drew upon Jewish bankers for money for their royal wars and the expansion of trade throughout the Mediterranean world, even to China and India, as in the case of Marco Polo.

Quality standards were enacted by Church and state as a means of preventing the sale of shoddy goods or short-weighting the customer. In brief, the Christian Church sincerely tried to apply Christian principles of love and jsutice to the everyday world of work and business.

The regulated economic system of the Middle Ages would be carried over into the modern age of national monarchies and embryonic capitalistic enterprises. From the 1500s until the 1700s in Western Europe all states held a firm grip over the conduct of banking and commerce in a system called mercantilism. Free capitalism, an economic system regulated by the natural forces of supply and demand rather than by the rule of the church and the state would not appear until the advent of the eighteenth century. In a sense the American and the French revolutions mark the establishment of free capitalism in the Western world. The Protestant Reformation would become one of the principal allies of the Adam Smith school of free enterprise.

In the later Middle Ages and the dawn of the Modern Age, or the time of the Renaissance in the fifteenth century, Catholic theologians began to accommodate the economic needs of Christian capitalists and merchants. A 1985 book by Jacques Le Goff, *Your Money or Your Life: Economy and Religion in the Middle Ages,* offers an interesting investigation of how the medieval church even in the thirteenth century was beginning to rationalize the validity of charging interest on loans. Normally a usurer would be condemned to hell for his sins, but Le Goff argues that the church used the idea of purgatory to permit usurers to escape punishment in hell. In purgatory the usurer could eventually be forgiven for his sin of greed.

Early in the history of the Church theologians had begun to find rational justifications for the making and possession of wealth. Poverty may be a virtue, but wealth, if properly used, can be a Christian virtue also. Bishop Clement of Alexandria (150–213) preached that God also blesses the rich, but riches should be used to help the poor and finance the charitable enterprises of the Church. God blesses both the rich and the poor. Augustine saw no evil in the prevailing Roman system of property ownership, including the buying and selling of slaves. Slaveowners were encouraged to be humane in their treatment of their slaves. The theologian Clement of Alexandria said Christians should acquire property honestly so that the Church could finance its undertakings. Riches were good; only their misuse was evil. Clement urged Christians to follow the Aristotelian standard of the golden mean, to be neither greedy nor ascetic.

Tertullian, another Alexandrian theologian, wrote *Rich Man's Salvation,* in which he said that to acquire wealth was to serve God, a point of view that business interests no doubt applauded. Augustine added his blessing to the accumulation of wealth by saying that both the clergy and the laity could acquire riches and still be good Christians. Augustine warned against the evils of greed, the exploitation of the poor, and the abuse of slaves, however. Christian love should be made manifest in the conduct of economic affairs.

By the eleventh century the Church was well on its way to becoming one of the wealthiest institutions in Christendom. Wealthy persons upon their death bed would bequeath their property to the church in the expectation that heavenly rewards would follow. Bishops and abbots became wealthy landowners from gifts and bequests, thereby causing these clerics to become feudal lords in the prevailing feudal system of land ownership. Bishops became the vassals of superior lords and barons, and in turn they became overlords to lesser vassals and their manorial holdings. It was difficult for a bishop to separate his spiritual duties from his temporal obligations to his superior feudal lord. Since the church was forbidden to go to war bishops were forced to hire feudal lords and their armies to protect their estates. Thus the clergy and even the popes were forced to compromise their religious commitments by making arrangements with kings and nobles for protection against invading enemies, be they Christian or Muslim. It is estimated that by the fifteenth century that the church owned from 25 to 50 percent of all of the land in Western Europe, all depending on the country in qustion.[2]

In 1376 it was reported that in England the clergy received five times the revenue of the king. With so much wealth, the church required the services of a large army of bureaucrats, tax collectors, and land overseers to conduct its worldly business interests.

At no time, even in the twentieth century, has the Roman Catholic church given its blessing to any system of free capitalism, which totally rules out all controls over the conduct of business and labor. Natural law could never replace God's law in the realm of economics. Neither did the church ever concede that charging interest was legitimate. Thomas Aquinas argued that interest was contrary to the laws of reason and nature. The Third Lateran Council (1170) ruled against the charging of interest on loans, a rule reaffirmed by the Council of Lyons (1274). However, the church, including even Thomas Aquinas, relaxed the rigid prohibition of all interest charges by declaring that a lender was entitled to a fee for the labor involved in making the loan, which for all practical purposes was an interest charge.

The involvement of the church in the worldly affairs of business and property ownership provoked conflicts with kings and criticism from churchmen, who believed that poverty was still the way of life for a Christian. One conflict between royalty and the papacy occurred when King Louis VII of France levied a tax on church lands to support the Second Crusade in 1146. The church responded in the Lateran Council of 1179 by saying that no king could tax church property without the consent of the local bishop. In 1188, Philip Augustus, king of France, imposed a tax on church lands to support the Third Crusade, a tax called the Saladin Tithe. Pope Boniface VIII issued a papal bull (*Clericos Laicos,* 1208), which forbade any king to tax church property without the consent of the pope, a position that was reaffirmed by the Lateran Council of 1215. These conflicts between church and state over the power of taxation and the exercise of political control over Christian nations became a major factor in causing the Protestant Reformation.

Within the Christian Church there were always certain voices decrying the virtues of riches and deploring the involvement of the church in affairs of the world. The church was sacrificing its spiritual function for the pursuit of evil mammon. John Chrysostom, bishop of Constantinople (398–404), wrote a *Homily on Timothy,* in which he decries the evil of riches, for it made Christians evil like Jews and heretics. The Donatist heresy of the third and fourth centuries proclaimed that riches were evil, and that only poor clergymen could administer the sacraments properly. They claimed that to live in the world was to choose eternal death. The Franciscan Order was organized in the thirteenth century as a protest against the growing wealth of the papacy as well as of the total church. The fourteenth-century Hussite and Albigensian heretics protested the moral degeneracy of the papacy and the church, which was attributed to the debasing effects of wealth.

The Church as Bastion of Civilization

The critics of medieval Catholicism should never overlook the fact that most clergymen were sincere, devoted Christian leaders. Corrupt popes and bishops were the exception, not the rule. The church was the one great civilizing force in Europe, redeeming its people from barbarism and ignorance. It was the church and its monasteries that restored to Western Europe the culture of the Greek and Roman civilizations. It was the church that built the universities and libraries, that preserved the ancient manuscripts, that encouraged the best scholars to give their minds to the discovery of new truths. The church was a beacon for civilization in a very dark world. The church was responsible for healing the sick, caring for the poor and the crippled, and protecting the weak and oppressed from the ravages of war and feudal violence. The church attempted to minimize the prevalence of war and personal violence, that is, to practice the commandment, "Thou shalt not kill." The church encouraged the acceptance of a chivalric code of relationships among all men, and between men and women. Romantic legends relate how chivalric knights were sworn to protect the church, to aid the weak and needy, to love children, and to respect womanhood and female virginity. The church attempted to forbid simulated war games, the mock battles in which reckless knights engaged in bouts of jousting and tournaments. These games were forbidden by the Tenth Ecumenical Council in 1139. Also beginning in the eleventh century the church sought to minimize the constant warfare so characteristic of the feudal system. First the church preached the "Peace of God," an ideal that would spare the members of the clergy and the monasteries from violent attacks, especially on church property. The Peace of God was offered to travelers, merchants, and pilgrims who, when under attack, could seek asylum in a church or monastery. Even criminals who were fugitives from the law might be protected by the Peace of God.

At the same time the church sought to minimize the constant state of feudal warfare by imposing upon the ruling lords and kings the "Truce of God," by which they would not wage war during the holy seasons of Advent and Lent. During the twelfth century more ambitious projects for peace were discussed, such as proposals that all wars among Christians should be adjudicated by the pope, or even that the pope should have the power to forbid all wars among Christians and that defiance of a papal ban would bring excommunication to the offending king or prince. Needless to say such extreme antiwar measures remained concealed in the archives of the papal court.

Even to this day the Catholic church has been a forceful voice speaking on behalf of world peace, the United Nations, and world disarmament, especially the outlawing of all nuclear weapons. In the area of social justice and welfare the church for years has been on the side of labor in its struggle for recognition and fair working conditions. The church has long supported reform measures for social welfare legislation. Pope John XXIII in 1962 issued a statement, *Mater et Magister Pacem in Terris,* that gave support to a broad program of welfare legislation for the poor, the children, and the elderly. The Protestant churches, by contrast, were most reluctant to support President Franklin Roosevelt's New Deal reforms and President Lyndon Johnson's program of social justice. This is not to deny, however, that many Protestants did support the New Deal reform measures wholeheartedly.

20

Varieties of Religious Experience: Love

Human beings have many ways to worship their God or gods, to demonstrate their love for divinity. Most Christians worship by attending weekly services at church, plus family prayers at home, and some people attend Bible study and prayer sessions during the week. For the majority, the emotional depth of commitment to God is slight, rarely reaching the point of an all-absorbing expression of love. A small number of Christians will enter the ministry, devoting their lives to the service of God. Even fewer may enter a monastic order where body, heart, and soul are exclusively dedicated to God's service. In a small minority of congregations, Christians are encouraged to believe that if they can generate a most intense feeling of emotion, called love for God, then they will truly know their God and Christ. The Shakers, the Pillars of Fire, the holy rollers, and other pentecostal Protestant churches value the expression of great spiritual emotion as a sign of God's presence in their being and in their church. However, other Christian churches, such as the Quakers, also feel deep emotions but refrain from any outward, visible signs of their love for Christ.

Christian love may come to a person suddenly, as in the case of John Wesley, a warming feeling in the heart, or in the case of the Apostle Paul, who on the road to Damascus had his sunstruck vision of the Christ. No intellect is involved, and the wisdom that comes to the devotee is by way of prayer and meditation practiced over long periods of time. Then, suddenly there comes to consciousness, intuitively it seems, visions, dreams, and voices; some claim to have heard voices of truth from God. Such Christian love for God is the way of the mystic.

Love is the central message of the Christ. He said that to love one's neighbors as oneself is the second commandment. The first commandment is to love God with all of one's heart and mind. However, in the English language the word "love" is an elusive word with many different meanings, some contradictory. There is love that is innate and never needs to be learned, the love we call sex, and the need for food and survival. But there are other expressions of love that we

279

can learn as children, such as love of family, love of friends and neighbors, love for persons who are not of our race or nationality, and above all love for our God and our church.

Whatever form love takes, all love experiences have two elements in common. First love always gives pleasure to the lover. Love satisfies some human need or desire. A lover seeks to embrace the object of love. The object might be a person, a thing, an idea, a symbol like a flag, or the image of God. Television has shown pictures of Iranian men flagellating themselves until blood blows, while demonstrating their love of Mohammed and their religious leaders. They must experience pain, but they must experience greater joy in their religious fervor, which wipes away the pain.

True love must be given freely, without the use of any pressures or compulsion from outside forces. A love relationship dies when love, no matter how good the objective may be, is forced upon the object of love. In a sense love is selfish, for unless the love relationship is pleasurable to the lover there will be no true love. Sacrificial love, love so total that all self-interests have been submerged in a love experience for other persons, yields to the lover a sense of joy from personal pride and social acceptance from his or her social group. Few persons would ever love God or Church if personal ego drives were not rewarded. Membership in a religious body rewards the person wtih a sense of power, a sense of pride and importance, a feeling that one is among the best of one's kind, and, above all rewards, the promise that one's soul will have eternal peace in heaven.

Three different forms of love can be identified in the Christian tradition. There is the love of God or Christian love, sometimes known as the Greek word for love, *agape*. Then there is a less noble form of love, but like Christian love one devoid of all sexual connotations, called Platonic or romantic love. The least noble form of love is sexual or erotic love, the love that is synonomous with sex. Each of these loves deserves a more detailed analysis.

Agape

Christian love or agape originally meant a love relationship among Christian men and women who, in sharing a common meal, for example, experienced a most meaningful measure of fellowship as they gave their lives to the service of their Christ and God. Later the term agape was broadened to include all of mankind who could be brought together in a love relationship with God and with each other. Agape is sacrificial love, such as the love Jesus had for all of mankind. According to Christian theology, Jesus' love was so generous that he was willing to die as a price to free man from sin. Agape or Christian love is shown in the parable of the Good Samaritan. It is the love that causes a Christian to rescue the drowning victim, to give his clothes to the naked beggar, or, in a million ways, help the less fortunate neighbor. The total commitment to a life of Christian love is expressed in St. Paul's list of Christian virtues, where he declares love to be the greatest virtue of all (1 Corinthians 13). It is the love that enables some of us to be canonized as saints. Today it is a love exemplified by St. Francis, Mother Teresa, or Gandhi. Such love is given freely with no expectation of any reward. If Christianity has any mission to fulfill, it is that the world may know that through Christian love someday in the future all of humankind may live in a world of peace, justice, and brotherhood.

Sexuality vs. Christian Dogma

Erotic love includes all forms of sexual behavior, from sex in marriage to many other forms of sexual behavior, heterosexual and homosexual, that are beyond the pale of acceptance in the Christian Church. The Christian attitude toward human sexuality brought a revolutionary change in how humans were to view sexual behavior. Almost all cosmic societies and pre-Christian religions gave the gods' blessings to human reproduction and even sanctioned the use of sex for personal pleasure if indulged in the marital relationship. The Judaic tradition gave sex a holy place in God's creation so long as it was within the marriage. The Song of Solomon glorifies man's love for woman, an erotic love that was later interpreted by Christians as a symbol for the love relationship between God and his people. Among the pre-Christian cultures and religions only the Greek Stoics and the Jewish Essenes considered sex impure and deemed an ascetic, sex-free life to be preferable to God.

From the first days Christian theologians and the leaders of the Church, beginning with St. Paul, deprecated human sexuality. The best expression of Christian virtue was to refrain from all sex and remain a virgin until death. Mary, the virgin mother, became the model for the ideal woman. St. John in the book of Revelation, glorified the 144,000 virgins in heaven. St. Jerome and St. Augustine warned mankind against falling prey to the devil and sex. Women were thought to be more sexual and more evil than men. Eve, the first woman, was the original temptress, the ally of Satan, and she destroyed the perfect Garden of Eden. Eve was a fallen woman, no better than a common prostitute. St. Jerome deemed marriage only a little better than fornication. St. Paul said it was better to marry than to burn, but it was best not to marry. If marriage and sex were to be evaluated by the early Christian Fathers on a scale of moral value ranging from one to ten, ten being total chastity, St. Paul would give marriage five points, St. Jerome two points, and both would give sex outside of marriage no points. The veneration of the Virgin Mary also expressed the Christian view that sex was evil. The perfect Christian should live in a monastery, free from the sins of the world and sexual temptations. Yet the Church needed new members, children, so the Church was forced to compromise its extreme position on sexual abstinence. The Church, therefore, found virtue in the Jewish commandment to "be fruitful and multiply" and decided to give marriage the status of a divine sacrament.

Historians have sought to discover the reasons for the Christian abhorrence of sex.[1] Although the Christian Church owes much to its Jewish heritage, it cannot trace its antisex bias to Judaism. Jesus, being a good Jew, never condemned marriage, nor did he speak openly against homosexuality, although he never condoned it. Jesus even found sympathy for a fallen woman, Mary Magdalene. He never admonished his disciples to leave their wives and follow him. Some scholars even believed that Jesus might have been a married man.

The only Jewish sect that advocated and practiced chastity was the monastic Essenes, a group about which Jesus and John the Baptist had knowledge, if not personal associations. Even St. Paul never commanded his bishops or elders to practice celibacy or refrain from marriage. He did recommend that his bishops not remarry when they became widowers (1 Timothy 3).

By 300 church leaders universally condemned sexual behavior of all kinds as being evil. Why this change? Perhaps it was in response to the several pagan religions then in existence that glorified sexual activity as a divine blessing. Or perhaps it was the influence of two competing religious groups for the souls of the Roman people, namely the Gnostics and the Manicheans, both of whom denounced sex as vile. Augustine's views against sex were accepted by St. Gregory of Nyssa, Tatian, St. Ambrose, and Origen. Yet all had to admit that sex for procreation was necessary for the survival of the church. The important Council of Nicea in 325 permitted the clergy to marry, but some leaders, like Eusebius, urged the clergy not to have sexual intercourse with their wives.

However, eight hundred years later the Roman Catholic Church was issuing decrees that forbade the clergy to marry. The Second Lateran Council in 1139 was one of the first councils to issue a ban on clerical marriages. Pope after pope during the twelfth and thirteenth centuries issued bans against clerical marriages. Such bans were difficult to enforce and no one knows how many priests and bishops, even popes, kept mistresses and fathered children. The Eastern Orthodox Church never ruled against priests being married. Married men have always been accepted into the clergy. But the Roman Catholic Church in this day has never compromised its position on clerical marriage. The ban on married clergy, as well as the ban on women in the priesthood was made a part of canon law by the Council of Trent in 1546.

With the advent of the intellectual movement called the Renaissance in the fifteenth and sixteenth centuries the medieval way of life and the role of the Roman Catholic Church were not only threatened, but doomed to experience an irreversible change. Since then Western Europe has experienced momentous changes in its outlook on moral standards, the role of the church, and most significantly on the right of all people to have the freedom to express and to act upon their personal views and choices of lifestyle.

A revolution in sexual attitudes and behavior has occurred since 1860. Churches are divided over how to control an excess of sexuality in our modern society. No one denies that sexual instruction for the young is necessary. Shall it be given at home, or by the church, or by the public schools? Both conservative Catholics and Protestants oppose sex clinics and classes in the public schools. Responsibility for sex instruction, they maintain, belongs to the home and the church. The advent of AIDS has persuaded many conservatives, like former surgeon general C. Everett Koop, that sex education in the school is now necessary, even to the degree that school clinics should provide condoms for teenage students.

Science has also changed public and religious attitudes about abortion. Both Jewish and Christian ethics have always taught that abortion was a grave sin, even likened to murder. Modern science has made abortions relatively safe and cheap. An abortion pill, like the birth control pill, is on the market in France and other countries and under testing in the United States. No doubt this drug will be sold soon in the United States unless the abortion opponents are successful in blocking its sale and use. If this is the state of abortion technology, convenient and safe, many conservatives fear that the abortion pill will be just another form of birth control.

The case against abortion in America rests on the premise that a fetus is a human being entitled to all of the guarantees provided for in the U.S. Constitution. The issue comes down to the question, "When does the fetus become a person?" Antiabortion advocates, especially the Roman Catholic Church and the fundamentalistic Protestant churchs, reply that the fetus becomes a person at the moment of conception. Those persons and churches that believe that abortions are not always acts against God's law assert that the mother has the moral and legal right to opt for an abortion up to the time when the fetus meets the Aristotelian standard of "viability," or within the first trimester. There is general consensus among medical professionals and the more liberal Christian churches that a fetus has no chance of survival in the first trimester, or even the second trimester. Hence there is no reasonable argument against the right to an abortion. Except for the most extreme antiabortionists, there is also general consensus that abortions can be performed much later in the pregnancy in the severe cases of rape, incest, and risk of death to the mother. However, both those who oppose abortion and those who believe that abortions are acceptable agree that abortion should never be used as a substitute for contraception.

Romantic Love

In the later Middle Ages the Christian Church accepted a more human, less ascetic definition of love, one that is named romantic, platonic, or chivalric love, a love relationship between men and women in which the sexual element is submerged, if not eliminated totally. Between the sexes the ideal relationship is one in which compassion and concern for the welfare of the other person is expressed without any need for sexual satisfaction. The woman should remain a virgin until marriage, symbolic of the divine element in the female. The man is obligated to respect her virginity, yet adore her, love her, as if she were a virgin saint. The medieval troubadours sang songs of romantic love in which knights on horseback would come to the rescue of a ravaged woman, after which a deep love relationship would develop between the saved and the saver. Medieval tales have been told by writers through the centuries about the adventures of these "angelic" romantic lovers who lived in the days of feudal chivalry.

The era of romantic love reflected the Christian spirit of love and kindness, but the songs and legends of romance also heralded a spirit of independence from the rigid morality of the medieval Church. The German minnesingers and the French troubadours sang songs celebrating the heroic deeds of brave knights in battle who fought for their lordly masters with loyalty and also defended their Church and God with the same devotion. In battle, the knights were sworn to protect, even above master and Church, the weak and defenseless woman and her child. Women in the songs and sagas of the medieval troubadours were a message of personal freedom, a freedom that may have been inspired by the return of the Greek classics and their plea for the rights of humans to explore freedom and expand their right to make their own decisions. At first the church was reluctant to endorse the new concept of love, for to promulgate the idea that people could make their own decisions about life's issues threatened to undermine the authority of the Church. Later the leaders of the Church realized that the message of the troubadours and of the authors of chivalric tales was a Christian message, for they also exhorted men and women to practice virtue, charity, and peace. By the eleventh century the traditions of feudal knighthood, the initiation of a young man into knighthood, had become a religious rite. Knights were sworn to defend the feudal lord and their Lord God in heaven. It would be the chivalrous knights who would go to fight the infidel for possession of the Holy Land.

The songs of the troubadour encouraged marriages made on the basis of the free choice of marriage partners. Arranged marriages were discouraged. Love between the sexes was to be less a matter of the glands and more a free decision of the heart. The husband was to look upon his wife as the image of the Virgin Mary, to be treated with respect and equality. Yet the romantic lover seemed to be free to love women other than his wife, but always the extramarital relationship was to be lived on the same plane of idealized love for a pure woman.

The songs and tales of romantic love, a common theme in Western literature, relate a love relationship that is not entirely human, nor wholly divine. It is a love that combines the Christ-like love with the purified form of human love as might be portrayed in a Greek statue. The physical body has been transmuted into an idealized image of a God-like human. Romantic love tales adore nature, the beauty of the forests and hills, the divine presence to be found in the birds and squirrels, in the manner that St. Francis loved all things of nature.

In his *Occidental Mythology* Joseph Campbell offers meaningful insights into the symbolic meanings of many of the romantic tales. In the Tristan and Isolde story there is the message that parents should no longer dictate the marital choices of their children. Isolde was to be married on orders from her parents to King Mark. Her real love was for Tristan. By accident both lovers drank a love potion that Isolde's mother had given to her to drink so that she would love King Mark. So the die was cast that Isolde should love Tristan and not King Mark.

The story of the Holy Grail, the legendary cup or chalice from which Christ had drunk wine at the Last Supper, and which was said to have been brought from heaven by neutral angels, relates how brave knights sought to find this lost holy object. The Grail represents the highest form of spiritual virtue to which man can aspire. In seeking to find the Grail, mankind is seeking to achieve the Christ-like, ideal life on Earth. However, the Grail must be found by oneself, not with the aid of a Church and its clergy and sacraments. One Grail legend relates how one day the Grail King left his castle and on the way he met a Muslim Knight. Being enemies they engaged in a battle during which the Muslim was killed by the Grail King. But the Grail King was castrated by the Muslim's lance. Thus Campbell concludes that the Muslim represented nature or natural man. He was proof that natural man cannot be separated from spiritual man. Both elements of man must live together in a state of balanced harmony.

Another seeker of the Grail was the German knight Parzifal, the Great Fool. Parzifal was neither saint nor devil. He was a man permitted to grow up in a natural manner, a good knight who obeyed his vows of loyalty and compassion for others. He, too, found the Grail by himself.

Then there is the tale of Sir Galahad, who was brought to the court of King Arthur dressed in red armor on the day of Pentecost. Galahad represents the Holy Spirit, the divine element, and his long search for the Grail tells mankind that salvation must be found in one's own manner and by one's own efforts.

One revolutionary theme in the romantic tales is a new vision of womanhood. Earlier in the Christian tradition woman was equated with Eve, the one who gave to the human race original sin. She was a creature not to be trusted. Sometimes she seemed to be more the ally of the Devil than of the Christ, hence it was logical that womankind be forced to submit to the will of father and then husband. But the new woman is to be the equal of her husband. Even better, she will become endowed with that divine element that equates her with the Virgin Mary. In a French romance, the tale of Aucassin and Nicolette, is related the true meaning of romantic love. Aucassin had been placed in prison by his father for falling in love with Nicolette. She goes to visit him in prison, and Aucassin says to her, "Woman cannot love man as man loves woman; for woman's love is in the glance of her eye, and the blossom of her breast, and the tip of the toe of her foot, but the love of man is set deep in the hold of his heart, from which it cannot be torn away." This is not to say that woman's love does not also come from the heart; but Aucassin is declaring love for Nicolette's soul as well as her body.

In the Arthurian legends there is the story of a platonic love relationship between Lancelot and Queen Guinivere, who is married to the king. However, since it is a nonsexual relationship it is a love affair that meets the standards approved by the troubadours.

A Christianized version of romantic love is the one portrayed by Dante in his *Divine Comedy*. Dante relates his love for Beatrice, a girl he had known since she was nine years old. Throughout her life of twenty-nine years, and even though she marries a Florentine nobleman, Dante continues to sing songs of love for her. In *Purgatory,* canto 30, Dante meets Beatrice, whereupon the angels sing the sacred phrase from the Song of Solomon, 4:8–9, "Come with me from Lebanon, my spouse, come with me from Lebanon. . . . Thou hast ravished my heart, my sister, my spouse." Beatrice to Dante is divine, the personification of the Virgin Mary, yet she represents a woman of the world, man's helpmate, his lover, and a woman who has earned her place among humans as divine being, equal with her man.

One of the romantic traditions that has been retained down to modern civilization is the chivalric social code, sometimes dubbed the "Emily Post" code, which expects men to place women in a special place of honor, to defer to their wishes, to treat them as "ladies" in the manner of a Sir Walter Raleigh removing his coat so that his Queen Elizabeth might cross a puddle of water without spoiling her shoes. It is a code of common courtesy that says "Ladies go first" or "Please take my seat."

21

Varieties of Religious Experience: Mysticism

From the beginning of time mankind has sought to know God and the mysteries of the universe. God may be discovered by pursuing a program of rational, intellectual study that may lead to a decision to commit one's life to God. God may also be discovered in a flash of intuition or emotional enlightenment. However, in the real world of everyday life, most Christians were born into the faith. They were reared in a Christian family that responds to the pressures of a Christian culture and society. Perhaps the one personal decision many Christians have is to decide with which of a hundred churches he or she should finally affiliate.

Most Americans believe in God; some polls suggest as many as 90 percent. Most people say they believe in a heaven after death. About 50 percent are affiliated with some Christian church, although the records indicate that only 25 or 30 percent attend church services regularly. The traditional preparation for becoming a Christian is to be in a Christian family, and attend a church school or Sunday School to learn Bible lessons, pray on certain occasions, attend worship services, support the church and its charities, and best of all to live such a life that the neighbors can say, "There goes a Christian." Those persons who wish to pursue a Christian career in the services of the church will attend colleges and theological seminars in which a diligent and rational study of theology and Scripture will be followed. Many additional hours will be spent in prayer and the observance of the rules and rituals prescribed by the particular Christian denomination.

A minority of Christians throughout the history of the Church have said there is a better way to know God, that is, by way of mysticism. Every religion from primitive times to the present has had a mystical element somewhere within its structure. It may well be that the mystical element is the core of all religions, not the pursuit of rational study and dialectical debate. Oriental religions, like Hinduism and Buddhism, tend to be more mystically oriented than Judaism and

Christianity. But these faiths, and Islam also, have had their share of mystical believers.

Mysticism is defined usually as union with God through a process of meditation or a trancelike emotional experience. The word *mysticism* comes from the Greek verb meaning "initiated into secret rites," and refers to knowledge of God that is inward, secret, and mysterious. Other definitions of mysticism include "a state of consciousness beyond ordinary experience through a vision of transcendental reality," or "the immediate awareness of the relationship with God."

Mystics operate on different levels of behavior. If the test of being a mystic is declaring that one has seen God, and that the experience is real, then a person who under the influence of a drug like peyote and as a result has trancelike visions of God or some other unearthly being such as angels or demons might be called a mystic. If a spirit-filled body is compelled to have visions, or to dance and leap in religious ecstasy, then that person might be a mystic. When the disciples of Christ saw the risen Christ they must have had a real experience that convinced them that Christ was really present. John Wesley relates that his final call to serve God came one evening in London as he passed a small chapel and heard a minister reading from Martin Luther's preface to Paul's book of Romans. The message so "warmed his heart" that Wesley became the founder of the Methodist Church.

I recall a visit to a holy roller tent meeting in Boulder, Colorado. Here I saw excited Christians jumping up and down, shouting meaningless words, at least for me, and few of the spiritually possessed were actually rolling on the ground as if they were in agony. In a Quaker meeting the members sit silently while awaiting a word from God befored someone arises and witnesses a message from God to the other Quakers present.

The one criterion for describing a mystical experience is that the knowledge of God comes instantly, intuitively, emotionally without any apparent preconscious, rational planning to know God. The truth comes from the heart, not the mind. The truth about God may come in an intense emotional experience or it may come while sitting quietly alone in prayer and meditation. The presence of God is more than an image of a picture; God becomes a living person or force, one that is present in the moment of life. At an advanced stage of mystical development, the person becomes a part of God, or so he or she believes, and the person can say with conviction, "I am with God."

No priests, or sacraments, or church services, or governments are necessary for the mystic to know God. Church leaders have reason to be wary of too many mystical Christians lest the institution of the Church cease to serve any worthwhile function. Fortunately for the Church, very few persons have the capacity or the will to practice a mystical religion. It takes much time, more time than busy working people have to give to meditation. Even more difficult is the need to put aside all worldly matters and discipline the body and spirit, in the manner of Hindu yoga exercises, to the degree that only the spiritual world has reality.

Christian Mystics

A few Christian mystics have left their marks on the Christian Church. Most of them lived in the prescientific age of the Western world. An early Christian mystic is reported in the book of the Acts, named Dionysius the Areopagite, a Neo-Platonist. He believed that God was beyond human understanding and could be known only in a mystical way. St. Augustine expressed the same Neo-Platonic way to God. The only way was through contemplation in silence while seeking to find the inner light of the soul. Better-known mystics of the Middle Ages were Meister Eckhart (1260–1327), St. Bernard of Clairvaux (1091–1153), and St. Francis of Assisi (1181–1226). Eckhart believed that one can know the God that dwells within by releasing the conscious mind and body from the spiritual aspects of the human being. As for the Buddhist, knowledge of God for Eckhart comes when all physical desire is eliminated, all sensual feelings and mental comprehensions are annihilated. Then God's truth comes to light. Bernard of Clairvaux, a monk and theologian, taught a more practical form of mysticism in which the soul is united with God by intense concentration on the lives of Jesus and the Mother Mary by the adoration of their images and the expression of one's love through the singing of hymns. In a series of songs he referred to Christ as the bridegroom of the Soul, the one to whom man must give his complete and ultimate love.

But of all medieval mystics the one most loved and known is St. Francis of Assisi. It is said of St. Francis that he saw in a vision the figure of the crucified Christ, after which he dedicated his life to serving God in poverty and charity while preaching to as many people as possible the message of God's love. The mystical nature of St. Francis was revealed when he perceived God to be within all of nature's creatures, almost a Spinoza form of pantheism. He sang the glory of Brother Sun, Sister Moon, brother birds and animals, and all other creatures. He even sang the praises of Sister Death. St. Francis' love of Christ was shown when he built a creche in his village of Greccio to celebrate the birth of Jesus. His friends saw in St. Francis the incarnation of Christ, for his manner of living was one of sacrifice, poverty, and ascetic self denial. No words describe St. Francis better than those in his prayer, "Lord, make me an instrument of your peace."

Other medieval mystics include Thomas à Kempis and St. Teresa of Avila. Thomas à Kempis (died 1471) wrote a popular book on mysticism, *The Imitation of Christ*. It presented the theme that in order to know Christ more than church worship and study were required. Ultimate knowledge of Christ comes only as one loves the Christ and sees in him the model for all of human life on earth.

St. Teresa (1515–1582) came from Avila, Spain. She offered a set of seven meditations and prayers that could give one union with God. Her mystical message displeased the church, which forced her to submit to trial by the Inquisition.

A contemporary mystic, St. Ignatius of Loyola, the founder of the Jesuit order, saw in his "spiritual exercises" the way by which the human soul could be released from the body so that it might drive the Christian to serve God with all of his heart.

Protestants minimized the mystical approach to God, although certain leaders and sects followed the mystical path. The Pietistic Evangelical churches in Germany and the Quakers and Methodists in England placed value in the mystical power of the Holy Spirit. Count von Zinzendorf (1700–1760) was a mystical leader of the German Moravian Brethrens. He was one of several persons to influence John Wesley to break with the Church of England and create his own Methodist movement. Another German mystic, Jacob Boehme (1575–1624), considered to be the greatest of the Protestant mystics, founded other Separatist or Baptist sects. He knew that God was beyond human comprehension. God was to be known only in a mystical vision through intense prayer and devotion.

22

The Catholic Clergy and the Evolution of the Religious Orders

The clergy of the Catholic church is divided into two groups. The "secular clergy," comprising the popes, cardinals, bishops, and parish priests, serve the worldy aspects of the church in its mission to save the souls of mankind. The secular clergy live and work in the everyday world of men and women as they engage in their daily tasks of earning a living and managing a family.

The second group is known as the "regular clergy," the clergy who live by prescribed rules (*regulae*) in isolated communities apart from the sinful world. These communities are the monasteries for the men and the convents and nunneries for the women.

The monastic orders are dedicated to the fulfillment of two functions. One is to purify the soul, which might soon meet Christ in the Second Coming. Since the world is evil and the human body is polluted by original sin, the person most ready to be with Christ in heaven is the one who by sacrificial living has rid his or her body of its evil nature. The other function is to carry out Christ's commandment to love others by rendering charity to the poor and oppressed and enlisting unsaved souls into the embrace of the church. The monastic orders have been the most dedicated of all Christian soldiers to spreading the gospel and bringing the City of God to earth.

Many of the leaders of the Roman church have come from the ranks of the regular clergy, such men as thomas Aquinas, twenty-four of the popes, and the majority of the saints, including St. Francis, St. Dominic, St. Ignatius of Loyola, and St. Teresa of Avila. Some of the most troublesome critics of the church have also been monks, including Erasmus and Martin Luther.

The Rise of Monasticism

The earliest Christian monks chose to live by themselves, alone on a mountain-top or in a desert cave in Egypt. The more extreme and harsh the living conditions, the more pain and deprivation suffered by the human body, it seems, the better cleansed and more ready for entry into heaven would be the human soul. Typical of these extremely ascetic Christians were the hermits who lived in remote places, isolated from the world, where in their loneliness they could devote every hour of the day to prayer and meditation while the flesh of the body suffered starvation, disease, filth and vermin, and the torturous pain of desert heat or mountain chill. One of these first hermits was St. Anthony of Egypt, who about 270 withdrew to the desert along the Nile River to live in a cave. Many zealous Christians soon came to share his way of salvation. Many of these saved souls in Egypt were destined to organize the Egyptian branch of Christianity, known as the Coptic Church. By 300 some three hundred "eremetic" cells or hermitages were operating in Egypt.

In Asia Minor other hermits sought to find salvation in the manner of St. Anthony. One hermit, St. Simeon, the Stylite, lived for thirty-seven years perched on a mountaintop near Antioch. Year after year St. Simeon would add earth to his resting place, where he lived and slept, until a pillar was formed eight feet high. His body covered with filth and vermin and actually dying of starvation, St. Simeon would stand on his feet for hours preaching to the many followers who would come to hear him. The sacrificial, almost suicidal lifestyle of the hermits was a price that some Christians were willing to pay for salvation.

A more moderate, practical form of ascetic living was developed. It was a way by which men and women, living separately in a monastery or a convent, could live a life of sensual denial and, even better, be able to render some useful service to fellow Christians at the same time.

One of the first monasteries was formed by St. Pachomius in Egypt about 330. His monastery required that devotees live by strict rules of conduct and prayer. The fact that St. Pachomius permitted both men and women to live together compromised the vow of chastity. This tempting relationship was corrected by the later monastic orders. All monks and nuns, no matter to what order they belonged, were sworn to take three vows on admission to membership: poverty, chastity, and obedience. One of the first permanent monastic orders to be formed, the predominant order in the Greek Orthodox Church to this day, is the Basilian Order. St. Basil, the founder, lived in Caesarea, Palestine, about 360. He had lived first as a hermit, but so many people wished to join him in fellowship that he decided to bring them together in a monastic community. St. Basil used the rules of St. Pachomius as the governing rules of his monastery. However, he separated the sexes by providing convents for the women. Although the daily routine of the monks and nuns required them to spend more hours in prayer, meditation, and study than doing anything else, time was allotted for doing the daily housekeeping tasks and farming. Study and prayer, plus a few hours of common labor, replaced the hermit's devotion to suffering physical pain and isolation from the world. The Basilian Order was noted for its reluctance to use punishment or violence to secure obedience to its rules or the laws of the Church.

An example of a Basilian monastery still operating today is the monastery of St. Catherine, built at the base of Mt. Sinai in 452. It was build, so legend says, where monks found the body of St. Catherine, who had been killed in Alexandria by the Roman emperor Maxentius because she had refused to renounce her Christian faith. Hence the monastery was built in her memory. Today it is a Muslim mosque, but twenty Christian monks are still permitted to live there. The monks live by the rules of St. Basil, which prescribe several hours of daily prayers, the first prayer beginning at 4 A.M. and lasting for two hours. Three fasting days per week require abstinence form eating meat. Tobacco and alcohol are forbidden. Wine can be used on festival days. All lights are out by 10 P.M.

In the fifth century a less restrictive form of monastic order was organized in Italy by St. Benedict. This order became the pattern of organization for all monasteries in the West. St. Benedict (480–544) was born in Nursia, Italy. For three years he lived a hermit's life, but then he found it unsatisfying. Like Jesus, he attracted several followers. These were organized into twelve communities with twelve men in each community. The number twelve is an obvious reference to the twelve disciples of Jesus. Benedict's first monastery, and the one best known, was built on top of Mt. Cassino, between Rome and Naples. Mt. Cassino is remembered well by many American soldiers in World War II as the scene of a bloody battle between the German troops entrenched on top of the mountain and the American assault soldiers below. The American victory opened the way for Allied forces to occupy Rome and soon remove Italian participation in the war.

The Benedictine Rules or constitution sets the pattern for all later monastic orders supported by the Roman Catholic Church. The rules permitted the monks to engage in useful work as well as spend four to five hours daily in prayer and study. There was still time left for performing the daily chores, doing farming to produce food, spinning and weaving cloth materials, and later such useful labor as copying manuscripts, collecting and studying ancient classics, and administering to surrounding communities by teaching children and rendering aid to the sick and to the poor. Thus the monasteries became an important link between the ancient Greek and Roman cultures and the fifteenth-century Renaissance. Later convents would be built for women. All candidates who served in a monastic order took the three vows—poverty, chastity, and obedience—and made a commitment to life-long service to their order and the Church. Monasteries were ruled by an abbot, who, like a bishop, was empowered with almost absolute control. Although abbots were elected by their fellow monks, this did not permit shared decisionmaking power. From the beginning the Church was determined that all monastic orders be subject to the control of the secular clergy, namely, the popes and bishops. The Council of Chalcedon in 451 placed the monasteries under the control of the local bishops. The emperor Justinian I ordered the monks to deliver all personal property to the Church and never to return to the outside world. By the sixth century, monasteries in both the East and West had become an integral and important element in the operation of the Christian Church.

Any evaluation of the work of the monks and nuns would have to conclude that they were the most dedicated of all Christian servants. No other group of Christians were more Christlike than the members of the monastic orders. In the Dark Ages the monasteries were the centers of learning and culture. They were the havens of rest and refuge for the sick, the weary traveler, the fleeing victim of war or poverty. They were the best weapon against illiteracy and cruel barbarism and violence. Monasteries were truly beacons shining in an age of superstition and ignorance. There is no better example of an ideal Christian monk than that of St. Bernard of Clairvaux, a twelfth-century teacher of Pope Eugenius III. In his *On Considerations* he tells of instructing Pope Eugenius not to forget that he was the successor to Peter the Apostle, as well as to the Roman emperor, but that his mission was to follow the way of Christ, not that of Caesar.

However, over time, certain monks and bishops succumbed to the evils of the world and became less than Christlike. As recipients of wealth and land bequeathed to them by rich landowners, many orders became very wealthy. One historian reports that among eight monastic orders one-fifth of the wealth of the times was held by Christian groups committed to the vow of poverty.[1] Some abbots, like bishops, lived life like feudal lords, often indulging themselves in worldly pleasures or spending more time managing their estates than attending to God's business.

As a result, new monastic groups were born as reforming orders more dedicated to restoring monasticism to the original ideals of St. Basil and St. Benedict. One of these reforming orders, the Cistercians, rose in 1098 to reform the Benedictine Order. The vows were to be taken seriously, especially the vow of celibacy. For the next two centuries, the Cistercians established their houses across Western Europe, particularly on the frontier edges of civilization. The Cistercians were akin to the American pioneers who ventured forth into the wilderness, breaking ground, bringing civilization to the barbarian frontiers. They were the patrons of lowly peasants, teaching them better farming methods and bringing some of their sons education and even allowing them to study for clerical positions in the Church. However, more of the monks came from the ranks of the wealthy and the nobility than from the peasantry.

Near the time of the millennium other monastic orders were founded. The Clunian Order (910) and the Carthusian Order (1084) are examples in France. Later and more successful orders to be founded were the Franciscans and the Dominicans in the thirteenth century, and in the sixteenth century the Hospitalers of St. John (1517), the Theatines (1524), the Augustinians (1565), and the Ursuline Order of Nuns (1535). This sixteenth-century revival of monasticism arose in response to the Protestant Reformation and the need to correct the several abuses then existing in the Catholic church. The most powerful and successful order to combat the heresy of Protestantism was the Jesuit order, the Society of Jesus.

The Franciscans and the Dominicans came into being during the reign of Pope Innocent III, when papal power had attained its greatest strength. It was also a time when the clergy seemed to be slipping into a state of indifference to the sacred ideals of the church and paying more attention to the business and pleasures of the secular world. Members of these two orders were monks in the sense that all were required to take the vows of poverty, chastity, and obedience. However, these new orders differed from the previous orders in that the monks, now called friars or brothers, were permitted to go out into the world preaching, teaching, proselytizing, healing the sick, and caring for the poor, services that were to be conducted outside of the monastery walls.

The Franciscans

The founder of the Franciscan Order was Francis of Assisi, born in 1182 into a family of wealthy Italian merchants. At first young Francis aspired to become a soldier knight, but he was destined to become the most devoted and famous soldier of the cross. St. Francis, as he would become, has been proclaimed the one Christian who most closely replicated the ideal life as represented by Jesus. In 1209 he was "called" to follow Christ in the manner of Christ's command in Matthew 28:19–20. In a few years Francis had attracted many followers, so he organized them into a fellowship for Christian service. He prepared a set of governing rules in 1209 that were approved by Pope Innocent III. Not only did Francis exemplify the virtues of poverty and chastity, but he also introduced a mystical, almost pantheistic, love of all things in nature into the Christian system of theology and worship. Seeing God in all living creatures, Francis preached to the birds and animals, the trees and the rivers, and all things of nature. He wrote songs in praise of the wonders of God's creation, as for example his "Canticle of Brother Sun." It is no wonder that his birthplace, Assisi, has become one of the most popular shrines to which pilgrims come to pay homage. In 1926, the seven hundredth anniversary of his death, two million pilgrims visited his shrine at Assisi. The Christian Church, even the Protestants, have given St. Francis a place of honor alongside Christ and the Apostles. One of the famous Franciscan missionaries to America was Father Junípero Serra, who founded the first mission in California, now in San Diego. Franciscan missionaries were to be found in all parts of the Americas, Asia, and Europe. St. Francis had a great influence on Clara of Assisi, who joined the clergy to follow his example and founded an order for women known as the Poor Clares. No monastic order did more than the Franciscans to bring to the world Christ's message of love and peace for all of mankind.

The Dominicans

Another reforming order of friars, the Dominicans, was founded by St. Dominic (1170–1221). His order was blessed by Pope Innocent III for the primary purpose of extirpating the Albigensian heresy and spreading the gospel to other parts of the world. St. Dominic failed to persuade the Albigensians to return to the Catholic fold and the pope ordered a crusade against them. French kings and nobles eagerly used the occasion to seize their lands, but the Albigensians persisted. Finally Pope Gregory called a court of Inquisition into session in 1233 to prosecute the heretics. The heresy was finally destroyed a century later, in 1330.

St. Dominic was born in Castile, Spain. First he joined the Augustinian Order and served as a teacher. At about the age of thirty be became aware of the Albigensian heresy, so as a step to combat them, he organized the Order of Preachers to destroy it. His order, as other monastic orders, lived by the three vows of poverty, chastity, and obedience. Members were to beg for their food. No order was more zealous in defending the church against any perceived enemy. So zealous were its members in pursuing heretics that their contemporaries nicknamed them the "Hounds of God," a play on the name "Dominican." The Dominican Order grew rapidly after 1215, so that by the time of Dominic's death over five hundred devoted missionaries had joined the order.

The Jesuits

Later in the sixteenth century, there arose a new order of friars, the Jesuits, that was even more vigorous and unrelenting in the pursuit of heretics and conversion of the non-Christian world. The founder of the Society of Jesus was Ignatius Loyola. He was born in 1491 in the Basque country of Spain. His parents belonged to the nobility so as a young man he was destined to become a soldier. During a battle at Pampolona in 1521 he was wounded and hospitalized. In the hospital he read two books that would change his life. One was on the life of Christ, the other on the lives of the Christian saints. Loyola left the hospital determined to organize a band of Christian knights who would wage war against Satan and all other enemies of the church. In 1522 Loyola took the vow of chastity, after which he visited the famous shrine of the Virgin Mary at Monterrart, near Barcelona, Spain. Here he gave his sword to the Madonna and became a hermit. For several months he fasted and tortured his body as penance for his sins. In his solitude he had visions of Christ and with instructions from Christ he wrote the guidebook for his future order, *The Spiritual Exercises*. In 1532 Loyola became a priest, after which he journeyed to Rome and Jerusalem. Then for seven years he studied at the University of Pisa and at a Spanish university. Later he went to the University of Paris to study and while there organized a prayer study group among his friends. The text used for study was his own *Spiritual Exercises*. One of Loyola's friends was Francis Xavier, the famous missionary to China, India, and Japan.

In 1540 the Jesuit order was approved by Pope Paul III. Loyola died at the age of sixty-five in 1556. In 1662 both Loyola and Francis Xavier were canonized as saints.

The Jesuit order is regulated by the "Institutes," the constitution for the order. The Institutes are a combination of the *Spiritual Exercises* and other instructions on how the Jesuits are to live. Loyola valued education greatly, and from the onset of the order a rigorous and demanding educational program was required of all initiates. Throughout its history, the Jesuits have established a worldwide reputation for quality education in all levels of schools that they support, from elementary school to graduate university level of education.

Jesuits take the customary monastic vows, but the vow of obedience is directed especially to the pope and the commanding general of the order. The Jesuits were truly the soldiers of the cross, for their organization used a military form of discipline and unquestioning obedience to superior officers. When a Jesuit was ordered to go he went, whether it be on a crusade, a pilgrimage, a missionary journey to far off China or the Philippines, or to defend the church. Jesuits were disciplined to speak correctly, to use the proper gestures, and to dress according to the rule book.

The first war in defense of the church was waged against Protestant rebels. It was the Jesuits, allied with Catholic monarchs in Spain and Austria, who were able to stem the advance of Protestantism and save southern Europe for the Roman Catholic Church. The best known of the Jesuit scholars was Peter Canisius, who wrote in defense of Catholicism. His one best-known book is the *Catechism* (1555), in which he answers some 211 questions posed by critics of the church.

Jesuit missionaries were instrumental in the founding of many educational institutions throughout the world. In 1553 a Jesuit mission was established in Sao Paulo, Brazil. Jesuit schools and missions would be established throughout Latin America, especially among the native people. The first Jesuit college was founded at Coimbra, Portugal, in 1542. Today it is the State University of Portugal. In 1552 a college was established in Rome that is now the Papal Gregorian University (Collegio Romano), a school devoted to the education of priests. The college curriculum was unique for its day, since it combined theological studies with the classical liberal arts.

In 1581, Pope Gregory XIII proclaimed the Jesuits the best instrument God had for fighting heretics. Critics of the church are fond of depicting the Jesuits as brutal allies of the Devil, as they seemed to delight in using every method of torture and violence against the enemies of the Church, the dissenters and the heretics. The Jesuits did acquire a questionable reputation for the manner in which the Inquisition in Spain was used to expel the Jews and Moors. Dissenters from Catholic dogma were punished severely. In 1633 the Inquisition condemned the scientist Galileo to death for his theory that the sun, not the earth, was the center of the solar system. Galileo recanted his heretical views so as to escape death. Galileo's confessor, the Jesuit Robert Bellarmine, believed that Galileo was correct about the sun, but he warned Galileo to keep quiet and deny his heliocentric theory of the universe.

During the eighteenth century the Jesuits lost favor with many European monarchs, scholars, and even the common people. They had become overly zealous and aggressive, too powerful and independent to be trustworthy. They were expelled from France, Spain, and Portugal. In 1773 Pope Clement XIV ordered that the Jesuits in Spain be suppressed after King Charles XII threatened to break with Rome and establish an independent Catholic church because of their activities. The Jesuit order became a victim of the French Revolution when laws were enacted that outlawed the Catholic church and all of its agencies, including the Jesuits. When Napoleon became emperor he restored the Catholic church in France by an 1801 concordat with Pope Pius VII, who in turn crowned Napoleon emperor of France. However, the church never regained its original status as an independent church, nor were the Jesuits recognized. Hencefore the Catholic church in France was more a national than a papal church. In 1814 Pius restored the Society of God to its former position of respect and power.

Even to the present the Jesuits continue to render dedicated service to the church, especially in Latin America. Recently Jesuit priests have joined revolutionary movements in Latin America seeking to overthrow the old feudal system of land ownership and dictatorial governments. The Jesuits, with other Catholic leaders, preach a brand of "liberation theology," which advocates a transfer of political power from the land-owning class to the masses of peasants. The irony is that many of the revolutionary groups liberation theology helps to sustain are inspired by Communist ideology, something that is anathema to the Catholic church. Another debated issue between the papacy and the Jesuits is birth control. Many of the priests see the need for some limitation of population in these impoverished, overpopulated countries in Latin America, Africa, and Asia. In 1968 Pope Paul VI issued an encyclical, *Humanae Vitae,* in which birth control was denounced vigorously. Only the rhythm method of contraception was approved. So Jesuits and the popes are not always in agreement on Catholic policies in the modern world. Yet the church and the Jesuits need each other. For almost five hundred years the Jesuits have been loyal and effective soldiers of Christ, and no doubt this relationship will continue long into the future. Of 140 Catholic universities in the world, 40 are operated by the Jesuits. The Catholic church needs the Jesuit order.

23

The Broken Body of Christ: The Eastern or Greek Orthodox Church

The Apostle Paul spoke of the Christian Church as being the body of Christ, eternal, unbroken, and for the benefit of all mankind. Yet before the first century had ended internal debates and divisions within the Christian body were already present. One group would proclaim itself to be the orthodox, the true faith, and all other groups who differed were branded as heretics. Human nature, being what it is, is prone to argument and division. Just as families have their internal strife, so do large bodies of humans organized into social institutions.

Until one Christian church, that is, one of the competing bodies, eliminated the other alleged Christian groups, until it had sufficient power to become the one true Church, then the body of Christ remained broken. The first phase in the struggle for internal Christian unity was complete when emperor Constantine in 323 recognized one of the Christian groups as the orthodox, state church of the Roman Empire. Armed with the power of the state even to execute dissenters, the orthodox Church extinguished most of the competing Christian groups by the seventh century. Only a few of the dissenters or heresies survived into the modern age, and they were on the fringe outposts of the Roman Empire in Egypt, North Africa, Syria, and Persia. Five heretical Christian groups refused to accept the primacy of the Roman church and the rule of the Roman Empire. The Monophysite church was established in Armenia, the Coptic Church in Egypt, the Abyssinian Church in Ethiopia, the Jacobite Church in Syria, and the Maronite Church in Lebanon and Palestine. Maronites accept that Christ had a dual nature but they have a different version of how the two natures are held together. The binding element is a special bond of moral will that they call "monotheism." The Maronites use the Roman Catholic sacraments and rites, but they refuse to accept the supremacy of the papacy.

The most serious division within the Christian body before Martin Luther occurred in 1054, when the Greek or the Eastern Orthodox Church split from the Roman Catholic Church. This division within the ranks of Christianity mirrored an original split within the Roman Empire itself, brought about seven centuries before, when the emperor Constantine moved the imperial capital from Rome to Byzantium, an ancient city on the Bosphorus, which he rebuilt and renamed Constantinople. In 330 the heart and central power of the empire was no longer in Western Europe. Hence the history of the Eastern Orthodox Church is inseparably entwined with the history of the Byzantine Empire. In the western part of the empire a vacuum was created when Rome was no longer the center of imperial wealth and power. Who would fill this vacuum of power? Many Germanic tribes sought to plunder the Roman provinces of their wealth after the fall of Rome in 410. German tribes invaded Italy and occupied the city of Rome. Other German tribes occupied and ruled the outlying provinces in England, Spain, France, and Germany. In time the several Germanic tribes were Christianized and gradually they became civilized communities and states with stable governments and populations. Some remnants of the Roman culture and government were adopted by the Germanic people, but in large measure they developed out of their own experiences new forms of government and new economic systems.

These years were the so-called Dark Ages of Western Europe. After the demise of the Roman Empire, civilization in the West declined precipitously, though Christianity and the remains of the Roman culture produced a better level of life than the former tribal character of the invading peoples. Christianity provided the cultural and moral foundations for the Germanic people, while the Germanic people developed the feudal system of government and tenure, and a social caste system of nobles and serfs.

The Eastern or Byzantine Empire after the sixth century ceases to play any important role in the life and government of Western Europe. Although the emperor Justinian, who ruled 527–565, did attempt to restore imperial control over the western provinces of Italy, Spain, and North Africa, after his death a sucession of weak emperors, some of whom murdered to get the throne, lost for all time any control over the rest of the former Roman Empire.

Most school children in the United States know little of the history of the Byzantine Empire or of the Eastern Orthodox Church. In the larger cities some children may know where a Greek church is to be found, or, at least, where a Greek candy shop or restaurant can be found. Western travelers to Istanbul (formerly Constantinople) will have visited Justinian's most noble church, the Church of Hagia Sophia. After the Turks conquered the Byzantine Empire in 1453 the Hagia Sophia became a Muslim mosque and the beautiful wall murals were covered with plaster. Today the church is a national museum and the wall murals have been restored along with the splendid stained glass windows. Until the Turkish conquest of the eastern empire, Constantinople was a center of commerce, wealth, and significant cultural enterprise. In fact western kings, princes, and merchants looked upon the eastern empire with greedy eyes. The Second Crusade was motivated more by a desire to take the riches and power of the eastern empire than by any desire to save the Holy Land from the Muslim infidels. For a thousand years the Byzantine Empire served as a fortified wall protecting Western Europe from Asiatic invaders: the Huns, the Tartars, and the Turks. But even more dangerous to Western Europe were the fanatically inspired men of Islam who conquered most of North Africa, Asia Minor, Persia, all the land to India, and then the lands of Eastern Europe to Hungary and Austria.

When the Byzantine Empire came under the rule of the Ottoman Turks, the Eastern Orthodox Church lost its base of power. The church and its patriarchs were now at the mercy of the Islamic empire. Henceforth the Turkish sultans would appoint the ruling patriarch of Constantinople, the head of the Eastern church.

The Division of the Church: Struggle for Supremacy and Controversy over Icons

The split between the eastern and Roman parts of Christendom came in July 1054, when the pope excommunicated the patriarch of Constantinople for heresy, and, in turn, the patriarch excommunicated the pope and his legates. After these mutual excommunications each church was to go its separate way, the Eastern church holding sway over Greece, the Balkans, Russia, Palestine, Egypt, and Syria, while the Roman Church remained supreme in western Europe. In the east the several different churches used the rituals and services of the Greek church even though the local churches outside of Greece used their native language and were subject to the rulers of their national states.

The division of Christendom was no sudden event. The roots of division began when the Fourth General Council ordered a ranking of the patriarchs of the Church, naming the bishop of Rome as number one and the patriarch of Constantinople as number two. The Council of Nicea in 324 had stated that all bishops or patriarchs were of equal status. The Eastern church never recognized the Roman pope as the supreme head of Christendom.

Another issue of contention was the matter of using icons of God, Christ, and other religious beings in worship services and church buildings. In the first two centuries the Christians refrained from the use of images or icons lest they be accused or worshiping pagan idols, forbidden by the Second Commandment. There was also a Judaic tradition that said God and divine beings were invisible, hence they could not be shown in paintings or in sculpture. During the third century this abhorrence of images disappeared and throughout Christendom pictures of sacred figures came into general use. Christian people began to venerate these images, especially of the Christ and the Virgin Mary, which were said to possess magical powers that could answer prayers, heal the sick, and bring fortune to the penitent. John of Damascus (675–749) offered a good rationale for the use of icons. He said that the likeness of God was revealed in the incarnation of the Christ, so it was no sin to have an image of the Christ displayed in the church.

But there were churchmen and theologians who retained doubts about the use of images. Some may have been influenced by the spreading Islamic religion, which forbade the depiction of human figures in sacred literature and buildings. In the Eastern church the opponents of icons persuaded Emperor Leo II (r. 711–741) to ban the use of icons. In two decrees in 729 and 736 Leo forbade all icons. The Roman Catholic Church protested. Pope Gregory II (r. 715-731) and Pope Gregory III (r. 731-741) both objected and the Roman Church continued to display icons. In one sense the controversy over icons was a major factor in causing the split in the Christian church. An Eastern empress, Irene, called the Second Council of Nicea in 787 to repeal the ban on icons, and the council did so. Other emperors wished to continue the ban on icons, so the struggle continued until another empress, Theodora, legitimized the use of icons in 843.

The break between the two parts of Christendom in 1054 was finalized over the issue of the supremacy of the papacy and the reluctance of the Western church and the Western kings and princes to accept the overlordship of the Byzantine emperor. When Charlemagne was crowned emperor of the Holy Roman Empire on Christmas Day in 800 by Pope Leo III, a strong signal was sent to the Byzantine ruler that the Western half of Europe was not to be ruled by the Eastern empire.

After the use of icons had been approved, artists were not free to present their own conceptions of religious art. Instead the church dictated both the subjects to be pictured and the style in which the images were to be portrayed. The subject matter was confined to spiritual matters, biblical scenes and characters, the holy persons, the Christ, the Virgin, the Apostles, and the saints. Natural scenes of landscapes and the everyday life of the people, rich or poor, were forbidden. Art must be symbolic, that which would elevate the spiritual aspects of man. The human figure should be pictured in drab colors, in postures where the body would be shown as being distorted, emaciated, elongated, or in any manner that would nullify all sensual aspects of the human body. Figures were painted in a two-dimensional perspective, a style most adapted to all murals and manuscripts. Sacred pictures were richly illustrated with dozens of religious symbols, which, in a shorthand style, told the viewer the significance of the picture. Such symbols as the cross, the fish, the lamb, St. Mark's lion, the vine, and the peacock (eternal life) were used abundantly. Many of the paintings had the subjects arranged in a triangular manner, the triangle representing the Trinity, with the most sacred person at the apex of the triangle. Medieval art was almost exclusively church art, and art was highly symbolic and stylized. The Roman church in the West broke away from these rigid patterns by the thirteenth century. Today the Eastern orthodox Church continues to use the flat, two-dimensional style of church art. The Western Roman Catholic Church, and the popes especially, encouraged a new form of art, one more natural and realistic, that portrays the human body in flesh tones and full-bodied curves. Landscapes begin to appear. Rivers, mountains, trees, and flowers appeared alongside the sacred persons. By the fourteenth century medieval art had begun to yield to the spirit of the Renaissance, the glorification of man and nature. It was the awakening of a new age that measured values not only in terms of God but in the minds of man and the God-given right of men to think and to create free of church interference.

Differences between the Roman Catholic and Eastern Orthodox Rites

The Eastern or Greek Orthodox Church today is the third-largest Christian denomination, with over 150 million followers. Ten million Orthodox Christians live in Greece. Nearly nine of ten Orthodox live in the countries of the former Soviet Union and Eastern Bloc. For years religious services were sharply curtailed. However, the Orthodox Church survived 150 years of Turkish rule, and it will undoubtedly survive the antireligious policies of the Communist nations.

In general, the Eastern Orthodox Church accepts the basic creeds of the Roman Church, such as the Nicene Creed, with a slight modification. The Nicene Creed concludes with the wording, "the Holy Spirit, who proceeds from the Father." The Eastern church accepts this as the correct form of the creed, while the Roman church has added the phrase, "and the Son." The Eastern church also rejects the doctrine of purgatory; hence extreme unction is given to the sick as well as to the dying. Other differences from the Roman Catholic Church are that the clergy may marry before ordination, but bishops must be celibate. In the Eucharist the Eastern church uses unleavened bread, which the Roman Church does not. But, over all, the Eastern and Roman churches accept Scripture as revealed truth, veneration of the Virgin Mary and the saints, and observation of the traditional holy days, although not always on the same days of the year.

The two Christian churches differ also in the structures used to govern them. First of all, the Eastern church never had the freedom of the Roman church to operate independently of the secular government of the nations in which it was located. It was always subjected to the rule of kings, czars, and sultans. There was never an opportunity for the patriarch of Constantinople to rule in a political sense over the Byzantine Empire, to become a major ecclesiastical and political ruler as did the Bishop of Rome. Even in church affairs the Eastern patriarchs were never able to become the supreme lawgivers. Always a Church council was declared to be the supreme source for all decisions. The seven great councils held between 325 and 787 were all declared to be the authoritative source for church doctrines and practices. The model for a church council was found in Acts 15:28, which describes the Council of Jerusalem.

One final difference between the two great divisions in Christendom is that the Eastern church has always placed higher value on the mystical and emotional aspects of religious worship. The Roman church services seem to be more controlled, more rational, and less given to emotional displays as seen in the church service, the ornamentation of the altars and church interiors, and the vestments worn by the clergy. The Eastern churches use more gold and colorful decorations. Easter is celebrated more joyously with music, song, and dance. The Eastern church places less stress on man's state of depravity and original sin. A happier mood seems to characterize the Eastern church. For example, since the Eastern church does not accept the idea of purgatory and penance, church theologians argue that sin is not a violation of moral law but a flaw in one's "godliness." The Eastern church also has a more generous attitude about the congregation participating in the Mass, since it permits the people to receive the wine as well as the bread.

The mystical element in Eastern theology is revealed in the belief that man as well as the Christ can be deified by the grace of God and the incarnation of Jesus as the Christ. The experience of deification is said to be accompanied by a miraculous burst of light, or a vision of light, or a vision, like that of St. Paul, of having seen the presence of the Christ. The greatest of the Eastern theologians to have any influence on Western Catholicism was Dionysius, the Pseudo-Areopagite, a disciple of Neo-Platonism. He wrote *Mystical Theology* in order to influence Catholic mystics like Bernard of Clairvaux and even Thomas Aquinas. The Eastern Basilian monks also reflect this respect for mystical experiences as having value over rational study for receiving knowledge about God.

Most monks in the Basilian orders are common laymen, not priests, who devote more time to prayer and meditation than monks in the Benedictine orders. The Basilian monks also serve as teachers, missionaries, writers, but most of them tend the monastery's needs of housekeeping, farming, and household manufacture.

The Eastern churches use a Greek cross floor plan, in which all arms are of equal length. Since the church building represents the universe, the four sides or arms are placed in alignment with the compass points, the East side representing Paradise and the west side the land of the dead who are awaiting the day of resurrection. The center of the church represents the earth, over which is the sky or the dome which so identifies a Greek church. In the church there are no pews, the congregation remains standing through the service.

Today the Eastern church is composed of fifteen self-governing church bodies, plus three autonomous groups in Finland, Japan, and Macedonia. The fifteen self-governing churchs are in Constantinople, Alexandria, Jerusalem, Antioch, Russia, Romania, Bulgaria, Georgia, Cyprus, the Czech Republic and Slovakia, Poland, Greece, Albania, and the Sinai.

In recent years some efforts have been made to effect a reconciliation between the Roman and Eastern churches. In 1964 Pope Paul VI met with the patriarch of Constantinople, Athenagoras, and in 1967 the patriarch returned the visit to Rome. In 1967 Pope John Paul II visited Constantinople, but for now any reconciliation seems far off. Two issues provide blocks to reconciliation. One is the refusal of the Eastern church to recognize the supremacy of the Roman pope; the other is the papacy's refusal to relinquish control over the Eastern Uniate churches in Romania, which use the Greek liturgy and rituals but do recognize the pope of Rome as the head of their churches.

24

The Broken Body of Christ: The Protestant Reformation

A Changing Society: Mercantilism, Wealth, Humanism, and Nationalism

The history of the Protestant Reformation, or, as Catholics prefer, the Protestant Revolt, is in many ways also the history of Western Europe from about 1400 to 1700. The Protestant movement arose from a complex of social and economic forces that had been in progress since 1400 or earlier. The one inevitable fact about life is change, even until death. By 1400 the old medieval system of feudalism and a church-ruled society in which the voices of angels uttered more truth than the pioneers of science was in disarray, if not doomed to oblivion. The papacy and the church were spending more time on the management of estates and political concerns than doing God's work.

The new modern age was brought to fruition gradually as new values replaced old ones. Political leaders and intellectuals began to worship a new set of values. No longer did Jehovah and the Christ represent the preferred value systems of modern man. More and more modern man became enamored of acquiring wealth and satisfying ego needs of here and now. Heavenly rewards could wait. Poverty might be good for monks and nuns, but for men and women of the world riches were better. Churches blessed the acquisition of worldly goods, and with wealth came the things that please the sensual desires of mankind: power, splendid lifestyles, wine and gold, but most of all, becoming the envy of one's neighbors. Even popes and bishops discovered that it was more blessed to be rich than poor.

If wealth was to be accepted as a good value, then the church and the state not only had to give their approval, but they also had to seek to remove the many restraints that inhibit the production and accumulation of wealth. New national monarchs knew that power is based on wealth, for it is money that

305

buys armies and weapons. The more the governments encouraged commerce and manufacturing, the more wealth there would be for the kings to tax. As national monarchs looked about them they saw huge estates of land owned by the church and the monasteries, tempting morsels to seize.

The kings of Spain, Portugal, France, England, and the Dutch Netherlands sponsored trading companies and explorers to discover new trade routes and sources of profitable trade. New lands were discovered as Columbus sought to find a westerly route to the rich spice lands of India. The Spanish monarchy became extravagantly rich from American gold and silver stolen from the Incas and Aztecs. From the fifteenth century on Western Europe experienced a burst of economic development. New towns arose, populated by displaced serfs from the feudal manors and dominated by a new social class, the bourgeoisie, or the middle class. With their wealth the middle class could force the despotic kings to share power with them, and, especially in England and the Netherlands, the seeds of parliamentary government were sown. The new middle class arose first in the Italian cities of Venice and Florence, where medieval trade with the east was first developed. The Crusades had been an important factor for the successful Venetian trade with the East. And in Florence a Christian banking business had begun to rival the Jewish bankers, thanks to the enterprising Medici family. By 1500 the center of commerce and banking was shifting northward to England and the Netherlands, and by 1700 these two nations had achieved a dominance over Spain and Portugal, and were to become the principal rivals with France for the control of Western Europe. These two countries also became the centers of commerce, urban life, and the promulgation of a new economic system, that of free capitalism. The foremost economist to portray the values of free capitalism would be an Englishman, Adam Smith, who wrote his classic treatment of free capitalism, *The Wealth of Nations,* in 1776.

Along with the growth of capitalism and the middle class came a new set of intellectual and moral values called humanism. Humanist intellectuals could not flourish until they had financial "angels" to buy the products of their work. As surplus wealth first developed in the Italian cities, it was to be expected that artists, scholars, and scientists would find financial patrons in Italy. This is no place to review the history of the Italian Renaissance of the fourteenth and fifteenth centuries. Suffice it to list a few familiar Italian Renaissance names: Petrarch, Boccaccio, Galileo, Raphael, Leonardo da Vinci, Michaelangelo, and Machiavelli. A century later the Renaissance thinkers were found in northern Europe, in England, France, and the Netherlands: Erasmus, Rabelais, Thomas More, Roger Bacon, Descartes, Rubins, Rembrandt, Copernicus, Kepler, Robert Boyle, Francis Bacon, and John Locke.

Humanism set out to free man's mind from the shackles of superstition and religious dogmatism so that truth could be found by reason and the application of reason through science. Man by virtue of his power of reason, freed from the stain of original sin, was quite competent to direct his own life. Priests and papal dictates were irrelevant. Reasoning men could even fashion their own paradise on earth, utopian socieities such as that conceived by the philosopher Francis Bacon. Humanism borrowed the values of the Greek philosophers, who placed man, not God, at the center of the universe. Man is the measure of all things. Nature is pure and good. The human body is noble and pure and artists should depict it in its full beauty, even in the nude, rounded, even voluptuous, and not in the medieval style of a body emaciated, distorted, covered by gray-tinted skin. Love between man and woman is good, and sex is not to be cast aside as something evil.

The humanists, as might be expected, met fierce opposition from the established authorities in both the church and the state. These free thinkers had to be brave men, willing to risk their lives for their heretical ideas, ideas which later become the foundation stones for modern science. Galileo and Copernicus barely escaped being burned at the stake.

Humanism also called out for the freedom of all humans to be masters of their own fate. The democratic process of popular voting, representative and constitutional government, and churches ruled by the people are all expressions of the humanist spirit.

Another value system arising from humanism is the spirit of nationalism, or popular pride and a sense of loyalty to a social group larger than the family, the clan, the tribe, or the feudal lord, pride in the national state, its language, its goals, and its preservation. No longer did people give their first loyalty to a pope or even a monarch, unless the monarch was seen as one of the people. National loyalty needed symbols to represent the new love objects, songs, flags, traditions and holidays, popular kings or presidents, and common goals, too many of which were expressed in bloody wars against perceived enemies. But of all of the possible national symbols to bind together these new nations, what better one could be found than to have a national church, a church using the national language and presided over by national priests, not foreign Italian clerics sent by the pope of Rome.

Prelude to Revolt: Corruption of the Church

By 1500 many Western European states were ready for a change in their religious affiliations, especially those states that were more urbanized and commercially developed, as in England, the Netherlands, Switzerland, and parts of France, Northern Germany, and the Scandinavian countries. Heretics and critics of the church had been successfully prosecuted before 1500, but by 1500 the Roman Catholic Church had been so weakened by internal dissension and corruption that it could no longer effectively suppress dissent. These dissenters constituted the clientele for the Protestant Reformation.

The opportunity for attacking the church and its clergy was provided by the degenerate state of papal leadership and a number of abuses that offended Christian leaders. The church had attained its greatest measure of spiritual and political power under Pope Innocent III in the thirteenth century. After his reign, the papacy went into a period of decline and corruption. As the papacy went so did many members of the clergy.

Only a few examples of papal degeneracy and clerical corruption can be given. When accusations are made against the medieval church, one must be careful not to conclude that by 1500 all popes and priests were corrupt. Corruption was not the rule, but it was convenient for the dissenters to damn all of the clergy for the sins of a minority. The church, for the most part, performed its Christian obligations, cared for the poor, educated some of the children, sanctified marriages and deaths, and gave moral leadership to a rather primitive society.

The most devastating charge made against the Church and the papacy was that the clergy, from the pope to the lowly priest, had become lazy and indifferent to its spiritual duties. The men of God were serving the gods of materialism more than Christ. Church services and rituals had hardened into routine exercises. It seemed that the dynamic spirit of the Christ had congealed into stagnation and immunity to change. No longer did the church seem to be willing and able to adjust to the new demands of a money-oriented society. Many parishes were said to be without priests, and all too often the available priests were illiterate and uneducated.

One critic of the church, Erasmus, a Dutch scholar, was both a loyal Christian and a critic of the church. He never left the church to become a Protestant. In his *Praise of Folly,* written in 1509, he severely castigated the church for its many abuses, such as the sale of indulgences, the use of magical charms and magical rites, and giving too much reverence to saints and pilgrimages when it would have been much better to worship a loving Christ. Erasmus mocked the use of rosary beads, calling them "the fumbling over beads." His view on theologians was expressed in this line from the *Praise of Folly*:

> As for the theologians, perhaps the less said the better on this gloomy and dangerous theme, since they are a style of man who show themselves exceeding supercilious and irritable unless they can heap up six hundred conclusions about you and force you to recant; and if you refuse they promptly brand you as a heretic.

In general the critics of the church condemned the veneration of saints, the belief that relics and pilgrimages could heal the sick and secure salvation in heaven, and that the sale of indulgences or pardons could release souls residing in purgatory. The use of magical and superstitious practices to delude the poor illiterate parishioners was a sinful act. Penance and purgatory were declared irrelevant to man's quest for salvation. Indulgences deluded the people into believing that all sins were pardonable. Even the rosary was a useless instrument for the salvation of the soul. In brief, the accretion of many "pagan" practices over the centuries had caused Christian people to put their trust not in God and Christ, but in superstitions, miracles, and magical words and gestures.

The clergy was charged with being overly concerned with the collection of tithes and the management of their estates. The possession of great wealth permitted some of the bishops to live in the manner of powerful feudal lords with fine homes and dress, riding to the hounds in the hunt, and always in the market for more estates and fatter coffers.

Even Catholic scholars agree that the popes of the fourteenth and fifteenth centuries were not paragons of Christian virtue. Many, like Pope Julian II, were capable, intelligent men, capable administrators, political governors, and leaders who would have made excellent kings or presidents, but who were failures as leaders of the Christian Church. Some popes were guilty of several sins, such as the sale of indulgences, the sale of church offices (simony), and placing their sons and nephews in high church offices (nepotism). Popes were accused of keeping concubines and bearing illegitimate children—who later would be made high church officials. Popes and bishops would rig the election of new popes and engage in all forms of political chicanery with national monarchs to secure favors for the clergy, most of all to secure military arms to fight papal wars and crusades.

Pope Nicholas V (1447–1459) was a Renaissance pope who did much to rebuild the city of Rome. He made plans for a new Vatican and a new church, St. Peter's Church. He supported famous artists such as Fra Angelico and Pirodella Francesca. He gave large collections of Greek and Roman manuscripts to the Vatican library. As a patron of the arts he is to be commended, but as a pope little can be said in his favor.

Pope Innocent VIII (1482–1492) arranged a marriage between his son and a daughter of the wealthy Lorenzo di Medici, a Florentine banker, who was given a bonus dowry in the form of a cardinalship for his thirteen-year-old son. This son later became Pope Leo X, who was noted for his costly military ventures. First he aided the Spanish Hapsburgs in their wars against France, then switched sides by making an alliance with Francis I, king of France. To win Francis's support Leo recognized the right of the king to appoint all church clerics in France to their offices. Leo was also known for his extravagant parties and carnivals. By war and party he bankrupted the papal treasury. Leo sold thirty-one cardinalships in 1517 for a profit of a half million ducats. In his behalf, Leo did support Renaissance artists and humanists generously.

Pope Alexander VI (1492–1503) came from the infamous Borgia family. He was the second Borgia to become a pope. He had much talent as a political leader and administrator, but as a pope he was a disgrace. He kept a mistress who bore him four children, of whom the best known were Caesar and Lucrezia Borgia. Caesar was made an archbishop at the age of seventeen and a cardinal at the age of eighteen. Lucrezia was married to the duke of Milan, a member of the powerful Sforza family. Eventually five Borgias became cardinals. Alexander kept a harem of boys and girls for his own pleasure. Worse, Alexander had sexual relations with his own daughter, a subject for much juicy Roman gossip.

If Machiavelli needed a living model for his prince he had a perfect one in the figure of Alexander VI. Machiavelli in his *The Prince* said, "Only a wily, treacherous despot could be a successful ruler over mean-spirited people." Justice and mercy were not in Alexander's or *The Prince*'s vocabulary.

Leo X, a Medici pope, was made a cardinal at age thirteen. He engaged in wars against the Spanish Hapsburgs, but during the wars against the Lutheran princes he deserted the French to help his Catholic allies, Charles V, emperor of the Holy Roman Empire and king of Spain. He sold indulgences abundantly to support his wars, his building program in Rome, and his luxurious lifestyle.

Perhaps something more damaging to the prestige of the papacy than immorality and corruption was the frequent involvement in wars and political intrigues with various Christian monarchs. The papacy had become a political football to be tossed between the kings of France and Spain and a number of Italian princes. Each political group sought to put its candidate on the papal throne. Moreover, the kings sought to secure from the papacy the right to tax church property and appoint all church officials. From 1328 to 1424 the papacy was a total disgrace to the Christian church. Pope Boniface VIII sought in 1296 to thwart all royal efforts to control church offices and revenues when he issued a bull, *Clericos Laicos,* forbidding kings to interfere in church affairs. Both English and French kings ignored the bull, and in 1302 Boniface issued another order, *Unam Sanctum,* which said that all kings were subject to papal orders. The kings ignored this order also. The conflict between national monarchs and the papacy reached a climax in 1303, when Boniface excommunciated the French king, Philip the Fair. France was placed under an interdict. King Philip marched upon Rome and arrested Boniface, who died in 1305, after which the French-controlled cardinals elected a French pope who moved the papacy to Avignon in France. For seventy years the papacy was located in France, an era known as the "Babylonian Captivity."

In 1377 a new pope, Gregory XI, moved the Vatican back to Rome, but the Italian cardinals refused to accept Gregory as the pope. In the next year the Italians elected one of their own, Urban VI, as pope. But the French cardinals refused to accept Urban; they elected Clement VI, who continued to rule the Church fromm Avignon. Now Christendom had two popes. A church council was called to meet in Pisa in 1409 to resolve the "Great Schism" within the papacy. The council elected a new pope, but now the Church had three popes, since the other two refused to resign. The Holy Roman emperor Sigismund called a council to meet in Constance in 1414, in which two popes were deposed and the third was persuaded to resign. A new pope, Martin V (r. 1417–14331), was elected. The council had hoped to effect some much-needed reforms but these efforts failed. The council did clip some of the papal powers by declaring that church councils were to be the supreme lawmakers.

The papacy continued its wayward ways until the time of Martin Luther. The handwriting was on the wall for both the popes and the church in general, for even as early as 1328, a Paduan writer, Marsilio, in a pamphlet, *Defensor Pacis,* denounced the papacy as being evil and declared that the national states should exercise control over the church. This was the theme of the Protestant Reformation.

A few critics of the church came from its inner circles. John Duns Scotus and William of Occam, thirteenth-century English theologians, opposed the introduction of rational thinking or scholasticism in the manner of Thomas Aquinas as a guide to finding Christian truth. Faith was the only path to true knowledge about God. A more dangerous critic was a Dominican friar of Florence, Italy, Savonarola (1494–1498). He became a moral crusader whose mission was to cleanse the church of corruption. He was a charismatic figure, a gifted speaker, able to command a public following. For four years in Florence he organized a moral crusade and made the city of Florence into a model Puritan community. The city became a veritable monastic theocracy in which the people were subjected to a regime of strict morality enforced by an army of roving spies who would arrest the errant citizen. Lewdness, drunkenness, gambling, prostitution, and all other forms of vice were outlawed. Rome was deemed "a deceitful, proud harlot." In a brief period Savonarola's moral tyranny became unacceptable to his own people, and soon Pope Alexander VI was persuaded to have Savonarola burned at the stake.

Pre-Reformation Dissenters: The Albigensians, Waldensians, Lollards, and Hussites

Other critics of the church preferred to make a clean break with Rome and leave it to organize their own brands of Christianity. One of these antichurch movements was the Albigensians or Cathari ("pure") rebels in southern France and northern Italy. The center of this movement was Albi, France. The Albigensians accepted the New Testament, especially the gospel of John. However, their theology was a mixture of orthodox Christianity, Gnosticism, and Manicheism. They believed that the world was composed of two elements, a nonmaterial element ruled by a god of goodness, who was the supreme God, and a material element ruled by Satan or Jehovah, who was evil. The Albigensians declared the Roman church evil and false. They considered themselves the true Christian church. The Albigensians lived in the manner of monks. They denounced the Virgin birth, the bodily resurrection of Christ, and the human element of the Christ—he was only pure spirit. All sacraments were rejected. The worship service used the New Testament; the Old Testament was banned as an evil book. They recited the Lord's Prayer during the service. The elect, or most pure members, dressed in white robes and refused to eat any meat. The less pure members could own property, eat meat, and marry. But since they were sinners they had to receive a special baptism before death called a "Consolation." It is no wonder that the Church banned the Albigensians as heretics and the popes ordered crusades against them by the Dominican friars. Popes Alexander III, Innocent III, and Gregory IX all preached crusades against these heretics. The crusades eventually won a victory when a French king sent an army under Simon de Montfort to crush the Albigensians in 1243. One should note that the majority of the group were urban merchants and poor, common people who, in the future, became the mainstay supporters of the kings and nobles who wished to be free from the control of the Church.

Another pre-Lutheran group of dissenters were the Waldensians, led by a merchant, Peter Waldo of Lyons, France, who in 1176 left his family and business to preach a gospel of poverty and asceticism. He took as the text of his message Matthew 20:21 in which Jesus tells his disciples to sell their goods, give them to the poor, and come and follow him. Waldo urged a friend to do likewise and so they were called the "Poor Men of Lyons." Waldo wished to restore the Christian church to its early, simple origins. He continued to use all of the seven sacraments except the Eucharist, which was reduced to a simple memorial service. He abolished the veneration of relics and saints and belief in purgatory, and denied the authority of the papacy. Baptism was only for adults. Women were accepted on an equal basis with men. All oaths were forbidden, as well as all participation in military service. In brief the Waldensians foreshadowed the coming of the more radical Anabaptist Protestants. However, any hope the Waldensians might have had to reform the church went down to failure when they were excommunicated in 1182 and shortly after destroyed by the armies of France and the papacy. A few survivors escaped to the Alpine regions of France and Italy.

A third heretical group arose in England under the leadership of John Wyclif (1330–1384). He was an Oxford scholar and a minor church official who wrote a series of pamphlets on "lordship" in which he called the popes false lords. Christians owe allegiance only to God, not to any pope. The national king should assume control of the church and its lands, leaving the clergy in charge of spiritual affairs only. The clergy should live in poverty and deny all wordly things. Wyclif's followers, called the "Lollards," were a throwback to the first-century primitive Christian Church. All members were their own priests and all were free to read the Bible. Hence Wyclif translated the Vulgate Bible into English. Only two sacraments were used, adult baptism and a memorial supper. Wyclif's followers came from the lower classes, and his movement was blamed for causing the Peasants Revolt in 1381, but this accusation was false. The Lollards were condemned as heretics by Pope Gregory IX, and soon they were gone from England. A few fled to Bohemia, where they became a part of the Hussite movement. Wyclif managed to escape the death penalty by dying, but his body was exhumed and burned so that Christian justice could be rendered.

In Bohemia, John Hus (1373–1415), inspired by the Lollard movement, organized a similar revolt against the church. At this time there was a close alliance between the English and the Bohemian monarchies. The Hussite dissenters were modeled after the Lollards. Their Bible was written in the Czech language. National monarchs should control the church and its lands. The priests were to live in poverty and they were given no special spiritual powers, since all poeple were deemed by God to be their own priests. Like other heretics, Hus was excommunicated and burned at the stake. To this day Hus remains a symbol of national pride for all Czechs. Later Hussites will be known as the Moravian Brethren, many of whom will come to America.

Church historians do not agree as to what influence these early heresies had upon the Protestant Reformation. Many of the reforms advocated by these groups were to become basic points of belief among the more radical Anabaptist Protestants. That the state should rule over the church was accepted by most of the more conservative Protestants. All agreed that the Bible and not the pope was the sole source of authority for the Protestant churches. The Lutheran movement introduced a new concept of salvation, won not by good works but by faith alone. The earlier movements continued to use the Catholic doctrine of salvation by good works.

Some Protestant leaders will claim that the Protestant revolt was inevitable, ordained from the beginning by God. But a good historian would say that the causes of the Protestant movement are to be found in a combination of conditions, including the stagnation and corruption within the Catholic church, the growing ambitions of national monarchs for land and power, plus a growing number of townsmen and merchants who wished to be rid of medieval restrictions on commerce and business and who preferred to give their allegiance and taxes to a national king than to a foreign pope. Moreover, the Renaissance spirit uttered by the voices and works of humanists inspired people to want freedom from religious restraints as well as from ruling despots, and in some of the Protestant messages people could hear voices speaking for personal freedom and more democratic governments in both church and state.

Martin Luther's Revolt

The events that triggered a successful revolt against the Roman church came in Germany on October 3, 1517, when an Augustinian Monk by the name of Martin Luther posted his *Ninety-Five Theses*—a list of problems the Roman church needed to address—on the door of the All Saints Church in Wittenberg. Luther had no intention of leaving his church, or creating a new Christian church. The theses were a statement of his concern that the corruption within the papacy and clergy would destroy the church if not corrected. Luther wanted them to return to their primary duties of shepherding their Christian flocks as Christ would have them do.

Luther was born in 1483, the son of a Saxon miner. As a young man he was well educated for the priesthood and soon he joined the Augustinian Order. Then he served as a professor at the University of Wittenberg. In 1511 he went to Rome to study, but what he learned most was that Rome and the papacy seemed to be rotten to the core. During adolescence Luther became conscious of his own sinful, sexual nature. He was plagued by sexual guilt feelings. At times he seemed to have been tortured to a point of a breakdown. The Devil, it seemed, had possessed Luther's soul, and Luther was determined to find some way to escape his clutches. Luther eventually believed he had found his road to salvation in Paul's letter to the Romans, in which is found the statement,

"By grace you have been saved through faith, and this is not your doing, it is a gift from God." In a 1519 debate with John Eck, a Catholic loyalist, Luther restated his belief in "justification by faith"—good works were not necessary to be saved.

The act that prompted Luther to post his theses was the papal practice of selling indulgences—remission of the temporal or purgatorial punishment for sin— to raise money to complete the building of St. Peter's Cathedral in Rome. A Dominican friar, John Tetzel, was sent to Germany by Leo X to sell these indulgences. Tetzel claimed that as soon as the coins rang in the money chest, the souls for which the money had been paid would bypass purgatory and go straight to heaven. Luther's theses condemned this fraudulent promise. In 1343 Pope Clement VI had proclaimed that the surplus merits earned by the saints could be used to pardon sinful souls in purgatory.

Pope Leo condemned Luther for his protests and ordered him to come to Rome and recant his sins. Luther refused to go. Luther continued his debate with the papacy when in 1519 he denounced the dogma of papal supremacy, and in 1520 he asserted that all church members were priests and that the assertion that the clergy had been given special spiritual powers by Peter was false. In "An Appeal to the German Nobility" Luther cited a statement from Paul in 1 Corinthians 12, that all church believers had received the same baptism as Christ and that all people were equal in the eyes of Christ and accordingly all could interpret Scripture for themselves. In 1520 Luther wrote "On the Liberty of a Christian Man," in which he outlined his theology for a new church based on the belief that salvation was justified by faith. In the "Appeal to the German Nobility" he called the German princes to reform the church within their provinces and to place the control of the clergy under the rule of the state. Because of his several writings in 1520, Luther was declared a heretic and ordered to appear before the Diet of Worms, the legislative body of the Holy Roman Empire, in 1521. Luther had many friends—German princes, nobles, and merchants—in the diet, so he refused to recant his disobedience of the pope. However, Luther did not want an open break with the papacy. He cautioned his friends to be patient and not do anything rash. Already the German peasants had attempted a revolt against their feudal masters in 1521 and Luther did not want to be blamed for this. Also the Anabaptists were beginning to form their own independent churches and this was not what Luther intended.

Luther was excommunicated and subject to the death penalty by being burned. But he was saved when his friend the duke of Saxoy took Luther into hiding at his castle in Wartburg. For a year Luther spent his time writing more books, translating the New Testament into German, and making plans for the future of his church. Later Luther translated the entire Bible into German, a work that became a standard by which all literary works in German would be measured.

In 1522 Luther returned to his professorship at Wittenberg, where he was proclaimed a national hero, safely protected from the wrath of the papacy and the pro-Catholic kings and princes. Luther sought to solidify his support from the North German princes by urging them to take control of the local churches and lands. He supported the efforts of the feudal nobles to suppress the Peasant revolts, and denounced the peasants in the most cruel and defamatory manner.

Luther broke further with the Church by renouncing his vow of celibacy and marrying a former nun, Katherine von Borea, in 1525. Luther was to have six children from this marriage, and his wife became a model for a Christian mother. Until his death in 1546 Luther kept busy writing, organzing the Lutheran Church, and, whether he wished to or not, becoming the apostle of the Protestant movement throughout Europe.

In 1529 Luther wrote a "Short Catechism," in which he outlined his theological differences with Catholicism. In 1530 he and his friend Philip Melancthon wrote the "Augsburg Confession," which is still used as the official creed of the Lutheran Church. Luther died with the knowledge that his church was destined to have a secure and permanent future.

For almost a hundred years the Catholics waged intermittent wars against the Lutheran defenders, all to no avail. The popes and the Catholic monarchs, especially the Hapsburg rulers of Spain and Austria, who traditionally were also the emperors of the Holy Roman Empire, went to war, but all they achieved was to retain southern portions of Europe, including southern Germany, for the Roman Catholic Church. The Lutheran defenders found their support among the Northern German princes, the Scandinavian monarchs, and the free cities of Germany, in which the middle classes were dominant. The Diet of Worms in 1521 had ordered all German princes to obey the pope and protect the church. But obedience did not follow, so in 1526 the Diet of Speyer yielded ground and permitted each prince to choose the religion for his state. Then in 1529 the Diet of Speyer once again ordered all princes to obey the pope and to persecute the heretics. As a result of this order the Protestant princes delivered a protest against the order, giving rise to the name "Protestant." Two years later the Protestant princes organized the Schmalkaldic League, a military alliance to fight the Catholic forces. After a series of wars, the first apparent victory for the Protestant allies came in 1552, when they defeated the forces of the papacy and Charles V, the Holy Roman emperor and king of Spain. A peace was arranged at Augsburg in 1555 that permitted each ruler to decide the religion for his state.

Religious wars were to continue until 1648 when, at the conclusion of the Thirty Years' War (1618–1648), the peace of Westphalia established the principle that each ruler could choose his country's religion. Northern Europe was destined to remain Lutheran and southern Europe to remain Roman Catholic. As a footnote, Protestants need to be reminded that probably their victory over the Catholics is mostly attributable to the fact that the Catholic Hapsburg forces were engaged in a more serious war against the Ottoman Turks, who threatened to conquer most of southeastern Europe, the Balkan countries, and even Hungary and Austria.

Today the Lutheran Church is found in ninety-two countries and has more than seventy million adherents. In 1593 Lutheranism became the state church of Sweden, and in 1537 the state church of Denmark, which then included the areas of Norway and Sweden.

Luther's Innovations in Ritual and Dogma

The changes in Christendom wrought by the Lutheran Church included, first, a complete break with the papacy in Rome by denying the doctrine that the pope was supreme. Luther saw a need for a strong head for the church, so he proposed that local kings and princes rule the Lutheran churches. Luther retained the clerical hierarchy of bishops, in which scheme the kings became the substitute for the pope. All clerical appointments were royal prerogatives. The clergy was no longer endowed with special spiritual powers by virtue of the sacrament of ordination. Priests and bishops were now lay servants who were not essential for the salvation of souls. The church was a community of believers who were in direct communion with God; hence there was no need for any priestly intercessors with God.

Luther preached that salvation comes from God's grace through the sacrifice made by Christ on the cross. Since salvation comes by way of faith there is no need for all of the sacraments, the veneration of saints and relics, and pilgrimages. The sacraments of penance, purgatory, and the sale of indulgences were all outmoded relics of a pagan past. Since each person is his or her own priest, it is imperative that all must read the Bible and find God's truth therein. Church worship is obligatory. In the Lutheran Church the congregation takes both the bread and wine in the Eucharist or communion service. Luther interpreted the Eucharist in such a way that its elements, the bread and the wine, did not undergo a miraculous transformation into the body and blood of Christ, which is the belief in the Catholic church. Although they remain their natural state, within them is the Holy Spirit, just as the element heat in a hot iron does not change the iron into some foreign substance. This interpretation is called "consubstantiation." The Lutherans use only two sacraments, baptism and the Eucharist.

The Lutheran Church retained most of the Catholic liturgy and ritual, except for using the local language. The clergy continued to wear special clerical vestments. The clergy could marry. The monasteries were abolished and their properties became royal possessions. Luther loved music, which in both vocal and instrumental songs became an important part of the worship service. Luther wrote thirty-six hymns. The best known is "A Mighty Fortress Is Our God." A Lutheran church has no images of Christ or other holy personages.

Luther's theology was vastly different from Catholic theology, for his way to salvation was by faith and not good works. A Christian is "born again" on profession that he or she is saved by the promise of God's grace as revealed in the death of Christ. Luther also opened the way for other persons to make new interpretations of the Christian message, hence he became a prophet to many later Protestant leaders. Luther has been described as a "God-intoxicated man," since he saw Christ as the central theme of Christianity. Manfred Barthel in his *The Jesuits* (p. 97) describes Luther's theology as, "By grace alone, by faith alone, by Holy Writ alone."

Although Luther won a victory over the papacy, he remains in the Catholic mind a heretic. But there are some signs of reconciliation between Catholics and Lutherans. It is said that Pope John Paul II prays earnestly that steps can be found to effect some reconciliation with the Lutherans.

What Luther started, John Calvin, King Henry VIII, John Wesley, and a host of other Protestant dissenters continued. Martin Luther was no social revolutionary, no man of the Renaissance. When he wrote "On Christian Liberty" he did not have in mind that all people are equal and that they should rule their lives in a democratic society. He did not preach the overthrow of the feudal class system, freedom for the serfs and slaves, or freedom for woman, who was still bound by tradition, law, and Christian duty to obey her husband and submit gracefully to his demands and desires. Except in his relations with the papacy, Luther was a man of the status quo.

25

The Splintered Body of Christ:
Protestantism after Luther

Ulrich Zwingli

After Luther's revolt in Germany, the Protestant movement spread to Switzerland, France, and Great Britain. In Switzerland the first successful new Protestant church was established by John Calvin. Before Calvin another reformer, Ulrich Zwingli, broke with the Catholic church in Zurich in 1484. Zwingli was a Catholic priest who left his church, married, and had four children. His disenchantment with the Catholic church was created when he read some of the critical writings of Erasmus. He joined Luther in condemning the several abuses being practiced by the papacy and the clergy. Like Luther, he declared the Bible to be the only source of authority for God's truth. Only two sacraments were valid—baptism and the Lord's Supper. Monasteries, pilgrimages, saints, relics, and clerical celibacy were all worthless for the salvation of man's soul.

For a few years Luther and Zwingli were friends, but in 1529, when Zwingli published his "Commentary on True and False Religions," Luther disputed Zwingli's idea that the Eucharist was only a memorial rite and that the physical presence of Christ was a myth. Luther disagreed with Zwingli when he proposed that the government of the church should be placed in the hands of the congregation rather than under the control of the clergy. Zwingli and Luther did agree that the church should be under the control of the civil government and that all citizens of a jurisdiction must be members of the state church. When the City Council of Zurich in 1529 put into action Zwingli's plan for a city-ruled church, war broke out between the Catholic and the Zwinglian cantons. In this war Zwingli was killed, following which, in 1531, a peace was arranged that left Switzerland divided between Catholics and Protestants.

John Calvin and the Rise of Calvinism in Switzerland, Scotland, the Netherlands, and France

Zwingli's work was to be continued by John Calvin, a much better theologian than either Luther or Zwingli. Calvin was born in France in 1509, educated at the University of Paris, and later forced to flee France because he supported the Lutheran movement. He fled to Basel, Switzerland, which was then a center for humanist studies. Here Calvin wrote his most important work, *Institutes of Christian Religion*. In 1536 Calvin was called to preach in Geneva, where he would carry out his life's work. In Geneva Calvin established a theocratic government in which the affairs of the city were controlled by Calvin's new church. Geneva became a model of Puritan sobriety in which the lives of all citizens were closely policed and all offenses punished severely. Geneva had acquired a new religion in which all people were expected to live the life of a monastic, with no pleasures: no sex except when used on rare occasions for procreation, no use of alcohol, no dancing or singing, no fun whatsoever. It was not surprising that many Genevans soon longed to return to the good old days of freedom in the Catholic faith.

Calvin was a God-possessed man who believed that his will was God's will. Man was born in sin and could be saved only by the grace of God. In fact man could never be certain that he could be saved, no matter how devout the person might be, since God had ordained that some souls were to be saved while others were not to be saved. This belief, preached also by St. Augustine, is the doctrine of predestination. It compromised severely the promise that through God's grace all men could be saved. Calvin's theocratic Geneva became the model for Puritanism in England and Scotland, and later in the New England colonies of the new world. In 1540 Calvin married a former nun who gave birth to five children, all of whom died in infancy. Calvin remained in Geneva until he death in 1564.

Calvin opened the way for more radical forms of Protestantism, which exist today as Presbyterian, Congregational, and Dutch Reformed Churches. In the Calvinist tradition the Bible is the sole source of authority. Men are hopeless sinners and only through faith, modified by predestination, can men be saved. Good works alone never save souls, but a saved person exhibits good works in his or her daily life by living the life of a loving, charitable Christian person. Calvin prescribed three necessary things for salvation: loyalty to his church, observance of the sacraments of the Lord's Supper and baptism, and obedience to the rule of the civil government. The government of the church was placed in the hands of a small body of presbyters, or elders, elected by the congregation, plus pastors and administrative aides called deacons. However, the governing board of the church, the synod or presbytery, was subject to the rule of the civil government. Calvin's measure of tolerance for Catholics or other non-Calvinist faiths, Jews or Moslems, was no better than the intolerance of the Catholic Inquisition.

The most commonly cited proof of Calvin's intolerance is his execution for heresy of Servetus, the doctor who discovered the pulmonary circulation of the blood. Servetus had denounced the Nicene Creed, the Holy Trinity, and infant baptism and so was guilty of heresy.

In the Calvinist church it seemed that God was the only one who had any freedom. The church service was typically Protestant in that there was a minimum of ritual and ceremony. Recitation of liturgy was replaced by an expanded moral exhortation or sermon to live the good life. Calvin broke with the traditional style of church architecture. Catholic and Lutheran, by replacing grand cathedrals with plain, unadorned, small buildings without steeples, stained glass windows, statues, wall murals, or any display of the cross.

In Scotland, Calvin had a friendly ally in the person of John Knox, who left Geneva to return to Scotland, and, with the aid of many Scottish nobles who wished to restore the Scottish church after it had been incorporated into the English kingdom, established a Calvinist church, the Presbyterian Church, in 1564. The Scottish church adopted Calvin's creed, enunciated in *The First Book of Discipline*. It also adopted the *Geneva Book of Common Prayer*. The Scottish synod had an equal number of pastors and elected presbyters, and the supreme ruler was the state government. For English Presbyterians the official creed is the Westminster Confession, drawn up by the English Parliament under the rule of Cromwell and the Puritans in 1643.

The Dutch Reformed Church was organized in the Netherlands in 1628. At that time the Netherlands was under Spanish rule, which sought to destroy the Calvinist church. In 1580 the Netherlands was placed under a papal interdict, which prompted a civil war. In 1584 the Dutch king, William of Orange, was murdered, but his efforts to save Calvinism forced a truce in which the northern provinces were left to remain Calvinist, and to become the independent state of the Netherlands.

In France the Calvinists, called the Huguenots, found their membership among the workers and merchants of French cities, especially in the south. In 1572, the French king, Charles IX, ordered some fifteen thousand Huguenots murdered, an act that for all practical purposes destroyed the Protestant movement in France. Some of the Huguenots fled to the American colonies. Those who remained in France were granted religious toleration when King Henry of Navarre issued the Edict of Nantes in 1598. Later French monarchies would continue to persecute Protestants, although many groups would survive. It should be noted that the victory over the Huguenots was more a defeat for the papacy than a victory, since the control of the monarchy over the Catholic church became more absolute, so that the church, in fact, became a national Catholic church.

Among the achievements of John Calvin is the recognition that he gave to the importance of education for creating a literate Christian body and an educated clergy. The Calvinist schools were at first operated by the churches, but since the church was under civil rule, a precedent was set for the establishment of state-operated, or public schools.

The Anglican Episcopal Church

Another Protestant church would find a home in England—the state church of England, the Anglican Episcopal Church. The English church was not born out of any serious theological differences with the Roman Catholic Church, but out of a desire of an English King, Henry VIII, to be master of his own kingdom, of the kingdom's church, and of the wealth of the church. The immediate event that prompted Henry to break with Rome was that he wished to be rid of his first wife, Catherine of Aragon, who he claimed was not able to give him a male heir, so that he could marry a young noble lady of the court, Anne Boleyn. She refused to beome his mistress, so marriage was Henry's only choice if he wanted to have her in bed with him. Henry VIII, who ruled 1509–47, was a most popular king, who possessed both intellectual talent and a Machiavellian genius for success in the game of politics, both domestically and in foreign relations. He made England a first-rate power that competed on even terms with the two dominant states in Europe, Spain and France. Henry was also a good Renaissance man who was well educated in the classics and who gave support to such scholars as Erasmus, John Colet, Richard Pace, and Thomas More, the author of *Utopia*. As a young king one of Henry's first acts was to found a "learning academy" to promote the study of the ancient philosophies and learning. Since Henry was the second son of Henry VII it was not expected that he would ever become the king, so he was educated to assume a role in the clergy. As a devout Catholic he wrote an attack on Luther's revolt against Rome, for which Pope Leo XI rewarded him the title, "Defender of the Faith."

Henry was no fool, nor was he a saint. His critics called him egotistical, power-hungry, and lust driven. As he broke with Rome he was called the anti-Christ bent on destroying Catholicism. What Henry failed to accomplish in his drive to make England a rich and powerful nation with a church led by the king was largely accomplished later by his daughter, Queen Elizabeth I.

Henry's desire to be rid of his first wife Catherine, who was the aunt of the powerful Charles V, king of Spain, was thwarted by Henry's inability to secure a papal annulment of the marriage. The pope might have been willing, but he was indebted to Charles V, who opposed the annulment of his aunt's marriage. In fact Charles's troops were occupying Rome at that time, 1527. Henry needed a divorce so his minister, Thomas Wolsey proposed that he call Parliament into session and enact a law separating the English church from papal control. So in 1529 Parliament placed the clergy under state control. In 1532 all tax payments to Rome were stopped, and the next year Parliament decreed that no divorce cases could be sent to Rome. At this point another minister of Henry, Thomas Cranmer, announced that the marriage to Catherine was null and void. In 1534 Parliament decreed by the Act of Supremacy that the king was now supreme head of the English church. Thomas More refused to accept this decision, for which he was executed in 1535. Henry proceeded immediately to seize all church properties, including monastic ones, which became a real boon to the King's treasury.

As the leader of the English church Henry proceeded to effect a new church creed and organization. In 1539 Parliament drafted the "Six Articles of Faith," which defined the structure of the new church. Three sacraments were retained: baptism, the Eucharist, and Holy Orders.

The definition of the Eucharist was neither the Catholic one of transubstantiation nor the Lutheran one of consubstantiation, but a less miraculous interpretation which declaims that no miracle had transpired, but that the communicant on faith believed at the time of taking the wine and the bread that the real presence of Christ was in the elements. Communicants took both the bread and wine. The Catholic beliefs in relics, saints, pilgrimages, confessions, and private masses were all retained. Services were conducted in English. A new translation of the Bible was ordered in 1537. The church retained the Catholic episcopal form of church government with the king as head of the church and a descending order of archbishops, bishops, and priests. All who remained loyal to the Catholic church were damned as heretics and subject to a death penalty; hence many Catholics fled England to freedom in the Netherlands.

With the death of Henry in 1547 the English church was left with an uncertain future. For over a hundred years the English church would continue to struggle before it found an established place among the world's religions. As the leadership changed so did the nature of the church. When Henry died his nine year old son, Edward, became the king. Being a minor, the monarchy was ruled by a regent, a brother of his mother, Jane Seymour. The regent belonged to the Somerset clan which adhered to the Calvinist church. So Parliament passed a series of laws from 1547 to 1549 that repealed the Six Acts and instituted more Protestant church practices. All were to receive the communion cup, images were removed from the churches, priests were permitted to marry, and more church property was taken by the state. A new prayer book, one still in use, was prepared in 1549.

When Edward died in 1533 he was succeeded by his half-sister, Mary, the daughter of Catherine and a staunch Catholic. Mary restored the Roman Catholic Church to its original state of power under the headship of the Roman pope. Now Protestants were persecuted and burned at the stake.

Fortunately for the Protestants, when Mary died in 1558 she was succeeded by her half-sister, Elizabeth, who restored her father's form of Protestantism in England. Elizabeth was a true woman of the Renaissance, a humanist, a supporter of the arts, one who had little interest in religion, and a devoted English monarch who was determined to make England the greatest nation in the world. She desired to effect a compromise between the pro-Catholic Christians and the radical Protestants. Like her father, she refused to accept papal rule over the church. In 1563 a basic statement of principles was drafted by Parliament, the "Thirty Nine Articles of Faith," which are still in effect. Elizabeth was declared the head of the church, its "Supreme Governor." Basically Elizabeth returned the church to its position under Henry VIII.

But the church still had many problems. The Catholics would seek to undo the Elizabethan settlement even though most were in exile. The Catholic faction placed its hopes on the Stuart, James I, who succeeded Elizabeth in 1603. Catholics felt that the time had come to destroy the Protestant heretics. Even though the Stuart kings, James I and Charles I, did their best to restore Catholicism, the Protestants were too powerful in Parliament to permit any movement toward Catholicism. Rather, the growing commercial Puritan interests in England moved in the other direction, toward a more radical form of Calvanism. Parliament, when controlled by the Puritan element under Oliver Cromwell in the period of 1649–58, enacted the abolition of all "popish" practices such as the belief in saints, images, relics, and pilgrimages. But there were now in England even more radical Protestants, the Anabaptist Christians, who in England were known as Separatists or Congregationalists. They would break away from the Church of England and have a church ruled by the congregation and with a worship service modeled after the first-century Christian church in Antioch. However, the Puritan church viewed the Separatists as heretics, and persecuted them. Many of the Separatists fled to the Netherlands for religious freedom and safety. Some of these "heretics" would come to America as our Pilgrim fathers.

The English people were relieved when Cromwell died in 1658. The Cromwellian era was a replica of the intolerably moral regime imposed by Calvin upon the Genevans. The Puritan forces had wished to overthrow the monarchy and set up a republican form of government with Cromwell as the president, or the "Protector" as he was called. The Puritans established a new prayer book based on the Calvinistic Westminster Confession. Bishops were replaced in church government by church councils or synods. But the Cromwell republic and Puritan rule ended with the passing of Cromwell and the accession to the throne of the moderate Stuart king, Charles II, in 1660. The Church of England was restored to power as it had been under Elizabeth, and after 1660 the church remained very much as it is in England today. When William and Mary came to the throne after the Glorious Revolution of 1689, England was to be ruled by a figurehead king with the actual power of government vested in the Parliament. By the Act of Toleration of 1689, all Christians excepting the Catholics were granted religious toleration. However, all taxpayers had to support the Church of England. The only serious challenge to the state church came from John Wesley and the Methodist movement in the eighteenth century. During the nineteenth century a small revival movement known as the Oxford Movement or Tractarian Movement sought to instill into a decadent church a new spirit of activity and dedication. The Oxford Movement was led by an Oxford fellow, John Keble, who in 1833 wrote a series of critical tracts about the Anglican Church. The best-known member of the Oxford group was John Henry Newman, who later became a convert to Catholicism. Basically the Oxford people wished to restore many Catholic practices to the English church, such as the use of the confessional, the veneration of saints, and regular periods of fasting. By 1880 the Oxford Movement had run its course, but it did leave a legacy of pro-Catholic bias within the Church of England. The church would become more tolerant of Catholics, who were finally granted toleration in 1828. Also thanks to the Catholic influence, the church assumed a more friendly attitude toward labor unions, labor legislation, and other forms of social welfare legislation.

Today there are over sixty million Anglicans in the world, three million in the United States, in the Protestant Episcopal Church of America.[1] In general the Church of England struck a compromise between Catholic formalism and ritual and the simplified or "purified" protestant churches. The English church is more tolerant of worldly pleasures than the Puritans or the Catholics. Birth control and sexual gratification in marriage are more accepted than by Catholics or Baptists.

The Church of England has its basic tenets of belief stated in its Book of Common Prayer. Three sacraments are recognized: baptism, the Eucharist, and penance. Salvation is found in doing good works and having faith in God's grace. Truth is learned from three sources: Scripture, reason, and tradition. Also accepted are belief in the Virgin Mary, the Holy Trinity, and the Resurrection. The Church takes a flexible position on the validity of angels, devils, spirits, and other supernatural phenomena, neither denying their existence nor proclaiming belief in these mysterious elements to be essential for Christian salvation. In many ways the Church of England has much in common with the Roman Catholic Church, and it may be possible to effect a reconciliation between the two churches. However, after thirty years of ecumenical talks the reunion date remains far off, one stumbling block being the role of the Pope in a reconciled church. Another and more important one, recently added, is the Church of England's recent decision to ordain women.

By 1600 three major Christian churches had left the fold of the Roman Catholic Church, the Lutherans, the Calvinists, and the Anglicans. A fourth group, the radical Anabaptists, were next to leave the Catholic Church.

The Anabaptists

This group of Protestants would splinter the body of Christ into thousands of parts. The Anabaptists may or may not be the descendents of the earlier Albigensians, Waldensians, and Hussites (the record is not clear) but the Anabaptists have many beliefs in common with these thirteenth-century heretics. The term anabaptist means "rebaptism," that is, the baptism of persons at the "age of reason," the onset of adulthood. This group arose first in Switzerland and adopted many of the beliefs of Zwingli, such as the conviction that all members are their own priests, and that each body of believers is free to govern itself. Popes and priests are irrelevant to the process of salvation. Zwingli is said to have coined the name "Anabaptist" for a radical group that preferred to be named the "Brethren in Christ." Although the Anabaptists orginated in Zurich they were soon persecuted and forced to flee to Moravia, southern Germany, Austria, and the Netherlands.

The first statement of Anabaptist belief, known as the Schaffhausen, was written in 1527 in southern Germany. Two of the most noted theologians were

Menno Simons (1496–1561) and Balthasar Hubmaier (1490–1528). Simons was the founder of the Mennonite Church in the Netherlands. It was there that the English Separatists met the Mennonites and adopted many of their "Baptist" beliefs, which were expressed in a document, "True Christian Faith," in 1541. Hubmaier was burned at the stake for heresy in Vienna in 1528.

The Anabaptists, like modern Baptists, professed a simple faith based on Scripture as the sole source of authority. They accepted, however, only the New Testament. Priests or clergy were irrelevant to the process of salvation. Worship services were simple, in a plain building, with a minimum of ritual, and a service confined to a sermon, hymn singing, prayer, and a memorial communion service each Sunday. The only other sacrament observed was adult baptism, by immersion of the body.

Most Anabaptists came from the lower classes, who sought a democratic form of church government and a lifestyle of poverty and communal sharing of all worldly goods. Church officials were elected in a democratic manner by members of the congregation. The democratic process was also to apply to the civil government. To protect the liberty of the church Anabaptists wanted a complete separation of church and state—a minimum of secular interference with their religious activities. As a rule, Anabaptists refused to take oaths or participate in any military action. For their nonconformist beliefs the Anabaptists were banned as heretics by the Diet of Augsburg in 1530, whereupon many fled to the Netherlands, where King William of Orange granted them a measure of religious toleration in 1577.

One distinguishing mark of the Anabaptists is the emphasis upon each saved person having received at the time of baptism an emotional, mystical experience of having been "born again." From the Anabaptist tradition arise the Protestant churches that proclaim that salvation is revealed by this sense of being resurrected from an old, sinful way of life to one of purity in the life of the Christ.

The heirs of the Anabaptist tradition are such modern American churches as the Baptists; the Hutterite Brethren; the German Baptists, or Dunkards, who came to America about 1723; the Mennonites, who went to Pennsylvania in 1653; the German Moravians, who became the United Brethren Church around 1735; and the Amish settlers in Ohio, Illinois, Indiana, and Iowa.

Socinians and Arminians

The Protestant Reformation unleashed a host of theological interpretations of the nature of the Christ and what the true Christian Church as conceived by God ought to be. Among the many voices speaking their views of the true church were two groups of humanist-oriented theologians who were never able to organize a separate church body that reflected their theological position. Two sixteenth-century critics of both the orthodox Catholic churchs and the major Protestant denominations, the Lutherans and the Calvininists, were the Socinians and the

Arminians. Both schools of thought reflected the Erasmian criticism of the major Christian churches—that they were overly dependent on revelation and mysticism as the source for discovering God's truth. They urged that more reliance be given to rational, logical means of truth seeking. Renaissance humanists had rediscovered the Greek passion for reason and the intelligence of man as being the proper routes to the discovery of truth. In the minds of these dissenters God had created both reason and revelation, and both were of equal worth. Revelation as found in scripture must be tested by the standards of reason. Although the Socinians and the Arminians differed in detail, in general they held many views in common. If rational tests are to be applied to the Christian theology, then Truth is limited to evidence that can be found in Scripture. Socinians rejected the Old Testament as being irrelevant to the nature and goals of Christ. The Arminians found the Old Testament valuable in that it contained the essence of Christian law, to which all Christians must give obedience. Both groups agreed that the true Christian church of the New Testament would be the church of the first century, before all the "papal trappings" had been added. Both groups rejected the theological concepts of original sin and predestination. The sacraments of baptism and the Lord's Supper had no mystical elements. They were only rites intended to educate the people about the nature of Christ.

Socinius (1539–1604) saw Christianity as a religion of law and promise. Jesus was stripped of most of his supernatural nature, hence his virgin birth was not recognized. Jesus was seen as a human person who set an example for all Christians to follow. Since the Old Testament contained no evidence by which to know the life of Jesus, it was rejected as being of no value. Jesus was a perfect moral and mortal man who became immortal only after his death. Jesus did not die to redeem mankind from sin. First of all, penalties for sins committed cannot be transferred from the guilty party to someone else. Hence God could not permit Jesus to bear the sins of others. Each person is responsible for his own acts, since God has deemed that all persons have free will to choose good or evil. Since Jesus was free of sin God could not punish him. His death on the cross was the choice that Jesus, with God's consent, made for himself. Immortality is given to man not because he deserves it, or earns it by professing belief that Jesus offers the way to salvation, but because man has willed to follow the lifestyle of a moral man, obedient to the law, just as Jesus had done on earth. Man is justified by good works, not by faith. Hence the proper Christian church is one in which Christian people are taught divine law and encouraged to follow the example set by Jesus, who lived the life of an obedient, God-fearing moral person.

Jacobus Arminius (Jacob Harmensen, 1560–16009) sought to provide a less radical interpretation of Christianity, although he had more in common with Socinus than Luther or Calvin. Arminius accepted the Old Testament as being a source of knowledge about divine law, which was the purpose for which Christ had founded his church. But Arminius believed that Jesus was more than a model person for Christians to emulate. His death and resurrection gave proof that Jesus was both God and man, and that he had died for the remission of the sins of man. He had not died for any sins that he had committed, but because God had willed that the sins of mankind were to be transferred to him for punishment. In God's system of divine justice all sins must be punished lest the social order end in chaos and anarchy. So Jesus is chosen by God to be punished for the many sins of mankind. Where Socinus had seen Jesus as a perfect model for mankind in the salvation process, Arminius believed that the death of Jesus on the cross was an essential ingredient in the formula for salvation. But the essence of Christianity was to be found not in any supernatural, mystical aspects of the divine will, but in teaching the people how to live good, rational, self-willed lives on earth. The Arminians would have no part of a church adorned with a host of mystical rites and rituals, ruled by a clergy especially endowed with the Holy Spirit and hence set apart from the congregation. In some respects one can discover in the Socinian and Arminian "heresies" some elements of modern liberal Protestant worship in a Unitarian or "process oriented" Methodist or Congregational church. The services are devoid of mystical rituals such as the miraculous transformation of the bread and wine into the body and blood of Christ. Priestly offices are no more than democratic measures for the orderly administration of a human institution.

The Methodists

A fifth Protestant church, the Methodist, arose in eighteenth-century England as a protest, reform movement within the Church of England. The Methodists remained within the English Church until the American Revolution, when the American wing of the movement broke away because it could no longer have a church ruled by English bishops and the English crown. Methodism came in response to the Industrial Revolution and the depressing conditions it created for urban workers and coal miners. The Methodists became the social conscience of England. As such they were pioneers in advocating social welfare legislation for laborers and the poor. They also devoted much time and money to setting up private welfare agencies in the urban centers to help depressed slum dwellers. The English church had little concern for the masses of poor people. It had become an agency to foster and protect the interests of the rich and the upper classes, those people who controlled it. J. R. Green has written of these conditions:

> Of the prominent statesmen of the time, the greater part were unbelievers in any form of Christianity, and distinguished for their grossness and immorality of their lives, and at the other end of the social scale lay the masses of the poor. They were ignorant and brutal to a degree which is hard to conceive, for the vast increase of population which followed the growth of towns and the development of manufacturers had been met by no effort for their religious or educational improvement. Not a new parish had been created. Hardly a single church had been built. Schools there were none, save the grammar schools of

Edward and Elizabeth. The rural peasantry, who were fast being reduced to pauperism by the abuse of the poor laws were left without moral or spiritual training of any sort. There was no effective police, and great outbreaks of mobs of London or Birmingham burned houses, flung open prisons, and sacked and pillaged at their will. In the streets of London gin shops invited every passerby to get "drunk for a penny, or dead drunk for two pence."[2]

Social and working conditions in English cities during the eighteenth and early nineteenth centuries have been well described by Charles Dickens in his many novels. Parliamentary commissions document in many volumes the horrendous working conditions in mines and factories. Women were exploited, working for slave wages in unsanitary sweat shop mills and factories. Working women, especially those in the coal mines, were regularly beaten and sexually abused. Children ten years of age worked in mines and factories ten or twelve hours a day, with little time for rest or meals. These conditions stirred the Christian conscience of the Methodists.

Sanitation in the cities was nonexistent. The gutters ran full with sewage and human and animal waste, yet for the poor, the open gutters were used for bathing and even for drinking water. It was no wonder that plague ran rampant and the life expectancy was twenty-five years. Most infants were dead before five years of age. A mother could give birth to a dozen or more children, and have only three or four survive to adulthood. Population growth remained static even though mothers, without benefit of birth control or abortions, gave birth regularly and frequently. The rule of life in England in 1700 or 1800 was to keep the women pregnant, and the workers ignorant. The prevailing economic theory was that of the economist David Ricardo, who announced that wages and working conditions were regulated by an "iron law of wages." The so-called law stated that a starvation level of existence was normal for the working masses since population growth always exceeded the demand for labor. So long as families had so many children the wage level was established by the laws of supply and demand. If supply was high, relative to demand, wages would be at subsistence level. It was a natural law, and nothing could be done about it until families had fewer children. Prisons were filled with debtors, and the streets teemed with the "ladies of the night." Poor workers found a mug of ale more refreshing than the prayers and sermons of unconcerned Anglican priests. When John Wesley and his brother Charles began preaching a new message of hope and care to the poor, many listened and became Methodists.

The founder of Methodism was born in 1703 and died at the age of eighty-eight, having lived a long life in Christian service and poverty. It is said that he gave away over $300,000, an astonishingly large sum of money in his day, to the care of the poor and sick. He was a small man, five feet four inches tall, and afflicted all of his life with a tubercular lung condition. Yet it seemed Wesley was endowed with indefatigable energy, both physically and spiritually. During his ministry of over fifty years he traveled, mostly on horseback, over

250,000 miles. He preached more than 42,000 sermons, often giving two or three sermons a day at places ten miles or so apart. At the age of eighty-three he was still preaching almost daily, and at the age of eighty-seven he preached three times in one day, often to crowds as large as thirty thousand in a day before microphones and loud speakers.

Wesley's parents were devout dissenters within the Church of England. Wesley's father, Samuel, was a poor priest serving a parish in Epworth. He was so poor that at one time he was imprisoned for indebtedness. The parents had nineteen children, John being number fifteen, an argument against abortion or contraception. Only ten children survived to adulthood. Wesley's father was an impractical dreamer, more given to poetry and song, than to being a good priest or a good provider for his family.

Wesley's mother, Susanna, was the mainstay of the family. Wesley credited his mother for his success. She was one of twenty-five children and a devoted mother who saw to it that her children were educated at home and in schools. John was her favorite child and she was determined to give him the best possible education. John was able to attend Oxford University on a scholarship in preparation to becoming a teacher. He was greatly interested in the classics and science, what there was in the way of science then, but he also found time for religious studies. He read Thomas à Kempis's *Imitation of Christ* and the works of St. Augustine. Wesley's favored book was Bishop Taylor's *Rules and Exercises of Holy Living and Dying*. While at Oxford Wesley and Charles, the author of over seven thousand hymns, plus a few friends formed the Holy Club, a prayer group. Other students nicknamed the club the "Methodists" because they were so faithful and disciplined in the performance of their religious studies and moral lifestyle.

Upon graduation from Oxford Wesley served for a few years as a tutor at Oxford. In 1726 he was ordained a minister in the Church of England. Henceforth he had to give every ounce of energy to the service of his church. In the Middle Ages Wesley might have joined a monastery, since he preferred to live a life of chastity and poverty, shunning worldly pleasures as a waste of time as well as being sinful. Wesley drafted a set of light rules to guide him in his daily life.

Wesley was an intellectual, a good scholar, and for his time a good theologian with better than a layman's acquaintance with eighteenth-century science. Yet, even more than a rational intellect, Wesley seems to have been motivated by a sense of feeling or intuition. A mystical experience was the best way to know God. He attributed his escape from death at the age of six to his mother, who had pulled him from a burning house, but also to God—he thought his life was saved by a miracle from God, or, as he said, "God had plucked a burning brand from the burning fire."

Wesley's great fear of ghosts and other supernatural beings, and his respect for the mystical element in religious experience undoubtedly played a role in his conversion experience. Like Paul on the Damascus Road, he was gripped by a sudden mystical experience. On his way home from a church service at St.

Paul's Cathedral he was passing by a small chapel on Aldergate Street when he heard a minister reading from Luther's *Commentary on Paul's Epistle to the Romans 3:16*, which said, "The spirit itself beareth witness with our spirit, that we are the children of God." He was so captivated by this message that he soon committed his life to Christian service. Soon after the Aldergate experience and after the death of his father in 1735, he and his brother embarked on a missionary journey to convert the Native American Indians and free the black slaves in Georgia. The journey was a failure. The Native Americans believed they had better gods than Christ, and the slaveholders were in no Christian mood to free what they considered property. Wesley had his first serious love affair in Georgia with a woman named Sophie Hopkey. However, Hopkey was in a hurry to marry and Wesley failed to meet the deadline, so Hopkey married another man. Later, at the age of fifty-one, John Wesley would marry a rich widow, Marie Vazeillo, who had several children. This marriage was in name only. They seldom saw one another, as Wesley was more married to his church than to his wife. When she died in 1781 it was said that Wesley endured the loss with a minimum of grief. Wesley did not encourage his ministers to marry, since family matters would detract from their church duties. However, he never forbade his clergy to marry.

Although his mission to America had been a failure, Wesley had a valuable learning experience on the way back to England. On board was a group of Moravian Baptists and one day when the boat was violently rocked by a storm he was puzzled by the fact that the Moravians did not seem to be afraid. What was the secret for their peace of mind? When he reached home he decided that he ought to know more about these Baptists, so he went to Germany, their home base, to study with a Moravian Baptist leader, Count Zinzendorf, a pietistic mystic. The secret was simply that the Moravian Baptists, in their mystical wisdom, were so certain that God would protect them in all times of peril that they had no need to be anxious.

Although Wesley felt that all Christians should experience the "heartwarming" effect, he was too rational a person to become a dedicated mystic. However, Wesley was convinced that the spiritual born-again experience was one of four sources for finding God's truth. The other sources of spiritual enlightenment were Scripture, reason, and tradition.

In the early 1740s Wesley began to travel about the English countryside preaching to villagers and coal miners his brand of Anglicism. He organized his followers into small cells called "societies" for the purpose of prayer and study. In 1744 he called a conference of representatives from the societies, which he called a "connexion." The connexion became the governing body for the Methodist movement. It was not yet a church, but only a dissident group within the Church of England. By 1770 Methodism had spread throughout England and even to the American colonies.

Wesley was a powerful speaker and a master organizer. He was assisted by several able associates, including his brother Charles; George Whitefield, a successful evangelist; Thomas Coke, and others. Wesley had little faith in democracy or that the masses of people control their own lives successfully. The people needed a strong "father" to discipline the Christian flock. Wesley imposed upon his congregation a semimilitary form of supervision by appointing a watchdog over each society, a supervisor who would report to Wesley any member who strayed from the path of righteousness.

The Methodist movement appealed most to the poor working classes, the peasants, factory workers, and coal miners. Later more and more middle-class urban people would join the Methodists. Although Wesley refused to be a rich man, he did not believe that riches in themselves were evil. He rejected the prevailing restrictions on charging interest or making a business profit. He realized that the Industrial Revolution and capitalism were changing the ways people thought and lived. He wanted to be in step with these new economic forces and policies. Wesley exhorted his people to work hard, save their money, earn as much money as possible, but give to God his share of the wealth.

As more people joined the Methodists, England's rulers and upper classes became alarmed that Wesley might provoke a social revolution. In 1738 Wesley was banned from the Church of England, but his movement continued to grow and he never accepted his banishment from the church. Wesley never had any intention of leaving the Church of England.

Methodists are known by two distinguishing marks: a liberal, not literal, interpretation of the Bible, and a commitment to social reform. Salvation is by faith and faith alone, but salvation is more than salvation for a person's soul. It includes salvation of the soul of the nation or the Christian community as well. Recall that Wesley gave four sources for discovering God's truth: Scripture, tradition, reason, and experience. In Wesley's theology, Scripture, the Bible, was the best source for truth. It was the inspired word of God, and all Methodists should be sufficiently literate to read and interpret the Bible for themselves. But Wesley never declared the Bible to be inerrant and written for all times. A reasoning Christian must realize that times do change and religious needs change along with them. It is from the Methodist Church that modern theology has gotten many of its theologians, even to the most radical interpretations of scripture by the process theologians.

The concept of tradition has caused the Methodists to accept the traditional Christian tenets of belief, such as those defined in the Nicene Creed. Methodists accept the belief in the Holy Trinity, the divinity of Jesus, and the Resurrection. The Resurrection event was probably one of the spirit and not the body. As for the Virgin Birth, Wesley was noncommital. Methodists' accept two traditional sacraments: baptism, both infant and adult, and the memorial Lord's Supper. Good Methodists must do good works, but they are not essential for salvation. Wesley found little value in the use of rituals, rites, and liturgy. Even dogmas and creeds were of minimal value. People are their own priests, free to choose salvation or not.

Wesley placed great value on rational thinking, but he did leave room for the mystical, charismatic expression of love for God. Not only does the Methodist

Church embrace members who are rational and science-oriented, but also those who in their hearts express this joy in strong outbursts of emotional feeling. That is, Methodism could claim the Pentecostal Nazarenes as well as the liberal rationalists and revisionists as good members. However, Wesley deplored the display of emotion during the worship service. Worship time should be used for prayer and meditation, not for wild dancing, loud singing, and speaking in mysterious tongues.

The first Methodists were strict Puritans, forbidding most forms of sensual and worldly pleasures. Gambling, dancing, illicit and extramarital sex, and the use of drugs and alcohol were strictly forbidden. Yet the forces of nature and social adjustment have permitted modern Methodists to take more modern positions on such issues as contraception, abortion, homosexuality, dancing, card playing, and Sunday baseball.

Wesley believed that the Holy Spirit should be a sufficient guide for proper conduct on the part of both the clergy and the laity. But in case the Holy Spirit failed to motivate proper Christian behaviorr, Wesley instituted a rigid form of discipline modeled upon the episcopal or bishopric form of church government. In England Wesley was the head of his church. In the colonies Wesley appointed subordinate agents called superintendents who were later designated as bishops. The ministers were appointed by the controlling bishop in a given area, and not elected by the congregation. Wesley, as mentioned earlier, had watchdogs supervising the behavior of the local clergy and church members, who, if caught in violation of rules, were punished severely. As Methodists adjusted over time to more democratic modes of control, such military forms of discipline would be abolished.

If there is one feature of Methodism that is most unique, it is that Wesley committed his movement to social reform and the improvement of the daily lives of the working classes of people. Wesley said that God had appointed him to preach to the poor and to create a new social order for them. The Methodist plan for reform takes the name of the social gospel. The social gospel need not come by way of strikes, social legislation, and revolution, but ought to come through the regenerated souls of Christian men and women.

If education and legislation were needed to pass labor laws, protective laws for women and children, and a more equitable distribution of wealth, then these measures were proper. Historian William Lecky claimed that the Methodist Church saved England from a political revolution. The Methodists supported schools for the children and adult working people, Sunday Schools for children who worked every day of the week, old folks' homes, orphanages, dispensaries to aid the sick, and local agencies to care for the unemployed and homeless. Reluctantly Methodists agitated to secure parliamentary legislation to abolish slavery, protect women and children working in the mines and textile mills, and legalize labor unions.

The Methodists supported an active missionary program in many parts of the world, and they did much to bring the Christian gospel to the isolated communities of America's western frontier. They were among the foremost champions of a democratic and free United States.

Wesley was an optimist who believed, like Rousseau, that man was created basically good, not evil, that man was a thinking being, capable of learning the good way of life and effecting changes for the good. Wesley said, "Love is the sole principle of action." He thought change was inevitable and that all of human society, including religion, must move with the changing events in the larger society. Life is an endless search for perfection, and change is the nature of the universe. Wesley realized that heaven on earth might be long in coming, but the struggle for perfection was worth the price. Wesley saw the need for better international relations and world peace. He said of war, "How shocking, how inconceivable a want there must have been of common understanding, as well as common humanity, before any two governors, or any two nations in the Universe could once think of such a method of decision."

By the time of Wesley's death in 1791 Methodism had been accepted by the Church of England and the English monarchy. By 1830 the Methodist Church had become one of the foremost churches in America. Methodists saw a vision that in the new nation, the United States, a democratic nation could become a model for the world, that slavery could be abolished, poverty and illiteracy could be wiped away, evil could be banished, and the greatest of evils, war, could be ended forever.

26

Post-Reformation Catholicism: Sixteenth to Twentieth Centuries

In the Aftermath of Revolt: The Catholic Counter-Reformation

Within a hundred years of the death of Martin Luther Roman Catholicism had stemmed the tide of Protestantism. The Roman Catholic Church had retained control of southern Europe, and its missionaries had carried the Catholic faith to the Philippines, Mexico, all of Central and South America, and the American Southwest. Approaches were being made in China and Japan. The recovery of the Catholic Church is the story of the Counter-Reformation.

Soon after the Lutheran revolt the papacy was occupied by a series of reform popes—Paul IV (r. 1555–1559), Clement VIII (r. 1592–1605), and Paul V (r. 1605–1621). In brief, the reforming popes pursued a common goal of restoring the papacy and the church to its former power and glory by a program of sincere devotion to the principles on which the church was founded. Traditional Catholic doctrines and dogmas were reaffirmed with almost no changes. Both the popes and church councils restated traditional Catholic dogmas with clarity and conviction. The Council of Trent (1545–1563), meeting in two sessions at different times, declared the pope to be infallible, that salvation is by faith and good works, that the seven sacraments are valid, that the veneration of the Virgin Mary and the saints is essential, and that the Mass is to be said in Latin.

The former papal abuses and immoral, extravagant lifestyles were ended. The clergy was ordered to respect the vows of chastity and poverty. The sale of indulgences and of clerical offices was forbidden. Papal power to appoint and control the clergy was reasserted. The papal curia and bureaucracy was reduced in size and the bureaucracy was reorganized into fifteen separate congregations. Plans were made to provide better seminaries and education for the priests. Better screening procedures were used to select young men for the priesthood. The Index of Prohibited Books was established in 1552 to censor the literature to be used in the church.

The papacy found a stalwart ally in the army of Ignatius Loyola and his Society of Jesus, the Jesuits. They were truly soldiers of the cross, serving as missionaries throughout the world, but rendering even greater service to the church as agents who spied out heretics and administered the courts of the Inquisition to suppress and execute the enemies of the church, heretics, Jews, Muslims, or anyone else.

But the papacy needed more powerful allies than even the Jesuits, and these were to be found among the Catholic monarchs in Spain, Austria, and the German states in the Holy Roman Empire. These monarchs organized the Catholic League to oppose the Protestant Schmalkaldic League during a long series of religious wars from 1552 to the end of the Thirty Years' War in 1648. As the Catholic forces were holding the tide against the Protestants in Central Europe they were forced to repel the approach of the Ottoman Turks into Austria, Hungary, and the Balkan states. The Catholics won an important victory for both Catholics and Protestants when the Turks were defeated in a battle at Lepanto in 1571.

Modern Challenges: Science, Capitalism, and the French Revolution

After 1600 the Catholic church faced a more threatening enemy than Protestants or Muslims, the rising tide of social and economic forces that would destroy the medieval way of life. Two of these dangers to traditional Catholicism and its dominance of Western civilization were the rise of science and rational philosophy and the rise of industrialism, which undergirds the capitalistic system of economy and modern democratic societies. Rational philosophers like John Locke and René Descartes undermined reliance upon faith and revelation as reliable sources for the truth. Scientists began to discover a world controlled not so much by God's laws as by the laws of nature. Isaac Newton projected a materialist universe governed and moved not by the hand of God but by precise and reliable forces in the universe, especially the force of gravity. Twentieth-century psychology revealed that man is motivated less by inner spiritual, God-given forces than by material hormones, glands, and psychic structures such as the ego. Science threatened to reduce man to a physical machine that responded to the needs of the earthly world with little concern for God and the eternal world. Evolution cast doubts upon the belief that man was a special creation of God. Man was reduced to being merely another animal creature, cousin to apes and reptiles.

The growth of capitalism, manufacturing, commerce, and the movement of people into urban centers meant the slow death of the feudal system, the landed nobility, the manorial villages, and the serfs bound to the soil as laborers for the nobles, estates. Urban dwellers, middle-class merchants and manufacturers, and the workers, skilled and unskilled, became aware of the joys of freedom, freedom from the terror of the Devil, freedom from excommunication, and freedom from the willful authority of pope and lord. The rise of capitalism, especially free capitalism, enhanced the drive for democracy in government and in society, and the combination of capitalism and freedom stimulated a craving for national independence from the papacy, the Holy Roman Empire, and the restraints of a universal church.

As noted earlier, the Protestant movement could never have succeeded without the support of national monarchs and the capitalist middle classes. The Catholic church received almost a mortal low during the French Revolution in 1789. All "papist" elements were eliminated from the new French society. Christ was replaced by Robespierre's "Supreme Being" or the Deists' "God of Reason." As in Russia in 1917 so the revolutionists in France believed that a new society could not be forged unless the power of the church was destroyed. The church in both France and Russia was seen as the ally of tyrannical, absolute monarchs, of the ruling noble classes and other forces that opposed capitalism, democracy, and science. In France the church was saved only because Napoleon overthrew the revolutionary extremists and effected a return to a more moderate regime. Part of the Napoleonic restoration was the restoration of the Catholic church in 1801, but now it was the national church of France, a church over which the papacy lost its power to appoint clergy and collect revenue. The pope had to recognize the validity of divorce when Napoleon forced him to grant a divorce from his wife, Josephine.

In 1865 the papacy announced in the *Syllabus of Errors* that all Church dogmas were true, including the dogma of the immaculate conception of the Virgin Mary, a dogma that had been first announced in 1854. In 1950 Pope Pius XII announced the dogma of the assumption of the Virgin Mary into heaven. As early as the eighth century a few theologians accepted this belief. Thomas Aquinas stated that he thought it was probable, but the church never declared it a dogma.

The papacy was forced to make some concessions to the growing importance of science for modern life, but any gestures toward the value of science in the search for spiritual truth were greatly limited. The church at first refused to accept the theory of evolution. The application of scientific methods to the study of Christian history was denounced. In his *In Rerum Novarum* of 1891 Pope Leo XIII (r. 1878–1903) denounced socialism as being a "Godless state furthering a murderous pestilence." This was at a time when much socialist doctrine was only what today we would call welfare statism.

By 1900 the papacy had lost all of its territorial possessions in Italy, which were incorporated into the Italian kingdom when it was created in 1870. Only a small area in Rome, the Vatican, was left to the church to retain as a sovereign, independent state. But the papacy never relinquished its claim to be supreme in matters of faith over all of Christendom when the doctrine of papal infallibility was reproclaimed in 1865.

The Church in the Twentieth Century

The Roman Catholic (and the Eastern Orthodox) Church suffered severe losses during the world wars. World War I caused the loss of Russia to the Eastern church. After World War II the Communist regimes caused the Roman church to lose control of Poland, Czechoslovakia, and Hungary, and the Eastern Church suffered losses in the Balkan states. Today the dissolution of the Soviet empire and the lifting of religious sanctions may give the church new life. In 1990 most religious groups were permitted freedom of worship.

When Pope John XXIII was elected to the papacy in 1958 the Catholic Church experienced a veritable and unexpected revolution when he called into session the Vatican Council of 1962. The council opened worship services to more of the congregation by allowing the faithful to participate more in the Mass, by permitting congregational hymn singing, and by allowing the Mass to be said in the vernacular language. Pope John encouraged ecumenical meetings with other religious groups, Protestants, Jews, and Muslims. He sought to find some measures to support Catholics in Communist countries, but he never relaxed his opposition to Communism. Nor did Pope John make any concessions to the idea that abortion, birth control, and divorce are evil. When John Paul II, the Polish pope, was elected to the papacy in 1978 a halt was brought to any measures that might liberalize the traditional doctrines of the church, although John Paul has persisted in promoting world peace and effecting some reconciliation with the Protestant Lutheran and English churches and with Judaism.

To the credit of the Roman Catholic Church it has maintained a consistent policy in recent times in behalf of Christian justice and human welfare for less fortunate people, a policy known as "social justice." Social justice has placed the power of the church on the side of labor unions, progressive social reformers, and proponents of social health insurance and old age retirement benefits. Pope Leo XIII in 1903 enunciated support for such principles as a just wage, the right of labor to have unions, and the need for a wide range of social legislation. Yet the church is reluctant to permit members of the clergy to engage in any form of direct action to secure these social benefits. Nor does the church give support to revolutionary movements that hope to overthrow the established order. In Spain the church supported the Franco regime, as opposed to the democratic forces. The papacy opposed clerical participation in Latin American revolutions that sought to overthrow the centuries-old rule of landed aristocrats and military dictators. Many of the Catholic clergy in Latin America support a brand of "liberation theology" that seeks to join forces with various democratic political movements to overthrow the old oppressive regimes, but the papacy is hesitant to support these clerical dissenters. Despite papal opposition the liberationists in Latin America continue to gain strength. In 1968 130 Catholic priests drafted a statement on liberation theology known as the "Medellin Conclusions," in which colonialism is denounced and support declared for the right of the people to enjoy justice, democracy, and human rights. In 1982 liberation theology was given a boost when eighty-five national churches met in Lima, Peru, to support the fight for democratic rights for the Catholic masses.

In the United States the Catholic church and its members are becoming a growing political force, especially since the election of a Catholic president, John F. Kennedy, in 1960. One issue that has mobilized Catholic political action is that of abortion. In 1982 the National Coalition of Nuns began an antiabortion campaign. A *Denver Post* poll in December 1985 revealed that 68 percent of Catholics favored contraception, 73 percent favored remarriage after divorce, 52 percent approved of marriage for the clergy, and 55 percent favored abortion in the case of rape and incest. However, these opinions do not reflect the official positions of the Catholic Church.

The abortion issue has been a problem for the Church since its inception. For the past fifteen centuries the Church has accepted the Aristotelian theory that the soul enters the fetus sometime after conception. One rule had it that this took place after forty days for males and ninety days for females. When the soul enters the developing fetus it is said to be "animated," after which human life has begun and an abortion would be an act of murder. From the time of Innocent III to Sixtus V it was held that only abortions of animated fetuses were immoral and illegal. Pope Sixtus V in 1588 declared all abortions after conception were illegal, which then became the official church policy. Pope Pius IX in 1869 reaffirmed the abortion policy of Sixtus V. In recent years the church has moderated its opposition to all birth control by approving the natural rhythm method.

The Catholic church in the United States in the past quarter century has been plagued by other troublesome issues, including the questions of permitting priests to marry, permitting women to serve in church offices, continuing the use of English instead of Latin in the Mass, and the declining enrollment in the clergy. There is a growing minority of Catholics who are expressing a desire for a more evangelistic, charismatic form of worship, one more typical of that used in Protestant evangelical and pentecostal churches. It is estimated that in the United States there are over three hundred thousand "charismatic Catholics." A more worrisome problem for the Catholic church is the growing number of dissatisfied Catholics in Latin America who are listening to the fiery sermons of evangelical Protestant ministers like Jimmy Swaggart. Some are deserting the Catholic church for a gospel they believe holds greater promise for freedom here and now.

Even the Protestant critics of the Catholic Church admit that the church has had a long and consistent policy of seeking a better world for the poor, the working people, and those who are handicapped and unable to survive in a competitive world on their own initiatives. Certainly no other Christian group, excepting the Quakers and churches of the German Brethren type, has a better record in opposing war, nuclear weapons, and seeking agencies to promote international accord and world peace. More and more Catholics and Protestants have found a common Christian mission in which all can unite in seeking an end to international rivalry and war.

27

Christianity in the Americas

The sixteenth century might be termed a landmark in Western history since it witnessed the decline of the Roman Catholic church and the rise of Protestantism. The 1500s also mark the decline of feudalism and a church-state-controlled economy. Capitalism, mercantilism, overseas explorations, colonialism, and the rising power of the urban middle classes belong to the centuries after 1500. In a sense the Western world experienced during this time a gradual evolution of new value systems to replace old ones. From a God-centered universe, the people of the West became enchanted with a Mammon-centered universe. The value of wealth, economic power, and sumptuous consumer spending replaced the sacred virtues of poverty and sensual denial.

The rise of the middle classes, who had the wealth to command power in society, in government, and in the Christian church, also enhanced the power of the newly emerging national monarchs in Spain, France, and England. Wealthy merchants and bankers joined forces with kings and their allies to wage war, expand trade, establish overseas colonies, and win for themselves power in government by forcing divine-right monarchs to share their power with the representatives of the capitalistic classes elected to parliaments of various types. By the 1600s even tiny Netherlands, ruled in large measure by middle-class merchants, was able to compete with the major powers for a share of world trade and European power. National monarchies, each one striving to outstrip the others for the dominant position in Western Europe, waged war after war from the sixteenth to the twentieth century. National armies and navies cost great sums of money, but from the growing ranks of capitalists and manufacturers kings were able to tax and borrow the funds for their military adventures. Moreover, the weapons of war became more sophisticated, more lethal, and more costly as cannons, guns, and gunpowder replaced the arrows and shields of the medieval knights.

The heightened costs of war stimulated the great powers to find new sources

341

of wealth, not at the foot of the rainbow, but somewhere beyond the horizon, where there were the trading riches of the East Indies and the hoards of gold and silver that native Americans had taken from the mines of Mexico and Peru. Africa, the East Indies, China, as well as the Americas became tempting areas for conquest, colonization, and exploitation for the benefit of European countries. If the greedy colonial powers had any guilt feelings about their enslavement of native peoples or the theft of their accumulated wealth, the Christian churches provided a ready rationalization that mollifed them. Colonialism was combined with a Christian missionary enterprise that was alleged to convert the heathen natives to salvation in the Christian faith.

Spanish Colonialism in Latin America and the American Southwest

After Columbus had discovered America, or at least a small part of it, in 1492, the Spanish monarchy lay first claim to the people and their wealth in America. Unfortunately the Vikings, who had come to North America centuries before, had lacked the foresight and the power to be the first claimants to America's wealth. The fruits of Columbus's discovery began to enrich the coffers of the Spanish monarchs when the conquistador Cortez came to Mexico with his army in 1519. Later more Spanish adventurers and colonial governors would come to establish Spanish provinces throughout Mexico, Central America, and much of South America.

Wherever Spanish rulers and armies went, the missionaries were soon to follow. The first Franciscan missionaries came to Mexico in 1526. Before long all of the major Catholic orders, Franciscans, Dominicans, Augustinians, and Jesuits, were engaged in converting the native Indians, in the process destroying in all possible forms the existing sacred temples, altars, and records of the extant Indian faiths. The Aztecs of Mexico permitted their religion to seduce them into accepting Christianity. The native people believed that Cortez was the reincarnation of their god Quetzalcoatl, who, according to their prophets, was expected to return to earth. So Cortez, the white god, accepted his divine position by conquering the Aztecs, enslaving the people, and destroying their sacred temples. Some natives were probably converted by the persuasive sermons of the missionaries, but most of these innocent people were converted by the sword. It was Spanish guns that imposed Christianity upon Latin America, a conversion that today leaves much of the native populations in Latin America with a Christian skin and an Indian heart. The Christian rulers and missionaries failed to recognize and respect the civilization of the Incas in Peru or the Aztec-Mayans in Mexico, civilizations which, in many respects, equaled the ancient civilizations in Egypt and Mesopotamia.

That the Spanish conquest of Latin America, excepting the region of Brazil, which was taken by Portugal, was a successful one seems apparent, since the prevailing language is Spanish, not counting hundreds of Indian dialects still in use, and the prevailing economic system is a feudal landholding system in which a few powerful landlords control vast estates which are worked by native laborers, whose status is little better than that of medieval serfs. Spanish colonial policy was to keep the native Indians in a state of poverty and illiteracy, subdued and Christian. A few lonely Spanish governors, bureaucrats, and soldiers found wives among the natives, from which marriages, or not, has come a mixed Spanish-Indian population, the "mestizo" class, the modern-day Mexican people.

Spain was most fortunate to find quantities of precious metals in America, all of which were easy to transport to the home country and to convert into buying power. For two centuries, until 1700, Spain prospered and became the first truly great power in Europe. The kingdom bought large armies and navies, and built cathedrals and palaces, endowed schools and art galleries. Spain's upper classes lived abundantly and splendidly. The rest of Europe prospered from the Spanish largesse as they sold Spain military supplies and consumption goods.

Not always was this new-found wealth a blessing. As the supply of gold increased so did inflation, and the rise of prices forced many poor people into poverty as wages lagged behind rising prices. In the long run the principal benefactors of Spanish wealth would be England and France, and to some extent the former Spanish province of the free state of the Netherlands. One unfortunate legacy of the Spanish gold prosperity was that other nations believed that they too could seize and take home riches in overseas lands with a minimum of effort or risk. England and France would find that the easy road to riches was an illusion.

Spanish explorers permitted Spain to lay claim to Florida and most of the present southwestern part of the United States. Except for a few mission stations and grants of land to Spanish noblemen, the Spanish control over these areas lasted for only a brief time before the United States claimed them, either by purchase, as in the case of Florida, or by settlement and conquest, as in the case of Texas, New Mexico, Arizona, and California.

As mentioned earlier, the Christian missionaries never succeeded in eradicating the native worship of the many native gods, goddesses, and spirits. It is remarkable how much of the religious worship among the Catholic people of Latin America is native in content and sometimes even form. The Christian God and saints have become identified with the ancient native deities. The Aztec chief god was also born of a virgin. Indian religious festivals were merged with Christian festivals. Indian dances and music became an integral part of the Christian service. The question is, Is Christianity in Latin America, for the majority of the natives, more Christian or more native Indian worship?

Anglicans, Congregationalists, and Puritans

The English not only transplanted their separate classes of society to the New World but also their various religions, both established church and dissenting sects. In Virginia, the Carolinas, and Georgia, where the large commercial plantations were to be organized, the ruling classes were the more wealthy proprietors and plantation owners who were most loyal to the English government, its traditions, and most of all to the Church of England. So in the South the one established, state-supported church was the Church of England. The dissenting churches, Catholic or Protestant, played little part in the conduct of these colonies. The Church of England in these colonies did attempt some missionary efforts to convert the native Americans, with almost no success despite the romantic story of how the Indian princess Pocahontas was married to a prominent Virginian, John Rolfe, and lived thereafter in England.

To the New England area came the dedicated English dissenters called the Puritans, those followers of Calvinistic Protestantism who wished to "purify" the Church of England of all "popish" practices. In England the Calvinists were divided between the Separatists, who wished to break away from the English Church completely, and a more moderate group of wealthier citizens who wished to remain within the Church of England but in a reformed church.

The Separatists were expelled from England as heretics in 1607. They found refuge in a more tolerant Netherlands, in Amsterdam, where they lived for a few years before sailing to American on the *Mayflower*. These Calvinist dissenters became our Pilgrim fathers, coming to a land of freedom under the auspices of the London Trading Company, the same company that had colonized Virginia. The Pilgrims had intended to land in Virginia, but winds and poor navigational aids brought them in 1620 to Plymouth Rock in Massachusetts.

The Plymouth colony was absorbed into the Massachusetts Bay Colony in 1691.

The Pilgrims did contribute to a sense of democratic behavior in America when they first drew up a statement of how the new colony was to be governed in the "Mayflower Compact" in 1620. As the civil government was to be ruled by the people, so also the church was to be ruled by the congregation. The Pilgrims established the Congregational form of worship in New England, which would also be adopted by the Puritan churches. Congregational worship did not mean that all residents of a locality were entitled to belong to the church. All Calvinist churches believed in predestination, which claimed that only the "elect" or saved could be church members. The method of determining who was elect and who was not was normally carried out by the ruling members of a church. A public profession of having been born again might suffice as proof, but more often it was how well a given person was perceived as a good Christian in the eyes of the ruling majority in the church. The Congregational churches, like the Baptists, believed that the civil government and the church should be separate entities. However, a thin line existed in Massachusetts between the two governments. Since the only church permitted in New England was the Congregational church, and since church membership and the ownership of some property were requirements for the right to vote in elections, the New England colonies were in a real sense church-ruled colonies.

The other Calvinist colony, the one that would dominate the religious and cultural life of New England and in a real sense determine the major value system and the religious life of the new United States, was the Puritan or Massachusetts Bay Colony. This colony was founded by a small band of dissenters, a thousand or so, mostly moderately well-off English people who wished to be free of the Church of England, not in theology, but only of its Mass and rituals. They were also desirous of an opportunity to prosper in America. The Puritan leader, John Winthrop, at the very outset laid down the basic principles upon which this new Zion was to be built. The model for the Massachusetts Bay Colony was the one built by John Calvin in Geneva. Winthrop proclaimed that now "the God of Israel is among us. . . . We shall be a city upon a hill." From the beginning there was no intention of separating church and state. Puritan society was to be ruled by God, or God's agent on earth, namely the Puritan church. Every aspect of life was to be determined by the rulers of the church. Church membership was limited to those who were said to be the "elected," and unlike the Pilgrim colony, where the ministers were given almost no voice in governing the church, in Massachusetts it was the clergy, with ruling elders, that ruled both the church and the state. Puritan rule was harsh and unrelenting, as it was in Calvin's Geneva. It seemed as though all persons were to become monks and nuns living under the stern eyes of God in a disciplined monastery. All forms of sensual pleasure were outlawed. Drinking, gambling, and dancing were taboo. Laws were passed forbidding all activity on the Sabbath. Even kissing one's wife on Sunday might violate the law. Hymns were sung in church without benefit of instrumental music. However, in reality the restrictions on worldly pleasures may not have been so repressive after all. John D'Emilio and Estelle B. Freedman in their book *Intimate Matters* suggest that these moral prescriptions were not observed by the masses of the people. Perhaps these rules were practiced by the most devout of the church members, those who ruled the colony, constituting about 20 percent of the total population.

The common people, the masses, had ample opportunities to find pleasure in saloons, gambling joints, and houses of prostitution. Moreover, since most young people married in the early years of adolescence, sex outside of marriage was no serious problem. It is true that women who violated the sexual mores were on occasions branded with the scarlet letter, and that witches were doused in the river or burned at the stake.

The Puritan state in Massachusetts was intolerant of any other religious group. The Puritan church was ordained by God to be the one and only true church. Cotton Mather, a prominent Puritan pastor and civic leader, could not understand why anyone would wish to have any other church. Diversity or pluralism in religion would destroy human society. Since man was the victim of original sin, not all souls could be guaranteed salvation. But one's best chance for salvation was within the confines of the Puritan church. Only church members could be saved, and even these good people could be saved only if they gave complete obedience to the laws of the church and of the state.

The Congregational Church continued to accept the basic theology of the Church of England, as stated in the Westminister Creed of 1649. However, the Puritans abolished the episcopal system of government in favor of the more democratic congregational form of government. The Congregational Church service was the simple form introduced by the Baptists. Worship was held in a small, simple white church building topped by a miniature steeple. Inside the congregation would listen to prayers, Bible readings, long sermons, often an hour or two in length, join in the singing of psalms and hymns, and participate each week in the ceremony of the Lord's Supper. Baptism was both by immersion and sprinkling. Puritans, like most people of their age, were firm believers in supernatural powers, such as angels, evil spirits, witches, miracles, and other mystical phenomena. Since all truth was contained in the Bible it was imperative that all persons should be literate. An educated congregation and clergy were high priorities among the Puritans.

Every century of Christian history experienced some form of religious emotionalism and revival of spiritual enthusiasm. So it was in New England during the first half of the 1700s, an era known as the "Great Awakening." This historic upsurge in American religious feeling was characterized by widespread ferment within and between denominations. It also forged some of the first sense of American colonial unity, and in this respect served as a basis for the approaching tide of discontent and rebellion. Three ministers who were the most active leaders of the Awakening experience were Jonathan Edwards, William Tennet in Pennsylvania, and George Whitefield, a Methodist minister, all of whom preached a message that Christ would soon appear on Earth, a message that had much influence among the frontier people who lived beyond the Alleghenies. Historian Martin E. Marty says, "The Great Awakening can be seen as a move toward the developing of modern religion in the West. At its heart was the notion of choice: you must choose Jesus Christ, must decide to let the Spirit of God work in your heart and—note well—you may and must choose this version of Christianity against that version.[1]

The Religious Mosaic of the Early Colonies

By the time of the American Revolution the English colonies were the home of many different religious groups. Rhode Island had been a refuge for radical Baptists expelled from the Massachusetts colony in 1636. Their two most prominent leaders were Roger Williams and Anne Hutchinson. The first Baptist Church in America was founded by Williams in 1639. The Baptist colony was the first to practice religious toleration and freedom of religious worship. Williams was certain that the Second Coming was near, but on a more realistic level he was certain that government was a curse of which the church should have no part. Government meddling in church affairs would make the church "a filthy dunghill and whorehouse of rotten and stinking whores and hypocrites."

Freedom for persecuted Catholics in England was provided when a Catholic, Lord Baltimore, was given an extensive land grant in what is now Maryland in 1634. This land grant for a proprietary colony was to be a haven for all persecuted Catholics in Europe. Lord Baltimore was forced to accept a policy of religious toleration, which in the long run would turn over control of the colony to a majority of Puritan immigrants. Relatively few Catholics came to Maryland since in England they represented a well-off class of landed noblemen. Probably not more than 20 percent of the people in Maryland were Catholic. In 1691 the proprietary charter was revoked, after which, Maryland became a royal colony.

A small colony of Swedish Lutherans located in what is now Delaware and New Jersey, which was then a part of the Dutch colony of New Amsterdam. After a series of conflicts with the Dutch rulers the Swedish Lutheran element was recognized as a separate group and free to worship. The English government took over the colony in 1664.

The first Jews came to America in 1654, mostly Shepardim from Spain. Most located in New Amsterdam. Before the American Revolution there were so few Jews in America as to never threaten the Christians, hence anti-Semitism was no serious problem. In fact the Jews and Jewish bankers became ardent supporters of the American Revolution.

As early as 1626 the Dutch West India Trading Company secured possession of the Hudson River valley and Manhattan Island. Along with Dutch fur traders came the Dutch Reformed Church. Although the Dutch governors and the church leaders preferred to make the Dutch Reformed Church the only church in the colony, other immigrants with their churches sought to establish a measure of religious freedom. Contention over the issue of religious freedom in the colony ended when it was taken over by the English in 1664 and the principle of religious freedom was recognized.

Of all of the English colonies, the one most tolerant and utopian was that of Pennsylvania. It was founded as a proprietary colony in 1681, when King Charles II gave William Penn a charter in payment for debts he owed to Penn's father. Penn was not destined to be a soldier like his father. Instead he was a visionary dreamer, educated at Oxford, who became interested in the Quaker religion. For attending Quaker meetings he was sent to prison, but he persisted in his love for the faith. He married a Quaker woman, and dedicated his land grant to the Quakers and all other persecuted people as a place of safety and freedom. In his "Holy Experiment" he invited, even solicited, the oppressed religious minorities of Western Europe to come to Pennsylvania. As enticing as religious freedom was, Pennsylvania also offered a plentiful supply of rich farmland that would profit the persecuted as well as the proprietor, Penn. So to Pennsylvania there came from England the Quakers and from Germany a number of Anabaptists, the German Baptists and the Dunkers. Even Catholics and Jews were welcome.

Another Calvinist church, the Scottish Presbyterian Church, also came to America. The Presbyterians originated from the Church of Scotland, organized by John Knox in opposition to the Catholic Stuart kings of England and Scotland. The first to come to America came from northern Ireland, Scotch-Irish folk who despised Irish Catholics. The Presbyterian followers first arrived in New England, New York, and Pennsylvania about 1670. The first Presbyterian Church was organized in Philadelphia in 1706. Presbyterians, for the most part, found that the good lands of the Atlantic Coast were already taken, so they became among the first pioneer settlers to move beyond the Allegheny Mountains. They became successful farmers and patrons of a most evangelistic, revival type of religion. The Presbyterians also brought a fondness for education, one evidence of which was their founding of the College of New Jersey at Princeton, the Princeton University of today.

Shortly before the American Revolution the English Methodists began sending missionaries to the colonies. The first of them came in 1765, when a small group of Irish Methodists led by Philip Embury and his cousin, Barbara Heck, came to New York City. Here they built the first Methodist church in America, the John Street Church, on Wall Street. At the same time other Methodists built churches in New Windsor, in Maryland, and in Philadelphia the St. George Church. The most powerful Methodist preacher was George Whitefield, an associate of John Wesley who became a major voice of revivalism in New England during the Great Awakening. Whitefield spoke to his "evil" audience by telling them, "You are ten thousand times more abominable in God's eyes than the most hateful, venomous serpent is in ours." Benjamin Franklin was so impressed with Whitefield's fiery sermons that on one occasion he was compelled to empty his pockets into the collection plate. Wesley disapproved of these emotional appeals, and over this issue the two friends parted company. The first annual Methodist Conference was called in 1773 by the most famous of early Methodist leaders in America, Francis Asbury. Most Methodists supported the American Revolution despite Wesley's disapproval. After the revolution the American Methodist Church cut its ties with the Church of England. In 1784 the Methodist Church of America was organized in Baltimore when Asbury called a conference of Methodist ministers to meet in the Loving Way Church. Here the Methodists adopted the "Thirty-Nine Articles of Faith" of the Church of England and the English *Book of Common Prayer* as their guides for the true faith. The Methodists also retained the English system of bishops to rule the church, an undemocratic form, but the prevailing system of church government before 1800. Hence the American Methodist Church would be named the Methodist Episcopal Church of America.

The Society of Friends, better known as the Quakers, hold a special place in the history of Pennsylvania, if not America. Most Americans can recall a box of cereal named Quaker Oats at the breakfast table with its picture of William Penn. The Quaker beliefs and services were so radical as to be rejected by Catholics and Protestants alike. Moreover, the Quakers had a social reform mission for the abolition of social injustice and war, policies which were not pleasing to either monarchs or the wealthy aristocrats then in control of politics in Western Europe. The Quaker movement has been described by Margaret Hope Bacon in *Mothers of Feminism* and Rufus Jones in *The Inner Light*. The Quakers saw no need for any formal church organization, government, rituals, or creeds. They believed that each person knows God from his or her own "inner light," the intuitive spirit of God that is in each one of us. The Quaker meeting house might be a member's home or a small, plain building, unadorned with images or stained glass windows. A member of the Society of Friends would worship with other friends in a quiet, meditative mood, without benefit of song or a minister to lead them in prayer or to give a sermon. Moments might pass before a word was uttered, and then a voice from one of the members would be heard as he or she arose to give witness to the moving spirit of God within his or her heart. Quaker women were once recognizable by their black bonnets and plain, dark-hued dress. The men wore broad-brimmed black hats and a full beard. Today Quakers wear modern clothes.

Most importantly Quakers are driven by their beliefs to effect change in their world. Although a small minority, they were in the vanguard of abolitionism, the women's rights movement, and labor union activism. Always they protested the injustices of the governments of the lands in which they lived, for governments promoted war, carried out capital punishment, and protected the inequality of the social classes. Quaker disdain for civil government is made evident by their refusal to swear to any oath other than to God. That the Quakers were persecuted severely could be expected since they saw no need for government, or prisons, or war, or the church as traditionally conceived.

Another radical group was called the Shakers, officially, the Union Society.[2] The Shakers were so named because their religious fervor was revealed by strong, emotional movements of the body, sometimes so strong as to cause convulsive rolling on the floor. The Shaker movement originated in England in 1741. The first Shakers to arrive in America came to Watervliet, New York, in 1774. They hoped that America would provide a safe haven from religious persecution.

The founder of the Shakers was a strange Manchester mill worker, Ann Lee, who, in a trance, came to believe that she was the Christ reincarnated as a woman who had come to Earth in the Second Coming. She and eight friends established a communal society that spread from New York to other Eastern states and the Ohio valley. By 1850, the Shakers had founded eighteen communities with about five thousand members. The few remaining Shakers live in one community in Maine.

Lee preached an apocalyptic message that the Christ would soon come to earth and establish his thousand-year reign. Until that day arrived, men and women should live a life isolated from the evil, material world. Urban centers must be shunned, as they are the Devil's work. Rural areas would provide a more secure home for believers. Hence, like the Jewish Essenes or Christian monastics, Shakers felt compelled to live a righteous life, isolated from the evil world, in a communal society in which all property and labor were shared equally. In the commune all members were privileged to share in governance, but once the rules were made, all were required to give absolute obedience to them. All members had to work according to their talents and abilities. The Shakers became famous for the quality of their crafts. Their furniture, woolens, water-resistant fabrics, and other items are treasured collectors' items today. Recently a Shaker rocking chair sold for over $50,000. Shakers were also pioneers in the growing and sale of garden seeds.

Not all of the Shaker day was given to labor. Almost equal time was devoted to prayer, meditation, and religious observances. The spirit world was as real to Shakers as the physical world. True wisdom could be derived from séances, visions, and trances.

Shakers abhorred sex as the apex of all human sin. Humans must never commit the unpardonable sin committed by Adam and Eve, namely, to engage in sexual intercourse. Marriage was forbidden, equated with prostitution. Although both men and women lived together, the sexes were rigorously segregated. Any increase in membership had to be only by recruiting adult members from the outside world, or by adoption, not by procreation.

The privilege of being able to enjoy eternal salvation required strict abstinence not only from sex, but from the use of tobacco and alcohol, and the wearing of flashy dress and jewelry. God, who is both male and female, loves plain people in a simple world.

The Development of Religious Toleration in Early America

As the twig is bent so grows the tree, an aphorism that applies to the evolution of the ideals and principles of American democracy. In America many different ethnic and religious groups were forced to live together in a state of equality and toleration lest they commit national suicide. The pioneer immigrants from Europe did not come to initiate a new social and political order. They came with their traditional values, moral codes, and social and religious institutions. Each church group believed that they were the chosen people of God, and that all groups should worship as they did. There was no concept of religious toleration, excepting that of the Baptists and the Quakers. All of the early colonies had a state-established church. Rhode Island, a state founded by the Baptists, was the one exception. As in England, only members of the state church could vote and participate in the government. All citizens had to pay taxes to support the official church. In 1689 England passed the Act of Religious Toleration, but it excluded Catholics and Jews, although, since both groups were so small in America before 1800, there was no serious problem of anti-Catholicism or anti-Semitism. Yet, somehow out of this background of religious intolerance, state-supported churches, and a class-divided, class-ruled society came the Declaration of Independence, the United States Constitution, the Bill of Rights, the disestablishment of all religions, the acceptance of a national policy of religious toleration, and the principle that all men (and eventually women also) are created equal.

The principle of religious toleration may have been generated by the teachings of Voltaire, Locke, Rousseau, and other enlightened men of the eighteenth century, including the French Deists and their American disciples, Thomas Jefferson, Tom Paine, James Madison, and Benjamin Franklin. It is true that there were a few signs in the Western world by 1700 that religious toleration was a sound policy. In France the Edict of Nantes in 1685 gave the French Protestants, the Huguenots, freedom to worship in a Catholic nation. In the Netherlands an act of toleration in 1581 gave all Christians except Catholics freedom of worship.

Religious toleration and freedom of worship were not born of any ideology, but out of the hard, realistic experience that in a world where people of many different faiths were forced to live side by side while striving to eke out a bare subsistence standard of living, religious persecution and wars were not productive. In 1784 Virginia was the first state to abolish the established church system and grant religious freedom to all people. Finally by 1833, when Massachusetts disestablished the Congregational Church, all of the American states had enacted acts of toleration and separation of church and state.

The Constitution of the United States had little to say about religion. In the First Amendment to the Bill of Rights there are provisions for freedom of worship and prohibition of the national government from ever establishing a state church. But all that applied only to the federal government in those pre–Civil War days. Religion was left to the states, and it was there that acts of toleration were to be passed.

Most Americans today believe that this nation was founded on the principles of the Christian faith, that this is a God-loving country ordained by God to be the chosen of all nations. The United States was intended to be ruled by Protestant Christians, not Catholics and Jews. Fundamentalist Christians maintain that this nation was founded on the principles of Protestantism and Puritan standards of morality. Therefore, they maintain, there should be prayer in the schools and Bible study in the classrooms. However, an unbiased student of the Constitution can find little support for the belief that this nation was intended to be the special preserve of a certain Protestant church. In the Declaration of Independence the only God to whom reference is made is the "Laws of Nature" and "Nature's God." These are deistic, not Christian, beliefs. The Constitution is silent on the matter of God or what kind of God is to be worshiped.

The concept of a democratic government owed its origins to certain English traditions and enactments that permitted some measure of popular participation in the government. There was the Magna Carta of 1215, the victory of the parliament over the monarchy when Cromwell established a republican form of government from 1649 to 1662, and the final victory of parliamentary forces that came with the Glorious Revolution of 1689. Those events were undoubtedly important beginnings, but democracy came to fruition in America out on the frontier when the colonists were forced to live thousands of miles from the center of power in London, and where the everyday decisions of local government had to be made by mutual consensus in a democratic manner.

In 1787 the new United States may have had dreams of a democracy, but its realization was more than a century away. As in England, so in the colonies and in the new United States the concept of democracy included only those persons who were male, endowed with a certain amount of property, and, in the South, white. Universal suffrage was nowhere to be found. The Founding Fathers did not choose to entrust the business of government to the illiterate, the poor, or to the female half of the populace. The Electoral College system of electing the president was designed to inhibit too much popular decision-making. Even the system of "checks and balances," which ensured that a president did not assume dictatorial power, also prevented too much popular control in the House of Representatives. America's Constitution makers had a genuine fear of the unrestrained mob, the masses who were so easily manipulated by unscrupulous politicians and clergymen.

One constructive legacy left by the Protestant colonists was the need for education, most of all public education. Protestants from the time of Martin Luther and John Calvin all preached the need for educated Christians who could read the Bible. Religious instruction in the home and in the church were always high priorities for Protestant Christians. In the colonies where the state and taxes supported the established church, it was easy to use public taxes to support public schools. The Massachusetts colony in 1647 was the first colony to require the establishment of a tax-supported system of public education. However, general acceptance of the idea that schools should be publicly supported out of tax revenues rather than by private family budgets did not gain general acceptance for elementary schools until about 1850, and for high schools not until the period after the Civil War, about 1875–80.

For two hundred years this nation has faithfully adhered to the principles of religious freedom and separation of church and state. For example, in 1962 the Supreme Court held that prayer in public schools, then a law in some twenty states, was unconstitutional. Most Americans today assert that the United States is a Christian nation, created and ordained by God to pursue its destiny in history and to be the dominant force in the Western Hemisphere, a destiny summed up in the nineteenth-century popular political battle cry, "Manifest Destiny." Proof that America is a Christian nation is found on U.S. coins, which have the phrase, adopted in 1864, "In God We Trust"; or in the pledge to the flag, which had the words "under God" inserted in 1954; or in the fact that all state legislatures and the Congress have chaplains to offer opening and closing prayers, chaplains who are usually from Protestant denominations.

But for the majority of Christian churches in the United States today more and more signs of religious tolerance and ecumenical relationships among all Christians and Jews are evident, despite the deep-seated hatreds expressed by the actions of bigoted Klansmen and Aryan Nation-type, Nazi-oriented fanatics, and lingering anti-Semitic biases among some of the fundamentalist Protestant churches.

28

Manifest Destiny and American Protestantism

Between 1800 and 1860 the new American nation entered into a time during which its national image both at home and abroad would be established. What the United States would represent to the outside world in the twentieth century would be determined in the pre–Civil War era. The future course of this nation, in large measure, would be built upon the New England Puritan model of politics, capitalism, morality, and religion.

From 1770 until after the War of 1812 America's energy was consumed by fighting for its freedom from England, fashioning state and federal systems of government, watching and fearing the progress of the French Revolution and the Napoleonic era, waging a second war against England in 1812, and trying to establish control over the territories between the Alleghenies and the Mississippi River. In this era there was no certainty that the United States would be able to survive the threats of territorial losses from either England or France.

By 1820 an era of stability and peace seemed to be on the horizon. Our pioneer nation seemed to have a chance to develop its economic resources, stimulate the development of industry in New England and other northern towns, expand its shipping and trade even to the Orient, and most of all, encourage the expansion of cotton plantations and slavery throughout the South, even to the Mexican territory of Texas. By 1830 a "Second Great Awakening" or religious revival permeated the Protestant churches, especially out on the western frontier in Kentucky, Tennessee, and the Ohio Valley. Between 1830 and 1850 America became the home for a number of idealistic, utopian experiments in the organization of communal societies that were both anticapitalist and anti–status quo Protestantism.

American Protestantism sought a religion that would give God's blessing to both democratic governments and the practice of a free capitalist economy. It was a religious setting in which the middle-class capitalists and people of wealth and property were to dominate the direction into which the new nation was to move. One phrase so characteristic of the mid-eighteenth century, and often spoken by preacher, editors, and politicians, was "Manifest Destiny." These two words simply said that God had ordained America to become the dominant power in the Western Hemisphere, and that the American people, in the words of Herman Melville, "are the peculiar, chosen people, the Israel of our time; we bear the ark of liberties of the world." God had determined that the United States should occupy and control all of the land from the Rio Grande River to the Canadian border, or even beyond, and from Atlantic to Pacific shore. Most of the rest of the Western Hemisphere, from the Mexican border to the Antarctic, was to be an American sphere of influence. All foreign powers were warned by the Monroe Doctrine of 1823 to stay out of the hemisphere, and, in turn, we would remain aloof from European affairs.

Manifest Destiny and the Oppression of Minorities

A question arises as to whose God had ordained all of this glorious future. The obvious answer is that it was the God of the dominant political force in the new nation, some form of the Calvinistic, Puritan religion. The Protestant mission was to win the West, develop its resources, convert or destroy the Native Americans, and thwart all foreign attempts to ever claim any part of the West, which rightfully belonged to the United States. All goals were achieved except the conversion of the Native Americans. Missionaries made a sincere effort to cause them to discard their traditional dress and put on Puritan bonnets and skirts, to exchange their native gods for Christ, and to become like white Americans, thrifty and productive capitalist farmers. But, in large measure, the effort was a failure. Native Americans were determined to cling to their gods, their customs, and values. Many did wear the cloak of a Christian on the outside, but in their hearts the gods of the mountain reigned supreme. Since the Native Americans could not be enslaved or Christianized, racial integration and intermarriage were unthinkable. The only solution left to the nation was to remove the Indians to the desert lands of the West, where they might starve, or to kill them, and during the mid-century the policy of President Andrew Jackson to remove Native Americans from their lands caused thousands of them to die. The story of how Christian America treated the native population is one of which Christ might have said, "I died on the cross in vain."

Then there was the problem of slavery, upon which the southern economy depended. The Christian conscience said, "Free the slaves." Northern Protestants said "Amen" to that, for their economy had found that slave labor was not profitable. But the southern Protestants replied that there is nothing in the Bible that says slavery is immoral or un-Christian. This is true, for the authors of the Bible lived in a pre-steam, pre-oil age, and there was no good substitute for slave labor.

Moreover, southern church preachers and elders rationalized that slavery was a blessing to the ignorant natives of Africa, for it gave them the opportunity to become civilized Christian people with appropriate rewards in heaven.

Before the American Revolution the few free black people in the North worshiped in white churches, but usually blacks were given places in the back of the church or in a balcony. Probably the Methodist Church was the one most friendly to black people. The first separate black church in America was organized by a Methodist minister, Richard Allen, in Philadelphia in 1793. He was to become the first bishop of the African Methodist Episcopal Zion Church. In 1820 the church split, with a second black church being organized, the African Methodist Episcopal Church. In the South the slave owners preferred to have their slaves worship in the white churches where the white masters could supervise their Christian behavior. Free black churches could become centers for antislavery propaganda and revolts.

During the 1830s and 1840s the American people experienced their first serious outbreak of "xenophobia," jingoistic hatred for alien peoples and cultures. An early form of Ku Klux Klanism came as early as 1798, when Congress passed the Alien and Sedition Acts which excluded dangerous aliens and their propaganda from entering the United States. These acts were directed against French radicals who might come to America. But the problem of undesirable aliens was not a serious one until large numbers of poor Irish Catholics arrived during the 1840s. The potato famine in Ireland caused thousands of poor farmers to leave and come to work in America. Their cheap labor was welcomed by urban employers and canal builders, but for most Americans, Catholics posed a threat.

The Jews never threatened the purity of the American nation or its religion until after 1880, when large numbers of them came from Russia to escape the pogroms. In 1800 only a few Jews, three thousand or so, lived in Boston, New York, Philadelphia, and Charleston. By 1830 most of the states permitted Jews to worship in their synagogues. South Carolina was the last to do so, in 1868.

So the Protestant campaign against undesirables concentrated its hatred on Irish Catholics. Riots against the Irish occurred in New York and other cities. Protestants fought Catholics and the Catholics retaliated. The chief issue of contention was that the Catholics wanted to organize their own parochial schools, and not send their children to the public schools. Protestants also thought the Irish were unfit to be Americans; they were too dirty, they drank too much, and they had too many children. In 1841 Samuel F. B. Morse, the inventor of the telegraph, organized an anti-alien party, the American Protestant Union, which in 1843 became the American Republican Party, and in 1854 the Know Nothing Party. The name came from the fact that when members were asked what they believed, they replied, "I know nothing." In 1849 another anti-alien party was formed, the Order of the Star Spangled Banner. All of these parties were basically anti-Catholic. Efforts were made to not hire Catholics, and almost everywhere Catholics could not vote or hold any public office. In 1856 the Know Nothing Party entered their candidate, Millard Fillmore, in the presidential race, but he was soundly defeated. This was a victory for American democracy and evidenced a sense of tolerance for non-Protestant groups.

The Second "Great Awakening"

Between 1830 and 1840 many Protestant preachers began to proclaim that the Second Coming was near, and that all Christians should prepare to meet their Christ. The return of the Christ had been promised in Scripture, and preachers could cite as proof 1 Thessalonians 4:16–17, 2 Thessalonians 2:8, and Revelation 20:4. Widespread talk of the Second Coming brought the Second Great Awakening in the American Protestant churches. This religious revival was most evident out on the frontier.

The most fervent revivalists of this era were Francis Asbury, the Methodist leader; Peter Cartwright; and Charles Finney. Asbury carried the Methodist faith to the frontier, where, like his mentor, John Wesley, he rode the circuits, preaching to many people in far-scattered communities. It is estimated that in his fifty years of ministry in America, Asbury traveled over 275,000 miles, mostly on horseback, preached over 16,000 sermons, and baptized untold thousands of souls. He crossed the mountains over sixty times while bringing his message to the isolated communities along the frontier from New York to the Carolinas and Kentucky. Asbury's method of circuit riding, holding revival camp meetings and preaching a fiery brand of "hell-fire and damnation" not only attracted many poor frontier people but set the pattern for the traveling missionaries of the Baptists and the Presbyterians.

After Asbury's death in 1815, the Methodist mission on the frontier was carried on by Peter Cartwright. He was an illiterate man who had been converted at a Methodist camp meeting in Kentucky in 1801. In 1802 he began his ministry, which he continued until his death in 1873. Cartwright's circuit took him from Kentucky to Illinois and all points in between. He preached over 14,000 sermons and converted over 12,000 persons. People came from miles around to hear Cartwright. The meetings might last two weeks or more and people would live in tents while awaiting the salvation of their souls. Whether souls were saved or not, it is said that the people had a good time exchanging gossip, catching up on the news, and meeting old friends and relatives. Cartwright's message was a simple one: "Be ye therefore perfect, even as your Father in Heaven is perfect." Perfect souls would build a perfect society and a perfect society would bring to Earth a Holy City, a new Zion. Cartwright not only saved souls. In Illinois he founded the state's system of public education and McKendrie College for training ministers. In 1846 he ran for Congress against Abraham Lincoln but lost.

Charles Finney, a Presbyterian evangelist and a powerful speaker, was the other great revivalist of the mid-1800s. His Christianity not only saved souls, but he was a foremost antislavery advocate and defender of equal rights for women. He was then founder and first president of Oberlin College in Ohio and a pioneer in American higher education because he opened college doors to both women and blacks on an equal basis. One story about Finney relates that he was so popular that one time in a Rochester, New York, revival, the meeting house became so crowded that its walls literally fell down.

The Great Awakening stimulated the churches to expand their missionary activities both at home and abroad. The American Bible Society was formed in 1815 to give Bibles to the poor wherever they lived. In 1826 the American Home Mission Society was organized to conduct missions on the frontier among Native Americans and pioneer settlers. In 1825 the American Tract Society was formed to spread the word of God throughout the nation. However, to have a Bible was of small value if the owner could not read. So many Protestants, especially the Methodists, organized Sunday Schools to teach adults reading skills. In 1824 the American Sunday School Union was organized to foster the spread of Sunday Schools. Methodists in the early 1800s became active proponents of tax-supported elementary schools. Massachusetts was the most active state in this respect. Horace Mann became the first state superintendent of schools in Massachusetts as well as in the nation, in 1837. He was also the first leader to establish a teachers college to train teachers for the public schools.

The revival spirit was instrumental in causing the several Protestant churches to become concerned about the sordid working conditions and the plight of the poor and other dependent persons. The women's rights movement began in a meeting at Seneca Falls, New York, in 1848 when a few women, led by Lucretia Mott and Elizabeth Cady Stanton, set in motion a campaign for equal civil rights for women. Puritan morality was expressed by a campaign against the use of alcohol when the American Society for the Promotion of Temperance was organized in 1826. Maine was the first state to enact a prohibition law against the use of alcohol, in 1851.

The expectation that the millennium had arrived or that it was soon to arrive caused new Protestant churches to be born. The ancient prophet Isaiah and the books of Daniel and Revelation had made clear that the Messiah would return some day. One group that was certain that the Second Coming was near was led by William Miller, a Baptist minister and a farmer. He predicted first that Christ would arrive on earth in 1814. Then he postponed the arrival until October 22, 1844, but Christ did not arrive then either. However, Miller's faithful followers remained confident that the Second Coming would arrive, and on that conviction a new church was founded, the Seventh-day Adventist Church. Like the Baptists, the Adventists adopted the first-century church as their model. Worship was held on the Jewish Sabbath, from sundown Friday evening until sunset on Saturday. Worship services were the plain, unadorned service of the Baptists, with Bible reading, prayer, sermons, and a few hymns. The basic creed of the Adventists is the promise that for a thousand years Christians will be in heaven with Christ, after which the earth will be purified by fire, the wicked will be resurrected and burned in hell, and the righteous will be raised up to a place on earth, Jerusalem, forever to live in peace.

At the same time another messianic church was founded, the Seventh-day Baptists, a church very similar to the Seventh-day Adventists. Adventists were zealous missionaries, and they have been noted for building schools and hospitals all over the world, and for providing quality educational and medical services. Like the Jews the Adventists eat only "kosher" food. They abstain from all flesh food, especially pork, and therefore follow a vegetarian diet. The Adventists pioneered in the production of cereal breads and breakfast foods. The familiar cereal names Post, Kellogg, and Graham crackers are all Adventist creations.

Another Protestant Church with millenarian expectations was the Disciples of Christ, also known as the Christian Church. The founders of the Disciples were Thomas Campbell and his son, Alexander. In 1809 they started a new church in Erie, Pennsylvania. Before the Campbell era a new church had been started by a Presbyterian minister, Barton Stone. The one purpose for having a new church was to reproduce the original Christian church as it was in Antioch. Hence the Disciples rejected all dogmas and doctrines that caused division within the Christian body. Basically the Disciples were an offshoot of the Baptists and so their services and beliefs resembled those of the Baptists. They accepted the Nicene Creed, the sacraments of baptism (adult baptism by immersion) and the memorial Lord's Supper. Church government was controlled by the congregation. Church membership was open to both men and women on an equal basis. The Disciples of Christ was one of the first churches to ordain women as ministers, in 1888. Being committed to the reestablishment of the first Christian church, it sought to heal the breaches among all Christians. The Disciples were always in the forefront of later ecumenical movements to unite the Christian body. They were more tolerant of Catholics than other Protestant groups, and they became leaders in the formation of the National Council of Churches and the World Council of Churches. Like the Methodists, the Disciples preached the virtue of living out the Christian life on earth; hence they were active promoters of the social gospel and social welfare legislation.

Joseph Smith and the Rise of the Mormon Church

Out of this religious ferment of the early 1800s came the Church of the Latter Day Saints, or Mormon Church.[1] The Mormon religion arose from the mystical experiences of Joseph Smith, who lived in Palmyra, New York. In 1820, as a boy of eighteen, while praying, Smith had a vision of angels, one of whom, Gabriel, told him that a new restoration of the gospel was in order. Christianity needed a new dispensation of faith, as recorded in Galatians 1:10. Another angel, Moroni, according to Smith led him to a place where gold plates had been buried in the year 421. The words on the plates were translated and became the Book of Mormon. It was printed in 1830. The Book of Mormon relates a thousand-year history of a lost tribe of Israelites who left Palestine and came to America to become the ancestors of the Native Americans. The leader of the lost tribe was Lehi. He had two sons, Laman and Nephi. The two brothers and their followers waged a long war won by the Lamanites. Nephi was killed. From the Lamanites came a series of prophets, the last one being Mormon and his son, Moroni. Smith claimed to be the heir to Moroni's spiritual position and rightfully was the prophet to restore the power of Israel on earth. Christ had visited New York after his resurrection. In a later revelation, Smith learned that he had been commissioned by Christ to form a new church. The Book of Mormon became the sacred scripture for this religion, along with the Bible. In recent years some critics of the Mormons have cast doubts upon the truth about the Book of Mormon. A friend of Smith, Martin Harris, is said to have written a letter in 1830 which said that the spirit Moroni arose from a white salamander while digging for the golden plates. In other words, Smith was portrayed as a religious faker, a charlatan. This letter has in no way caused Mormons to doubt the authenticity of the book of Mormon.

Joseph Smith believed that he was living in the age of the millennium, the last days before Christ returns, and that all Christians should make ready to meet the Christ. If Mormons obey the Scriptures they will reap a good harvest on earth as well as in heaven. The Mormons proposed to live in isolation from the sinful world so that they could build on earth a veritable Garden of Eden. This ideal is what the Mormons proposed to do in Utah.

Man, according to Smith, existed before time and will continue to exist forever. The study of family history and its ancestors is an important part of Mormonism. Mormons who have lived and died continue to live in a resurrected life. The family unit contains both the living and the dead, all of the blood relatives from time immemorial. The family unit never dies, hence the study of genealogy has placed the Mormon Church as the best single source of family histories in the world. Even family members who died long ago can be baptized and join their family members in heaven.

The Church of the Latter Day Saints had always been an object of persecution by other Christian groups. Its early history is one of constant oppression; Mormons were often forced to flee from place to place for religious peace and security. First they had to leave New York for Kirkland, Ohio, in 1831. In 1839 they were driven from Ohio to Illinois and Missouri. In 1844 Joseph Smith was killed by a mob in Nauvoo, Illinois. His successor, Brigham Young, in 1847 led his people, like Moses, to the safety of the Utah desert. The tale of the Mormon migration is much like that of the Eastern Native Amerians to Oklahoma about the same time, a tale of tears and hardships. A few remnants of the Nauvoo Mormons were left in Independence, Missouri, where a second branch of the church remains active today as the Latter Day Saints, Reorganized Church of Jesus Christ. In Utah the Mormons found peace and isolation from hostile neighbors. As a rule their relations with the Native Americans were also reasonably peaceful. In Utah the Mormons have prospered with diligence and hard work. It is estimated that today the Mormon Church has assets of $8 billion, making it the wealthiest Protestant Church in America.

Mormons conduct an extensive missionary enterprise all over the world. They have been most successful in Asia and Latin America. Today the Mormon Church has over six million members, two-thirds of whom live overseas. Every young Mormon man is expected to give two years' service in the mission field.

At the center of the Mormon Church is the family and its ability to reproduce. For many years polygamy was permitted so that the church might grow in population. By federal law polygamy was outlawed in 1890. The Mormon birth rate is twice that of the national average, a result of the church's stern opposition to the use of any form of contraception or abortion.

The Mormon Church has a strong Puritanical bias against sensual pleasures, sex, gambling, or the use of alcohol and tobacco. But more like the Puritans of New England, the Morman Church conceives of itself as being a theocracy in which the wisdom of the church's leaders must be the guidelines for all aspects of life in a Mormon community or state. Utah is nearly a church-ruled state, and a center of political and religious conservatism as reflected in the dominance of the Republican Party. The chief officer of the Mormon Church is its president. He has an advisory council of twelve membrs or apostles and a lesser council called the First Quorum of the Seventy. The Mormon president, like the pope, can issue pronouncements on faith that can change Mormon beliefs. For example, in 1978 the president received a revelation that black people, who had long been denied membership in the church, were eligible to become Mormons.

The road to salvation for a Mormon is to give complete obedience and loyalty to the church. Women cannot become priests or church leaders. Their role is to remain good wives and mothers. An evil woman can be banned from the church, with the result that all of her family members are excluded from heaven. All Mormons are to give a tithe, 10 percent of their income, to the church, a large tax that has made it possible for the church to support vast charitable and educational institutions, plus a wide array of hospitals and homes for the elderly and orphans. In many cases it has been able to refuse the federal program of Social Security benefits.

A unique aspect of Mormonism is the Temple, a sacred building like the one in ancient Jerusalem, which is not for worship, but used principally for marriage celebrations in which the bride and groom are married not just to each other, but also to their relatives in heaven. The church has no order of priests or ministers. Within the hierarchy of control, below the Council of Apostles, are a number of officers called patriarchs, high priests, bishops, elders deacons, and teachers. Services are typically conducted by a lay person with simple Baptistlike services of worship. Music and singing are featured. The Mormon Tabernacle Choir has achieved a worldwide reputation for its quality religious music.

A summary of Mormon beliefs would include the following:

1. Inerrant authority of the Scriptures, including the Book of Mormon, insofar as correctly translated.

2. The Holy Trinity is accepted but each element is a separate entity.

3. God and Christ were once human beings in the flesh.

4. Revelation is a continuing process. Life is a continuum from birth to death and into eternity. The living are united to the dead. A Mormon family is made up of the living members plus all of the ancestors from the time of Adam.

5. Salvation is a continuing process, never completed until a perfect soul arrives in heaven.

6. Original sin does not exist. Each person is responsible for his or her own salvation, which includes justification by faith and good works.

7. The two sacraments are baptism and the Lord's Supper. Baptism is by immersion, usually given to children about the age of eight. Unbaptized souls in heaven can be baptized also.

8. Literal resurrection of the physical body.

9. Full faith in the coming of Christ and the Millennium.

10. Church government is based on the patriarchal society as portrayed in the Old Testament. The church government is made up of only male members.

Unitarians, Transcendentalists, and the Movement for Social Reform

By 1840 the American republic seemed destined to become one of the world's greatest, richest powers. Ministers, publicists, and politicians all proclaimed that God had indeed blessed the nation. Cotton was king in the South. New England's textile mills were competing with England's mills because of cheap female labor, cheap water power, and able enterpreneurs. Northern cities were prospering from an extensive shipping industry and a growing fishing and whaling industry. Population was growing, the West was being won in the Ohio Valley and Texas, and family fortunes, like those of the Goulds and the Vanderbilts, were beginning to build a new social class of financiers and bourgeois elitists. America was showing the world that heaven could be built on earth. A combination of fortunate conditions, a land of rich natural resources, isolation from the turmoil of European wars and therefore no need for heavy military expenditures, the Puritan work ethic, and a capitalist system of free enterprise blessed by most of the Protestant Chuches, all working together made American a land of opportunity for fame and fortune.

But cracks were beginning to appear in this pretty picture of prosperity and achievement. Somehow the lofty promises of freedom and equality for all, as promised in the Declaration of Independence and the preamble to the Constitution, were not being realized. The great masses of workers and farmers were poor and were denied any real participation in the political process. Slaves were the property of their masters. And women, legally, were the property of their husbands. The distribution of the nation's wealth was growing more and more unequal. Social critics began a search for solutions to the increasing injustices in the body politic and in the social system. Some solutions were anti-Christian; some were socialistic; some were modifications of Christianity; and some hoped to find relief in some of the non-Christian religions such as Hinduism or Buddhism.

By 1830 a few American intellectuals ceased to have faith in the miracle of the Second Coming that would bring heaven to the American people. It would be better if we use our brains to create man-inspired and man-made solutions to the social ills. The validity of supernatural forces and truth by revelation must yield to better sources of knowledge, reason, and science. The eighteenth-century French philosophers of the Revolution, Rousseau, Voltaire, Diderot and the Deists, and the English philosopher John Locke, all were causing American thinkers to doubt the value of religion and the power of prayer. Yet not all men of wisdom agreed that science and reason alone could solve the nation's problems. Oriental religions revived the belief that in meditation good knowledge can be found. Immanuel Kant in his *Critique of Pure Reason* concluded that although reason and science are valuable in the search for truth, the highest, ultimate form of reason is intuition, a transcendental method to finding truth. Some men, like Henry Thoreau, living like a hermit on the shores of Walden Pond, rejected the Christian God and found, like the pantheists, the true God in all forms of nature. But the one message that came out of the rationalism of the Jeffersons and the Lockes, and even out of the pantheists and the Buddhists, was the conviction that God is within every human being, and that each person is equally divine and capable of creating a world of perfection, that is, the democratic ideal of freedom and equality for all people.

Out of this complex of romantic, idealistic, and rational thinking came a new American church, the Unitarian Church. It was never to become a large church, but it did have great influence in bringing social reforms to America. Its founder was William Ellery Channing (1780–1842). As a Congregational minister in Boston, Channing left his church because of its dogmatism and reluctance to admit that there were any social injustices in America. Unitarians rejected the belief in the divinity of Christ. He was only a great human being who gave to mankind the important message of love for all human beings. Such beliefs as the Virgin Mary, the saints, original sin, predestination, the Resurrection, and the Second Coming of Christ were all myths. If Christ left any message for the Church to fulfill it was that its primary mission was to effect on earth the many needed social reforms.

Closely related to the New England Unitarians was a new philosophical movement called "transcendentalism." The chief prophets of transcendentalism were Ralph Waldo Emerson, a former Congregational minister; Henry David Thoreau; Nathaniel Hawthorne; Bronson Alcott; Margaret Fuller; Orestes Brownson; and George Ripley. Margaret Fuller was the editor of a radical magazine, *The Dial,* and an important feminist crusader. George Ripley was the founder of a utopian community, Brook Farm, near Roxbury, Massachusetts.

Transcendentalists were influenced as much by the philosophy of Immanuel Kant as they were by the teachings of Jesus. Truth is to be found by way of meditation, and meditation reveals the truth since it springs from the heart of man, man's "oversoul," that divine spark in all of us that gives us wisdom and inspiration to do good deeds. Man is to be guided by the voice of the oversoul. Man is basically good provided he can be freed from the chains of tradition, superstition, the dogmas of the Church, and the laws of the civil government. The transcendentalists drew heavily upon their studies of Hinduism and Buddhism. If God dwells in the soul of man, then it is certain that man is born to be free, and that he has the capacity to fashion a perfect democratic society, one that gives to each citizen a life of freedom, prosperity, and harmony in a perfect union of all peoples.

The poet Walt Whitman, in his *Leaves of Grass* (1855) expresses the ideals of transcendentalism. Other poets, such as William Cullen Bryant, James Russell Lowell, and Emily Dickinson, praise the glories of nature and free people. Emerson's "Essay on Self-Reliance" has become America's best explanation for having confidence in the ability of free people to govern themselves and to build a good world for all. Emerson said of the oversoul, "Meantime within Man is the Soul of the Whole, the wise silence, the universal beauty, to which every part and particle is equally related; the eternal one. . . . We see the world piece by piece as the sun, the moon, the animal, the tree, but the whole, of which these are only the shining parts, is the Soul."

Thus there began in America about 1830 a concerted drive to set free the slaves and emancipate women. In the vanguard of social reform were the Quakers, the Methodists, the Unitarians, the transcendentalists, the romantic idealists, and the utopian socialists. The list of needed reforms reached beyond the issues of slavery and feminism. The evil of alcohol, mass illiteracy, horrible working conditions in factories and mines, especially for women and children, the rising feelings of hatred for Catholics and foreigners in general, the increasing divisions between the rich and the poor, prostitution, all required attention.

Most of the social injustices needed long years of education, the changing of social values, and the passage of much state and federal legislation. Perhaps a short cut to utopia could be found if people returned to a simple, communistic way of life in which they could live in small, self-sufficient communities, all living together in peace and equality, no one striving to be richer or better than anyone else. All conflicts would cease, and there would be no need for big governments, big armies, and big taxes. Perhaps more Americans could live in the manner of the Pennsylvania Amish or the Dunkers or the Mennonites, living in their isolated, self-sufficient communities. In Europe in the early 1800s certain utopian socialist communities were being organized. In France the best-known utopian socialist was Charles Fourier, and in England, Robert Owens, a wealthy industrialist.[2]

Fourier's philosophy came to America by way of Albert Brisbane about 1835. Brisbane had the support of America's best-known newspaper editor, Horace Greeley, and the New England transcendentalists. The Brook Farm community sponsored by the transcendentalists was modeled after the Fourier plan. Other

Fourier communities were established in New York, Michigan, Iowa, Wisconsin, and Ohio. One of the first communities, or phalanxes, as Fourier called his communities, was founded at Ripon, Wisconsin, in 1844. These communities were organized on the principle that labor is the source of all value and that the fruits of labor should be shared equally. All members of the community were guaranteed lifetime security. By 1860 all of the phalanxes were bankrupt and out of existence. Some critics say the utopian dream failed because too many members were lazy and refused to work; hence there were no profits. Others contend that the utopian communities did make a profit, that the people did work effectively, but outside employment paid better returns, hence the people left to find better-paying jobs in the capitalist world.

Robert Owens, a wealthy English industrialist, was appalled at the terrible effects of the Industrial Revolution upon the working people. He believed that more could be done by applying Christian ethics to the industrial scene than by trying to have Parliament pass reform legislation. In England, Owens set up a few utopian communities, but he thought he might have better success in the New World. So in 1825 he purchased a Rappist commune in Indiana and named it New Harmony.[3] The new community was based on both Christian and rational economic principles, such as those espoused by Fourier. Owens had no use for supernatural Christianity or the belief that the Bible had all of the answers. Members were recruited from many sources: intellectuals, idealists, teachers, Quakers, artists, poor farmers, and factory workers. The only commitment a member was expected to make was to denounce capitalism as evil and class divisions as un-Christian.

Within three years New Harmony was practically bankrupt. It was evident that if utopian socialism was ever to survive, then it must have some powerful, irresistible emotional force to bind the people together, a force akin to a spiritual one, or perhaps an all-consuming one like communism. It was evident, however, that American workers were not ready to accept the economic principle that all should share equally in the labors of all workers.

Another interesting experiment in utopian living-together was the Oneida community in New York. This group, the Perfectionists, was led by a young, well-educated minister, John Humphrey Noyes, who was convinced that the Second Coming of Christ had occurred one generation after the death of Christ, or with the beginning of the Christian Church. Mankind was now in a state of evolution moving toward a state of perfection. It was now the time that all Christians begin to live like saints in such a state. Man was under a divine injunction to live a pure, sin-free life, similar to the life of one in a monastery. So Noyes established a community in Oneida, New York, in 1831. At first, like the Shakers, he ordered that men and women should work together but that they remain celibate. Later Noyes had a revelation that since his people were then living in the kingdom of heaven celibacy was no longer required. Now a complex marriage arrangement was ordained in which there was to be a marriage of both sexes in spirit and flesh. The new marriage system was to symbolize the unity of all people in a Christian marriage, or in a life motivated by God's universal love for all men and women. As a result of this new revelation men and women were free to enjoy sex with one another. Neighbors around Oneida failed to understand that these sexual relations were pure and godly. Instead they condemned the community as being promiscuous and licentious. So Noyes and his community were forced to flee Oneida. In Fact, the sexual aspect of the Oneida community was not a free-love system at all. Sex was limited to procreation. The parents of the resulting children might be any members of the group; hence the children were regarded as being the children of all the members. Members of the community had equality but an absence of freedom. The community was ruled by a theocratic group of ministers with no input from the members. Noyes viewed his group as a family with him as the patriarchal father. All members were expected to spy on one another and to report any wayward acts. Worship services followed the Quaker model of remaining silent until one was moved by the Holy Spirit to speak. The disciplined, regimented life within the community did generate a quality type of crafts and other manufactured products. Furniture, textiles, and silverware were produced with precision and careful workmanship. Although the Oneida community has long since disappeared, it does remain as a stock company producing a high quality of silverware. As farmers the Perfectinoists were also excellent producers. The failure of the community can be attributed to the harsh discipline, the lack of personal freedom, and the attractiveness of good wages in outside employment. For a brief time the Oneidans were in the forefront of promoting social welfare, civil rights for women, opposition to slavery, and the encouragement of scientific experimentation. They were greatly interested in the current scientific developments of their time, such as eugenics for breeding a better human race, evolution, and the philosophy of positivism, which promoted the use of the scientific method of discovery.

America was not an ideal place for the building of ideal, utopian communities. Almost without exception they were all failures, and although they gave their support to the reform efforts of other groups, by themselves they made only a meager contribution to the advancement of conditions for the poor and the enslaved.

The pioneer efforts for social reform came from the efforts of the liberal Methodists and Congregationalists, the Quakers, the transcendentalists, the Unitarians, and the rational deists. By 1830 voices were crying out against slavery. One extreme position on slavery was spoken in the pages of the *Liberator,* a paper published by William Lloyd Garrison, who demanded the immediate abolition of slavery. The New England Anti-Slave Society joined Garrison in demanding freedom for the slaves and their immediate introduction into the American society as full and equal citizens. More moderate critics of slavery proposed a more gradual abolition of slavery. They hoped that in time the slave holders would realize that slave labor was both unproductive and un-Christian, and that they would free their slaves voluntarily without compensation. The names of the "gradualists" are many and some are most familiar names. Among these persons were Horace Greeley, Harriet Beecher Stow, the Quaker Grimke sisters, minister Wendell Phillips, Charles G. Finney, black writer Frederick Douglass, and another newspaper publisher, Elijah Lovejoy of Alton, Illinois, who was killed by a proslavery mob. The slave issue divided the churches. In 1845 the Baptists Church split into a Northern and a Southern Baptist Church. In 1846 the Methodist Church was split. By 1860 the only churches left in unity were the Catholics, the Episcopalians, and the Lutherans. The Congregational Church never divided over the slave issue, but individual churches did choose to support one side or the other.

By 1840 the Anti-Slave Society had over 150,000 members. In 1840 and 1844 the Liberty Party entered a candidate, James Birney, on an antislavery platform. In 1848 the Free Soil Party, which wished to ban slavery from the territories prior to their admission as states, had as its presidential candidate Martin Van Buren. In 1852 the Free Soil Party became the Republican Party, which in 1860 nominated Abraham Lincoln as its candidate. The Republican Party was pledged to preserve the Union, outlaw slavery in the territories, but divided over the issue of abolishing slavery. Voters were left with expectation that sometime in the future slavery would be abolished by law.

Concern for the workingman and the abominable conditions in the workplaces also received concern and agitation for improvements. In 1828 working men's parties were organized in New York City and Philadelphia. Nathaniel Hawthorne, editor of the *New York Post,* wrote in 1836, "Workingmen have the right to strike." Unitarians were vigorous proponents of labor unions and protective legislation. Labor unions were declared legal in Massachusetts in 1842.

Public education was also the concern of the liberal forces in America. By 1860 the reformers had secured public elementary education in most of the states. High schools were to wait until after the Civil War. Many church colleges were founded in the period preceding the Civil War. By 1860 there were thirty-four Methodist colleges. Emory College was founded in Georgia in 1837 and De Pauw University in Indiana in 1837. Both were Methodist colleges. Oberlin College was the most revolutionary, for its doors were open to both women and black students.

Puritan ethics condemned the use of alcohol, gambing, dancing, and most forms of sports. Any nonchurch activities on the Sabbath were banned by so-called blue laws. In 1816 the Methodist Church banned the use of alcohol by its members. After 1830 there were consistent campaigns waged against the use of alcohol but no prohibition laws were passed before 1869, when Maine became the first "dry" state in the Union. Prohibition laws eventually gave way to the need for the states and the federal government to secure taxes from the sale of alcoholic beverages.

Prison reform was on the liberal agenda. By 1852 twenty-one states had built more humane prisons. Women's rights advocates were campaigning for equal rights for women. The first organized effort to promote women's rights came in 1848, when a group of women met at Seneca Falls, New York, and drafted a "Declaration of Sentiments," modeled after the Declaration of Independence. Some of the pioneer leaders of the women's rights movement were Susan B.

Anthony, Harriet Beecher Stowe, Lucretia Mott, Elizabeth Cady Stanton, and the Grimke sisters of South Carolina.

In the period before the Civil War very little was accomplished in effecting reforms for workers, women, the poor, the sick and handicapped, and in reducing the social evils of drinking, prostitution, and gambling. Only the seeds of reform were planted, and it would be in the next century that the seed would grow into trees that bore fruit. Between 1830 and 1860 there was one all-consuming issue which threatened to divide, if not destroy, the new nation—slavery. Could the new republic, which held so much promise for the future, survive half free and half slave?

29

Post–Civil War Protestant Division and Unity

The Religious and Political Disunity
of the Nation following the Civil War

The Civil War in many respects left the nation more divided than it was before. The North still viewed the South as a land of rebellious traitors, while the South licked its wounds in deep anger for the needless destruction thrust upon its people when Gen. Sherman marched to the Atlantic Ocean leaving behind a swath of total destruction. Then followed the evil acts of the northern carpetbaggers, who came South to loot what was left of the Confederacy. In alliance with the freed slaves and the federal army, the northern-controlled state legislatures in the South made off with the meager resources left after the war.

A hundred and thirty years later most of the visible scars inflicted on the South have healed. But in the soul or the inner psyche of southern people there still remain doubts about northern goals and policies, doubts which cause misgivings, suspicions, and a reluctance to trust northern politicians in Congress.

After the Civil War the United States became a rich and powerful nation, and after World War I its preeminence in world affairs became evident. After World War II there was no other power in the world to challenge the supremacy of the United States. Today, in the 1990s, however, Americans are no longer certain they are the masters of the destiny of the world, as defeated Japan and West Germany have become major competitors in the world marketplaces.

The question arises: What role did the many different churches in the United States play in this achievement of world prominence? The Protestants were to become more and more divided as to which one bore the true stamp of Christian truth. Did the state of disunion among the Protestants after 1865 in no way impede America's rise to power? Perhaps this only indicates that religion was becoming a minor factor in the course of American histrory, and this loss of influence was a national benefit, as it permitted the forces of science and materialism to build great industries, discover new technologies, and release the makers of national policy from the ties of religious superstition and those traditional, but outmoded, values of the Middle Ages.

Public opinion polls in the past thiry years show consistently that the American people believe that we are a Christian nation, that God is on our side, and that "Manifest Destiny," that is, God's will and plan for America, continues to direct the course of American history. Alexander Solzhenitsyn, the Russian writer and critic of Communism, asserts that America is not a Christian nation. Rather it is a godless nation cast in the model of immorality, materialism, and self-greed.

Church statistics report that about half of the American people belong to some religious group, and that about one-fourth attend their churches or synagogues on a regular, weekly basis. Many Americans were dismayed in 1972 when the Supreme Court ruled that prayer in public schools was unconstitutional, a concession made in part to satisfy the objections to prayer made by the Mennonites and Jehovah Witnesses. One conclusion might be that Americans say they are Christians, but do not want to be judged on the basis of Christian principles.

In the United States today there are over eighty million Protestants, fifty-three million Catholics, six million Jews, and a small number of Moslems, Buddhists, and other religious groups. The *1985 Yearbook of American and Canadian Churches* lists 219 religious bodies. J. Gordon Melton and Robert J. Moore, in their *The Cult Experience Responding to the New Religious Pluralism,* estimate that there are more than eight hundred Christian bodies and six hundred non-Christian bodies. If all Protestant single churches, including store-front churches and home churches, are counted, then ten thousand more church bodies might be counted. The *World Christian Encyclopedia* lists 20,780 distinct Christian denominations in the world as of 1980, most of which are Protestant and in the United States.

In the United States worship is so free and generous that everyone should be able to find a church of his or her choice. Or if this is not possible, then everyone has the freedom to go and organize their own church. No church has the power to excommunicate members of other churches. No one can be labeled a heretic for not accepting the creed of any church. There is no end to the degree to which Protestant Christianity can be divided. However, many Protestant leaders are concerned that this multiplication of Christian churches will spell the doom of Protestantism, and if that disaster is to be avoided, then Protestants must come together in a spirit of reconciliation and unity.

The Conflict of Religion and Science

By 1860 the Western world was being oriented to think in terms of reason and science. The scientific method of study and research when applied to machines and technology won almost universal approval, for out of science came new wealth, a better standard of living for most people, and a place of power among the nations of the world. But when scientific analysis is applied to the Bible and the history of the Christian Church, many Christians (and before 1900 most Christians) rejected science as blasphemous and ungodly. Many people preferred to believe that more of God's truths could be found in myth and supernatural phenomena than in science. Perhaps Christians had good reason to be skeptical about the long-run effects of science upon religion. God might die, as Harvey Cox suggests in his book *Religion in the Secular City,* or as Richard Goodwin has stated in *The American Condition,* God-given values might be replaced by the ideas of Sartre, the French existentialist. Sartre said that freedom would become the foundation of all values: "In willing freedom we discover that it depends entirely upon the freedom of others, and that the freedom of others depends on our own." In other words man no longer needs to depend upon God or his church, or even the state for his own welfare.

Many Christians, especially fundamentalists, cannot accept such manmade value judgments. If "Man is the measure of all things," then the human condition would be reduced to Hobbesian bestiality. To deny the truths of such basic Christian beliefs as the Virgin Birth, the divinity of Jesus, and the Resurrection would be the death of the Christian Church. Anthony Fleur in his book *Did Jesus Rise from the Dead?* comments on the Resurrection experience by saying that in the mind of a scientist, or as expressed by the Scottish philosopher David Hume, what is not possible to happen in nature could not have happened. But Fleur cites the view of the modern theologian Karl Barth, that although the Resurrection cannot be proved by science, it is an event that must be accepted on faith. In science the tests of reason are valid, but in the realm of God's world truth is beyond understanding and so must be accepted on faith.

However dangerous it may be to permit science and reason to infiltrate into Christian thinking, in this modern world of rational thought and scientific analysis, science and reason will continue to cause division within the ranks of Christians. Two issues over which division most often occurs are evolution and abortion.

The Evolution Controversy

Charles Darwin published his *Origin of Species* in 1859, and ever since Christians have argued about the validity of the theory of evolution. The current conclusion of modern anthropologists is that the human race evolved from a common ancestor who lived first in central Africa and that Homo sapiens has been on earth for more than a hundred thousand years. Many people find it difficult to accept the view that humans are a part of the total chain of animal life, and that life is in a process of constant change. Some conservatives cannot conceive of a God who is not fixed, always the same. Whatever God is, that which God created is always in a process of change or evolution. Yet Christians should not lose sight of the fact that no matter what scientific explanation is given for the origin of the universe, the "big bang" theory or some other theory, there is still some yet unknown, unrevealed force that caused the big bang and evolution to occur, and that force can be called God, spirit, *elan vital,* or the oversoul. Pantheists, Native Americans, and environmentalists see in the theory of evolution a blessing, since all of life in nature is united in a common bond of creation and value. Evolution also lends support to the feminist movement in that evolution can find no evidence that men were created superior to women or women superior to men. Today most mainline churches have a liberal wing of members who accept the theory of evolution as a proper and Christian explanation of the origins of all life. The Unitarian-Universalist Church accepts evolution without reservation. However, for the conservative wing of mainline churches and the separate fundamentalist and pentecostal Protestant churches, the theory of evolution is anathema and the teaching of evolution in the public schools must be stopped.

In the early 1920s many southern states passed laws against the teaching of evolution in the public schools. These efforts were negated first by a famous evolution case tried in the courts of Tennessee, the Scopes trial in 1925. The famous Chicago lawyer Clarence Darrow took the side of the teacher who was accused of teaching evolution while the state had as its prosecutor the populist Christian orator and former presidential candidate William Jennings Bryan. Although Scopes and the evolutionists lost the case, Bryan and the antievolutionists became objects of ridicule in the North. Bryan was to die of a heart attack shortly after the trial. The antievolutionists were defeated in 1968, when the Supreme Court ruled against the states that outlawed the teaching of evolution.

Since then the campaign against the teaching of evolution has taken a new tack—antievolutionists claim that the biblical account of creation can be supported scientifically, and that therefore this new discipline, "creation science," should be allowed to be taught instead of, or at least alongside of, evolution.[1] Both theories should be permitted in the classroom. Two states, Arkansas and Louisiana, did pass laws requiring that creation science be taught in the public schools alongside scientific evolution. The Supreme Court struck down the Louisiana law in 1987.[2] Since then the fundamentalistic Christians are using pressure tactics on text book publishers to include a chapter on creationism in their biology texts.

Controversies over Contraception and Abortion

Science has provoked another divisive issue in Christian churches, and that concerns the matters of abortion and contraception. Form year one in the Christian church sex came under fire as being a major sin. From Paul to Augustine to Calvin to the Puritans, both the Catholic church and Protestant churches have sought to repress the human urge for sex and reproduction, while at the same time exhorting married couples to bear more children. A guide book on sex and marriage by O. S. Fowler published in 1870 taught married couples that sex in marriage was both godly and healthful, but that to violate the laws of nature (God) would undermine one's health, destroy human morality, and even destroy civilization. Sexual virtue was as innate in human beings as eating, so the author said.

In the twentieth century science has made possible almost fool-proof contraceptives and safe abortions. Thus sex can be had within marriage or outside marriage with little risk of pregnancy. The nation does face a serious moral dilemma. Puritan, Victorian moralists are correct when they charge that free, uncontrolled sexuality will result in an increase of sexual immorality and crime, so few people would advocate a "free-love" standard of morality. However, it is interesting to note that even many of the most conservative, most moralistic fundamentalists are proclaiming that sex in marriage is Christian, desirable for a happy marriage, should be used for nonprocreative pleasure, and that it promotes good health. Such ideas are found in a book, *How to Be Happy Though Married* by Tim Lahaye, a prominent fundamentalist and critic of "secular humanism."

The Puritan antipathy toward sex became a major issue after the Civil War, when the Comstock law was passed by Congress in 1873. This law forbade the circulation through the mails of any contraceptive information and devices. In 1965 the Supreme Court overturned residual state laws against contraceptives and opened the way for the public sale and use of all contraceptives. The birth control movement, despite the Comstock law, made headway in the period after 1880. Margaret Sanger led a campaign against the Comstock law in favor of birth control. She opened the first birth control clinic in Brooklyn in 1916. Her campaign on behalf of contraception grew out of her personal experiences as a nurse while working in the slum areas of New York City. She saw what painful burdens were placed upon poor women and families who could not control their family size. Sanger was also instrumental in securing money for research on the "pill."

A revolution in both sexual attitudes and behavior has occurred since 1960. Churches are divided over how to control an excess of sexuality in our modern society. No one denies that sexual instruction of the young is necessary. Shall it be done at home or in the school? Conservatives, Catholics and Protestants both, oppose any sex classes or clinics in the schools. All instruction is the responsibility of the home and the church. The advent of AIDS has persuaded many conservatives, like former surgeon general C. Everett Koop, that sex education in the schools is necessary, even to the extent that schools ought to provide condoms for protection against this fatal disease.

Science has also changed public and religious attitudes about abortion. Jewish and Christian ethics have always taught that abortion is a sin and even murder. Modern science has made abortions relatively safe and cheap. An abortion pill, like the birth control pill, is on the market in France. No doubt it will soon be sold in the United States unless abortion opponents are successful in preventing its sale. If this is the state of abortion technology, then many people will consider the abortion pill as another form of birth control.

The case against abortion rests on the premise that a fetus is a human being entitled to all of the protection guaranteed by the U.S. Constitution. The issue comes down to the question of when the fertilized cell becomes a viable fetus, that is, a potential human being that has life. Conservatives say that life begins at the moment of conception. More liberal Christians say that viability may not be until the embryo can sustain its life when freed from the mother's uterus. Scientists differ as to when viability occurs, but there is general consensus that there is viability after the second trimester of pregnancy. It was this belief that caused the Supreme Court in the *Roe* v. *Wade* decision of 1973 to declare that women should have the nearly unlimited choice of an abortion through the second trimester. This decision has caused pro-choice and anti-abortion activists to wage angry battles in the streets and before the White House. The Catholic church remains unalterably opposed to almost all abortions, except to save the life of the mother. More liberal Protestants would concede that there are cases where abortion might be justified. The Episcopal Church supports the right to have an abortion when the mother's life is in danger, and in cases of rape and incest, but never as a form of birth control. In general, Baptists, Presbyterians, and Methodists support that position. The United Church of Christ is pro-choice with no exceptions. The other Protestant churches—Lutherans, Missouri Synod, Mormons, and the many fundamental and evangelical churches—support the rigid position of the Catholic church. The absolute position of conservative Christians is reinforced by the belief that no only is a human body destroyed, but the soul that enters at the moment of conception is also destroyed. The nation remains severely divided. Public opinion polls indicate that regardless of which church members are polled, a slight majority generally supports the availability of legal abortion, that is, that a woman should be free to choose an abortion.

The Protestant Response to the Challenge of Science— Liberal Christianity and Evangelism

Scientific and rational philosophies in the nineteenth century have added to the conflicts within the Christian body. The more educated, liberal Christians find it difficult to accept the supernatural aspects of religion. The conservatives contend that the supernatural and the mystical elements of human thought are basic to the survival of all religions. If all of the supernatural phenomena were eliminated, there might be no room for God and religion in the scheme of human existence.

The pro-science, liberal Christians, would never be so extreme as to say that all of religion is a fairy tale or myth. Only atheists say religion should be declared dead and buried along with pagan idols and witchcraft. Liberal Christians would test the truth of the Bible by scientific analysis. Christian heroes would become the subject of objective biographers and historians. The liberal mainline churches that accept the process theology orientation would reject belief in the Virgin Mary, the bodily Resurrection, and the power of the saints to heal the sick. Liberals reject also the mystery that comes with the sudden conversion experience, the "born again" experience, with its mystical power to remake human nature in an instant. However, the evangelical, revival meeting type of conversion plays a major role in the purpose and goals of the fundamentalist Christians.

A major division within the Protestant church is over the issue of whether science should be permitted to dilute or even destroy a Christian's faith in the power of faith and mystery. A pioneer forerunner of a liberal Protestant religion was the minister Josiah Strong, who wrote two best-selling books, one in 1881, *Our Country, Its Possible Future and Its Present Crisis,* and in 1893 *The New Era, or the Coming Kingdom.* First Strong saw that science has a proper place in the study of and the explanation of religious matters. "God's methods are scientific, and if we are to be intelligent helpers of God, our methods also must be scientific."[3] He deemed it proper that the Christian Church be more concerned with life on earth than in heaven. Strong was a forerunner of the Christian social gospel of the twentieth century. But his greatest concern was that the Protestant church was becoming so divided that it would eventually culminate in self-destruction. Pluralism in religion was a deplorable condition. In 1892 Strong organized the Evangelical Alliance, an ecumenical movement to secure brotherhood and unity among the many Protestant denominations. But Strong made one serious error in the promotion of Christian love and brotherhood. He deplored the fact that so many alien immigrants, Catholics and Jews from Eastern Europe, and Orientals were coming to America. These non-Protestant elements would eventually destroy the very foundations of the American way of life. The future progress of the nation must be preserved for the dominant and best people, the white, Anglo-Saxon, Protestant people. Immigration of these un-American groups must be restricted, if not totally prevented.

Other theologians, contemporary with Josiah Strong, who gave impetus to the introduction of science and the social gospel into the Protestant Christian church were Lyman Abbott and Henry Ward Beecher. In 1897 Abbott published *The Evolution of Christianity,* which presented the thesis that religion and the churches must change as time passes. It is God that remains the only stable controlling force in mankind's struggle for existence. Beecher, pastor of the Plymouth Church in Brooklyn, wrote and spoke in defense of science and evolution. He thought that the Bible ought to be subject to the scrutiny of scientific historical analysis, that anti-Semitism was un-Christian, and that it was proper for the Church to support the rights of labor and women to share equally in America's bounty.

But in truth the new liberalism that encouraged the scientific element in religion and salvation by way of social action and legislation was not accepted by the great majority of Protestant Christians. The road to salvation was still the one promised by the Apostles and the early Christian theologians, the way of prayer, individual confession of sins, and conversion. And if the personal souls were saved, in due time the world and all humanity would be saved, if not on earth then in heaven, by the grace of God.

Throughout the nineteenth century, especially in the latter half, another era of revivalism was experienced. The one evangelist minister who did most to maintain America's faith in the goodness of the old-fashioned religion was Dwight Moody of Chicago. Moody grew up in Boston but he moved to Chicago in 1856. For his time Moody was the most popular of all evangelists. He organized his Bible Institute to train ministers who would go forth and preach the coming of the Lord, that the end of the world was near, that the Panic of 1893 gave notice that the return of Christ was near, and that man's only salvation from the coming disaster was to get "right" with God and pray. Moody had no use for science and evolution, or for the social gospel. In God's good time the fate of the poor and oppressed would be solved in God's way. It is no wonder that Moody and his fundamentalistic beliefs won the support of America's middle class and the rich and powerful industrialists, the Carnegies, the Armours, the Wanamakers, the Chicago McCormicks. Moody was a master of the revival style of preaching, of which lively gospel music was an integral part. Moody's success could not have been achieved without the fiery music of his song-writing colleague, Ira Sankey.

Probably Moody's most famous successor was Billy Sunday, who in the early 1900s traveled across the nation winning converts to the Lord. An ex-professional ball player, Sunday mastered the art of spiritual gymnastics. To witness one of his Sunday services was to see a man gyrating across the pulpit in leaps and bounds, waving his arms as if they were windmills, shouting and weeping, all to create an emotional frenzy among his audience. As a boy of six I heard Billy Sunday preach in Sterling, Colorado. Aside from his emotional outbursts, my young memory recalls only one remark, made when two women began to leave the church before the meeting was over, and Sunday shouted to the ushers in the rear, "Rope those heifers and bring them back."

Evangelists like Dwight Moody who preach that the Second Coming is imminent, that all should make ready for the advent of Christ, have continued until the present, and likely they will be present in the Christian churches a thousand years from now.

Hal Lindsey, the author of the *Late Great Planet Earth*, sold eighteen million copies in which he predicts that the Earth is in its last days before Armageddon, the war between the forces of good and evil, a war that will happen near Haifa, Israel. Jesus will come, a thousand years of peace will follow, and then Christ will come again after a Middle East dictator blows up the earth in a nuclear holocaust. In 1981 Lindsey published a second book, *Countdown to Armageddon,* also a best seller. Charles Berlitz in his *Doomsday 1999* predicted that Armageddon will occur in the period 1989–99. Bill Maupin in Arizona predicted that the Second Coming would occur on the fortieth anniversary of the founding of Israel, or May 13, 1988. It is interesting to note that these prophets of doom used to blame the end of the world and Armageddon upon Communism and the Soviet Union. Hence it is imperative that the Christian United States must save the world from evil enemies by building up a massive military defense. That approach will have to change now.

Social Activism

Should organized church institutions engage in political action to secure a better condition for the masses of the people? Some Christians sincerely believe that the church and the state should remain separate and never should the Church engage in political action. If its members choose to vote their religious convictions, then that is good and proper. But other Christians, the more conservative and traditional ones, believe that the social group is not a Christian's concern, despite Christ's injunction to be our brother's keeper. This group says that when all humans are saved by justification by faith, then the world will have peace and prosperity. The road to social justice and reform is by way of prayer and a personal commitment to obey the commandments and to do good to others. Unfortunately, the Christians who are reluctant to support reforms and welfare measures for the poor and the less able citizens have found support in the theory of evolution. If it is the law of nature, God's law, that only the fittest of the species should survive, then a good Christian should not interfere with God's law. The poor and the unfortunate people must suffer their pain and endure their fate as best as possible without any outside aid. This cruel version of evolution as applied to the social condition is most often attributed to the British sociologist Herbert Spencer, and his theory of social Darwinism, and the American economist William Graham Sumner.

However today social Darwinism has been largely replaced by a more Christian social gospel and by a belief that the state has a responsiblity to improve the condition of its less fortunate citizens, a view shared by most liberal Christian churches. The social gospel or social justice programs of the several Christian churches had its origins among the Jewish prophets, like Micah, who said, "The Lord requires of you to do justice, and to love kindness, and to walk humbly with your God." Jesus said to feed the hungry and clothe the naked. Throughout history the Christian church has tried to fulfill the commandment to feed the hungry, care for the poor, and protect the weak. The Roman Catholic Church has often taken seriously its mission to help the weak and secure a more just and equitable distribution of the world's wealth. Among the Protestants, the first church to dedicate its purpose to the aid of the poor and the improvement of the lot of the working class and of women was the Methodist Church. John Wesley said that God had anointed him to preach to the poor and to help them. The social-gospel concept came into being about 1900, when the nation was struggling with the problem of how to control big business and the robber barons. Both farmers and workers suffered in the panics of 1887 and 1893, and out of this suffering a reform political movement, the Populist movement, arose. William Jennings Bryan ran for the presidency in 1896 on the Populist ticket. Although not elected Bryan gave support to the idea that Christians should become involved in politics for the sake of the poor and less fortunate. Out of the Populist movement came the presidency of Theodore Roosevelt and his "trust busting" legislation. Now it became possible and Christian for government to legislate reforms on behalf of social justice and equality.

In 1908 the Methodist Church issued a social reform program, "The Bill of Human Rights," the social gospel program. Other churches, both Catholic and Protestant, adopted similar programs by 1914. Among the leaders for social justice were Bishop Francis McConnell of the Roman Catholic Church, and John R. Mott, a wealthy Methodist industrialist, active in the Young Men's Christian Association movement, who organized the Student Christian Federation, later also the World Student Christian Federation. Mott was an active supporter of the social gospel and of ecumenical movements to include all Christians and Jews, which efforts led to the formation of the Federal Council of Churches in 1908. Many other Christian men were allied with the social gospel movement, including Walter Rauschenbusch, a Baptist minister, a professor at the Rochester Theological Seminary, and one who worked among the poor people in New York's Hell's Kitchen area, where he learned that the Christian church must come to the relief of the poor in the slums of the American cities. He wrote *Christianity and the Social Crisis* in 1886 and *Christianizing the Social Order* in 1912. Probably no single theologian did more to make the Christian church aware of its social responsibilities than Rauschenbusch, who died in 1918. It should be noted that he had the financial support and friendship of John D. Rockefeller, all of which was of much benefit to his promotion of the social gospel. Closely related to the social gospel mission was the effort to promote world peace, especially after the outbreak of World War I in 1914. Among the prominent names in support of the peace movement were Reinhold Niebuhr, the German theologian who later dared to oppose the Nazi regime in Germany; Harry F. Ward, a Methodist who organized the Federation for Social Service in 1907; the Rev. Ernest Tittle of Evanston, Illinois; and a number of liberal ministers, such as Harry Emerson Fosdick, Ralph W. Sockman, and G. Bromley Oxman.

Separation of Church and State

After the Civil War one more issue dividing the nation's religious community was the matter of separation of church and state. The Fourteenth Amendment to the Constitution, passed in 1868, guaranteed that all citizens of the United States enjoyed all of the basic rights and freedoms cited in the Constitution and the Bill of Rights. Did the clause enunciating separation of church and state in the First Amendment also apply to the several states? The Supreme Court gave an affirmative answer in the case of *Everson* v. *Board of Education* in 1948.

The church-state issue provoked many sharp conflicts between Catholics and Protestants, Protestants and Jews. Especially bitter were the disputes between liberal Protestant and conservative Protestant churches. Where is that thin line of separation to be drawn? And who is to decide where to draw that line? The definitive answer is the Supreme Court of the United States. As to where the line of separation is to be drawn, the Supreme Court throughout the history of the nation has hewed closely to the principle of strict separation, or Jefferson's concept of a wall between church and state, which should be built high, wide, and without any serious cracks.

Today most religious bodies in the United States have formed associations or agencies to promote the interests of each group. Such bodies might be labeled "political action" bodies designed to influence public opinion and to lobby in state and national legislatures. Most of these church-related action groups have come into being since 1900. The Federal Council of Churches, composed of the liberal, mainline Protestant churches, and now called the National Council of Churches of Christ in the U.S.A., was first organized in 1908. The Jewish B'nai B'rith Anti-Defamation League was founded in 1913, and the U.S. Catholic Conference was formed in 1917. In 1920 the American Civil Liberties Union came into being to provide legal assistance to those persons and groups who believed that their civil rights had been injured. The Jewish people also organized the American Jewish Committee and the American Jewish Congress. Liberal Protestants and various Jewish organizations joined forces in 1928 to form the National Conference of Christians and Jews, a powerful agency in the campaign for civil rights and the prosecution of acts of anti-Semitism and acts of discrimination and persecution of the black people of the nation. Are the organized action groups representing many different religious bodies an infringement upon the separation of church and state provision?

Almost without exception no serious challenge has ever been directed against special-interest pressure groups, be they of a secular or a religious nature. A democracy must permit, even encourage, the free expression of both individuals and groups no matter how distasteful some of the voices may appear to opposing interest groups. Even the active participation of religious leaders, the clergy and rabbis, has been accepted by the American people. Among the black people the effort to secure their rights and freedom has been spearheaded by black churches and such ministers as Martin Luther King, Jr., Ralph Abernathy, and Jesse Jackson. Catholic bishops are often the most vocal and best spokesmen in defense of the Catholic position on public issues. And to name the Protestant ministers who led many campaigns in defense of their churches would fill a book. Even the active campaign of the Rev. Pat Robertson and his "700 Club" for the presidency in 1988 generated no serious criticism, nor did the active efforts of the Moral Majority, led by the Rev. Jerry Falwell, for the Republication candidacy of Ronald Reagan.

Since most religious bodies of all persuasions have their organized agencies to influence political action it may be impossible for state and national legislatures to render any final verdict on where that wall of separation is to be built. Therefore the Supreme Court has been left with that responsibility. The most critical periods of conflict between the several religious bodies seems to occur following wartime eras. This was the case after World War I and World War II. In order to prosecute war efforts most vigorously, propaganda techniques are used to arouse the public's sense of patriotism. The appeal to religion, the claim that God is on our side, tends to intensify the religious and emotional feelings of the people. After the war is over these strong emotional feelings of patriotism tend to be expressed against those citizens who seem to be unpatriotic and un-American, which at one time meant black people, Asiatics, Catholics, and Jews. After World War I strong anti-Semitic feelings were expressed, and the Ku Klux Klan revival gave voice to great hatred for blacks, Catholics, and Jews. The Protestant community was split over the evolution issue and the Scopes trial in Kentucky. But the high point of anti-Catholicism occurred in 1928, with the nomination of Alfred Smith, governor of New York, as the Democratic candidate for the presidency. Protestant extremists were heard to be crying, "the pope is taking over the White House." As the Catholic forces after World War II began to seek public tax money for the support of parochial schools, the conservative Protestants and many of the liberal Protestants organized campaigns against any tax support for parochial schools. The climax of these Protestant protests came in 1948, with the organization of Protestants and Other Americans United for Separation of Church and State, and the publication of an extremely anti-Catholic book by Paul Blanshard, *American Freedom and Catholic Power,* in 1958. The sale and influence of this book was a powerful weapon used to defeat any aid for Catholic schools in the state and national legislatures.

Prior to the Civil War the issue of separation of church and state remained relatively subdued. Protestants outnumbered Catholics and Jews by overwhelming numbers. Moreover, the Protestants were generally not divided over the main issues, except over slavery. By 1850 most of the states had disestablished their state churches and had accepted the principle of tax-supported public elementary schools. A few southern states lagged behind on this matter. The general attitude was, if Catholics want their own schools, let them pay for them out of their own pockets. Protestants were quite content to send their children to public schools knowing that the school boards and the teachers were solid Protestants who would maintain a Protestant-oriented curriculum and a Puritan standard of student ethics. For proof of this one need only pick up a copy of a *McGuffey Reader,* which was widely used in the public schools before 1860.

Excepting slavery, only two pre–Civil War issues aroused any religious concerns. One was the sale and use of alcoholic beverages. Puritan Protestants viewed the use of alcohol as one of the deadly sins. Irish Catholics, Episcopalians, and Lutherans were much less concerned about alcoholic abuses. However, the prohibition forces did win one victory before 1860, namely when the state of Maine went dry in 1851.

The other issue concerned diplomatic representation to the Vatican in Rome. For nineteen years, 1848–1867 the United States sent a minister to the Vatican. But after the Civil War Protestant zealots opposed such concessions to the Catholics and finally forced President Andrew Johnson to withdraw the papal embassy. Only in 1983 was an ambassador sent to Rome again, a concession made by President Reagan to draw support from Democratic Catholics. It should be noted that the bitter conflicts between Catholics and Protestants were greatly diminished after the election of John F. Kennedy, a Catholic, to the presidency in 1960.

After 1920 the most serious conflict between Protestants and Catholics arose over the issue of aid to church schools. Between the fundamentalist Protestants and the liberal Protestants the issue was, to what extent could religious education and practices be permitted in the public schools? After 1900 large numbers of both Catholics and Jews had come to the United States from areas in Eastern Europe. As a result both groups had enlarged their numbers and their ability to speak with some force in state and local politics. Thus these groups were in a position to challenge the long-dominant voice of Protestants in the national arena of politics. This is one reason why so much legislation and so many court decisions occurred in the period after 1920.

Fortunately for the peace of the nation the Supreme Court decisions were accepted by the parties involved as fair and just decisions according to the judicial traditions of a democratic nation. Moreover, since 1950 both Protestant and Catholic groups have become sufficiently wise and tolerant to sit down together in an ecumenical session and attempt to resolve their differences in a friendly manner. Even the Christians have extended a welcoming hand to Jewish synagogues, thereby causing the American religious scene to offer the hope and promise that a truly Christian-Jewish fellowship can soon become a democratic reality.

In general the Supreme Court has maintained the Jeffersonian concept of a wall of separation, one that adheres to a strict exclusion of religion from public schools. As a rule the courts have accepted a traditional policy that churches should not be taxed by any government for all property used for religious and educational purposes. Any church property used for commercial profit is taxable, a decision rendered in 1984 against the Unification Church led by Sun Myung Moon. Also churches must pay the Social Security taxes for their employees, a decision that has angered many of the fundamentalistic churches, causing some of them to refuse to pay these taxes.

One of the first basic decisions affecting the issue of separation of church and state came in 1947, with the *Everson* v. *Board of Education* decision that public funds might be used to transport children to church schools. Protestants saw in this decision a crack in the wall of separation, but this concession to religious education has been maintained. A more basic decision came in 1948, when the Supreme Court ruled in the *McCollum* v. *Champaign Board of Education* that no religious instruction could be permitted in the public schools. Even released time for religious education conducted on off-school premises was disallowed. However, in 1952, in the *Zorach* case, the Supreme Court did approve of the released time policy for religious education when done outside school property.

In 1962 in the case *Engel* v. *Vitale,* the court outlawed the practice of prayer in any form, even silent, in the public schools. In 1863 in the *Abington School District* v. *Schempp* case, the Supreme Court ruled against Bible reading in the public classroom. In 1962 the Republican party included in its platform a provision for the use of prayer in the public schools. In 1966 and 1984 abortive attempts were made in Congress to amend the Constitution so as to permit prayer in the public schools.

Since 1960 both Catholic and conservative Protestant churches have sought to secure some form of public support for their church schools. In the 1973 case of *Levitt* v. *Committee of Public Education and Religious Liberty,* the court ruled against any form of tax aid to private and parochial schools. Since then various church groups have sought to circumvent this decision by advocating the use of credit vouchers by which any parent can use equivalent tax funds for the education of his or her children in any school of choice, public or private. So far this effort has not been successful.

In 1943 the Jehovah's Witnesses won a victory for their beliefs when the Supreme Court held that members of this church did not have to salute the flag, or say the pledge to the flag, or serve in the military. This decision applies to anyone who claims that his or her conscience or religious convictions are violated by a requirement to salute the flag and serve in the military.

Since 1980 fundamentalist Protestants who have failed to have Bible study and prayer inserted in the public schools have sought to achieve somewhat the same goals by charging that the public school curriculum and faculty are antireligious, even atheistic. These conservative groups cite as evidence that the public schools are teachings "secular humanism" in courses on social science, humanities, and science. The teaching of Darwinian evolution is considered most offensive. Since a direct attack on these "irreligious" subjects has failed the test as judged by the Supreme Court, the newest tactic is to have state legislatures require the teaching of "creation science" either as a substitute for scientific evolution or as a science subject that should be given equal space and time in the classroom along with scientifically based biology courses. In 1982 an Arkansas law that required the teaching of creation science was struck down by the Supreme Court. In 1987 a similar law in Louisiana was declared unconstitutional. Although the conservative religious forces in the nation have failed to have their agendas accepted by the Supreme Court they have not given up hope that soon they will prevail and win the battle against the liberals. In 1990 they achieved one victory when the Supreme Court authorized the right of religious student organizations to hold meetings in the public schools along with such other student groups as pep clubs and drama societies. Liberal Christians and Jews are alarmed by this crack in the wall of separation.

The Religious Makeup of the American Populace

In 1987 two sociologists, Wade Roof and William McKinney, made a study of American churches. They published it as a book entitled *American Mainline Religions.* From 1972 to 1984 surveys were conducted by the National Opinion Research Center to discover the membership composition of the major groupings of American religions. The results:

1. Mainline churches (American Baptists, American Lutherans, United Presbyterians, United Methodists, Episcopalians, United Church of Christ, and Disciples of Christ) accounted for 32.9 percent of all Christian memberships.

2. Conservative Protestants totaled 15.8 percent (this group includes Southern Baptists, 9.2 percent; Pentecostals, 2.5 percent; and others, 4.1 percent).
3. Roman Catholics: 25 percent.
4. Jews of all groups: 2.3 percent.
5. All other churches: 8.0 percent.
6. No religious preference: 6.9 percent.

During the time after 1950 the mainline churches in the Protestant faith suffered significant losses in membership. Some declined as much as 10 percent in a single decade. On the average the conservative Protestant churches increased their membership as much as 100 percent, while the Roman Catholics gained about 25 percent.[4]

The study reports also what percentage of church members attend services regularly. The national average was 46 percent with the Jehovah's Witnesses having a 77 percent attendance, Mormons 64 percent, conservative churches 58 percent, Roman Catholics 55 percent, mainline Protestants 40 percent, and Unitarian-Universalists 22 percent. In terms of the educational level of the church memberships the Jews ranked first, then the mainline Protestants. The Catholics were average, and at the lower end of the scale were the conservative protestant and the black churches. When members were asked if they believed in a life after death, the national average affirming that belief was 77 percent. Nonchurch members replied with only 44 percent believing, and Unitarian-Universalists with 43 percent. On the upper end of the scale the conservatives replied 89 percent affirmatively, mainline Protestants 83 percent, Roman Catholics 75 percent, and black members 72 percent.

Of some importance is the matter of where in the United States these various groups tend to be concentrated. The nation today has a mobile population, so the degree of one group being most populous in one section of the country is less likely than it was a hundred years ago. Yet some regional differences remain. The Mormons dominate the areas of Utah, Arizona, and Idaho. The Lutherans tend to be concentrated in the Midwest, around the Great Lakes areas, and predominantly in rural and small town localities. The southern tier of states shows a heavy concentration of conservative Protestants, especially the Southern Baptists. The Roman Catholics are primarily in urban industrialized areas, those cities around the Great Lakes, the Ohio Valley, and in New York City. Episcopalians are mostly in large cities, and rather evenly distributed in both northern and southern cities. The Jews and Unitarian-Universalists are usually concentrated in large cities in the Northeast. Mainline Protestants are widely distributed across the nation, both in the cities and in rural areas. The liberal Protestants tend to be found largely among the well-to-do middle classes, the more educated people, and, as a rule, are apt to live more in the suburbs of large cities than in the central city. Black Protestants are found largely in the rural areas of the South and in the northern industrial cities such as New York, Chicago, Philadelphia, Detroit, Cleveland, Gary, and Pittsburgh.

Among the new Protestant groups, the largest single one is the Assemblies of God, with over eleven thousand churches and two million members in the

United States, sixteen million overseas. It has become a significant force in the religious life of America. The Assemblies of God was formed in Phoenix, Arizona, in 1914. Between 1979 and 1985 the membership of the church increased 23 percent. Originally the Assemblies of God was popularly known as the "Holy Rollers."

Fundamentalism

After the Civil War, and more so after 1900, Protestantism became increasingly divided. New Protestant churches came into being. The liberal churches, those adhering to liberal and scientifically oriented theologies were labeled by the conservatives as being anti-Christian, pro-atheistic, and heretical. These conservatives, many of whom left the mainline churches, became known as the "fundamentalists."[5] In a series of statements issued in 1909 and known collectively as "The Fundamentalists" there began a formal recognition of this conservative wing of Protestantism, the heir of the Moody form of Protestantism. Over a period of ten years over three million copies of these fundamental statements were circulated. Theological seminaries and church publishing houses were brought into being to spread the fundamental gospel. The World's Christian Fundamentals Association was organized to combat the evils of modernism and science in religion. Some writers have credited Dwight Moody as being the father of fundamentalism, for at the Niagara Conference of Protestant Conservatives in 1985 five principles were adopted: inerrancy of the Bible, the Virgin Birth, the deity of Jesus, the atonement of Jesus on the cross, and the physical resurrection of Jesus and his eventual bodily return to Earth at the time of the Second Coming. In brief, all fundamentalists accept these five basic elements of belief. In addition, fundamentalists believe that it is proper for Christians to engage in political action to promote their beliefs and to put an end to the heresy of secular humanism, communism, and the existence of evolution ideology and abortion.

Within the ranks of the fundamentalists there is a more extreme group that calls itself the Christian Reconstructionists. Their ultimate goal is to establish a theocratic state by all possible means, including propaganda, religious conversion, and political action. A few would even support revolutionary violence. They would have America resemble a state similar to the one Iran has had under the control of the radical Shiite Moslems and the Ayatollah Khomeini. The Deuteronomic code of morals would be enforced. Women would be confined to the home under the rule of their husbands. The church would govern the state and the governors would be the ministers.[6]

Today a principal center of the fundamentalists is Jerry Falwell's church in Lynchburg, Virginia. Wheaton College, outside of Chicago, is also a major center for educating fundamentalist ministers. Fundamentalist churches for the most part are found among the Southern Baptists and other southern denominations. Bob Jones University in South Carolina is another center for training fundamentalist ministers. Tim LaHaye, a Baptist minister, has been a successful publicist for fundamentalist views in his books and television programs. He says that no secular humanist should be permitted to hold any public office, and that at least 25 percent of all government jobs should be given to conservative Protestants.

If the fundamentalist churches should gain control of the United States, and they did their best to do so when Ronald Reagan was elected president in 1980, they would place the Bible ahead of the Constitution. A Puritan society would be reborn in which women would be confined to the home, abortions and contraceptives would be outlawed, extramarital sex and prostitution would be banned, and children would attend publicly funded church schools. Feminist movements would be regarded as subversive, anti-Christian organizations. Public funds now supporting social and welfare programs would be used to support a strong military program. The fundamentalists are among the most ardent proponents of national defense and military action to keep America strong.

It is interesting to note that the same fundamentalists who are so opposed to science in religion have no hesitation to use the best of modern electronic technology in the fields of communication to promote and evangelize their religious views.

Among certain fundamentalist groups anti-Semitic attitudes seem to have been replaced in recent years by an ardent pro-Israel point of view. Critics of the fundamentalists are puzzled when they see rabbis being invited to speak from church pulpits and the fundamentalist ministers conducting tours to Israel. Moreover, it seems strange that these churches have become active lobbyists in favor of financial and military support for the state of Israel. Such support began in the early 1980s, when Menachem Begin came to power in Israel. From about 1965 to the present certain fundamentalists and evangelical church leaders, such as Jerry Falwell, Jimmy Swaggart, and Pat Robertson, have endorsed a pro-Israel support policy. A most radical group of fundamentalists, called the Temple Mount Faithful, have raised funds for the destruction of the Islamic mosque in Jerusalem, the sacred Dome of the Rock, so that the third Jewish Temple might be build on this site, the site of the original Jewish Temple.

The explanation for this anomaly in the attitude of the fundamentalists toward the Jews and Israel has been given by Robert Friedman, a longtime journalist working in the Middle East. Friedman believes that for the fundamentalists the establishment of the state of Israel in 1948 has fulfilled biblical prophecy. The advent of Israel marks the beginning of that time when the world will be destroyed by war or some other divine catastrophe. The Jews, for the most part, will be killed. Then Christ will return to earth and rule as king over the kingdom of God. All surviving Jews will become Christians. So Israel and its rebirth in Palestine hails the day when Christianity will triumph over all other faiths in the world.

More than half of the American Protestants are fundamentalists, either belonging to some form of a conservative fundamentalist or evangelical church or remaining within the mainline churches. Since 1870 most of the new denominations in the United States have been organized under the banner of the evangelical churches. In brief, the evangelicals wish to recover and to expand the kind of religion which our forefathers enjoyed, a religion which feels the inward voice of God directing their daily lives, a religion expressed more in emotion and feelings than in reason and science, with little concern for social causes, international peace movements, and ecumenical programs to unite the Christian fellowship or to join with non-Christian religions for the sake of world peace and brotherhood.

The Pentecostal Movement

Closely related to the evangelical church movement is the rise of the Pentecostal form of Protestantism. Beginning in the 1890s a revival movement prompted many Protestants to seek to return to the primitive Christian church of the first century. A traditional date for the birth of the Pentecostal movement was when students at Bethel Bible College in Topeka, Kansas, in 1900, were given an assignment to find evidence to support baptism by the Holy Spirit. The students concluded that the best evidence for baptism was that the baptized person could speak in tongues, *glossolalia*. The students were so excited about their discovery that some began to speak in tongues, in the manner of the New Testament Pentecostals. Methodists, because of John Wesley's "heart warming" experience at Aldersgate, were especially susceptible to the Pentecostal movement. According to most historians, the first truly Pentecostal church was founded in Topeka, Kansas, at Bethel College by Charles Fox Parham in 1900. His disciple, William T. Seymour founded a second black Pentecostal church in Los Angeles in 1906. In brief, the evangelicals and the Pentecostals expressed their religious beliefs in exciting revival meetings and church services where there was an abundance of "hell fire" preaching, lusty singing of gospel tunes, swaying of arms and body, often shouted "amens" from the congregation, and occasionally voices speaking out in unknown, unintelligible sounds. The black churches in America use a very similar form of exciting worship service. There is a minimum of Bible study but what the mind misses the heart more than compensates for.

The evangelical spirit caught on after 1900 and continues to grow. From out of the Methodist Church came another Church of the Nazarene in 1908, founded in Pilot Mound, Texas. An offshoot of Methodism was "Good News" Methodism, a small group based in Wilmore, Kentucky, site of the Asbury Theological Seminary. By 1985 evangelical and Pentecostal churches were all over the world, the largest single group being the Assembly of God Churches. Jimmy Swaggart's television ministry has brought the Assembly of God's mission to Latin America and the Orient. The single largest evangelical church is in South Korea, with a membership of over a hundred thousand people. If television audiences are included, the evangelical and Pentecostal churches and their cobelievers in the mainline churches may total almost three hundred million followers. It is estimated that in the United States the memberships of the evangelical churches outnumber those in the Pentecostal churches by two to one.

In a biography of Oral Roberts, David Harrell summarizes the tenets of belief for the Pentecostal churches:

1. The ability to speak in tongues (Acts 1:5, 2:1–4, 8:16–17, and 10:44–46).
2. Divine healing is a part of God's plan (Matthew 8:16–17 and Mark 16:14–18).
3. The sign of total sanctification is made evident by an intense, instantaneous awareness that the Holy Spirit has entered the body (Acts 26:18).
4. Belief in the Second Coming of Christ, or in the "dispensational premillennialism" (1 Thessalonians 4:15–18 and Matthew 24:29–49).
5. A Puritan type of morality as revealed by a plain lifestyle, wearing no jewelry, abstaining from alcohol and tobacco, and rejecting such sinful pleasures as gambling and dancing.

The belief in dispensational millennialism developed in the mid-nineteenth century when a British theologian by the name of John Nelson Darby came to the United States and announced that he had discovered a new interpretation of the millennium experience as described in Revelation, chapter 20. He concluded that all of human history from the time of creation to the end of time after the millennium could be divided into seven stages. In each stage God makes a new covenant with his people. Christians had now entered the sixth stage, the last one before Christ returns to Earth. Soon the end of the world will be upon all Christians, after which the seventh stage would arrive, and Christ would return to earth to establish the kingdom of God.

In general Protestant evangelicals accepted the Darby concept of how the millennium would arrive. Dwight Moody preached the dispensational or premillenian interpretation of the eschatological doctrine of Christianity, a belief that holds that Christ will return to earth before the millennium, the thousand-year period of theocratic rule on earth.

During the 1900s another interpretation of Revelation came into the evangelical message of the final days, a view known as postmillennialism. This interpretation was more hopeful and optimistic. No longer were human beings seen as hopeless sinners doomed to suffer the torments of sin and pain before Christ would come to restore them to a state of glory and eternal happiness. Postmillennial theology asserts that the kingdom of God on earth is already in progress. Christians are being redeemed from sin and are being restored to a state of perfection. As Christians are redeemed so a new society of Christlike virtue, justice, and love is being created. It should be noted that the creation of a Christian society is not achieved through political action, only by the action of being a "born again" baptized Christian. Christians are now in the last dispensation. After a thousand years of striving for perfection, Christ will return to claim his bride, the Christian Church and its followers.

The Jehovah's Witnesses

One group that has placed all of its religious convictions in one basket labeled "the Second Coming of Christ" is the Jehovah's Witnesses. The members of this faith prefer to call their church building an assembly hall, or the kingdom hall. The name of the denomination is taken from Isaiah 63:12, "You are my witnesses with Jehovah, and I am God." For the Witnesses the Bible is inerrant and the only guide to salvation. The Witnesses operate as an incorporated body, which includes a Tract Society and the Watchtower Bible Society. The founder of the Witnesses was Charles Taze Russell, who in 1884 incorporated his movement, hence the Witnesses are sometimes called the "Russellites."

The Witnesses are primarily concerned with preparing as many souls as possible to meet their Lord in the Second Coming. Every member is obligated to be a personal witness, a missionary. Like the Mormons, they are often seen going from door to door in the cities distributing their Watchtower tracts and books, encouraging people to come to kingdom hall and receive the message that Christ has arrived. Russell proclaimed that in 1914 Christ became king in heaven and he cast out Satan, which set off a chain of catastrophic events in the world, the first one being the outbreak of World War I. Although Christ is not visible to the human eye his presence is revealed in the outbreak of these terrible disasters on earth. So people must now prepare for a thousand-year period in which Christ will rule over the earth. At the end of a thousand years death and hell will be destroyed. Only 144,000 souls will enter heaven (Revelation 7:4). The remaining billions of souls on earth will continue to live forever on earth, and earth will become a heaven. All evil will be gone and the righteous will live in one world, one nation in peace, after their resurrection from their graves (Micah 4). The New Jerusalem will be built in today's Palestine, in Jerusalem.

The Jehovah's Witnesses have no clergy or ruling elders. All members, men and women, can be ordained to speak, yet the women do seem to play an inferior role in the church. No sabbath is observed, but the members meet on Sunday for Bible study. They have no seminaries, but each member studies to become a pastor in fact, witness to God's truth, which all people should have the opportunity to hear and to read.

The Worldwide Church of God

Another religious body which was founded on the expectation that Christ is soon to return is the Worldwide Church of God. Its founder, Herbert Armstrong, left a career in business that had suffered repeated failures to turn to the business of doing God's work in 1926. Armstrong made a serious study of the Bible in the hope that he could unravel its mysteries. After several years of study he formulated a creed for his new church. The tenets of belief were published in

1934 in a magazine called *Plain Truth*. This magazine was distributed free of charge across the nation and even across the world.

The Worldwide Church and its beliefs are very strange to most Christians. The claim is made that all other Christian churches, Protestants and Catholics, are in error. From the beginning the Christian church was led astray by Simon Magus and his Gnostic heresy. The true Christian church was born on Pentecost Day, A.D. 33, when Christ appeared to 120 disciples in Jerusalem. Armstrong claimed that the true heir of the Christian church is his Worldwide Church of God. This true church developed in Smyrna, was kept alive by the French Waldensians during the Middle Ages, and then was brought to America in the nineteenth century when a Baptist sect settled in the Willamette Valley of Oregon. The Worldwide Church became the successor to this Oregon group when it was established in 1931. The mission of the Worldwide Church is to save the world from war and disunity. God will bring forth on earth a worldwide constitution and government, a theocracy that derives its power from God and will erase from the earth all poverty, disease, famine, war, and every other form of human peril. Armstrong accepted all of the biblical prophecies about the Apocalypse as told in the books of Daniel and Revelation. He saw no symbolism or mythology in the message of Revelation. The Second Coming is inevitable. The war of Armageddon will occur and Satan will be defeated. For a thousand years Christ will rule over the world and its capital will be in Jerusalem. The world will be divided into twelve provinces and the Apostles will govern them. Second in command under Christ will be Daniel. The resurrected saints will become the new world's bureaucrats. After a thousand years a second judgment will be rendered and all condemned souls will be given a second chance for salvation. Eventually the reign of Christ will prevail all over the world and for eternity.

The Worldwide Church rejects the idea of the Trinity. It claims that the Christian Church is one family in which God, Christ, and all believers are equal members in God's family. The church is ruled by a body of elders that administers the finances and conducts a most simple form of church service. Since there is no clergy the church members, the laity, are in charge of all worship services.

Christian Scientists

A nineteenth-century church most unlike either the conservative or mainline Christian Churches was Mary Baker Eddy's Christian Science Church, or the Church of Christ Science. One must not take the term "science" as being indicative that she was uniting science and religion into some form of a new Unitarian type church. Far from it, as the Christian Science repudiates the very basis of scientific thought, that is, that the universe is a physical, material fact of reality and subject to the rules of natural law and mathematics. The Christian Science world is one of mysticism in which, like Plato, reality is in the invisible world of God or Idea. Mary Baker Eddy had since youth suffered pain from a spinal injury. Medical science did not seem to give her relief so she sought out quack doctors, like a hypnotist by the name of Quimby and a minister who preached a brand of Swedenborg mysticism. She also began to study the Bible for clues to the faith healing process practiced by Jesus. After she married she wrote a book on mental health and in 1875 published her masterwork, *Science and Health with the Key to the Scriptures*. This book, along with the Bible, became the Scripture for the Christian Scientists. In 1879 Eddy established the first Christian Science Church, the mother church in Boston, which became the center of authority for the church and the source of a most respectable newspaper, the *Christian Science Monitor*. Scholars who wish objective reporting of world news will resort to the *Monitor* almost as frequently as to the prestigious *New York Times*.

Eddy found relief from pain in her search for healing by way of the Scripture. She wished to share this "good news" with all other people. Medical doctors were not happy as Christian Science practitioners competed with them for business. Scientists scoffed at Eddy's absurd ideas. Most other Christian Churches mocked her beliefs in faith healing as well as her ideas about the nature of the universe. But her church survived criticism and grew, so that in every American town of any size a person could find a small building or a room that houses a reading room open to the public free of charge. In most cities and towns over 10,000 a Christian Science Church could be seen, identifiable by its domed room made in the image of a classical Greek temple.

Christian Science views the physical world and the human body as illusions. Reality is in the spirit, or God. God is no divine person, but the divine principle of all that exists, including the human mind and body. When the person's mind is in tune with the divine principle then healing will follow. In the body of Jesus was the divine principle and so his healing miracles were not miracles at all. These acts of healing the sick and raising bodies from the dead resulted from the fact that Jesus was only fulfilling the divine law of nature or of God. The curse that man suffers evil and disease stems from all material aspects of life. If one reads and interprets divine Scripture correctly then all human illnesses can be healed. Christian Science teaches one how to heal the broken body. The Holy Trinity is not the Father, Son, and the Holy Spirit, but life, truth, and love. Through perfect prayer healing can be effected. Prayer is not a petition for God's help, but a plea for spiritual understanding of God's power. The more specialized instruction must come from a professionally trained practitioner, who is neither a physician nor a minister. This person not only instructs in the healing process but also conducts the worship services. Until recently practitioners were denied access to hospitals, or to performing surgery or dispensing drugs, but within limits they can practice medicine and receive Medicare payments. Death is only for the irrelevant, physical part of the body. That which is real, the part of us which is God, will live forever.

Christian Science healing has caused great debate and skepticism. No doubt there are certain psychosomatic ailments that Christian Science and mental healing can cure, but when Christian Science attempts to heal broken bones and cure cancer then cause for doubt becomes legitimate. Faith healing is a common belief and practice among charismatic and Pentecostal Christians. The ministry of the television evangelist Oral Roberts includes belief in faith healing. The Assemblies of God Churches accept that faith healing is true. In 1977 the Episcopal Church issued a new prayer book. It gave sanction to the practice of the "laying on of hands" in the conduct of healing services.

Isms and Cults

During the 1970s a number of semireligious cults in the United States promoted nonmedical healing programs. One was the transcendental meditation cult introduced from India by Maharishi Mahesh Yogi. Basically this cult's program was a form of Hindu yoga in which instruction was given as to how to breathe properly and how to meditate by reciting over and over a mantra while in a state of deep sleep or a trance. Stress, so prevalent in our high-paced, competitive society, can probably be relieved by transcendental meditation, but as a cure for most ills the cult promoted a fraud.

From Japan came Zen Buddhism in the 1960s, which also claimed to be able to reduce stress and promote good health by learning how to breathe properly and practice meditation in the lotus position, which then would destroy personal ego drives, after which the person could become master of self and thereby able to endure the pains and pressures of the external world.

In the 1980s one more health cult appeared, one that seemed to be based more on magic and occult phenomena than on any scientific facts. This cult, the New Age cult promoted by the actress Shirley MacLaine, has had a popular acceptance. MacLaine's book on the subject doubled its sales in five years after 1980. Not only was her book widely received by ordinary people, but business executives, movie stars, stock brokers, and other prominent people began to accept New Age principles. Whatever the New Age cult may be, it is not Satanism, atheism, or some form of Hindu mysticism. Probably it is a form of Christianity in which Christ is stripped of his divinity. If anything, New Age ideology resembles a form of pantheism in which God is found in all things. The New Age cult employs a mixture of psychology, religion, and superstition to build a program guaranteed to provide good health and success. It is estimated that Shirley MacLaine has made over a million dollars from her promotion of the New Age program. The New Age message says that modern science offers little hope for health and wealth. Better routes to success are found in the occult, magic, and the unseen cosmic forces known by astrologists. Healing is done by using the techniques of primitive man, using witchdoctors, shamans, divination, sorcery, the magic found in pyramidal structures and in crystals. Special Tibetan bells, herbal teas, and Viking runes are all useful sources for finding the good life. Moreover, all humans are a part of God and nature (pantheism) and hence mankind is under moral obligation to protect the envirnoment and all of God's creatures. The New

Agers hope also to be able to communicate with the spirits of our ancestors and with creatures on planets in outer space. New Age teachers or gurus are called "channelers." One channeler, Jo An Karl, claims that she married St. Peter and was persecuted with him in Rome. Shirley MacLaine has related that her channeler convinced her to go to Lake Titicacao in Bolivia, where she met passengers on board an alien spaceship.

Christian churches view the New Age movement with suspicion, but it is not likely that they will suffer any great loss of membership to the New Age cult. It is estimated that there are over five hundred cults in the United States, a third of them in California.[7]

Another cult is the Church of Scientology, founded by L. Ron Hubbard in California in 1959. Hubbard is said to have made a million dollars a week from his writings and lectures.[8] Hubbard is the author of the key guide book for the cult, *Dianetics: The Modern Science of Mental Health,* published in 1950. Hubbard was a science fiction writer who says that he discovered new secrets of the mind by which he could improve one's health and business success, all for a fixed fee. Dianetics holds that the mind has two parts, the analytic or rational part, the conscious mind, and a reactive or intuitive mind that protects us from danger, a mind that might be compared to Freud's id. The reactive mind causes our psychoses and neuroses. To heal this mind Hubbard believes that one must bring the forces stored in the reactive mind, "engrams," to the surface of consciousness. Thus rational behavior would be restored. Special techniques are required such as a system of questions and answers called "auditing." Also a special machine similar to an electrocardiograph is used to develop a superego and thereby effect cures for disease, poverty, and other afflictions. The key to health is to overcome evil spirits that came to earth seventy million years ago when Xenu, the ruler of all of the planets, proceeded to reduce the world's population by exploding a volcano. In this volcanic explosion a host of evil spirits was released to plague and destroy the human population. Basic Scientology is a form of religion that holds that man is a spiritual being quite separate from his physical body. If the body can be rid of the engrams in the reactive mind, then the ego or analytic mind can restore the person to its pure spiritual state of being.

The number of cults and other strange religious bodies is innumerable. There is the Pillars of Fire Church, founded by Alma White in Denver in 1910. There is also the Four Square Gospel Church founded by Aimee Semple McPherson in Los Angeles in 1927. The Four Square Gospel Church follows an extreme form of charismatic evangelicalism in which faith healing is practiced and the message from the pulpit is preparation for the Second Coming, preached in a style of high dramatics, using all of the emotional appeals known to the theater. McPherson was a Hollywood movie star who probably made more money preaching her gospel than she could have made in the movies. I saw one of her revival meetings in Denver in 1925, and it was the equal of any Broadway production. McPherson, a beautiful woman, dressed in the white robes of an angel, truly hypnotized an audience of two thousand, after which hundreds approached the stage, where she blessed them and prayed for them. How many crippled and ailing souls were healed that night is unknown.

Another church in the United States founded by a married couple, Charles and Myrtle Fillmore, is the Unity Church. The Fillmores believed that they could improve on Mary Baker Eddy's Christian Science faith healing mission. The Fillmores had come to Colorado for their health, and while there they conceived of a plan to restore a person's health by faith healing. The Unity Church subscribes to the idea that God dwells within each person and that heaven and hell exist here and now on earth. God is love and God has the secret formula for good health. If one follows the laws of God or nature (pantheism can be found in the Unity faith) then one can gain a state of good health. No one need doubt that the miracles performed by Jesus were real, for Jesus was only following the laws of God. The Unity movement became quite popular in the 1890s, but today, although it survives, it attracts little support from the Christians in the United States.

Two imports from the Orient have attracted a good amount of public attention in recent years, the Unification Church (the "Moonies") and the Hare Krishna movement.

From Korea came a charismatic preacher, Sun Myung Moon, who in the 1960s came to the United States and said that he was the "Lord of the Second Advent," a reincarnation of Christ. Moon, a former Presbyterian, believed that the United States was the proper place to receive the new Messiah, the third Adam, the second Christ. His theology was a mixture of Christianity, old Korean beliefs, and the creations of Moon's own mind. Jesus had achieved spiritual salvation, but he had failed to reach a physical salvation. He would bring to earth a perfect social system, a perfect marriage and family life, and a world freed of evil and Communism. If people could come together and live in a communal relationship, sharing their wealth and living in a relative state of poverty, perfect happiness and godliness could be achieved. Moonies have been recruited from among the young people of the country, where, so the critics argue, these young recruits have been brainwashed to leave their families and occupations to go to live in a disciplined community ruled by Moon. Although the Unification Church preaches a lifestyle of poverty, Moon lives in luxury. The Moonie communes, about a hundred persons in each commune, live a monastic type of life, working hard on the Moonie farms, or in fishing factories, business establishments, contributing their earnings to their church while living an ascetic life, abstaining from sex, alcohol, and drugs, and worshiping their leader, Moon. The Unification Church owns much property.

The Unification Church has been under fire from other Christian groups and the law enforcement agents of the United States and California. The church has been accused of brainwashing and kidnapping young people, of deceiving its membership, and of failing to pay its share of taxes. One practice that has outraged the Christian people of the nation has been its practice of holding mass weddings for its young members. In 1982 a mass wedding of over two thousand couples was held in Madison Square Garden in New York City. Moon made the marital choices. The couples were told that they would have to wait over three year before they could consummate the marriage. In 1989 the California Supreme Court held that the Unification Church and Moon were liable for deceiving the members, a verdict upheld by the U.S. Supreme Court. Ted Patrick has written a critical account of the "Moonie" church, *Let Our Children Go.*

The Hare Krishna movement has become familiar to many Americans who travel by air, for airports are common sites for them to sell their publications and solicit funds to support their mission. This movement came to the United States from India in the 1960s when a guru, A. C. Bhaktivedanta Swami Prabhypada, began to recruit members for the Hare Krisha movement. Like the Moonies the Hare Krishnas sought to recruit young people who might be interested in new and exotic religions, and who would be eager workers for the cause. The basic belief of the Krishnas is that Lord Krishna is the supreme personality through whom the person's soul can be united with the universal soul, Brahman, or God, or absolute truth. The human soul is a part of Brahman, the individual soul and the universal soul are one. Krishna, also pure soul, dwells within the human soul. Man is both soul and body, and man's duty is to purify his soul so that it can unite with Krishna and Brahman.

Soul purification is achieved by the usual Hindu processes, through meditation, the practice of yoga, living on a vegetarian diet, refraining from alcohol and gambling, abstinence from sex except for procreation, and spending much time in reading the Hindu scriptures, the Bhagavad Gita. Time must be reserved for soliciting funds and doing some work for pay, while dressed in the saffron garb of a Buddhist monk. Hare Krishnas regard themselves as being self-sufficient, with no need for parents or the external society. The sole purpose of life is to follow *bhakti,* the rules of discipline by which the impure body can be restored to purity and to Brahman.

Black Churches of America

One American church with a separate existence and mission is the black Protestant churches. Before 1920 almost all black worshipers were in Protestant churches, the great majority being in either a Baptists or a Methodist Church. Today blacks are increasingly finding more support for their drive for freedom and equality, especially for a good education for their children, within the Roman Catholic Church. It is estimated that there are now two million black Catholics and a thousand black parishes. It should be said that the black parishioners are not always comfortable with the staid formalism of a Catholic service, for in the black religious tradition the typical service has followed the evangelical style of much emotion, singing, and audience participation.

The largest black denomination is the National Baptist Convention, USA, with over five million members. There are also two other Baptist groups and three Methodist conferences that total over twelve million members. Within the urban ghettoes of the large urban centers there are thousands of small storefront churches that provide religious outlets for many poor black families.

Before the American Revolution the free blacks and the slaves normally worshiped in white churches. During the early 1800s separate black churches were organized in the North, most of them being either Methodist or Baptist. Until the Civil War the slaves, for the most part, worshipped with their masters, where they could be supervised. Where separate black churches existed they were apt to become centers for revolt. It was in their own churches that the slaves could, at least, dream of freedom.[9] After the Civil War the blacks were free to have their own churches. By 1900 two-thirds of the black churches were either Baptist or Methodist. It is unnecessary to say that the great majority of black congregations worshiped in simple, humble buildings, served by an uneducated minister who worked six days a week at some form of labor and preached to his people on the seventh day. But too many white Americans have failed to understand what the black churches have meant to their people. In slavery the church was the sole source of hope and redemption from slavery. After the Civil War the free black churches also gave hope and courage to the millions of blacks who continued to live in a virtual state of slavery or peonage, working the plantations for meager wages. In the post–Civil War era it is true that northern churches and philanthropists contributed money and leadership to build Negro colleges and welfare agencies. It is true that the civil rights movements of the 1960s and since had great support from the liberal Protestant and Catholic Churches, plus millions of other liberal citizens who joined various human rights organizations to secure through legislation the promise found in the American Constitution and spelled out in the Fourteenth and Fifteenth amendments. But no white American can dismiss or deny that black people, through their churches, played a major role of self-help in securing what political and economic gains they have received since 1960.

Throughout American history the black churches have been one of the few avenues through which black people could voice their cry for freedom. Black ministers like Martin Luther King, Jr., Hosea Williams, Jesse Jackson, Ralph Abernathy, and Malcolm X and Elijah Mohammed of the Black Muslims, have all played a major role in the march for freedom. Such black organizations as the National Urban League, the National Association for Colored People, Operation PUSH, the Southern Christian Leadership Conference, the Students for a Democratic Society, and the Student Non-Violent Coordinating Committee all share an important part in giving to the black people their political freedom and civic equality, at least in the eyes of the law, opening doors for equal opportunity for education at all levels, and gaining a chance to secure a fair share of the labor market. More and more middle-class blacks are making their way into the American capitalist system with their own businesses. In the area of television and entertainment the names of Bill Cosby, Oprah Winfrey, Louis Armstrong, Mohammed Ali, Sammy Davis, Jr., and hundreds of others have become household names and friends in most American homes.

Black people have miles to travel before they are accepted on an equal basis in white America. Racial bias and racial conflicts continue to mar the American Dream. But more and more white America accepts the reality of life that America is a plural society in which there is no room for anti-Semitism, anti-Catholicism, and most of all no room for holding on to the myth of black inferiority and white, Aryan supremacy.

For the unforeseeable future, a century or more, white and black Americans will pursue separate lives in the areas of social relations, marriages, church activities, and friendships. The two races will work together, participate together in community activities and in political campaigns, but after the work day is over, each will leave to go home to a largely racially segregated community. This lifestyle is still the one most preferred by both white and black Americans. Before blacks can accept white Americans on an open and trustworthy basis, they must first find their own identity as a race of people with a noble heritage.

Black leaders in church and politics have yet to make a decision as to whether to achieve their unfulfilled goals of equality by means of political action, education, and passive nonviolence, as advocated by Martin Luther King, Jr., or by the gun, as advocated by the Black Panthers or, occasionally, Louis Farrakan of the Nation of Islam. The devastating failure of the Black Panther party in 1969–70 demonstrated that the road of violence is futile in the face of the power of the great white majority in the United States. Blacks and whites since 1970, despite all-too-frequent incidents of racial violence, are learning the art of cooperation as more and more blacks assume positions of leadership in the nation. Black city mayors, black governors, and even black presidential candidates, are all becoming acceptable to more and more white Americans.

Moves toward Unity

Since the beginning of the twentieth century leaders in both Catholic and Protestant churches have begun to see the folly of agitating the divisions within the Christian body. Painfully, few brave Christians have dared to speak out on behalf of the common bonds among the Christians. It is time to bring to a halt the growing number of Protestant denominations. It is time to seek reconciliation with the Roman Catholics, and to offer to the Jews the hand of brotherhood. Protestant denominations have begun to come together in a denominational unity. The northern and southern Methodists joined together in 1939, and in 1969 the Methodists united with the United Methodist Church of today. In 1984 the northern and southern Presbyterians united to form the present Presbyterian Church U.S.A. In 1957 the New England Congregational Church joined with the German Evangelical and Reformed Churches to form the current United Church of Christ.

In 1961 the Unitarian and the Universalist churches united to make the Unitarian-Universalist Association. In 1918 the northern and southern Lutheran churches came together as the United Lutheran Church. In 1962 this Lutheran

Church joined with the Augustana Evangelical Lutheran Church to form the Lutheran Church of America. In 1988 the church incorporated other Lutherans, the American Lutheran Church, and the Association of Evangelical Lutheran Churches. It is the fourth largest Protestant denomination, with over five million members.

Not only have Protestant denominations come together in unity, since 1908 the several major Protestant denominations have begun to cooperate in a national campaign to promote the social gospel and to minimize the doctrinal bickerings of past decades. In 1908 the National Council of Churches of Christ in America was formed. It was modified and became the National Council of Churches in 1950. This alliance of mainline Protestant Churches did not include the Catholics and the fundamentalist-evangelical churches. The National Council of Churches did play a significant role in the achievement of the many social welfare reforms and civil rights gains since 1960. The council's support of these liberal legislative measures aroused the wrath of the conservative groups in the nation who, in their anger, charged that these Christians had sold out to the socialists and Communists. Although the Roman Catholics were not in the National Council of Churches they have moved to approach Protestant groups in attempts to understand one another better and to work together for social welfare measures under the umbrella of the Democratic party. Pope John XXIII and the Vatican Council of 1962 opened the door for better relations between Catholics and Protestants. Protestant Churches around the world now have an association by which their international concerns can be addressed in the World Council of Churches, formed in Amsterdam in 1948.

Since the Civil War, when large numbers of Jewish immigrants came from Eastern Europe, the American nation has been plagued by serious anti-Semitic outbreaks and nasty propagandistic charges that they are "Christ killers," communists, greedy bankers who are intent on controlling the business of the world, subversive elements willing to sell out America, like Judas, for a price, and on and on. Intelligent American citizens, Christian or not, realize that these anti-Semitic charges are foolish and untrue. In self-defense the Jewish people organized the Anti-Defamation League of B'nai B'rith in 1913. In 1929 Christians and Jews moved a step further by forming a joint effort to educate the public and build a more friendly attitude toward one another, an association called the National Conference on Christians and Jews. In 1948 the World Council of Churches denounced anti-Semitism. In 1961 the council declared that the Jews were not responsible for the death of Jesus, a view shared by the Vatican Council in 1962. In 1987 both the United Presbyterian Church and the United Church of Christ agreed that the Jews were not "Christ killers." These churches also acknowledged that the Christians were not the successors to the Jews by having made a new covenant with God that replaced the Jewish covenants. The Jewish covenants had never been broken. The Vatican Council of 1962 declared that Christians and Jews were communities elected by God and each one was of equal worth in God's eyes.

The fires of racial and religious hatred that were so violent in the post-World War I era, when the Ku Klux Klan from 1921–25 threatened to gain control of several state governments, have been dampened by concerted efforts to promote in the schools educational programs on behalf of tolerance as promised in the American Constitution, by nationwide enactment of anti-discrimination laws, and by vigorous prosecution of bigots in state and federal courts. But the ashes still smolder, all of which means that the enlightened leaders of all faiths, both white and black, must continue to teach and practice the gospel of love and mutual aid.

In the American Constitution it is stated clearly that this country is to operate on the principle of strict separation of church and state. It cannot be denied that each religious group has a political agenda that it expects, or at least hopes, its members will remember to vote for when they enter the polling booth. Even the less politically motivated evangelical churches have interests that are to be served at election time. It would be an interesting exercise in imagination if the United States had a parliamentary system of government in which many parties participated, not just two or three, as is currently the case. Many of the states in Western Europe have a Christian political party, even two or three Christian parties. What would the platform of the liberal, mainline Protestant churches be? Catholics might have their party, the fundamentalists would have their party, the blacks their party, and even so small a group as the Jews might attempt a party. The platform of a political party derived from the liberal, mainline Protestant churches might include the following planks.

1. Freedom for all persons to worship or not worship any God or gods that they choose to worship. Implementation of full religious toleration, a precious human right, which had its first application in the Netherlands under William of Orange in 1577, and a practice that has not been accepted by Catholics and the conservative Protestant churches. No tax support for privately operated schools.

2. Unity and peace among all nations. Not only should the Christian churches find unity and peace among themselves, but religious conflicts between non-Christian religions and Christian churches should cease. And what is good for the religions of the world holds true for the economic and political relationships among the many nations of the world. Although a world state remains a utopian dream, Christian support is given to all of the world agencies and federations that intend to promote mutual cooperation among all nations. Support should be given to the United Nations and its several subagencies. International justice through the World Court should be used when international disputes cannot be settled by mutual diplomatic negotiations or by arbitration. No sovereign nation should be free to reject the verdict of the court. Cultural exchanges, foreign travel, and fair trade agreements are all in the interest of Christian peace. Christian love rejects the use of war, and only in extreme cases of violation of the canons of justice could the use of war be justified, as perhaps in the case of World War II.

3. Concern for the protection of the global environment and all of God's creatures on earth. Many Christians are accepting a pantheistic concept of the

universe, a concept that finds God in all things, living and not living. Man shares with the plants and animals a common bond in a common divine element, and each part of the environment requires respect and care on the part of the dominant species of God's creation.

4. Respect and enforcement of those basic human rights, God-given rights, that all humans on earth should share. The concept of Christian human brotherhood is meant to embrace all peoples, all nations, all races, and all social and economic classes, the rich and the poor alike, all on an equal basis in the eyes of God and the law.

5. Women must be freed from the chains of an ancient paternalistic tradition that began with Adam or whenever mankind first established a family and a society. There have been a few societies in which the female members were dominant, a matriarchal system, which is probably no better than a male-controlled social system. But the majority of human societies have been male dominated. Women should share equally with men in the direction of the family and the government of the nation. Emancipated women should be given the option to choose the size of the family, which means the right to use contraception and in dire circumstances even abortion. In the operation of the Christian church women should share equally with men the right to make decisions and to serve as priests or ministers of their churches. The Methodist church in 1980 appointed its first female bishop. Other mainline Protestant churches are ordaining women to serve in the pulpit. The feminist movement, which secured the Nineteenth Amendment guaranteeing female suffrage has a positive role to play in Christian society. The equal position of women must be recognized both by the laws and the courts so that women's personal lives may be secure from abuse from either husbands or predatory males.

6. The Christian gospel of love demands the social gospel, by which conditions for all persons on earth takes precedence over the salvation of souls for an eternal life in heaven. That is not to say that soul salvation is not basic to the mission of the Christian church. The social gospel endorses labor unions and labor legislation, civil rights for all segments of the society, health protection for all regardless of personal income, a place of safety and minimum comfort for the aged, the homeless, the widowed, and the abandoned or orphaned child.

7. An end to all forms of bigotry, discrimination, and persecution that may be practiced in the name of a superior race, or by any group that has antipathy toward any religion, social class, political affiliation, or economic creed. Any movement or group of persons that is motivated to destroy by violent methods, even though they be Christian in name, are not worthy of peace and the hand of Christian fellowship.

In brief, a mainstream Christian political platform might even aspire to bring to earth the City of God while promising to good and righteous Christians that their souls will be assured a place in heaven.

Epilogue

Most modern anthropologists would agree that since the first signs of human habitation on earth religion has been a major component of human culture. It is almost a truism to say that the human species has always had some form of religion—an acceptance of the belief that there are creative forces in the universe beyond the control of human intelligence, at least up until the present age. Religion has played a major role in the determination of how humans have lived with one another and with the natural environment. Although the specific forms and beliefs may differ from one human group to another, all religions, those of today and of prehistoric man, exist because they satisfy the needs for human survival, the security of life. All humans, as other animal species on earth, must secure those elements that provide for the sustenance and reproduction of life, that is, food, shelter, protection from the catastrophic events in the natural environment, security from the lethal weapons of other humans, peace of mind, the satisfaction of human wonder about the numerous puzzlements in the world, and even some hope for survival after death.

So long as religion can provide some measure of satisfaction for the security of the human person, security for the body, mind, and emotions, and no other means of satisfaction can be found to offer better, happier means, then religion will continue to play a basic role in the conduct of human life. What the future is for the continuation of religious systems may be debatable, but a cynic who might suggest that the death of the gods is imminent is probably a most unwise person.

However, there are critics of religion today who dare to suggest that religion is a dying institution; that it has no meaning for the modern, scientifically oriented person; and that only foolish, superstitious persons living in the Dark Ages have any need for religious beliefs. Many people who are actively involved in today's science and technology professions, those who know firsthand the marvels of discovery and knowledge, have little need for the solutions and answers that religion can offer for their many problems and questions. If modern science and technology can do for humans what religion has done in the past, then what need is there for the obsolete, outdated priests, prophets, and their gods?

The prophets of doom for religious institutions cite as evidence for their prediction the apparent decline in religious activity and participation by those persons in our Western European nations and in the United States and Canada who profess to be members of Christian churches or Jewish synagogues but who rarely attend worship services or support their religious bodies financially. American citizens proclaim their nation to be a Christian nation, but no more than a fourth attend church services regularly. The moral ethical standards by which the nation's life is regulated seem to follow the patterns set forth by the popular culture— the movies, television, the marketplace, and the heroes and heroines of politics, sports, and Wall Street—rather than by the Ten Commandments.

All of the major world religions have one message to give to their followers and that is to love your neighbor as you would be loved, to be a compassionate, forgiving person. No single commandment is more essential to the peace and survival of the human race than the one to "Love your neighbor." Yet in *The Compassionate Beast: What Science Is Discovering About the Human Side of Humankind,* a recent study by prominent sociologist Martin Hunt of human compassion and how "love thy neighbor" is conceived and propagated, not a word is mentioned about the role of religion in the development of the love motive in the human personality. Hunt suggests that the compassionate aspect of mankind arises from an instinctual motivation to reduce conflict among the human species. In order to survive mankind must love others and avoid conflict. He suggests that parents are the most effective transmitters of the compassionate spirit to their children, but the agents of God are not mentioned.

Does religion have a future, especially among the people who live in the modern, industrialized world where the values of science, technology, materialism, and the satisfaction of immediate needs are given the highest priority in our scale of values? Despite the predictions that in the evolutionary process over time religion and the worship of supernatural forces will become obsolete and useless, the reality that religion is still alive and active tends to refute the dire predictions of the cynics. Religious worship continues to serve many of the needs of mankind everywhere in the world today. The best efforts of Communism to stamp out the evil opiate of religion in the Soviet Union, Eastern Europe, and China never did more than cover the skin of the nation's people with a cloak of atheism, while under the skin, in the heart of the people, the traditional hunger for God lived on. Once the communist rule was broken and replaced, the old familiar religious traditions and beliefs became openly and widely practiced again. Until mankind can find better answers to such questions as to how the universe and life began, how life evolves or changes over millions of years of time, what the future holds for the earth, why humans must live in pain and sorrow and die in famine, disease, and war, and when life is over what happens to the human soul, if there is one, then the future of religious institutions as servants to the needs of mankind seems assured.

What some critics suggest are signs that religion is dying may only be signs that the old forms of religion are changing. It is probably safe to say that in all of the major world religions dissident groups have emerged to declare that the traditional forms of belief have become obsolete, that they are no longer in tune with the changing social and economic conditions in the world, and therefore that the religion of the people needs to be reinterpreted and changed. The anti-change group may declare that the dissidents are heretices or the enemies of the faith, that they are destroying that which God has ordained, and that if the reformers are not stopped, then the faith will disappear forever, after which God may punish us. And theologians may assert that any creation from or by the gods is permanent and unchangeable. Nonetheless, the historical fact is that all religions do change, although the rate of change may be glacial. All of the major world religions are today not the same as they were a thousand or three thousand years ago. Out of Hinduism came Buddhism, Sikhism, and Jainism. In both Hinduism and Buddhism there are numerous sects that retain the basic concepts of the faiths but differ in the details of worship practices, rituals, and the modes for attaining unity with God. Among the followers of Islam there are the Sunnis, the Shiites, the Sufis, and others. And among the Christians, the body of Christ has been broken into a thousand pieces, especially since the Protestant Reformation. In a democratically organized nation, as in the United States, with no political power to enforce the sanctions of any one church group, it is reasonable to expect that all religious bodies will change and new ones will arise. Probably each group will believe that it is the one and true expression of God's will. Within the ranks of the Christian churches new concepts and values are being given to women. New values are being given to the "Good Samaritan" ideal when certain Christian groups find merit in the values of socialism, social legislation by the state, and the freedom for families to limit the size of the family. In modern Israel Judaism is beginning to expand its concept of what people should be embraced in the fellowship of the "Chosen People." The concept of who should enjoy the love of the Jewish people is being expanded to embrace all of the human race.[1]

The pace of change for most, if not all, of the major world religions may accelerate in the years ahead as more and more of the nations become dependent upon one another for their survival. Today's economic life is no longer confined to the territorial limits of any given country. Commerce and financial investments are becoming international in scope. Communication and travel mechanisms are so convenient and instantaneous that any nation may have as its neighbor a nation that is on the other side of the world. English more and more is becoming the international language for discourse in both economic and political areas. If the nations are to survive and they are forced to recognize the reality that this world is becoming *one world,* if this planet, earth, is ever to realize an end to conflicts and wars, especially those wars fought in the name of God—crusades, jihads, and "just wars"—then the many nations of the world must become allied by economic and political systems with centralized agencies, like the United Nations, or other regulatory international bodies. The vision of a world state is not a fantasy of an intoxicated mind. A study of history shows how humans have enlarged their area of kinship and loyalty from tribes to feudal states, to national states, and, in the twentieth century, to embryo confederations of states under the aegis of organizations ranging from the League of Nations to the United Nations.

As nation states struggle to find the will and skill to effect on earth systems by which they can cooperate and act in peace, live according to rules and laws that have been enacted by mutual consent, then inevitably the several world religions will need to accommodate this new world order of tolerance and peace.

If the world religions are to meet the needs of the future, one further change is needed: the development of a new attitude toward the rate of population growth and the use of the natural resources provided by the earth. In general all religions bless reproduction as a sacred obligation. "Be fruitful and multiply" says the Bible. So long as the human race was subjected to the deadly hazards of disease and famine, and unlimited rate of reproduction was essential to maintain even a stable population. But many of those hazards have been eliminated by science and technology. Humans are now threatened by the excess of population growth.

Another biblical injunction states that mankind should dominate the planet earth. Many of the resources of the earth are finite and not replaceable. Modern industrial societies in the past century have consumed these resources at a reckless pace. Even more serious is that the production of goods for human consumption and war has filled the atmosphere, the rivers, and the land with toxic poisons that endanger the health and life of all people on earth. The people who worship the gods of nature in the cosmic forms of religion, as do the Native Americans, reverse the Christian concept of the relationship of man to the earth. Instead of man dominating the earth, the earth is to control man, or at least man must live in harmony with nature. To love and protect the environment must become an imperative equal to the one that commands all people to love one another as themselves.

Religious systems do change, but reluctantly and painfully. Religious convictions are embedded deeply within the hearts of mankind and in the very souls of the social group, family, and nation. Hence any change in belief comes at an agonizingly slow pace. During the French Revolution the period of the Reign of Terror abolished the Christian church and substituted the worship of reason. A few years later, when Napoleon came to power, the Christian churches were restored. In Eastern Europe and the Soviet Union the Communist regimes were committed to the abolition of religion, the opiate of the people. But after seventy years it is clear that their efforts failed to extinguish the human desire to worship God.

Throughout human history the missionaries and soldiers of Christian nations have conquered so-called barbarian people and forced upon them the Christian faith. Most often the religions of the conquered people were never removed from the hearts and minds of the people. Instead a compromise was effected by the conqueror and the conquered by which the Christian forms of belief and worship became a veneer that covered the traditional forms of worship among the conquered people, which they continued to use after the conquest. Christianity in Africa has had to bless many of the beliefs and rituals of the several native African religions, just as the conversion of the Germanic tribes caused Christianity to incorporate into its religion many of the Germanic beliefs and festivals. Other mission-oriented religions, Buddhism and Islam, experienced the same intermingling of their religious practices with those of the people who were converted or subdued.

As religious institutions evolve over long periods of time, is it possible that the human race might have one, universal faith? If the day should ever arrive when the vision of the peace-loving romantics, philosophers, and prophets of a one-world state is realized—that all people on earth will live under a common law and government—then it would be reasonable to expect that this society would need one form of religion. The Bahai faith, which came out of Persia (Iran) in the late nineteenth century, had as its prime objective the formulation of universal faith that combines into one religion the common elements of the five principal world religions. In a hundred years the faith has attracted so few adherents that hardly anyone in any nation of the world can recall ever meeting a Bahai worshiper.

The Bahai vision of a world religion is not without realism. One who studies comparative religions soon finds many common elements and objectives among all faiths, including those we call "primitive" or "cosmic." All religions serve mankind for one primary purpose, that is, to enhance and promote the security of the human race. Hence all religions seek to protect humans from killing each other and from being killed by uncontrollable and unpredictable forces of nature. Mankind so dreads the enemy known as death, the destroyer of life, that all religions generally attempt to show that death is not the end of existence. Science cannot protect us from death, so mankind is forced to resort to the gods for protection, and if this is impossible, then mankind must have the security of a good and peaceful life after death. Therefore, all religions command the faithful to avoid injury in any form to their neighbors, mental harassment, physical violence, war between tribes and nations. And we must never call upon the gods to inflict punishment upon other humans. To love your neighbor is a universal commandment among most religions. Furthermore, all religions seek to reduce those human appetites that arouse people to commit violence or injury to their neighbors. Those basic motivations that cause the human species to place self-interests above the group interests, such desires as sex, greed, power over others, or other ego drives that threaten the peace of the social group, must be either mitigated or removed.

If mankind could ever learn to control those negative impulses which endanger human survival, then the visions of prophets and romantics might be achieved on earth. This is not the place to review the history of utopian societies. Plato, the Greek philosopher, had a vision of an ideal society when he wrote his *Republic*. St. Augustine believed that the Christian church could become the "City of God" on earth. Buddha envisioned a perfect society if mankind could through the act of meditation suppress all of the ego drives that possess most humans. Muhammad foresaw the coming of a heaven on earth if all people would follow his words as given to him by Allah. In the sixteenth century Thomas More conceived of an ideal state, Utopia, ruled by benevolent priests. And in the seventeenth century Francis Bacon wrote his *New Atlantis,* in which an idealistic philospher conceived of the possibility of building a perfect world of peace and security.

The history of the eighteenth and nineteenth centuries abounds with utopias, novel experiments designed to create a perfect world on earth. Some were motivated by religious beliefs and others were distinctly secular in nature, almost in defiance of religious values, since they hoped to find in socialism panaceas for the ills and pains of mankind. There were the utopian socialists of France, England, and the United States, men like Charles Fourier, Robert Owen, Ralph Waldo Emerson, and Alfred Noyes. Such religious groups as the Quakers, the Shakers, the Mormons, and many others had visions that perfect societies living in peace and brotherhood could become models of how people ought to live together, if not in a large, extended group, then in small, self-contained, monasticlike groups. In a sense Karl Marx hoped that a perfect worldwide society could be achieved through the gospel of Marxist socialism or communism. Edward Bellamy and Aldous Huxley are among more recent visionaries who dared to dream of a more perfect world.

The vision of a perfect society on earth in which all races, all classes, and all religions might live in peace, without the fear of war, disease, and poverty is not yet on the horizon. This dream may never be realized, yet no cynic can deny that the people of the world are being drawn closer together by the ties of fast communication and transportation, economic interdependency, more common use of a single language such as English, the exchange of modes of dress and recreation, the bonds of scientific discovery, which know no national boundaries, and the expansion of knowledge across the world of how people live and how all people share common goals and needs.

However, that time when all people can share in common more of the world's riches as might be provided by an international community of many states or one state, a world of international peace and mutual cooperation, will never be realized so long as the religions of the world contend that each is the one and only expression of the voice and will of God, that their true, orthodox faith can never be compromised by acknowledging that other faiths are also the true expression of God's plan for the human race, even if in different form.

The religious bodies in the United States have learned to live within the limits prescribed by the nation's Constitution. There is no one state-supported church, all religions must respect the separation of church and state, and all religious groups must tolerate the right of all others to practice freely their special forms of religious expression. If this democratic ideal of religious behavior could be accepted by all religions worldwide, then truly the goal of world brotherhood could be more easily and quickly made reality on earth.

Acknowledgments

The author expresses his gratitude to two persons who reviewed the original manuscript, Dr. Earl K. Hanna, former pastor of the Arvada, Colorado, United Methodist Church, Chaplain of Rose Hospital, Denver, and moderator of a weekly "process theology oriented" radio program. Also recognized is Dr. Thomas Roby, Professor of Humanities, Kennedy-King College, Chicago, Illinois.

The Jefferson County Library System, especially the Arvada Branch, was most helpful in providing the resources for writing this book.

Acknowledgments

Bibliography

World Religions in General

Armstrong, Karen. *A History of God.* New York: Ballantine Books, 1993.

Berry, Gerald L. *Religions of the World.* New York: Barnes and Noble, 1956.

Campbell, Joseph. "Transformation of Myth Through Time." Based on television series by Stuart Brown and William Fill. New York: Harper and Row, 1990.

Campbell, Joseph, with Bill Moyers. *The Power of Myth.* New York: Doubleday, 1988.

Cavendish, Richard. *The Great Religions.* New York: Arco, 1980.

Cavendish, Ruth, ed. *Encyclopedia of Mythology: Man, Myth and Magic.* New York: Marshall Cavendish, 1985.

Champion, Selwyn Gurney, and Dorothy Short. *Readings from World Religions.* Greenwich, Conn.: Fawcett, 1951.

Eliade, Mircea. *The Encyclopedia of Religion,* 16 vols. New York: Macmillan, 1987. An indispensable resource.

———. *A History of Religious Ideas: From Gautama Buddha to the Triumph of Christianity.* Chicago: University of Chicago Press, 1982.

Ellwood, Robert S. *Many Peoples, Many Faiths.* Englewood Cliffs, N.J.: Prentice-Hall, 1987.

Hinnels, John R., ed. *A Handbook of Living Religions.* New York: Penguin, 1984.

Hutchinson, John A. *Paths of Faith.* New York: McGraw Hill, 1975.

James, William. *The Varieties of Religious Experience.* New York: Penguin, 1982.

Katagawa, Joseph M., ed. *The Comparative Study of Religions.* New York: Columbia University Press, 1958.

King, Ursula, ed. *Women in the World's Religions, Past and Present.* New York: Paragon House, 1989.

Kraemer, Ross Shepherd. *Her Share of the Blessings.* New York: Oxford University Press, 1992.

Küng, Hans. *Theology for the Third Millennium: An Ecumenical View.* New York: Doubleday, 1988.

———. *Christianity and the World Religions: Paths to Dialogue with Islam, Hinduism and Buddhism.* Garden City, N.Y.: Doubleday, 1986.

Noss, John. *Man's Religions*. New York: Macmillan, 1980.

Parrinder, Geoffrey, ed. *World Religions from Ancient History to the Present*. New York: Facts on File Publications, 1971.

———. *A Dictionary of Non-Christian Religions*. Philadelphia: Westminster Press, 1971.

Pelikan, Jaroslav, ed. *The World Treasury of Modern Religious Thought*. Boston: Little, Brown, 1990.

Severy, Merle, ed. *Great Religions of the World*. Washington, D.C.: National Geographic Society, 1971.

Sharpe, Eric J. *Comparative Religion: A History*. New York: Charles Scribners' Sons, 1975.

Smith, Huston. *Religions of Man*. New York: Harper and Row, 1958.

Wolcott, Leonard, and Carolyn Wolcott. *Religions Around the World*. Nashville, Tenn.: Abingdon Press, 1967.

Chapter 1—A Universal Human Experience

Angeles, Peter A. *The Problem of God*. Amherst, N.Y.: Prometheus Books, 1980.

Baha'i World Faith. Wilmette, Ill.: Baha'i Publishing Trust, 1971.

Einstein, Albert. *The World as I See It*. London: Watts and Co., 1935.

Guthrie, Stewart Elliott. *Faces in the Clouds: A New Theory of Religion*. New York: Oxford University Press, 1993.

Kaufmann, Walter. *The Faith of a Heretic*. New York: Doubleday, 1961.

Küng, Hans. *Does God Exist?* New York: Doubleday, 1978.

Parsons, Keith M. *God and the Burden of Proof*. Amherst, N.Y.: Prometheus Books, 1988.

Ruse, Michael, ed. *But Is It Science?: The Philosophical Question in the Creation-Evolution Controversy*. Amherst, N.Y.: Prometheus Books, 1988.

Strahler, Arthur N. *Understanding Science*. Amherst, N.Y.: Prometheus Books, 1992. See chapters 11 and 14.

Tinder, Glenn. "Can We Be Good Without God?" *Atlantic Monthly*, December 1989, pp. 69–85.

Trefil, James. *Reading the Mind of God*. New York: Charles Scribners' Sons, 1989. See chapters 10, 12, and 15.

Chapter 2—Prehistoric Cosmic Religions

Attenborough, David. *The First Eden: The Mediterranean World and Man*. Boston: Little, Brown, 1987.

Barzun, Jacques, ed. *Records of Civilization: Sources of Japanese Tradition*, vol. 54. New York: Columbia University Press, 1960. See chapters 2 and 13 on Shintoism.

Breeden, Stanley. "The First Australians." *National Geographic*, February 1988, pp. 62ff.

Brown, Karen McCarthy. *Mama Lola: A Voodoo Priestess in Brooklyn*. Berkeley: University of California Press, 1991.

Brown, Michael H. *The Search for Eve*. New York: Harper and Row, 1990.

Campbell, Joseph. *Primitive Mythology*. New York: Penguin, 1987.

Davidson, Ellis. *Gods and Myths of Northern Europe*. New York: Penguin, 1965.

Davis, Wade. *The Serpent and the Rainbow.* New York: Simon and Schuster, 1985. Good account of voodooism.

Eliade, Mircea. *Cosmos and History.* New York: Garland Press, 1985.

———. *Shamanism.* Princeton, N.J.: Princeton University Press, 1964.

Erdoes, Richard, and Alfonso Artiz, eds. *American Indian Myths and Legends.* New York: Pantheon, 1984.

Esterbrook, George. "Are We Alone?" *Atlantic Monthly,* August 1988, pp. 25ff.

Evans-Pritchard, E. E. *Theories of Primitive Religion.* New York: Oxford University Press, 1968.

Frazer, James G. *The Golden Bough: The Roots of Religion and Folklore.* New York: Crown, 1981.

Freuchen, Peter. *Book of the Eskimo.* New York: Fawcett, 1981.

Gumbatis, Marija. *The Language of the Gods.* San Francisco: Harper and Row, 1989.

Gilpin, Laura. *The Enduring Havaho.* Austin: University of Texas Press, 1968.

Goer, Joseph. *How the Great Religions Began.* New York: Signet, 1856.

Goode, William J. *Religion Among the Primitives.* Glencoe, Ill.: Free Press, 1951.

Harrod, Howard L. *Remembering the World Plains Indian: Religion and Morality.* Tucson: University of Arizona Press, 1987.

Hawkins, Jacqueline. *Man and the Sun.* New York: Random House, 1962.

Hori, Ichiro. *Folk Religion in Japan: Continuity and Change.* Chicago: University of University Press, 1983.

Leeming, David. *The World of Myth.* New York: Oxford University Press, 1990.

Kluckhom, Clyde. *Navaho Witchcraft.* Boston: Beacon Press, 1967.

Loh, Jules. *Lords of the Earth: A History of the Navajo Indians.* New York: Crowell-Collier Press, 1971.

Lowie, Robert H. *Primitive Religion.* New York: Grosset and Dunlop, 1952.

McFadden, Steven. *Profiles in Wisdom.* Santa Fe, N.M.: Bear and Company, 1991. See chapter 5 on shamanism.

National Geographic, October 1988, pp. 440–99. Article on prehistoric cave art and the search for modern man.

Parrinder, Geoffrey, ed. *African Traditional Religions.* Westport, Conn.: Greenwood, 1970.

Rigaud, Milo. *Secrets of Voodoo.* San Francisco: City Lights Books, 1985.

Rosenberger, Boyce. "What Made Humans Human?" *New York Times Magazine,* April 8, 1984, pp. 80ff.

Simpson, Jacqueline. *Everyday Life in the Viking Age.* New York: Peter Bodrich Books, 1987.

Sokyo, Ono. *Shinto: The Kami Way.* Rutland, Vt.: Charles E. Tuttle and Company, 1962.

Stone, Merlin. *When God Was a Woman.* New York: Harcourt Brace Jovanavich, 1977.

Trefil, James. *Dark Side of the Universe: A Scientist Explores the Mysteries of the Cosmos.* New York: Charles Scribners' Sons, 1988.

Tyler, Edward R. *Primitive Culture.* London: T. Murray, 1871.

Walsh, Roger N. *The Spirit of Shamanism.* Los Angeles: Jeremy P. Tarcher, 1990.

Wilford, John Noble. "Artistry of the Ice Age." *New York Times Magazine,* May 21, 1978, pp. 47ff.

Wright, Ronald. *On Fiji Island.* New York: Penguin, 1986.

Yazzie, Ethelan, ed. *Navajo History.* Tsaile, Ariz.: Navajo Community College, 1971.

Chapter 3—River Valley Religions: Babylon and Egypt

Campbell, Joseph. *Oriental Mythology.* New York: Penguin, 1962.
———. *Occidental Mythology.* New York: Penguin, 1964.
Cerny, Jaroslav. *Ancient Egyptian Religion.* London: Greenwood, 1979.
Frankfort, Henri. *Ancient Egyptian Religion.* New York: Columbia University Press, 1948.
Gardner, John C. *Epic of Gilgamesh.* New York: Alfred A. Knopf, 1984.
Gumbatas, Marija. *The Language of the Goddess.* San Francisco: Harper and Row, 1989.
Hawkins, Jacqueline. *Man and the Sun.* New York: Random House, 1962.
Hooke, Samuel. *Middle Eastern Mythology.* New York: Penguin, 1963.
Ions, Veronica. *Egyptian Mythology.* New York: Peter Bodrich, 1980.
Langdon, S. *Babylonian Epic of Creation.* New York: Oxford University Press, 1923.
Sanders, N. K. *The Epic of Gilgamesh.* New York: Penguin, 1960.

Chapter 4—The Greek Gods and the Hellenistic Cults

Campbell, Joseph. *Occidental Mythology.* New York: Penguin, 1964.
Coolidge, Olivia. *Greek Myths.* Boston: Houghton Mifflin, 1949.
Grant, Michael. *The Formation of the Western World: A History of Greece and Rome.* New York: Charles Scribner's Sons, 1991.
———. *Myths of the Greeks and Romans.* New York: New American Library, 1962.
Graves, Robert. *Greek Myths,* 2 vols. New York: Pelican-Penguin Books, 1955.
———. *The Greek Myths.* Mount Kisco, N.Y.: Moyer Bell, 1988.
Guthrie, W. K. C. *The Greeks and Their Gods.* Boston: Beacon Press, 1950.
Highwater, Jamake. *Myth and Sexuality.* New York: Penguin, 1990.
Nilsson, Martin P. *Greek Popular Religion.* New York: Columbia University Press, 1948.
Sandback, F. H. *The Stoics.* New York: W. W. Norton, 1975.
Taylour, Lord William. *The Mycenaeans.* New York: Frederick A. Praeger, 1964.

Chapter 5—The Greek Gods Become Roman

Grant, F. C. *Ancient Roman Religion.* New York: Macmillan, 1957.
Grant, Michael. *A Social History of Greece and Rome.* New York: Macmillan, 1993.
Ogilivie, R. M. *Romans and Their Gods in the Age of Augustine.* New York: W. W. Norton, 1970.
Sardi, Marta. *The Christians and the Roman Empire.* Norman: University of Oklahoma Press, 1986.
Wilkens, Robert L. *The Christians as the Romans Saw Them.* New Haven, Conn.: Yale University Press, 1984.

Chapter 6—The Chinese Way of Life: Taoism and Confucianism

Barzun, Jacques, ed. *Records of Civilization: Sources of Japanese Tradition,* vol. 54. New York: Columbia University Press, 1958. See chapter 18 on Confucianism.
Biofeld, John. *Taoism: The Road to Immortality.* Boulder, Colo.: Shambala Press, 1978.
Campbell, Joseph. *Oriental Mythology.* New York: Penguin, 1962.
Ching, Julia. *Probing China's Soul: Religion, Politics and Protest in the Peoples' Republic.* San Francisco: Harper and Row, 1990.
———. *Christianity and Chinese Religions.* New York: Doubleday, 1989.
Creel, H. G. *Chinese Thought from Confucius to Mao-Tse-Tung.* Chicago: University of Chicago Press, 1971.
Dreher, Diane. *The Tao of Peace.* New York: Donald I. Fine, 1990.
Goodrich, Carrington. *Short History of the Chinese People.* New York: Harper and Row, 1963.
Harrison, Lawrence. *Who Prospers?* New York: Basic, 1992. See chapters 3, 4, and 5 on how Confucianism molded Chinese culture.
Latourette, Kenneth S. *China.* Englewood Cliffs, N.J.: Prentice-Hall, 1964.
Li, Dun J. *The Ageless Chinese: A History.* New York: Charles Scribners' Sons, 1965.
Mitchell, Stephen. *Tao Te Ching.* New York: Harper and Row, 1988.
Reischauer, Edwin O., and John K. Fairbank. *East Asia: The Great Tradition.* New York: Houghton-Mifflin, 1960. See chapter 3 on Confucianism.
Waley, Arthur. *Analects of Confucius.* New York: Random House, 1989.
Welch, Holmes. *Taoism: The Parting of the Way.* Boston: Beacon Press, 1966.
Wingtsit, Chan. *Religious Trends in Modern China.* New York: Columbia University Press, 1953.

Chapter 7—Hinduism

Ashby, Philip H. *Modern Trends in Hinduism.* New York: Columbia University Press, 1974.
Barzun, Jacques, ed. *Records of Civilization: Sources of Indian Tradition,* vol. 56. New York: Columbia University Press, 1958.
Bonner, Arthur. *Averting the Apocalypse: Social Movements in India Today.* Durham, N.C.: Duke University Press, 1990. Excellent glossary of Hindu terms.
Campbell, Joseph. *Oriental Mythology.* New York: Penguin, 1962.
Chatterji, Jagodish C. *The Wisdom of the Vegas.* Wheaton, Ill.: Theosophical Publishing House, 1973.
Godden, Jon, and Rumer Godden. *Shivas Pigeons: An Experience in India.* New York: Alfred A. Knopf, 1972.
Greenfield, Robert. *The Spiritual Supermarket.* New York: E. P. Dutton, 1975. Good reference on the Hare Krishna movement
Groslier, Bernard, and Jacques Arthaud. *Angkor: Art and Civilization.* New York: Praeger, 1966.
Mayo, Katherine. *Mother India.* Westport, Conn.: Greenwood Press, 1970.
Morgan, Kenneth W., ed. *The Religion of the Hindus.* New York: The Ronald Press, 1953.
Munro, Eleanor. *On Glory Road.* London: Thames and Hudson, 1987.
Naipul, V. S. *India: A Wounded Civilization.* New York: Random House, 1978.

Organ, Troy Wilson. *Hinduism: Its Historical Development.* Westbury, N.Y.: Barron's Educational Service, 1974.

Prabhavavanda, Swami, and Christopher Isherwood. *The Song of God: Bhagavad-Gita.* New York: Mentor, 1961.

Renon, Louis, ed. *Hinduism.* New York: George Braziller, 1962.

Rice, Edward. *The Ganges.* New York: Four Winds Press, 1979.

Wilson, Henry. *Benares.* London: Thames and Hudson, 1985.

Wolpert, Stanley. *India.* Berkeley: University of California Press, 1991.

Zachner, R. C. *Hindu Scriptures.* New York: McKay, 1992.

Zimmer, Heinrich. *Myths and Symbols in Indian Art and Civilization.* New York: Harper, 1946.

———. *Philosophies of India.* Princeton, N.J.: Princeton University Press, 1951. Also a good reference for Buddhism and Jainism.

Chapter 8—Buddhism

Aitken, Robert. *Encouraging Words: Zen Buddhist Teachings for the Western World.* New York: Pantheon, 1991.

Anderson, Walt. *Open Secrets: A Western Guide to Tibetan Buddhism.* New York: Viking, 1979.

Barzun, Jacques, ed. *Records of Civilization: Sources of Japanese Tradition,* vol. 54. New York: Columbia University Press, 1958. See chapters 5 and 8.

Bechert, Heinz, and Richard Gombruchi. *The World of Buddhism.* London: Thames and Hudson, 1984.

Bunce, W. K., ed. *Religions in Japan.* New York: C. E. Tuttle, 1981.

Campbell, Joseph. *Myths to Live By.* New York: Viking, 1972. See chapter 7.

Conze, Edward. *Buddhism: Its Essence and Development.* New York: Harper-Collins, 1959.

Dumoulin, Heinrich. *Zen Buddhism: A History,* 2 vols. New York: Macmillan, 1990.

Greenfeld, Robert. *The Spiritual Supermarket.* New York: E. P. Dutton, 1975.

Jayatillake, K. N. *The Message of the Buddha.* New York: The Free Press, 1974.

Kitagawa, Joseph M. *Religion in Japanese History.* New York: Columbia University Press, 1966.

Pye, Michael. *The Buddha.* London: Duckworth, 1979.

Rice, Edward. *The Ganges.* New York: Four Winds Press, 1974.

Robinson, Richard H., and Willard L. Johnson. *The Buddha Religion: A Historical Introduction.* Belmont, Calif.: Wadsworth Publishing Company, 1982.

Ross, Nancy Wilson. *Buddhism: A Way of Life and Thought.* New York: Alfred A. Knopf, 1980.

Schulberg, Lucille. *Historic India.* New York: Time Life Books, 1968.

Shapiro, Richard. "The Spiritual Life of Japan." *New York Times Magazine,* November 23, 1986, pp. 110-13.

Thich, Nhat Hanh. *Old Path, White Clouds.* Berkeley, Calif.: Parallax Press, 1991. Biography of Buddha based on Mahayana texts.

Tworkov, Helen. *Zen in America.* San Francisco: North Point Press, 1989.

Zimmer, Heinrich. *Philosophies of India.* Princeton, N.J.: Princeton University Press, 1951. Part 3, chapter 4.

Chapter 9—Sikhism

Clark, John Archer. *The Sikhs.* Princeton, N.J.: Princeton University Press, 1946.
Cole, Owen, and P. S. Sambhi. *The Sikhs.* London: Rutledge, Chapman and Hall, 1986.
McLeod, W. H. *Sikh History, Religion and Society.* New York: Columbia University Press, 1991.
———. *Guru Nanak and the Sikh Religion.* Oxford: Clarendon Press, 1968.
O'Brien, Conor Cruse. "Holy War Against India." *Atlantic Monthly,* August 1988, pp. 54ff.

Chapter 10—Jainism

Tobias, Michael. *Life Force: The World of Jainism.* Berkeley, Calif.: Asian Humanities Press, 1991.
Zimmer, Heinrich. *Philosophies of India.* Princeton, N.J.: Princeton University Press, 1967. See pp. 217–62 on Jainism.

Chapter 11—Zoroastrianism

Bharucha, Ervad Sheriarje Dalabhai. *Zoroastrian Religion and Customs.* Flushing, N.Y.: Asia Book Company, 1928.
Boyce, Mary. *Zoroastrianism: Its Antiquity and Constant Vigor.* Costa Mesa, Calif.: Mazda Publishers, 1984.
Darmesteter, James. *The Zend Avesta of Zarathustra.* Edmonton, Wash.: The Near Eastern Press, 1984.
Duchesne, Guillemen Jacques. *Symbols and Values in Zoroastrianism.* New York: Harper and Row, 1966.
Hawkes, Jacqueline. *Man and the Sun.* New York: Random House, 1962.
LoPate, Philip. *The Rug Merchant.* New York: Viking Penguin Press, 1988.
Pangborn, Cyrus R. *Zoroastrianism: A Beleagured Faith.* New York: Advent, 1982.
Yamauchi, Edwin M. *Persia and the Bible.* Grand Rapids, Mich.: Baker Book House, 1990.
Zachner, R. C. *The Dawn and Twilight of Zoroastrianism.* London: Weidenfeld and Nicolson, 1961.

Chapter 12—Judaism, Mother of Monotheism

Adler, Morris. *The World of the Talmud.* New York: Schocken Books, 1963.
Alter, Robert, ed. *The Literary Guide to the Bible.* Cambridge, Mass.: Harvard University Press, 1987. A basic reference.
Arendt, Hannah. *Antisemitism.* New York: Harcourt Brace, 1968.
Blau, Joseph L. *Modern Varieties of Judaism.* New York: Columbia University Press, 1966.
Brook, Stephen. *Winner Takes All: A Season in Israel.* London: Hamish Hamilton, 1990. Good account of everyday life in Israel.

Brown, Salo W. *A Social and Religious History of the Jews,* 18 vols. New York: Columbia University Press, 1937. The author died in 1989 and never finished the final two volumes.

Cohen, Arthur, and Paul Mendes-Flohr, eds. *Contemporary Jesish Religious Thought.* New York: The Free Press, 1988.

Cornfeld, Gaalyan. *Archaeology of the Bible.* New York: Harper and Row, 1976.

Eban, Abba. *Heritage: Civilization and the Jews.* New York: Summit, 1984.

Feinsilver, Rabbi Alexander, ed. *The Talmud for Today.* New York: St Martin's Press, 1980.

Fox, Robin Lane. *The Unauthorized Version: Truth and Fiction in the Bible.* New York: Alfred A. Knopf, 1992.

Friedman, Richard E. *Who Wrote the Bible?* New York: Summit, 1987.

Friedman, Robert J. *Zealots for Zion.* New York: Random House, 1992.

Gordis, Robert. *Love and Sex: A Modern Jewish Perspective.* New York: Hippocrene Books, 1988.

Grant, Robert M., and David Tracy. *A Short History of the Interpretation of the Bible.* Philadelphia: Fortress Press, 1984.

Harris, Liz. *Holy Days: The World of a Hasidic Family.* New York: Macmillan, 1986.

Hertzberg, Arthur. *The Jews in America: Four Centuries of an Uneasy Encounter: A History.* New York: Simon and Schuster, 1989.

Idel, Moske. *Kabbalah: New Perspectives.* New Haven, Conn.: Yale University Press, 1988. Good study of Jewish mysticism.

Johnson, Paul. *A History of the Jews.* New York: Harper and Row, 1987. Excellent glossary.

Josipovic, Gabriel. *The Book of God: A Response to the Bible.* New Haven, Conn.: Yale University Press, 1988.

Langmuir, Gavin K. *History, Religion and Antisemitism.* Berkeley: University of California Press, 1990.

Liebman, Charles S, and Steven M. Cohen. *Two Worlds of Judaism.* New Haven, Conn.: Yale University Press, 1990.

Martin, Bernard. *A History of Judaism,* 2 vols. New York: Basic, 1974.

Meyers, Carol. *Discovering Eve: Ancient Israelite Women in Context.* New York: Oxford University Press, 1988.

Patai, Raphael. *The Seed of Abraham.* Salt Lake City: University of Utah Press, 1986.

Peters, F. E. *The Children of Abraham: Judaism, Christianity, Islam.* Princeton, N.J.: Princeton University Press, 1983.

Plaut, Rabbi W. Gunthem, ed. *The Torah: A Modern Commentary.* New York: Union of American Hebrew Congregations.

Potok, Chaim. *The Promise.* New York: Simon and Schuster, 1967. The story of a Jewish boy who studies the Talmud.

Powel, Ernest. *The Labyrinth of Exile: A Life of Theodore Herzl.* New York: Farrar, Straus and Giroux, 1989.

Romer, John. *Testament: The Bible and History.* New York: Henry Holt, 1988

Roth, Cecil, and Geoffery Wigoder, eds. *Encyclopedia Judaica,* 17 vols. Philadelphia: Coronet Books, 1972.

Russel, D. S. *Between the Testaments.* Philadelphia: Fortress Press, 1960.

Safire, William. *The First Dissident: The Book of Job in Today's Politics.* New York: Random House, 1992.

Scalamonte, John D. *Ordained to be a Jew.* Hoboken, N.J.: KTAV Publishing House, 1992. Good glossary on Judaism.

Shanks, Hershel, et al. *The Dead Sea Scrolls after Forty Years.* Washington, D.C.: Biblical Archaeology Society, 1992.

Shenker, Israel. *Coat of Many Colors.* New York: Doubleday, 1985. A popular summary of Judaism.

Smith, Morton. *Palestinian Parties and Politics that Shaped the Old Testament.* New York: Columbia University Press, 1971.

Sunderland, Jabez Thomas. *The Bible: Its Origin, Growth and Character.* New York: G. P. Putnam, 1893.

Viorst, Milton. *Sands of Sorrow.* New York: Harper and Row, 1987. Good account of the divisions within Judaism.

Wilson, Ian. *Exodus: The True Story Behind the Biblical Account.* San Francisco: Harper and Row, 1985.

Christianity in General

Bokenkotter, Thomas S. *A Concise History of the Catholic Church.* New York: Doubleday, 1990.

Broderick, Robert C., ed. *The Catholic Encyclopedia.* Nashville, Tenn.: Thomas Nelson, 1976.

Chadwick, Henry. *Atlas of the Christian Church.* New York: Facts on File, 1987.

Cowie, Leonard W. *The March of the Cross: An Illustrated History of Christianity.* New York: McGraw-Hill, 1962.

Dowley, Tim, ed. *Eerdmann's Handbook to a History of Christianity.* Grand Rapids, Mich.: William B. Eerdmanns Publishing, 1977.

Gonzales, Justo L. *The Story of Christianity.* San Francisco: Harper and Row, 1984.

Johnson, Paul. *A History of Christianity.* New York: Atheneum, 1976.

Latourette, Kenneth Scott. *Christianity Through the Ages.* New York: Harper and Row, 1965.

———. *History of Christianity,* 2 vols. San Francisco: Harper, 1975.

McDonald, William J., ed. *New Catholic Encyclopedia,* 16 vols. New York: McGraw-Hill, 1967.

McManners, John, ed. *The Oxford Illustrated History of Christianity.* New York: Oxford University Press, 1990.

Mason, Caroline, and Pat Alexander, eds. *Picture Archive of the Bible.* New York: Lion Publishing, 1987.

Patterson, Orland. *Freedom in the Making of Western Culture,* vol. 1. San Francisco: Basic Books, 1991. See pp. 293–401 on the development of the concept of freedom in Christianity.

Pelikan, Jaroslav, ed. *World Treastury of Modern Religious Thought.* Boston: Little, Brown, 1990.

Walker, Williston. *History of the Christian Church.* New York: Macmillan, 1985.

Chapter 13—The Advent of Christianity

Anderson, Hugh. *Reflections of Several Historians and Theologians on the Life of Jesus.* Englewood Cliffs, N.J.: Prentice-Hall, 1967.

Brandon, S. G. F. *Jesus and the Zealots: A Study of the Political Factors in Primitive Christianity.* New York: Charles Scribners Sons, 1968.

———. *The Trial of Jesus of Nazareth.* London: Bateford, 1988.

Brown, Raymond E. *The Birth of the Messiah,* 2d ed. Garden City, N.Y.: Doubleday, 1993.

Bultman, Rudolf. *Jesus Christ and Mythology.* New York: Charles Scribners Sons, 1981.

Cassels, Louis. *The Real Jesus: How He Lived and What He Taught.* New York: Doubleday, 1968.

Charlesworth, James H., ed. *Jesus and the Dead Sea Scrolls.* New York: Doubleday, 1992.

Crosson, John Dominic. *The History of Jesus: The Life of a Mediterranean Jewish Peasant.* San Francisco: Harper, 1991.

Cullen, Murphy, "Who Do Men Say That I Am? Interpreting Jesus in the Modern World." *Atlantic Monthly,* December 1986, pp. 37–65.

Cullman, Oscar. *Jesus and the Revolutionaries.* New York: Harper and Row, 1970.

Fosdick, Harry Emerson. *The Man from Nazareth.* New York: Harper, 1949.

Funk, Robert W., and Roy W. Hoover. *The Jesus Seminar: The Five Gospels.* New York: Macmillan, 1994. The fifth gospel is the recently discovered gospel of Thomas.

Grant, Michael. *Jesus: A Historian's View of the Gospels.* New York: Macmillan,, 1973.

Küng, Hans. *Interpretation of Jesus, His Life and Message.* New York: Doubleday, 1984.

Maccoby, Hyam. *The Sacred Executioner: Human Sacrifice and the Legacy of Guilt.* New York: Norton, 1983.

Mack, Burton L. *The Last Gospel: The Book of Q.* San Francisco: Harper, 1993.

Meier, John P. *A Marginal Jew: Rethinking the Historical Jesus.* New York: Doubleday, 1991.

Mitchell, Stephen. *The Gospel According to Jesus.* New York: Harper-Collins, 1991.

Muggeridge, Malcolm. *Jesus: The Man Who Lives.* Washington, D.C.: Regnery Gateway, 1976.

Neusner, Rabbi Jacob. *A Rabbi Talks with Jesus.* New York: Doubleday, 1993.

Ostling, Richard N. "Who Was Jesus?" *Time,* August 15, 1988, pp. 34–40.

Olmstead, A. T. *Jesus in the Light of History.* New York: Charles Scribners and Sons, 1942.

Pelikan, Jaroslav. *Jesus Through the Centuries.* New Haven, Conn.: Yale University Press, 1985.

Sanders, E. P. *Jesus and Judaism.* Philadelphia: Fortress Press, 1985.

Schillebeeckx, Edward. *Jesus: An Experiment in Christology.* New York: Crossroads, 1983.

Schonfield, Hugh J. *Those Incredible Christians.* New York: Bernard Geis Associates, 1968.

Schweitzer, Albert. *The Quest for the Historical Jesus.* New York: Macmillan, 1964.

Sheehan, Thomas. *First Coming: How the Kingdom of God Became Christianity.* New York: Random House, 1986.

Smith, Morton. *Jesus the Magician.* New York: Harper, 1981.

Tillich, Paul. *The Future of Religion.* New York: Harper and Row, 1966.

Trueblood, Elton. *The Humor of Christ.* New York: Harper and Row, 1964.

U.S. News and World Report, December 21, 1992, pp. 79–89. Contains good interpretations of the life of Jesus by modern historians.

Vermes, Geza. *Jesus the Jew: A Historian's Reading of the Gospels.* Minnapolis, Minn.: Fortress-Augsburg Press, 1981.

Wells, G. A. *The Historical Evidence for Jesus.* Amherst, N.Y.: Prometheus Books, 1982.

Wilson, A. N. *In Jesus, A Life.* New York: W. W. Norton, 1992.

Chapter 14—The Pauline Church of the First Two Centuries

Barnkamm, G. *Paul.* New York: Harper and Row, 1971.

Maccoby, Hyan. *The Mythmaker: Paul and the Invention of Christianity.* San Francisco: Harper and Row, 1986.

Meeks, Wayne A. *The First Urban Christians: The Social World of the Apostle Paul.* New Haven, Conn.: Yale University Press, 1983.

Morton, Andrew. *Paul, the Man and the Myth: A Study in the Authorship of Greek Prose.* London: Hodder and Staughton, 1966.

Pagels, Elaine. *The Gnostic Paul.* Philadelphia: Fortress Press, 1979.

Raetzel, Calvin J. *The Letters of Paul.* Atlanta, Ga.: John Knox Press, 1982.

Schillebeeckx, Edward. *Paul, the Apostle.* New York: Crossroads, 1983.

Schonfield, Hugh J. *Those Incredible Christians.* New York: Bernard Geiss Associates, 1968.

Chapter 15—The Formation of the Christian Church—A.D. 100 to 400

Bentley, James. *Secrets of Mount Sinai.* New York: Doubleday, 1986.

Carey, George, ed. *The Message of the Bible.* Batavia, Ill.: Leon Library, 1988.

Carmichael, Joel. *Birth of Christianity: Reality and Myth.* New York: Hippocrene Books, 1989.

Chadwick, Henry. *History of the Church,* vol. 1. New York: Penguin, 1968.

———. *Heresy and Orthodoxy in the Early Church.* Brookfield, Vt.: Ashgate Publishing, 1991.

Fox, Robin Lane. *Pagans and Christians.* New York: Alfred A. Knopf, 1986.

Franck, Irene M., and David M. Brownstone. *The Silk Road, A History.* New York: Facts on File, 1986. See pp. 216–24 on the Manicheans.

Grant, Frederick C. *Hellenistic Religions: The Age of Syncretism.* New York: Macmillan, 1953.

Frend, W. H. C. *Martyrdom and Persecution in the Early Church: A Study of a Conflict from the Maccabeans to the Donatists.* Garden City, N.Y.: Anchor, 1967.

———. *The Rise of Christianity.* Philadelphia: Fortress Press, 1984.

Gager, J. G. *The Social World of Early Christianity.* Englewood Cliffs, N.J.: Prentice-Hall, 1975.

Goguel, Maurice. *The Primitive Church.* New York: Macmillan, 1964.

Grant, Frederick C. *Roman Hellenism and the New Testament.* New York: Charles Scribners Sons, 1962.

———. *The Economic Background of the Gospels.* New York: Oxford University Press, 1926.

Grant, R. M. *Gnosticism and Early Christianity.* New York: Columbia University Press, 1959.

Grant, R. M. *The Rise and Triumph of Christianity in the Roman World.* San Francisco: Harper, 1980.

Guignebert, Charles. *The Early History of Christianity.* New York: Twayne Publishers, 1927.

Hardy, Edward R. *Christian Egypt: Church and People: The Copts.* New York: Oxford University Press, 1952.

Herrin, Judith. *The Formation of Christendom.* Princeton, N.J.: Princeton University Press, 1987.

Hoffmann, R. Joseph, ed. *The Origins of Christianity: A Cricial Introduction.* Amherst, N.Y.: Prometheus Books, 1985.

Larue, Gerald A. *The Supernatural, the Occult and the Bible.* Amherst, N.Y.: Prometheus Books, 1990.

Layton, Bentley. *The Gnostic Scriptures.* New York: Doubleday, 1987.

Legge, Francis. *Forerunners and Rivals of Christianity from 330 B.C. to 330 A.D.*, 2 vols. New Hyde Park, N.Y.: University Books, 1965.

Pagels, Elaine. *Adam, Eve, and the Serpent.* New York: Random House, 1988.

———. *The Gnostic Gospels.* New York: Random House, 1979.

Phillips, G. A. *Eve: The History of an Idea.* San Francisco: Harper and Row, 1984.

Peters, F. E. *The Harvest: A History of the Near East from Alexander the Great to the Triumph of Christianity.* New York: Simon and Schuster, 1970. Chapter 17 good on the Gnostics.

Robinson, James M., ed. *The Nag Hammadi Library in English.* New York: Harper and Row, 1977.

Ross, C. Randolph. *Common Sense Christianity.* Cortland, N.Y.: Occam Publishers, 1989.

Schonfield, Hugh J. *Those Incredible Christians.* New York: Bernard Geis Associates, 1968.

Sheehan, Thomas. *The First Coming: How the Kingdom of God Became Christianity.* New York: Random House, 1988.

Tyson, Joseph B. *The New Testament and Early Christianity.* New York: Macmillan, 1984.

Wakin, Edward. *A Lonely Minority: The Modern History of Egypt's Copts. The Challenge of Survival for Four Million.* New York: Morrow, 1963.

Wilken, Robert. *Christians as the Romans Saw Them.* New Haven, Conn.: Yale University Press, 1984.

———. *The Myth of Christian Beginnings: History's Impact on Belief.* Garden City, N.Y.: Doubleday, 1971.

Chapter 16—Islam

Alireza, Marianne. "Women of Saudi Arabia." *National Geographic,* October 1987, pp. 423–53.

Dawood, N. J. *The Koran.* Baltimore: Penguin, 1961.

Denny, Frederick M. *An Introduction to Islam.* New York: Macmillan, 1985.

Esposito, John L. *Islam: The Straight Path.* New York: Oxford University Press, 1990.

Glubb, John. *Life and Times of Muhammed.* Lanham, Md.: Scarborough House, 1970.

Hitti, P. K. *History of the Arabs.* New York: Macmillan, 1964.

Hourani, Albert. *A History of the Arab People.* Cambridge, Mass.: Harvard University Press, 1991.

Ibn, Ishaq. *The Life of Muhammed*. London: Oxford University Press, 1967.

Jelloum, Tahar Beb. *The Sand Child*. New York: Harcourt Brace, 1989.

Lamb, David. *The Arab: Journey Beyond the Mirage*. New York: Random House, 1987.

Levy, R. *The Social Structure of Islam*. London: Cambridge University Press, 1957.

Lewis, Bernard. *Islam and the West*. New York: Oxford University Press, 1993.

Mackey, Sandra. *The Saudis: Inside the Desert Kingdom*. Boston: Houghton Mifflin, 1987.

Matise, Ruthven. *Islam in the World*. New York: Oxford University Press, 1984.

Mottahedeh, Roy. *The Mantle of the Prophet*. New York: Simon and Schuster, 1985.

Naipaul, V. S. *Among the Believers: An Islamic Journey*. New York: Random House, 1981.

Patai, Raphael. *The Arab Mind*. New York: Charles Scribners Sons, 1983.

Pipes, Daniel. *In the Path of God: Islam and Political Power*. New York: Basic, 1985. Excellent glossary.

Robinson, Maxine. *Islam and Capitalism*. New York: Pantheon, 1973.

Schimmel, Annemarie. *Islam*. Albany: State University of New York Press, 1992. Good account of the Sufis, pp. 101–20 and the Islamic saints, pp. 121–26.

Shah, Idries. *The Way of the Sufi*. New York: E. P. Dutton, 1969.

Shipler, David K. *Arab and Jew*. London: Penguin, 1987.

Wright, Robin. *In the Name of God: The Khomeini Decade*. New York: Simon and Schuster, 1989.

Chapter 17—Roman Catholic Orthodoxy, 400–1200

Allegro, John M. *The Dead Sea Scrolls and the Christian Myth*. Amherst, N.Y.: Prometheus Books, 1984.

Augustine, St. *The City of God*. New York: Modern Library, 1950.

Barr, William Henry. *Self-Contradictions of the Bible*. Amherst, N.Y.: Prometheus Books, 1987.

Bede. *A History of the English People*. New York: Penguin, 1955.

Bentley, James. *Secrets of Mount Sinai*. Garden City, N.Y.: Doubleday, 1986.

Bultmann, Rudolph. *The History of the Synoptic Tradition*. New York: Harper and Row, 1963.

Brown, Peter. *Augustine of Hippo*. New York: Dorset Press, 1987.

———. *The Body and Society: Men, Women, and Sexuality in Early Christianity*. New York: Columbia University Press, 1988.

Cain, Terry. *What Your Minister Is Afraid to Tell You About the Bible*. Saratoga, Calif.: R and E Publishers, 1993.

Cambridge History of the Bible, 3 vols. New York: Cambridge University Press, 1970.

Crossan, John D. *The Historical Jesus*. San Francisco: Harper, 1991. Excellent on the book of Daniel.

Eusebius. *The History of the Church from Christ to Constantine*. New York: Dorset Press, 1965.

Fosdick, Harry Emerson. *The Man from Nazareth as His Contemporaries Saw Him*. New York: Greenwood, 1978.

Fredricksen, Paula. *From Jesus to Christ: The Origins of the New Testament: Images of Christ*. New Haven, Conn.: Yale University Press, 1988.

Frend, W. C. *The Rise of Christianity.* Minneapolis, Minn.: Fortress Press, 1984.

Grant, F. C. *The Economic Background of the Gospels.* New York: Oxford University Press, 1926.

Grant, Robert. *A Historical Introduction to the New Testament.* New York: Harper and Row, 1963.

Jonas, Hans. *The Gnostic Religion.* Boston: Beacon Press, 1958.

Keller, Werner. *The Bible as History.* New York: Bantam, 1974.

Knoles, George H., and Rexford K. Snyder, eds. *Readings in Western Civilization.* New York: J. B. Lippincott, 1951.

Latourette, Kenneth Scott. *The First Five Centuries.* New York: Harper and Brothers, 1937.

Larue, Gerald A. *The Supernatural, the Occult and the Bible.* Amherst, N.Y.: Prometheus Books, 1990.

Mitchell, Stephen. *The Gospel According to Jesus.* New York: Harper Colins, 1991.

Pelikan, Jaroslav. *Memory and Eternity in the Thought of St. Augustine.* Charlottesville, Va.: University of Virginia Press, 1986.

Schonfeld, Hugh J. *Those Incredible Christians.* New York: Bernard Geis Associates, 1988. See chapter 13 for a good analysis of the book of Revelation.

Smith, Morton, and R. Joseph Hoffmann, eds. *What the Bible Really Says.* Amherst, N.Y.: Prometheus Books, 1989.

Spong, John Shelby. *Rescuing the Bible from the Fundamentalists.* San Francisco: Harper, 1991.

Watts, William, ed. *Confessions of St. Augustine.* London: William Heinemann, 1919.

Chapter 18—The City of God on Earth: Temporal Church Power

Baldwin, James. *A Calendar of Saints.* New York: Facts on File, 1987.

Barraclough, Geoffrey. *The Medieval Papacy.* New York: W. W. Norton, 1979.

Brown, P. R. L. *The Cult of the Saints.* Chicago: University of Chicago Press, 1981.

Carroll, Michael. *The Cult of the Virgin Mary.* Princeton, N.J.: Princeton University Press, 1986.

Cheetham, Nicholas. *Keepers of the Key.* New York: Charles Scribners Sons, 1983.

De Rosa, Peter. *Vicars of Christ: The Dark Side of the Papacy.* New York: Crown Publishing, 1988. A critical, well-documented history of the papacy. Pages 273–438 good on doctrines concerning family and sex.

Goodwin, Malcolm. *Angels: An Endangered Species.* New York: Simon and Schuster, 1990.

Hasler, A. *How the Pope Became Infallible.* New York: Doubleday, 1981.

Schaf, Philip, and Henry Ware, eds. *A Select Library of Nicene and Post-Nicene Fathers of the Christian Church.* Grand Rapids, Mich.: Wm. Eerdmanns Publishing, 1956.

Chapter 19—Daily Life in Medieval Christian Europe

Anderson, Bonnie, and Judith Zinsser. *A History of Their Own: Women in Europe,* vol. 1. New York: Harper and Row, 1988.

Boswell, John. *The Kindness of Strangers: The Abandonment of Children in Western Europe from Late Antiquity to the Renaissance.* New York: Pantheon, 1988.

Bullough, Vern, and J. Brundage. *Sexual Practice in the Medieval Church.* Amherst, N.Y.: Prometheus Books, 1982.

Gies, Francis and Joseph. *Marriage and the Family in the Middle Ages.* New York: Harper and Row, 1987.

———. *Life in a Medieval Village.* New York: Harper and Row, 1990.

LeGoff, Jacques. *Your Money or Your Life: Economy and Religion in the Middle Ages.* New York: Zone Books, 1988.

Pagels, Elaine. *Adam, Eve, and the Serpent.* New York: Random House, 1988.

Tawney, Richard. *Religion and the Rise of Capitalism.* Glouchester, Mass.: Peter Smith, 1962.

Weber, Max. *The Protestant Ethic and the Spirit of Capitalism.* New York: Charles Scribners Sons, 1958.

Wood, Michael. *In Search of the Dark Ages.* New York: Facts on File, 1987.

Chapter 20—Varieties of Religious Experience: Love
Chapter 21—Varieties of Religious Experience: Mysticism

Bulfinch, Thomas. *Bulfinch's Mythology.* New York: Modern Library, 1958.

Campbell, Joseph. *Creative Mythology.* New York: Penguin Books, 1968. Chapter 4.

Eliade, Mircea. *Encyclopedia of Religion,* vol. 9. Article on love.

Fox, Robin Lane. *Pagans and Christians.* New York: Alfred A. Knopf, 1987. Chapter 11.

Herlihy, David. *Medieval Culture and Society.* New York: Harper and Row, 1968.

Huizinga, John. *The Waning of the Middle Ages.* New York: Doubleday, 1954.

James, William. *The Varieties of Religious Experience.* New York: Dolphin Books, 1960.

Keen, Maurice H. *Chivalry.* New Haven, Conn.: Yale University Press, 1986.

Nygren, Anders. *Agape and Eros: A Study of the Christian Idea of Love.* New York: Harper and Row, 1969.

Pelikan, Jaroslav. *The World Treasury of Modern Religious Thought.* Boston: Little, Brown, 1990. Essays by Anders Nygren on St. Augustine's reflections on agape and eros.

Underhill, Evelyn. *Mysticism.* New York: Doubleday, 1990.

Wilhelm, James J., and Laila Zamuelis, eds. *The Romance of Arthur.* New York: Garland Publishing, 1984.

Zarwetsky, Irving I., and Mark P. Leone, eds. *Religious Movements in Contemporary America.* Princeton, N.J.: Princeton University Press, 1974. Pages 255–71 on mysticism.

Chapter 22—The Catholic Clergy and the Evolution of the Religious Orders

Duckett, Eleanor. *Monasticism.* New York: Dorset Press, 1990.

Fox, Robin Lane. *Pagans and Christians.* New York: Alfred A. Knopf, 1987. Chapter 7.

Lawrence, C. H. *Medieval Monasticism: Forms of Religious Life in Western Europe in the Middle Ages.* New York: Longmans, 1989.

Levi, Peter. *The Frontiers of Paradise: A Study of Monks and Monasteries.* New York: Atlantic-Grove, 1988.

Chapter 23—The Broken Body of Christ:
The Eastern or Greek Orthodox Church

Atiya, Aziz A. *History of Eastern Christianity*. Milwood, N.Y.: Kraus, 1980.
Franzius, Enno. *History of the Byzantine Empire*. New York: Funk and Wagnalls, 1967.
Gage, Nicholas. *Hellas, a Portrait of Greece*. New York: Villard Books, 1987.
Garvey, John. "Religion: Eastern Orthodoxy." *Atlantic Monthly*, May 1989, pp. 30–37.
Herrin, Judith. *The Formation of Christendom*. Princeton, N.J.: Princeton University Press, 1987. Chapter 8 on iconoclasm.
Norwich, John J. *Byzantium: The Early Centuries*. New York: Alred A. Knopf, 1989.
Severy, Merle, and James L. Stanfield. "The Byzantine Empire." *National Geographic*, December 1983, pp. 709–75.

Chapter 24—The Broken Body of Christ:
The Protestant Reformation

Bainton, Roland H. *Here I Stand: A Life of Martin Luther*. New York: Abingdon Press, 1990.
———. *The Reformation of the Sixteenth Century*. Boston: Beacon Press, 1952.
Chadwick, Owen. *Pelican History of the Chrisitan Church*, vol. 3. New York: Penguin, 1964.
Cowie, Leonard W. *The Reformation of the Sixteenth Century*. New York: Putnam, 1970.
Elton, G. R., ed. *The New Cambrige Modern History*, vol. 2. New York: Cambridge University Press, 1965.
Dillenberger, John, and Claude Welch. *Protestant Christianity*. New York: Charles Scribners Sons, 1954.
Estep, William R. *Renaissance and Reformation*. Grand Rapids, Mich.: William Eerdmanns Publishing, 1986.
Friedenthal, Richard. *Luther, His Life and Times*. New York: Harcourt Brace Jovanovich, 1970.
Hillebrand, Hans J., ed. *The Reformation*. New York: Harper and Row, 1964.
Hordern, William E. *Layman's Guide to Protestant Theology*. New York: Macmillan, 1968.
Huizinaga, John. *Erasmus and the Age of Reformation*. Princeton, N.J.: Princetone University Press, 1984.
Hulme, E. M. *The Renaissance and the Protestant Reformation* and *The Renaissance and the Catholic Reformation*, 2 vols. New York: AMS Press, 1914.
Oberman, Heiko O. *Luther: Man Between God and the Devil*. New Haven, Conn.: Yale University Press, 1989.
Pelikan, Jaroslav. *Reformation of the Church and Dogma, 1300–1700*. Chicago: University of Chicago Press, 1985.
Simon, Edith. *Luther Alive: Martin Luther and the Making of the Reformation*. New York: Doubleday, 1968.
Walker, W. *John Calvin: The Organizer of Reformed Protestantism, 1509–1564*. New York: G. P. Putnam, 1906.

Chapter 25—The Splintered Body of Christ: Protestantism after Luther

Bowsma, William J. *John Calvin: A Sixteenth-Century Portrait.* New York: Oxford University Press, 1988.

Brockney, William H. *The Baptists.* New York: Greenwood Press, 1988.

Burtner, Robert W., and Robert E. Chiles, eds. *John Wesley's Theology.* Nashville, Tenn.: Abingdon Press, 1954.

Dickens, Arthur G. *English Reformation.* University Park: Pennsylvania State University Press, 1991.

Jordan, Anne Devereau, and J. M. Stifle. *The Baptists.* New York: Hippocrene Books, 1990.

Kraybill, Donald B. *The Riddle of Amish Culture.* Baltimore: Johns Hopkins University Press, 1989. Good survey of the Anabaptist movement.

McGrath, Alister E. *Life of John Calvin: A Study in the Shaping of Western Culture.* Cambridge, Mass.: Basil Blackwell, 1990.

McNeil, John T. *On God and Political Duty.* New York: Macmillan, 1956.

———. *The History and Character of Calvinism.* New York: Oxford University Press, 1954.

Norwood, Frederick A. *Source Book of American Methodism.* Nashville, Tenn.: Abingdon Press, 1982.

Pudney, John. *John Wesley and His World.* New York: Charles Scribners Sons, 1978.

Scarisbrick, J. J. *Henry VIII.* Berkeley: University of California Press, 1968.

Smith, Lacey Baldwin. *Henry VIII: The Mask of Royalty.* Boston: Houghton Mifflin, 1971.

Chapter 26—Post-Reformation Catholicism: Sixteenth to Twentieth Centuries

Bartel, Manfred. *The Jesuits: History and Legend of the Society of Jesus.* New York: William Morrow, 1984.

Berger, Joseph. "Being Catholic in America." *New York Times Magazine,* Auguest 23, 1987, pp. 22ff.

Berryman, Philip. *Liberation Theology: Essential Facts about the Revolutionary Movement in Latin America and Beyond.* New York: Pantheon, 1987.

Briggs, Kenneth A. "Using the World as a Pulpit." *New York Times Magazine,* October 10, 1982, pp. 25ff.

Broderick, James. *The Origins of the Jesuits.* Chicago: Loyola University Press, 1989.

Cleary, Edward, ed. *Born of the Poor: The Latin American Church Since Medellin.* South Bend, Ind.: University of Nortre Dame Press, 1990.

Daniel-Rops, Henri. *The Catholic Reformation.* New York: E. P. Dutton, 1926.

Dickens, Arthur G. *The Counter-Reformation.* New York: W. W. Norton, 1979.

Forest, Jim. *Religion in the New Russia.* New York: Crossroad, 1990. A publication of the World Council of Churches on new opportunities for all Christian groups.

Gallup, George, Jr., and Jim Castelli. *American Catholic People: Their Beliefs.* New York: Doubleday, 1987.

Greeley, Andrew M. *The Catholic Myth: The Behavior and Beliefs of American Catholics.* New York: Charles Scribners Sons, 1990.

Hennessey, James. *American Catholicism: A History of the Roman Catholic Community in the United States.* Milwaukee, Wis.: Marguette University Press, 1981.

Hoffman, P. "The Jesuits." *New York Times Magazine,* February 19, 1982, pp. 24–29.

Janelle, P. *The Catholic Reformation.* Milwaukee, Wis.: Bruce Publishing, 1941.

McDonough, Peter. *Men Absolutely Trained: A History of the Jesuits in the American Century.* New York: The Free Press, 1992.

Reese, Thomas J. *Archbishop: Inside the Power Structure of the American Catholic Church.* San Francisco: Harper and Row, 1989.

Sweeney, Terrence. *A Church Divided: The Vatican Versus American Catholics.* Amherst, N.Y.: Prometheus Books, 1992.

"Synod of Bishops Report, 1985." *New York Times,* December 8, 1985, pp. 6ff.

Wille, David. *God's Politician: Pope John Paul II and the New World Order.* New York: St. Martin's Press, 1992.

Chapter 27—Christianity in the Americas

Ahlstrom, Sidney E. *A Religious History of the American People.* New Haven, Conn.: Yale University Press, 1972.

Bacon, Margaret Hope. *Mothers of Feminism: The Story of Quaker Women.* New York: Harper and Row, 1987.

Butler, Jon. *Awake in a Sea of Faith.* Cambridge, Mass.: Harvard University Press, 1990. Denies that Protestantism promoted democracy in colonial America.

Gaustad, Edwin, ed. *A Documentary History of Religion in America,* 2 vols. Grand Rapids, Mich.: William E. Eerdmann, 1982–83.

Gura, Philip F. *A Glimpse of Zion's Glory: Puritan Radicalism in New England, 1670–1680.* Middletown, Conn.: Wesleyan University Press, 1984.

Handlin, Oscar and Lillian. *Liberty and Power, 1600–1760.* New York: Harper and Row, 1986.

Hudson, Winthrop. *Religion in America.* New York: Charles Scribners Sons, 1965.

Langdon, George D., Jr. *Pilgrim Colony: A History of New Plymouth, 1620–1691.* New Haven, Conn.: Yale University Press, 1966.

Lippy, Charles H., Robert Choquette, and Strafford Poole. *Christianity Comes to America, 1492–1776.* New York: Paragon House, 1992.

Marty, Martin E. *Pilgrims in Their Own Land: 500 Years of Religion in America.* Boston: Little, Brown, 1984.

———. *Righteous Empire: The Protestant Experience in America.* New York: Dial, 1970.

Melton, Gordon J. *Encyclopedia of American Religion.* Detroit, Mich.: Gale Research, 1989.

Miller, William Lee. *The First Liberty: Religion and the American Republic.* New York: Alfred A. Knopf, 1985.

Newman, Cathy. "The Shakers' Brief Eternity." *National Geographic,* September 1989, pp. 303–25.

Olmstead, Clifton E. *History of Religion in the United States.* Englewood Cliffs, N.J.: Prentice-Hall, 1960.

Sperry, Willard L. *Religion in America.* New York: Cambridge University Press, 1946.
Stein, Stephen J. *The Shaker Experience in America.* New Haven, Conn.: Yale University Press, 1992.
Sweet, W. W. *Religion in Colonial America.* New York: Charles Scribners Sons, 1972.
———. *Religion in the Development of American Culture, 1765-1840.* New York: Charles Scribners Sons, 1952.

Chapter 28—Manifest Destiny and American Protestantism

Andrews, Edward D. *The People Called Shakers.* New York: Oxford University Press, 1989.
Brodie, Fawn M. *No Man Knows My History: The Life of Joseph Smith, the Mormon Prophet.* New York: Alfred A. Knopf, 1971.
Coates, James. *In Mormon Circles: Gentiles, Jack Mormons and Latter-Day Saints.* Reading, Mass.: Addison-Wesley, 1991.
Cohen, Daniel. *The Spirit of the Lord: Revivalism in America.* New York: Fourwinds Press, 1975.
Ferguson, Charles W. *Organizing to Beat the Devil.* New York: Doubleday, 1971. Methodism in the United States.
Friedman, Robert J. *Zealots for Zion.* New York: Random House, 1992. Pages 142-52 and chapter 5 on fundamentalism.
Handlin, Oscar and Lillian. *Liberty in Expansion, 1760-1850.* New York: Harper and Row, 1989.
Heineman, John, and Anson Shupe. *The Mormon Corporate Empire.* Boston: Beacon Press, 1985.
Hudson, Winthrop E. *American Protestantism.* Chicago: University of Chicago Press, 1963.
Klaw, Spencer. *Without Sin: The Life and Death of the Oneida Community.* New York: Pilgrim Press, 1993.
Krauthammer, Charles. *Cutting Edge.* New York: Random House, 1983. Review of the millennium forecasts.
Lindsey, Robert. "The Mormon Growth, Prosperity and Controversy." *New York Times Magazine,* January 12, 1986, pp. 19-46.
McCord, William. *Voyages to Utopia.* New York: W. W. Norton, 1989.
Schoumatoff, A. "The Mountain of Names." *New Yorker,* May 13, 1985, pp. 51ff.
Sims, Patsy. *Can Somebody Shout Amen.* New York: St. Martin's Press, 1988. Good on revivalism in America.
Stokes, Anson, and Leo Pfeffer. *Church and State in the United States.* New York: Harper and Row, 1964.
Troelsch, Ernst. *The Social Teachings of Christian Churches,* 2 vols. Chicago: University of Chicago Press, 1981.
Weinberg, Albert K. *Manifest Destiny: A Study of Nationalist Expansion in American History.* Baltimore: Johns Hopkins University Press, 1935.

Chapter 29—Post–Civil War Protestant Division and Unity

Anderson, Robert M. *Vision of the Disinherited: The Making of American Pentecostalism.* Peabody, Mass.: Hendrickson, 1992.

Armstrong, Herbert W. *Mystery of the Ages.* New York: Dodd, Mead, 1985.

Atachk, Jon. *A Piece of Blue Sky: Scientology, Dianetics and L. Ron Hubbard, Exposed.* Secaucus, N.J.: Carol Publishing, 1990.

Bailey, Kenneth K. *Southern White Protestantism in the Twentieth Century.* New York: Peter Smith, 1964.

Balomer, Randall. *Mine Eyes Have Seen the Glory.* New York: Oxford University Press, 1989. An eyewitness account of evangelical meetings and church services.

Barr, James. *Beyond Fundamentalism.* Louisville, Ky: Westminster Press, 1984.

Belloh, Robert N., and Frederick E. Greenspahr, eds. *Uncivil Religion: Inter-Religious Hostility in America.* New York: Crossroads, 1987.

Berryhill, Michael. "The Baptist Schism." *New York Times Magazine,* June 9, 1985, pp. 88ff.

Biornstadt, James. *Sun Myung Moon and the Unification Church.* Minneapolis: Bethany House, 1981.

Blanshard, Paul. *American Freedom and Catholic Power.* Boston: Beacon Press, 1958.

Bloesch, Donald G. *The Future of Evangelical Christianity.* Garden City, N.Y.: Doubleday, 1983.

Bloom, Harold. *The American Religion.* New York: Simon and Schuster, 1992.

Bromley, David G., and Anson Sharpe. *Strange Gods: The Great American Cult Scare.* Boston: Beacon Press, 1981.

Bryan, Mike. *A Skeptic Revisits Christianity: Chapter and Verse.* New York: Random House, 1991. An observation on a Southern Baptist seminary.

Conway, Flo, and Tim Siegelman. *Holy Terror: The Fundamentalists' War on America's Freedoms in Religion, Politics, and Our Private Lives.* New York: Dell, 1984.

Cornwall, John. *The Hiding Places of God.* New York: Warner, 1991. Study of modern cults and supernatural phenomena.

Cox, Harvey. *Religion in the Secular City.* New York: Simon and Schuster, 1984.

Creus, Mickey. *The Church of God: A Social History.* Knoxville: University of Tennessee Press, 1990.

Cruse, Harold. *Plural But Equal: Blacks and Minorities in America's Plural Society.* New York: Morrow, 1984.

D'Antonio, Michael. *Fall from Grace.* New York: Farrar, Straus-Geroux, 1988.

———. *Heaven on Earth: Dispatches from America's Spiritual Frontier.* New York: Crown Publishers, 1992.

D'Emilio, John, and Estelle Friedman. *Intimate Matters: A History of Sexuality in America.* New York: Harper and Row, 1988.

Epstein, Daniel Mark. *Sister Aimee: The Life of Aimee Semple McPherson.* New York: Harcourt Brace Jovanovich, 1993.

Etird, James M. *End-Times: Rapture, Anti-Christ, Millennium.* Hashville, Tenn.: Abingdon Press, 1986.

Falwell, Jerry. *Listen, America.* Garden City, N.Y.: Doubleday, 1980.

Ferraby, John. *All Things Made New: A Comprehensive Outline of the Bahai Faith.* Wilmette, Ill.: Bahai Publishing Trust, 1960.

Frazier, E. Franklin. *The Negro Church in America.* New York: Shocken, 1964.

Frazier, E. Franklin, and C. Eric Lincoln. *The Negro Church in America: The Black Church Since Frazier.* New York: Schocken, 1974.

Frye, Roland M., ed. *Is God a Creationist? The Religious Case Against Creation Science.* New York: Charles Scribners Sons, 1983.

Galanter, Marc. *Faith Healing and Coercion.* New York: Oxford University Press, 1988.

Gallup, George, Jr., and Jim Castelli. *The People's Religion: American Faith in the '90s.* New York: Macmillan, 1989.

Greenfield, Robert. *The Spiritual Supermarket.* New York: E. P. Dutton, 1975.

Griffin, David R. *A Process Christianity.* Phildadelphia: Westminster Press, 1973.

———. *Varieties of Postmodern Theology.* Albany: State University of New York Press, 1989.

Haden, Jeffrey K., and Charles E. Swann. *Prime Time Preachers, The Rising Power of Televangelism.* Reading, Mass.: Addison-Wesley, 1986.

Harrell, David E. *Oral Roberts.* Bloomington: Indiana University Press, 1985. Good study of Pentecostalism.

Hartshorne, Charles, and William L. Reese. *Philosophers Speak of God.* Chicago: University Chicago Press, 1976. Good on process theology.

Hopkins, Charles H. *The Rise of the Social Gospel in American Protestantism, 1865–1915.* New Haven, Conn.: Yale University Press, 1940.

Higgins, Nathan I. *Black Odyssey.* New York: Pantheon, 1977. Good review of the black churches.

Küng, Hans. *Theology for the Third Millennium: An Ecumenical View.* New York: Doubleday, 1988.

Lewis, Norman. *The Missionaries.* New York: McGraw-Hill, 1989.

Lincoln, C. Eric and Lawrence H. *Mamiya. The Black Church in the African-American Experience.* Durham, N.C.: Duke University Press, 1990.

Luker, Kristin. *Abortion and the Politics of Motherhood.* Berkeley: University of California Press, 1984.

Marsden, George. *The Shaping of Twentieth-Century Evangelism, 1870–1925.* New York: Oxford University Press, 1980.

———. *Understanding Fundamentalism and Evangelicanism.* Grand Rapids, Mich.: William Eerdmanns, 1990.

Martin, Walter. *The Kingdom of Cults.* Minneapolis, Minn.: Bethany House, 1985.

Marty, Martin E. *Modern American Religion, 1893–1919,* 2 vols. Chicago: University of Chicago Press, 1986 and 1991.

Marty, Martin E., and R. Scott Appleby, eds. *The Glory and the Power: The Rapid Rise of Fundamentalism in the 1990s.* Boston: Beacon Press, 1992.

Melton, J. Gordon. *Encyclopedic Handbook of Cults in America.* New York: Garland Press, 1986.

Melton, J. Gordon, and Robert J. Moore. *The Cult Experience: Responding to the New Religious Pluralism.* New York: Pilgrim Press, 1982.

Needleman, Jacob, and George Baker, eds. *Understanding the New Religions.* New York: Seabury Press, 1978.

Neuhaus, Richard J. *The Naked Public Square: Religion and Democracy in America.* Grand Rapids, Mich.: William Eerdmanns, 1986.

Ochshorn, Judith. *The Female Experience and the Nature of the Divine.* Bloomington: Indiana University Press, 1981.

Poloma, Margaret M. *The Assemblies of God at the Crossroads*. Nashville: University of Tennessee Press, 1989.

Price, Lucien. *Dialogues of Alfred North Whitehead*. Boston: Little, Brown, 1947.

Rusher, William R. *The Rise of the Right*. New York: William Morrow, 1984. What the conservatives hope to gain.

Russell, Jeffrey Burton. *The Mephistopheles: The Devil in the Modern World*. Ithaca, N.Y.: Cornell University Press, 1986.

Shinn, Larry D. *Dark Lord: Cult Images and the Hare Krishnas in America*. Louisville, Ky.: Westminster Press, 1987.

Silk, Mark. *Spiritual Politics: Religion and America Since World War II*. New York: Simon and Schuster, 1988.

Stone, Ronald H. *Reinhold Niebuhr: Prophet to Politicians*. New York: Abingdon Press, 1972.

Synan, Vinson. *The Holiness-Pentecostal Movement in the United States*. Grand Rapids, Mich.: William Eerdmanns, 1971.

Tillich, Paul. *The Future of Religion*. Edited by Gerald C. Brauer. New York: Harper and Row, 1966.

———. *The Socialist Decision*. New York: Harpers, 1977.

Torrey, R. A., ed. *The Fundamentalists: A Testimony to the Truth*. Grand Rapids, Mich.: Baker Bible House, 1980.

Wade, Wyn Craig. *The Fiery Cross: The Ku Klux Klan in America*. New York: Simon and Schuster, 1987.

Whitehead, Alfred North. *Process and Reality*. New York: The Free Press, 1978.

Williams, Daniel Day. *What Present Day Theologians are Thinking*. Westport, Conn.: Greenwood Publishers, 1978.

Wills, Gary. *Under God: Religion and American Politics*. New York: Simon and Schuster, 1990.

Zaretsky, Irving I., and Mark P. Leone, eds. *Religious Movements in Contemporary America*. Princeton, N.J.: Princeton University Press, 1974. Analysis of Scientology, pp. 547–87, Hare Krishnas, pp. 463–78, and Jehovah's Witnesses, pp. 700–21.

Endnotes

Chapter 1—A Universal Human Experience

1. William James, *Varieties of Religious Experience,* pp. 31–32.
2. Joseph Campbell, *The Power of Myth,* p. 214.
3. Harvey Cox, *Religion in the Secular Society,* p. 137.
4. *New York Times Magazine,* June 10, 1984, pp. 30–32.
5. *New York Times Magazine,* August 21, 1988, p. 23.
6. *Graduate Education Monitor,* University of Colorado, Boulder, Colorado, Fall 1987.
7. *National Geographic,* October 1988, pp. 436–37.

Chapter 2—Prehistoric Cosmic Religions

1. MacDonald Harris, "Welcoming the Sun," *New York Times Magazine,* March 15, 1987, p. 20.
2. Merlin Stone, *When God Was a Woman,* p. 29. Also chapters 5 and 8.
3. Good accounts of shamanism are found in Mircia Eliade, *Shamanism,* and Peter Freuchen, *The Eskimo.*
4. See Sandra Widener, "The Peyote Path to God," *Denver Post Magazine,* June 16, 1985.
5. Stanley Breeden, "The First Australians," *National Geographic,* February 1988, p. 62.
6. *Time,* November 10, 1986, pp. 78–79.

Chapter 3—River Valley Religions: Babylon and Egypt

1. A useful work on the Egyptian religion is Veronica Ions, *Egyptian Mythology,* 1986.

Chapter 4—The Greek Gods and the Hellenistic Cults

1. H. W. Robbins and W. H. Coleman, *Western World Literature,* p. 136.

Chapter 5—The Greek Gods Become Roman

1. R. J. Fox, *Pagans and Christians,* p. 422.
2. Geoffrey Parrinder, ed., *World Religions,* p. 160.

Chapter 6—The Chinese Way of Life: Taoism and Confucianism

1. J. Li Dun, *The Ageless Chinese,* p. 184.
2. Ibid., pp. 373–85.
3. John Biofeld, *Taoism: The Road to Immortality,* p. 187.
4. National Geographic Society, *Great Religions of the World,* p. 127.
5. *New York Times,* February 7, 1993, p. 10.

Chapter 7—Hinduism

1. Hans Küng, *Christianity and the World Religions,* p. 183.

Chapter 8—Buddhism

1. Jacob E. Conner, "The Forgotten Ruins of Indo-China," *National Geographic,* March 1912, pp. 209–71.
2. Thich Nhat Hanh, *Old Path White Clouds,* p. 232–33.
3. J. Barzun, ed., *Records of Civilizations: Sources of Japanese Traditions,* vol. 54, p. 93.
4. Ibid., p. 261.

Chapter 9—Sikhism

1. Sandra Widener, "Another Path to God," *Denver Post Empire Magazine,* December 16, 1984.

Chapter 11—Zoroastrianism

1. For more information on this subject, see Jeffrey Burton Russell, *Mephistopheles: The Devil in the Modern World.*

Chapter 12—Judaism, Mother of Monotheism

1. William H. Stiebing, Jr., *Out of the Desert? Archaeology and the Exodus-Conquest Narratives* (Amherst, N.Y.: Prometheus Books, 1989), p. 92.
2. Charles R. Krahmalkov, "Exodus Itinerary Confirmed by Egyptian Evidence," *Biblical Archaeology Review* 20, no. 5 (September-October 1994): 54–62.
3. See Wilens, *The Christians as the Romans Saw Them,* pp. 137–43.
4. See John Crossan, *The Historical Jesus,* p. 239, and Robin Lane Fox, *The Unauthorized Version,* pp. 331–37.
5. Melvin Konner, "Symbolic Wound," *New York Times Magazine,* May 8, 1988, p. 58.
6. K. L. Bo and J. Howe, *We Live There Too,* pp. 210–11.

7. *Denver Post,* October 28, 1987, C–3:5.

8. For more information about Hasidism, see Liz Harris, writing in a series of September 1985 articles in the *New Yorker*; Elie Wiesel, *Souls on Fire*; Harry Rabinowicz, *Hasidism, the Movement and Its Masters,* 1988; and Martin Buber, *Tales of the Hasidim.*

9. See Charles Krauthammer, *Cutting Edges* (1983), and Wolf Blitzer, *Between Washington and Jerusalem* (1985).

Chapter 13—The Advent of Christianity

1. Werner Keller, *The Bible as History,* pp. 355–58.

2. Morton Smith, *Jesus the Magician,* p. 8.

3. In addition to the several authors who have been cited above a few more names should be added: Thomas Sheehan, *The First Coming,* p. 52; Michael Grant, *Jesus, an Historian's Review of the Gospel,* pp. 9, 72–73; and Stephen Mitchell, *The Gospel According to Jesus,* pp. 17–28.

4. Hans Küng, *Christianity and World Religions,* p. 95.

5. James Bentley, *Secrets of Mount Sinai,* pp. 138–40, 185–86.

6. Paul Tillich, *The Future of Religions,* p. 93.

Chapter 14—The Pauline Church of the First Two Centuries

1. James Charlesworth in his study of the Dead Sea Scrolls believes that the Essenes had little or no influence on the teachings of Jesus. *Jesus and the Dead Sea Scrolls,* p. 37.

2. Fran Schumer, "A Return to Religion," *New York Times Magazine,* April 15, 1984.

Chapter 15—The Formation of the Christian Church—A.D. 100 to 400

1. John Romer, *Testament: The Bible and History,* p. 196.

2. Many sources relate the history of the Church in its first four centuries. Among the most useful are Robin Lane Fox, *Pagans and Christians,* 1966, W. H. C. Frend, *The Rise of Christianity,* 1984, and F. C. Grant, *Roman Hellenism and the New Testament.* A basic source for this period is Kenneth S. Latourette, *History of Christianity.*

3. R. M. Grant, *Gnosticism and Early Christianity,* and H. Jonas, *The Gnostic Religion,* are also useful accounts of Gnosticism.

4. Irene M. Franck and David M. Brownestone, *The Silk Road, a History,* 1986.

Chapter 16—Islam

1. Many books have described the life of a Muslim woman who lives in the twentieth century. A few recent books might be suggested for further reading: Nanal El Saadow, *The Hidden Face of Eve: Women in the Arab World,* 1982; Marianne Alireza, "Women of Saudi Arabia," *National Geographic,* October 1987; and Tahar Ben Jelloun, *The Sand Child,* 1988. *The Sand Child* is the story of an Arabic girl whose father did not want a girl child, so he tries to pass her off as the boy he desired.

2. Sandra Mackey, *The Saudis: Inside the Desert Kingdom,* 1987.

3. Albert Horani, *History of the Arab People,* pp. 155–56.

4. Two good reports on conditions in Iran are Michael Fisher, *Iran,* and Florence Smith, *Iran.*

Chapter 17—Roman Catholic Orthodoxy, 400–1200

1. Hugh Schonfield, *The Incredible Christians,* chapters 8 and 11.
2. For current interpretations on the book of Revelation see James Bentley, *Secrets of Mount Sinai,* pp. 170–71; John D. Crossan, *Historical Jesus,* pp. 9 and 239; and Robin Lane Fox, *The Unauthorized Version,* pp. 346–47.
3. John Romer, *Testament: The Bible and History,* p. 308.
4. G. H. Knoles and R. K. Snyder, *Readings in Western Civilization,* p. 206.
5. Mircea Eliade, *History of Religious Ideas,* vol. 2, pp. 195–96.

Chapter 18—The City of God on Earth: Temporal Church Power

1. G. H. Knoles and R. K. Snyder, *Readings in Western Civlization,* p. 261.
2. Brand Blanshard, *Reason and Belief,* 1975, pp. 456–63.
3. For a list of many relics see Paul Johnson, *History of Christianity.*

Chapter 19—Daily Life in Medieval Christian Europe

1. Frances and Joseph Gies, *Marriage and Family in the Middle Ages,* p. 346.
2. Paul Johnson, *History of Christianity,* p. 221.

Chapter 20—Varieties of Religious Experience: Love

1. A good analysis has been made by Terence Sweeney in *A Church Divided: The Vatican versus American Catholics,* 1992.

Chapter 22—The Catholic Clergy and the Evolution of the Religious Orders

1. Paul Johnson, *History of Christianity,* p. 235.

Chapter 25—The Splintered Body of Christ: Protestantism after Luther

1. A good account of the American Episcopal Church is found in Paul Wilkes, "The Episcopalians," *New York Times Magazine,* September 1, 1985.
2. J. R. Green, *A Short History of the English People,* p. 107.

Chapter 27—Christianity in the Americas

1. Martin Marty, *Pilgrims of the Land,* p. 109.
2. An excellent, scholarly treatment of the Shakers can be found in Stephen J. Stein, *The Shaker Experience in America.*

Chapter 28—Manifest Destiny and American Protestantism

1. For a good account of the Mormon Church, see John Heineman and Anson Shupe, *The Mormon Corporate Empire*, 1985.

2. See William McCord, *Voyages to Utopia*, 1989, chapter 4, for a good review of utopian socialism.

3. George Rapp, a German preacher, had founded a commune in Indiana in 1814 and named it Harmonie. It prospered, but the celibate, German-speaking community did not get along well with its frontier neighbors, and by 1825 they were ready to sell the commune and join another successful Rappite community in Pennsylvania.

Chapter 29—Post-Civil War Protestant Division and Unity

1. For discussions of the evolution issue today, see Roland M. Frye, ed., *Is God a Creationist?: The Religious Case Against Creation Science* (New York: Scribners, 1985); Arthur N. Strahler, *Understanding Science* (Amherst, N.Y.: Prometheus Books), chapter 14.

2. Stephen Jay Gould, "The Verdict on Creationism," *New York Times Magazine*, July 19, 1987.

3. Martin Marty, *Modern American Religion*, vol. 1, p. 23.

4. *Time*, April 5, 1993.

5. See Robert I. Friedman, *Zealots for Zion*, pp. 142–52 and chapter 5 for a good review of fundamentalism. Another good source on fundamentalism is George Marsden, *Fundamentalism and American Culture*.

6. For a good study of the Christian Reconstructionists see Gary North, *Unconditional Surrender*. North's father-in-law is a chief apostle of this extreme group.

7. Fergus M. Bordewich, "California's Thriving Cults," *New York Times Magazine*, May 1, 1988.

8. Irving I. Zaretzky and Mark P. Leone, eds., *Religious Movements in Contemporary America*, pp. 547–87.

9. See Harold Cruse, *Plural But Equal*, p. 305.

Epilogue

1. Charles S. Liebman and Steven M. Cohen, *Two Worlds of Judaism*, 1990, pp. 133–47.

Name Index